Introduction to Programming with Visual Basic

RALPH DUFFY

North Seattle Community College

Introduction to Programming with Visual Basic™

Copyright © 1995 by Que® Corporation.

Library of Congress Catalog No.: 95-068937

ISBN: 0-7897-0247-9

98 97 96   4 3 2

Interpretation of the printing code: the rightmost double-digit number is the year of the book's printing; the rightmost single-digit number, the number of the book's printing. For example, a printing code of 95-1 shows that the first printing of the book occurred in 1995.

Screens reproduced in this book were created using Collage Plus from Inner Media, Inc., Hollis, NH.

Introduction to Programming with Visual Basic™ is based on Visual Basic™ 3.

Publisher: David P. Ewing

Publishing Manager: Chris Katsaropoulos

Product Marketing Manager: Susan J. Dollman

Managing Editor: Sheila B. Cunningham

Cover photograph of basalt columns courtesy of John Lythgoe/Master File

Dedication

To Bucky, the babies, and Hsiau-Hua

Acquisitions Editor

Diane E. Beausoleil

Senior Editor

Jeannine Freudenberger

Copy Editors

Karen Dodson
Beth Hux
Virginia D. Noble

Book Designer

Paula A. Carroll

Production Team

Mona Brown
Charlotte Clapp
Mary Ann Cosby
Terrie Deemer
Mike Dietsch
Paula Lowell
Brian-Kent Proffitt
Jill Tompkins
Mark Walchle
Dennis Wesner

Indexer

Greg Eldred

Composed in *1 Stone Serif* and *MCPdigital* by Que Corporation.

About the Author

Ralph Duffy holds a B.A. from the University of Michigan and an M.S. from Pennsylvania State University. He has worked as a statistical consultant and a programmer/analyst for Pennsylvania State University, the Indiana University School of Medicine, and Purdue University. He is currently an instructor in the Computer Information Systems Department of North Seattle Community College.

Mr. Duffy also is the Director of the IBM Technology Transfer Center in Seattle. This Center, in cooperation with Microsoft Corporation, provides training in computer applications for the faculty and staff of colleges throughout the Northwest, including the University of Washington and Seattle University. Mr. Duffy is the author of *Excel 4 for Windows SmartStart, Excel 5 for Windows SmartStart, Paradox SmartStart*, and *dBASE III Plus SmartStart*, and co-author of *Paradox for Windows SmartStart*, all published by Que Education & Training.

Preface

Que Education & Training is the educational publishing imprint of Macmillan Computer Publishing, the world's leading computer book publisher. Macmillan Computer Publishing books have taught more than 20 million people how to be productive with their computers.

This expertise in producing high-quality computer tutorial and reference books is evident in every Que Education & Training title we publish. The same tried and true authoring and product development process that makes Macmillan Computer Publishing books bestsellers is used to ensure that every Que Education & Training textbook has the most accurate and most up-to-date information. Experienced and respected college instructors write and review every manuscript to provide class-tested pedagogy. Quality-assurance editors check every line of programming code in Que Education & Training books to ensure that the code is accurate and that instructions are clear and precise.

Above all, Macmillan Computer Publishing and, in turn, Que Education & Training have years of experience in meeting the learning demands of computer users in business and at home. This "real world" experience means that Que Education & Training textbooks help students understand how the skills they learn will be applied and why these skills are important.

A Distinctive Approach to Learning Visual Basic

Introduction to Programming with Visual Basic brings a unique approach to learning Visual Basic. Whether you are new to programming or have already programmed in another language, this text provides one of the fastest and easiest ways available to learn to write programs for Windows. If you are experienced with Windows, you know that Windows is a much more interesting environment for programming than traditional operating systems, which do not use a graphical user interface. And writing Visual Basic programs will give you a deeper insight into how Windows applications like Word for Windows and Excel operate.

Introduction to Programming with Visual Basic is a textbook employing an easy-to-follow, step-by-step approach to learning Visual Basic in a college-level course. Because *Introduction to Programming with Visual Basic* concisely covers the most important topics and covers them completely when they are introduced, you become a productive programmer very rapidly.

Following are some of the distinctive features of the book:

- Each chapter begins with a set of objectives.

- Margin icons show where each objective is covered and help you focus your learning.

- Key terms are defined in the margin next to where they are first used in the text.

- Frequent illustrations will aid your learning.

- Many hands-on exercises are interspersed throughout the chapters at the points where doing the exercise can best clarify the immediately preceding discussion.

- The early chapters are designed to build quickly the "critical mass" of material necessary for you to start programming on your own.

- The student disk in the back of this book contains many projects that illustrate simply and clearly the controls and programming statements covered in the associated chapter.

- Questions at the end of the chapter point out important concepts in the chapter and enable you to verify your understanding of the material.

- Most of the chapters end with several programming projects that involve the topics covered in the chapter. Your instructor will probably require you to complete all or some of these projects.

How This Book Is Organized

Each chapter follows the same general format. A chapter overview comes first and then the chapter objectives are listed. Each hands-on exercise section is set off from the rest of the text by a different color background. Each chapter ends with a summary that reviews the most important points in the chapter and the questions and projects that test your understanding.

In the body of each chapter, care has been taken to ensure that you can read the book as you are working in your computer lab and when you are studying without a computer. Illustrations show how the computer screen should look after certain actions are taken. Frequent references are made to useful help topics, tips, and examples available in Visual Basic's excellent on-line Help facility. As you read each chapter, run the sample programs stored in the corresponding directory on the student disk.

The early chapters carefully build your confidence and understanding without causing you more frustration than, unfortunately, is inevitable when you program. The rest of the chapters move more rapidly to explain some of the more advanced topics in Visual Basic.

Chapter 1, "An Introduction to Programming for Windows," explains the fundamental concepts of programming and identifies what is "new and different" about programming for Windows.

Chapter 2, "How to Use Visual Basic to Create Your First Program," covers starting and exiting from Visual Basic (VB); describes the components of the VB environment; and tells you how to write, save, and run your first VB program.

Chapter 3, "Using Forms and Some of the Most Commonly Used Controls," describes the uses, properties, and events of forms. The chapter also introduces three of the most useful VB controls: Command Button, Text Box, and Label controls.

Chapter 4, "Using More Controls and Creating Graphics," teaches you about the Check Box, Option Button, Image, Picture Box, and Frame controls. You learn how to modify properties in VB code, draw and animate shapes, and capture graphics for use in your program. This chapter also introduces control arrays.

Chapter 5, "Programming in Visual Basic," explains, in depth, the types of files that make up a complete VB application. You learn what is happening inside your computer when you run a VB program, what kinds of procedures are used in a VB project, and the way to call procedures. The chapter also defines variables and strings and explains the data types used in VB.

Chapter 6, "Building a Complete Application," walks you through the creation of a text editing program for Windows. You learn how to create access keys and use control arrays. You create an executable file from your VB project and take the steps necessary to enable the user to run the program by double-clicking an icon in Windows Program Manager.

Chapter 7, "Program Flow and Decision Making," teaches you how to use both conditional and unconditional branching in your programs. Conditional testing with the If-Then and Select Case statements is covered, as well as looping in a program by using the For-Next, While-Wend, and Do-Loop statements.

Chapter 8, "Testing and Debugging Your Program," gives invaluable advice about an approach to proper programming and about using VB's built-in debugging tools to test your program, identify problems in your code, and correct these problems quickly.

Chapter 9, "Using Arrays and Data Structures," shows you how to create and use both fixed and dynamic data arrays, how to open and read a VB sequential file, how to set up user-defined data types, and how to pass arrays and records to procedures.

Chapter 10, "Learning to Use More Controls and Functions," explains the List Box, Combo Box, Scroll Bar, and Timer controls. The chapter explains many useful built-in VB functions, random-number generation, input boxes, and message boxes.

Chapter 11, "Designing Custom Menus," tells you everything you need to know about creating menus and using them in your programs.

Chapter 12, "Processing Files," explains how to create VB programs that read and write sequential, random, and binary data files on your disk. You learn how to use the Common Dialog control to make your programs more flexible. The chapter also explains VB functions that enable you to manage the directory structure and files on your disk and to use the Drive, Directory, and File List Box controls.

Chapter 13, "Using the Grid Control," shows you how to use the Grid control to display information, let the user select information in a grid, and create spreadsheetlike applications.

Chapter 14, "Using the Data Control to Interact with Databases," explains how to use one of the most important controls in VB—the Data control with data-aware controls to enable the user to create applications that can display, modify, add, and delete records in a database.

When you complete your study of this textbook, you will have had a complete introduction to Visual Basic programming for Windows and will have created many useful programs. We at Que Education & Training hope you enjoy this text!

Conventions Used in This Book

This book uses a number of conventions to help you learn the program quickly.

Step-by-step exercises are given a light screened background to set them off from the rest of the text. Information you are asked to type is printed in **boldface and red**. Access keys for menus, commands, and options appear in **boldface and red** in exercises, (**V**iew) and in boldface elsewhere (**V**iew). Keys you press are shown in **boldface and red** in the exercises (**Enter** or **Alt+F4**).

DOS commands, file names, and file paths usually appear in all uppercase characters.

Program code lines, keywords, names of variables, procedures, events, methods, and other code items appear in a `special typeface` so that they stand out from the rest of the text.

A code instruction too long to fit on one line on the page is printed with a line-continuation character (➡), which indicates that the instruction continues on the following line. When you see this character, continue to type one long line of code in the VB code editor.

Acknowledgments

Que Education & Training is grateful for the assistance provided by the following reviewers: Ron Bass, Austin Community College; William Eddins, York College of Pennsylvania; Donnavae Hughes, North Harris College; Arthur Husionica, University of Maryland; Dr. William A. Newman, University of Nevada/Las Vegas; James A. Sherrard, Jefferson Community College; and Sue Welsch, Sierra Nevada College. And thank you to our technical editors, Russell L. Jacobs, Software Alchemy, and Bryan Gambrell, Que.

The author gratefully acknowledges Jeannine Freudenberger, Senior Editor, for her work in managing this project, and editors Ginny Noble, Karen Dodson, and Beth Hux for their excellent work on the text. And many thanks to Chris Katsaropoulos for his guidance in the conception of this book and to Lisa Proctor for her help in developing this project.

Trademark Acknowledgments

An Instructor's Manual (ISBN 0-7897-0271-4) is available to the adopters of *Introduction to Programming with Visual Basic*, upon written request. Please submit your request on school letterhead to your local representative or to S. Dollman, Macmillan Computer Publishing, 201 W. 103rd Street, Indianapolis, IN 46290-1097.

Contents at a Glance

1 An Introduction to Programming for Windows 1

2 How to Use Visual Basic to Create Your First Program 25

3 Using Forms and Some of the Most Commonly Used Controls 55

4 Using More Controls and Creating Graphics 93

5 Programming in Visual Basic 123

6 Building a Complete Application 161

7 Program Flow and Decision Making 205

8 Testing and Debugging Your Program 243

9 Using Arrays and Data Structures 283

10 Learning to Use More Controls and Functions 315

11 Designing Custom Menus 351

12 Processing Files 385

13 Using the Grid Control 415

14 Using the Data Control to Interact with Databases 455

Index 491

Table of Contents

1 An Introduction to Programming for Windows   **1**

Objectives 1

Programming Languages 2

Translation Programs: Compilers and Interpreters 4

Which Programming Language Is the Best? 4

Interface 5

The Standards of the Windows Interface 6

What Is Visual Basic? 6

Why Write a Program? 7

    Programming for Fun 7

    Programming Small Utilities 7

    Programming as a Profession 7

        Independent Programmer 7

        Working as a Programmer for a Business or a Software Company 8

Problem Solving with the Computer 9

Programming Tools: Flowcharts and Pseudocode 11

    Flowcharts 11

    Pseudocode 11

Introduction to Programming Statements 13

    Overview of Programming Statements 13

    Variables 14

    Program Flow 16

    Types of Programming Language Statements 16

        Comments 16

        Assignment Statements 18

        Input Statements 18

        Output Statements 19

        Conditional Statements 19

        Case Statements 20

        Loops 20

Windows Object-Oriented Event-Driven Programming 21

Chapter Summary 22

Test Your Understanding 23

    True/False 23

    Short Answer 23

    Projects 24

        Project 1:   Learning More about Programming 24

        Project 2:   Learning More about Flowcharts and Pseudocode 24

        Project 3:   Researching Software Products 24

Project 4:   Learning about Career Opportunities 24
Project 5:   Exploring Programming Literature 24
Project 6:   Drawing a Flowchart 24

2 How to Use Visual Basic to Create Your First Program   25

Objectives 25
Starting Visual Basic 26
Learning the Parts of the Visual Basic Program Development Environment 27
    The Form 27
    The Properties Window 28
    The Project Window 29
    The Toolbox 30
Removing and Adding Custom Controls 31
Using Controls as You Develop Your Application 31
    Sizing a Control 33
Understanding the Menu Bar 34
    Access Keys 35
    Shortcut Keys 35
    The Window Menu 37
Getting Help 37
    Your Own Private Tutor 38
    Learning by Example 38
Starting and Ending Program Execution 39
Understanding the Toolbar 39
Customizing Visual Basic through the Options Menu 40
    The Environment Options 40
    Project Options 41
Creating Your First Visual Basic Program 42
    Defining the Problem 42
    Designing the Program 42
    Preparing to Create the Program 43
    Revisiting the *Caption* and the *Name* Properties 47
    Attaching Code to an Object 47
    Entering Code in the Code Window 47
Quitting Visual Basic 50
Chapter Summary 51
Test Your Understanding 51
    True/False 51
    Short Answer 51
    Projects 52
        Project 1:   Using the VB Tutorial 52
        Project 2:   Opening Windows 52
        Project 3:   Exploring the Help System Glossary 52
        Project 4:   Searching for Help Topics 52
        Project 5:   Using Context-Sensitive Help 52
        Project 6:   Creating a Simple Form 53
        Project 7:   Writing a Calculator Program 53

3 Using Forms and Some of the Most Commonly Used Controls   55

Objectives 55

Adding Forms to Projects 56

Changing a Form's Appearance and Behavior 56

    Types of Properties 57

    Properties Related to Forms 57

    Color Properties 58

    Text Properties 59

        The *Caption* Property 59

        The *Name* Property 59

    The Size and Location Properties 60

        Left and *Top* 60

        Height and *Width* 60

    The *BorderStyle* Property 61

    The *Visible* Property 61

Using the Control Menu 62

    The Picture Properties 62

        The *Icon* Property 63

        The *Picture* Property 63

    The *WindowState* Property 64

    Other Properties 65

Revisiting the Calculator 65

    Planning Changes to the Form 65

Understanding Events That Happen to Forms 67

    The *Load* Event 67

    The *Unload* Event 69

Using the Controls in Your Toolbox 70

    Working with Controls in Your User Interface 70

    Adding Controls to a Form 71

    Setting Control Properties 71

    Changing Control Properties at Run Time 72

    Learning Commonly Used Properties of Controls 73

        The *Name* Property 73

        The *Caption* and *Name* Properties 76

Changing the Appearance of Your Text 77

    Understanding and Changing Fonts 77

        Changing Fonts 77

    Changing Other Text Appearance Properties 78

        The *Alignment* Property 78

        The *Value* Property 79

        The *Enabled* Property 79

        The *Visible* Property 79

        The *TabIndex* and *TabStop* Properties 79

        The *MousePointer* Property 81

Understanding Frequently Used Controls 81

    Command Buttons 82

Properties of the Command Buttons 83

Events of the Command Button Control 83

The Label Control 83

Properties of the Label Control 84

The Events of the Label Control 85

Text Boxes 85

Text Box Properties 86

Common Events of the Text Box Control 87

Chapter Summary 88

Test Your Understanding 88

True/False 88

Short Answer 89

Projects 89

Project 1:   Building a User Interface 89

Project 2:   Creating Forms 90

Project 3:   Creating a Stock Analysis Input Form 91

4 Using More Controls and Creating Graphics   93

Objectives 93

The Check Box Control 94

Properties of the Check Box Control 94

Check Box Events 95

The Option Button Control 95

Properties of the Option Button Control 96

Option Button Events 96

The Image Control 96

Displaying Pictures in an Image Control 97

The *Stretch* Property 97

Image Control Events 98

The Picture Box Control 98

Special Properties of the Picture Box Control 99

Events of the Picture Box Control 100

The Frame Control 100

Special Properties of the Frame Control 101

Events of the Frame Control 101

Introduction to Graphics 101

Using Foreground and Background Colors 102

Using the Line and Shape Controls 102

The Line Control 103

The *Name* Property 103

The Location Properties: *X1, Y1, X2, Y2* 103

The *BorderWidth* Property 104

The *BorderColor* Property 104

The *BorderStyle* Property 104

The *DrawMode* Property 105

The *Visible* Property 105

The Shape Control 106

The *Shape* Property 106

Location Properties: *Left, Top, Height,* and *Width* 107

The *Name* Property 107

Border Properties 107

The *BackColor* Property 107

The *BackStyle* Property 107

The *FillColor* and *FillStyle* Properties 107

Understanding Persistent Graphics and the *AutoRedraw* Property 108

Moving Pictures at Run Time 109

Copying Controls 111

Using Graphical Components from Windows in Your User Interface 112

Creating Toolbars with Buttons That Click 115

Chapter Summary 118

Test Your Understanding 119

True/False 119

Short Answer 119

Projects 120

Project 1:   Using Animation and Icons to Launch a Rocket 120

Project 2:   Exploring a Sample VB Program 122

Project 3:   Creating and Using Icons 122

5 Programming in Visual Basic   **123**

Objectives 123

Here's How VB Programs Work 124

Form Files 124

Code Modules 124

The AUTOLOAD.MAK File 125

How the Program Runs and Stops 125

Specifying the Start-Up Form 125

Including the *Sub Main* Procedure 126

Stopping the Program 126

A Quick Summary 126

Where Should the Code Go? 127

Procedures 128

Event Procedures (Event Handlers) 128

General Procedures 129

Sub Procedures and *Function* Procedures 130

Why Have More Than One Code Module in a Project? 131

The Mechanics of Writing Code 131

Sprinkling Your Code with Comments 131

Breaking Up Your Code 132

Organizing Your Code with Tabs 132

Declarations of Variables 133

Using Text and Numbers in a Program 133

What Are Variables? 133

Data Types 134

Numeric Variables 135

Strings 136
The Variant Data Type 137
Declaring Variables 138
How Do You Declare a Variable? 139
The Scope of a Variable 140
    Local Variables 141
    Module-Level Variables 141
    Global Variables 142
A Program to Illustrate the Scope of Variables 142
Static Variables 143
Storing Values in Variables 145
Getting Values Out of Variables 145
    Doing Math 145
Turning Digits into Text and Vice Versa 146
Manipulating the Characters in a String 147
Gluing Together Pieces of Text 147
Trimming Unwanted Text 147
Manipulating Strings 148
Calculating the Length of a String 148
Finding Text in a String 148
Pulling Out Part of a String 149
Putting It All Together 149
Using Character Values 150
Passing Variables to Functions and Procedures 152
Learning about Constants and Declaring Them 153
Chapter Summary 154
Test Your Understanding 154
    True/False 154
    Short Answer 155
    Projects 156
        Project 1: Writing Code for a Form 156
        Project 2: Writing Code for a Password 157
        Project 3: Writing Code to Calculate Ratios 157
        Project 4: Writing a Program to Convert Temperatures 159
        Project 5: Writing a Program to Calculate Area and Volume 160

6 Building a Complete Application   161
Objectives 161
Introducing Ted, a Text Editor Application 161
Defining Ted's Text Box Properties 162
Designing Ted's User Interface 164
Writing Ted's Event Procedures 167
Examining the *Form_Load* Procedure 167
Initializing the Check Boxes 169
Activating the Font Attributes 170
Using *Not* to Toggle a True/False Property Value 170
Using the *SetFocus* Method 171

Understanding Selected Text 173
Understanding the Cut, Copy, and Paste Buttons.................................. 174
Disabling Command Buttons 177
    Understanding the *Enabled* Property 177
    Using the General Procedure *BlankText*... 177
Invoking *BlankText* from Event Procedures 179
Viewing the Available Events... 182
    Viewing the Programmer-Defined Procedures 183
    Viewing the Event Procedures 183
Using Access Keys 184
    Creating Access Keys in Visual Basic 184
Working with the Form as a Text File 185
    Viewing TED.FRM 185
    Understanding the Text File 188
    Printing the Text File 188
    Modifying the Text File 189
Using Control Arrays 189
    Advantages of Control Arrays 189
    Creating a Control Array 190
    Working with the *Index* Property 190
    Using *Index* in Event Procedures 194
Printing and Running Ted from the Program Manager.......................... 197
Chapter Summary 201
Test Your Understanding 201
    True/False 201
    Short Answer 202
    Projects 203
        Project 1: Using Two Forms in a VB Project............................ 203
        Project 2: Using VB's Help on Functions 204

7 Program Flow and Decision Making   205
Objectives 205
Branching... 206
    Labels and Line Numbers 206
        Labels.. 206
        Line Numbers 207
    Unconditional Branching with *GoTo* 207
    Conditional Branching with *On-GoTo* 209
    The *On Error GoTo* Statement 210
Ending Program Execution 210
Conditional Testing... 211
    Testing with the *If* Instruction 211
        Single-Line *If*... 211
        Adding an *Else* Clause to *If-Then*....................................... 212
        Then and *Else* Clauses 213
        Types of Testing Expressions.. 214
        The Relational Operators... 215

Compound Testing Expressions 216
The Logical Operators 216
Nested *If* Instructions 217
Multiline *If* 218
Testing with *Select Case* 220
Looping 222
Using *For-Next* Loops 223
Using the *Step* Clause 225
Bypassing the Loop 226
Syntax of *For-Next* 227
Using Variables in a *For* Instruction 227
Excluding the Counter Variable in a *Next* Instruction 228
Placing a Loop in a Single Line 228
Using the Counter Variable 228
Nesting *For* Loops 229
Common Traps in *For* Loops 230
Terminating Loops with the *Exit For* Statement 231
Using *While-Wend* Loops 231
Using *Do-Loop* Loops 233
The *Exit Do* Statement 236
Using Nested *Do-Loop* Statements 237
Chapter Summary 238
Test Your Understanding 239
True/False 239
Short Answer 239
Projects 240
Project 1:   Writing a Program in Which the User Enters a Number .. 240
Project 2:   Writing a Program That Prompts the User to Enter
             Characters in a Text Box 241
Project 3:   Writing a Program That Displays the Number of Times a
             String Occurs 241
Project 4:   Writing Program Versions That Count and Display Specified
             Letters in a String 241
Project 5:   Writing a Program with Four Text Boxes 241
Project 6:   Writing a Program That Uses Integer and Prime
             Numbers 242

8 Testing and Debugging Your Program 243

Objectives 243
The First Computer Bug 244
Interactive Testing and Debugging 244
A Debugging Philosophy 245
Dealing with Run-Time Errors 248
Finding a Logic Error 252
General Debugging Tips 252
Debugging Execution Errors 253
Debugging with the Debug Window 254
Ways to Enter Break Mode 254

Viewing the Debug Window 255
Typing Instructions in the Debug Window 255
Using the Debug Window with Applications That Are Running 256
Interrupting a Program with Ctrl+Break 256
Resuming a Program 256
Debugging Logic Errors 257
Introducing VB's Debugging Tools 258
Tracing a Program 258
Setting Breakpoints 260
Watching a Program 261
Specifying a Watch Expression 261
Viewing the Watch Pane 262
Editing and Deleting a Watch Expression 263
Using Watchpoints 263
Using Instant Watch 263
Using Calls 264
Other Debugging Tools 265
Using the Set Next Statement 265
Using the Show Next Statement Option 266
Using *Stop* 266
A Summary of Debugging Tools 266
Error Handling and Error Trapping 267
Using Error Trapping 268
Enabling Error Trapping 269
The TRAPERR Application 269
Using *On Error GoTo 0* 271
The *On Error Resume Next* Instruction 271
Returning from an Error Handler 271
Writing an Error Handler 273
Using the *Err* and *Erl* Functions 273
Using the *Err* Statement 274
Simulating Errors 274
Using the *Error$* and *Error* Functions 275
A Philosophy of Error Handlers 276
Chapter Summary 277
Test Your Understanding 278
True/False 278
Short Answer 278
Projects 279
Project 1:   Using the Debug Window to Keep Track of a
Variable's Value 279
Project 2:   Practicing with VB's Debugging Tools 281

9 Using Arrays and Data Structures   283
Objectives 283
Working with Arrays 283
A Sample Program with Arrays 285

Understanding How ACE Works 288

Placing Data into Arrays 289

Dimensioning Arrays with *Dim* 290

Specifying the *As* Clause 291

Omitting the *As* Clause 291

Defining the Subscript Range 291

Declaring Multiple Arrays 292

Where to Put *Dim* Instructions 292

Changing the Base Subscript—*Option Base* 292

Using Variables and Constants as Array Dimensions 293

The Scope of Array Declarations 293

Declaring Arrays with *Static* and *Global* Instructions 294

Creating Static Arrays 294

Declaring Procedures with the *Static* Keyword 294

Declaring Fixed-Sized Arrays in Nonstatic Procedures 295

Creating Global Arrays 295

Table Lookup—A Sample Program with Arrays 295

Using the AREACODE Application 296

Understanding How AREACODE Works 299

Using Multidimensional Arrays 300

Fixed and Dynamic Allocation 302

Declaring Dynamic Arrays 302

Allocating a Dynamic Array with *ReDim* 303

Reallocating a Dynamic Array with *ReDim* 303

Erasing Arrays—The *Erase* Instruction 304

Declaring a Dynamic Array with *ReDim* 305

Using User-Defined Data Types 305

Defining a Record 306

User-Defined Types versus Variant Type Arrays 307

Declaring Variables of a Record Type 307

Referring to the Components of a Record Variable in Code 307

Passing Arrays and Records to User-Defined Procedures 307

Passing an Array 308

Passing a Record 308

Chapter Summary 309

Test Your Understanding 309

True/False 309

Short Answer 310

Projects 311

Project 1:   Writing a Program That Sorts Data Items 311

Project 2:   Rewriting the Program in Project 1 312

Project 3:   Writing a Program That Reads Letters into an Array 312

Project 4:   Writing a Program That Stores Numbers in Arrays 312

Project 5:   Rewriting the Program in Project 4 312

Project 6:   Writing a Program That Plays Tic-Tac-Toe 312

10 Learning to Use More Controls and Functions   **315**

Objectives 315
The List Box and Combo Box Controls 316
    Choosing between a List Box and a Combo Box 318
    Methods for List Boxes and Combo Boxes 319
    Properties of Controls for Both List Boxes and Combo Boxes 319
    Special List Box Properties 320
    Special Combo Box Properties 320
    Events of Both the List Boxes and Combo Boxes 321
Scroll Bar Controls 321
    Special Properties of Scroll Bars 321
    Events of the Scroll Bars 322
The Timer Control 323
    Properties of the Timer Control 323
    The Event for the Timer Control 324
The *Asc* and *Chr$* Functions 324
    Creating Line Feeds 325
The *Format$* Function 325
    Formatting Numeric Values with *Format$* 325
    Understanding Multipart Format Strings 326
    Using the Predefined Formats 327
    Formatting Dates and Times with *Format$* 327
Numeric Functions and Statements 327
    Trying the Examples in This Chapter 329
    Using the Rounding Functions 329
    Rounding Numbers 330
    Using Random Numbers 330
    Returning Random Numbers with *Rnd* 331
The Financial Functions 332
    Calculating a Loan Payment 332
    Determining Principal and Interest 333
Type Conversion 333
    Mixing Data Types 334
    Numeric Type Conversion 334
        Numeric Conversion with the Variant Data Type 335
        Explicitly Setting the Data Type of a Variant Variable 335
        Special Variant Values: Empty and *Null* 335
        Testing the Numeric Data Type of a Variant Variable 336
The *InputBox$* Function 336
    Understanding the *InputBox$* Function 336
    Specifying the Optional Parameters 337
The *InputBox* Function Used with Variant Variables 338
The *MsgBox* Function 338
    Understanding the Syntax of the *MsgBox* Function 339
    Specifying the *Options* Parameter 339
    Specifying the Default Button 340

Displaying an Icon 340
Changing the Modality 340
The *MsgBox* Statement 341
The DIALOGBX Example—No Forms Needed 342
Understanding How DIALOGBX Works 345
Chapter Summary 346
Test Your Understanding 347
True/False 347
Short Answer 347
Projects 348
Project 1:   Writing a Program That Displays the Time in a Label 348
Project 2:   Writing a Program That Simulates a Lottery Drawing 348
Project 3:   Modifying the Ted Application Developed in Chapter 6 . 349
Project 4:   Writing a Program That Contains No Forms 349
Project 5:   Writing a Program That Obtains a Table of Monthly
Payments 349
Project 6:   Writing a Program That Contains a List Box and a
Text Box 349

11 Designing Custom Menus   351

Objectives 351
Using the Menu Design Window 352
Available Tools 352
Menu Outline 353
Creating a Menu Application 354
Specifying an Access Key 356
Understanding Indentation 358
Designing a Menu Structure 361
Editing a Menu 362
Adding Menu Options 363
Adding Separator Bars 364
Using an Ellipsis to Indicate a Dialog Box 365
Polishing the Appearance of Menus 366
Adding a Shortcut Key 366
Using the *Enabled* Property 368
Coding Menu Options 370
Adding Code for Menu Procedures 371
Programming the Style Menu 373
Programming the Additional Properties 375
The *Checked* Property 375
The *Enabled* Property 378
Creating a Menu Control Array 379
Completing the Sample Application 381
Chapter Summary 382
Test Your Understanding 382
True/False 382
Short Answer 383
Projects 384

Project 1: Adding Menu Choices to Ted 384
Project 2: Adding Help and Exit Menus to Greeter 384

12 Processing Files   385

Objectives 386
Using the File Controls 386
    The File List Box Control 387
    The Directory List Box Control 388
    The Drive List Box Control 388
    Making File Controls Work Together 388
File and Directory Management in Visual Basic 389
Visual Basic's File-Processing Functions 390
Using Data Files 390
Using Data Files—General Concepts and Techniques 391
    Using the *Open* Statement 391
    Using the *Close* Statement 392
    Reading and Writing Data 392
Using Sequential Files.. 392
    Creating a Sequential File 393
        Opening the File 393
        Writing the Data 394
        Closing the File 394
    Appending to a Sequential File 395
    Reading a Sequential File 395
        The *Input #* Statement.. 396
        The *EOF* Function 396
        Using the *Line Input #* Statement 397
    Other Sequential File Tools... 397
    Example of a Sequential File 397
Using Random Files 398
    Designing a Random File 399
        Creating Text Fields in a Random File 399
        Creating Numeric Fields in a Random File 400
        A Sample Record 400
    Using a Random File with User-Defined Data Types...................... 401
        Defining the Record Variable 401
        Opening the File 401
        Writing Records with *Put* 402
        Reading Records with *Get* 403
        Closing the Random File 403
    Example of a Random File Program 403
    Using *Seek* and *Loc* with Random Files 404
    Using the *EOF* Function with Random Files 404
Using Binary Files 405
    Working with a Binary File 405
        Opening the File 405
        Reading and Writing Data 405

Closing the File 406
Using the *Seek* Statement 406
Using the *Seek* and *Loc* Functions 407
Using the *EOF* Function 407
Using the Common Dialog Box Control 407
The *Action* Property 408
Additional Properties of the Common Dialog Box 408
The *FileName* Property 409
The *Filter* Property 409
The *CancelError* Property 410
Chapter Summary 411
Test Your Understanding 412
True/False 412
Short Answer 412
Projects 413
Project 1:   Writing a Seminar Registration Application 413
Project 2:   Enhancing the Seminar Registration Application 414

13 Using the Grid Control   415

Objectives 415
Understanding the Grid Control 416
Understanding Grid Characteristics 416
Displaying Pictures 417
Controlling the Grid's Appearance 417
Setting Grid Properties 417
Row, *Col*, and *Text* 418
FixedRows and *FixedCols* 418
Rows and *Cols* 419
Selecting Cells 422
Enabling the User to Select Cells 424
Understanding the *Clip* Property 424
Using the *ColWidth* and *RowHeight* Properties 425
Using the *ColAlignment* and *FixedAlignment* Properties 426
Displaying Pictures in a Grid 428
Understanding the *TopRow*, *LeftCol*, and *ScrollBars* Properties 428
Understanding the Limitations of *TopRow* and *LeftCol* 429
Displaying Scroll Bars 429
Understanding the *HighLight* and *GridLines* Properties 429
Using the Grid Events *RowColChange* and *SelChange* 430
Using the *AddItem* and *RemoveItem* Methods 430
Understanding the PhoneBook Application 431
Working with the Command Button Array 435
Understanding the *UnSelect* Procedure 438
Understanding the *DeleteGridLine* Procedure 439
Creating the Floating Text Box 441
Method 1:   Using the *KeyPress* Event 441
Method 2:   Using a Text Box and a Grid Combination 442

Recognizing the Desire for Cell Editing 443
Writing and Reading the Data File 446
    Storing and Loading Large Amounts of Data When You Use a Grid 447
    Understanding the *SaveFile* Procedure 447
    Understanding the *LoadFile* Procedure 449
Chapter Summary 451
Test Your Understanding 451
    True/False 451
    Short Answer 452
    Projects 452
        Project 1:   Modifying a Program to Allow a User to Enter Data 452
        Project 2:   Writing a Program to Create a Spreadsheetlike
            Application 452
        Project 3:   Writing a Program for a Game 453

14 Using the Data Control to Interact with Databases   **455**
Objectives 456
Understanding Databases 456
Building the Database for the Sample Application 459
Understanding the Data Control 466
    Using Bound Controls 468
Building the Sample Application 469
Using Code with Data Controls 476
    Understanding the *Recordset* Property 476
    Understanding How the Delete Button Works 480
Using Queries with Single and Multiple Tables 480
    Relating Two Tables 485
Other Database Tools 487
Chapter Summary 487
Test Your Understanding 488
    True/False 488
    Short Answer 488
    Projects 489
        Project 1:   Entering Data into an Access 1.1 Database 489
        Project 2:   Adding Capabilities to the Seminar Registration
            Program 489
        Project 3:   Adding the Capability to List Registrant Data for All
            Seminars 489
        Project 4:   Adding Other Listing Capabilities 489
        Project 5:   Placing a Second Data Control on the Form 489

Index   **491**

CHAPTER 1

An Introduction to Programming for Windows

The most popular programs now being written for personal computers are Windows programs. This book teaches you how to write Windows programs using the Visual Basic programming language. Visual Basic provides the fastest and easiest way to write Windows programs—and it's the most fun. This first chapter explains some concepts with which you may not be familiar if you have never programmed before. If you are already an experienced programmer, you will probably want to skip this chapter and begin with Chapter 2.

Objectives

By the time you have finished this chapter, you will be able to

1. Understand What a Computer Program Is

2. Understand What a Programming Language Is and How It Is Used to Write a Program

3. Realize Why You Might Need to Write a Program Yourself

4. Outline the Steps Involved in Planning and Writing a Windows Computer Program

Program
A set of instructions telling a computer what to do; also referred to as software.

5. Understand the Logical Structures Used in Structured Programming

6. Understand the Most Commonly Used Types of Programming Statements

7. Understand the Basic Concepts Involved in Windows Programming

A **program** is a set of instructions that tells a computer what to do. This set of instructions, written by a computer programmer, is also called software. Just as a novel is a series of sentences properly arranged to form a complete story, a computer program is a series of statements designed to make your computer perform specific tasks. Anything you do with a computer—write reports, perform calculations, draw, or even play games—cannot be done if the proper programs are not loaded on your computer.

System software
Programs that enable the running of other programs.

Application software
Programs that perform useful tasks for you on the computer.

User
Someone who uses a computer to accomplish a specific task.

Without programs, your computer is just metal and plastic taking up space on your desk. That fact is the reason that computer programs are becoming an indispensable part of our lives. Some fundamental programs, like DOS and Windows, are called **systems software**. These programs enable the running of other programs, called **applications software**, that let us do useful things with our computers. Commercial applications software—like Word for Windows, Quicken, Excel, and a multitude of games—is written by programmers at Microsoft, Lotus, Borland, and other corporations.

The people who use these commercial applications programs to get work done or to have fun are referred to as **users**. For example, a secretary who uses a commercial word processing program to type letters and reports uses the computer and its programs. But the secretary is not a programmer because he or she does not write programs. If you want to write your own applications programs, you must first learn a programming language. Then you can be both a programmer and a user.

Programming Languages

Central processing unit (CPU)
The chip that processes program instructions and tells the computer what to do.

Machine language
The language understood by a CPU.

Programming language
A language used to create instructions for a computer.

Translation program
A program written to transform programming language statements into machine language.

Programmers would have a much easier time if programs could be written in standard English sentences. Unfortunately, this is not yet the case. Any computer understands only one language, and that language is totally different from English. The brain of a computer is an integrated circuit called the **central processing unit** (abbreviated **CPU**). The CPU can execute only instructions stored in the form of its own **machine language**. Machine language is a series of 0s and 1s (binary numbers). These binary numbers represent a program's instructions to the CPU. Machine languages, however, are difficult to learn and cannot be efficiently used by humans to write programs. So, to enable people to write instructions for a CPU, programming languages were developed.

There are many **programming languages**. Some commonly used programming languages are Ada, Pascal, C, C++, Visual C, Visual Basic, QBASIC, COBOL, and FORTRAN. Much of current commercial software development uses these languages. Programming languages use a few English words along with algebraic and mathematical symbols.

The program instructions you enter in a programming language are translated into machine language instructions for the CPU to execute. How does this translation process occur if the computer's CPU still understands only its machine language?

The answer is that another program has been written to perform the programming language to machine language translation. This **translation program**, written by expert programmers, is in machine language. The need for an accurate translation of your program is the reason that the rules of a programming language like Visual Basic are so strict. If you do not follow the programming language rules, the translation program will get so confused that it can't continue. The translation program then stops and produces error messages. Don't worry, though, the programming mistakes you make won't hurt your computer.

The process of writing a program in a programming language is referred to as
...ding. Remember, you write in a programming language, and you must follow
...es because another special computer program has to **translate** your pro-
...ing language statements into the central processing unit's machine lan-
...You might think of a computer's CPU chip as a genius who understands
...aelic. This genius will patiently wait to try to help you until you get your
...3asic program right.

...our program is translated into machine language, a computer can exe-
... instructions. The computer programs you buy (Windows, Excel,
...rfect, Quicken, and others) were originally written in a programming
...e. They were translated into machine language before being placed on
...d sent to your computer store. Your computer can run a program in the
...machine language. When the computer starts executing a program's
...instructions, we say that the computer is **running the program**.

...in a program is called a **bug**. If the computer finds such a big error in
...gram that the computer cannot continue executing your program, we
...our program has "blown up." Obviously, this is not something you
...appen, so you must be very careful both when writing and when
...a program.

...nake two types of programming errors. **Syntax errors** are errors in
...f the language itself. **Logical errors** are errors that result from a fault
...sign of the program. Logical errors are usually the toughest kind of
...d and fix in a program. Logical errors can be avoided *only* if you are
..., systematic, and thorough in your thinking processes. *The computer*
...logical errors in your program. Obviously, this fact is comforting be-
...ow that the only logical errors in your program are errors that you
...urself.

...I agree, maybe it is just a small comfort. It is certainly not fun to
...arelessness pointed out to us. And it is certainly very frustrating to
...n front of your computer trying to fix your program. But get used
...ty is that if your program doesn't work, there are no excuses. You
...stood. You have been careless. You have placed errors in your pro-
...have to find and fix them.

...gram has errors, you must find them. This process is called **de-**
...program. Visual Basic has a built-in debugger to help you quickly
...s in your code. Using the debugger and developing a plan for
...nd identification is discussed in Chapter 8, "Testing and Debug-
...ogram."

Programs that are without errors themselves and that can handle any predictable
user error are called "bullet proof." Such programs are desirable but hard to
achieve. Even more desirable are programs that, from the design stage on, are
developed in such a way that no bugs are ever introduced. Errorless programs
happen only if you build them carefully and systematically at all stages of program development. To help you think thoroughly and systematically, some

steps to follow when writing a program are recommended later in this chapter. In a sense, these steps are a kind of quality-assurance program for your programs. Your goal is zero defects from start to finish of your program.

The aspect of computer programming that first shocks and then frustrates students is the care and precision with which they must plan and then write their programs. Computers can't read your mind or make any assumptions. They will carefully do exactly what you tell them—if you tell them clearly and completely. Writing a computer program is in some ways like opening a combination lock. You have to do all the right things in exactly the right order or the combination won't work. And don't forget, when writing a program, you must observe all the rules of the programming language you are using.

Translation Programs: Compilers and Interpreters

Source code
The typed program instructions that you create.

Program statements in a programming language like Visual Basic are called **source code** because they are the source of the computer's instructions. A programmer must use either a compiler or an interpreter to translate programming language statements into **machine code** (machine language statements).

Machine code
Machine language statements.

The primary difference between a compiler and an interpreter lies in the way they translate and execute a program. A **compiler** translates the entire program into machine language. If no programming language errors (syntax errors) are found during translation, the compiler saves the machine code in a disk file. Then your whole program can be run without the need for any additional translation. If you want to run the program again, you simply run the machine code in the disk file; you do not need to translate again. Another advantage of compiler translation is that the resulting machine code runs on the computer much faster than the machine code produced by an interpreter. The compiler optimizes the code for speed in execution. The disadvantage of a compiler is that the programmer must wait until the entire program has been compiled before any programming language syntax error (no matter how small) is identified by the translator.

Compiler
A program that translates an entire program from programming language into machine language and saves the machine language in a disk file.

Interpreter
A program that translates a program from programming language into machine language by translating and executing one statement at a time.

An **interpreter**, on the other hand, reads, translates, and executes the statements one at a time. Interpreters usually check the syntax of your programming language statements as soon as you type them. Any programming language errors in a program statement are revealed immediately, and you can correct them. The disadvantage of interpreters is that the computer executes your program slowly. Furthermore, the translation process must be done each time you run the program because the interpreter does not save the executable machine code version of your program interpreter.

Which Programming Language Is the Best?

Why are there so many programming languages? Is one language better than another? The answer is both yes and no. Each language was developed to perform a particular function. One language may be best for calculating charts of the results of particle physics experiments; another language may be best for creating business reports. The language you choose for a project is determined by the language's suitability for the task.

Remember that some programs can be run on a personal computer that uses only DOS, but other programs also require Microsoft Windows. The most popular programs for personal computers are Windows programs because they are designed to use the Windows interface. Visual Basic was designed to be the easiest language to use to write a Windows program.

Now, you need to understand what a user interface means and why it is important.

Interface

User interface
The way a program looks and the way the user interacts with the program.

Graphical user interface
An interface that communicates by means of pictures and other graphical objects.

The way a program looks and feels to its users is important for its success. **User interface** is the general term designating how the program looks on the user's screen and the way in which the user communicates with the program. **Graphical user interfaces** (**GUIs**) communicate with the user by displaying pictures and other standard objects. The user responds to the graphical display by using the mouse or typing at the keyboard.

An application program has a poor interface if its screens are garishly colored, confusing, or unpleasant to look at. The interface is poor if it lacks proper information to guide the user. On the other hand, a program has a good interface if its screens are clearly organized and logical, with functions easily accessible and displayed in a standard way.

Most application programs consist of a series of steps that implement the cycle:

INPUT —> PROCESSING —> OUTPUT

The user provides input values, the program performs the proper processing on the input, and (usually) the program displays the resulting output. Of course, the whole point of a program is to produce the proper output for a given input. If the user is confused by the program's interface and provides incomplete or incorrect input, you can be sure that the program will either "blow up" (stop) or produce incorrect output: "Garbage in ... Garbage out."

Therefore, one of your main goals as a programmer is to make your program easy for the user to use correctly. Your program's interface should also display and label the output clearly. Your screen design should be readable, easy on the eyes, and unobtrusively colored. The instructions should be logical and easy to understand. Instructions that can be readily comprehended are called intuitive. The more intuitive a program is, the easier it is to use. If necessary, you should provide a special Help screen for the users to access. As its name suggests, a Help screen provides useful information and tips on the program for the user.

The Standards of the Windows Interface

Since the dawn of computing, programmers have been inventing their own interfaces. This practice resulted in confusion, and users of popular applications software packages found that each program's user interface was different. Microsoft Corporation has introduced a set of standards for any application program sold as a Windows program. Microsoft specified the standards for the user interface that programmers must follow. Programmers can save time by writing Windows-compliant programs (programs that follow the Windows standard) because the programmers don't have to develop a unique interface for each application. Visual Basic includes all the programming tools required to create good Windows-compliant user interfaces.

Since Microsoft introduced the Windows standards, the confusion and lack of a common and consistent interface is ending. Windows-compliant programs offer users an enormous advantage. After a user learns the conventions of the Windows standard interface, she or he can operate other Windows-compliant programs with relative ease.

What Is Visual Basic?

Visual Basic was developed from Microsoft's QBasic, but Visual Basic has many extra features. The *Visual* part of Visual Basic comes from the fact that it can produce a Windows-compliant user interface. Basic stands for *Beginners All-Purpose Symbolic Instruction Code*. Its name seems intimidating, yet BASIC has been a starting point for many programmers. It was developed for mainframe computers at Dartmouth College in the 1960s and has been subsequently rewritten for personal computers. BASIC may lack some of the sophisticated features of programming languages like Pascal, C, and C++, but it is much easier to learn and is excellent for writing programs. A new BASIC programmer can understand and begin writing programs in a relatively short time. For example, the following QBasic program displays a message and the sum of three numbers.

Listing 1.1 A simple program written in QBasic.

```
' QBASIC program to
' Print the sum of three numbers

Print "The sum of 7 + 3 + 5 is ";
Print 7 + 3 + 5
```

Programs can be as simple as the short example shown in Listing 1.1 or as complex as those used by NASA to control space missions. A program to control the flight of a space shuttle may contain hundreds of thousands of programming language statements. The complexity of a program depends on the job it must perform.

Walk into any software store, and check the shelves. You can find computer programs of every type, size, description, and price. Word processing, spreadsheet, database, project management, personal organizers, data communications, computer-aided design, and game programs are all available.

Why Write a Program?

Many commercially available programs are excellent, some are adequate, and a few are not worth the disks they are stored on. With such an enormous number of programs available, you may wonder why new programs are needed. All computer programs are written to help use a computer to solve a problem (or for you to entertain yourself). There are several good reasons why you might write a program, three of which are discussed in the following sections.

Programming for Fun

You can use your programming skills in a variety of ways for your own enjoyment, the amazement of your friends, and the confusion of your enemies. Many programmers like to write additions to existing software that either correct a problem or offer easier, more elegant ways of accomplishing the program's functions. You can also design your own games, instruct your computer to issue a greeting when you turn it on, catalog your collection of CDs, or keep track of your friends' and relatives' birthdays. You can even have a birthday card automatically printed and ready for mailing a few days in advance.

It is a wonderful feeling of accomplishment when you run your first program and see that it actually works!

Programming Small Utilities

Utility
A program that performs a specific task.

Perhaps the most common reason to write a program is to create a small utility. A **utility** is a program that does a specific task or tasks. Utilities solve a problem or fill an immediate need. Examples of utilities are a short program that calculates a formula, a program that reads a text file and formats it for a printer, and a program that rearranges data in a file. Programs in this category may not have polished user interfaces, but they get the job done.

Programming as a Profession

A glance at the employment section of a city newspaper will show you that many programming jobs are available. Basically, these jobs are of two types; the independent programmer and the programmer employed by an organization.

Independent Programmer

You may discover an area for which no computer programs exist or where the existing software is inadequate. As an independent programmer, you must be able to analyze the situation and determine whether a program can perform the task faster and more efficiently. If so, the situation is a perfect candidate for your programming skills.

For example, consider the fictional company International Croquet Mallet Corporation (ICMC)—based in Dallas. You learn that ICMC distributes croquet mallets worldwide and therefore receives funds not only in dollars but in escudos, francs, marks, rubles, and guilders. These funds are kept in the countries where the payments are made until the dollar ratio is high enough to permit the company's maximum benefit on the exchange rate. The company's accountants check the exchange rate daily and notify the company when they feel that a transfer of funds should occur. The company managers then execute the transfer.

You could offer to assist this company by writing a program that automatically scans the exchange rates and identifies those countries whose currency has increased in dollar value. If the company's foreign funds in one country and the currency exchange rate with that country have reached a certain level, your program could direct an electronic funds transfer from the foreign bank to the company's U.S. account. The program would then calculate the amount of profit made on the exchange.

Instead of using the labor of several professionals, one employee can operate the program and accomplish the transfers in a matter of seconds rather than hours. There is no longer a need for lengthy and complex manual calculations and record keeping; your program stores all the information in a file that can be retrieved at any time.

Working as a Programmer for a Business or a Software Company

It would be a kinder world if programmers could write only personally enjoyable and fulfilling programs. The vast majority of programs, however, are written to meet the specific requirements of the company employing the programmer. In these cases, the problem has been identified; the programmer's task is to find the solution. Your programming skills are defined by how well the program you write deals with these solutions.

Suppose that you are employed as a programmer by ICMC, which produces croquet mallets of various lengths and colors. Suppose that the company's senior managers want to know the lengths and colors that sell best in certain countries. Your task is to write a program that scans the orders, breaks down the data into the necessary categories, and prints the information in a clear and concise form.

For this project, you may be asked to write the program on your own. For a larger, more complex project, you may be part of a team of programmers working together. As a member of a programming team, you may be responsible for one small portion of the program, which will be integrated with the work of your colleagues.

Problem Solving with the Computer

Problem definition
A clear statement of the problem to be solved.

All the programming that has been mentioned involves problem solving with the computer. In a programming language class, you will learn to program when your instructor gives you problems to solve. But you should not begin immediately to code your program. Rather, you first have some thinking to do about the problem. This step in the programming process, often called **problem definition**, can save you a great deal of time.

Whether you are coding a program to solve a problem at school, on your job, or at home, your first step should always be to define the problem clearly. If you cannot *write out* a clear description of the problem in English, you don't understand the problem well enough to create your program. And you won't suddenly gain clarity *as* you code your program. What you will do is waste time solving some other problems and then going back to start over again. Work smart. Write out the problem description completely. Once you know where you have to go, you can jot down *in English* a plan to get you there. This process is called program design.

Program design
A written sketch of the interface screens and the steps a computer program must accomplish.

During the **program design** phase of the programming process, you sketch out what you will need on your user interface screens and write out, in English, the steps that your computer program must accomplish to reach your goal—a solved problem. *Strongly resist the urge to start coding your program immediately.* Once you start coding, you will be caught up in the idiosyncrasies of the programming language. You won't be able to focus on making a plan to reach your goal. Remember the old programmer's motto: Prior Planning Prevents Poor Programming.

Follow a proven strategy; divide your work into these steps and conquer:

1. Understand your problem.

2. Design your problem solution (the program design) logically by thinking it through step-by-step and writing it out carefully.

3. Code the program in a programming language.

4. Test the program, and debug it.

In the next section, the crucial program design process is reviewed in more detail.

When you have completed an assigned reading in this text, you will have a general understanding of the kind of Visual Basic statements you will need to use in the next programming assignment. When you receive the assignment, be sure to write out your own description of the task your instructor has set for you (the problem definition). Then write an English outline of exactly what the program will do. You can verify your understanding with your instructor if necessary.

Algorithm
A list of the steps needed to solve a problem.

Remember, your Visual Basic code will implement a series of steps that follow the INPUT —> PROCESSING —> OUTPUT cycle. So, before you start entering programming language statements, you need to plan your work by listing and (optionally) numbering the steps involved. These steps are called your **algorithm**. An algorithm is like a logical recipe for the processing in a program. As you think through and write out the steps (your algorithm) that will produce the desired output from a given input, you also need to sketch what the program's input and output screens will look like.

You will move back and forth between planning the processing steps (called "constructing your algorithm") and creating the input and output screens. As you work on the algorithm, you usually realize that you need some additional pieces of information from the person using the program. Your sketch of the input screen must be modified to include a clear way for the user to enter the additional information. Program and input screen design are discussed in more depth throughout this text.

Note the emphasis on planning your program and sketching the input screen *before* you start to use the programming language. This point is very important. Writing a program can be a difficult and complicated process—especially when you are beginning to learn a programming language. Whenever you are faced with a problem, you should break it down into a series of smaller (and usually simpler) steps. Because you need to understand this process very well, here is a review:

1. Think through the logical steps the computer must follow in your algorithm, and sketch the input and output screens.

2. Try to "play computer" with your algorithm. Try to step back and look at the steps in your algorithm with fresh eyes. Don't "see" anything that isn't there. Don't assume anything or skip steps. Follow each step and verify that you have, in fact, solved your problem.

Only after you have completely finished the program design should you begin coding your input and output screens and your algorithm in the programming language. If you start coding before you have completely designed your program, any code you enter will come to control the whole design of the program and all your thinking (the tail will wag the dog).

Instead of efficiently focusing on one step in program design at a time, you will spread your concentration thin. You will always have "Just one more bug to fix but I know what it is." Four days of hard work later, you will still have "Just one more bug to fix but I know what it is." You will actually slow program design, create errors due to awkward and contorted logic, and greatly increase programmer frustration. Don't forget the programmer's motto: "When you are neck deep in alligators, it's hard to remember that your original objective was to drain the swamp."

Programming Tools: Flowcharts and Pseudocode

Computer science has produced a number of tools to help you think through your algorithm. Two of these tools are flowcharts and pseudocode.

Flowcharts

Flowchart
A graphical representation of your program plan.

Most beginning programming classes teach you how to create a flowchart. A **flowchart** is a blueprint (graphical representation) of your program plan. A flowchart details the major steps, decisions, and branches that determine how your program runs.

In this chapter, you will see several examples of flowcharting. The examples, however, will generally use pseudocode to illustrate an algorithm. You will find that sketching a flowchart is a real aid to thinking through a tricky part of your program design.

Pseudocode

Pseudocode
A kind of structured English that resembles programming code.

Many programmers combine flowcharts with pseudocode. **Pseudocode** is a kind of structured English that lends itself to program design. Pseudocode is easily converted into code in any programming language.

Pseudocode is another way of creating an outline of what a program should do. It is a program instruction written in plain English. The short program in Listing 1.1 might originally have been outlined as follows:

> Print a message.
> Calculate the sum of three numbers.
> Print the result.

When you write the actual program, you replace the preceding sentences with real programming language statements that tell your computer to perform the tasks described. Outlining your program in pseudocode is an excellent way to see the task as a whole and provides you with much of the information you need to write the actual code. Pseudocode statements are not usually numbered. However, if you find it helpful to number the steps, do so.

After the outline is complete, you have an overview of how your program code should work. Now you are ready to start coding your program language statements.

Figure 1.1 illustrates the techniques of flowcharting and pseudocode and shows the program-logic structures you will use frequently.

Figure 1.1

Examples of sequence flowcharts and pseudocode.

Sequence Flowchart

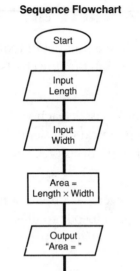

Sequence Pseudocode

Input Rectangle Length
Input Rectangle Width
Calculate Area = Length × Width
Output Label for Result
Output Area

IF-THEN-ELSE Flowchart

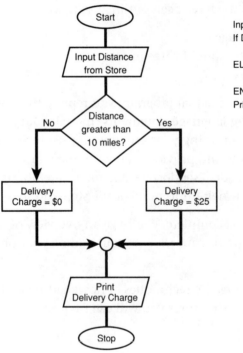

IF-THEN-ELSE Pseudocode

Input Distance from Store
If Distance > 10 miles THEN
    Delivery Charge = $25.00
ELSE
    Delivery Charge = $0.00
END IF
Print Delivery Charge

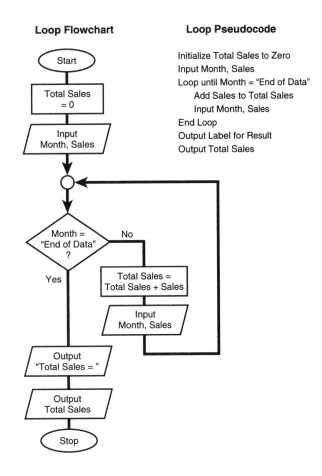

Loop Flowchart

Loop Pseudocode

```
Initialize Total Sales to Zero
Input Month, Sales
Loop until Month = "End of Data"
    Add Sales to Total Sales
    Input Month, Sales
End Loop
Output Label for Result
Output Total Sales
```

Introduction to Programming Statements

The first part of this chapter introduces you to the general purpose of and steps involved in programming. This section defines and describes many types of statements and shows you how they are used to create computer programs.

Learning to program is a hands-on experience. Reading theory and looking at examples can help you, but seeing the results on your computer screen drives home the theory. This chapter begins by showing you some program examples written in pseudocode. In later chapters, you see actual Visual Basic examples.

Overview of Programming Statements

This section provides an overview of various programming statements. These examples are designed to help you see how the statements look in a program. You will also be shown the logic of the statements in pseudocode and flow-charts.

Programming statement
A specialized set of instructions that tell a computer how to perform a task.

Programming statements are specialized sets of source code instructions that tell a computer how to perform a task. These statements are executed one after another until the program ends. To help you better understand programming statements, the following lines show how the AddSum program (from earlier in the chapter) would look in pseudocode.

> Print a message showing what is being added.
> Calculate the sum of three numbers.
> Print the result.

Hard coded
Values in a program are said to be hard coded if there is no way for the user to enter a different set of values.

You can see that a program modeled from the preceding pseudocode doesn't really do much. Because the example requires no input from a user, it has no real user interface. The numbers to be added are **hard coded**; that is, the user cannot add any numbers other than the numbers coded into the program, for this example, 7, 5, and 3. The output produces a message and the number *15* on a line by itself, with no explanation of what that number means. By adding some input and output statements to this program, you can make it more useful. The following pseudocode shows the AddSum program with some additional statements:

> Display to the user a short description of what this program does.
> Display what input it expects.
> Ask for the first value.
> Store the first value and call it A.
> Ask for the second value.
> Store the second value and call it B.
> Ask for the third value.
> Store the third value and call it C.
> Add the three stored values together and store the result as SUM.
> Display the message "The Sum of the numbers that you entered is:" to the user.
> Display the value of SUM to the user.

With just a few additions, the program this pseudocode describes has gained a measure of flexibility. A user can now total any three numbers by running this program.

Two of the most important things programs do are receive input and produce output. As the programmer, you decide what kind of input your program needs and what output the program produces.

By having your program ask the user for the data it requires to run, you have eliminated guesswork on the part of the user. Otherwise, the user is faced with an empty screen and no explanation of what input the program expects.

Variables

A variable is a fundamental element of any programming language. You may recall from basic algebra that a variable is something that changes. For example, in the equation: $X = Y + 5$, the variables (X and Y) can hold different values, and when Y changes, so does X. Think of X or Y as a box (in computer memory) that can hold a number. You (or the computer) can place any single value in this box. A current value of Y (for example, 10) will remain there until you change or remove it. While Y is 10, X will contain 15. If you enter a new value for Y, say 35, the old value (10) is cleared from the variable (the computer's memory location). The variable Y now contains only the number 35. The variable X will, as a result of the computation, now contain 40.

Variable

A named area in RAM that stores a value.

When programming a computer, you use variables in much the same way that you use them in algebra. A **variable** is an area the computer sets aside for you in the computer's internal memory (RAM). The data stored in a variable may change. You refer to the memory location in your program by using the name of the variable. Just as in algebra, if you have a program variable named Y, visualize an empty box marked Y. This box, which represents a location in computer memory, can accept (contain) only one item at a time. Each numeric memory address or location in your computer's RAM can be considered a box.

Identifier

A variable name.

Computers usually have millions of memory locations. When coding in a programming language, you assign an **identifier** (variable name) to each of these locations. Using identifiers to represent specific locations in memory is much easier than using actual numeric memory addresses. If the user enters a new value for the variable when he or she runs the program, the old value is replaced by the new value. When you use a variable name in a program, the computer substitutes the actual contents of the memory location for the variable name. In Visual Basic, you simply enter an equation as you do in algebra: for example, $X = Y + 5$.

The expanded pseudocode example in the preceding section asked the user for values and then stored them in the computer's memory. These values are stored in variables. Specifically, data values are stored in memory at different locations. The computer is capable of manipulating variables and changing their values.

The variables in the AddSum pseudocode example are named A, B, C, and Sum. In such a short program, you can easily remember what type of information each variable is supposed to hold and what each is used for. As a program grows, however, keeping track of variables with such short names becomes much more difficult. You can give variables names that help you remember the purpose they serve in your program. Instead of A, B, and C, for example, you could name your variables `FirstNumber`, `SecondNumber`, and `ThirdNumber`.

Longer names make your program much clearer to any programmer who tries to read and follow it—and clearer to you if you have to go back and revise your code six months or a year after you wrote it. A more detailed discussion of variables can be found in Chapter 5, "Programming in Visual Basic."

Program flow
The order in which statements are executed in a program.

Branching
Changing the order in which statements are executed.

Conditional statement
A program statement that causes control of the program to jump to a different point.

Figure 1.2
A linear flowchart for the original AddSum program.

Program Flow

The examples in this chapter have been executed in a linear fashion—the statements are performed in order from top to bottom. The order of the statements never varies.

As programs become more complicated, however, you will sometimes want to change the **program flow** (the order in which statements are executed) based on the value of one of the variables or the occurrence of a specific event. Changing the order in which statements are executed is called **branching**.

You can use pseudocode or flowcharts to design the flow of the program. The program statement that causes control of the program to jump to a different point is called a **conditional statement**. You learn more about conditional statements in Chapter 7. Figure 1.2 shows a flowchart of the original AddSum addition program. Notice that it is linear and has no branches.

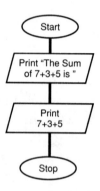

Figure 1.3 shows a flowchart of a program, similar to the AddSum program, that branches on a certain condition. You can see where the program branches based on the value of the variable.

Types of Programming Language Statements

As you write programs, you use different types of programming language statements. The following sections explain the most common types of statements. Those included are comment, assignment, input, output, conditional, case, and loop statements.

Comments

Comment
An annotation or explanation of code.

A **comment** is an annotation or explanation of code and is an important part of a programmer's toolbox. Writing comments along with your code can help you, or anyone else who reads your program, understand what each section of your program does. Many programmers start coding by entering all their pseudocode statements as comment statements. This practice enables them to see the steps in their plan on-screen as they enter their program. They follow each pseudocode statement with the programming language statements that implement that pseudocode step. This excellent programming practice is highly recommended.

Figure 1.3
A branching flowchart for the revised AddSum program.

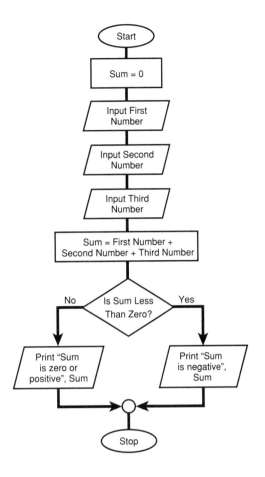

In Visual Basic, you indicate the beginning of a comment with an apostrophe ('). Everything that follows until the end of that line is considered part of the comment, and your program ignores it. Rem, short for remark, is another way to mark a comment in Visual Basic. The following lines show examples of the two forms comments can take in Visual Basic:

```
'This is a program comment
Rem This is a program comment too.
```

You should use comments liberally throughout your programs. Commenting a ten-line program might seem like overkill; but as you learn more and your programs grow longer, having a record of what you were *intending* to do when you wrote each section of code becomes essential. Careful commenting and documentation can simplify revisions later. Comments aid both you and others who may be working on your program. To someone seeing your program for the first time, your comments are like a road map indicating what each section is supposed to do.

Commenting can also help you find and remove program bugs. Many times you can find a bug by checking the comments to see what the program is supposed to be doing at a certain point; then you can see whether the code matches the comment. This practice is especially useful when you are first learning to program. Remember, you can enter your pseudocode program plan as comments. Then, under each comment, you fill in the Visual Basic statements that implement the pseudocode in the comment.

Assignment Statements

Assignment statements assign values to a variable. You can assign both numbers and text to variables, as shown in the following examples. An equal sign (=) is used to make an assignment. Text must be enclosed in quotation marks. A short explanation of the code follows each example:

```
A = B
```

Places the contents of variable B into variable A.

```
Total = SubTotal + Tax
```

Adds the contents of the variables and places the result into a variable named Total.

```
Name = "Lloyd Elm"
```

Places a character string (what is inside the quotation marks) into the variable Name.

You can assign the contents of any variable to a variable of the same type. Variable types are discussed in Chapter 5, "Programming in Visual Basic." You can evaluate an expression and set a variable equal to it. The most commonly used arithmetic operators used in programming are + (addition), – (subtraction), * (multiplication), / (division), and ^ (exponentiation).

Input Statements

All programming languages have input statements. Input statements bring data into a program. A program to generate a customer's bill requires input statements. The user enters each item a customer ordered. Then the program instructs the computer to total the order, save the order on disk, and print the order on the printer.

The input statement requests data, and the program then processes this data to produce the desired output. The following pseudocode represents a program that would accept and print item descriptions, prices, and quantities ordered until the user enters the word *END*.

> Display the program title on-screen.
> Display the program instructions to the user.
>
> BEGIN:
> > Ask the user for an item description, price, and quantity ordered.
> > Input the variables Item, Description, and Quantity.
> > If Item equals the word END, end the program.
> > Otherwise, print Item, Description, and Quantity on the printer.
> > Go back and repeat, starting from the word BEGIN.

Whenever a program receives input interactively (from a user), you must include a good user interface. The interface does not have to be fancy, but it should give the user a clear idea of what he or she must do next to make the program perform correctly.

Input comes from many different places. It can come from files on your hard drive or floppy disk drives, a keyboard, mouse, graphics tablet, trackball, touch screen, modem, fax card, or numerous other sources.

Reading a file
Getting information from a disk file.

The preceding pseudocode represents a program that requests user input from the keyboard. For this application, keyboard input is fine. On many occasions, however, you must retrieve information from a disk file. Getting information from a file is called **reading a file**. Storing information in a file is called **writing to a file**. Chapter 12, "Processing Files," provides a more detailed discussion of storing and retrieving data.

Writing to a file
Storing information in a disk file.

Output Statements

Regardless of how good your program logic is, nobody will know it if your program has no output statements. You could say that the purpose of a program *is* its output. A program must display its results. However, *output* means more than printing to the screen. Just as input statements can receive input from different sources, output statements can send output to screens, printers, disk files, modems, or even to a sound card so that your computer can tell you the results by voice. All programming languages have instructions to do output in some form. For example, Visual Basic programmers can use the keyword `Print` to send output to the screen. In the following chapters, this text covers screen, printer, and disk file output statements.

Conditional Statements

If (you can't stand the heat) Then stay out of the kitchen.

Conditional statement
A statement that evaluates a condition and then takes an action based on that condition.

This statement is a **conditional statement**. Its name comes from the fact that it evaluates a condition and then takes an action based on that condition. If the words or expressions within the parentheses evaluate to *true*, the part of the statement following the word `Then` is executed. If the expression within the parentheses evaluates to *false*, whatever action comes after `Then` is ignored. The program continues with the next statement following the `If`-`Then` statement.

You can expand this example by adding another condition:

If you can't stand the heat, Then stay out of the kitchen, or Else put the roast in the oven.

The `Else` statement provides another option if the condition is false.

In the first case, only one action can be taken. If you can't stand the heat, then you stay out of the kitchen. With the `Else` option, you are given one action if you cannot stand the heat and another action if you can.

In the pseudocode example shown in the discussion of input statements, the variable `Item` was tested to see whether it contained the word `End`. In Visual Basic, you could code this statement as

```
If (Item = "End") Then End
```

`If`-`Then` statements are discussed further in Chapter 7, "Program Flow and Decision Making."

Case Statements

Case statement
A shortened conditional statement.

Case statements are a shorthand way of writing conditional statements. If you have a long or complicated expression to evaluate and you must compare it to two or more conditional values (two or more tests on the expression), you can replace the series of If-Then tests with one Select Case statement. The following example shows a program that uses a series of If-Then conditional statements:

```
If (FirstName$ = "Sally") Then
    Print "Hi Sally!"
    End
End If

If (FirstName$ = "David") Then
    Print "Yo, Dave!"
    End
End If

If (FirstName$ = "Cassie") Then
    Print "Where's Sally?"
    End
End IF
```

The following code example uses the Select Case statement to perform the same task as in the preceding example.

```
Select Case FirstName$
    Case "Sally"
        Print "Hi Sally!"
    Case "David"
        Print "Yo, Dave!"
    Case "Cassie"
        Print "Where's Sally?"
End Select
```

The Select Case statement decreases the size of the program and makes the code clearer and more efficient. Select Case statements are very useful when the program needs to check input against a fixed list of values.

Clarity is one good reason for using a Select Case statement. Another reason is that the expression you are testing is evaluated only once, rather than once for every If statement; this factor makes your program run faster. The more complicated the test expression is, the more time you save by using Select Case statements. Chapter 7, "Program Flow and Decision Making," explores Select Case statements in more detail.

Loops

Loop
A statement that causes the computer to repeat an action or actions until a specified condition is met.

A **loop** causes the computer to repeat the execution of a statement or set of statements until a condition you have specified has been met. A looping structure either begins or ends with the test of a condition. There are several kinds of loop statements, and you can control the flow of your program by using them. The previous pseudocode example of an order entry program contains a loop. The program continues accepting and printing item descriptions, prices, and quantities ordered until the user enters the word End. When the user enters End, the program "drops out" of the loop.

Visual Basic has four different ways to set up a loop in a program. Loops are discussed in more detail in Chapter 7, "Program Flow and Decision Making."

Windows Object-Oriented Event-Driven Programming

Object
Identifiable shape (a window, scroll bar, or command button) on a computer screen.

Object-Oriented Programming (OOPs)
The type of programming necessary to use Windows graphical objects like command buttons, scroll bars, and menus.

Event
An action that occurs to an object while a VB program is running.

Event-driven programming
A type of programming in which the user of a program determines the next procedure by causing an event to occur to an object.

Procedure
A group of statements in the Visual Basic programming language.

As you know from having used Windows, the user can provide input by typing from the keyboard and by using a mouse to click buttons, manipulate scroll bars, and make choices from lists or menus. A language used to write programs for Windows must be capable of creating all the standard **objects** you see when you use Windows or a program for Windows. Visual Basic for Windows was designed to write programs for Windows. Other languages—such as QBasic, FORTRAN, COBOL, and Pascal—don't have the capacity to generate or respond to a Windows-type interface. This fact means that designing the screen (or screens) that provide input for a Windows program is more important (and challenging) than designing the user interface for a DOS program.

The user interface is not all that is different about programs that use a graphical user interface. When you write programs using Visual Basic, you will be writing programs that are *object-oriented* and *event-driven*. **Object-Oriented Programming (OOPs)** is something new. Visual Basic does not meet all the technical criteria to be called a "true" object-oriented language. Nevertheless, if you have written programs in other (non-GUI) languages, you will immediately see that Windows programming is different. The user manipulates on-screen objects, such as buttons, icons, and menus, to trigger the running of the program.

In Visual Basic, the objects that appear on the user interface screen have associated programming language code that belongs to the object. As a result, the program code is not all in one big chunk (as it is with DOS programs). Rather, as illustrated in figure 1.4, pieces of code can be scattered to a variety of locations. The VB program referenced in figure 1.4 would consist of three form modules and two code modules. (Form modules and code modules are discussed in Chapters 2 through 5). Pieces of code could be placed in any of these locations. All the pieces of code must work together to produce a properly functioning program. This fact is one reason why a written plan of your program is so important.

The reason that the objects (buttons, scroll bars, menus) have Visual Basic code associated with them is that they must be capable of responding to user-generated **events**. That fact has given rise to the term **event-driven programming**. For example, if you have used a Windows program like WordPerfect for Windows or Microsoft Access, you know that these programs have toolbars containing icon buttons. When you, the user, click one of the button objects, you provide input to the program. You generate an event (the clicking of that particular button). What the program does then is determined by the programming language statements that execute in response to your click event. These statements are called a **procedure**. Programmers have already written these event-handling procedures for the users.

Figure 1.4
Categories of
locations in which
Visual Basic code
can be placed.

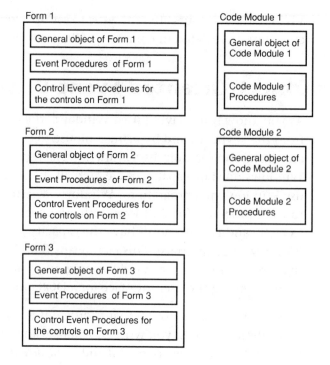

Click event
Occurs to an object
(like a menu choice)
when, as the pro-
gram is running,
the user clicks the
object.

The user "drives" a program by generating a **Click event** to the particular button object. Most Windows objects, like buttons or scroll bars, have a set of many
different events to which they can respond. However, what happens if you (the
programmer) do not write a Visual Basic code procedure to handle the occurrence of a particular event? Exactly nothing! Why is that?

Well, if a user clicks a button, and there are no program statements to tell the
computer what to do in response to that particular button's Click event, the
computer does what it is told—nothing.

But suppose that you, the programmer, do write procedure code to handle the
occurrence of a Click event to that button. Now when the Click event occurs,
the computer does what you have told it—in the procedure—to do in response
to the event. You could have the computer open or save a file, print a document,
or perform any of the many operations possible for a computer.

**Event
procedure**
A procedure associ-
ated with an object
and a particular
action occurring to
that object.

To write a program that makes the computer perform a complicated series of
actions, you will still write large "hunks" of code. This part of programming is
just like programming in the old days. However, you will also write smaller modules of code that are attached to objects on the Windows screen. These modules
are the **event procedures** (event handlers) for that object.

Chapter Summary

In this chapter, you have learned that a program is a set of instructions that tell
a computer what to do. Programs must be carefully planned before they are written in a programming language like Visual Basic. There are various programming
languages you can learn in order to write programs. Programming languages

make programming a computer easier, but they must be translated into the CPU's machine language. Users are people who don't write programs; they use programs written by others. Types of commercial programs include spreadsheets, word processors, desktop publishing programs, and databases. However, many more such programs remain to be written—perhaps by you.

You have learned how to get input to and output from your program by using programming statements. You learned the importance of adding comments to your code so that you and others can understand what each segment of code is supposed to do and to aid in debugging and revising your code. You also learned about conditional and looping statements to control program flow. You have seen how assignment statements change the values of variables inside the program.

In Chapter 2, you are more fully introduced to Visual Basic and the Visual Basic programming environment. Soon you will start learning how to design input screens and write and run your first Visual Basic program.

Test Your Understanding

True/False
Indicate whether the statement is true or false.

1. A computer's CPU can execute a statement written in Visual Basic.

2. When given a programming assignment, it is a good idea to go immediately to a computer and start typing your Visual Basic program so that you waste no time.

3. Variables can hold only numbers.

4. The arithmetic operator used to show multiplication in a program statement is ×.

5. In a Windows program, all programming language statements are written together in one large group.

Short Answer
Answer the following questions.

1. What are the two types of language translators?

2. Write a statement in pseudocode that performs a test of a condition where two possible actions can be taken.

3. What are the two tools usually used to design a logical plan for a program?

4. What are the two general types of errors found in a computer program and how do they come to be in the program?

5. List the most commonly used types of programming language statements and provide examples of each.

Projects

Project 1: Learning More about Programming

To learn more about the history of computer programming and programming languages, look up these topics in the references in your library.

Project 2: Learning More about Flowcharts and Pseudocode

To learn more about flowcharting and pseudocode, consult some library books on program design and programming languages like BASIC.

Project 3: Researching Software Products

Visit a local computer or office supply store to learn about the commercial software products they sell.

Project 4: Learning about Career Opportunities

To learn about careers in computing, check the employment section of your Sunday paper. What skills are they looking for?

Project 5: Exploring Programming Literature

Computing magazines carry many articles on programming and programming languages. Do a literature search to find articles on topics like Visual Basic, object-oriented, and event-driven programming.

Project 6: Drawing a Flowchart

Draw a detailed flowchart to diagram the steps necessary to open your car door, start the car, and begin driving.

CHAPTER 2

How to Use Visual Basic to Create Your First Program

Visual Basic (sometimes abbreviated as VB) offers a simple approach to programming for Windows. With Visual Basic, you can quickly and easily create programs that combine a professional appearance with powerful features that enable you to take full advantage of your computer system.

In this chapter, you actually start using Visual Basic. You learn what you need in order to run a program you have constructed. You also learn how to take advantage of the Visual Basic program development environment, and you learn some basic commands you will use whenever you work with Visual Basic. You even create your first Visual Basic program with the lessons in this chapter. You begin by examining what you need to design a program using Visual Basic.

Objectives

By the time you have finished this chapter, you will be able to

1. Start Visual Basic

2. Identify the Components of the Visual Basic Programming Environment and the Functions of These Components

3. Place, Size, and Position Controls on a Form

4. Identify the Functions of the Most Frequently Used Items in the Visual Basic Menu Bar

5. Understand the Functions of the Toolbar

6. Customize the Visual Basic Program Development Environment

7. Write, Save, and Run a Visual Basic Program

8. Exit Visual Basic

Starting Visual Basic

There are a variety of ways to start Visual Basic. The easiest way, if you are already in Windows, is to double-click the VB program icon in the Visual Basic program group of the Program Manager. You can, however, use other ways to start a Windows program, including the following:

- Double-click VB.EXE in the File Manager.

- Choose **R**un from the **F**ile menu in the Program Manager, and then enter **VB.EXE** (with its installed path) at the command line.

Regardless of how you start Visual Basic, the same items appear on your screen. These items represent the Visual Basic program development environment. You are now in the Program Design mode of VB. (Visual Basic has two other modes, Run and Break, which are discussed in later chapters.)

The tools used to design the user interface and enter the program code appear on the screen. Figure 2.1 shows an example of how your screen may appear.

Figure 2.1
What you see after starting Visual Basic.

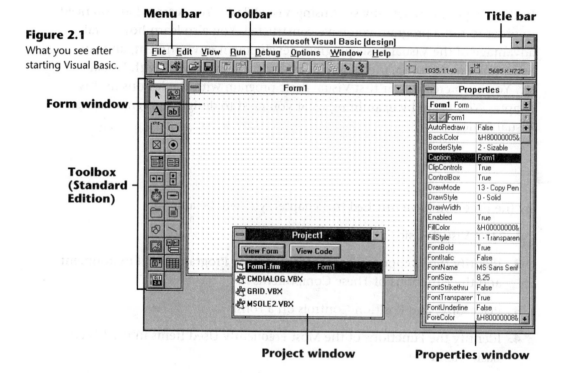

Because the windows in the VB programming environment can be moved around, your screen may appear somewhat different from the figure. Visual Basic has two editions: the Professional Edition and the Standard Edition. The Professional Edition has a larger on-screen Toolbox than the Standard Edition. The Toolbox is described later in this chapter. Before going any further with Visual Basic, you need to identify the major parts of the Visual Basic program development environment.

Learning the Parts of the Visual Basic Program Development Environment

Once opened, Visual Basic overlaps all other windows on your screen. For example, notice that the regular Windows desktop is still visible in the background of figure 2.1. Most VB programmers minimize the Program Manager window after they have started VB. This step reduces the clutter on the background of your screen.

The VB program development environment has only a few main elements. These elements are shown and labeled in figure 2.1. The major windows within the VB environment (Form, Project, Properties, and Toolbox) can be moved, sized, and minimized in the same way that any window can. These windows often blot out (overlap) each other. You can move a window to the "top of the pile" by clicking any visible part of the window with your mouse. You can also use the VB **W**indow menu or a function key to bring another VB window to the top.

Each element used in the VB program development environment performs a valuable function. You explore these elements and discover their purposes in the following sections.

The Form

Form

A display area on which you place controls when you are in Design mode; becomes the application's window when the program is run.

The most prominent element of the Visual Basic program development environment is the blank **form** that appears in the middle of your screen (see figure 2.2). Forms enable you to see how your program's window will look on-screen when your Visual Basic program is running. In the Program Design mode, you see a grid of dots on the form. The grid is displayed to help you line up your controls on the form. In the Run mode—when your program is executing—the dots disappear.

Figure 2.2

A blank form.

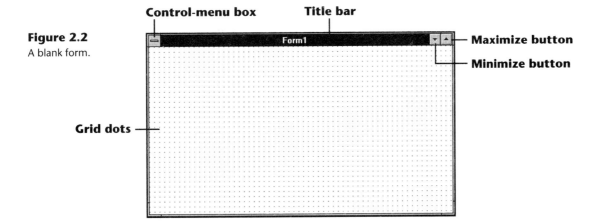

Remember, when you create a form, you are developing your program's on-screen window. Applications written in Visual Basic usually include at least one form. Visual Basic's way of getting you started is to present a blank form on which you can immediately begin working. This form usually becomes the first on-screen window the user who runs your program sees. Usually, only one form at a time appears on the user's screen.

Caption
The words that appear in the title bar of a Visual Basic application's window.

The blank form that is on your screen has a default name of Form1 and a default caption of Form1. The Name property of a form is the identifier that Visual Basic uses to refer to that form. In a Visual Basic application, all the objects—both forms and controls—must have names. What appears on the title bar of the form is called its **caption** in Visual Basic terminology. By default, Visual Basic uses Form1 as both the Name property and the Caption property for this first form. Don't confuse the name and the caption; they are two different attributes of many Visual Basic objects. The difference between the Name property and the Caption property of a form is explained in Chapter 3.

Property
An associated set of attributes for each object used in Visual Basic.

Name and Caption are two examples of object **properties**; in this case, the object is a form. In Visual Basic, every object (such as a form) has an associated set of attributes called properties. The properties of an object determine how the object will look and behave when the Visual Basic program is run on a computer.

Other properties of a form include Size, Color, and Location on the screen. As you will see, different types of objects have different sets of properties. The properties of a form or any other object in your Visual Basic application can be viewed and changed if necessary by using the Properties window. This window, which is also part of the Visual Basic environment, is discussed in the next section.

You can close or resize the form so that it does not overlay the other elements of the screen. You close the Form window by double-clicking the Control-menu icon in the upper-left corner of the form, just as you close any window within Windows. You resize the form by clicking and dragging its border.

The Properties Window

Properties window
A window in Visual Basic that lists the properties of the form and the controls in the form.

Another major part of the Visual Basic environment is the **Properties window**, shown in figure 2.3. This window lists the properties of the controls—on-screen objects, such as buttons—that you have placed in a form, as well as the properties of the form itself. Each control and each form has its own Properties window. Only one object's Properties window is shown at a time. The Properties window enables you to design your program's user interface.

Remember, when you run a program, the form becomes a window on the user's screen. The controls become the objects in the window. The user performs actions, such as typing text in a text box object or clicking the form or a command button. These actions generate events and provide input to the program.

An object (either a form or the controls on a form) and the information in the Properties window have a reciprocal relationship. The Properties window shows the properties of only one object at a time. That object is the one that is currently selected. The information in the Properties window changes as you select different objects on the form or as you use the mouse to change the size or location of an object.

Figure 2.3
The Properties window.

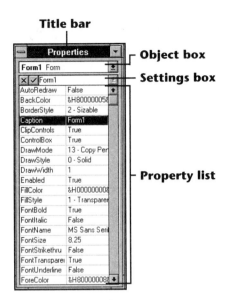

Title bar

Object box

Settings box

Property list

To select the form itself, click in an area of the form not occupied by a control. When you modify the information in the Properties window, your changes are automatically reflected in the object. The full purpose and meaning of the Properties window will become clearer after you work through Chapter 3.

The Project Window

Project
All files associated with a Visual Basic application.

In Visual Basic terminology, a **project** refers to all the files associated with a VB application. In other words, a project is a group of forms, code modules, and custom controls used by a particular Visual Basic program. A project and a program are synonymous. Each Visual Basic program solves a different problem. Each program, therefore, usually has several different forms with different controls on them and different VB program code.

MAK file
A special VB project file containing the names and disk locations of all files for that project.

A Visual Basic program, therefore, usually consists of a collection of files rather than just one file. For example, one VB application may need three different forms. Each form is stored in a separate disk file. The names and disk locations of the files are stored in a special project file called a MAK file. The project's **MAK file** is VB's record of what files you need to run your application.

The contents of the MAK file—the pieces and parts of a program—are displayed in the Project window, which is shown in figure 2.4. You can use this window to add files to your project or to delete files. If you have several forms, you can move between them by selecting a form in the Project window and then clicking the View Form button at the top of the Project window.

Figure 2.4
The Project window.

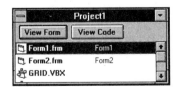

As you work through the various projects in this book, you will learn more about how the Project window helps you manage all the parts of your program. If you have code modules or forms that you want to use in several projects, you can. After you have saved a file, you can add the same form, code module, or custom control to any number of projects. Just remember that any changes you make to a form in one project will appear in the other project the next time the form in the other project is opened.

The Toolbox

When you work in Visual Basic, you see a collection of buttons in a window along the left side of the screen. This window is called the **Toolbox**. The buttons in the Toolbox, called **controls**, represent objects you can place on your forms. These objects implement your program's user interface. When the program is running, users perform actions on controls, thereby controlling what the program does. The Professional Edition Toolbox contains all the controls in the Standard Edition's Toolbox plus some others. Figure 2.5 shows the Standard Edition Toolbox, and figure 2.6 shows the Professional Edition Toolbox.

Toolbox
A collection of buttons in a window at the left side of the screen. They enable you to place controls on a form.

Controls
Objects placed on a form by using the buttons in the Toolbox.

Figure 2.5
The Standard Edition Toolbox.

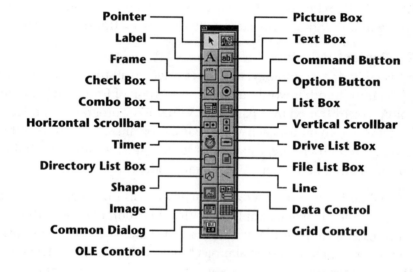

Figure 2.6
The Professional Edition Toolbox

If the Toolbox does not appear on your screen, you can display it by selecting the **T**oolbox menu item from the **W**indow menu. You also use this menu option to hide the Toolbox.

Regular controls
Controls built into Visual Basic.

The Visual Basic Toolbox contains two types of controls: regular and custom. The controls built into Visual Basic are **regular controls**. All the controls in the Standard Toolbox shown in figure 2.5 are regular controls *except* the Grid, Common Dialog, and OLE controls.

Custom controls
Controls the programmer can add to a project.

Any remaining controls in the Toolbox are **custom controls**, which are not built into Visual Basic. You add custom controls to your project by including a special file, which contains the control. These files have a VBX extension and are found in the WINDOWS\SYSTEM subdirectory. When you look at your Toolbox, custom controls don't look any different from regular controls, and you use them the same way—by placing them on a form. The Professional Edition Toolbox has more custom controls than the Standard Edition.

Removing and Adding Custom Controls

One of the first actions you may want to take is to change the custom controls available in the Toolbox. To reduce clutter in the Toolbox and shorten the time needed to load your project, you may want to remove any unused controls. Custom controls are stored in files that have a VBX extension. To remove a custom control, from the Project window, select the file name representing the control. Then from VB's **F**ile menu, choose **R**emove File. The file name is removed from the Project window, and the custom control is removed from the Toolbox.

To add a custom control to your project, select A**d**d File from VB's **F**ile menu. After you supply the file name for the control, the file name is added to the Project window, and the appropriate button for the control appears in the Toolbox.

By tradition, custom control files are kept in Windows' SYSTEM subdirectory. Many third-party control providers, however, create their own directories and store their custom control files there when controls are installed. Third-party custom controls are advertised in *Visual Basic* magazine and other Windows programming magazines. These third-party add-on custom controls enable you to do things in your application that you cannot do with Microsoft's controls.

Some custom control files contain more than one control; for example, THREED.VBX contains six custom controls: a 3-D frame, a 3-D option button, a 3-D check box, a 3-D command button, a 3-D panel, and a 3-D group pushbutton. If a file contains multiple controls, you cannot choose which controls in that file you want loaded—you can load all or none of them; it's up to you.

Using Controls as You Develop Your Application

When you use a control in your program, you place it on a form. There are two ways to place a control: double-clicking and drawing. When you use the mouse to double-click the control in the Toolbox, VB places the control in the center of the form. You move a control to its proper position on a form by clicking and dragging with your mouse. You can then make changes to the control as necessary by changing its properties in the Properties window.

To draw the control, first select it by using the left mouse button to click the control in the Toolbox. (Make sure that you don't double-click; double-clicking puts the control on the form as described in the preceding paragraph.) Next, place your mouse pointer over the form on which you want to draw the control. Point to the position where you want a corner of the control placed. Now, press and hold down the left mouse button and drag diagonally down and to the right. As you move the mouse, you see an outline that represents the size and position of the control you are drawing. When you release the mouse button, the control appears in the size you have drawn. In later projects, you will need to place one control in (on top of) an existing control. The double-click method does not work properly in this situation. You must draw the second control on top of the first.

Placing Controls in a Form

Make sure that Visual Basic is on-screen and in Design mode. Refer to figure 2.5 for the names of the controls, if necessary. To practice placing controls on a form, follow these steps:

1 Double-click (use the left mouse button) the Text Box tool in the Toolbox.

A text box (Text1) appears at the center of your form.

2 Place your mouse pointer on the center of the text box.

3 Press and hold down the left mouse button.

4 Move your mouse so that the text box is dragged to the upper-right corner of the form.

5 Release the mouse button.

The text box now appears in the upper-right corner of the form.

6 Click the left mouse button once on the Text Box tool in the Toolbox.

7 Place the mouse pointer (now a cross hair) in the upper-left area of the form.

8 Press and hold down the left mouse button.

9 Drag the mouse down and to the right until the second text box (Text2) is about twice as large as Text1.

10 Release the mouse button.

11 Place the mouse pointer (now an arrow again) on the first text box (Text1).

12 Click the left mouse button.

Selection handles appear around the Text1 text box (see figure 2.7).

Figure 2.7
The selection
handles around
the Text1 text
box.

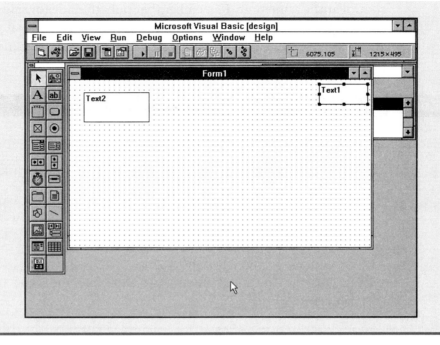

Sizing a Control

Sizing handles
Small solid squares
appearing at inter-
vals around the
outside of the
control, used to size
the control.

Notice that when you select a control that has already been placed on a form, eight **sizing handles** appear around the outside of the control. These handles look like little solid squares, as shown in figure 2.8. A selected form does not have sizing handles because the form is sized by dragging its border.

Figure 2.8
Sizing handles on a
selected control.

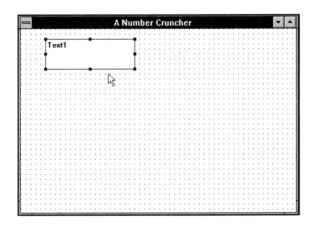

To change the size of a selected control, point to one of the sizing handles, and press and hold down the left mouse button. The mouse cursor changes to a double-headed arrow. As you move the mouse in one of the directions indicated by the arrow, the size of the control changes in that direction.

Basically, if you drag one of the sizing handles on the sides of the control, you move that side left, right, up, or down. If you drag one of the sizing handles in the four corners, you can move the handle diagonally and move two sides of the control at the same time. Remember that only the side (or sides) associated with the sizing handle is moved; all other sides retain their original position. Usually, after you have sized and positioned a control, you will set some of its other properties by using its Properties window.

Sizing Controls

To practice sizing a control, do the following:

❶ Place the mouse pointer on the sizing handle (the black square) at the lower left corner of Text1.

❷ Press and hold the left mouse button, and drag the mouse until the lower-left corner of Text1 is approximately at the center of the form. Then release the mouse button.

❸ Practice moving and sizing the two text boxes until you are comfortable with this technique.

If you have placed a control on your form and later decide that you don't want it in your program; you can easily delete the control.

Deleting Controls

First, make sure that VB is in Design mode—not Run mode. The mode is displayed in the VB window's title bar. To delete a control on a form, click the control with your mouse to select the control. The dark sizing handles appear to show you that the control is selected. Press the Delete key to delete the control.

To delete both text boxes, follow these steps:

❶ If Text1 is not selected, click it. Sizing handles appear around Text1.

❷ Press and release the **Delete** key. Text1 is deleted.

❸ Click Text2 to select it.

❹ Press and release the **Delete** key. Your form should now be empty.

Understanding the Menu Bar

The **menu bar** is the row of menu names under Visual Basic's title bar, as shown in figure 2.9. You can select menus with either the mouse or the keyboard. To select a menu with the mouse, just point to the menu name, and click the left button. A pull-down menu appears; you can then make a choice from that menu. Some menu items are executed immediately, but others require more information from you before the item can be executed. A menu item followed

Menu bar

The row of menu names under the Visual Basic title bar.

by an ellipsis (...) indicates that choosing the item does not execute the command immediately. You will see either another menu or a dialog box, as when you accessed the Print dialog box using **F**ile **P**rint.

Title bar   **Menu bar**

Figure 2.9

The menu bar appears at the top of your screen.

While you are using Visual Basic, not all menu items are applicable at all times. Menu items normally appear as black text. When you can't use a menu item, it is *grayed* (not enabled). You can still see the item, but you can't select it. Items are grayed rather than removed so that you can remember menu item locations.

You can also choose from menus by using the keyboard. This technique is explained in the next section.

Access Keys

Access key

The key you press in combination wtih the Alt key to choose a menu or option.

Notice that the first character of each menu name in the menu bar is underlined. The underlined character is the **access key** for that menu. (In some other programs, these access keys are called *hotkeys*.) To activate a menu, you press and hold the Alt key, and then press the corresponding access key. For example, to pull down the **F**ile menu, press and hold the **Alt** key, and then press **F**.

After you pull down a menu, notice that each menu item also has an access key. The access key for a menu item, however, isn't always the first letter because many menu items start with the same letters. If the first letter were always underlined, the access keys wouldn't be unique. (The access key would still work. Windows would simply cycle through all the menu items with that particular access key, highlighting each, and you would have to press the Enter key to execute the option you wanted.) For rapid access, reduced confusion, and ease of use, the creators of VB have defined other letters in many menu items as the access keys. The underlined letter within a menu item is always the access key for that menu item.

Selecting a menu item by using an access key is even easier than selecting a menu. Just press the access key *without* pressing the Alt key. For example, to select the **N**ew Project menu item, while the **F**ile menu is open, press **N** without using Alt. What could be faster?

Shortcut Keys

Shortcut key

A key or key combination that provides a faster way of selecting menu items.

As their name implies, **shortcut keys** provide an even faster way of selecting menu items. Pull down the **F**ile menu again, as shown in figure 2.10. Notice the four menu items that have additional text on the right side of the menu list.

For example, the **P**rint item has Ctrl+P next to it. This text shows the shortcut keystrokes to access that menu item directly without having to pull down the **F**ile menu and then select **P**rint. The plus sign (+) between the two keys signifies that the first key should be pressed and held while the second key is pressed.

Figure 2.10

The File menu.

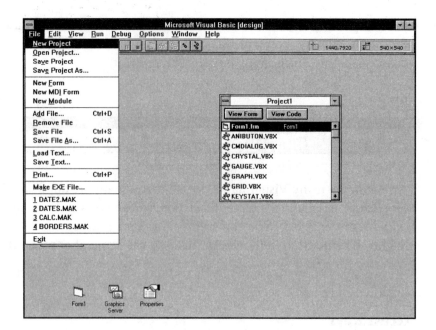

Function keys

Special keys, either across the top or on the left side of the keyboard, assigned operations to speed your work in Visual Basic.

Although some shortcut keys are assigned for compatibility with other Windows programs (such as Alt+F4 for **F**ile E**x**it), the rest are assigned based on frequency of use. The operations performed most frequently are assigned to **function keys**. These are the special keys across the top or on the left side of your keyboard; each one begins with the letter *F*, as in F1, F2, F3, and so on. Operations assigned to function keys are handy because they require only a single key press. You will appreciate this feature while you are getting started with Visual Basic. For example, the first function key, F1, instantly invokes the on-line help.

Using the Print Dialog Box

In this exercise, you access the Print dialog box. You later use this dialog box to print the controls, properties, and Visual Basic code in your project. Now you have nothing to print, but you can practice using menus. Make sure that you are in the Design mode of Visual Basic. Then do the following:

❶ Click the **F**ile menu. The menu drops down.

Note that the shortcut key combination for **P**rint is Ctrl+P.

❷ Click **P**rint.

The Print dialog box appears. You have nothing to print yet.

❸ Click the Cancel button.

The Print dialog box disappears.

❹ Press and hold down the **Alt** key; then press **F** (the underlined letter in **F**ile).

❺ Release the **Alt** key (or leave it down—it really doesn't matter), and press **P** (for **P**rint key).

The Print dialog box appears. Click the Cancel button.

Now try the shortcut key combination for the **File Print** command.

6 Without any menus pulled down, press and hold down the **Ctrl** key.

7 Press **P**.

The Print dialog box immediately appears.

8 Click the Cancel button.

2

Note: *If you pull down a menu or get a dialog box by accident, press the **Esc** key.*

The Window Menu

As mentioned in this chapter, when you're using Windows, the desktop screen can become cluttered. Whole windows sometimes seem to be buried under a mass of overlapping windows. The **W**indow menu provides a quick way to activate and display several windows involved with the Visual Basic environment. You can use this menu to reactivate a previously disabled or minimized window or simply to "dig out" a buried window.

Not all items in this menu are always available. The availability of an item depends on the current mode (Design, Run, or Break) and on the other windows visible. For example, you cannot activate the Properties window while in Run mode. When a menu item appears gray (dimmed), it is not currently available.

When you select an option from the menu, the selected window moves to the foreground and becomes the active window. You can begin using the window immediately. Table 2.1 gives a brief description of the most frequently used submenu options available from the **W**indow menu.

Table 2.1	Frequently Used Window Menu Options
Option	**Function**
Procedures	Opens a dialog box from which you can select any procedure you want to view or edit. The shortcut key is F2.
P**r**oject	Opens the Project window.
Pr**o**perties	Opens the Properties window. For more information on this window, see the next several chapters. The shortcut key is F4.
Toolbox	Opens the Toolbox, from which you can select graphics controls to place on a form.

Getting Help

Visual Basic offers an extensive Help system that is accessed by choosing the **H**elp menu. Some of these features include searching for topics or key words, cutting and pasting code examples from Help screens to your programs, and using hypertext-type links in which special highlighted words in one Help screen open related screens. Help screens function like ordinary windows. Not only can you move a Help window around the desktop, you can resize, maximize, and reduce it to an icon.

The VB Help systems works the same way the Help systems in others Windows applications work. You choose Help from the menu, choose the topic you need, and follow the instructions on the Help screens. VB does have two unique features, discussed in the following two sections. You can work through a special on-line tutorial, or you can learn by looking at special examples.

Your Own Private Tutor

To see a quick on-line tutorial of some Visual Basic features, choose **L**earning Microsoft Visual Basic from the **H**elp menu. The screen shown in figure 2.11 appears.

Figure 2.11
The Learning
Microsoft Visual
Basic screen.

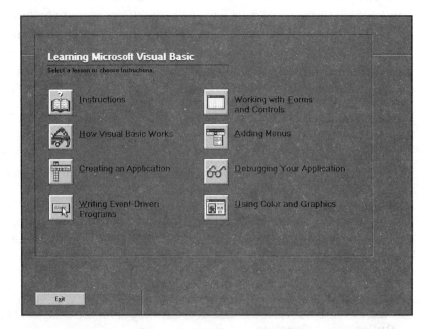

Learning Microsoft Visual Basic is an interactive slide show that contains seven lessons concentrating on different themes in Visual Basic. Learning Microsoft Visual Basic walks you through some Visual Basic features with a graphical display of information. You can run Learning Microsoft Visual Basic at any time.

Learning by Example

Sometimes the best way to understand how something works is to look at an example. Microsoft provides quite a few good examples with Visual Basic. These examples are located in the SAMPLES subdirectory under the directory in which VB is installed (usually C:\VB). You open an example program in the SAMPLES subdirectory by using the **F**ile **O**pen command. By opening an example project and examining its components, you not only get a different perspective on the Visual Basic programming process, but you also find some clever techniques for accomplishing common programming tasks.

Starting and Ending Program Execution

The **R**un menu contains the commands to run your VB program and to end it. The **S**tart option starts the execution of your program. F5 is the shortcut key to start a program. The **E**nd option terminates execution of the program. You can also start a program by clicking the Run button on the Toolbar. To stop a running program, click the End button on the Toolbar. If a menu item with an associated Toolbar button is grayed, the Toolbar button will also be grayed.

Understanding the Toolbar

The **Toolbar** is another important part of the VB environment. The Toolbar is the row of picture buttons under the menu bar (see figure 2.12). The icons on the faces of the buttons represent the action taken when you press that button. For example, the button with an icon of an open file folder represents opening a project (a MAK file).

Figure 2.12
The Toolbar.

└ **The Toolbar**

Toolbar
The row of picture buttons below the menu bar.

Each Toolbar button represents a frequently performed action that is also available from the menu system. Using these buttons makes performing actions faster and easier. By clicking a Toolbar button, you immediately activate the indicated command. For example, instead of opening the **F**ile menu and selecting Sa**v**e Project, you can click the Save Project button in the Toolbar. You can think of the Toolbar as a collection of shortcut buttons. Whether you use the menu commands or click the Toolbar, Visual Basic performs the same action. The method you use is a matter of personal preference.

The Toolbar contains five groups of buttons. You use the first group (starting from the left) to add new forms or modules—the basic project building blocks—to your project file. You use the second group to open or save a project. The next group accesses the Menu Design dialog box (covered in Chapter 11) and the Properties window. You use the fourth group to start, pause, or stop the execution of your application while designing or debugging. And you use the last Toolbar button group for debugging, which enables you to execute your application by stepping through it, to set breakpoints, and to view the values contained in variables. (These terms may sound foreign now, but you will find more information on debugging in Chapter 8.)

You may find that you don't use the Toolbar and prefer the additional screen space for other purposes. You can hide the Toolbar by selecting **T**oolbar from the **V**iew menu. Notice that when the Toolbar is visible, a check mark appears to the left of the menu item, and when the Toolbar isn't visible, there is no check mark. This is Visual Basic's way of telling you whether the Toolbar is on or off.

Customizing Visual Basic through the Options Menu

Given the same office, no two individuals will organize it the same way. John may like his desk by the window, and Jane may prefer hers facing the door. The Visual Basic programming environment is so advanced that it enables you to customize virtually any aspect of the VB environment. Some of the changes you make may apply only to your current project, but other changes will apply to all your projects. You customize VB by using the **O**ptions menu.

By adjusting the values of various settings available with the **O**ptions menu, you can change the way Visual Basic looks and works. The **O**ptions menu opens to reveal two submenus: **E**nvironment (controls various Visual Basic settings) and **P**roject (controls the way some options work on the current application). The following sections describe some of the options available from these two submenus.

Environment options
A group of options used by VB to control how the programming environment works.

The Environment Options

Visual Basic uses a group of options, collectively referred to as **environment options**, to control how the VB programming environment operates. To access these options, you choose **E**nvironment from the **O**ptions menu. The Environment Options dialog box appears; it contains options that apply to all your projects (see figure 2.13).

Figure 2.13
The Environment Options dialog box.

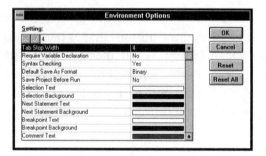

The first option you may want to change is Default Save As Format. Microsoft recommends setting this option to Text, which instructs Visual Basic to save your forms and form code in a special Text format that you can read and modify using any editor or word processor. Form files (whether they are in Text or Binary format) have the extension FRM. The Windows Notepad program is great for editing MAK files and Text format FRM files. A file saved using the Binary option is readable only by Visual Basic.

One advantage of saving forms in the Text format is that if a file is corrupted (for whatever reason), you may be able to salvage it by editing the corrupt portion with a regular text editor. You also can print and modify the files directly by using an ASCII editor like Notepad. You can enter VB code using Notepad if you have a computer without Visual Basic loaded.

The advantages of saving files in Binary format don't outweigh the advantages of the Text format. If you save files in Binary format, your projects load slightly faster because VB must first convert the files saved in Text format to Binary format (internally) before VB can use the files. In addition, project files stored in the Binary format consume somewhat less disk space than if they were stored in Text format. This factor may not be a real drawback, however, because all but the largest Visual Basic projects take relatively small amounts of disk space.

The second environmental option you may want to change is Save Project Before Run. You should always save your project on disk before you run it. When this option is set to Yes, Visual Basic prompts you when you are about to run your project without saving the changes you have made. Then you can save your project to disk. This prompt helps ensure that you don't lose any work if your program crashes as a result of the changes you have made. Of course, you can save your program to disk before you run it without having set the Save Project Before Run option. You use the **F**ile Sa**v**e Project command or the Save Project button in the Toolbar.

Other environment options can be changed, although these changes are not necessary at this point. Any changes you make to your environment are immediate. As soon as you close the Environment Options dialog box, the changes are made. By clicking the Reset All button, you can restore the values of all settings to their default values. When you finish making any changes, you click OK to accept the new values and close the dialog box.

Project Options

The **P**roject submenu of the **O**ptions menu presents three options of use when you are working on a particular application. Project options affect the application you're currently writing. To change the options for the current project, choose the **P**roject option from the **O**ptions menu. The Project Options dialog box appears (see figure 2.14). At this point in the course, there is no reason for you to change any of these options.

Figure 2.14
The Project Options dialog box.

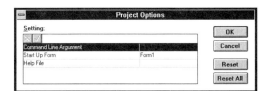

Of the three options presented in the Project Options dialog box, the one you are most likely to change later is the Start Up Form option. Every program has a starting point, and your Visual Basic programs can start in only one of two places: with a form or with a Visual Basic procedure (discussed in Chapter 5).

Most of your programs will use a form as their starting point. When you start Visual Basic, you see a blank Form window on-screen. You can change which form is displayed when you start Visual Basic by changing the Start Up Form Project option. The start-up form can be any form in your project. By default, VB uses Form1 as the start-up form. Typically, the only time a procedure is used as the starting point is when your project contains no forms.

The last Project option is Help File. Most Windows programs have an on-line Help file similar to Visual Basic's. If you have a Help file for your application, you can use the Help File option to identify this file for Visual Basic. Designing a custom Help file requires the Professional Edition of Visual Basic. The process of developing help files is beyond the scope of this book.

Creating Your First Visual Basic Program

Controls enable you to add functionality to your applications with minimum effort. Earlier in this chapter, you learned what controls are, and you learned how to use them in a form you are developing. You are about to see how quick and easy Visual Basic makes Windows programming through the use of controls.

Defining the Problem

For your first project you will make something simple yet useful—a calculator. The first step is to define what you want the project to accomplish. This calculator will be simple; it will do one thing—add two numbers. The user will enter two numbers and then signal the program to perform the calculation. Because this program is introductory, it will not offer a full range of calculating tools. Thinking through and writing out this description of what you want to accomplish is called problem definition.

To accomplish the specified goal, your program must

- Provide a way for the user to enter the numbers to be added

- Provide a way for the user to trigger the addition operation

- Display the result of the addition for the user

Designing the Program

The first step in converting the problem definition to a workable program design is to identify how many forms you will need. Because in this program you need to collect only a small amount of input and display a small amount of output, you need only one form.

The second step is to decide whether you must provide choices to the user so that the user has the option to do a variety of different things with the program. If so, you will usually need to create menus that list the options for your program. This program provides no options. Two numbers are entered and added, and the result is displayed. Therefore, no menus or other controls allowing a choice of options are needed.

The third step in program design is to identify the controls that will be required on the forms to accept input and display output. The Text Box control is the one that users can type data in. You need two text boxes: one to hold the first number and one to hold the second number. The Label control is used to display output. You will need one Label control to display the result of the addition.

The fourth step in program design is to decide what controls are needed to trigger events. You need a way for the user to signal the computer that he or she wants the numbers added and the result displayed. A Command Button control is easy to use for this purpose as long as its Caption property is set to display a word or phrase that explains what happens when the button is clicked.

Now, the plans for your user interface are complete. The next step is to decide what processing steps are necessary to convert the input to the desired output. These steps will be expressed in Visual Basic code when the program is finished. At this point, however, you should express your plan in pseudocode like this:

> Event handler for the command button click.
>
> Set the Caption property of the Label to the result of adding the Text properties of the two text boxes.
>
> End the event.

You can do all these tasks easily with Visual Basic. Your user interface will look like the sketch in figure 2.15. Now you will take a look at how you go about implementing this calculator program.

Figure 2.15
A sketch of the user interface.

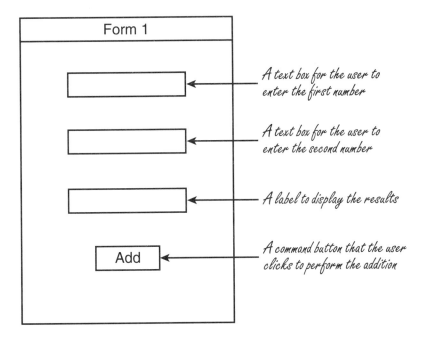

This program design sketch is detailed enough to guide you as you construct your user interface.

Preparing to Create the Program

To begin your project, you need to start with a clean VB programming environment slate. The best way to do this is to choose **N**ew Project from the **F**ile menu. Make sure that the Toolbar and the Toolbox are displayed, using the techniques covered earlier in this chapter. Your Project window should contain only one form—Form1.

After you have cleaned your slate, you are ready to create a Visual Basic program. To begin, you will follow these general steps:

1. Place on the form the controls that are necessary to define the user interface.

2. Write the Visual Basic code necessary to produce the desired results.

You will always follow this procedure regardless of the type of Visual Basic program you are creating. These two steps are covered in the following sections.

Defining the User Interface

You define the interface for your calculator in the Form window. When you start a new project, the Form window is completely empty. You define the interface by placing controls within the form, as indicated earlier in the chapter. Check the design sketch in figure 2.15; you need to model your interface from this sketch.

To create your calculator interface properly, follow these steps:

1 Size the form to the approximate size (approximately four inches by three inches) desired for the program window when the program is running.

Sizing the form is easy. Just use the mouse to size the edge of the window, as described earlier in this chapter. Make the Form window the size you want your calculator to be when the program runs.

Next, you define two Text Box controls to hold the two numbers that will be added together.

2 Double-click the Text Box control in the Toolbox, and move the first Text Box control up near the top of the form. You can use the mouse to move and resize the control so that it is positioned properly.

3 Double-click the Text Box control in the Toolbox again, and move the second Text Box control up under the first Text Box control.

Figure 2.16 shows how these should be positioned and sized in your Form window.

Figure 2.16
Positioning the
text boxes.

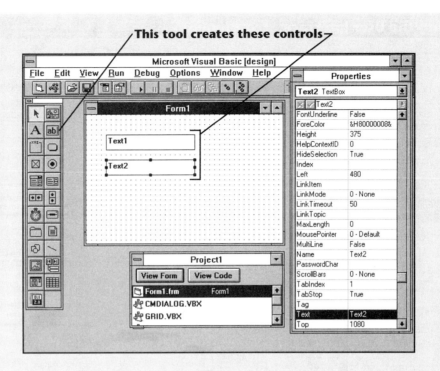

Next, you define a Label control to display the result of the addition. Use a Label control rather than a Text Box control because users cannot type in a label as they can in a text box.

❹ Double-click the Label control in the Toolbox. Position this control a little below the second text box.

Figure 2.17 shows how this control should be sized and positioned on the form.

Figure 2.17
Positioning the
Label control.

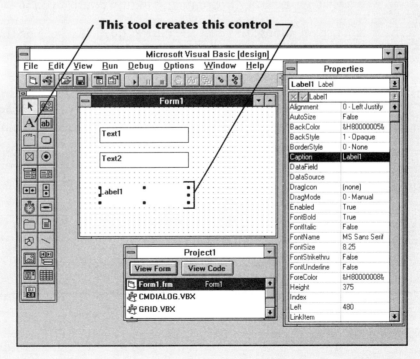

(continues)

Defining the User Interface   (continued)

Then you define a Command Button control that will enable the user to trigger the addition and display the result in the Label control.

5 Double-click the Command Button control in the Toolbox. Position this control below the label as shown in figure 2.18.

Figure 2.18
Positioning the command button.

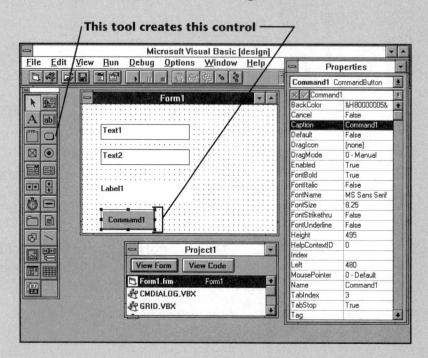

As the final stage in defining the user interface, you need to change the text that appears on the Command Button control you just placed in your form.

6 Use the mouse to select the button (just click it). The sizing handles appear around the control.

7 Choose the Caption property in the Properties window.

Notice that the value of this property is currently Command1, which is the default text on the button. You need to change the value to Add.

8 If necessary, scroll to the proper location in the Properties window, and then double-click the Caption property.

9 Type **Add**, and press **Enter**.

The text on the command button changes to Add.

This step completes the design of the user interface for your first program.

Revisiting the Caption and the Name Properties

Remember the difference between the Caption and the Name properties? The Caption property refers to the text used to identify the object to the user; this text appears on the user's screen. For a form, this text appears in the title bar of the Form window. For other objects (such as command buttons), the text appears on the object itself. You can change the Caption property as you see fit.

The Name property is the name by which the object is known (referred to) inside the VB program code. The user never sees the name of an object. Only programmers are aware of the name of an object because that is how the object is referred to in Visual Basic code. Why would you ever want to change the Name property rather than use the default supplied by Visual Basic? Because as you develop larger and more complex programs, you will want to use object names that are meaningful in the context of what the object does.

Sometimes you will want to give the same name to the Caption and the Name properties for an object. Then you can just glance at the user interface screen to see the name of a control. This practice makes writing code a less error-prone and faster process. For small programs (such as this calculator project), you will probably never need to worry about changing the Name property.

Your user interface is now complete, and you are ready to write the program code.

Attaching Code to an Object

As indicated earlier, the calculator must add the two numbers contained in the text boxes and display the result in the label area. You want the program to perform the addition each time the command button is chosen. (You choose a command button by clicking it.) This action causes a Click event to occur for the command button. If there is code in the command button's Click event procedure, that code is executed.

Code window
The Visual Basic window that you open when you want to type VB code into your program or when you want to view the program statements already in your program.

The programmer enters in the **Code window** the program code to be executed when a certain event happens.

To access the Code window for the command button's Click event, double-click the Command Button control in your form. The Code window appears, as shown in figure 2.19.

Entering Code in the Code Window

The empty Sub procedure for the Visual Basic code that handles the Click event is already positioned in the Code window. You just have to "fill in the sandwich" between the first and last lines of the Sub procedure. The Click event is the event that most frequently occurs to a command button object, so the Code window initially displays the empty Click event procedure.

Notice that the Sub procedure says Command1_Click. The name of an event procedure first gives the Name property of the object involved in the event. The Name property is followed by an underline and then the event type. The Code window for *any* object initially displays the empty Sub procedure for the event that most frequently occurs to that object. You can change to a different object or different event by using the selection boxes at the top of the Code window.

Figure 2.19

The Code window.

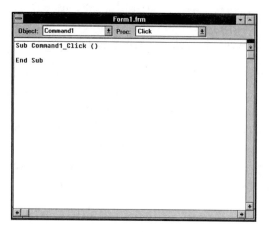

Notice the two selection boxes (Object and Proc) at the top of the Code window. You use the left one (Object) to indicate the object to which this procedure is being attached (in this case, the command button); you use the right box (Proc) to indicate the event to which this code applies (in this case, to a mouse click).

Coding an Event Procedure

Because these settings are correct, you can now start typing the Visual Basic procedure you want executed when the user clicks the command button. Follow these steps:

❶ The insertion point should already be positioned between the top and bottom Sub procedure lines.

❷ To add the values of the numbers in the two text boxes and store the result in the label, enter the following single line of code:

```
Label1.Caption = Val(Text1.Text) + Val(Text2.Text)
```

This program line may not make much sense to you—particularly if you have not programmed before. Basically, you are entering an equation. The part to the left of the equal sign (Label1.Caption) indicates what value you are assigning the Caption property of Label1 (the default Name property assigned by Visual Basic to the Label control object that you placed on the form). In Visual Basic, properties are written to the right of the object to which they apply . The object and the property are separated by a period. You read Label1.Caption as "The caption property of the object Label1."

Two other object names are used in this equation: Text1 and Text2. These are the names of the two Text Box control objects placed in the form. The Text property contains the number the user types in the control. Val() is a function that makes sure that what the user types is a value (a number that can be added). You learn about functions in Chapters 5 and 10.

In plain English, the equation says

> Make the contents of the Label control object equal to the contents of the first Text Box control object plus the contents of the second Text Box control object.

Don't be scared off by this formula; by the time you work through this book, you will be able to construct this type of equation easily. By the way, the uppercase letters in the equation are used for readability. Visual Basic is not sensitive to differences between upper- and lowercase letters except when they are inside quotation marks.

After you enter the code line, close the Code window to get it out of the way while you run the program. And . . . that is all there is to entering your program code to handle the Click event!

Figure 2.20 shows what your final program's user interface screen should look like.

Figure 2.20
The finished calculator.

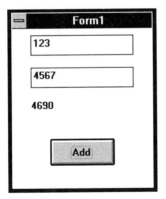

Running and Testing Your Program

To run the calculator, click the Start button in the Toolbar, press **F5**, or select **S**tart from the **R**un menu.

To add numbers and display the sum, follow these steps:

❶ Type a number into the first text box.

❷ Press the **Tab** key (on your keyboard) to move the insertion point to the second text box.

❸ Type a number into the second text box.

❹ Click the command button.

Note: *When computers display information on-screen, the information always looks correct; but it could be 100 percent wrong. Always test your programs with a range of numbers, and verify the results with your hand calculator. If your program passes the test, you can use it with confidence. If you click this button with no values, it will generate an error.*

The program you just created is not yet a stand-alone Windows program because it can be run only from within the Visual Basic environment—not from Windows. In Chapter 6, you learn how to turn a VB program into a full-fledged Windows program that can be run from the Windows Program Manager by clicking its icon.

Make file
The programmers' name for the MAK, or project, file.

You should save your work to disk often. In fact, you may save your work many times while you are working on a Visual Basic program. If you don't save your work, you will lose it when you exit Visual Basic or Windows or if a problem occurs in your computer. When you save your work, you are prompted to supply a file name and a name for the MAK file. Programmers call this a **make file**, although you (and they) know that it is a project file. This file contains the file names of the components displayed in the Project window.

Saving Your Work

You can save your project to your hard disk or a floppy disk at any time; just choose Save Project from the File menu. If you are saving this project for the first time, you are prompted for a file name to use for both your form and your project. All you have to do is provide a name. Be sure to remember the eight-character limit for file names in Windows. For this example, use the name **CALC**. When you press **Enter**, Form1 and the controls it contains are saved in a file with the name CALC.

Next, you are asked for the name to use for your MAK project file. You can use the same name as you did for the module file—**CALC**. Then press **Enter**.

Quitting Visual Basic

When your work is saved, you can exit Visual Basic the same way you quit any other Windows program. The most common methods are

- Use the mouse to double-click the Control-menu icon (the gray box at the left end of the title bar).

- Choose the Exit option from the File menu.

Either method closes all the Visual Basic windows and returns you to the Program Manager.

Chapter Summary

In this chapter, you have learned how to use and customize the Visual Basic program development environment. In particular, you explored the Toolbar, Toolbox, menu bar, Form window, Project window, Properties window, and Code window. You also constructed and ran a simple Visual Basic project.

In the next chapter, you learn a great deal more about writing programs in Visual Basic.

Test Your Understanding

True/False
Indicate whether the statement is true or false.

1. You place controls on a form when you are in the Design mode of Visual Basic.

2. Your VB program is saved in one file.

3. The properties of the selected object are displayed in the Properties window.

4. A form becomes a window when a VB program is run.

5. The Command Button control is an example of a custom control.

6. Custom controls are stored in disk files with the extension FRM.

7. If a project contains three forms, you will be asked to provide four file names the first time you save the project.

8. In VB code, an object name is followed by a period and then by an event.

9. The Text property of a Text Box control can be set only in Design mode.

10. A form must have a file name that is the same as its Caption property and its Name property.

Short Answer
Answer the following questions.

1. Describe why you might use a Text Box control instead of a Label control in a Visual Basic program.

2. List the ways in which you can start Visual Basic.

3. What is the function of the Project window?

4. What is the function of the Properties window?

5. What is the function of the Toolbox window?

6. What is the function of the Code window?

7. Explain how to access the Code window.

8. Explain the use of the two items (Object and Proc) at the top of the code window.

9. List the ways in which you can start the run of a Visual Basic program.

10. What is the function of the Options menu?

Projects

Project 1: Using the VB Tutorial

Complete the seven lessons in the Visual Basic on-line tutorial "Learning Visual Basic."

Project 2: Opening Windows

Start Visual Basic. Close the Form, Project, Properties, and Toolbox windows. Now perform the actions necessary to make each window appear on-screen again.

Project 3: Exploring the Help System Glossary

Start Visual Basic if it is not already running. In VB's **Help** menu, choose **Con**tents. Click Glossary, and look up the definitions of any VB terminology that you have encountered in this chapter but are still not clear on. Then exit from VB's Help system.

Project 4: Searching for Help Topics

1. Start Visual Basic if it is not already running.

2. In VB's **Help** menu, choose **Search** for Help On. Then in the Search dialog box, type **form**, and click the **Show** Topics button. Click the **Go** To button. If your computer is attached to a printer, when the form Help screen appears, chose **File** and then **Print** topic.

3. Click the **Search** button at the top of the Help window.

4. In the Search dialog box, type **code** and then click **Show** Topics. Double-click Guidelines for Entering and Editing code.

5. Chose **File** and then **Print** topic.

6. Exit from VB's Help system.

Project 5: Using Context-Sensitive Help

Start Visual Basic if it is not already running. Then click once on a tool in your Toolbox. Press the **F1** key to access the Help screen for that tool. Print the Help screen.

Project 6:   Creating a Simple Form

1. Start a new project in Visual Basic.

2. Delete any custom controls from the project.

3. Add three text boxes and two command buttons. Change the `Caption` property of each button. Use whatever caption you want. Change the `Text` property of the text boxes so that they are blank (empty).

4. Save the project. Save the form in Text format.

5. Switch to Windows Notepad, and load and print first the MAK file and then the FRM file in your project.

Project 7:   Writing a Calculator Program

Write a Visual Basic calculator program that will let the user enter two numbers. The program should then add the two numbers, subtract `number2` from `number1`, divide `number1` by `number2`, and multiply the two numbers. The program should display the results of each computation in four separate labels when the user clicks a button with the caption `Compute`. The program should indicate which of the results came from the addition, which from subtraction, and so on. Save the project as **C2P5**.

Using Forms and Some of the Most Commonly Used Controls

Chapter 3 introduces the use of forms in a Visual Basic project. You have learned that forms and their controls are the foundation of Visual Basic programs. You used a form when you created a simple Visual Basic program. (Although you can create a Visual Basic program without forms, it is rarely done.) In this chapter, you learn about forms, their properties, and their events. You also learn about three of the most frequently used Visual Basic controls: the Command Button control, the Text Box control, and the Label control. You see how you can use these controls in a program, and you learn about their most important properties and events. You also learn more about writing Visual Basic code.

Objectives

By the time you have finished this chapter, you will be able to

1. Add Forms to a Project

2. Understand the Most Useful Properties and Events of Forms

3. Modify the Properties of Forms in Design Mode and in Visual Basic Code

4. Understand the Properties and Events That Are Common to Most Controls

5. Understand the Functions, Properties, and Events of the Command Button, Text Box, and Label Controls

Adding Forms to Projects

Your Visual Basic programs can contain as many forms as you need. The number of forms needed is determined by the number of different windows required by a program. You add a new form to your project by choosing **N**ew Form from the **F**ile menu or by clicking the Toolbar's New Form button. The New Form button is the leftmost button on the Toolbar, and on its face is an icon of a form.

When you instruct Visual Basic to add a new form, a new Form window appears on-screen, and the default form caption appears in the title bar for the Form window. The default caption is always Form1, Form2, Form3, and so on. Each time you create a new form, the number at the end of the caption is incremented. Later in this chapter, you learn how to change the default name and caption for a form.

Changing a Form's Appearance and Behavior

You probably will never use a form without altering its appearance. You may want the form to be a different size or color. Or perhaps you want a thick border or maybe a thin one. Visual Basic provides many form properties that can make your applications more functional, interesting, and enjoyable to use.

When you open a project file, you may see only the Project window; the Form window may be closed. In this case, click the View Form button at the top of the Project window. To change a form's properties, you use the Properties window, shown in figure 3.1 (refer to Chapter 2 for additional discussion). If the Properties window is not visible on your screen, you can display it by pressing **F4** or choosing **P**roperties from the **W**indows menu.

Figure 3.1
The Properties window.

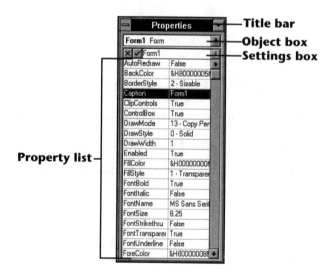

The Properties window displays a list of characteristics and specifications for a selected form or for a selected control within a form. Because properties are associated only with forms and controls, the **P**roperties item on the **W**indow menu is not valid unless a form or a control is selected. If the **P**roperties menu item is grayed or if the F4 key has no effect, you must select either a form or a control before you can display the Properties window.

The property names are listed in the left column of the Properties list box; the current values of the properties are listed in the right column. You can browse through the list of properties the same way you browse through any list box. Move one item at a time by using the keyboard's up- and down-arrow keys or by clicking the up- or down-pointing arrow on the scroll bar to the right of the list. Move a page at a time by pressing the Page Up and Page Down keys or by clicking in the scroll bar at the right side of the window.

The top text box (the Object box) in the Properties window is a drop-down list of all the objects in the active form. The Object box itself always contains the name of the selected object (Form1 in figure 3.1). The second text box (the Settings box) is used to modify the value for the selected property (Caption in figure 3.1). Double-click the property name in the Properties list box to move the name into the Settings box and modify the property's value.

Clicking the X button at the left of the Settings box cancels a setting modification in progress. Clicking the check mark button at the left of the Settings box or pressing the Enter key accepts the modification. Some properties with a set of alternatives (like Yes or No, or 1, 2, 3) can be changed by double-clicking the property in the Property list.

Types of Properties

Design-time properties
Properties listed in the Properties window; the initial values are set while the project is being designed.

The properties you see listed in the Properties window are referred to as **design-time properties**. This term means simply that you set the initial values while you are designing your project. Other properties associated with forms are not available from the Properties window. These properties are called **run-time properties**, and they can be modified only when a program is running. Run-time properties are modified through the use of Visual Basic programming commands rather than with a tool, such as the Properties window.

Run-time properties
Properties not available from the Properties window; can be modified and used only when a program is running.

One example of a run-time property is ActiveControl. This property specifies the control on your form, that has the focus (the control that is currently selected). Because ActiveControl makes sense only at run time, you won't find it listed in the Properties window.

Properties Related to Forms

The best way to understand the purpose of different properties is to take a look at what the properties do. The following sections introduce you to many of the properties related to forms. Some of these properties are also properties of controls. Remember, these are the properties you will most likely use as you get started with Visual Basic.

A few other properties are also introduced. Many people are overwhelmed by the quantity and variety of different properties available. Don't worry. Just because Visual Basic provides a property doesn't mean that you have to change it. In fact, in most instances, your form will be just fine if you use the default property values. As your experience grows, you will learn about the other properties. And as your needs grow, you will come to appreciate the versatility offered.

If you forget the purpose of a property or if you simply want to learn more about a property, select that property in the Properties window, and press **F1**. This key accesses the Visual Basic Help system, displaying context-sensitive help about the selected property.

Color Properties

Color can be a most effective means of communicating. Color can add variety and spice to a program. For example, you may want to color code your forms as a way to indicate their purposes; you could use pale yellow for a data-entry form and light green for an output form. When you start placing controls on your forms, you can also modify the controls' colors. For example, if you use a control that displays a numeric value, you may want negative values to be displayed in red.

The properties that control the colors of a form and a control are

- BackColor. Sets the background color of a form or control. The default color is white.

- ForeColor. Sets the color used in a form or control to display text or graphics. You will not often change this property for a form. You will often change the BackColor and ForeColor of text boxes and labels.

- FillColor. The color used by the VB application at run time to fill patterns and shapes in the background of a form or in a control.

- BorderColor. Specifies the color used to display the border of certain controls. BorderColor is not a property of forms.

If you search the VB Help system topics, you will find Help screens with information about these four properties. You will also find information on changing these properties in Visual Basic code. The Usage section of a VB Help screen always shows you how to refer to a property in Visual Basic code.

In Windows, colors are referred to by number. The value of a color property is always a number that represents the amount of each of the three primary colors (red, green, and blue) used to make up that color.

Fortunately, Visual Basic doesn't force you to use numbers to enter colors. If you double-click any color property in a Properties window, you see a palette of colors from which you may choose (see figure 3.2). The palette contains 64 colors. The first 48 are predefined; you define the last 16. When you select a color, its number is automatically placed in the selected color property in the object's Properties window.

The 64-color palette used to define colors can be composed of any set of 64 colors drawn from as many colors as your hardware supports. If your video card is capable of displaying more than 16 million colors, for instance, the palette can consist of any 64 of those 16 million colors.

Figure 3.2
Choosing a color
from the palette.

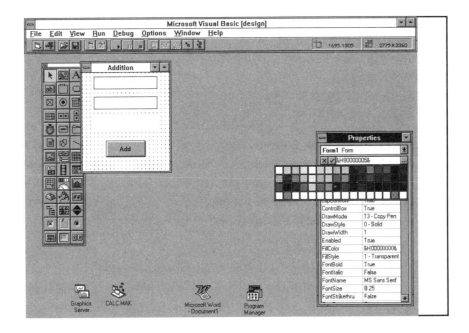

The fact that you can easily add many colors to a form makes getting carried away with your color scheme easier. You should use color only in a functional way; don't use so much color that it is distracting.

Text Properties

In Chapter 2, you learned how the Name and Caption properties relate to forms and objects. To understand these properties fully, you need to know more about them.

When a new form is added to your project, its two text properties, Caption and Name, are automatically set to default values. You see these values in the top line of the Settings box in the Properties window. Most Visual Basic programmers, however, change these defaults to reflect the proper title and purpose of the form.

The Caption Property

Most Windows programs display some descriptive text in the title bar of the application's window. Sometimes this text is as simple as the name of the program. Most of the time, however, the text is the name you decide to assign to the dialog box your form is defining. When you design programs with Visual Basic, you use the Caption property of the form to control the text displayed in the form's title bar.

To change a form's caption, double-click the Caption property in the Properties window. Then type the text you want to appear in the form's title bar. The text you type immediately appears in the title bar.

The *Name* Property

If your application contains more than one form, you should assign a unique name to each form. Don't use the default name assigned by Visual Basic. The name is used primarily to refer to a form (in Visual Basic program procedures) or to refer to the controls within the form. For instance, if you change the name of a form from the default (such as Form1) to a descriptive name (such as GetInput), you will have a much better idea of what the form is for when you refer to it from other parts of your program. This name will identify the form in the Project window. Using descriptive names for your forms makes it easier to remember the purpose of each form in your project.

Note: *A form's* Name *property does not refer to the file name by which the form is stored. You specify the file name in the File Save dialog box when you save the form module. The file name is not a property of the form. It is simply the name used by the operating system to reference the FRM file in which the form is stored. The file name also appears in the MAK project file.*

The Size and Location Properties

Because forms represent program windows or dialog boxes that appear when your program is running, the form must have a size and a location that indicate at least where the form appears on the screen and the form's dimensions. The various size and location properties determine the form's dimensions and its position on-screen.

Note: *The default measurement for size and location in VB is Twips (1,440 twips equal 1 inch). Twips are a unit of measurement developed by Microsoft so that VB objects can be displayed on a variety of different computers. In the printing industry, a point is 1/72 of an inch. This measurement is used to describe the size of a print font. The name Twip comes from the fact that a Twip is one-twentieth of a point.*

The size and location properties are Left, Top, Height, and Width. Together these four properties define the location and size of a form. In the following sections, you learn more about these properties.

Left and Top

The Left and Top properties specify the location of the form's left and top edges, respectively. In effect, these two properties define the location of the upper-left corner of the window. Although you can manually enter coordinates in the Properties window, simply dragging the form with the mouse is much easier. As you move the Form window, the values of the Left and Top properties are automatically updated to reflect the new location.

Height and Width

Visual Basic could have been designed with Right and Bottom properties in addition to Left and Top, but it wasn't. A more sensible way is to specify the upper-left corner and then specify the height and width of the window in relation to that corner. The use of the Height and Width properties works this way. Therefore, your program code can move the window by resetting Top and Left without accidentally altering the window's size.

When combined with the Left property, Width determines where the right side of the form is. Given the Top property, Height determines where the bottom of the form is. As with the Top and Left, using the mouse to modify the height and width of the Form window is much easier than entering the values manually.

The *BorderStyle* Property

Borders define the boundaries (edges) of a window or a dialog box. Visual Basic enables you to specify the border type by using the BorderStyle property. You can choose any of the following four different border types for your Form windows: None, Sizable, Fixed Double, or Fixed Single.

If you choose None as a BorderStyle, the window will not have a border; you will have no demarcation between the window and the surrounding desktop. This style may be fine if the form's BackColor is a different color from the Windows desktop. If the BackColor and the Windows desktop are the same color, your controls themselves will appear to be lying on the desktop instead of in a window.

The most common type of border is the Sizable border, the default. If you choose Sizable for BorderStyle, the user can change the size of the window when your program is running. Sometimes a changeable window size is not appropriate. For example, if your form will be used as a dialog box, you will want to use a fixed border.

The Fixed Double border type typically is used when designing dialog boxes. If you use the Fixed Double border type, the size of the window cannot be changed. (The user can still move the form, but the size remains the same.)

Finally, the Fixed Single border is used primarily to design windows (not dialog boxes) whose size you want to remain stable. Again, although the user can move the window, the window cannot be modified in size.

Note: *When you use the* Fixed Single *and* Fixed Double *border styles, the Minimize and Maximize buttons are not displayed on the form. These border styles do not, however, omit the Minimize and Maximize items from the window's Control menu. To remove Minimize and Maximize from the Control menu, set the* MinButton *and* MaxButton *properties to False.*

Most programmers double-click properties like BorderStyle when they want to change the property in the Properties window. Double-clicking enables programmers to "step" quickly through the list of available settings. For properties with multiple options, the second drop-down list at the top of the Properties window is enabled, and you can select from the drop-down list.

The border-style changes you make to your forms are not evident until you run your program. The reason is simple: If the border changed at design time and you selected a border type other than Sizable, you would have no way to resize the form during design.

The *Visible* Property

The form's Visible property determines whether the form is visible when it is loaded into the workspace of your program. The default value for this property is True, although you can also set it to False. (These are the only two settings.)

The Visible property enables you to indicate the initial condition of the window. While you are running the program, you can use other program instructions to change the property "on the fly." This kind of instruction typically is used when your application contains several forms and you want to control the display of those forms as you switch from one to another. You hide one form and show the next form. The screen doesn't get cluttered, and you can designate which form gets the attention of the user.

An example in VB code that uses the Hide and Show methods to change the Visible property is

```
Form1.Hide
Form2.Show
```

Using the Control Menu

In Windows, a Control menu appears when you click the Control-menu box, which is at the left end of a window's title bar (see figure 3.3). Visual Basic enables you to designate whether the menu appears at all.

Control-menu box

Figure 3.3
The Control-menu box.

Earlier in this chapter, you learned that you can use the MinButton and MaxButton properties to indicate whether the Minimize and Maximize menu items appear on the Control menu; you should use these properties if you are designing a window whose size you don't want changed. Setting these properties to False means that the menu items won't be displayed.

The ControlBox property turns the Control menu off entirely. If this property is set to False, the Control-menu box will not appear on the window. Use the False setting when you are designing dialog boxes instead of windows.

The Picture Properties

Pictures add pizzazz to your form, and Windows provides an excellent environment for working with graphics. Visual Basic gives you the tools to add graphics to your form through the use of two properties. The Icon property enables you to control which icon is displayed when the form is minimized, and the Picture property provides a method of adding a picture to the form itself.

In Windows, a form icon and a program icon are different. The form icon is displayed when the window defined by the form is minimized. A program icon is displayed when the program resides in a group in Program Manager, waiting to be executed. You set the form icon by using the Icon property; you set the program icon when you make an executable program file, as discussed later in this text.

The *Icon* Property

The Icon property determines which icon is displayed when the form is minimized. The default icon for Visual Basic forms is not very attractive, but you can assign any icon you want. Figure 3.4 shows a simple example of the difference between the stock Visual Basic form icon and a custom icon.

Figure 3.4
Examples of stock and custom icons.

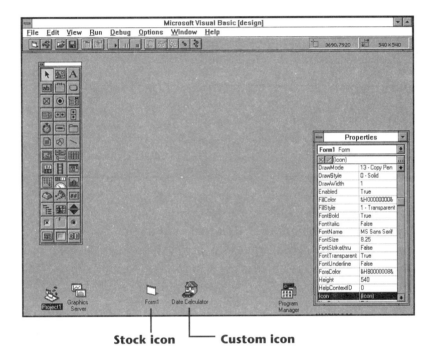

Many icons are provided with Visual Basic in the VB\ICONS subdirectory. The icons are all shown in Appendix B of the *Programmer's Reference* (provided with the Visual Basic software package).

The *Picture* Property

You can place an image—an icon, for example—directly on the form itself by using the Picture property. The image is placed as a background in the form, beginning at the upper-left corner. You can use the IconWorks program found in VB\SAMPLES to view the icons available in VB\ICONS. You can also use IconWorks to draw your own icon. You can then save it in a disk file and place your icon in a form or a graphics control. Figure 3.5 shows an example of a picture placed in a form.

In Chapter 4, you learn how to capture any image from your Windows screen and paste it into a form or graphics control.

Visual Basic recognizes four picture types. Table 3.1 lists their names and file extensions.

Figure 3.5

An example of using a picture in a form.

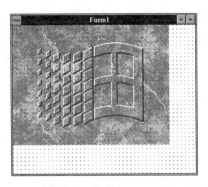

Table 3.1   Picture File Formats

Format	Extension
Bit Map	BMP
Device Independent Bit Map	DIB
Windows Metafile	WMF
Icon	ICO

Pixel

The smallest picture element that a device can display on-screen.

Bit maps represent a picture by storing the value of each **pixel** in that picture. (Pixels are the smallest units that make up the images you see on a screen.) The larger the picture being stored, the larger the size of the BMP or DIB file representing it. Bit-mapped files don't scale well. If you plan to stretch or shrink the size of the picture, consider using a metafile.

An icon, or ICO file, is a special type of bit-mapped file. These files are graphic images that are limited to 32 pixels wide by 32 pixels high. Icons can, however, be stretched when placed in an Image control, as you learn later in this chapter.

Metafiles represent a picture by depicting the way the picture is drawn. The WMF format offers two advantages over bit maps. First, the WMF format is usually more efficient with regard to storage space. Second, metafiles are not as distorted by changing their size from the size of the original picture. Unless you will be doing a great deal of graphics programming with VB, the characteristics of the various image files are not important for you to memorize.

The *WindowState* Property

A form in Microsoft Windows can appear in one of three states: maximized (filling the entire screen), minimized (as an icon at the bottom of the screen), or normal (filling a portion of the screen). The WindowState property determines whether the form is shown maximized, minimized, or normal at run time.

Three values are available for this property: 0 (the default value, the form appears in normal size), 1 (the form is minimized, shrunk to an icon), and 2 (the form is maximized). If you modify the value at design time, the form's appearance does not change until run time.

The WindowState property you set in the Properties window sets only the initial window condition. You can change the condition while the program is running (using programming commands), or the user can change the condition by minimizing, maximizing, or restoring the window size.

Other Properties

Forms have quite a few additional properties. You can learn more about these properties by clicking the property in the Properties window and pressing **F1** for context-sensitive help. For an in-depth look at additional properties, refer to Que's *Using Visual Basic 3*, Special Edition.

Revisiting the Calculator

Now that you know more about forms and the ways you can use properties to control forms, you are ready to put the information to work. The best way to do this is to look again at the Visual Basic project you started in Chapter 2. In the following exercises, you change some of the form and control properties in this project.

Opening the Project

Before you can make changes to your calculator program, you must load it from disk either by clicking the Open icon on the Toolbar (third icon from the left) or by choosing **O**pen Project from the **F**ile menu. You see a dialog box where you can specify the project to open.

You may remember from Chapter 2 that the project file name was CALC. Thus, you should open the file CALC.MAK. Everything will be in the same condition it was when you last saved your project.

Planning Changes to the Form

Applying the information learned in this chapter, suppose that you decide to make the following changes:

- Modify the caption shown on the title bar of the calculator.
- Change the form's border so that the user cannot resize the window.
- Change the program's icon to something representative of your calculator program.
- Change the background color of the form to light blue.
- Modify the default information shown in the text boxes and label.
- Change the foreground color of the label to red.

Making Changes to the Form

To make these changes, make sure that Visual Basic is loaded and that you have opened CALC.MAK; then follow these steps:

❶ To make the first change, select the form (use the mouse to click the Form window title bar). Then press the **F4** key to make the Properties window active.

❷ To change the form's Caption property, double-click the Caption property in the Properties window. This step places the property's current value in the editing area of the Settings box at the top of the Properties window.

❸ Replace the default form caption (Form1) by typing a more descriptive name; type **Addition**. This word appears in the Settings box.

❹ Press the **Enter** key, or click the check mark button at the left of the Settings box. (The button with an X at the left of the Settings box cancels an entry in progress).

Notice that when you type the new caption, it appears immediately in the Form window title bar.

❺ Change the form's BorderStyle property to 3 Fixed Double by double-clicking the property in the Properties window until the correct setting appears.

You will not see any immediate difference in how the Form looks. However, the window will behave differently when the program is executed.

❻ Now change the form's Icon property. If you double-click the property, you can choose the icon file you want to use.

Use the MISC18 icon, which is a plus (+) sign, because the calculator will perform addition. Make sure that the icon properties file to use is VB\ICONS\MISC\MISC18.ICO, and then press **Enter**.

❼ Change the form's background to light blue by double-clicking the BackColor property and clicking one of the light blue colored squares in the palette.

❽ Use the mouse to select the first of the Text Box controls in the form.

❾ Change the Text property so that it is empty (the default is Text1). Double-click the Text property in the Properties window. The default Text property appears in the editing area of the Settings box at the top of the Properties window. Press the **Backspace** key to clear the Text property. Press the **Enter** key.

❿ Use the same technique to empty the Text property of the Text2 text box.

⓫ To make the same change in the Label control, select it, and then modify the Caption property. Delete the default value (Label1) so that nothing appears in the label.

⓬ Change the color of the caption that will be displayed in the label. Double-click the `ForeColor` property, and click one of the red squares in the color palette.

⓭ After making these changes, save the project on disk as **C3PROG**.

⓮ Run the modified program, enter numbers, and note the changes.

Understanding Events That Happen to Forms

There are 23 different events that can occur to forms, but many of these events are rarely used by programmers. In other words, the procedures to handle these events are left empty; no code is inserted in them. Visual Basic's Help contains explanations of all 23 form events. The events for which programmers most frequently code event handlers are the `Form Load` and `Unload` events.

The *Load* Event

Form loading

The loading of a form into memory, where it becomes available to a program.

You cannot use a form at run time until the form is loaded. **Form loading** means that the form is placed into memory, where it becomes available to your program. Your program code can then start using the form and the controls that are on it.

When is a form loaded? One form, called the start-up form, loads as soon as your program starts running. How can you define which form is the start-up form? The following exercise covers this topic.

Specifying the Start-Up Form

To specify a start-up form, follow these steps:

❶ Open the project in Visual Basic, and choose **O**ptions **P**roject. This command displays the Project Options dialog box (see figure 3.6).

Figure 3.6
The Project Options dialog box.

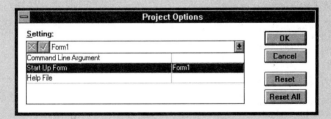

❷ Click Start Up Form, and use the **S**etting drop-down list to choose the form you want to be the start-up form.

❸ Choose OK.

When you try this exercise, you will notice that, in addition to being able to choose one of the project's forms to be the start-up form, you also can choose Sub Main as the start-up form. Sub Main isn't a form; it's a section of code in a BAS module. You learn more about Sub Main in a later chapter. For now, just understand that no form has to load right away or show up on-screen if you don't want it to. Form1 (the first form in a new project) will be the start-up form unless you specify another form.

What is useful about the Load event? The Load event is a good time to execute the code that sets up the controls on a form. For example, suppose that you want the program to check the disk for a registration file or to fill a list box with values when the form is loaded. To accomplish either of these actions, you should insert the necessary program code into the Load event for the form. If you want some code to execute as soon as you start the program, insert that code into the Load event for the start-up form.

This technique is illustrated in the code for the Load event in the project EVENTS.MAK, which you can find on your student disk in the CHAPT3 subdirectory.

Using the Load Event

This exercise shows how to use the Load event. Follow these steps:

❶ Open the project EVENTS.MAK which is your student disk in the CHAPT3 subdirectory.

❷ To display Form1, open the Project window, choose EVENTS.FRM, and click the View Form button.

❸ In the Project window, choose the View Code button (or double-click any blank area of Form1).

❹ Examine the code for the Load event (see figure 3.7).

Figure 3.7
The code for the Load event of Form1.

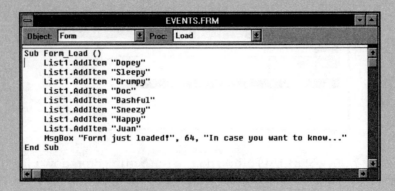

❺ Run the program, and click the OK button in the message box that appears on the display.

⑥ Examine the program's window, and notice that the list box is filled in.

⑦ End the program.

Now that you know how to make things happen when a Load event occurs, consider the Unload event.

The *Unload* Event

Unload
To remove a form from memory.

Forms take up memory. To conserve memory, you can remove from RAM any forms that the program isn't using. To remove a form from memory, you **unload** it. You can unload the form by executing a line of code that generates an Unload event for the form:

Unloading *Form1*

3

If you double-click a form's Control menu when the program is running, an Unload event is generated for the form, and the form goes away. If you need to have the program execute some code when a form is unloaded, add the code for the form's Unload event, as follows:

```
Sub Form1_Unload ()
       'put the code that you want executed here
End Sub
```

In EVENTS.MAK, the Unload procedure for Form1 includes a line of code that displays a message box when the Unload event occurs.

① Open EVENTS.MAK, if it is not already open.

② Open the code window for Form1, click the Proc drop-down list, and choose the Unload procedure from the list. You should see the code shown in figure 3.8.

Figure 3.8
The Unload event procedure for Form1.

When you close the program by double-clicking its Control menu, or choose Close from the Control menu, an Unload event occurs. When that event occurs, the program displays the See ya! message box.

As mentioned , other events are also associated with forms, but Load and Unload are enough for now.

Using the Controls in Your Toolbox

In Chapter 2, you learned about the Toolbox, which is the repository of all the controls you can use in your Visual Basic programs. The Toolbox does not need to be displayed when you are programming in Visual Basic, but it is helpful when you are designing your forms. If the Toolbox is not on-screen, choose **T**oolbox from the **W**indow menu to display Visual Basic's Toolbox.

This section discusses some of the most commonly used controls. First, the text explains some of the common properties for these controls. Some of these properties are the same ones that you learned about in the discussion of form properties. Then the chapter discusses the individual controls, their special properties, and their most frequently occurring events.

Working with Controls in Your User Interface

In Chapter 2, you learned how to start working with the building blocks of Visual Basic programs—controls. For example, you learned that when the Toolbox is displayed, you can place a control in a form using either of these methods:

> In the Toolbox, double-click the tool that represents the control you want to place in your form. This method places the control in the center of the form.

> In the Toolbox, click the tool that represents the control you want to use in your form. This method selects the tool. Then use the mouse to draw the control in the form. This technique is most frequently used when drawing controls inside a Frame control or inside a Picture Box control.

You can use certain techniques when working with controls in the Design mode. You can change properties, delete controls, move controls, and resize controls. Before you can take any action with regard to a control on a form, you must first select the control. To select a control, point to it in your form, and then click it once.

You move a control the same way you move other objects in Windows. After you have selected the control by clicking it, use the mouse to point to the object. Then click and hold down the mouse button. As you move the mouse, the control also moves. When you release the mouse button, the control is "dropped" at that location.

To resize a control, you use the black sizing handles that appear around it when it is selected. To change the size of the control, point to one of the sizing handles with the mouse, click and hold down the mouse button, and move the mouse. When the control is the right size, release the mouse button. To delete a control, select the control you want to delete, and then press the Delete key. Just be sure to modify any VB program code that may have referred to the control. If you don't, you may get errors when you later try to run the software.

Adding Controls to a Form

After the Toolbox is displayed, you can start using it to add controls to your forms. Adding controls to your projects is a three-step process:

1. You add the required controls to the form.

2. You set the properties of the controls.

3. You attach any necessary code (code to handle the occurrence of the event) to the controls' event procedures.

Each step is important to the development of your programs. The first two steps can be particularly time-consuming, especially if your program does quite a bit of user interaction. The first step is done exclusively with the Toolbox. The second step is usually done with the Properties window in Design mode. However, when your program is running, Visual Basic statements can also set the properties of controls. The final step involves actually creating programming code.

The easiest way to understand how to do the first two steps is to get a firm grasp on the different controls you have available. Each control is designed to provide you with a special set of user interface and programming capabilities. Of course, there is some overlapping of properties and functions for the controls. But after you know what the controls are, you can pick the right one for the right job and then set the properties of that control. In the next several sections, you learn about different types of controls available in Visual Basic and about their properties.

Setting Control Properties

As you worked through the first section of this chapter, you learned about forms and their properties. Properties also apply to controls. Many controls have some of the same properties as forms. For example, controls have names. Most controls have widths and heights and `BorderStyles`, `Visible`, `BackColor`, and `ForeColor` properties. Many of the controls you use in Visual Basic can have dozens of properties associated with them. These properties are listed in the Properties window, and they differ (to some degree) based on the type of control you are using.

Most of the properties associated with controls are intuitive in nature. When you change a control's property, the behavior or appearance of the control changes accordingly. As you work through the examples in this book, you will learn more about the individual properties of many controls.

To list every possible property for every possible control would be virtually impossible—the possible combinations could number well into the thousands. Thus, it is far more valuable for you to learn how to discover more about properties on your own. That way, if you run across a property that is not described in this book, you can still get information about it.

Learning about a Property

The best way to get information about a property is to follow these steps:

❶ Select the object (form or control) whose properties you want to change or learn more about.

❷ In the Properties window, select (click) the property in question.

❸ Press the **F1** key, which results in Visual Basic's displaying context-sensitive help about the property.

Later in this chapter, you learn about some of the more common control properties and learn how to use them.

Changing Control Properties at Run Time

You can set properties when you design a form or a control and then change them as your program is running. Usually, you set the initial property values in Design mode and then change a few of them when your program is running.

To alter a particular property of a control while your program is running, your program instructions must use the following format:

```
form.control.property = value
```

Make sure that what you substitute for the form and control correspond to the Name property assigned to the form and control whose property you are changing. Specification of the form is necessary only if the program code is referring to a control in a form different from the one currently selected. For example, if Form2 is active and you want to refer to text in text box 3 in Form1, you would code:

```
Form1.Text3.Text
```

As a second example, consider the Enabled property (explained more fully later in this chapter). When you first design your program, you can set the control as enabled or disabled. You may want this state to be changed as your program is running, however. If you want to change the Enabled property of a control named Command1 in a form named Form2, you use the following program line:

```
Form2.Command1.Enabled = False
```

As you will learn after using Visual Basic for a while, each control was developed to meet a particular programming need. For example, the primary purpose of a Label control is to display short pieces of information that cannot be changed by the user while the program is running. For text boxes, the primary purpose is to display or accept large amounts of text. This text can be entered in the Properties window in the Design mode. And when the program is running, the text can be entered by the user from the keyboard or read by the program from a file.

Visual Basic refers to the property most closely associated with the control's primary purpose as the control's value. (This value is not the same as the Value property). The benefit of knowing this fact is that when your program is running, it can change the value of the control without your needing to indicate explicitly which property you are changing. For example, the following two lines of code perform exactly the same action because the Caption property is the Label1 control's value:

```
Label1.Caption = "Last Name"
Label1 = "Last Name"
```

Table 3.2 lists some Visual Basic controls and their default properties.

Table 3.2 Controls and Their Values	
Control	**Value**
Check Box	Value
Frame	Caption
Label	Caption
Option button	Value
Text Box	Text
Timer	Enabled

Learning Commonly Used Properties of Controls

Some properties are shared by many controls. These properties are also the most commonly used and modified properties. This section discusses these properties.

The *Name* Property

Every control in an application must have a unique Name property. In any application, you can simply accept the default names that Visual Basic assigns to the controls (and to the forms). In applications with several controls, however, modifying their names to be more descriptive of their purposes is a good idea.

Whenever you place a control on a form, Visual Basic assigns the control a default name. That name consists of a base name followed by a number. For example, the first command button you place on a form is given the name Command1. If you place additional command buttons on the form, the default names are Command2, Command3, and so on. The second column in table 3.3 shows the default name and the function of each control type.

Table 3.3 The Toolbox Controls				
Control	**Default Name**	**Name Prefix**	**Chap. Num.**	**Description**
Picture Box	Picture1	pic	8	Provides a rectangular area in which graphics can be displayed.
Label	Label1	lbl	8	Displays text that the user cannot directly modify at run time.

(continues)

Table 3.3 Continued

Control	Default Name	Name Prefix	Chap. Num.	Description
Text Box	Text1	txt	8	Displays text that the user can directly modify at run time.
Frame	Frame1	fra	8	Provides a rectangular area in which other controls can be placed as a group.
Command Button	Command1	cmd	8	Responds to a user click to activate a requested event.
Check Box	Check1	chk	8	Displays an X or an empty box to indicate the current state of a True/False option, and responds to a user click to toggle the choice.
Option Button	Option1	opt	8	Displays a bullet if an option is selected; this control typically appears in groups to enable the user to choose from mutually exclusive options.
Combo Box	Combo1	cbo	8	By combining the features of both a text and a list box, the user can specify data by typing a value or selecting an appropriate value from a drop-down list.
List Box	List1	lst	8	Displays a drop-down list of values, from which the user can select one value.
Horizontal Scroll Bar	HScroll1	hsb	8	Provides a visual mechanism for the user to select a particular value from a continuous range of possible values.
Vertical Scroll Bar	VScroll1	vsb	8	Similar to the Horizontal scroll bar, but with a vertical orientation.
Timer	Timer1	tmr	8	Triggers an event when a specified time period elapses.
Drive List Box	Drive1	drv	25	Provides a list of the PC's available disk drives, enabling the user to select one.
Directory List Box	Dir1	dir	25	Provides a list of paths and directories, enabling the user to select a path.
File List Box	File1	fil	25	Provides a list of files, enabling the user to select one.
Shape	Shape1	shp	11	Provides a tool for drawing two-dimensional geometric shapes.
Line	Line1	lin	11	Provides a tool for drawing straight lines.
Image	Image1	img	11	Provides a rectangular area in which graphics can be displayed; this control is similar to, but simpler than, a picture box.
Data	Data1	dta	28	Supports databases, including compatibility with commercial products such as Microsoft Access.
Grid	Grid1	grd	26	Displays data in rows and columns.
OLE	OLE1	ole	31	Provides a data link with an external OLE (Object Linking and Embedding) compliant application.

If an application has five command buttons named Command1 through Command5, it's difficult when looking through the code to recognize immediately how each command button operates. Instead, you may want to assign more descriptive names, such as OKButton, QuitButton, DeleteButton, and so on. That way, when the control name appears in code, the command button being referenced is obvious.

In VB code, you use a control's name to reference the individual control. For example, the following instruction modifies the Caption property of the command button named Command2:

```
Command2.Caption = "Click Me Now"
```

Visual Basic (and you) use a control's name when referring to one of the control's event procedures. For example, the Click event handler procedure for the command button named Command2 would be named

```
Command2_Click ()
```

The BackColor property is available for command buttons but does not really change the color of the button. I don't know why Microsoft did this. Command buttons will always be gray.

How Event Procedures for a Control Are Named

Once you modify a control name, Visual Basic automatically creates for the control's event procedures templates using the new name. For example, if you change the name of Command1 to QuitButton, Visual Basic renames the template for the control's Click event procedure from Command1_Click to QuitButton_Click.

Be very careful about modifying the Name property *after* writing event procedures. If you modify the Name property of a control for which you have already written an event procedure, Visual Basic does *not* rename the existing event procedure. Instead, the old event procedure is placed in the general declaration section of the form, and a stub for the new named event procedure is created.

For example, suppose that you have written a Command1_Click event procedure. Then you change the name of Command1 to QuitButton. The Command1_Click procedure is no longer considered to represent an active event and is moved to the form's general declaration section. Visual Basic creates a new template (without any program instructions) for the QuitButton_Click event procedure. You must rewrite the program code for the new Click procedure. (You can, of course, cut and paste the instructions from the old procedure into the new one.)

In any case, if you are going to modify the Name properties of controls and forms, you should do so *before* writing any associated event procedures.

Recommended Naming Conventions

You can give your controls names up to 40 characters long. The name can contain letters, digits, and underscore characters but must begin with a letter. You cannot have any blank spaces in a name. It is generally considered good programming practice to give your forms and controls descriptive names. Doing so helps make the program code easier to read—which is especially important when debugging. The more controls you have in an application, the more important this advice is.

Name Prefixes

When renaming controls, you are free to use any names. One common renaming scheme uses a three-letter prefix immediately followed by a descriptive name. The prefix identifies the control type. For example, the prefix for a command button is *cmd*. Using this scheme, you might write the name cmdQuit instead of QuitButton.

The advantages of this scheme are as follows:

- The prefix immediately identifies the type of control. Any time you see in the program code a control name that begins with *cmd*, for example, you know that the control is a command button.

- The prefixes ensure that controls of the same type appear together in the Code window list. In the Object box of the Code window, the controls and forms of a project are listed alphabetically. If you systematically use the suggested prefixes, the command buttons appear listed together. Similarly, each of the other types of controls is listed in a group. When you look through the list of controls, you can quickly identify every command button in the application.

The third column in table 3.3 shows the prefixes for a naming scheme in popular use.

The *Caption* and *Name* Properties

Some properties are so common in their use and are properties of so many controls that they deserve special treatment and discussion. In this section, you learn about these properties and ways their use can enhance your programs.

Captions are used as on-screen identifiers for many different types of controls. This property applies to Command Button, Label, Check Box, Option Button, and Frame controls.

Visual Basic also allows you to create access keys for use with captions. Most Windows programs use access keys on command buttons or other controls. Access keys, represented on-screen by an underlined letter, indicate that you can select the control by pressing the Alt key in combination with the underlined letter.

You can create your own access keys by using the ampersand (&) character when setting the Caption property. For example, suppose that you want to set the caption for a command button to the word *Go* and you want the access key to be Alt+G. Set the Caption property equal to &Go. The ampersand indicates that the following character (the *G*) is the access key. Visual Basic takes care of the rest—when your program is running, the *G* will be underlined, and the program will automatically recognize what to do when Alt+G is pressed.

The `Caption` property is used to display small amounts of information to the user. Some controls (such as the Text Box and Combo Box controls) are used to display larger amounts of information. In these cases, text that is displayed by the control is assigned to the control's `Text` property. To change what is displayed in a text box, change its `Text` property.

This displayed text is easily altered in appearance if you do not like the way the default settings look. To change the appearance of the contents of the `Text` property, you change properties discussed in the following section.

Changing the Appearance of Your Text

One of the strongest features of Windows is the attractive way in which it can present information. Visual Basic, through Windows, gives you complete control over how your text looks on-screen. If you are using a control that displays text, you can use Visual Basic to modify how that text is presented.

3

Understanding and Changing Fonts

Font
A particular style of type.

The word **font** refers to the style of type (characters) used in the display of information. Each font has distinguishing characteristics, such as the typeface, which refers to the general appearance of a character; the type style (such as italic or boldface); and the type size (how large the character appears). To change the appearance of text on your controls, Visual Basic provides several different properties. For example, the following instruction makes the caption of `Label1` appear in italics:

```
Label1.FontItalic = True
```

By default, the value of `FontItalic` is False.

Changing Fonts

By default, Visual Basic uses the MS Sans Serif font for all the controls you create. If you want to specify a different font, just change the `FontName` property.

The fonts available to Visual Basic depend on the fonts installed on your computer system. Visual Basic knows which fonts are installed; therefore, at design time, you can select from a list of available fonts. If you distribute your application to others, you must make sure that they have the same fonts available on their system. If they don't, your program will not appear the same to them as it does to you. The simplest solution is to use the default MS Sans Serif font. This very readable font is available on all Windows 3.0 and Windows 3.1 systems.

TrueType fonts
Fonts constructed so that they can be scaled without losing their good appearance.

With the introduction of Windows 3.1 came the inclusion of a new font technology called TrueType. **TrueType fonts** are constructed in such a way that they can be scaled without losing their good looks—in many ways TrueType fonts are a competitor to PostScript fonts. If your program requires using fonts of many different sizes, consider using TrueType fonts.

You are not limited to using fonts supplied with Windows. In fact, thousands of different fonts can be purchased from many different sources. If you choose to use a font from a third-party vendor, you should be aware that most vendors do not allow you to redistribute their fonts. They require each user to purchase a copy. If you intend to distribute your applications to others, be sure to take this fact into account when selecting the fonts you use.

Changing Other Text Appearance Properties

Besides specifying the type of font to use, you also can use Visual Basic to control how that font looks. Table 3.4 describes other properties that can be used to modify text used in your controls.

Table 3.4	Visual Basic Text Properties	
Property	**Value**	**Result**
FontBold	True False	Text appears in bold. Text appears normal.
FontItalic	True False	Text appears in italics. Text appears normal.
FontSize	A number	The size of each text line in points. Each point is approximately 1/72 of an inch.
FontStrikethru	True False	Text appears with a line horizontally through the middle of it. Text appears normal.
FontTransparent	True False	Background shows through text. Text blocks background.
FontUnderline	True False	Text appears underlined. Text appears normal.

The *Alignment* Property

If you have used a word processor for any length of time, you already know that there is more than one way to align text in a document. Although not quite as versatile as a word processor, Visual Basic also enables you to align the text within various controls. Primarily, this capability applies to any displayable text set with the Caption or Text property.

The Alignment property is applicable to the Label, Text Box, Check Box, and Option Button controls. Table 3.5 lists the various Alignment property settings you can use. You should note, however, that not all these settings are available for all controls. For example, you cannot center check boxes and option buttons.

Table 3.5	Visual Basic Alignment Options
Alignment	**Meaning**
Left Justify	Align the text at the left side of the control.
Right Justify	Align the text at the right side of the control.
Center	Center the text within the control.

The *Value* Property

Controls like check boxes and option buttons can be either on or off, True or False. The `Value` property enables you to indicate the initial setting for the control. If you set the `Value` property to either 1 or True (depending on the control), the control is shown on the form as selected. You can also change the `Value` property at run time by using VB code.

The *Enabled* Property

The `Enabled` property regulates the user's run-time access to a control. This property can have the value True or False, with True as the default value.

Many controls can be either enabled or disabled at run time by using the `Enabled` property. If this property is set to True (the default), the control is available to be operated by the user as the program is running. If the `Enabled` property is set to False, the control will be visible to the user but inoperable. When your program is running, the control appears dimmed or grayed to indicate to the user that it cannot be accessed. When disabled, a control does not respond to any user-generated events, such as a mouse click.

In code, you can set the value of `Enabled` to False to disable a control temporarily. When you want the user to regain access to the control, change the value back to True.

The *Visible* Property

Another property that is common to many different controls is `Visible`. The `Visible` property determines whether the user can see the control at run time. When the value of `Visible` is False for a control, the control is hidden from view. When hidden, a control does not respond to any user-generated events. Your VB program code, however, can access it.

In general, you should avoid using the `Visible` property as a way of restricting the user's options. Controls that suddenly disappear and then later reappear tend to confuse users. Users might think that an application which is working just as you programmed it is not performing correctly. To make a control temporarily unavailable, set the `Enabled` property to False rather than set the `Visible` property to False. This setting leaves the control in place on the user's screen.

The *TabIndex* and *TabStop* Properties

The tab order has to do with the order in which different controls are selected when your program is running and the Tab key is pressed. At run time, one and only one control can be the currently selected control. In Windows terms, we say that the control has the focus.

Focus
The control that will respond to keyboard actions is said to have the focus.

The **focus** means that the control will respond to keyboard actions. If a Text Box control has the focus, the insertion point appears in that text box. Whatever characters the user types will be directed by Windows from the keyboard into that one text box. If a Command Button control has the focus, pressing the Enter key or the space bar "clicks" the button. In general, while any Windows application is running, the user can repeatedly press the Tab key to move the focus from one control to the next. The values of each control's `TabIndex` and `TabStop` properties determine how this tabbing operates.

Normally, Visual Basic sets the tab order equal to the sequence in which you added controls to your form. At design time, Visual Basic assigns a `TabIndex` value of 0 to the first control you place on the form. As you add more controls to the form, the `TabIndex` value of each new one increases by one. At run time, pressing Tab moves the focus from one control to another, based on the consecutive values of the `TabIndex` property. Thus, if you have six controls on a form, the `TabIndex` can be any value between 0 and 5, inclusive.

The `TabStop` property can have a True or False value, with True as the default. When the value of `TabStop` is set to False for any control, it is bypassed in the tab order at run time. In other words, the user cannot get access to the control with the Tab key. In such a case, however, the control retains its `TabIndex` value.

At design time or at run time, you can modify the values of a control's `TabIndex` and `TabStop` properties. By doing so, you alter the run-time tab order, which modifies the sequence in which the controls get the focus when the Tab key is pressed.

At design time, few of us create controls in the proper sequential order as we build our program, so we often have to change the default tabbing order. If you do change the value of `TabIndex` for a control, Visual Basic automatically adjusts this value for the other controls to reflect your modification. Visual Basic ensures that the controls' `TabIndex` values always range from 0 to N minus 1, where N is the total number of controls on the form.

Although all controls have a `TabIndex` property, some of them cannot receive the focus at run time. Some controls, such as a Label control, can be given a tab order, but that fact does not mean that the user can select the control by using the Tab key. For most purposes, it makes no sense for the user to select these types of controls.

The following controls cannot receive the focus at run time: Label, Timer, and disabled or hidden controls. In such cases, the controls retain their `TabIndex` values but are bypassed in the tab order at run time. Labels and Timers cannot receive the focus, so these two controls do not have a `TabStop` property.

If you have a control on your form that you don't want (or need) the user to be able to select with the Tab key, you can set the `TabStop` property for that control to False. However, neither the `TabStop` nor `TabIndex` property will have any effect if the user selects a control by clicking.

The Importance of *TabIndex* and *TabStop*

As you now know, the tab order of all the controls in an application is determined by the values of their `TabIndex` properties. Recall that the tab order refers to the sequence in which each control gets the focus as the user presses the Tab key.

For applications that require the user to type information in different places on the form, the tab order can be important. Keep in mind that some users prefer to run an application without using the mouse. Such users are likely to be touch typists, who are comfortable with their fingers on the keyboard.

You can check the tab order of the controls on a form without using the Properties window to examine the TabIndex values. Simply press Tab repeatedly, and watch the focus move from one control to the next in the order that each was placed on the form.

Once a form is designed, you may want to change the values of TabIndex to update the tab order. These two ordering schemes are the most commonly used:

Reading order. Set the tab order from left to right, from up to down. With this scheme, the focus moves in a logical, natural order through adjacent controls.

Order of importance. Set tabbing to move from one control to another in the order the user would most likely want. That is, controls in which input is likely to be typed are early in the tab order. Controls not likely to be used appear later in the order.

Note: *Although it is not a Windows standard, many users like to move through a series of text boxes by using the Enter key. Users want to be able to type a value in the first text box, press Enter, and have the insertion point move to the next text box just as it does when they press Tab. By writing VB code statements, you can enable the user to use the Enter key for this purpose. In a later section of this chapter, you are shown how to do this. You use the Visual Basic* SendKeys *function in a program procedure. The use of the* SendKeys *function is explained in VB's Help facility.*

The *MousePointer* Property

The MousePointer property determines the run time shape of the mouse pointer while it is over the control. For most controls, the default shape is the arrow. For text boxes, however, the default shape is the I-beam, which signifies the text insertion point. By setting the value of MousePointer to appropriate numeric values, you can make the pointer take on one of several shapes, including hourglass, cross hair, I-beam, or sizing arrow.

Understanding Frequently Used Controls

You can use many different controls in your Visual Basic programs. In fact, if you look at VB's Standard Edition Toolbox, you will notice that it includes 22 different controls you can place in your form. The Professional Edition Toolbox contains 38 tools. Obviously, not all controls will be used in your programs. In fact, in most of your programs, you will only use a few of these controls.

The following sections introduce you to several of the most commonly used controls in the Toolbox. Several of these controls will already seem familiar—you used them in earlier chapters when you were developing the calculator program. If you need detailed information on all the Visual Basic controls, refer to Que's *Using Visual Basic 3*, Special Edition.

Command Buttons

Command Button controls are probably the most frequently used. They have a 3-D look that invites the user to "press them" by clicking. When clicked, command buttons appear to move in and then back out, like a push-button on a piece of electronic equipment. This click generates what is called the Click event. Command buttons usually have Visual Basic code written to handle their Click events.

In the Toolbox, the Command Button control is represented by a rectangle with rounded corners and a shadow (see figure 3.9). You can use the techniques described in Chapter 2 to place a Command Button control in your form. Figure 3.9 shows the Toolbox from the Professional Edition. The Toolbox in the Standard Edition has fewer controls, but the tools have the same graphic and create the same control.

Figure 3.9
The Command Button control.

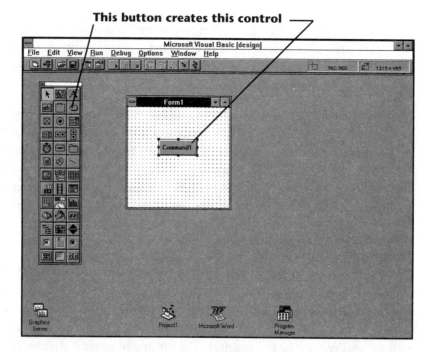

The first Command Button control placed on your form will have the word Command1 on its face; this word is the default caption. A second command button's caption will be Command2; the third will be Command3, and so on. The default Name property is assigned by VB in the same manner. To change the caption, change the value assigned to the Caption property for that Command Button control. To change the default name, alter the control's default Name property in Design mode. Remember, you should always assign a unique and meaningful name to each control. You can modify the Name property only in Design mode, not in Run mode.

Typically, a command button represents a task that is activated when the user clicks the button. The user can activate a command button by clicking it. Alternatively, when the command button has the focus, the user can press Enter or the space bar.

Properties of the Command Buttons

The Default and Cancel properties are unique to command buttons. If you set the value of Default to True for a command button, that button activates whenever the user presses Enter. The effect is the same as clicking the button. The default button appears with an outline that is darker than the other command buttons. One common use of the Default property is to create an OK button for a form. To create such a button, just specify its Caption property as OK, and set its Default property to True.

Similarly, the Cancel property determines which command button activates when the user presses Esc. If you set the value of a command button's Cancel property to True, that button activates whenever the user presses Esc. Be careful when you use this property. Visual Basic does not provide any visual cue to indicate which command button, if any, has the Cancel property. The primary purpose of this property is to create a command button labeled Cancel, which activates when the user presses Esc. Keep in mind that if you set the Cancel property to True for some other button, the user may not understand what happens when the Esc key is pressed.

The initial values of Default and Cancel are False for every command button. Only one command button can have a Default value of True. If you set Default to True for one command button, Visual Basic automatically sets the Default to False for every other command button. Similarly, only one command button can have a Cancel value of True.

The Value property for a command button indicates whether the button is selected. True means yes, and False means no. If you set Value to True in program code, the command button's Click event activates. The BackGround color of a command button will always be gray.

Events of the Command Button Control

The primary event for a command button is the Click event. This event activates whenever the user clicks the command button or, alternatively, whenever the user presses Enter (or the space bar) when the command button has the focus.

The Label Control

Visual Basic's Label control is named appropriately. As the name suggests, a label typically provides a heading or other annotation on the form. One common use of a label is to identify a control, such as a text box, which does not have its own Caption property. Use a label wherever you must provide a description of another control.

You can also display brief text with labels. A simple answer, such as Yes or No, or the result of a numerical calculation is easy to display using a label. Use a label to display text that you don't want the user to be able to change when the program is running. That is why you used a Label control (rather than a Text Box control) in your calculator program example.

In the Toolbox, the Label control is represented by a large capital letter *A*. For an indication of which tool to use and what you are creating, see figure 3.10.

This button creates this control

Figure 3.10
The Label control.

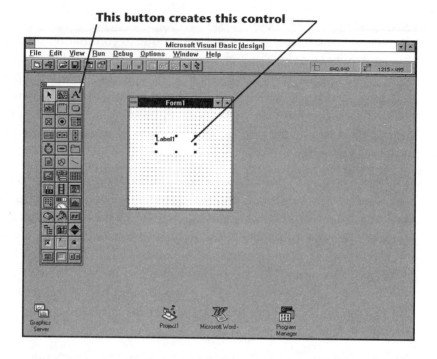

Properties of the Label Control

The Caption property determines the text string displayed in the label. At run time, the caption is visible on the form. Although most label captions are short, you can use a caption up to one thousand characters in length.

With the Alignment property, you can specify how the caption aligns in the label. The value of Alignment can be 0 (left-aligned), 1 (right-aligned), or 2 (centered). The default value is 0.

Instead of Alignment, you can use the AutoSize property to specify whether Visual Basic automatically resizes a label's border to fit its caption. The default value is False, which means that the size of the label is fixed. In this case, the text at the end of a long caption will not be visible if it does not completely fit within the label's border.

If you change the value of AutoSize to True, Visual Basic automatically adjusts the label's Height and Width properties so that the caption is not surrounded with wasted space. Then you can modify its Left and Top properties to relocate the resized label anywhere on the form.

The WordWrap property is unique to Label controls. The value of this property determines how the label resizes when AutoSize is True. When WordWrap is False (the default value), caption text does not wrap. If necessary, the label expands horizontally to encompass the caption text. If WordWrap is True, however, the width of the label remains fixed. If necessary, the caption text wraps to multiple lines, and the label expands vertically to enclose the complete caption.

The `BorderStyle` property determines whether a visible border appears around the label. The default value is 0, which specifies that no border appears at run time. If you set the value to 1 (`Fixed Single`), a thin, black rectangular border appears around the label.

The `BackStyle` property specifies whether objects behind the label are visible. The default value is 1 (Opaque), which prevents objects behind the label from showing through. If you change the value to 0 (Transparent), any background object, such as a picture, shows through the label.

The Events of the Label Control

Labels usually display headings, so you generally don't write event procedures for Label controls.

Text Boxes

Suppose that you want to display a large amount of text or you want the user to be able to edit text or enter text as the program is running. In these cases, you should use a Text Box control instead of a Label control. The primary purpose of most text boxes is to provide a means for the user to type necessary input while an application is running. At run time, the user can click a text box and begin typing text. Unlike labels, text boxes don't have the `Caption` property.

Text boxes can hold as many as 32,000 characters; the `MaxLength` property setting determines the maximum number of characters. Text boxes offer a special set of properties for dealing with a large quantity of text. The text box has a `MultiLine` property so that as text is entered into a text box, the text will wrap just as text wraps in a word processing program. When the `MultiLine` property is on, you can use the `Alignment` property to left-justify, right-justify, or center text. The `ScrollBars` property enables you to attach built-in scroll bars to the text box so that the user can scroll text in the text box when your program is running. Users can cut, copy, and paste text in a text box.

Exploring the Text Box Properties

To learn more about the properties of the text box, draw a text box on a form, and follow these steps:

1 Select the text box, and press the **F4** key to bring its Properties window to the front.

2 Click a property in the Properties window, and press the **F1** key for Help on that topic. In the Toolbox, the Text Box control is represented by the lowercase letters *ab* within a rectangle. For an indication of which tool to use and what you are creating, see figure 3.11.

(continues)

Exploring the Text Box Properties   (continued)

This button creates this control

Figure 3.11
The Text Box control.

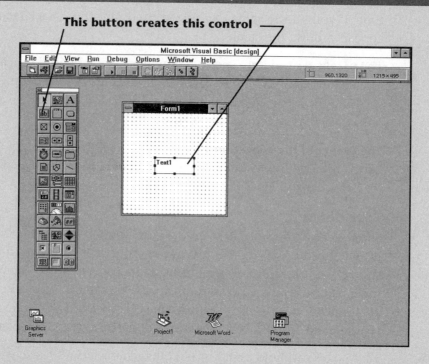

By default, Visual Basic assigns the name of the text box to the Text property. The first Text Box control placed on your form contains the word Text1, the second contains Text2, the third contains Text3, and so on. To change this text, change the value assigned to the Text property for the Text Box control. To remove any text from the text box, delete the text in the control's Text property in the Properties window. To remove text from a text box as your program runs, set the text box's Text property to "" in Visual Basic code. For example,

```
TextBox1.Text = ""
```

Text Box Properties

A few properties are unique to text boxes. These properties are used to control the way information is displayed in the text box.

When you place a new text box on a form, the text box, by default, shows only a single line of text—regardless of how tall you make the text box. You can still browse through the text using the arrow keys, but only the one line is displayed. To have Visual Basic display more than one line in a text box, set the MultiLine property to True.

Because text boxes allow a user to enter large amounts of text, you may need to limit their input. After all, why let the user enter 200 characters if you need only 5? To limit the length of the input, set the MaxLength property to the desired length.

When MaxLength is set to 0 (the default), the text box can hold any amount of text up to about 32,000 characters. If you set MaxLength to any positive nonzero value, you limit the number of characters that can be entered to that value. After the limit is reached, your system beeps when more keys are pressed.

You can also use text boxes for getting passwords from the user. For example, the user may need to enter a password before he or she can access information in your program. The `PasswordChar` property comes in here. Normally, this property is not set; it is empty. If you change `PasswordChar` to a character, that is the character displayed when the user starts typing. Thus, if you have set `PasswordChar` to the letter X, when the user types a five-character password, all the user sees is XXXXX in the text box. Internally, however, Visual Basic tracks exactly what was typed.

For text boxes (unlike labels), the default value of `BorderStyle` is 1 (`Fixed Single`), which produces a thin line around the box.

The `ScrollBars` property determines whether the text box displays scroll bars. The default value is 0, which means that no scroll bars appear on the text box. Other values are 1 (horizontal scroll bar), 2 (vertical scroll bar), and 3 (both scroll bars). You typically set the value of `ScrollBars` to 2 or 3 when `MultiLine` is True.

With the `ScrollBars` property, you can create a text box with a fixed size and position on the form but accept large amounts of text from the user. For example, if you set the value of `ScrollBars` to 1, the user can type text past the right edge of the control. The text box scrolls horizontally to accommodate every new character. With both vertical scrolling and `MultiLine` enabled, typed text that reaches the right edge of the text box wraps down to the next line.

By default, when the mouse pointer is over a text box, the pointer shape changes to the I-beam. By clicking the left mouse button, you cause the I-beam to act as a text insertion point—the text cursor moves to the location of the I-beam. You can use the `MousePointer` property of the text box to change the pointer shape.

Common Events of the Text Box Control

The main event for text boxes is the `Change` event. This event occurs any time the value of the `Text` property is modified. The change can come when the user types text or when the program code modifies the value of the `Text` property. A `Change` event occurs each time the user adds or removes one character from a text box. You can use the `Change` event to monitor or respond to each character a user types. You can use the `SendKeys` function (see VB's Help) to prevent a user from typing certain characters into a text box. If you want to prevent a user from entering text in a text box after a certain point in your program, at that point, your code should contain a statement like this:

```
Text1.Enabled = False
```

The `GotFocus` and `LostFocus` events trigger when the text box gets the focus or loses it, respectively. For a text box, `GotFocus` occurs when the user tabs to or clicks in the text box. `LostFocus` occurs when the user tabs away from the text box or clicks another control. You see a blinking cursor in the text box when it has the focus. Text boxes also respond to `KeyDown`, `KeyUp`, and `KeyPress` events. These events occur when the user presses a key while the text box has the focus.

One frequently used example of code for the KeyPress event allows a user to enter text into a text box and then move to another text box (in the tab order) by pressing the Enter key rather than the Tab key. The following event procedure shows you how to move through the tab order by pressing the Enter key (the ASCII code for the Enter key is 13):

```
Sub Text1_KeyPress (KeyAscii As Integer)
    If KeyAscii = 13 Then SendKeys "{Tab}"
End Sub
```

Chapter Summary

In this chapter, you have learned a great deal about the properties of forms and controls. You learned how to add new forms to your project and change the appearance and behavior of forms and controls. You learned how to change the color, location, size, border, Text, Visible, Enabled, and Picture properties of forms and controls. You saw how to change form and control properties when designing and when running your program.

You were taught how to use commonly used controls—Command Button, Label, and Text Box. Now that you have a good understanding of how to use forms and several controls, you are ready to learn more about Visual Basic controls, graphics, and program code in Chapter 4.

Test Your Understanding

True/False
Indicate whether the statement is true or false.

1. The Picture property of a form enables you to place a picture at the top center of the form.

2. The maximum number of forms that you can use in a project is seven.

3. Any property of a form or control that can be changed at design time can also be changed at run time.

4. The Icon property of a form determines which icon can be used in the Picture property of a form.

5. The Form Load event is frequently used by programmers to contain Visual Basic code.

6. The Text Box control does not have a BorderStyle property.

7. The Click event is the most frequently used event for a Label control.

8. Every control in an application must have a unique Name property.

9. Some properties in the Properties window can be changed in value by double-clicking the property name.

10. The Text Box control can have attached scroll bars that enable the user to scroll through large amounts of text.

Short Answer

Answer the following questions.

1. List the steps that you would go through to add a new form to a project and change its background to red at design time.

2. Write the Visual Basic code that would change to EXIT the caption of a command button named Command4 on Form2.

3. Write the Visual Basic code that would cause an icon in C:\WINDOWS\MYICON.ICO to be displayed as the Picture property of Form1.

4. What properties can you change in the Properties window of a Text Box control to change all the possible display characteristics of the text in that Text Box control?

5. When would you use a Text Box control in a project rather than a Label control?

6. What are the most important events for a Label control?

7. Explain the properties that determine the size and location of a Text Box control on a form.

8. List the border styles that you can set for a form, and explain how they differ.

9. Explain what the Visible and Enabled property settings are and how they affect a control. How are these properties different in their effect?

10. What are the limitations Visual Basic places on the Name property of a control? Do upper- and lowercase letters make a difference?

11. In what property of a Text Box control is user input placed when the program is running?

12. Define *focus*. How does an object get the focus? How can you change the tab order? Are any events associated with the focus?

13. How could you prevent a user from typing text into a Text Box control?

14. What is the function of the MultiLine property of a Text Box control?

15. Explain the use of the Default property of a command button?

Projects

Project 1: Building a User Interface

In this project, you build the user interface for a calculator program that you will complete in a later chapter. Create the form and controls shown in figure 3.12. The title of the window the finished program displays should consist of your first and last names and **PROJECT 1**. The window should be three inches high by five inches wide. The background color of the form and all Label controls (if any) whose content does not change should be light blue. The background color of any text boxes you use or any labels whose content can change as the program runs should be white.

Name all controls using the prefixes shown in table 3.3. Give the command buttons the same names as their respective Caption properties. Make sure that the tabbing order is set so that the user can enter data with the maximum efficiency. The user should not have to click a text box to be able to enter text into it.

Save the form and the project as **C3P1**. Then use the **File Print** command to access the Print dialog box. In this dialog box, make sure that the **All** option button is selected and the **Form** and Form **Text** check boxes are checked. Then click the OK button to print your form.

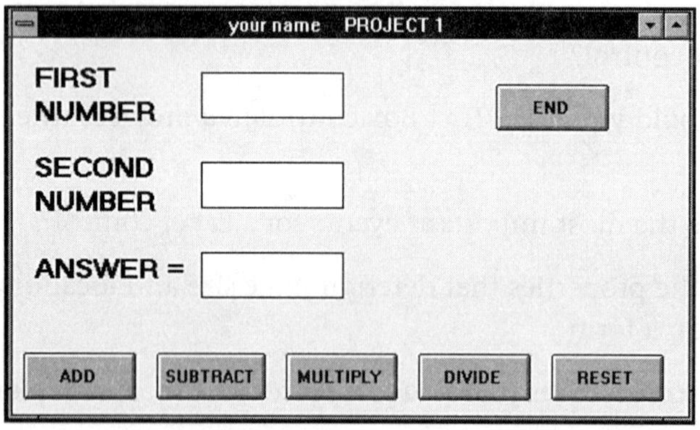

Figure 3.12
The PROJECT 1 form.

Project 2:   Creating Forms

In this project, you create two forms. The first form will provide security for the information available in the second form. Assume that the second form will display data in a database. In order to avoid unauthorized access to the database, the first form will be displayed on-screen until the correct password is entered. Then the second form should be displayed. When the user enters the password, the * character should be displayed rather than the actual character entered.

After the user has entered the password, the user should click the VIEW DATA button, and if the password is correct, the data form should be displayed. At this point in the development of the project, don't worry about testing for the correct password. Simply place the buttons on the form, and change their Caption and Name properties. Name all controls using the prefixes shown in table 3.3. Give the command buttons the same names as their respective Caption properties.

Refer to figure 3.13 to see how the first form (the password form) should look. Refer to figure 3.14 to see how the second form should look. The background of the first form should be dark blue, and the words *CTC DATABASE SYSTEM* should be in light blue. Use the default colors for the rest of the controls on both forms. The password entry form should be the first form to appear when you run the program. It should fill the whole screen when the program runs. It should not display a Control-menu box; it should not be resizeable, and it should not display Minimize and Maximize buttons.

Figure 3.13
The PROJECT 2
password form.

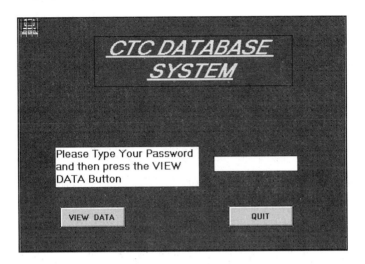

Figure 3.14
The second
PROJECT 2 form.

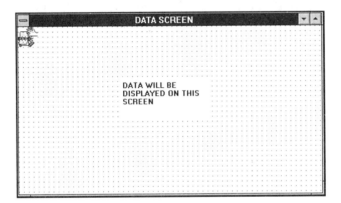

The icon found in VB\ICONS\MISC\SECUR03 should appear in the upper-left corner of the password form. The icon found in VB\ICONS\OFFICE\CRDFLE11 should appear in the upper-left corner of the second form, and this same icon should be displayed when this form is minimized and the program is running.

Do not enter any VB code; you will do this in a later project. Simply create the user interface by setting up the necessary forms and controls and their properties. Save the forms as **C3P2A** (the first form), **C3P2B** (the second form), and the project as **C3P2**. Then use the **F**ile **P**rint command to access the Print dialog box. In this dialog box, make sure that the **A**ll option button is selected and the **F**orm and Form **T**ext check boxes are checked. Then click the OK button to print your form.

Project 3:   Creating a Stock Analysis Input Form
In this project, you create the Stock Analysis input form shown in figure 3.15. The user should be able to enter the five data values. The user should not have to click in a text box in order to enter data in it. The user should be able to move through the boxes from top to bottom by using the Tab key.

Figure 3.15
The PROJECT 3 form.

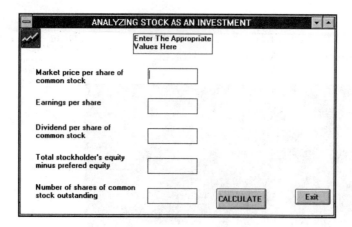

The background of the form should be pale yellow. The background color of the areas in which the user types data should be white. The background of the command buttons should be their default gray. The background of the other controls should be pale yellow. The icon found in VB\ICONS\OFFICE\GRAPH03 should appear at the upper-left corner of the form. When the program is running and the form is minimized, the same icon should represent the program.

Do not write any VB code to implement any of the functions of the program. Simply build the user interface. Name all controls using the prefixes shown in table 3.3. Give the command buttons the same names as their respective Caption properties. Save the form and the project as **C3P3**. Then use the **File** **P**rint command to access the Print dialog box. In this dialog box, make sure that the **A**ll option button is selected and the **F**orm and Form **T**ext check boxes are checked. Then click the OK button to print your form.

CHAPTER 4

Using More Controls and Creating Graphics

As you have learned, the Toolbox contains the standard objects that represent the user interface elements in Windows. In Visual Basic, these objects are called controls, and when you place controls on a form, they provide a way for your program to accept input and display results.

In this chapter, you learn how to use additional controls effectively and how to manipulate the properties associated with these controls. By the time you reach the end of the chapter, you will be able to create a more professional-looking user interface for your programs. As you learn how to use the graphics controls available in the Toolbox, you learn also how to use Visual Basic to create simple animation effects.

Objectives

By the time you have finished this chapter, you will be able to

1. Understand the Most Important Uses, Properties, and Events of the Check Box, Option Button, Image, Picture Box, and Frame Controls

2. Modify the Properties of These Controls in Design Mode and in Visual Basic Code

3. Use These Five Controls in a Visual Basic Program

4. Draw and Animate Shapes and Lines on a Visual Basic Form

5. Capture Graphics Elements of the Windows Environment and Make Them Part of Your Program's User Interface

6. Use Control Arrays

The Check Box Control

Check box
A square box that you select to toggle an option on or off.

Sometimes you need only a yes or no answer from the user. Check Box controls are perfect for collecting simple input such as Yes or No, True or False, and On or Off. **Check boxes** are used in many different Windows programs. These boxes consist of a small square that you can turn on or off; when the square is selected (clicked by the user), an X appears in it. When the check box is deselected, the square is empty.

In the Toolbox, the Check Box control is represented by a square containing an X. For an indication of which tool to use and what you are creating, see figure 4.1.

Figure 4.1
The Check Box control.

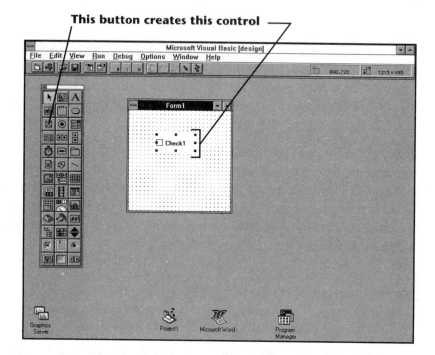

The first Check Box control placed on your form contains the word Check1, which is a default caption. The second Check Box control's caption is Check2, the third is Check3, and so on. To change the caption, you change the value assigned to the Caption property for the Check Box control.

An important feature of check boxes is that they do not present mutually exclusive choices. When the check boxes are grouped, the user can select any, all, or none of the check boxes. For example, a text editor can contain check boxes for Italic, Bold, and Underline. The user can select these options in any combination, including none of them or all of them.

Properties of the Check Box Control

The state of a check box is represented by the Value property. Value works differently with a check box than with an option button. For a check box, Value can be 0, 1, or 2. When Value is 0 (the default), the check box is deselected, and the square is empty. When Value is 1, the check box is selected, and an X appears inside the square. When Value is 2, the control appears gray or dimmed. You set

Value to 2 to signal the user that the option presented in the check box is not currently available.

Check Box Events

The primary event used with check boxes is the Click event. Unlike an option button, a check box does not respond to a DblClick event.

The Option Button Control

The option button is a cousin of the check box. Option buttons permit the selection of one option from several choices. Although the use of a single check box may make sense, option buttons always appear in groups of two or more. A group of option buttons includes all the option buttons in a form or a Frame control. When your program is running, clicking one of the option buttons automatically turns off the others. For this reason, option buttons are sometimes referred to as being mutually exclusive—only one of them can be selected at a time.

Option button
A round button that you select to turn an option on or off.

An **option button** appears as a little circle with a text description beside it. When the option is selected, a black dot appears in the circle. When the option is not selected, no dot appears.

Typically, several option buttons are grouped together to represent mutually exclusive choices. One button in the group is always selected. When the user selects a different button in the group, Visual Basic automatically deselects the previously selected button. All option buttons that you place directly on a form are considered part of a single group. You can select only one such option button at any time.

You can group option buttons by placing them in a frame. All option buttons placed in a frame are considered to be one separate group. A form can have several frames, each housing a separate group of option buttons. The Frame control is discussed later in this chapter.

Generally, you display a group of option buttons vertically. At run time, Visual Basic selects the first option button you placed in the group (you can change this default in your program code). As a rule, you should place option buttons from the top down, with the uppermost button representing the one the user is most likely to select.

In the Toolbox, the Option Button control is represented by a circle with a dot in it. For an indication of which tool to use and what you are creating, see figure 4.2. (Note, however, that you will usually be creating a group of option buttons, rather than the single button shown in this figure.)

The first Option Button control placed on your form contains the word Option1, which is the default caption. The second Option Button control's caption is Option2, the third is Option3, and so on. To change the caption, you change the value assigned to the Caption property for the Option Button control.

4

This button creates this control ⎯

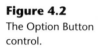

Figure 4.2
The Option Button
control.

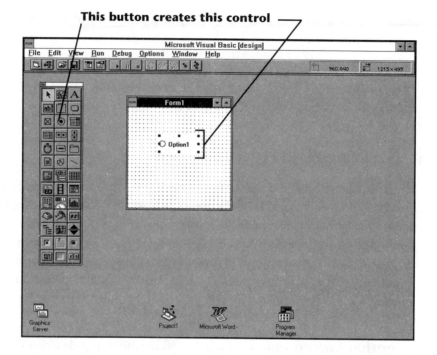

Properties of the Option Button Control

You can specify the state of an option button with the Value property. When Value is set to True, the button is selected. When Value is False, the button is deselected. Keep in mind that whenever you set a button's Value property to True, Visual Basic automatically sets Value to False for the other option buttons in the group.

You use the Caption property to specify the text title that appears beside the button. The caption can contain as many as 255 characters, with additional characters dropped. The title can appear to either the left or the right of the button, as determined by the value of the Alignment property. The default value is 0, which specifies that the title appears to the right of the button. If you change the value of Alignment to 1, the text appears to the left.

Option Button Events

For option buttons, you most often use Click event handler procedures to respond when the user clicks one of the buttons.

The Image Control

The effective use of pictures and icons can enhance any application. The Image control on the Toolbox is designed for displaying images, which are stored in disk files. You can display pictures and icons in forms or in Image controls. The default name for the first Image control you place on a form is Image1. Subsequent Image controls are named Image2, Image3, and so on. Figure 4.3 shows which tool you use and what you create.

Figure 4.3
The Image control.

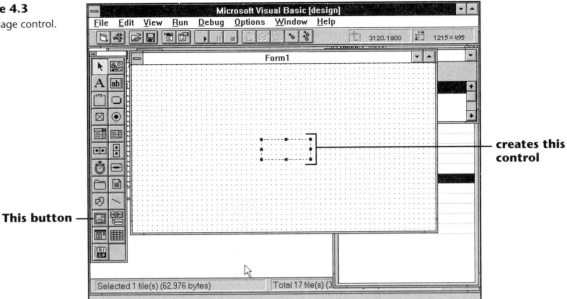

This button —

creates this
control

Displaying Pictures in an Image Control

To display a picture in an Image control, assign a file name to its `Picture` property, just as you do with a form. You can load the picture at design time with the Properties window or at run time with a `LoadPicture` statement. For example, the following instruction loads a bit-mapped file into the `Image1` control:

```
Image1.Picture = LoadPicture("C:\WINDOWS\LEAVES.BMP")
```

Whenever you load a picture into an Image control, the control resizes to fit the size of the picture.

The *Stretch* Property

The `Stretch` property is unique to Image controls. It can be used to make the picture inside the Image control larger or smaller. The default value of `Stretch` is False. When `Stretch` is False, the control resizes to fit the picture you load. In other words, the size of the picture determines the size of the Image control. If you then resize the control, the picture will not shrink or expand to fill the control. If you make the control smaller, you crop off part of the picture. If you enlarge the control, the picture remains at its original size, fixed at the upper-left corner of the control.

If you set `Stretch` to True, the loaded picture resizes to fit the new size of the control. That is, the picture and the control expand or shrink together. You can take advantage of this effect to lengthen or narrow a picture horizontally, vertically, or both. Not only can you make a picture larger or smaller, but you also can stretch the picture to make it "fatter" or "skinnier."

You resize an Image control either at design time by moving the control's sizing handles or at run time, in VB code, by modifying the values of the control's `Height` and `Width` properties.

Image Control Events

The Image control is designed to be a container for pictures and often does not have any associated VB event handler procedures that contain code. The procedure for the `Click` event is the most frequently used. You can use images as picture buttons in a program, and you can load an Image control with a picture of the function performed when the control is clicked. For example, an Image control that saves a file when the control is clicked could contain one of VB's disk icons. Image-control picture buttons, however, do not have the "click in, click out" feature that command buttons have. You can indicate that an image-control picture button has been selected by changing its `BorderStyle` in the `Click` event. You do this in VB code with a statement like the following:

```
Image1.BorderStyle = 1
```

Later in this chapter, you learn how to use an Image control inside a Picture Box control to create the clicking effect.

The Picture Box Control

Picture Box
A control that can contain a graphical image, other controls, or a drawing area for graphical methods.

A **picture box** acts as a container for a graphics image. The image can be a bit map, an icon, or a metafile stored in a disk file. (All three are types of Windows pictures.) A picture box can also display output from graphics methods such as `Line` and `Circle`, as well as text created with the `Print` method. Furthermore, a picture box can contain other controls, such as Option Button, Shape, and Line controls. Figure 4.4 shows the Picture Box control in the Toolbar.

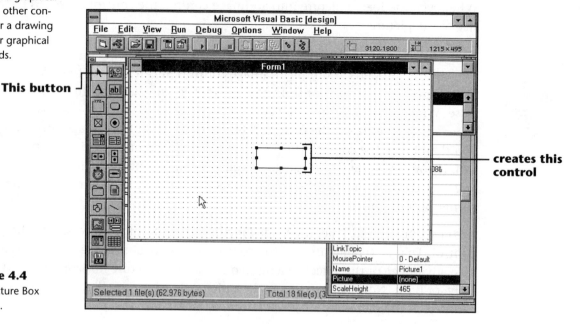

Figure 4.4
The Picture Box control.

Special Properties of the Picture Box Control

When a picture box displays an image, the `Picture` property specifies the name of the graphics file. The picture box can display graphics files in bit map, icon, or metafile format. Such file names typically have BMP, ICO, and WMF extensions, respectively.

At design time, you use the Properties window to set the value of `Picture` to the graphics file you want to use. At run time, you set a value for `Picture` with the `LoadPicture` function. For example, the following instruction loads a bit-mapped file into the `Picture1` control:

```
Picture1.Picture = LoadPicture("C:\WINDOWS\CARS.BMP")
```

When you assign `Picture` at design time, a copy of the image is saved with the form. As a result, you can run the saved FRM file on any computer, even one without the original graphics file. If, however, you set `Picture` at run time with the `LoadPicture` function, the application must have access to the graphics file to display the image. If you compile the application to an executable file, the image is not stored in the EXE file. To display the image successfully, you must have the graphics file available in the host computer at run time.

The picture box has a `FontTransparent` property. If the value of `FontTransparent` is True, the contents of the picture box show through the text. If the value is False, the text obscures any background graphics.

By default, the extra portions of the graphics image are clipped if it is larger than the picture box. If, however, you set the value of the `AutoSize` property to True, the picture box automatically resizes to display the entire image.

The `Align` property is unique to the picture box. When the value of this property is 0 (the default), the picture box appears on the form at the location determined by its `Height`, `Width`, `Left`, and `Top` properties.

When `Align` is 1, however, the picture box moves to the top of the form and expands horizontally over its entire width. Similarly, when `Align` is 2, the picture box moves to the bottom of the form and expands horizontally. You typically use `Align` to create a picture box that acts as a toolbar at the top of the form or as a status bar at the bottom.

The `CurrentX` and `CurrentY` properties of the picture box specify the current horizontal and vertical coordinates of the drawing pen. These properties indicate where in the control the next drawing method begins. These properties are not available from the Properties window at design time but can be referenced in program code at run time.

The `DrawMode` property indicates the type of Drawing tool used in creating graphics with the Visual Basic drawing controls, such as Shape and Line, or the graphics methods, such as `Circle`. The `DrawStyle` and `DrawWidth` properties specify the style and width of the drawn line, respectively. When two-dimensional shapes are created, the `FillColor` and `FillStyle` properties specify the color and pattern, respectively, that are used inside the shape. (These properties and the drawing pen are explained more fully later in this chapter.)

Events of the Picture Box Control

The `Paint` event is unique to picture boxes. (`Paint` is defined for forms but not for any other control.) The `Paint` event is triggered when part or all of a picture box is reexposed after it is hidden by another window. If the value of `AutoRedraw` is set to True, repainting and redrawing are automatic, so you usually don't need to write code for any `Paint` events. Another event unique to picture boxes (and forms) is `Resize`. This event occurs whenever the size of the picture box changes.

For picture boxes, the `Change` event occurs whenever the `Picture` property changes. The picture box can respond to many of the common events you have used with other controls. For more information, consult the VB Help topic Picture Box.

The Frame Control

The Frame control acts as a container for other controls, typically option buttons or check boxes. In the Toolbox, the Frame control is a small rectangle with an xyz at the top (see figure 4.5). As noted earlier, when option buttons are placed in a frame, those buttons are mutually exclusive. If the user selects one button, Visual Basic automatically deselects the others in the frame. Placing option buttons inside frames allows you to have multiple independent groups of option buttons on a form.

Figure 4.5
The Frame control.

This button ———

creates this control

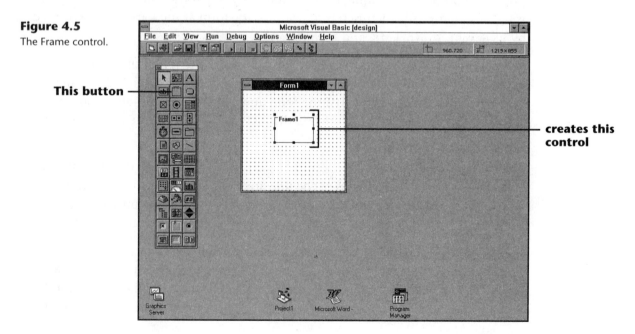

Frame
A rectangular area on-screen that contains other controls.

To group controls in a **frame**, you must first place the frame on the form. Then you draw the controls inside the frame. You cannot place a control inside a frame by double-clicking the control's button in the Toolbox. You must click the control's button in the Toolbox and then move the mouse pointer into the frame. Press and hold down the left mouse button, drag the pointer over an area inside the frame, and then release the button.

Once you have controls placed in a frame, they are fixed relative to it. If you move the frame, the controls move with it. When you place a control inside a frame, the control's Left and Top properties are specified relative to the upper-left corner of the frame.

The first Frame control placed on your form contains the word Frame1, which is the default caption. The second Frame control is Frame2, the third is Frame3, and so on. To change the caption, you change the value assigned to the Caption property for the Frame control.

Special Properties of the Frame Control

A frame appears as a rectangular border with a caption near the top. The Caption property specifies the caption text. Although most captions are short, a caption can contain up to 255 characters (any excess characters are dropped). The caption appears along the top border of the frame, beginning near its upper-left corner.

Events of the Frame Control

Because the frame acts as a container for other controls, the frame itself does not respond to many events. Instead, action in a frame is usually centered in one of the enclosed controls. For more information, consult the VB Help topic Frame Control.

Introduction to Graphics

In Visual Basic applications, you create graphics with three types of tools:

- *Line and Shape controls.* These controls, available from the Toolbox, create straight lines and two-dimensional shapes, such as boxes and rectangles. As you develop the user interface for an application, you can use these controls at design time to enhance the application's appearance. The Line and Shape controls work on forms, picture boxes, and frames. This portion of the chapter explains how to use these controls.

- *The graphics methods.* The graphics methods, such as PSet, Line, and Circle, appear in your program code. With these methods, you can draw points, lines, and two-dimensional shapes at run time. The graphics methods work on forms and picture boxes.

- *Pictures and icons.* As noted earlier in this chapter, the effective use of pictures and icons can enhance any application. These graphics images are stored in disk files. You can display pictures and icons in forms, picture boxes, and Image controls.

Foreground color
The color of the pixels in a drawn object.

Background color
The color of all the background pixels.

Using Foreground and Background Colors

In a discussion of graphics, the terms **foreground color** and **background color** are important. The foreground color is the color of the drawn object. You draw a red circle, for example, by turning each pixel of the circle into red. In this case, red is the foreground color. The background color, naturally enough, is the color of all the pixels other than the drawn object. When you start a new project, the default form has a white background.

For forms and most controls, the `ForeColor` property specifies the foreground color, and the `BackColor` property specifies the background color.

Using the Line and Shape Controls

With the Line and Shape controls, you can draw straight lines and various two-dimensional shapes. These controls are available from the Toolbox. You can place Line and Shape controls on a form, picture box, or frame. Figure 4.6 shows the Line and Shape controls in the Toolbox.

Figure 4.6
The Line and Shape controls.

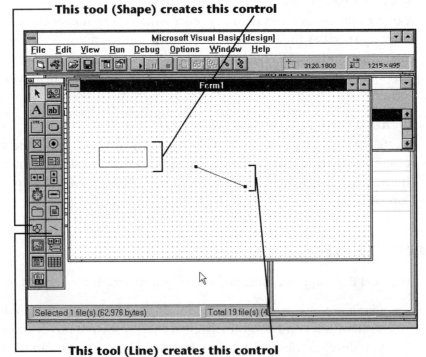

This tool (Shape) creates this control

This tool (Line) creates this control

The primary use of these two controls is to enhance a form's visual appearance. Usually, you place these controls on a form or picture box at design time and keep the controls fixed (relative to their containers) while the program runs. As with all controls, Line and Shape controls have a `Name` property. At run time, your program code can reference Line and Shape controls and their properties. However, compared to most of the other controls in the Toolbox, Line and Shape controls have limited functionality. Note some of their limitations:

*   *Line and Shape controls have no events.* As a result, the controls can't respond to system or user-generated events at run time.

- *Line and Shape controls have a limited set of properties and methods.* Although you rarely do so in practice, you can modify the property values of these controls at run time to create various visual effects.

- *Line and Shape controls cannot receive the focus at run time.* The controls have no `TabIndex` property. At run time, the user cannot access the controls with the mouse or keyboard.

The Line Control

A Line control displays a straight line. The line can be horizontal, vertical, or diagonal. At design time, a Line control has two sizing handles, one at each end of the line. By moving these handles anywhere on the form (or other container holding the Line control), you can create a line of any length, location, and angular orientation.

A few well-placed lines can greatly enhance a form's appearance. For example, figure 4.7 shows a survey form that contains some Line controls with labels and check boxes.

Figure 4.7

A form containing Line controls.

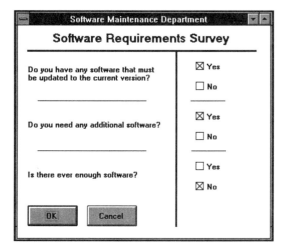

Line controls have 13 properties: `BorderColor`, `BorderStyle`, `BorderWidth`, `DrawMode`, `Index`, `Name`, `Parent`, `Tag`, `Visible`, `X1`, `X2`, `Y1`, and `Y2`. You can set values for these properties at design time and also modify their values in program code at run time. (The `Parent` property is an exception; `Parent` is not available at design time but can be read at run time.) The following sections describe the most important of these properties.

The *Name* Property

By default, Visual Basic names the first Line control on a form `Line1`. Subsequent lines are named `Line2`, `Line3`, and so on. At design time, you can modify a default name by changing the value of the control's `Name` property.

The Location Properties: *X1, Y1, X2, Y2*

The `X1`, `Y1`, `X2`, and `Y2` properties determine the location of the line relative to its container. Line controls are the only controls that have these properties. (Line controls do not have the `Left`, `Top`, `Height`, and `Width` properties supported by most other controls.)

The values of X1 and Y1 specify the horizontal and vertical coordinates, respectively, at one end of the line. Similarly, X2 and Y2 specify the coordinates at the other end of the line. Remember that unless you have modified the container's Scale-related properties, the values of Y1 and Y2 increase if you move the line downward toward the bottom of the container. If X1 and Y1 are both 0, one end of the line is at the upper-left corner of the container.

Line controls do not support the Move method. If you want to move a line at run time, your program code can modify the values of X1, Y1, X2, and Y2 as appropriate. For example, the following instructions move one end of a Line control named Line1 350 twips to the right and 200 twips upward:

```
Line1.X2 = Line1.X2 + 350
Line1.Y2 = Line1.Y2 - 200
```

The Move method is explained later in this chapter.

The *BorderWidth* Property

The BorderWidth property determines the thickness of the drawn line. The default value is 1, which specifies the minimum line thickness. To get wider lines, you can increase the value up to a maximum of 8192.

The *BorderColor* Property

The BorderColor property determines the color of the drawn line. The default value is the standard Windows drawing color, normally black. At design time, you can select the value of BorderColor from the color palette. At run time, you can modify a Line control's color by changing the value of this property in program code.

In program code, you can assign to BorderColor any numerical value that represents a color. The easiest way to do this is with the RGB function or the QBColor function. To learn more about these functions, consult VB's Help facility. For example, the following instruction changes the color of the Line3 control on MyForm to green:

```
MyForm.Line3.BorderColor = QBColor(2)    'green
```

Notice that this instruction specifies the form and the control. If you omit the form designation, Visual Basic assumes the current form. Alternatively, if CONSTANT.TXT is loaded into the application, you can assign the value of BorderColor with one of the color constants from that file.

The *BorderStyle* Property

A drawn line does not have to be solid. By modifying the value of the BorderStyle property, you can draw a line in one of several styles. Table 4.1 shows the various styles that correspond to the values of BorderStyle. The settings in this table are valid for both the Line control and the Shape control.

Table 4.1 Values of *BorderStyle* for the Line and Shape Controls	
Value of ***BorderStyle***	**Drawing Style**
0	Transparent
1	Solid (the default style)
2	Dashed
3	Dotted
4	Dash-dot
5	Dash-dot-dot
6	Inside solid

BorderStyle values of 1 and 6 produce solid lines. The distinction between these values is not important for the Line control but is meaningful for shapes. For more on this topic, see the section "The Shape Control" later in this chapter.

The values of BorderWidth and BorderStyle are not independent. If BorderWidth is greater than the default value of 1, the resulting line is solid regardless of the value of BorderStyle. In fact, if BorderWidth is greater than 1 and if BorderStyle has a value other than 1 or 6, Visual Basic automatically resets the value of BorderStyle back to the default value of 1.

The *DrawMode* Property

You can think of Visual Basic as drawing each line with a pen. By default, this pen draws the line in the color specified by BorderColor. If you modify the value of DrawMode, however, you can make the pen produce special drawing characteristics. The color of each point in the drawn line depends on the pen color *and* the color of the background pixel on which each point in the line is to be drawn.

The default value of DrawMode, for example, is 13. This setting represents the simplest situation—each point in the line is just the pen color. If DrawMode is 4, Visual Basic applies the Not operator to the pen's color code. The result is a line of the "opposite" pen color. If DrawMode is 6, Visual Basic applies Not to the color code of the pixel to be drawn on. The resulting color is the "opposite" of the background color. For example, if a form's background color is black, the line will be white. If you change the form's background color to red, the line will become a green-blue color. A lime green background color will produce a purple (grape) colored line.

The *Visible* Property

As with other controls, the Visible property determines whether the Line control is visible at run time. A value of True (the default) makes the line visible; False makes the line invisible. The value of Visible affects only run-time visibility. If you set Visible to False with the Properties window, the control remains visible at design time.

The Shape Control

A Shape control displays a two-dimensional enclosed figure. Six different geometric shapes can be drawn. At design time, a Shape control has the conventional six sizing handles that appear with most controls. By moving a shape's handles, you can stretch the shape to any size you want.

Figure 4.8 shows an example of each of the different shapes you can draw with the Shape control. In this figure, each shape is drawn with different property values. As explained in the following sections, you can adjust these property values to produce a variety of visual effects.

Figure 4.8

Six examples of the Shape control.

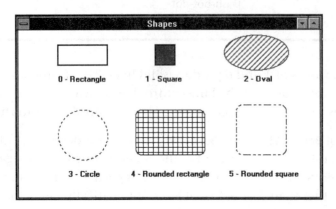

Although each shape drawn with the Shape control produces an enclosed two-dimensional figure, you cannot use the resulting shapes as containers for other graphics.

With the exceptions of the X1, Y1, X2, and Y2 properties, Shape controls have the same properties as Line controls. In addition, Shape controls have these properties: BackColor, BackStyle, FillColor, FillStyle, Left, Top, Height, Width, and Shape. The following sections describe the differences between the Shape control properties and the Line control properties.

The *Shape* Property

The value of the Shape property determines which of the six possible shapes the Shape control displays. In figure 4.8, the value of the Shape property is indicated below each of the six shapes. Table 4.2 lists the possible shapes. The default value of Shape is 0, which produces a rectangle.

Table 4.2 Values of the *Shape* Property	
Value of the Shape Property	**Resulting Shape**
0	Rectangle
1	Square
2	Oval
3	Circle
4	Rectangle with rounded corners
5	Square with rounded corners

Location Properties: *Left, Top, Height,* **and** *Width*

Like most controls, the Shape control supports the Left, Top, Height, and Width properties. The values of Left and Top specify the control's location relative to its container.

Although you cannot use the Move method at run time to move a Line control inside its container, you can use this method at run time to move a Shape control inside its container. If you do, Visual Basic adjusts the values of Left and Top as necessary.

The *Name* **Property**

By default, Visual Basic names the first Shape control on a form as Shape1. Subsequent Shape controls are named Shape2, Shape3, and so on.

Border Properties

The BorderColor, BorderWidth, and BorderStyle properties affect the perimeter of the drawn shape. For the most part, these properties work for Shape controls as they do for Line controls. The values of BorderStyle presented earlier in table 4.1 are valid for shapes as well as lines.

When the value of BorderWidth is greater than 1, you need to define whether the height and width of the control include the border, and exactly where the border begins and the interior area ends.

The *BackColor* **Property**

The BackColor property determines the color of the shape's enclosed area. You can assign a value for this property in one of the ways you assign values for other color properties: with the color palette at design time, with a color code constant, or with the RGB or QBColor function at run time. Consult Visual Basic's Help for information on these functions.

The *BackStyle* **Property**

The BackStyle property specifies whether the background behind the Shape control is visible. The default value is 1 (opaque), which means that the color specified by the BackColor property obscures anything from showing through the shape. If you change the value of BackStyle to 0 (transparent), the background shows through the shape. This background may be a solid color or may contain graphics, such as a picture. When BackStyle is set to transparent, the value of BackColor is irrelevant.

The *FillColor* **and** *FillStyle* **Properties**

The FillColor property specifies the color used to fill the shape's enclosed area. As with other color properties, you can assign a value for this property with the color palette at design time, with a color code constant, or with the RGB or QBColor function at run time. The FillStyle property determines the manner in which the color is applied. Table 4.3 shows the eight possible values of FillStyle and their resulting effects.

Table 4.3 *FillStyle* Effects	
Value of *FillStyle*	**Resulting Effect**
0	Solid fill
1	Transparent
2	Horizontal lines
3	Vertical lines
4	Upward diagonal (lines go up toward the left)
5	Downward diagonal (lines go down toward the left)
6	Cross-hatched with horizontal and vertical lines
7	Cross-hatched with diagonal lines

When `FillStyle` is 1 (the default), the background shows through, and the value of `FillColor` is irrelevant. When `FillStyle` is 0, a solid color fills the shape. In this case, the effect is the same as when the `BackStyle` property is set to opaque. The other values of `FillStyle` produce a pattern inside the shape. In figure 4.8, the value of `FillStyle` is 5 for the Oval.

Understanding Persistent Graphics and the *AutoRedraw* Property

In the course of running most Windows applications, individual windows become temporarily obscured and then later reexposed. Your Visual Basic applications are no exception.

A form or picture box can become momentarily concealed in a number of ways. For example, a dialog box may open, a form can be resized and minimized, or you may move one window temporarily over another. When several applications are running simultaneously, it's normal for one application to cover up another application temporarily.

Whenever a window is reexposed, the contents of that window must be redrawn. Windows automatically handles this redrawing process for everything except graphics drawn at run time with the graphics methods.

Persistent graphics
Graphics that automatically regenerate when their container is reexposed after being covered.

When a form or picture box container is covered and then reexposed, you usually want that container to appear just as it did before being covered. If the graphics in the container automatically regenerate themselves, such graphics are called **persistent graphics**.

Forms and picture boxes have an `AutoRedraw` property. By default, the value for this property is False. If, however, you set a container's `AutoRedraw` property to True, Visual Basic automatically creates persistent graphics for that container.

`AutoRedraw` affects only the graphics drawn with such graphics methods as `PSet` and `Circle`. Whether `AutoRedraw` is True or False, Windows automatically regenerates the controls and pictures you place in a form or picture box. A Line or Shape control is not affected by the value of its container's `AutoRedraw` property. A line or shape persists even if its container's `AutoRedraw` property is False.

The following sections describe in detail how you use the Line and Shape controls.

Moving Pictures at Run Time

You can dynamically move a picture within a form by loading the picture into an image or picture box container and then moving the container with program instructions. If you modify the values of the container's Left and Top properties, the picture moves accordingly. For example, the following instructions move an Image control named MyImage 500 twips to the right and 250 twips upward:

```
MyImage.Left = MyImage.Left + 500

MyImage.Top = MyImage.Top - 250
```

Visual Basic provides the Move method to simplify moving a form or control with a single instruction. You can also change the size of the moved object. Notice that only the left parameter is mandatory. For example, the following instruction moves the upper-left corner of a picture box to location 300, 400:

```
MyPicture.Move 300, 400
```

This next instruction moves the picture box to a location 500 twips to the right and 750 twips downward from its current location:

```
MyPicture.Move Picture1.Left + 500, Picture1.Top + 750
```

The following instruction doubles the height and width of the picture box:

```
MyPicture.Move Picture1.Left, Picture1.Top, 2 * Picture1.Width,
➡ 2 * Picture1.Height
```

After the Move method relocates or resizes the object, Visual Basic updates the values of the object's Left, Top, Width, and Height parameters accordingly. For more information on the Move method, consult VB's Help facility.

Creating Simple Animation

You can achieve simple animation by using a program loop to move an object repeatedly. To see how this type of animation works, try the following exercise. This code assumes that you have VB and Windows loaded on drive C. If VB and/or Windows is located on another drive, modify the code to reflect VBs location.

❶ Start a new project, and place two Image controls anywhere on the form.

❷ Create the following Form_Load event procedure:

```
Sub Form_Load ()

    Form1.Caption = "Click form to see animation"


    Image1.Move 600, 240
    Image1.Picture = LoadPicture("C:\WINDOWS\ARCHES.BMP")
```

(continues)

Creating Simple Animation (continued)

```
            Image2.Move 5000, 1920
            Image2.Picture LoadPicture("C:\VB\ICONS\MISC\MISC26.ICO")
End Sub
```

This procedure loads a picture into each Image control. The first picture is the Arches bit map. The second picture is an icon representing a woman.

If you installed Visual Basic in the standard way, these picture files should be in the directories indicated in the `LoadPicture` instructions. If your files are in different subdirectories, substitute the correct directory paths in the `LoadPicture` instructions.

Notice how this procedure uses the `Move` method to position the two Image controls correctly on the form.

3 Now create the following `Form_Click` event procedure:

```
Sub Form_Click ()
    Dim Delta As Integer
    Delta = 4    'Change value to adjust movement rate

    Do
        Image2.Move Image2.Left - Delta
    Loop Until Image2.Left < 1320

End Sub
```

This procedure uses the `Move` method to move the icon of the woman incrementally. Each time the `Move` instruction executes, the Image control moves a small distance to the left. The value of `Delta` specifies, in twips, the incremental distance.

4 Run the application. At first, the woman appears outside the arch, as shown in figure 4.9.

Figure 4.9
The woman is outside the arch.

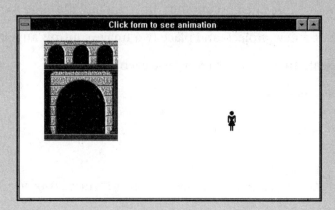

⑤ Click anywhere on the form, and the woman "walks" until she disappears under the arch (see figure 4.10).

Figure 4.10
The woman has walked under the arch.

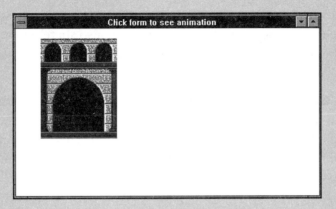

The speed and smoothness of the animation depend on the value of `Delta`. When `Delta` is larger, the picture moves faster but with a jerkier motion. If you reduce the value of `Delta`, you get a smoother, slower movement.

The animated movement of an Image control tends to cause flicker in the moving picture. Pictures in Picture Box controls, however, tend to move without this flicker. To see the difference, modify the application to use two picture boxes rather than two Image controls.

To make this modification, replace the two Image controls with two picture boxes at design time. In the program code, change each occurrence of `Image1` to `Picture1`. Similarly, change `Image2` to `Picture2`. Specify `AutoResize` to be True for both picture boxes. When you run this modified application, the flicker should be gone (or at least greatly reduced).

Copying Controls

When you have one control on a form, you can add additional controls of the same type by copying the existing control to the Clipboard and pasting as many copies as you need. This technique is called creating a **control array**. One advantage of this technique is that the copies have properties identical to those of the source control. If you need several controls with identical properties, set the properties of the original control before copying it to the Clipboard.

Control array
A group of controls of the same type that share a common name and event procedures. Each control in the group has a unique index number that identifies it.

When you begin to copy and paste a control, Visual Basic warns you that you already have a control on your form with that name (for example, `Command1`). No two controls on a form can have exactly the same name. If you paste a copy of a control in a form, Visual Basic begins creating a control array for the control and changes its name. VB names the original control `Command1(0)`. The second control is named `Command1(1)`, the third is named `Command1(2)`, and so on.

After the copy of the control is pasted in your form, all its properties are identical to those of the original control with one exception—the `Name` property. `Name` has been changed by Visual Basic to include the next available numeral for this type of control. This change is necessary because, as noted, no two controls of the same type can have the same name unless they are part of a control array. Only the Name property is changed, not the Caption property.

A control array enables several controls of the same type to share properties and a single name. The controls in the array can also share one section of code. For now, don't create any control arrays. In Chapter 6, you learn more about and actually use a control array.

Using Graphical Components from Windows in Your User Interface

You can insert pictures into a form, an Image control, or a Picture Box control by using the **P**aste command from the **E**dit menu. This command copies the contents of the Windows Clipboard into the form or control you have selected. But how do the pictures get into the Clipboard in the first place? You use the **E**dit Cu**t** or **E**dit **C**opy command to place selected text or a picture in the Clipboard. You can use the Clipboard Viewer application to see the current contents of the Clipboard. Virtually all Windows applications support the Cu**t**, **C**opy, and **P**aste commands from the **E**dit menu.

In Windows, pressing the Print Screen key places a "snapshot" of your screen into the Clipboard. You can then paste this snapshot into your Visual Basic application. Usually, you won't want the whole screen in your application (unless you are writing a tutorial program that teaches how to use an application like Word for Windows or Excel for Windows). What you will want to do is "cut out" one button, icon, or picture for your application. To do this, you use the Windows Paintbrush application. The technique is to place your Clipboard snapshot into Paintbrush, edit the snapshot or cut out just that part of the picture you want in your application, and copy the piece to the Clipboard. You then paste the piece of the snapshot into your VB application.

In review, you use the following steps to capture a screen and then cut out a picture for your program:

1. Bring up on-screen the picture you want in your program.

2. Press **Print Screen**. (Alt+Print Screen captures the active window only.) The picture is now in the Clipboard. The mouse pointer will not be shown.

3. Start Paintbrush, maximize it, and use the **E**dit **P**aste command to place the screen shot into Paintbrush. (Paintbrush is located in the Program Manager Accessories group.)

4. Click either of the Selection tools in the top row of the Paintbrush Toolbox. Usually, you will want to use the rectangular tool at the top right of the Toolbox.

5. Carefully click and drag the selection cross hair over just that part of the picture you want to keep. The selection is surrounded by a dashed line.

6. Choose **E**dit **C**opy to place the selection into the Clipboard.

7. Press **Alt+Tab** (or use the Task Manager in the Control-menu box) to switch to Visual Basic.

8. In your program, select the form or control into which you want to place the captured picture. (Selection handles should appear around a selected control.)

9. Choose **E**dit **P**aste. Now the picture is in your application.

10. Save the project. Then, if you subsequently make a mistake, you won't have to do the work again.

Placing a Picture into a Form's *Picture* Property

In this exercise, you place the Windows logo into the upper-left corner of a Visual Basic form. Before you begin, start the Paintbrush application and begin a new project in Visual Basic, using the **F**ile **N**ew Project command. Then practice using Alt+Tab to move among the various running applications.

4

❶ In the Program Manager window, pull down the **H**elp menu, and choose **A**bout Program Manager. The About Program Manager dialog box appears (see figure 4.11).

Figure 4.11
The About Program Manager dialog box.

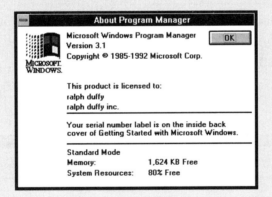

❷ Press **Print Screen**. The screen you see is now in the Windows Clipboard. You can verify this fact by starting the Clipboard Viewer application in the Main program group.

❸ Click OK in the About Program Manager dialog box.

❹ Switch to Paintbrush by pressing **Alt+Tab**.

❺ Make sure that the Paintbrush window is maximized so that it will hold as much of the Clipboard's contents as possible.

❻ Choose **E**dit **P**aste. The About Program Manager dialog box screen appears in the Paintbrush window (see figure 4.12).

(continues)

Placing a Picture into a Form's *Picture* Property   (continued)

The Selection tool

Figure 4.12
The Paintbrush window.

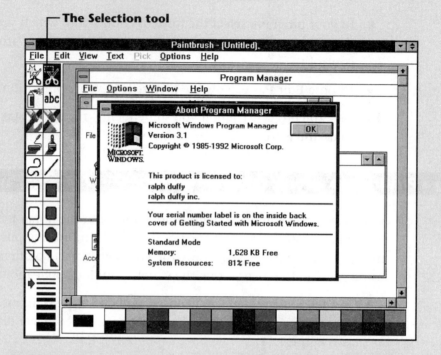

7 Click the Selection tool (it is in the upper-right corner of Paintbrush's Toolbox). The mouse pointer becomes a black cross hair.

8 Click and drag the cross hair from the upper-left corner to the lower-right corner of the Windows logo. Now your screen should look like figure 4.13. Notice the dashed line surrounding the selected Windows logo.

Figure 4.13
The dashed line shows what will be copied into the Clipboard.

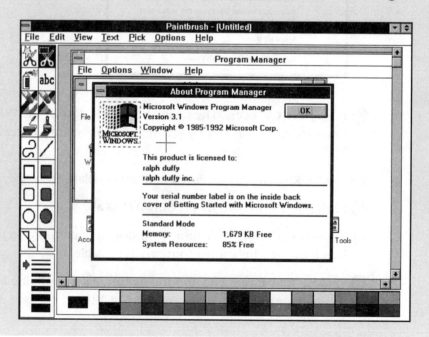

9 Choose **Edit** **C**opy from the Paintbrush menu. The Windows logo is now in the Clipboard.

10 Use **Alt+Tab** to switch to Visual Basic.

11 In VB, choose **Edit** **P**aste.

The contents of the Clipboard are pasted into the Picture property of the form. Your screen should now look like figure 4.14.

Figure 4.14
The Windows logo pasted into your VB form.

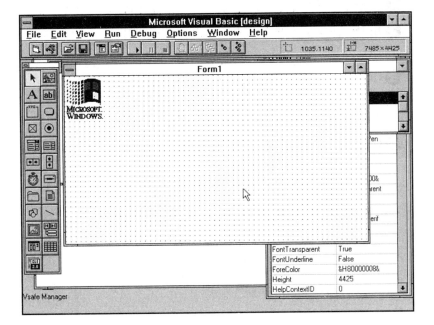

4

Creating Toolbars with Buttons That Click

Most Windows applications contain a Toolbar with buttons offering shortcuts for the menu commands. These buttons contain pictures that indicate the functions of the buttons. The buttons click in and out just as command buttons click. In a Visual Basic program, you create the Toolbar with the Picture Box control. The individual buttons in the Toolbar are Image controls that are drawn on the picture box. Pictures are then placed in the Image controls to show their functions.

If you are a good (and patient) artist, you can create the pictures by using Paintbrush, IconWorks, or another graphics program. To show that a button in the Toolbar has been clicked, you can change the image's border or its color. However, by using the copy-and-paste technique presented in the preceding section, you can capture the images of the buttons used in other applications and make them part of your application's user interface.

In the following exercise, you use this technique to place a File Open button in a Toolbar. After you have done this exercise, you will have the skills necessary to create a more complete Toolbar with many buttons. However, you will have to wait until you have finished some of the later chapters in this book before you will know how to write the code for the Click event procedures for the buttons. In fact, so that you won't be confused with complicated Visual Basic statements, the Click event procedure for the button in this exercise will be left empty.

Placing a Button in a Toolbar

Now complete the exercise to capture "clicked out" (button is up) and "clicked in" (button is down) pictures for your application's Toolbar.

1 In your form, add a picture box at the top of the form.

2 In the picture box, draw three Image controls. Set the Visible property of two of the Image controls to False.

3 Copy into the Clipboard the picture of the button you want clicked out (when it is up). Then paste the picture into the Image control whose Visible property is True.

4 Capture the picture of the button when it is "clicked in," copy the picture into the Clipboard, and then paste it into one of the Image controls whose Visible property is False. Figure 4.15 shows both buttons.

Figure 4.15
"Clicked in" and "clicked out" buttons.

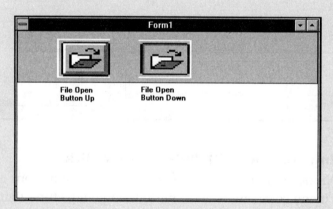

Note: *When capturing the picture, before you press the Print Screen key, you need to place the mouse pointer on the button that you want to be "clicked in." Then press and hold down the left mouse button so that the on-screen button stays "clicked in." Now press the Print Screen key. Pause and then release the mouse button. If you check the contents of the Clipboard, you will see that you have captured the picture of the clicked-in button without the mouse pointer.*

5 In the button-up image's MouseDown event, first move the image's picture into the third Image control (its Visible property is False). This image functions as a "holding area" for the button-up picture.

Note: *If you have many buttons in your Toolbar but only one will be "clicked in" at a time, you need only one invisible image to function as a holding area. You will need, however, a button-up and button-down pair of Image controls for each button you place in the Toolbar.*

6 In the button-up image's `MouseDown` event, move the button-down picture into the Image control that is visible (the one that has been called the button-up Image control).

7 In the button-up image's `MouseUp` event, move the picture (the button-up picture) now in the holding area back into the button-up Image control.

Sound complicated? Well, maybe it is at first. But after you practice the operation a couple of times, you will see how easy it is. Most students like the effect and think it's well worth the effort. Once you have captured the button-up and button-down pictures, all you are doing is swapping the pictures back and forth between Image controls in sync with the user's mouse clicks.

One thing that you should look at is how Windows actually creates the effect of the button clicking in and out. You can clearly see the effect when the pictures of the buttons are in the Clipboard. Use the Clipboard Viewer application in the Program Manager Main group to check the contents of the Clipboard. You will see that the lines at the outside of the button change color when the button clicks in. That is the only difference between a button that is "up" and one that is "down." You can create your own button pictures in IconWorks.

The following exercises illustrate some of the topics covered in this chapter. You will need to start Visual Basic before you begin the exercises.

Seeing How a Toolbar Operates

In this exercise, you explore an application, provided on your student disk, that illustrates the operation of a simple toolbar. The functionality of the buttons has not been implemented. You learn how to do that later in this book. In this exercise, concentrate on understanding how the click effect of the button is implemented.

1 Load the program TOOL1.MAK from the CHAPT4 directory on the student disk.

2 Run the program to see how the buttons on the toolbar work.

3 In Design mode, identify each of the controls on the form, and examine their properties.

4 Find the event procedures that have been coded for each of the objects. Is there code in the general object of the form? Are there event procedures for the form?

5 Choose **File Print**.

6 In the Print dialog box, choose the **Form**, Form **Text**, and **Code** check boxes. Then choose the **All** option button.

7 Click the OK button.

Examine the printout you produced to make sure that you understand this application.

Seeing How a Status Bar Operates

In this exercise, you explore an application, provided on your student disk, that illustrates the operation of a status bar at the bottom of a window. A menu item enables the user to indicate whether he or she wants the name of a button to be displayed in a label under the button. Again, the functionality of the buttons has not been implemented. This program also illustrates the use of the mouse movement events.

① Load the program TOOL2.MAK from the CHAPT4 directory on your student disk.

② Run the program to see how the status bar explains the function of each button as you point to it.

③ Choose the menu item (Tool Tips) that displays the name of each Toolbar button on which you place the mouse pointer.

④ In Design mode, identify each of the controls on the form, and examine their properties.

⑤ Find the event procedures that have been coded for each of the objects. Is there code in the general object of the form? Are there event procedures for the form?

⑥ Choose **File Print**.

⑦ In the Print dialog box, choose the **Form**, Form **Text**, and **Code** check boxes. In the Print dialog box, choose the **All** option button.

⑧ Click the OK button.

Examine the printout you produced to make sure that you understand this application.

Chapter Summary

In this chapter, you learned about check boxes, option buttons, images, picture boxes, frames, lines, and shapes. You learned how to use a Frame control to group other controls. You learned how to place pictures in forms, images, and picture boxes. The chapter showed you how to create simple animation, toolbars, and status boxes. You were also introduced to the concept of a control array. In the next chapter, you learn more about writing Visual Basic code.

Test Your Understanding

True/False
Indicate whether the statement is true or false.

1. Forms, picture boxes, and Image controls can display pictures.

2. An Image control does not have a Click event.

3. You cannot place other controls over a picture box.

4. The Line and Shape controls each have a Click event.

5. When you are using the Line control, the BorderWidth property determines the thickness of the drawn line.

6. The Stretch property of the Image control, when set to a value of True, lets you make a picture in the control larger or smaller.

7. A form can contain only one group of option buttons.

8. Check boxes are mutually exclusive; when one is checked (selected), the others must not be checked.

9. The Value property of an option button indicates whether that button has been selected.

10. The best way to place an Option Button control on a Frame control is to double-click the Option button tool in the Toolbox.

Short Answer
Answer the following questions.

1. Write the Visual Basic code to cause an Option Button control named Option1 to be the selected option button in a group.

2. Write the Visual Basic code to cause an icon in the file C:\WINDOWS\ YOURICON.ICO to be displayed as the Picture property of a Picture Box control.

3. List the steps you would follow in Design mode to place the icon mentioned in question 2 in the currently selected Image control and then to allow it to be resized.

4. What is a control array? How is a control array created?

5. Explain the function of the BorderStyle property of the Line and Shape controls.

6. Explain the function of the Shape property of the Shape control. What are the valid settings for this property, and what is the effect of each setting?

7. Explain the function of the FillStyle property of the Shape control. What are the valid settings for this property, and what is the effect of each setting? How is FillStyle different from FillColor and BackStyle?

8. Explain how a picture can be moved around in a form at run time. Explain the controls, events, and methods involved.

9. Explain the steps needed to capture the picture of a File Save button to use in a VB program. What controls, methods, and events are needed?

10. Explain what controls are needed to create a toolbar with three buttons that click up and down. How many of each type of control are needed? What special properties must be set? Write a line of code that will move a button-up picture into a control that currently contains a button-down picture. In which event should this code be placed?

11. What controls, events, code, and methods have to be included in a frame to create a status bar?

Projects

Project 1:   Using Animation and Icons to Launch a Rocket

In this project, you use simple animation and the icons available in VB to launch a rocket. Figure 4.16 shows the icons you use.

Figure 4.16
The on-screen components.

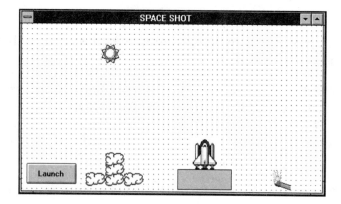

Several of the icons must be placed in Image controls with the Stretch property set to True so that the icons can be resized. The icons shown in figure 4.16 are the following:

VB\ICONS\INDUSTRY\ROCKET.ICO

VB\ICONS\ELEMENTS\CLOUD.ICO

VB\ICONS\ELEMENTS\FIRE.ICO

VB\ICONS\ELEMENTS\SUN.ICO

The complete listing of all VB icons is found in Appendix B of *Visual Basic Programmer's Guide*. You create the launching pad with the Shape control (see figure 4.17).

When the user clicks the Launch button, the fire icon should appear under the rocket, as shown in figure 4.18. Then the rocket should "blast off" (see figure 4.19). Finally, the rocket should steadily move up the screen and become smaller (see figure 4.20). Save this project as **C4P1**, and print the form text and code.

Figure 4.17
Ready to launch.

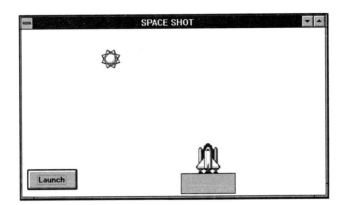

Figure 4.18
We have ignition!

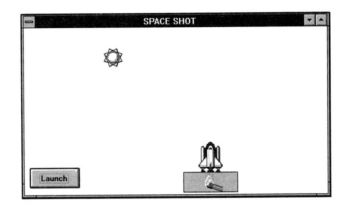

Figure 4.19
Lift off.

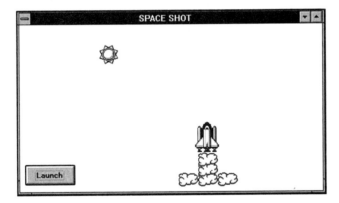

Figure 4.20
The rocket climbs
steadily into the sky.

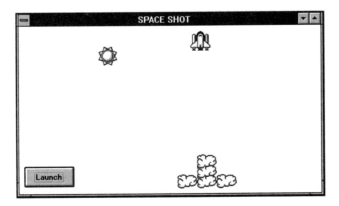

Project 2: Exploring a Sample VB Program

In this project, you explore one of the sample VB programs that Microsoft provides with Visual Basic. These sample programs are in subdirectories under VB\SAMPLES. You use the **File O**pen Project command to load the programs; then you can explore how the programs work and print them. Microsoft provides these programs to show you how to use VB. The programs are a gold mine of programming information. The program you load, study, and then modify in this project is designed to illustrate the use of some of the controls and the control arrays. Load the CONTROLS.MAK program from the SAMPLES subdirectory.

When you run CONTROLS.MAK, you have the choice of running several different routines. The four options you need to learn well in this project are **C**heck Box, **N**umber System, **S**croll Bars, and Control **A**rray. There are a few code statements and functions that you have not yet encountered in this text (but you will). Use the VB Help facility to learn about anything that you don't understand. After you have run and explored each of these four options, print the Check Box form and its code. To do this, highlight CHECK.FRM in the Project window. Then Choose **File P**rint. In the Print dialog box, click the **Cu**rrent option button. Then click the **F**orm, Form **T**ext, and **C**ode check boxes. Finally, click the OK button.

Your job is to create a running version of just this part of the CONTROLS project. Then you add a third check box that will let you enter underlined text in the text box. Test the program; save it on disk; and print your form, form text, and code. Then replace the check boxes with option buttons grouped on a Frame control. This version of the program should let you enter only bold, italic, or underlined text. Again, save your project as **C4P2**, and then print the form, form text, and code.

Project 3: Creating and Using Icons

In this project, you explore the creation and use of icons by using the ICONWRKS sample application. You do not need, at this point, to understand how the code in this program works. What you do need to know is how to use its icon viewer to browse through the icon libraries in the VB\ICON subdirectory. In addition, you need to know how to use ICONWRKS to construct your own custom icon.

Use the **File O**pen Project command to load the ICONWRKS.MAK program from the VB\SAMPLES subdirectory. Use the program's **H**elp menu to learn how to use the program to view and create icons. Browse through the icon library by using the icon viewer. Load the icon of your choice into the IconWorks Editor. Make some modifications to the icon and then save it to your floppy disk as **C4P3**. (*Don't* save the modified icon back into the VB Icons library.) Then create your own custom icon, and save it on your floppy disk (*not* the VB icon library).

Start a new project, and place two Image controls in the form. Set the `Stretch` property of these controls to True. Set the `Picture` property of the first image so that it displays the VB icon you modified using ICONWRKS. Set the `Picture` property of the second image so that it displays the custom icon you created using ICONWRKS. Resize the images so that each one is about one inch square. Then print the form and save your project as **C4P3**.

CHAPTER 5

Programming in Visual Basic

When you program in Visual Basic, you perform two activities. You build your user interface by creating forms that contain controls. Then you type your VB program instructions. As you create the forms and add controls, VB sets up the event procedures you may need. VB creates the empty event procedures for each form and each control in the form; you just need to add the code. You now know about forms, controls, events, and methods. But what about that Visual Basic program code? Deciding where all that code is supposed to go can be pretty confusing.

Probably the most frequent task any program performs is manipulating text and numbers in some way. When you place text in a text box, you are working with text. When you click a scroll bar (increment its value), you are working with numbers. You have to learn to work with text, numbers, variables, and other types of data if you want to write programs with any programming language, including Visual Basic.

In this chapter, you learn how a VB program is put together and where you put different types of program code. You also learn about using variables and constants in your programs. This chapter prepares you for programming in Visual Basic.

Objectives

By the time you have finished this chapter, you will be able to

1. Identify the Types of Files in a VB Project

2. Understand What Happens When You Run a VB Program

3. Understand Event, Form-Level, and Code-Module Procedures

4. Understand What Causes the Execution of Code in Event, Form-Level, and Code-Module Procedures

5. Determine When to Place Your VB Code in an Event, Form-Level, or Code-Module Procedure

6. Understand What a Variable Is and Use One

7. Understand Data Types

8. Work with Strings in a VB Program

9. Call a Procedure

10. Understand What a Named Constant Is and Use One

Here's How VB Programs Work

To understand how you put together a Visual Basic program, you need to understand how a VB program works. First, you need to understand the types of files that make up a VB program.

Form Files

As you work on a project, its forms are stored in files, one form to a file. The controls that reside on the form are also saved in the form's file. You can use any valid DOS file name for a form's file name, and the form file has the file extension FRM. The form files that make up a project are listed in the Project window (see figure 5.1). When you want to work with a form, you simply select that form from the Project window and then choose the View Code or the View Form button, depending on whether you want to view the form's Code window or the form itself.

Figure 5.1
The Project window listing various types of files.

Form module
Contains controls and all the VB code associated with the controls and the form itself.

In addition to the form and its controls, the form file contains the Visual Basic statements that make up any procedures you have written for the form's events, including events that apply to the form and those that apply to specific controls on the form. A simple project could contain only a single form, and all the program code could be contained in the form file. Therefore, the Project window would show only a single form file. Because form files contain code, they are called **form modules**.

Code Modules

Form files are not the only types of files you can find in a Visual Basic project. In addition to form modules (FRM files), your project can contain code modules. The code module contains the general procedures and functions that are part of your program; the code module can hold from zero to many procedures. Each procedure must have a unique name. You learn more about procedures later in this chapter. Code modules do not contain forms or controls.

If procedures are already in the form file, why do you need these other files and procedures? The event procedures and functions that you write for a form are sometimes not the only procedures, functions, and other program code that you need to write for a program.

If you have functions that are common to many of your forms, for example, you should not duplicate them in each form. Doing so increases the size of your application and also makes it difficult for you to manage the code-writing and debugging processes. If you have an error in the same code in four different forms, you will have to change the code four times.

Code module file
A BAS file that contains all the procedures and variable declarations accessible to all your forms.

How do you avoid duplicating a procedure in each form that needs it? Just create a **code module file** (BAS file) that contains all the procedures and variable declarations that need to be accessible to all your forms. Your project can include form files and one or more code module files. You learn more about code modules and variable declarations later in this chapter.

The AUTOLOAD.MAK File

VBX file
A file containing all the code necessary to make custom controls work.

You may never use some of the custom controls that come with Visual Basic. If you want to prevent VB from automatically loading specific **VBX files** each time you start a new project, make a backup copy of AUTOLOAD.MAK, located in the Visual Basic directory (see figure 5.2). Then start Notepad, and open the file AUTOLOAD.MAK. Delete the line(s) in AUTOLOAD.MAK that list the VBX file(s) you do not want Visual Basic to load each time it starts a new project.

5

Figure 5.2
Notepad with AUTOLOAD.MAK opened for editing.

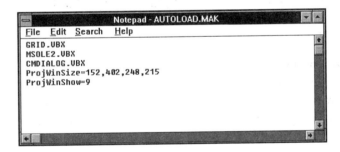

You can also include files like CONSTANTS.TXT in your projects by adding their names to the AUTOLOAD.MAK file. Then resave AUTOLOAD.MAK, and restart Visual Basic.

How the Program Runs and Stops

In addition to knowing what goes into a Visual Basic program, you should understand how a VB program works, at least in general terms. You need to understand which code is executed first when the program starts. This code is the entry point, or starting point, for your program.

Specifying the Start-Up Form

You read about the start-up form in Chapter 3. You can assign one of the forms in your program as the start-up form. If a form is assigned as the start-up form, it is loaded as soon as the program starts.

When should you assign a form as the start-up form? If your program uses a main program window and you want that window to display immediately when the program starts, assign it as the start-up form. In the Load procedure for the form, add any statements that you want to have executed as soon as the program starts. These statements may set up variables, load other forms, fill in items in list boxes, or perform other start-up tasks.

Including the *Sub Main* Procedure

You can also assign a Sub procedure called Main as the start-up form (although it isn't a form at all). Sub Main is a procedure just like any other procedure you create. The only differences are that its name is Main and it is located in a code module (a BAS file)—not in a form. If you assign Sub Main as the start-up form, no forms load automatically when the program starts. Instead, the statements in Sub Main execute.

You can have only one Sub Main in a program. If your project contains more than one module file, only one of the module files can contain a Sub Main procedure.

In the Sub Main procedure, you should include any statements that you want to have executed when the program starts. Think of Sub Main as the Load procedure for a program. If you need to set up some variables or perform other actions before any forms are loaded, include the statements in Sub Main to perform those actions; then assign Sub Main as the start-up form. If your program uses an INI file to store its settings, for example, you may need to add to Sub Main some code that causes your program to read the INI file to determine how the program should run, which form it should open, and so on.

Stopping the Program

At some point, you will want your program to stop. If the user chooses **File Exit** from your program's menu, for example, the program should stop. Use the Visual Basic End statement to end the program. Here's a sample Sub procedure for an mnuFileExit menu choice. Assume that the name mnuFileExit has been assigned to **E**xit in the **F**ile menu of your program:

```
Sub mnuFileExit_Click()
    'if the user clicks File, then Exit, end the program
    End
End Sub
```

Another way to end the program is to include the End statement in the main form's Unload procedure. When the form is unloaded, either by your program's unloading it through code or by the user's closing the window (form), the End statement in the Unload procedure will execute, ending the program.

A Quick Summary

The following list provides a quick summary of what happens in the life of a VB program:

1. The program starts and automatically loads the start-up form, executing the statements in the start-up form's Load procedure.

At this time, the statements in the `Sub Main` procedure are executed if you have assigned `Sub Main` as the start-up procedure.

2. An event occurs, either because you generate the event in your program code or because the user performs some action (like clicking a button) that triggers the event.

3. If you have written a procedure to respond to the event, the code in that procedure executes. If no procedure code for the event exists, the program waits for the next event to occur.

4. When the user finishes with the program, she or he performs some action—such as choosing E**x**it from the program's **F**ile menu, clicking a command button, or closing the start-up form—to end the program. The `End` statement, which you have placed in the appropriate place in the program code, is then executed and terminates the program.

Where Should the Code Go?

Part of the process of planning and creating a program includes deciding what procedures are needed and where you should put them. Later in this chapter, you can work through a specific example and design a program. For now, read about the categories of code routines you can add to a program and where that code should go. Figure 5.3 gives you a graphical representation of how you can structure a program's code.

5

Figure 5.3
Where program code can be placed.

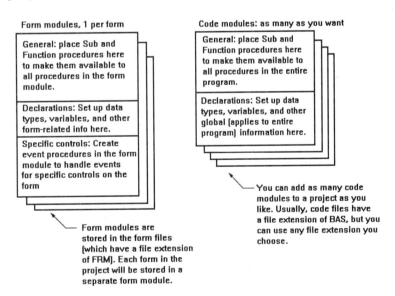

But first, you need to understand what a VB code procedure is.

Procedures

By now, you probably understand that a procedure is a group of Visual Basic statements that have a unique name, like Form1_Load, Command1_Click, txtEntry_Change, FileOpenProc, Main, and so on. Your program executes the statements in a procedure to perform the various actions that the program is designed to perform. Procedures are placed either in a form module or in a code module, based on the type of procedure it is.

Event Procedures (Event Handlers)

Event procedure
A procedure associated with a particular control and event.

An **event procedure** is associated with a particular control and event. The name of the event procedure should indicate this relationship. The procedure executes when the particular event happens to that control. The procedure named txtEntry_Change, for example, executes when the text in the text box named txtEntry changes. When that text changes, a Change event is generated, causing the procedure txtEntry_Change to be executed. Notice that the event procedure's name consists of the name of the control, followed by an underline, followed by the name of the event.

Event procedures enable you to handle specific events for a control or form. Event procedures execute only when the event with which they are associated occurs or when you specifically cause the event to occur by executing an appropriate statement in your program.

As an example, here are two instances in which the procedure btnEnd is executed:

- The user clicks the button named btnEnd, generating a Click event for the button.

- Your program executes the statement btnEnd_Click in another procedure.

Because event procedures are associated with specific events occurring within a form, event procedures are placed in the form module that contains the control associated with the event. If you have code statements that you want executed only if a user performs an action to a control, place that VB code in an event procedure. If you have code that you want executed only when an event occurs to a form, put that code in the appropriate event procedure. For example, if you have code that you want executed when Form1 is loaded, place the code in the Form1_Load event procedure that Visual Basic has ready for you (see figure 5.4).

Remember that the event procedures you have coded execute only when a particular event happens to a given object. Remember also that *before* you start writing any program code, you should give a form or control the name you will use to refer to that form or control in VB code. You give an object a name by setting the object's Name property in the Properties window.

Figure 5.4
The Code window for the Form_Load event.

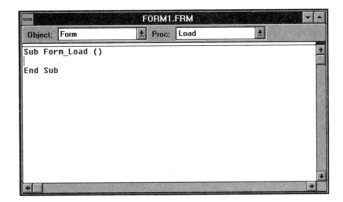

The names of Visual Basic forms, controls, procedures, variables, and constants must conform to the following rules:

- They must begin with a letter.

- They must contain only letters, numbers, and the underscore character. Punctuation characters and spaces are not allowed.

- They cannot be longer than 40 characters.

Reserved word
A word that only Visual Basic can use, part of the Visual Basic language.

- The names of items you declare in your code cannot be a VB **reserved word**. Reserved words are words (such as If, Loop, and Show) that only VB can use as part of the VB language. Your program will have an error in it if, for example, you use the name Loop for a form.

For a complete list of reserved words, see Appendix F of the *VB Language Reference*, which is included in the box with the VB program disks from Microsoft.

General Procedures

General procedure
A procedure not associated with a specific object or event.

A **general procedure** is not associated with a particular object and event. Instead of being executed when the event occurs to the specified control, a general procedure executes only when your program directs it to execute. In programming terms, we say that your program "calls" the general procedure by name.

General object
The area of a form module or a code module in which all general procedures are entered.

General procedures are useful when you need to make a set of VB statements available to other procedures. That way, you don't have to write the same code over and over again in different locations. General procedures that will be used within a form are placed in the general object of that form. The **general object** is the area of a form module or a code module in which all code not associated with a particular object (that is, general procedures) is entered. In the declarations section of the general object, form-level or code-module-level variables and constants are declared. Global variables and constants can be declared only in the declarations section of a code module's general object. Procedures that are going to be used in several *different* forms or several *different* code modules (BAS modules) must be placed in the general object of a code module.

You access a form's general object by double-clicking the form to open the Code window of the form. Then you select (general) from the Object drop-down list and type the name of the procedure and the lines of code that constitute the procedure. When you view the code in a code module, you automatically have access to the general object of the code module. You can immediately type the name of the general procedure and the lines of code that constitute the procedure.

Sub Procedures and *Function* Procedures

You can create two types of general procedures: Sub procedures and Function procedures. Both types of procedures work much the same way, but they have some differences. Sub procedures do not return a value, but Function procedures do return a value. That difference can be confusing to a nonprogrammer, so a short explanation is provided.

Subprogram
A self-contained program, a Sub procedure.

A Sub procedure (sometimes called a **subprogram**) is a self-contained procedure. When a Sub procedure executes, some of its statements may calculate values or perform other tasks, and the Sub procedure may set the properties of controls or forms being used by the program. The Sub procedure, however, does not generate and return a single value that represents the sum of its efforts.

Function procedure
A procedure that generates a return value.

A ***Function* procedure**, however, does generate a return value. Think of a Function procedure as a magic black box. You pour some information into the box; the box works on the information for a while and then produces an answer. That answer is the return value of the Function procedure. To sum it up, a procedure calls a Function procedure and passes it some information; the Function procedure runs through its paces, chewing on the information, and returns the value to the procedure that called it. In a later chapter, you learn how to pass values to Function and Sub procedures.

If you are writing a procedure that calculates values internally or just sets properties of controls but doesn't pass a value back to the procedure that called it, you probably should use a Sub procedure. If you need to write a self-contained procedure that evaluates information that you pass to it and returns a value, create it as a Function procedure. Use a function if you need an answer returned or if you need to know whether the function completed successfully.

You create a Sub procedure by typing the key word Sub followed by the name of your procedure. The Sub procedure ends with the End Sub statement. You create a Function procedure by typing the key word Function before the name of the function. The Function procedure ends with the End Function statement. You can also create empty templates for the two different types of procedures by choosing **N**ew Procedure from the **V**iew menu. The New Procedure dialog box opens (see figure 5.5).

Figure 5.5
The New Procedure dialog box.

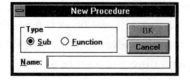

You select the type of procedure you want and then type its name in the **N**ame text box. Your last step is to choose OK.

The procedures in a form can be called only by other procedures within that form. When you want a procedure to be available to only the procedures in a form, place the procedure in the form module, either as an event procedure or as a general procedure. If you need to call the procedure from another form, move the procedure to a code module.

Before you start creating procedures, though, think about how you are going to name them. Because procedures in a form module are available only within their form, they can have the same procedure names as procedures in other forms. For example, two forms can both have a `Form_Load` procedure. Procedures in code modules, however, must have unique names. You can't use the same name for two different procedures within a code module (or in more than one code module).

Why Have More Than One Code Module in a Project?

A project can contain many code modules. By using multiple code modules, you can add a logical structure to your project while you are working on it. You might put all the general procedures related to calculation in one code module, for example, and place all the procedures related to output display updating in another code module. You could place all your global variable declarations and global named-constant declarations in a third code module.

When your program is running, whether your procedures and global declarations are contained in a single code module or in many code modules makes no difference. All the procedures are combined when the program is compiled, just as if they came from a single code module.

5

The Mechanics of Writing Code

You have written a little bit of code in previous chapters but without much explanation of what you were doing. In this section, you learn about some of the mechanics and conventions used in writing Visual Basic program code.

Sprinkling Your Code with Comments

Comment

Text that explains what the program code is doing.

In program code, a **comment** is a bit of text that explains what the program code is doing. By adding comments to your program, you make it much easier for you or someone else who will be working with your source code (the program code that you write) to follow the logic of the program. If you put a program away for a few weeks and then begin working on it again, comments in the code help you easily pick up where you left off.

Comments can be on lines of their own, or you can add comments at the end of a statement. To add a comment, precede the comment with an apostrophe ('). Here are some examples of comments in a procedure:

```
Sub TaxCalc ()
    'This is a comment on a line by itself.
    'The next line displays a value in a text box
    txt1.Text = "Enter Income Tax Here"
    txt2.Text = "Pay This Amount" 'This is a comment on the same line
End Sub
```

In this example, the comments are shown in italics. When you add comments to your program, however, the comments appear on-screen in a different color from the program statements. By default, Visual Basic displays comment text in green, but you can specify a different color if green doesn't suit you. To specify a different color for comment text or for other options, choose **O**ptions **E**nvironment. In the Environment Options dialog box, click Comment Text in the list box, and choose a color from the Settings drop-down list (see figure 5.6). Choose OK to make your changes take effect.

Figure 5.6

The Environment Options dialog box.

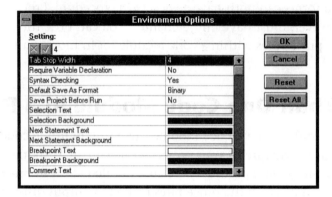

Make liberal use of comments in your code. Even if you remember right now what a program statement is for, you may forget two months from now when you want to make a change to the program. If you have comments in the code, you won't have to spend time trying to remember how your program works, what its variables represent, and so on. In a work environment, other programmers will find your program easier to understand if you have included meaningful comments.

Breaking Up Your Code

Normally, your program statements are added to a procedure one line at a time, with each statement on its own line:

```
Text1.Text = "This is one statement."
Text2.Text = "This is another statement."
Form1.Show
Form2.Hide
```

Organizing Your Code with Tabs

Using tabs to organize your program's code and to help you visualize the logical flow of the program is a good idea. Tabs are particularly useful in helping you understand the flow of a decision structure or loop structure. You read more about these types of control structures in Chapter 7, "Program Flow and Decision Making." For now, here is an example of some code that uses tabs to show the organization of the control structure:

```
Sub NestedControls ()

Text1.Text = "Beginning count routine"
If Choice = 1 Then
```

```
        For x = 1 to 1000
                Text2.Text = "Counting characters..." + Str$(x)
        Next x
    End If
    Text1.Text = "Count completed."

    End Sub
```

Pressing the Tab key shifts the statement to the right to the fifth character in the line. Visual Basic does not insert a tab character; instead, VB inserts spaces into the line. Using the Tab key to structure the appearance of your code makes it much easier to read the flow of the program's logic. You may also want to add a blank line at the beginning and end of a Sub or Function procedure, as shown in the preceding example, to make determining where the procedure begins and ends easy.

Declarations of Variables

While you were working with some of the earlier VB programs, you may have noticed the word (*declarations*) in the Proc drop-down list of the Code window of the general object of a form or code module. The declarations section of a module is for declaring constants, types, variables, and DLL procedures. You can't place any executable statements (like a Sub or Function) in the declarations section.

Constants, types, and variables are explained later in this chapter. For now, you just need to understand that the declarations section is where you declare (define) information that your program will use.

DLL procedures are not covered in this text, although you should know that you can call functions that are stored in Windows DLL files. Visual Basic cannot handle many complex tasks directly, but the Windows API (Application Programming Interface) does provide functions that handle these complex tasks. For example, you cannot make a Visual Basic program window "float" on top of the display when it doesn't have focus, but you can cause it to behave that way by using a call to one of the Windows DLLs. For more information on calling procedures that are stored in DLLs, see *Using Visual Basic 3*, Special Edition, published by Que Corporation.

Using Text and Numbers in a Program

Your programs will often be required to process text (like people's names) and numbers (like the radius of a circle or scores on a test). To process text and numbers, you will need to use Visual Basic variables in your program.

What Are Variables?

Variable
A symbol(s) that represent(s) value(s) which can be altered.

Variables in a program are just like the variables you learned about in algebra class. Variables are used as symbolic containers for information. The following code uses variables named fred and x to store two numbers. The code also uses a loop to execute a statement 12 times. A Loop structure is a special Visual Basic code construction that enables the program to execute a group of statements conditionally (such as a certain number of times):

```
Sub Example ()
    'First, set fred equal to 12
    fred = 12

    'Next, start a loop that will repeat until a counter is equal
    'to fred

    For x = 1 to fred
        'Put the value of x in a text box
        Text1.Text = x
    'Increment x by 1 and do it all again
    Next x

End Sub
```

The first line of the procedure stores the numeric value *12* in a container (a variable) named fred. The value of fred is used in the second statement as a "stopper" value. The For-Next loop executes 12 times; it starts with x equal to 1 and then displays the value of the variable x in Text1. The Next x statement increments x by 1 and the For-Next loop repeats with a value for x of 2. The For-Next loop continues to repeat until x is equal to fred, or 12.

You can tell from the example that variables are just symbols that represent values. They're just like named containers for information.

Data Types

There are many different types of data: numbers, text, dates and times, and currency. In addition, there are also different types of variables that can contain numeric data. These statements may seem confusing at first, but this section clears up some of that confusion. First, look at table 5.1. It shows the data types that you can use in Visual Basic.

Table 5.1   Visual Basic Data Types

Type Name	Description	Type-Declaration Character	Range
Integer	2-byte integer	%	-32,768 to 32,767
Long	4-byte integer	&	-2,147,483,648 to 2,147,483,647
Single	4-byte floating-point number	!	-3.402823E38 to -1.401298E-45 (negative values) 1.401298E-45 to 3.402823E38 (positive values)
Double	8-byte floating-point number	#	-1.79769313486232D308 to -4.94065645841247D-324 (negative values) 4.94065645841247D-324 to 1.79769313486232D308 (positive values)
Currency	8-byte number with fixed decimal point	@	-922337303685477.5808 to 922337303685477.5807

Type Name	Description	Type-Declaration Character	Range
String	String of alpha-numeric characters	$	0 to approximately 65,500 65,500 characters
Variant	Date/time, floating-point number, or string	(none)	Date values: January 1, 0000 to December 31, 9999; numeric values: same as Double; string values: same as String

Figure 5.7 shows the relationships among the categories of VB data types.

Figure 5.7
The eight funda-mental data types.

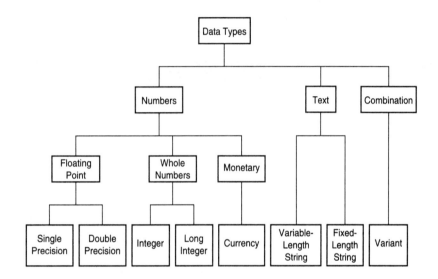

Visual Basic's Help facility contains much useful information on variable types.

Numeric Variables

Integer
A whole number without a decimal fraction.

Because it may have been a while since you had a math class, you may need a review. An **integer** is a whole number without a decimal fraction (places after the decimal point). The Integer and Long data types are virtually the same, except that the Long data type can store larger numbers (either positive or negative) than the Integer type. The Long type uses twice as much RAM as the Integer type to store its value. Remember, variables are a way of referencing the contents of memory locations.

Real number
A number that has a fractional part.

The Single and 0 data types also are used for numbers, but they can contain a decimal fraction, like 342.9987. Both Single and Double variables store **real numbers** (numbers that have a fractional part). A Single data type is a single-precision value, and a Double data type is a double-precision value. The Double type variable can contain larger numbers and numbers with more decimal places than the Single data type because the Double type uses twice as much memory to store its value.

The Currency data type also can contain a number, but it is fixed at four decimal places. If you calculate a Currency variable using numbers with more than four decimal places, the value will be rounded to four decimal places.

Remember, any number in a variable that will be used in calculations must be stored in a numeric type variable.

Strings

A String data type contains alphanumeric characters (letters, numbers, punctuation marks, and so on). Your name is a string. The text "This is a string" is a string. The characters "123456" make up a string.

Visual Basic provides many ways to manipulate a string. You can convert numbers in a string to a single number so that it can be used in a calculation. You can concatenate strings ("glue" them together), trim characters out of a string, and much more. String manipulation is explained later in this chapter. Strings cannot be used in a calculation; if you try this, you will get a `Data type mismatch` message from Visual Basic.

Exploring Data Types

Take a moment to play with a small program that displays different data types in a text box. The VARIABLE.MAK project is a program that displays a selection of buttons. When you click a button, a value appears in the Value text box, and its data type is displayed in the Type text box.

To understand more about data types, follow these steps:

1 Open the project VARIABLE.MAK, which is in the CHAPT5 directory on your student disk.

2 Run the program. Figure 5.8 shows the program's form.

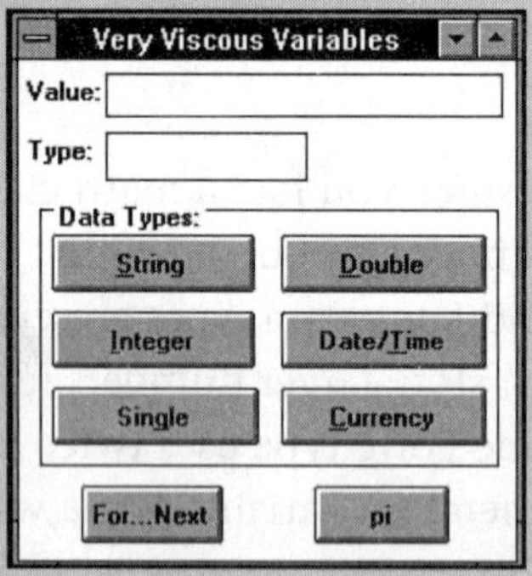

Figure 5.8
The form for VARIABLE.MAK.

3 Click the String button. A String data type appears in the text box.

4 Click the Integer button. An Integer data type appears in the text box.

5 Click the Single button. A Single data type appears in the text box.

6 Click the Double button. A Double data type appears in the text box.

7 Click the Date/Time button. The current date and time appear in the text box.

8 Click the Currency button. A Currency data type appears in the text box.

9 End the program.

The program has no problem displaying all the different data types in the same text box because Visual Basic converts the data as necessary to display it in the text box.

Run the program again, and click the buttons until you are comfortable with your understanding of the different data types. Remember, controls are not variables. Keep the project VARIABLE.MAK open. You use it again in the next few sections.

The Variant Data Type

The default data type is called the Variant data type. A Variant data type can hold a date/time value, an integer, a floating-point number, currency, or a string. If you create a variable in your program but don't explicitly specify its type, it will be created as a Variant type.

Variant data types are chameleon variables—they can freely change type. If you create a variable and store the value 3 in it, Visual Basic represents the number as an Integer type. If the variable later changes value to *3.14159*, Visual Basic stores the value as a Double. The variable is still recognized as a Variant type, although Visual Basic changes the way the variable is represented internally (in RAM) to the Variant type.

5

Working with Variant Data Types

Use VARIABLE.MAK to test the way a Variant data type can change. Follow these steps:

1 Run the program, and click the pi button. The Value text box displays 3, and the Type text box displays Integer.

The values change to 3.14159 and Double, respectively.

2 End the program.

The procedure for the pi button sets pi to 3 and displays it in the Value text box. This change causes the Type text box to display the Integer data type. The procedure changes pi to 3.14159, which causes pi's variable type to change to Double.

Because a Variant type variable can represent many different types of data, there are some potential problems you may experience when trying to manipulate and use a Variant type variable. Later in this chapter, you read about some of those potential problems.

Declaring Variables

When you create a variable, you declare it. You can declare a variable explicitly or implicitly. Assume that the variable named TaxRate hasn't been defined yet in your program. Your program executes the following statement:

```
TaxRate = 0.2
```

When VB executes that statement, the variable TaxRate is created *implicitly*. The statement implies that you want to set a memory location called TaxRate to 0.2. However, you haven't explicitly declared what type of variable TaxRate should be. What data type is TaxRate? Variables are created using the Variant type unless you specify otherwise. So TaxRate is a Variant type variable represented internally as an Integer.

To declare a variable *explicitly* as a specific data type, use the Dim statement. Here's the format for the Dim statement when it's used explicitly to declare a variable:

```
Dim varname As vartype
```

varname specifies the name of the variable, and *vartype* specifies the variable's data type. Here are some examples that explicitly declare different variable types:

```
Dim fredStr As String

Dim fredInt As Integer

Dim fredSing As Single

Dim fredDoub As Double

Dim fredCurr As Currency
```

Take a few moments to experiment with declaring variables. In the following exercise, have a look at the declarations section of the code to examine the Dim statements contained in it. Then eliminate the Dim statements, and see how the program is affected.

Declaring a Variable Explicitly with *Dim*

To declare a variable explicitly, follow these steps:

❶ Continue working with VARIABLE.MAK, and open the Code window.

❷ From the Object drop-down list, choose (general).

❸ From the Proc drop-down list, choose (declarations).

❹ Examine the Dim statements, and note that they explicitly declare a selection of the variables that are used elsewhere in the program.

❺ Turn the statements into comments by adding an apostrophe (') in front of each Dim statement.

❻ Run the program, and click the six data type buttons in turn.

Note that the data types no longer match the button names—the Single, Double, and Currency buttons all generate a Double variable.

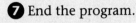 End the program.

You can see that unless you explicitly declare a variable type, you don't have much control over the type of variable it becomes. In some cases, implicitly declared variables inherit the expected data type. If you store a date or time in a variable, for example, it will become a Date/Time variable because no other variable type can store that type of data.

When should you declare a variable explicitly with the Dim statement? Whenever you want to force the variable to be treated as a specific type, declare it explicitly. Remember that the program can interpret the value 432.5234 as a Single, Double, Currency, or even String data type. If you want to make sure that the variable which will contain that value is treated as a Currency data type, declare the variable explicitly as a Currency type.

How Do You Declare a Variable?

Besides using the Dim statement to declare a variable as a specific type, you can declare a variable explicitly as a specific type by using a type-declaration character at the end of the variable's name.

Look at table 5.1 again, and notice the column titled "Type-Declaration Character." If you add one of the listed type-declaration characters to the end of a variable name when you create the variable, it will be created as that specific type of variable. If you use no type-declaration character, the variable is created as a Variant data type.

For example, if you want to define a variable as a String data type, add the dollar sign ($) at the end of the variable name:

```
thisOne$ = "This is a string!"
thisOtherOne$ = "45"
yetAnother$ = "3.14159"
```

An important point to note is that in the case of strings, you must enclose the string in quotation marks when you create it. The following statement would generate the error message Type mismatch when the program runs because you create a String variable and then attempt to store a number in it:

```
yetAnother$ = 365
```

Issuing this statement is like trying to perform mathematical operations with String data.

Now you know how to declare a variable implicitly and explicitly, either using type-declaration characters or the Dim statement. But where should the declaration go? That depends on how you want to use the variable. Where you declare a variable—in an event procedure, in the general declarations section of a form, or in the general declarations section of a code module—determines the variable's scope.

The Scope of a Variable

Scope

Area within a program in which a variable is accessible.

The **scope** of a variable refers to its visibility (or accessibility) within the project. A variable that you create implicitly in an event procedure has a scope that is limited to that procedure. Only statements within the same procedure know that the variable exists and can access it. A statement in any other procedure cannot use that variable.

Furthermore, if you use the same variable name in a different event procedure, Visual Basic will set aside another new, separate memory location for that variable. You will then have two variables with the same name, but they will contain two different values.

Sometimes you will need to use a variable with a broader scope. You may need a variable to be available to all procedures in a form module or even to all the procedures in the whole application. The following list explains the types of scope that variables can have and also explains how to create variables with different scope:

- *Local variables.* Local variables have a scope that is limited to the procedure in which they are created.

  To create a local variable, you can declare it within a procedure by using the Dim, Static, or ReDim statement. You also can create the variable implicitly as a Variant data type just by using it on the left side of an equal sign in the procedure. If a variable isn't declared outside of the procedure in which it is created, it is local to that procedure.

- *Form-level variables.* Form-level variables are visible (accessible) to all the procedures in a form. Any procedure in the form can use the variable.

  To create a form-level variable, use the Dim statement to declare the variable in the declarations section of the general object in that form.

- *Code-module-level variables.* Module-level variables are visible (accessible) to all procedures in a code (BAS) module. Any procedure in the module can use the variable.

  To create a code-module-level variable, use the Dim statement to declare the variable in the declarations section of the module.

- *Global variables.* Global variables are visible to all procedures throughout the entire project. Any procedure in the program, regardless of which form or code module the procedure comes from, can use the variable.

  To create a global variable, use the Global statement to declare the variable in the declarations section of any code module.

Local Variables

A **local variable** is used when you need to store some temporary information that doesn't have to be accessible outside of the procedure. Every procedure in your program could have a local variable named Total, for example, and each procedure can set Total to a different value without affecting any of the other procedures because you have as many different memory locations named Total as you have procedures. Local variables declared implicitly or explicitly with Dim remain in existence only as long as the procedure in which they are created is executing. When the procedure ends, the variable is gone. For a programmer, this situation can be confusing. Be careful when you use duplicate variable names. Having local variables with the same name can lead to bugs in your program.

You can create local variables that exist for as long as the application is running by creating the variables with the Static statement. Static variables are explained shortly.

Here are three examples of statements within a procedure that create local variables:

```
Sub ThreeLocalVars ()
    Dim ProductName as String
    Acount% = 2
    FirstName$ = "Phineas"
End Sub
```

For Acount% and FirstName$ to be local variables, they cannot be declared with a Dim statement in the module's general declarations section. Doing so would make them module-level variables.

Module-Level Variables

Module-level variables are available to all procedures within a single code or form module. If you have a module named FUBAR.BAS that contains 20 procedures, each of those 20 procedures can access module-level variables that are defined within the module. If the project also has a module named FERGIE.BAS, none of the procedures in FERGIE.BAS can see or use the module-level variables in FUBAR.BAS.

You use module-level variables when you want to share information among different procedures *within* a module. If all the procedures for a form need to use the same variable, create the variable as a module-level variable for that form module.

Module-level variables are available longer than local variables. A module-level variable remains in existence as long as the program is running. If a form is unloaded, its module-level variables still remain in existence and retain their values. You can use a form's module-level variables even after the form is unloaded.

To create module-level variables, add a Dim statement in the declarations section of the form or code module in which the variables will be used. For example, the following statements could be used to declare variables:

```
Dim DistanceX As Double

Dim AcountNumber

Dim Population As Long
```

Global Variables

Global variable
A variable that is available to every procedure in every form and code module in the program.

Global variables are available to every procedure in every form and code module in the program—you can use global variables anywhere in the program. If you want to have the user input his or her name, for example, and use that name in the title of every form in the program, you can create a global variable to contain the name.

To create a global variable, you must declare it in the declarations section of a code module by using the Global statement:

```
Global Samples As Long

Global DistanceY

Global Assignments As Double
```

Global variables *cannot* be declared in a form module—they must be declared in the declarations section of any code module. If your program uses more than one code module, it's a good idea to declare all your program's global variables in one code module. You might even name the module GLOBAL.BAS to help you remember where your global variables are declared.

A Program to Illustrate the Scope of Variables

You may be confused at this point about scope. What you need is a good example. The sample project SCOPE.MAK illustrates variable scope. The program consists of two forms (see figure 5.9).

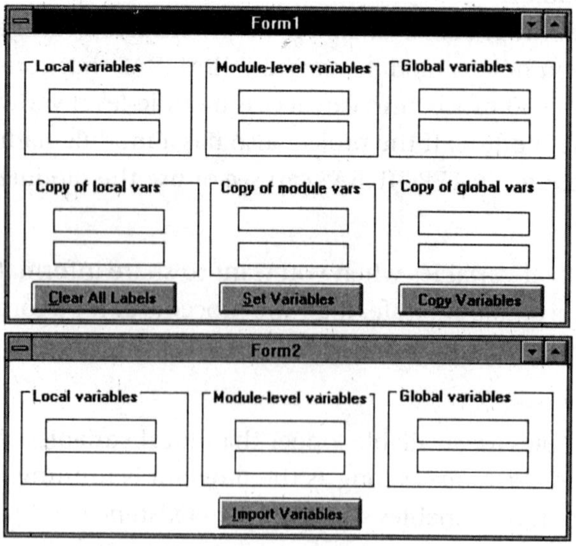

Figure 5.9
The Scope forms.

The **C**lear All Labels button clears the contents of all labels in both forms. The **S**et Variables button sets the value of two local variables, two module variables, and two global variables and then displays them in the top row of frames. The Co**p**y Variables button attempts to copy all the variables to corresponding labels in the second row of frames. The **I**mport Variables button on Form2 attempts to copy all the variables from Form1 to Form2.

Understanding Scope

To experiment with the scope of variables, follow these steps:

1 Open the sample project SCOPE.MAK, which is in the CHAPT5 directory of your student disk.

2 Run the program, and click **S**et Variables. The first row of frames should fill with values.

3 Click the Co**p**y Variables button. The module variables and global variables appear in the second row of frames.

4 Click the **I**mport Variables button on Form2. The global variables appear in Form2.

5 End the program.

What's going on in this program? The local variables are set within the Click event procedure for the **S**et Variables button. Because they are local variables, they aren't visible (and don't exist) outside of that procedure. When you click the Co**p**y Variables button, the local variables aren't copied to the second row. Why? The procedure that copies the variables is a different procedure from the one that sets the local variables. Local variables cannot move from one procedure to another, so the copy procedure can't copy them.

The module variables, however, are copied when you click the Co**p**y Variables button. The procedure that sets the variables and the procedure that copies the variables are in the same module, so one has no problem using module-level variables set by the other.

The global variables also copy because they're global variables. They can go any-where—be used anywhere in your project.

What about the **I**mport Variables button? When you click that button, only the global variables are imported into Form2. Why? The local variables on Form1 can't come over because they're from a different procedure. The module variables can't come over either, because Form2 and Form1 are different modules. The global variables, however, come over.

Take some time on your own to wander around the code for SCOPE.MAK and figure out where and how all the variables are declared.

Static Variables

Module and global variables exist as long as the program that created them is running. When the program ends, the module and global variables are destroyed. Local variables, however, vanish as soon as the procedure that created the variables ends.

Static variable
A local variable that exists as long as the program runs.

Sometimes it's necessary to make a local variable exist longer than its procedure is running. You do this by declaring the variable as a **static variable**. A static variable persists as long as the program runs, just like module and global variables. Even though its value persists, however, the static variable is still a local variable and can be accessed only by the procedure in which it is contained.

Assume that you want to write a function that accumulates a total. The variable that keeps track of the running total must be static to make it persist after the function ends. Here is a sample function to accumulate a total:

```
Function Accumulate(someNumber)
     Static runningTotal
     runningTotal = runningTotal + someNumber
     Accumulate = runningTotal
End Function
```

The next time the Accumulate function executes, the previous value of runningTotal is increased by adding the value of someNumber to it. If runningTotal were *not* declared as a static variable, it would be reset to zero each time the function was executed.

To make all the variables in a procedure static variables, add the Static keyword before the Sub or Function heading:

```
Static Function Calculate_Tax(Income)
```

By adding the Static keyword before the procedure heading, you eliminate the need to declare variables as static within the procedure itself.

Figure 5.10 summarizes the scope of Visual Basic variables.

Figure 5.10
The scope of VB variables.

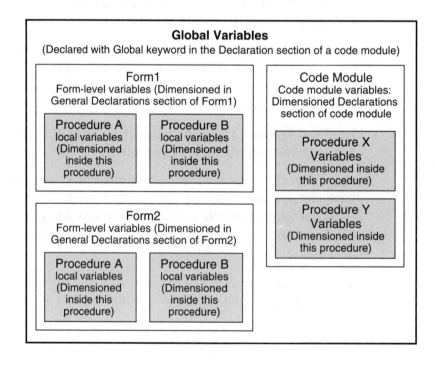

Storing Values in Variables

A variable isn't useful if you don't put some information in it. There are several ways to store information in a variable. Often, you assign a value to a variable by using the following syntax:

```
varname = value
```

To store some text in a String variable, for example, you might use statements like these:

```
FirstName$ = "Jane"

yourName$ = "Bill Gates"

InterestingNumber = 37.473
```

You can also assign a value to a variable by setting it equal to the value of a control. This method is frequently used in Visual Basic programs because user input is gathered by the controls. Then the input is transferred into variables before being used in calculations. Suppose that you want to read the contents of a text box called Text1 and store the value in a variable called HoldArea$. Here is the statement you use:

```
HoldArea$ = Text1.Text
```

If the text box is located in a different form, you add the form name in front of the control name:

```
HoldArea$ = Form2!Text1.Text
```

You also can set a variable equal to the value of another variable of similar type:

```
cakes$ = pies$

NewXvalue% = OldXvalue%

LastName$ = UserInput$
```

Getting Values Out of Variables

If you store a value in a variable, you may want to get that value out again to use it. To place the value of a variable into a text box, for example, you use the following statement:

```
Text1.Text = cakes$
```

Doing Math

You can do all sorts of math operations in a Visual Basic program. The math operators that you use are much the same as the ones you use in everyday math. The following list describes the operands and gives examples:

Operand	Function
+	Adds two operands.

```
result = ((thisNumber + thatNumber) + 1)
```

—	Subtracts one operand from another and also returns the negative value of an operand.

```
result = firstNum — secondNum
negResult = — result
```

| * | Multiplies two operands. |

```
result = PI*Radius*Radius
JointTax = ((husbandsTax + wifesTax) * 1.15)
```

| / | Divides two operands and returns a floating-point result (a number with a decimal fraction). |

```
floatResult = millimeters / 2.54
```

| \ | Divides two operands and returns an integer value. The decimal fraction, if any, is truncated. |

```
intResult = thisNumber \ thatNumber
```

| ^ | Raises an operand to a power of an exponent. |

```
result = 10 ^ 3
```

| Mod | Returns the modulus, or remainder, of the division of two operands. |

```
justFraction = thisNumber Mod thatNumber
```

Turning Digits into Text and Vice Versa

Sometimes you need to convert a number (digits) into a string. If you want to store the value of a Numeric variable in a String variable, for example, you have to perform a conversion. The Str$() function converts a number to a string. The value may not look any different after the conversion, but it is different to the computer because it is stored differently in the computer's memory. You cannot do math with strings even when they contain digits.

Here is an example of a small procedure that executes a loop ten times. In each iteration of the loop, the variable counter is incremented by one. The value of counter is converted to text and concatenated on the end of a string:

```
For counter = 1 to 10
    countText$ = Str$(counter)
    theString$ = "I am counting..." & countText$
Next counter
```

You can simplify the procedure a little by combining the two statements inside the For-Next loop:

```
For counter = 1 to 10
    theString$ = "I am counting..." & Str$(count)
Next counter
```

You don't actually have to convert a number to a string to concatenate it to a string. The & operator automatically concatenates the number as if it were a string.

You do not need to convert a number to a string in order to display it in a label or text box. Visual Basic converts the number for you. Just set the value property of the control equal to the Numeric variable or numeric value:

```
Label1.Caption = someNumericVar

Text1.Text = 435.1957
```

If you need to convert a String or the Text property of a Text Box control to a number for use in a calculation, you use the Val() function. The following example converts the contents of the text box Text1 to a number:

```
someNumber = Val(Text1.Text)
```

If the string contains other characters besides numbers, VB returns a value of zero if the first character is not a number. If the first character is a number, Visual Basic returns the value of as many numeric characters as there are at the beginning of the string. If the string is "342-Hello", for example, the Val function returns the value *342*.

Manipulating the Characters in a String

You can manipulate text (character strings) in a Visual Basic program. This section covers some of the most common operations you will want to perform on strings.

Gluing Together Pieces of Text

You can concatenate (join) two strings to form a single string. Assume that your program contains two text boxes in which the user enters his or her first and last names. You want the program to create a string that contains the text "Hello, " (note the space after the comma) with the user's first and last names. You can use the & operator to concatenate the strings:

```
message$ = "Hello, " & Text1.Text & Text2.Text
```

What if the first and last names are stored in variables instead of text boxes? Just specify the variable names instead:

```
message$ = "Hello, " & firstName$ & lastName$
```

What if you have a String variable and want to concatenate something to the end of it, but you don't want to create a new variable? Use a statement similar to the following:

```
listOfPeople$ = listOfPeople$ + you$
```

Trimming Unwanted Text

Visual Basic has a few functions that trim the leading and trailing spaces off a string. When you use the Str$() function to convert a number into a string, for example, Str$() adds a leading space to the string if the number is positive. The Str$ function reserves a space for the sign of the number and then omits the plus sign. (VB adds a minus sign if the string is negative.) You might need to remove the leading space to use the string, so you will have to trim the leading space.

The LTrim and LTrim$ functions trim the leading spaces from a string. The difference between the two functions is that LTrim returns a Variant data type, and LTrim$ returns a String data type. Here are some examples of statements that trim the leading spaces from a variable named WordStorage:

```
Answer$ = LTrim$(WordStorage)

Answer = LTrim(WordStorage)

someString$ = "This is a string " & LTrim$(WordStorage)
```

The `RTrim` and `RTrim$` functions perform virtually the same functions as the `LTrim` and `LTrim$` functions, except that they trim trailing spaces from the string (spaces at the end, not the beginning):

```
Answer$ = RTrim$(WordStorage)

Answer = RTrim(WordStorage)

someString$ = "This is a string " & RTrim$(WordStorage)
```

What if you want to trim both leading and trailing spaces from the string? You don't have to use both the `LTrim` and `RTrim` functions. Instead, just use either the `Trim` or `Trim$` function. Both functions trim the leading and trailing spaces from a string in one operation. `Trim` returns a Variant data type, and `Trim$` returns a String type:

```
Answer$ = Trim$(WordStorage)

Answer = Trim(WordStorage)

someString$ = "This is a string " & Trim$(WordStorage)
```

Will you ever have to trim the spaces from a string? Sure you will. When you start dealing with file records and random access (see Chapter 12, "Processing Files"), you are going to end up with extra spaces on strings that you store in your data files. You get these spaces because all random-access records are the same length, but the strings you store in them will be different lengths. Visual Basic pads the strings with spaces to make them all the same size. The functions covered in this section will help you get rid of those added spaces.

Manipulating Strings

You may run across a situation in which you need to pull out a portion of a string. Assume that your program prompts the user to enter his or her full name in a text box and stores the name in the variable `fullName`. You then want to extract the user's first name and last name and store them in separate variables named `firstName` and `lastName`. In this situation, you can use three functions to get the job done.

Calculating the Length of a String

The first function is the `Len()` function. `Len()` returns the number of characters in a string. You can use `Len()` to determine the number of total characters in the user's first and last names, including the space between them.

Finding Text in a String

The second function you need is the `InStr()` function. `InStr()` returns the character position of the first occurrence of one string within another string. In the code shown in the following section, "Putting It All Together," `InStr()` locates the first space in the string, which marks the end of the first name and the beginning of the last name.

Pulling Out Part of a String

The other function you need is the Mid$() function. Mid$() returns a portion of a string based on a starting character position and ending character position that you specify.

Putting It All Together

Following is the completed procedure, with comments. Figure 5.11 shows the relationship between some of the variables used in the procedure and the string fullName.

Figure 5.11
What all those variables mean.

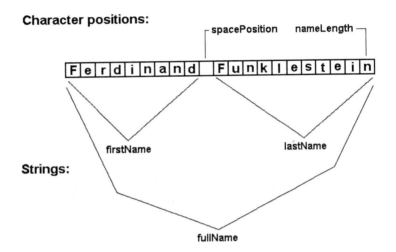

Here's the completed function:

```
Sub SplitName (fullName)
    'Determine the length of the string fullName
    nameLength = Len(fullName)
    'Locate the space between the first and last names and store
    'the character position in the variable spacePosition
    spacePosition = InStr(1, fullName, " ")
    'If spacePosition is 0, there are no spaces in the name
    If spacePosition = 0 Then 'user entered only a first name
        'Display fullName in the First name label
        Label2.Caption = fullName
        'Clear the Last name label
        Label3.Caption = ""
    Else 'Otherwise, there is a space in the name
        'Determine the length of the last name by subtracting the
        'character position of the space from the total
        'string length
        lastLength = nameLength--spacePosition
        'Determine the length of the first name by
        'subtracting the
        'length of the last name, plus 1 for the space, from the
        'total name length
        firstLength = nameLength--(lastLength + 1)
        'Pull the first name out by clipping out the
        'portion of fullName
        'from character 1 (the start) to the length of
        'the first name
```

5

```
                    firstName = Mid(fullName, 1, firstLength)
                    'Pull the last name out by clipping out
                    'the portion of fullName
                    'from one character to the right of the
                    'space to the length of the  last name
                    lastName = Mid(fullName, spacePosition + 1, lastLength)
                    'Put the first and last names in their respective labels
                    Label2.Caption = firstName
                    Label3.Caption = lastName
                End If
                'Display the number of characters in the name
                Label9.Caption = nameLength & " characters"
            End Sub
```

Take a moment to run the program called STRINGY.MAK that uses this procedure. Figure 5.12 shows the form for STRINGY.MAK.

Figure 5.12
The form for
STRINGY.MAK.

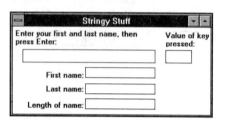

Working with Text

To work with the project, follow these steps:

❶ Open the project STRINGY.MAK, which is in the CHAPT5 directory of your student disk.

❷ Run the program, and enter your first and last names in the text box. Examine the information that appears in the other labels.

❸ End the program.

When you press **Enter**, the SplitName procedure executes. This procedure pulls the first and last name strings out of the full name and displays them in their appropriate labels. Read the next section to find out how the program knows that you pressed the Enter key.

Using Character Values

Without going into a long discussion about the subject, I will tell you simply that alphanumeric characters have a numeric value associated with them. These values are called the ASCII values. The ASCII value of the uppercase letter *A*, for example, is 65. The ASCII value of lowercase *a* is 97. A space is 32, and Enter is 13.

STRINGY.MAK is a program that uses the ASCII values of characters. When you press a key, STRINGY displays in a label the ASCII value of the character you pressed. STRINGY also checks the value of each character you press to determine whether you have pressed the Enter key. If you have pressed the Enter key, STRINGY calls the `SplitName` procedure to split your name into first and last names. All these events happen in the procedure `Text1_KeyPress`.

The `KeyPress` event occurs for a control whenever you press a key with the control active. Each time you press a key in the text box in STRINGY, a `KeyPress` event occurs for `Text1`. The ASCII value of the key that was pressed is passed to the event procedure as an Integer data type.

Two functions in the procedure `Text1_KeyPress` work with ASCII values. These functions are `Asc()` and `Chr()`. The `Asc()` function returns the ASCII value of the first character in a string expression. In this example, `Asc()` returns the ASCII value of the character you pressed.

The `Chr()` function creates a character string from the ASCII value specified as the argument to the function. If a program issues the statement `char$ = Chr(65)`, for example, the variable `char$` is set to the letter *A* because ASCII 65 represents the letter *A*.

Here is the complete `Text1_KeyPress` procedure:

```
Sub Text1_KeyPress (KeyAscii As Integer)
     'Create a character using the value KeyAscii
     'and store it in charPressed
     charPressed = Chr(KeyAscii)
     'Find the ASCII value of the character stored in charPressed
     'and store it in charVal
     charVal = Asc(charPressed)
     'Put the ASCII value of the character in Label6
     Label6.Caption = charVal

     If KeyAscii = 13 Then        'You pressed Enter...
          SplitName (Text1.Text) '...so execute the SplitName
                                  'function
     End If
End Sub
```

Why create the `charPressed` and `charVal` variables in the function? The only purpose they serve is to give you an example of the `Asc()` and `Chr()` functions. If all you want to do is place in `Label6` the value of the character that the user pressed, you already have the information you need—the value of `KeyAscii`.

Therefore, this procedure performs the same function and is much simpler:

```
Sub Text1_KeyPress (KeyAscii As Integer)
     Label6.Caption = KeyAscii
     If KeyAscii = 13 Then
          SplitName (Text1.Text)
     End If
End Sub
```

You can manipulate text in many other ways, but the functions explained in this chapter cover the most common methods. Visual Basic also has many built-in functions that perform mathematical and financial calculations for you. In Visual Basic, you can even write your own functions. You will read more about built-in and user-written functions in Chapter 10.

Passing Variables to Functions and Procedures

Arguments are expressions, constants, or variables that are passed to a procedure. Consider the following function:

```
Function Accumulate(someNumber)
      Static runningTotal
      runningTotal = runningTotal + someNumber
      Accumulate = runningTotal
End Function
```

The variable someNumber is an argument that is passed to the procedure. The procedure then uses that argument to perform some action. How is the argument passed to the function? It's passed by the procedure that calls the function. Here is a simple procedure that passes two numbers to the Accumulate function; one using a variable and the other a value:

```
Sub TotalIt()
      myNumber = 12
      Accumulate(myNumber)
      Accumulate (36)
End Sub
```

When you name a procedure that uses arguments, you specify the names of the arguments and their data types in the procedure heading. In the following procedure heading, a single argument named someNumber will be passed to the function:

```
Function Accumulate(someNumber)
```

Your procedure may require more than one argument. Here is a function that adds three numbers together:

```
Function SumThreeNums(number1, number2, number3)
      SumThreeNums = number1 + number2 + number3
End Function
```

But wait! How do you know what the data type is for number1, number2, and number3? By default, arguments are passed as Variant data types. You can, however, specifically define the data type of an argument by declaring its type in the procedure heading. Here is a function that uses three arguments, all of different data types:

```
Sub Example3 (myName As String, myAge as Integer, myPay as Double)
      message$ = "Your name is " & myName
      newAge% = myAge + 1
      money# = myPay * 4.5
EndSub
```

Passing by value

Making a copy of a variable so that the original variable is not changed.

When you pass a variable to a procedure by the method in either of the preceding two examples, the variable itself is passed to the procedure. The procedure could then change the value of the variable. Sometimes, that's a bad situation: changing the value of the variable could make the variable unreliable. Instead of passing the variable itself, you can pass a copy of the variable. This process is called **passing by value**. Any changes the procedure makes affect only the copy of the variable, not the variable itself.

How do you pass a variable by value? Just add the `ByVal` keyword when you declare the argument in the procedure heading:

```
Function SumTwoNums(ByVal number1 As Double, ByVal number2 As Double)
    SumTwoNums = number1 + number2
End Function
```

It's good programming practice not to modify the value of arguments within a function. You can either declare the arguments `ByVal` or store the arguments in new variables and then modify the new variables. Calling functions and procedures is discussed in more depth later in this text.

Note: *You cannot add or delete arguments inside the parentheses of a form's or a control's event procedure. You cannot pass information to an event procedure. Windows and VB are the only entities that can pass arguments to an event procedure. You can pass arguments only to user-created* Sub *procedures.*

Learning about Constants and Declaring Them

Constant
A preset named storage location that never changes during the running of a program.

You can also use named constants in your programs. **Constants** are like variables that you preset and never change. Programs are easier to understand when you store a number that you will use in calculations in a named constant. Then your calculation can use the named constant. An example would be storing 0.075 in a constant named SALESTAX. Visual Basic has stored many named constants in a file named CONSTANTS.TXT. You can add this file to your projects. A good programming practice is to name constants in all capital letters and variables with some lowercase letters. Then when you are looking at your program a year later, you know immediately what is a variable and what is a constant.

Do you remember the VARIABLE.MAK project from earlier in this chapter? It contains a procedure that displays a number that looks suspiciously like pi. Pi has the constant value of about 3.14159265. Assume that you want to use pi in many different procedures in your program. Just declare it as a constant by using the `Const` statement:

```
Const PI = 3.14159265

Const SHAPE_ONE = "Square"

Const YES = 1

Const NO = 2
```

Constants, like variables have a scope—local, module-level, or global. When you declare constants keep in mind the following rules:

- *Local constants.* To make a constant available only in a procedure, declare the constant within the procedure with the `Const` statement.

- *Module-level constants.* To make a constant available within all procedures in a form or code module, declare the constant in the declarations section of the module with the `Const` statement.

- *Global constants.* To create a constant that is available to all procedures in the program, declare the constant in the declarations section of any code module using the `Global Const` statement. You cannot declare a global constant in a form module.

How do you use a constant? Just refer to its name as if it were a variable. To multiply a value times a constant called `PI`, for example, you might use this statement within a procedure:

```
circumference = PI * diameter
```

In this example, `circumference` and `diameter` are variables, and `PI` is a constant. When the program comes to that statement, it simply replaces the `PI` constant with whatever value you have assigned to `PI`.

Use constants whenever you can because constants can make modifying a program much easier. What if the world suddenly spins off axis and the value of pi changes? All you have to do is make one change to the statement that defines the constant `PI`, and your program will calculate correctly again. You also eliminate the possibility of entering the value of pi incorrectly in a couple of procedures—it's easier to spell *PI* than to enter *3.14159265* each time you want to use pi in a statement.

Chapter Summary

In this chapter, you were introduced to the fundamentals of writing a VB program. You have learned the types of files that make up a VB project and in which of these files you should declare variables and constants and write code. You have learned how to use variables, constants, and data types. The importance of the scope of variables and constants is explained. You have also learned how to write your own procedures and functions. You were introduced to the techniques of calling procedures. You learned to use many more of VB's built in functions.

In the next chapter, you create a complete and useful VB project. You also make your VB program an executable file and add it to a program group in the Program Manager window.

Test Your Understanding

True/False
Indicate whether the statement is true or false.

1. It is a good idea to begin writing code for a form or control even though you have not yet given to either the name you plan to use in your program code.

2. A MAK file contains all the procedures, forms, controls, and code modules in your projects.

3. Only variable declarations can be placed in the general object of a form.

4. Global constant and variable declarations must be placed in the general declarations section of a code module.

5. The event procedures in a form can be executed from a code-module procedure.

6. Every Visual Basic program must have a start-up form.

7. A file named AUTOLOAD.MAK determines which files are placed in the MAK file of a new project.

8. Procedures are a group of Visual Basic statements that have a unique name.

9. All procedures must start with the word Sub and end with the End Sub statement.

10. General procedures in a form can be run from any procedure in your project.

11. Most event procedures are also general procedures.

12. The values stored in the variables you use in an event procedure are available to all the procedures in a project.

13. If you place a number that a user types in a text box into a Variant type variable, you can use that number in mathematical calculations.

Short Answer
Answer the following questions.

1. What is the absolute minimum number of files required in a runnable VB program's Project window?

2. With reference to question 1, what would be the file type of each file listed in the program's Project window?

3. With reference to questions 1 and 2, what would be the start-up form (list all possibilities) for the runnable program?

4. When would you put a procedure in the general object of a form? When would you put a procedure in a code module (BAS file)?

5. How is a variable different from a constant?

6. What is meant by the *scope* of a variable? Do constants have a scope?

7. How is a variable that is declared in your program related to memory locations (RAM addresses) inside your computer?

8. List the categories of variable scopes (for example, local variables), and explain how they are declared in a VB program.

9. How is an Integer type variable different from a String type variable? How is a Variant data type different from the other data types?

10. How do you declare a variable type? What is a type-declaration character and how is it used? Give three examples that use a type-declaration character and three examples that declare a variable type without using a type-declaration character.

11. How could you make sure that someone (competent in VB) reading the statements in your program will recognize immediately the type of variables involved? How can someone distinguish immediately between variables and constants?

12. What is a static variable?

13. How do you convert a number in a String variable to a value that can be used in a calculation?

14. Assume that an individual's first name and last name are stored in two different String variables. You need to join them in one String variable with a space between the first and last names. Write the VB statements that store the first and the last names in two different variables and then join them in a third variable (with a space between them).

15. What statement trims unwanted blank characters from the right of a string?

16. Write the VB statement that finds the number of characters contained in a String variable `CompanyName$`.

17. Convert the following expressions into VB statements. Remember the order of mathematical operation, and use parentheses when necessary to enforce this precedence:

$$X = \frac{4 + 6}{5 \times 7}$$

$$V = \frac{1}{3}\pi r^2 h \qquad (\pi = 3.1415)$$

$$P = \frac{F}{(1 + i)^n}$$

$$D = \sqrt{(10 - 5)^2 + (12 + 3)^2}$$

Projects

Project 1:   Writing Code for a Form

Refer to the user interface that you completed in Project 1 of Chapter 3 (C3P1). Write the code to do the following:

1. When the ADD button is clicked, add the first and second numbers entered by the user and display the answer.

2. When the SUBTRACT button is clicked, subtract the second number from the first number and display the answer.

3. When the MULTIPLY button is clicked, multiply the first and second numbers and display the answer.

4. When the DIVIDE button is clicked, divide the first number by the second number and display the answer.

5. When the RESET button is clicked, clear the text boxes and the label for the answer. Place the focus on the first number's text box.

6. When the END button is pressed, the program should end (use VB's End statement).

7. Do not perform calculations if either number input text box is empty (the Text property = ""). Make visible a label that asks the user to complete entry of the numbers and then test again to make sure that both the first and second numbers have been entered. Use an If-Then statement for this purpose.

8. Save the program on disk as **C5P1**.

9. Test the program with different numbers, and when you are sure that it is working properly, print the form, form text, and code.

Project 2:   Writing Code for a Password

Use the forms that you created for Chapter 3, Project 2 (C3P2). Assume that the correct password is ParaMount.

1. Write the code to test for the correctness of the password entered when the VIEW DATA button is clicked (use an If-Then statement).

2. If the password is correct, the second form should appear on the screen. If the password is incorrect, the first form (the password form) should remain on-screen.

3. When the QUIT button is clicked, the program should end (use VB's End statement).

4. Save the project on disk as **C5P2**.

5. Test the program. When the program works properly, print the form, form text, and code.

Project 3:   Writing Code to Calculate Ratios

Use the form you created in Project 3 of Chapter 3 (C3P3). Write the code to perform the following calculations:

1. When the input values have been entered and the CALCULATE button is clicked, the following ratios should be calculated:

5

$$\text{Price/earnings ratio} \quad = \quad \frac{\text{Market price per share of common stock}}{\text{Earnings per share}}$$

$$\text{Dividend yield} \quad = \quad \frac{\text{Dividend per share of common stock}}{\text{Market price per share of common stock}}$$

$$\text{Book value per Share of common stock} \quad = \quad \frac{\text{Total stockholder's equity – preferred equity}}{\text{Number of shares of common stock outstanding}}$$

Use an indicator variable that you set to Yes in the Change event for each of the data input text boxes to test whether the user has entered data in that text box. If a text box is empty (has not changed), make visible a label that tells the user to complete data entry in that text box. Only when the user has changed the data in every data input box should the program complete its calculations. Before each run of the program or each set of calculations, the indicator variable must be reset to No.

2. After the ratios have been calculated, clear from the screen the tables, text boxes, and buttons used for data entry.

3. Display and label the results of the calculations. Create and add to the form the controls necessary to do this.

4. When the user clicks the Price/earnings label, the following help should be displayed in a label:

   `Indicates the market price of one dollar of earnings.`

   When the user double-clicks this label, it should disappear.

5. When the user clicks the Dividend Yield label, the following help should be displayed in a label:

   `Shows the proportion of the market price of each share of stock returned as dividends to stock holders each period.`

   When the user double-clicks this label, it should disappear.

6. When the user clicks the Book value label, the following help should be displayed in a label:

   `Indicates the recorded accounting value of each share of common stock outstanding.`

   When the user double-clicks this label, it should disappear.

7. Save this program as **C5P3**. Test your program, and when it is correct, print the form, form text, and code.

Project 4: Writing a Program to Convert Temperatures

In this project, you write a program that converts Fahrenheit temperature to Celsius temperature and vice versa. The user will enter the temperature to be converted into a labeled text box (see figure 5.12). Version one of this program should use a command button to indicate that the conversion is from Fahrenheit to Celsius and a second command button to indicate that the conversion is from Celsius to Fahrenheit.

Figure 5.13

The Temperature
Conversion Form.

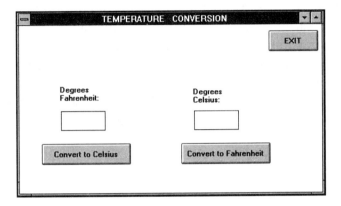

A second version of this program should eliminate the command buttons. The program should convert Fahrenheit to Celsius if the user has caused the KeyPress event to occur to the Fahrenheit text box. The program should convert Celsius to Fahrenheit if the KeyPress event has occurred to the Celsius text box.

The formulas to use are

$$\text{degrees Celsius} \quad = \quad \frac{5}{9}(\text{Fahrenheit degrees} - 32)$$

$$\text{degrees Fahrenheit} \quad = \quad \frac{9}{5}\text{ Celsius degrees} + 32$$

Test values are

Degrees C	Degrees F
1000	18032
100	212
78	172.4
0	32
−22	−7.6

You should use ICONWRKS to create an icon in a form that opens the program. This icon should be representative of temperature measurement or conversion from Fahrenheit to Celsius. This form (name it ABOUT) should also explain the purpose of the program and tell how to use it. Note that these user instructions will differ for the two versions of the program. When the user clicks the ABOUT form, it should disappear, and the input/output form for the program should appear.

Save the first version of the program as **C5P4A**. Save the second version as **C5P4B**. Print all forms, form text, and code for both versions.

Project 5:   Writing a Program to Calculate Area and Volume
Optional: For students with a background in mathematics

In this project, you create a program that enables the user to calculate the area and volume of four different geometric shapes.

The program first enables the user to indicate which one of the four shapes is involved in the calculations. Then the program displays an input form that requests the values required in the formulas for that particular shape. When the user has finished entering the input data, the program calculates and displays the volumes and areas. Do not worry about the units of measure involved; simply enter and display the numeric values. When the user has seen the result, he or she clicks a NEW button to return to the Shape Selection screen. A QUIT button lets the user exit the program. Use these abbreviations:

R = Radius
H = Height
A = Major semiaxis
B = Minor semiaxis
Pi (use the Greek letter) = 3.14159

The shapes and corresponding formulas (use this version of the formulas) are

Right Circular Cylinder:

$$\text{Area} = 2\pi RH$$

$$\text{Volume} = \pi R^2 H$$

Right Circular Cone:

$$\text{Area} = \pi R \left(R + \sqrt{R^2 + H^2}\right)$$

$$\text{Volume} = \frac{1}{3}\pi R^2 H$$

Sphere:

$$\text{Area} = 4\pi R^2$$

$$\text{Volume} = \frac{4}{3}\pi R^3$$

Prolate Spheroid

$$\text{Area} = 2\pi A^2 + \frac{\pi B^2}{\sqrt{\frac{A^2 - B^2}{A}}}\ \text{Ln}\left(\frac{1 + \sqrt{\frac{A^2 - B^2}{A}}}{1 - \sqrt{\frac{A^2 - B^2}{A}}}\right)$$

$$\text{Volume} = \frac{4}{3}\pi A^2 B$$

CHAPTER 6

Building a Complete Application

In this chapter, you use what you learned from the preceding chapters to create a working application. The emphasis is on the step-by-step building of an application. The application you develop is a multiline text editor that features cut-and-paste and font-attribute-selection capabilities. The core of the application is a Text Box control containing the text that is edited.

Objectives

By the time you have finished this chapter, you will be able to

1. Modify Property Values at Run Time

2. Initialize an Application with the `Form_Load` Event

3. Understand the Relationship between Event Procedures and General Procedures

4. Create Access Keys

5. Use Control Arrays

6. Create an EXE File

7. Set Up an EXE File That Can Be Run Using an Icon in Program Manager

Introducing Ted, a Text Editor Application

The text editor you develop in this chapter is similar to the Notepad utility that comes with Windows. The application is known as Ted (*Text ed*itor). The controls used in the application are a text box, three check boxes, and four command buttons.

To create Ted, you first start a new project:

❶ Choose New Project from the File menu.

❷ Double-click the Text Box control in the Toolbox to place a text box in the center of the form. The sizing handles for the text box should be visible. If the handles are not visible, click inside the text box so that they appear.

❸ Use the sizing handles to enlarge the text box to approximately twice its original width and height. Don't worry about its exact size and location. At this point, it's important only that you have a form containing a text box.

Defining Ted's Text Box Properties

Ted uses the Text, MultiLine, and ScrollBars properties of the text box. Table 6.1 summarizes these properties.

Table 6.1	Ted's Text Box Properties	
Property	**Default Value**	**Description**
Text	Text1	Specifies the text contained in the edit area
MultiLine	False	Specifies whether the text box can display multiple lines
ScrollBars	0 (none)	Specifies whether the text box contains horizontal or vertical scroll bars (or both)

The Visual Basic controls have quite a bit of built-in functionality when the program is in Run mode. You can, for example, delete the contents of the text box. First start the program, and move the cursor to the text box's upper-left corner. Then hold down the Del key until all the text is erased.

Type some words in the text box. Continue typing until the text cursor reaches the right edge of the box. Notice that as you continue typing, the cursor stays at the right edge and scrolls the preceding text to the left to accommodate the new typed characters.

By repeatedly pressing the left (or right) arrow key, you can move the cursor to the left (or right) edge of the text box and scroll the previously typed text into view. The Home and End keys move the cursor to the beginning and end of the text, respectively.

Press **Enter**. Visual Basic beeps, but nothing happens. Because the value of the `MultiLine` property is False, the text box does not display multiple text lines. Thus, pressing Enter does not move the cursor down to the next line.

You can select a block of characters. Hold down the left mouse button as you drag over a block of characters. Then release the button. Another method is to hold down the **Shift** key as you use the **arrow** keys to move the cursor. The selected characters appear highlighted in a different color. Press **Del**, and Visual Basic deletes the selected characters from the text box.

Another built-in feature of text boxes is word wrap. This feature is activated when you set the value of the `MultiLine` property to True. When you come to the end of a line, the text automatically moves to the next line. This feature is common to word processors.

You will find that you use the `Multiline` property frequently when you use text boxes. At run time, a Label control can automatically resize itself to fit the amount of text in its caption when the `AutoSize` property is set to True. However, text boxes do not have this property. Therefore, because the size of the text box cannot be changed as a program is running, the text inside the text box must be arranged to fit within the box.

Understanding Word Wrap

Stop the application. Select the text box by clicking it. Then open the Properties window (press **F4**). Find the `MultiLine` property, and change its value from False to True.

Run the application again. Type some text, and watch what happens when you reach the right edge of the text box. The text wraps down to the next line of the text box. Continue typing until the box contains several lines.

Notice that the text box automatically implements word wrap. That is, the lines break at the boundaries of whole words, not just at the first character that reaches the right edge (see figure 6.1).

6

Figure 6.1
A text box
demonstrating
word wrap.

Even though word wrap is enabled, you can press Enter at any time to force the cursor down to the next line. If you continue typing past the lower border, the text box automatically scrolls upward to accommodate the new text.

Adding Scroll Bars

Your next step is to add scroll bars to your application. Stop the application, and follow these steps:

1 Open the Properties window for the text box, and click the ScrollBars property.

2 Click the right arrow of the Settings box, to drop down the available choices for this property. The default value is 0 (no scroll bars). Other values are 1 (horizontal scroll bars), 2 (vertical scroll bars), and 3 (horizontal and vertical scroll bars). Change the value to 2 (vertical scroll bars).

3 Run the application again. Scroll bars appear on the right edge of the text box.

4 Type several lines of text so that the contents of the text box scroll past the bottom edge. Use the scroll bar to move the contents of the text box vertically through the editing area.

5 Stop the application.

Designing Ted's User Interface

The next step in creating Ted is to design the user interface. You must place the various controls on the form and set the design-time property values. Figure 6.2 shows the finished interface. (Every time you start the application, the text box will again display the default Text1.) As the figure shows, Ted's form contains four command buttons and three check boxes, in addition to the text box.

Figure 6.2
Ted's user interface.

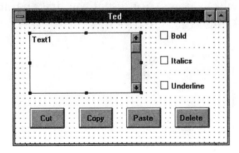

Creating Ted's User Interface

Using the Toolbox, place four command buttons and three check boxes on the form. (The Check Box control is the Toolbox icon that resembles a square with an X inside.) Using the Properties window, assign the property values shown in table 6.2.

Table 6.2   Design-Time Property Values for Ted

Object	Property	Value
Form1	Caption	Ted
	Height	3300
	Left	1185
	Top	1440
	Width	5370
	Name	frmTed
Text1	Height	1455
	Left	360
	Top	240
	Width	2775
	Name	txtTed
Command1	Caption	Cut
	Height	495
	Left	360
	Top	2040
	Width	855
	Name	cmdCut
Command2	Caption	Copy
	Height	495
	Left	1560
	Top	2040
	Width	855
	Name	cmdCopy
Command3	Caption	Paste
	Height	495
	Left	2760
	Top	2040
	Width	855
	Name	cmdPaste

(continues)

Creating Ted's User Interface   (continued)

Table 6.2	Continued	
Object	**Property**	**Value**
Command4	Caption	Delete
	Height	495
	Left	3960
	Top	2040
	Width	855
	Name	cmdDelete
Check1	Caption	Bold
	Height	375
	Left	3600
	Top	120
	Width	1215
	Name	chkBold
Check2	Caption	Italics
	Height	375
	Left	3600
	Top	720
	Width	1215
	Name	chkItalics
Check3	Caption	Underline
	Height	375
	Left	3600
	Top	1320
	Width	1215
	Name	chkUnderline

Notice that the Name property for each object begins with a three-letter prefix. The prefix identifies the object type: frm for form, txt for text box, cmd for command button, and chk for check box. After the prefix, the rest of the name helps describe the object. For example, chkBold is the check box used to indicate whether boldface text is desired. This naming convention helps identify clearly each object in the subsequent code.

The interface is now designed. Run the application. Click one of the check boxes a few times. Notice that a large X toggles on and off in the check box. If you click a command button, it looks as if it has been pressed into the form. These visual capabilities of check boxes and command buttons are built into the controls.

At this stage, of course, clicking a check box or command button doesn't actually *do* anything. To add functionality to your applications, you must write program code in the event procedures. You do this next.

Writing Ted's Event Procedures

The event procedures are the engine of any application. When you write event procedures, you give life to an application—you determine how it responds to anything taking place in its environment. The following sections examine the various event procedures necessary to make the Ted application work. The approach is incremental: You add more procedures and code as you build the application piece by piece.

Examining the *Form_Load* Procedure

Each time you start the sample application, the contents of the text box read `Text1`. It is much better if the editing area is blank when the application begins. That way, the user has a clean slate with which to begin editing.

You can clear the contents of the text box by using the Properties window to change the value of the `Text` property at design time. This method works, but there is another way. You can change the value of the `Text` property with a program instruction. Just set the value of the `Text` property to the empty string (`""`). The necessary instruction is

```
txtTed.Text = ""
```

Notice the syntax for referring to a property: the object name (`txtTed` in this case) followed by a period and the name of the property (`Text` in this case). The instruction makes sense. But where do you put the instruction?

The `Form_Load` event procedure is a natural location. When you first run an application, Visual Basic loads the form into memory and then displays it onscreen. The process of loading the form generates a `Form_Load` event. Program instructions in the `Form_Load` event procedure execute when the application begins. Therefore, the `Form_Load` procedure is the place to initialize an application.

6

Adding the Initializing Code to the *Form_Load* Procedure

If you have the application running, stop the application to return Visual Basic to Design mode. You can then use any of the following techniques to open the Code window in preparation for writing program instructions:

Press F7.

Choose Code from the View menu.

(continues)

Adding the Initializing Code to the *Form_Load* Procedure   (continued)

Click the View Code button on the Project window. (If the Project window is not visible, choose Project from the Window menu.)

Double-click the form or any object on it.

As you have seen in previous chapters, the Code window has two boxes, labeled Object and Proc. Now work through the following steps:

❶ Click the down arrow to the right of the Object box to view its list of objects defined in the application. In this drop-down list, click Form.

❷ Click the down arrow to the right of the Proc box. You see a drop-down list containing all the events recognized by the form. Click Load. The Code window now displays the Form_Load event which, for the moment, is nothing but the following empty procedure stub (template):

```
Sub Form_Load ()


End Sub
```

The Form_Load event is the default event for a form. If you double-click the form, the Code window opens with the Form_Load event visible.

❸ In the procedure template for Form_Load, type the instruction that clears the text box. The following is the result:

```
Sub Form_Load ()

    txtTed.Text = ""        'Blank contents of text box

End Sub
```

❹ Run the application. Notice that the contents of the text box are now blanked out (see figure 6.3).

Figure 6.3
Ted with a blanked-out text box.

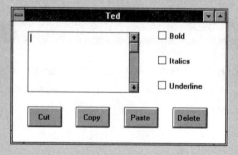

So far, your application has no bugs. Stop the application. You are now ready to establish the initial font property settings for the text box.

The Ted editing program supports bold, italic, and underline emphasis in the text box. You can choose some or all of these font attributes at any time.

Initializing the Font Attributes

Visual Basic uses the `FontBold`, `FontItalic`, and `FontUnderline` properties to indicate whether a font attribute is active. A value of True means that the text has that attribute; False means that the text does not have that attribute. Suppose that when Ted begins, you want to turn off all the font attributes. Add the following instructions to the `Form_Load` event procedure:

```
txtTed.FontBold = False
txtTed.FontItalic = False
txtTed.FontUnderline = False
```

By default, the value of only one of these attributes—FontBold—is True; the other two are False. (You can verify these values by checking the properties in the Properties window.) As a result, you don't need to set the values of `FontItalic` and `FontUnderline` to False in the `Form_Load` procedure. Including these instructions, however, doesn't hurt. They clarify that all the special font attributes are off when the application begins.

Checked
A check box displaying an X to indicate that the corresponding attribute is selected.

Initializing the Check Boxes

Each check box indicates whether one of the font attributes is active. The check box displays an X when the corresponding attribute is active. In this case, the box is said to be **checked**. Otherwise, it is blank.

Visual Basic uses the `Value` property to specify whether the check box is checked. `Value` is not, however, a True/False property. Instead, Value can be 0 (unchecked), 1 (checked), or 2 (dimmed). The value of 2 creates a gray text box. You can use this value to indicate that the box itself is currently inactive.

6

Setting the Value Properties

The font attributes are not active when Ted begins, so you want each check box to be blank. To blank each check box, add the following instructions to `Form_Load`:

```
chkBold.Value = 0
chkItalics.Value = 0
chkUnderline.Value = 0
```

The completed `Form_Load` event procedure is as follows:

```
Sub Form_Load ()
   txtTed.Text = ""          'Blank contents of text box

   txtTed.FontBold = False
   txtTed.FontItalic = False
   txtTed.FontUnderline = False

   chkBold.Value = 0
   chkItalics.Value = 0
   chkUnderline.Value = 0
End Sub
```

Activating the Font Attributes

When the user clicks a check box, you want it to become checked, and the contents of the text box to have the corresponding font attribute. For example, when the user clicks the Italics check box, it should become checked, and the contents of the text box should appear in italics. If the user clicks the Italics check box a second time, it should become unchecked, and the contents of the text box should no longer appear in italics.

You have already seen that each time you click a check box, Visual Basic automatically toggles it between checked and unchecked. You don't need to write any program code to get that effect.

Using *Not* to Toggle a True/False Property Value

Concerning the font attribute in the text box, you must write program code to toggle the corresponding property value between True and False. For example, when the Underline check box is clicked the first time, you want the value of `txtTed.FontUnderline` to change from False to True. The next time the check box is clicked, `txtTed.FontUnderline` should once again become False.

Several ways exist to code such an instruction. The following instruction toggles the value of the `FontUnderline` property between True and False:

```
txtTed.FontUnderline = Not (txtTed.FontUnderline)
```

Writing a *Click* Procedure

By placing the `Not` instruction inside the `Click` procedure for the Underline check box, you can underline the text inside the text box. To do this, access the Code window for the Underline check box. Then complete the following event procedure:

```
Sub chkUnderline_Click ()
    txtTed.FontUnderline = Not (txtTed.FontUnderline)
End Sub
```

This code is all you need to implement underlining. Now you should run the program to check whether there are any problems (bugs) up to this point. Run the application, and type an entry in the text box. Then click the Underline check box a few times. The check box toggles between checked and unchecked. At the same time, the contents of the text box toggle between underline and normal font. Figure 6.4 shows an example of underlined text.

Figure 6.4

An example of underlined text.

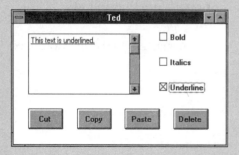

Using the *SetFocus* Method

As long as the Underline box is checked, any new text you type in the edit area appears underlined. Notice, however, that after you click the Underline check box, the blinking text cursor does not appear inside the text box. To type new text, you must move the pointer inside the text box and click to reposition the cursor.

In Visual Basic, the term **focus** refers to the active object. When you click a check box, it has the focus. When you see the blinking cursor inside the text box, you know that the text box has the focus.

For Ted, you want the focus to move to the text box after a check box is clicked. That way, the user can immediately type new text (or use the arrow keys to move the cursor) without having first to click inside the text box.

Visual Basic provides the `SetFocus` method for just this purpose. Recall that a Visual Basic **method** specifies a particular action performed on an individual object. (To find out which methods are available for a control, click the control's icon in the Toolbox, and then press the F1 key. Finally, click the word *Methods*, appearing in green, near the top of the control's Help screen.)

The syntax for a method uses a dot to separate the object that is acted on and the action that is taken:

```
object.method
```

This syntax tells Visual Basic to apply the action specified by `method` to the object designated by `object`. The following instruction, for example, uses the `Print` method to display a message on `Form1`:

```
Form1.Print "Here I am."
```

To set the focus to the text box `Text1` so that all typing would appear in it, you would use this code:

```
Text1.SetFocus
```

Focus

In Windows, at run time, the capability of one object (such as a window, form, or control) to receive mouse clicks or keyboard input. The focus can be placed on an object by the user or by application code.

Method

A prewritten procedure, internal to VB, that acts on an object.

6

Adding the *SetFocus* Instruction

Stop the application, and add the `SetFocus` instruction to the `chkUnderline` event procedure. The updated event procedure is as follows:

```
Sub chkUnderline_Click ()
    txtTed.FontUnderline = Not (txtTed.FontUnderline)
    txtTed.SetFocus
End Sub
```

Run the application again, and notice what happens when you click the Underline check box a few times. The focus seems never to leave the text box. As a result, you can type new text without having first to click inside the text box.

Actually, when you click the check box, the focus moves to it. The `SetFocus` method in the `Click` procedure, however, immediately moves the focus back to the text box.

Note: *You are using the "code a chunk and test it immediately" technique. You should always use this technique when developing your own programs. Another good technique is to save your program periodically as you are working on it. You shouldn't wait until your program is finished to save it. Save the program as soon as you have done more work than you want to do over again. That way, if you have a problem and lose the version of your program in RAM, for whatever reason, you don't have to start over from scratch.*

Saving Ted

To save Ted's form as a disk file, choose the Save File **As** option from Visual Basic's **F**ile menu. When the Save File As dialog box opens, save the form as **TED.FRM**. (If you specify the name as simply **TED**, Visual Basic automatically adds the FRM file extension.) Be sure that you specify the directory path correctly so that the file is saved in your intended directory. You will probably want to save the file on a disk in drive A or B.

Figure 6.5 shows the Save File As dialog box. Notice the check box that reads **S**ave as Text. This check box is on the right side of the dialog box. If you don't choose this option, the form is saved in a compressed binary format. Choose the **S**ave as Text option. Then click OK (or press **Enter**) to save the form as a disk file named TED.FRM.

Figure 6.5
The Save File As
dialog box.

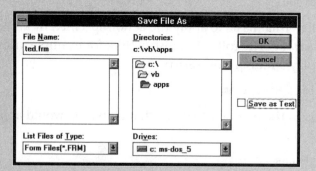

Next, choose the Sa**v**e Project As option from the **F**ile menu. When the Save Project As dialog box opens, specify **TED.MAK** as the file name. (If you specify the file name simply as **TED**, Visual Basic automatically adds the MAK file extension.) Again, be sure that you specify the directory path correctly.

Once you have Ted saved on disk, you can later load the application back into Visual Basic with the **O**pen Project option from the **F**ile menu.

Writing the *Click* Procedures for the Other Check Boxes

In a similar way, create the event procedures for the Bold and Italics check boxes. Stop the application if it is running, and create the following two event procedures by entering them in the Code window for each control:

```
Sub chkBold_Click ()
    txtTed.FontBold = Not (txtTed.FontBold)
    txtTed.SetFocus
End Sub

Sub chkItalics_Click ()
    txtTed.FontItalic = Not (txtTed.FontItalic)
    txtTed.SetFocus
End Sub
```

This code is all you need to make the three check boxes work. Run the application, and click various combinations of the check boxes. Notice that you can activate some or all of the text attributes in any combination.

Figure 6.6 shows an example of the Bold and Italics text attributes.

Figure 6.6
The Bold and Italics attributes are activated.

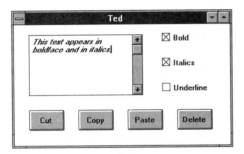

Coding the Delete Command Button

Next, you must write the program code to make the command buttons work. The Delete button is a good place to start. When the user clicks this button, the entire contents of the text box should be deleted. You need only set the `Text` property of the text box to the empty string. The event procedure is as follows:

```
Sub cmdDelete_Click ()
    txtTed.Text = ""
    txtTed.SetFocus
End Sub
```

As with the check boxes, this event procedure uses `SetFocus` to reactivate the text box after the user clicks the Delete button. Try running the application. Type something in the text box; then click the Delete button. The entire contents of the text box are erased.

The next step is to program the other three buttons. To do that, you must first understand how Visual Basic treats selected text.

Understanding Selected Text

A text box has built-in capabilities for selecting text. As you learned earlier, the user can select a block of text with the mouse or the keyboard.

6

To help you work with selected text, Visual Basic provides three text box properties: SelLength, SelStart, and SelText (see table 6.3).

Table 6.3	Properties Associated with Selected Text	
Property	**Data Type**	**Description**
SelLength	Numeric	Specifies the number of characters selected; value is 0 if no text is selected.
SelStart	Numeric	Specifies the character position at which the selected text begins; a value of 0 indicates the first character.
SelText	String	Specifies the selected text; value is the empty string if no characters are selected.

Because these properties do not appear in the Properties window, you cannot set their values at design time. You can set them only at run time in your program code. If a text box contains selected text, the value of SelLength indicates how many characters are selected, the value of SelStart indicates the character position of the first selected character, and the value of SelText is a string consisting of the selected characters. For example, if you set SelStart to 5 and SelLength to 3, the text box appears with the sixth, seventh, and eighth characters highlighted.

If you modify the value of SelText, Visual Basic replaces any currently selected text with the new specified string value and sets the value of SelLength to 0. The result is that the contents of the text box are modified but no text is selected. If the text box does not contain any selected text when an instruction modifies the value of SelText, the new specified string is inserted at the character position specified by the value of SelStart.

For Ted, you must write program instructions to make the command buttons work correctly. As it turns out, you need to modify only the value of SelText.

Understanding the Cut, Copy, and Paste Buttons

The Cut, Copy, and Paste buttons work with selected text. Before writing the event procedures for these buttons, you need a clear understanding of exactly what these buttons should do.

When the user clicks the Cut button, any selected text is deleted from the text box and placed in a temporary memory location similar to the Windows Clipboard. The Copy button places a copy of the selected text in the temporary memory location but does not alter the selected text in the text box. With either Cut or Copy, the current selected text replaces any previous text in the temporary memory location.

The Paste button pastes any text in the temporary memory location back into the text box. The pasted text replaces any currently selected text in the text box. If the text box contains no selected text when Paste is clicked, the pasted text is inserted at the current cursor position.

Declaring a Form-Level Variable

To implement the temporary storage location, you can store the cut or copied text in a string variable. Then when the Paste button is clicked, the stored text can be retrieved from this variable.

Name this variable `ClipText`. The variable must be available to all Ted's event procedures. As you know, you can create a form-level variable by declaring it in the *general declaration* section of the form. Follow these steps:

1 Press F7 to open the Code window.

2 In the Object box, choose (general), the first item in the drop-down list.

3 In the Proc box, choose (declarations).

4 Type the following instruction:

```
Dim ClipText As String
```

This instruction declares that `ClipText` is a variable of the string data type.

By placing the variable instruction in the form's general declarations section, you can read or set the value of `ClipText` in any of the form's event procedures.

Coding the Cut Button

You want to store a copy of the selected text in the `ClipText` variable when the user clicks the Cut button. You must also delete the selected text from the text box. You can accomplish these objectives with two program instructions that take advantage of the `SelText` property:

```
ClipText = txtTed.SelText
txtTed.SelText = ""
```

The first instruction places a copy of the selected text into `ClipText`. If no text is selected, the value of `ClipText` becomes the empty string. The second instruction deletes any selected text from the text box. These instructions go in the `Click` procedure for the Cut button.

Create the following event procedure:

```
Sub cmdCut_Click ()
    ClipText = txtTed.SelText
    txtTed.SelText = ""
    txtTed.SetFocus
End Sub
```

6

The `txtTed.SetFocus` instruction moves the focus back to the text box when the Cut button is clicked.

Coding the Copy Button

The Copy and Cut buttons are similar. The only difference is that with Copy, the selected text is not deleted from the text box. Add the `cmdCopy_Click` procedure:

```
Sub cmdCopy_Click ()
    ClipText = txtTed.SelText
    txtTed.SetFocus
End Sub
```

Notice that this procedure does not reset the value of the text box's `SelText` property to the empty string. When the user clicks the Copy button, the selected text is copied to `ClipText` but also remains in the text box.

Coding the Paste Button

As explained earlier, when an instruction modifies the value of `SelText`, the string specified in the instruction replaces any text that is currently selected. If no text is currently selected, the specified string is simply inserted at the position of the cursor. In both cases, Visual Basic deselects the entire contents of the text box. (The value of `SelLength` is set to 0 to indicate that no text is selected.)

Therefore, to make the Paste button respond appropriately when clicked, all you need to do is set the value of `SelText` to the current value of `ClipText`:

```
Sub cmdPaste_Click ()
    txtTed.SelText = ClipText
    txtTed.SetFocus
End Sub
```

At this point, Ted is functional. Try running the application and experimenting with the command buttons. Notice that if you select some text and then click Cut, you can immediately recover the selected text by clicking Paste. Figure 6.7 shows Ted in use.

Figure 6.7
Ted is working.

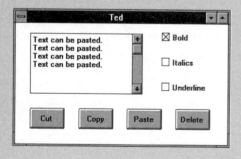

What happens if you click the Paste button when some text is highlighted in the text box? You find that the contents of `ClipText` *replace* the currently selected text. This standard Windows behavior is built into the text box.

Disabling Command Buttons

Although Ted works correctly, several possible refinements can make it a more polished application. One embellishment is to disable a command button when its use doesn't make sense.

For example, when ClipText is empty, clicking Paste is meaningless because there is no stored text to paste. ClipText is empty when the application begins. Also, ClipText becomes empty if you click Cut or Copy when no text is highlighted. Similarly, if the text box has no contents, the Cut, Copy, and Delete buttons cannot produce any meaningful effect. In this situation, however, ClipText *could* contain text, and the Paste button would be meaningful.

Understanding the *Enabled* Property

Visual Basic has a way to disable command buttons. The Enabled property of a command button determines whether it responds to any user events. The Enabled property can have the value True or False. When True, the button is enabled and responds normally to user-generated events, such as a click. True is the default value of Enabled. When Enabled is False, however, the button does not respond to any user-generated events. The button's caption appears dimmed (or grayed) as a visual cue to the user that the button is disabled.

With Ted, you can take advantage of the Enabled property to disable command buttons in appropriate situations. You need to add program instructions that modify the value of Enabled for the various command buttons, depending on the current context of the text box.

For example, when the application first begins, all four command buttons should be disabled. After all, with no text in the text box, you cannot copy, cut, or delete anything. Furthermore, ClipText contains the empty string, so you have nothing to paste either.

In fact, whenever the contents of the text box become blank, the Cut, Copy, and Delete buttons should be disabled. Whenever ClipText is the empty string, the Paste button should be disabled. You can write a user-defined procedure to disable the command buttons. The program code can invoke this procedure when the application begins and any other time that the contents of the text box become blank.

Using the General Procedure *BlankText*

You can create a user-defined procedure named BlankText. This procedure disables the Cut, Copy, and Delete buttons. It also disables the Paste button if ClipText contains the empty string. The following is the BlankText procedure:

```
Sub BlankText ()
    cmdCut.Enabled = False
    cmdCopy.Enabled = False
    cmdDelete.Enabled = False

    If ClipText = "" Then
        cmdPaste.Enabled = False
```

6

```
        Else
            cmdPaste.Enabled = True
        End If
    End Sub
```

Where in the program code do you put this procedure? Such procedures go in the form's general section. You will recall that Visual Basic uses the term *general procedure* to refer to a user-defined procedure.

Adding the *BlankText* Procedure

Follow these steps to add `BlankText` to Ted's program code:

1 Press **F7** to open the Code window.

2 In the drop-down list for the Object box, choose (general).

3 Choose **New Procedure** from the **View** menu to open the New Procedure dialog box.

4 Type **BlankText** in the Name section.

5 Choose **Sub**.

Sub is the default option (see figure 6.8).

Figure 6.8
Specifying the BlankText procedure in the New Procedure dialog box.

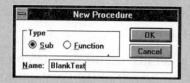

6 Click OK or press **Enter**.

Visual Basic provides a template stub for the procedure as follows:

```
Sub BlankText ()

End Sub
```

7 Type the following procedure:

```
Sub BlankText ()
    cmdCut.Enabled = False
    cmdCopy.Enabled = False
    cmdDelete.Enabled = False

    If ClipText = "" Then
        cmdPaste.Enabled = False
    Else
        cmdPaste.Enabled = True
    End If
End Sub
```

You have now created a general procedure named `BlankText`. If you click the down arrow to the right of the Proc box, you see `BlankText` in the list of procedures. The procedure uses a block `If-Then-Else` instruction to take different actions depending on the value of `ClipText`.

The `If` instruction tests the contents of `ClipText`. If `ClipText` is the empty string (that is, there is no text to paste), the procedure disables the Paste button.

If `ClipText` does *not* contain the empty string (there is some text to paste), however, the `Else` clause goes into effect. The instruction in the `Else` clause enables the Paste button.

Invoking *BlankText* from Event Procedures

`BlankText` now exists at the form level along with the event procedures. You can invoke `BlankText` from any event procedure by using Visual Basic's `Call` instruction:

```
Call BlankText
```

The `Call` keyword is optional. All you need to invoke `BlankText` is the following simple instruction:

```
BlankText
```

Modifying *Form_Load*

When the application begins, the text box is blank, and `ClipText` is empty. You want the four command buttons to be disabled. Now that the `BlankText` procedure is defined, you can invoke it in the `Form_Load` event to disable the command buttons.

The following is the revised event procedure. The only modification from the earlier version of `Form_Load` is the second program instruction, which invokes `BlankText`. Add the `BlankText` line to make `Form_Load` appear as follows:

```
Sub Form_Load ()
    txtTed.Text = ""          'Blank contents of text box
    BlankText

    txtTed.FontBold = False
    txtTed.FontItalic = False
    txtTed.FontUnderline = False

    chkBold.Value = 0
    chkItalics.Value = 0
    chkUnderline.Value = 0
End Sub
```

Now run Ted. The four command buttons all appear dimmed (see figure 6.9).

(continues)

6

Modifying *Form_Load* (continued)

Figure 6.9
The four command buttons are dimmed.

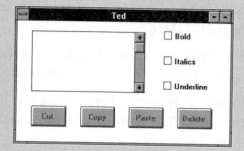

Type some text in the text box. Notice that the command buttons remain disabled.

You obviously need to do more programming—whenever there is text in the text box, the Cut, Copy, and Delete buttons should always be enabled. Stop the application.

Enabling the Command Buttons

To enable the command buttons when the user types in the text box, Visual Basic provides the Change event. The Change event triggers whenever the contents of the text box are modified. For example, typing new characters in or deleting any from the text box triggers the Change event. Selecting text, however, or simply moving the cursor does not generate a Change event. The Change event also triggers any time a program instruction modifies the contents of the text box by changing the value of its Text property.

Create the following txtTed_Change event procedure:

```
Sub txtTed_Change ()
    If txtTed.Text = "" Then
        BlankText
    Else
        cmdCut.Enabled = True
        cmdCopy.Enabled = True
        cmdDelete.Enabled = True
    End If
End Sub
```

The procedure uses a block If-Then-Else instruction to take different actions, depending on the value of the txtTed.Text property. The If instruction tests whether any text is in the text box. If it is empty, the procedure calls the BlankText procedure and terminates.

If the text box contains some text, however, the Else clause goes into effect. The three instructions in the Else clause enable the Cut, Copy, and Delete command buttons.

Try running the application again. Notice that as soon as you type something in the text box, the Cut, Copy, and Delete buttons are enabled. Click Delete. The four buttons are again disabled, thanks to the `txtTed_Change` event procedure.

You can also delete the text box's contents by selecting all the text and pressing **Del** or by moving the cursor to the upper-left corner of the text box and then holding down the **Del** key until the entire contents of the text box are deleted.

An empty text box is not necessarily a sign that the Paste button should be disabled. The contents of the text box can be empty even though `ClipText` contains some text.

Verifying the Paste Button

Type several characters in the text box. Select a few characters so that a portion of the text in the box is highlighted. Click Copy to place a copy of the selected text in the `ClipText` variable.

Now click Delete to clear the contents of the text box. Notice that the Paste button becomes enabled but the other three buttons are disabled.

Click Paste to transfer a copy of the saved text into the text box. Notice that doing so enables the remaining command buttons. Paste remains enabled also. You can, therefore, paste additional copies of the saved text by clicking Paste repeatedly.

Save your project onto your disk again so that the files are updated to reflect the changes you have just made.

Ted is close to completion. One more detail with the Cut and Copy buttons, however, requires attention. Now that you have added code to enable and disable the command buttons, you will find that Cut and Copy don't work quite properly. If you cut or copy some text when the Paste button is disabled, it does not become enabled.

Refining the Code for the Cut and Copy Buttons

Most likely, you saw the effect just described when verifying the Paste button in the preceding section. If not, you can see the effect if you start the application, type a few lines into the text box, and then select some of the text. Now click Cut or Copy. Notice that the Paste button does not become enabled. (The Paste button should become enabled, because the cut or copy operation placed text in `ClipText`.)

(continues)

Refining the Code for the Cut and Copy Buttons   (continued)

To correct this problem, just add the following instruction to the `Click` procedures for both the Cut and Copy buttons (insert this code above the line that invokes the `SetFocus` method):

```
If ClipText <> "" Then cmdPaste.Enabled = True
```

The `<>` operator means "not equal." This instruction enables the Paste button when the contents of `ClipText` are not equal to the empty string.

The following are the updated event procedures:

```
Sub cmdCut_Click ()
    ClipText = txtTed.SelText
    txtTed.SelText = ""
    If ClipText <> "" Then cmdPaste.Enabled = True
    txtTed.SetFocus
End Sub

Sub cmdCopy_Click ()
    ClipText = txtTed.SelText
    If ClipText <> "" Then cmdPaste.Enabled = True
    txtTed.SetFocus
End Sub
```

You may wonder why the `Click` procedure for the Cut button doesn't check whether the contents of the text box have become empty. After all, when the entire contents of the text box are highlighted, clicking Cut clears the box. You might expect the `cmdCut_Click` procedure to call `BlankText` when the contents of the text box are deleted.

Actually, the necessary code is contained in the `Change` procedure for the text box. When you select some text and click the Cut button, a `Change` event triggers for the text box. The code in the `Change` event procedure invokes `BlankText`. This situation is one example of a single action triggering multiple events. Here, when you click the Cut button, a `Click` event occurs for it. The cut, however, changes the text in the text box. Thus, a `Change` event for the text box occurs, as well.

Viewing the Available Events

You can use the Code window to view all the available events for a form or control. Just open this window when Visual Basic is in Design mode. For example, in the Ted application, double-click a control (or the form) to open its Code window. Then click the down arrow to the right of the Proc box. You see a drop-down list that shows all the available events.

Events listed in boldface are those for which you have already written an event procedure. Figure 6.10 shows the Code window and event procedure list for the Cut command button.

Figure 6.10

The Code window for the Cut command button.

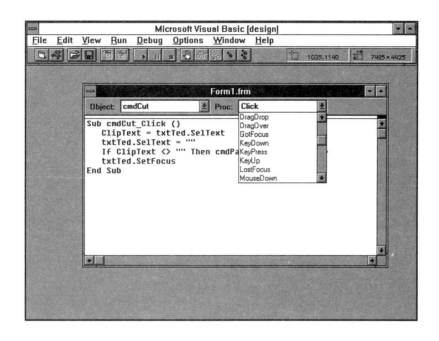

Viewing the Programmer-Defined Procedures

To see any program code not associated with an event procedure, click the down arrow to the right of the Object box in the Code window. Click (general), the first item in the drop-down list. Now click the down arrow to the right of the Proc box. The drop-down list contains the names of the general procedures. For Ted, the only general procedure is BlankText. Notice that the drop-down list also contains the item (declarations). Click this item to see the form-level declarations. Ted has only one such declaration:

```
Dim ClipText As String
```

Viewing the Event Procedures

You can cycle through an application's event procedures by repeatedly pressing **Ctrl+up arrow** or **Ctrl+down arrow** when the Code window is open. With each keystroke, the next coded event procedure (or the general declarations section) scrolls into view.

Another way to view an application's existing event procedures is with the View Procedures dialog box. Open the Code window (press **F7**); then press **F2**. Figure 6.11 shows this dialog box for Ted.

6

Figure 6.11

The View Procedures dialog box for the Ted application.

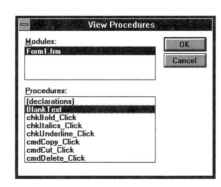

The View Procedures dialog box lists all the event procedures for which program code has been written. To bring any procedure into view, double-click its name. Alternatively, you can select the procedure name from the list by clicking it. Then click OK.

Using Access Keys

Access key
A key you press in combination with the Alt key to choose a menu or option.

Ted is now a fully functional application. The event procedures are complete. That fact doesn't mean, however, that you cannot improve the application. You can add access keys to the command buttons and check boxes. An **access key** is a key you press in combination with the Alt key to activate a command button, check box, or other element of an application. Many Windows applications, including Visual Basic, use access keys.

Creating Access Keys in Visual Basic

In a Visual Basic application, you can create an access key for any control that has a Caption property. You need to make only a small modification to the value of each control's Caption property. Put an ampersand (&) in front of the character you want to designate as the access key.

For example, you can make *C* the access key for the Copy button by changing its Caption property to &Copy. Similarly, you can make *B* the access key for the Bold check box by changing its Caption to &Bold.

Notice that, once you make *C* the access key for the Copy button, a small problem arises with the Cut button. You can't use the same access key for two different controls, so *C* cannot function this way for Cut. Instead, *t* is a reasonable choice for the Cut button's access key. The Caption becomes Cu&t.

Adding Access Keys to Ted

To add access keys to Ted's four command buttons and three check boxes, open the Properties window, and change the Caption properties as table 6.4 shows.

Table 6.4 Access Keys for the Ted Application

Control	Access Key	Value of *Caption* property
chkBold	B	&Bold
chkItalics	I	&Italics
chkUnderline	U	&Underline
cmdCut	T	Cu&t
cmdCopy	C	&Copy
cmdPaste	P	&Paste
cmdDelete	D	&Delete

That is all you need to do. Visual Basic takes care of the rest. When you run the application, each access key appears underlined. (The ampersand character is not displayed.) Furthermore, you don't need any additional program code to make the access keys functional.

Run the application. Figure 6.12 shows an example of Ted in use.

Figure 6.12
Ted has access keys.

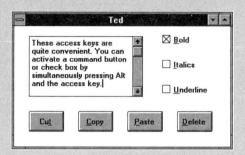

Notice that each access key is underlined. If you press **Alt** with one of the access keys, you activate the corresponding command button or check box.

For example, press **Alt+D** to delete the contents of the text box. The effect is the same as clicking Delete. Furthermore, by pressing **Alt+U** several times, you toggle underlining on and off—the same as clicking the Underline check box several times in succession.

Ted is now a polished application. Of course, you can always add more functionality. For example, to make Ted a professional text editor, you might add options to save the contents of the text box to a disk file and load them back into the box. To find out how to do this, see Chapter 12, "Processing Files." Save your project again to disk.

Working with the Form as a Text File

When you save a form as a text file, you can view it with a word processor or text editor. The file consists of a readable description of the form. The description enumerates each control on the form, including all associated property values and a complete listing of every general and event procedure. This description provides a concise representation of the form, so it's a valuable debugging aid. To work with the text description of the form, you must have saved the FRM file with the **S**ave as Text option.

Viewing TED.FRM

Although it is not necessary for you to view the text file now, if you want to view it, you can load it into any word processor or text editor. For example, you could switch to the Windows Notepad program in the Accessories group. Then you could use Notepad to open the file TED.FRM (being sure to specify the correct disk drive and directory). The text file for TED.FRM would appear as follows:

```
VERSION 3.00
Begin Form frmTed
   Caption          =    "Ted"
   Height           =    3300
   Left             =    1185
   LinkTopic        =    "Form1"
   ScaleHeight      =    2895
   ScaleWidth       =    5250
   Top              =    1440
   Width            =    5370
   Begin CheckBox chkUnderline
      Caption          =       "&Underline"
      Height           =       375
      Left             =       3600
      TabIndex         =       7
      Top              =       1320
      Width            =       1215
   End
   Begin CheckBox chkItalics
      Caption          =       "&Italics"
      Height           =       375
      Left             =       3600
      TabIndex         =       6
      Top              =       720
      Width            =       1215
   End
   Begin CheckBox chkBold
      Caption          =       "&Bold"
      Height           =       375
      Left             =       3600
      TabIndex         =       5
      Top              =       120
      Width            =       1215
   End
   Begin CommandButton cmdDelete
      Caption          =       "&Delete"
      Height           =       495
      Left             =       3960
      TabIndex         =       4
      Top              =       2040
      Width            =       855
   End
   Begin CommandButton cmdPaste
      Caption          =       "&Paste"
      Height           =       495
      Left             =       2760
      TabIndex         =       3
      Top              =       2040
      Width            =       855
   End
   Begin CommandButton cmdCopy
      Caption          =       "&Copy"
      Height           =       495
      Left             =       1560
      TabIndex         =       2
      Top              =       2040
      Width            =       855
   End
```

```
      Begin CommandButton cmdCut
         Caption        =    "Cu&t"
         Height         =    495
         Left           =    360
         TabIndex       =    1
         Top            =    2040
         Width          =    855
      End
      Begin TextBox txtTed
         Height         =    1455
         Left           =    360
         MultiLine      =    -1   'True
         ScrollBars     =    2    'Vertical
         TabIndex       =    0
         Text           =    "Text1"
         Top            =    240
         Width          =    2775
      End
   End
End
Dim ClipText As String

Sub BlankText ()
   cmdCut.Enabled = False
   cmdCopy.Enabled = False
   cmdDelete.Enabled = False

   If ClipText = "" Then
      cmdPaste.Enabled = False
   Else
      cmdPaste.Enabled = True
   End If
End Sub

Sub chkBold_Click ()
   txtTed.FontBold = Not (txtTed.FontBold)
   txtTed.SetFocus
End Sub

Sub chkItalics_Click ()
   txtTed.FontItalic = Not (txtTed.FontItalic)
   txtTed.SetFocus
End Sub

Sub chkUnderline_Click ()
   txtTed.FontUnderline = Not (txtTed.FontUnderline)
   txtTed.SetFocus
End Sub

Sub cmdCopy_Click ()
   ClipText = txtTed.SelText
   If ClipText <> "" Then cmdPaste.Enabled = True
   txtTed.SetFocus
End Sub

Sub cmdCut_Click ()
   ClipText = txtTed.SelText
   txtTed.SelText = ""
   If ClipText <> "" Then cmdPaste.Enabled = True
   txtTed.SetFocus
End Sub
```

```
Sub cmdDelete_Click ()
   txtTed.Text = ""
   txtTed.SetFocus
End Sub

Sub cmdPaste_Click ()
   txtTed.SelText = ClipText
   txtTed.SetFocus
End Sub

Sub Form_Load ()
   txtTed.Text = ""           'Blank contents of text box
   BlankText

   txtTed.FontBold = False
   txtTed.FontItalic = False
   txtTed.FontUnderline = False

   chkBold.Value = 0
   chkItalics.Value = 0
   chkUnderline.Value = 0
End Sub

Sub txtTed_Change ()
   If txtTed.Text = "" Then
      BlankText
   Else
      cmdCut.Enabled = True
      cmdCopy.Enabled = True
      cmdDelete.Enabled = True
   End If
End Sub
```

Understanding the Text File

The format of the text file is relatively straightforward. The first line lists the version number of Visual Basic. Then the design-time property values of the form are listed. Following that, each control is named, along with its property values. The controls are listed in alphabetical order, as are the properties of each. The listed properties include those of the location (Top, Left, Height, and Width), and any set to nondefault values at design time.

The TabIndex property, shown for each control, specifies the tab order. The tab order determines the sequence in which each control gets the focus if you repeatedly press the Tab key. The general declarations section follows the list of each control's property values. For Ted, the general declarations section consists of the single Dim instruction, which declares the variable ClipText.

Next comes a complete list of the general and event procedures. Notice that Visual Basic arranges these procedures in alphabetical order, as for the lists of controls and properties.

Printing the Text File

To print a listing of the text file, all you need to do is print the file as you print any other text document. Just use the normal printing capability of the word processor or text editor with which you are viewing the file. In Windows

Notepad, for example, you print a file by choosing **P**rint from the **F**ile menu.

You can also use Visual Basic's **F**ile **P**rint command to print a listing of the text associated with a form.

By printing the file, you get a hard-copy archive of the form. If you ever lose the TED.FRM file, you can regenerate the application from the information on the printed listing.

Modifying the Text File

Once you have a form's text file loaded into a word processor or text editor, you can actually modify the description of the form. For example, you can change some property values or modify an event procedure. You can even add a new control or event procedure. After you modify the file, you can save the file again under either the old name or a new one. Be sure that the word processor or text editor saves the file in ASCII (text) format, not in any special proprietary format specific to either of these two systems. If you use Notepad, it will always save your text files properly.

When you later load the modified file back into Visual Basic, your modifications are immediately implemented. With this technique, you can "program" Visual Basic applications in your word processor.

Using Control Arrays

Often, a Visual Basic application has several controls of the same type that perform similar functions. For example, Ted has three check boxes that manipulate the font attributes. Each of Ted's three check boxes has a name: `chkBold`, `chkItalics`, and `chkUnderline`. To enable each check box to respond to the `Click` event, you wrote three separate event procedures: `chkBold_Click`, `chkItalics_Click`, and `chkUnderline_Click`.

Control array
A group of controls that share the same name and event procedures. Each control in the group has a unique index number that identifies it.

Visual Basic provides an easier way, however, to work with groups of similar controls: the control array. A **control array** is a group of controls that share the same name. Each member of the control array is called an **element** of the control array. Each individual control in this type of array is distinguished by a separate value for its `Index` property.

A control array always contains controls of the same type. For example, a control array can consist of command buttons, check boxes, or labels. However, you cannot have a single control array comprised of a command button, a check box, and a label.

Element
A single member control in a control array.

Advantages of Control Arrays

With control arrays, you can realize several advantages:

- *Your program code can manipulate a group of controls more efficiently.* For example, you can create a program loop that in a few lines of code, modifies the property values for every element of the control array.

- *Several controls can share the same event procedures.*

- *You can write a single event procedure for each type of event.* For example, one `Click` procedure is all you need to make *every* element of the control array respond to the `Click` event. In this way, the elements of a control array can share program code.

- *You can add or delete elements of a control array at run time.* Sometimes, you want to add or remove a control while the application is running. By using Visual Basic's `Load` and `UnLoad` statements in program code, you can add or remove elements of a control array at run time. The only way to add or remove controls at run time is by using a control array. You must first create the control array at design time. Then you can write program code to add elements to and remove them from this array.

Creating a Control Array

You create a control array by assigning the same name to two or more controls that have already been placed on the form. When you use the Properties window to assign the same value of the `Name` property to two or more controls, Visual Basic opens a dialog box that asks whether you want to create a control array. By clicking Yes, you establish a control array. As explained in the preceding chapter, you can also create a control array by copying and pasting it through Visual Basic's **E**dit menu. The third way to create a control array is to assign a value to the `Index` property of a control.

Working with the *Index* Property

Your program code needs a way to reference the individual controls in the control array, because all its elements have the same name. That's the job of the `Index` property.

Each element of a control array has a different `Index` value. `Index` values start at 0 and increase incrementally. In other words, `Index` is 0 for the first element of the control array, 1 for the second element, 2 for the next, and so on.

When working with the Properties window, you may have seen `Index` in the list of properties. `Index` has meaning only for control arrays. When you first place a control on a form, its `Index` property has no value. When you create a control array, however, Visual Basic assigns a specific value of `Index` to each element.

You can modify `Index` values at design time with the Properties window. By assigning a value to `Index` for any control, you immediately establish it as belonging to a control array.

In program code, you reference an element of a control array by enclosing its `Index` value in parentheses. For example, suppose that you establish a control array named `cmdButtons`, which consists of three command buttons. The `Index` values for the three controls are 0, 1, and 2. The following instruction assigns a new caption to the third command button:

```
cmdButtons(2).Caption = "My Index is 2"
```

The array name is immediately followed by a set of parentheses. In the parentheses, a numeric value specifies the element of the array.

Creating a Simple Example of a Control Array

To learn how to use control arrays, you should use a simple test program; don't try them for the first time in a large, complicated project. This exercise demonstrates several aspects of control arrays. You create a simple application containing a control array of three command buttons.

Be sure that you have saved Ted before starting. You pay another visit to Ted later in this chapter.

Start by creating a new project. Choose New Project from the File menu. Then follow these steps:

1 Double-click the Command Button icon in the Toolbox to place a command button near the center of the form. Visual Basic assigns the default name Command1 to this control.

2 Stretch the control horizontally to approximately twice its initial width. (Don't worry about being exact.)

3 Place the control near the upper-left corner of the form.

4 Add two more command buttons to the form; stretch each one to approximately the same width as the first.

Place these controls in a vertical column below the first control.

The two new command buttons have the default names Command2 and Command3. Figure 6.13 shows the form at this stage.

Figure 6.13
Three command buttons are placed on the form.

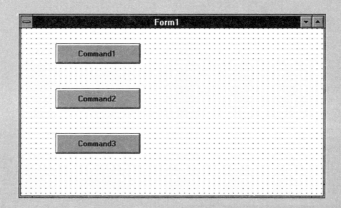

5 Click Command1 to select it. Press F4 to open the Properties window. Change the value of the Name property to cmdButtons.

6 Click Command2. Open the Properties window, and change the value of the Name property to cmdButtons. Visual Basic opens a dialog box that asks whether you want to create a control array (see figure 6.14).

(continues)

6

Creating a Simple Example of a Control Array   (continued)

Figure 6.14
The dialog box that asks whether you want to create a control array.

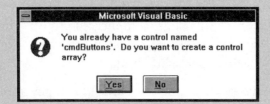

⑦ Choose the Yes option.

Notice that in the Properties window, the Object box reads cmdButtons(1) CommandButton. The parentheses indicate that this control is part of a control array. The 1 inside the parentheses indicates that the value of Index for this control is 1.

You can verify this value of Index by searching through the Properties window to find this property and checking its value. Similarly, if you open the Properties window for the upper-left command button, you see that its Index value is 0.

⑧ Click Command3. As with the other two command buttons, change the value of its Name property to **cmdButtons**. Index is 2 for this control.

⑨ In the Properties window, click the down arrow to the right of the Object box. Notice that the drop-down list shows the various elements of the control array (see figure 6.15).

Figure 6.15
The Object list in the Properties window.

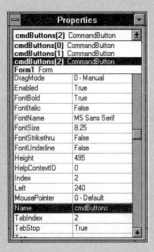

⑩ Press **F7** to open the Code window. Select the Click procedure for cmdButtons. Notice that the Sub instruction in the procedure template now appears as follows:

```
Sub cmdButtons_Click (Index As Integer)
```

Ordinarily, the parentheses inside a Click event procedure do not contain any parameters. Here, however, Index As Integer appears inside the parentheses. This phrase specifies Index as a parameter of data type Integer. As a result, when the Click procedure activates, Visual Basic passes Index to the procedure. In the procedure, you can use the Index parameter to determine which element of the control array was clicked. In this way, a single Click event procedure works for all elements of the control array.

⓫ Create the following event procedure:

```
Sub cmdButtons_Click (Index As Integer)
   cmdButtons(Index).Caption = "You clicked me!"
End Sub
```

Notice how the instruction in the event procedure uses Index to modify the caption of the clicked command button.

⓬ Run the application. When you click any of the three command buttons, its caption changes to You clicked me!

⓭ Stop the application, and reopen the Code window to the Click procedure for the command buttons. Modify the right side of the Caption instruction as follows:

```
Sub cmdButtons_Click (Index As Integer)
    cmdButtons(Index).Caption = "I'm Index #" & Str$(Index)
End Sub
```

Here, the Str$ function converts the numeric value of Index into a string value. As such, the right side is entirely in string format, as required by the Caption property.

⓮ Run the application again. When you click one of the command buttons, the new caption displays the Index value for the control.

In figure 6.16, the top two command buttons have been clicked. Stop the application. Save the form as **C5E1** and the project as **C5E1**.

Figure 6.16
Two command buttons display their new captions.

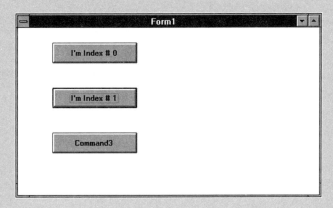

Creating a Simple Example of a Control Array (continued)

15 Print the project by choosing **File Print**.

16 In the Print dialog box, choose the **All** option button.

17 Click the **Form**, Form **Text**, and **Code** check boxes.

18 Click the OK button.

Using *Index* in Event Procedures

When you are writing event procedure for a control array, Visual Basic always adds the Index parameter with the phrase Index As Integer. The As Integer qualification specifies that Index is a parameter that has an integral numeric value.

In the event procedure, you can test the value of Index to determine which element of the control array triggered the event. For example, you might write an instruction like the following:

```
If Index = 1 Then Beep
```

This instruction beeps the speaker only if the control with an Index value of 1 triggers the event.

So far, you have worked exclusively with event procedures that normally do not contain any parameters. As you learn throughout the book, some events always contain specialized parameters.

For example, the KeyPress event occurs when the user presses a key while a control has the focus. Consider the KeyPress event for a command button named MyButton. Here, MyButton is not part of a control array. In the Code window, the Sub instruction for this event appears as follows:

```
Sub MyButton_KeyPress (KeyAscii As Integer)
```

KeyAscii has a numeric value indicating the key that was pressed. If MyButton is a control array, however, the Sub instruction appears as follows:

```
Sub MyButton_KeyPress (Index As Integer, KeyAscii As Integer)
```

In this case, Visual Basic passes both the Index and KeyAscii parameters.

The point here is not to explain KeyPress but rather to emphasize that Visual Basic adds the Index parameter to *any* event procedure associated with a control array.

Modifying Ted to Use a Control Array

Recall that the Ted application has three check boxes that manipulate the bold, italic, and underline font attributes. The check boxes have the names chkBold, chkItalics, and chkUnderline, respectively. When designing Ted, you could have created a control array for these three check boxes. In this case, a single Click procedure would manipulate the font attributes for all three buttons.

You can change Ted and convert the check boxes from ordinary separate controls into a control array.

First, to load Ted back into the Visual Basic environment, choose **O**pen Project from the **F**ile menu. When the dialog box opens, specify the file TED.MAK. Be sure that you specify the proper drive and directory path to the file. If the form is not visible after the file loads, open the Project window. (If the Project window is not visible, choose **P**roject from the **W**indow menu.) To see the form, click the View Form button in the Project window.

Follow these steps to turn the three check boxes into a control array named chkFontStyle:

1 Open the Properties window, and find the check box at the top. This check box is currently named chkBold.

2 Change the value of the Name property to **chkFontStyle**.

3 Open the Properties window for the chkItalics check box.

4 Change the value of Name to **chkFontStyle**. You specified the same name as an existing check box, so Visual Basic opens the dialog box that asks whether you want to create a control array.

5 Choose **Y**es to confirm that you want to create a control array.

6 Open the Properties window for the third check box. As with the other two boxes, change its Name to **chkFontStyle**.

You now have a control array named chkFontStyle. If you examine the values of Index in the Properties window, you find that the values are 0, 1, and 2 for the three check boxes, moving from top to bottom.

7 Open the Code window for the chkFontStyle Click event procedure. Visual Basic provides the following template for the event procedure. Notice that Index is present as a parameter:

```
Sub chkFontStyle_Click (Index As Integer)

End Sub
```

(continues)

6

Modifying Ted to Use a Control Array   (continued)

8 Write the code for the Click event procedure. You can write a series of If instructions as follows:

```
If Index = 0 Then txtTed.FontBold = Not (txtTed.FontBold)
If Index = 1 Then txtTed.FontItalic = Not (txtTed.FontItalic)
If Index = 2 Then txtTed.FontUnderline = Not
➡ (txtTed.FontUnderline)
```

As explained in the next step, another way is to use Visual Basic's Select Case statement.

9 Create the following procedure:

```
Sub chkFontStyle_Click (Index As Integer)
    Select Case Index
        Case 0
            txtTed.FontBold = Not (txtTed.FontBold)
        Case 1
            txtTed.FontItalic = Not (txtTed.FontItalic)
        Case 2
            txtTed.FontUnderline = Not (txtTed.FontUnderline)
    End Select
    txtTed.SetFocus
End Sub
```

Here, the Select Case-End Select block examines the value of Index and executes the appropriate instruction, depending on the value. The Select statement is explained in the next chapter.

10 Open the Code window for the Form_Load procedure. The final three lines of the procedure initialize the Value properties for the three check boxes:

```
chkBold.Value = 0
chkItalics.Value = 0
chkUnderline.Value = 0
```

11 These three lines must be modified to use the name of the control array. Modify the final three lines of the procedure as follows:

```
chkFontStyle(0).Value = 0
chkFontStyle(1).Value = 0
chkFontStyle(2).Value = 0
```

Note: *You no longer have controls named* chkBold, chkItalics, *and* chkUnderline, *so you may wonder about the fate of the* Click *procedures that you previously defined for them. After all, you cannot have a* chkBold_Click *event procedure if you don't have a* chkBold *control. You can verify that the old event procedures no longer exist. Open* *the Code window, and examine the Object list. The list doesn't even contain the old control names, so their* Click *procedures are no longer event procedures.*

Visual Basic does not discard the old procedures; instead, the system moves them to the general procedures section. As such, they are no longer event procedures but are similar to the user-defined procedure BlankText. *The old procedures cannot be called by system events, but you can write program code to invoke one of them explicitly.*

To verify that the procedures are intact, choose (general) in the Object list. Then drop down the list in the Proc box. You see the old Click *procedures. The old* Click *procedures are no longer used in the modified Ted application, so it's a good idea to delete them completely. You may forget about them and try to use variable names or control names from the old event procedures. This error can cause problems in your program. To delete these old procedures, open the Code window for each procedure one at a time, and delete each in its entirety.*

In Form_Load, you can use a loop to initialize the Value properties. For example, you can write a For-Next loop as follows:

```
For J = 0 To 2
    chkFontStyle(J).Value = 0
Next J
```

For-Next loops are described in the following chapter. Such a loop hints at the power inherent in control arrays. For a control array with only a few elements, there's no particular advantage to writing a loop rather than a series of individual assignment instructions. However, suppose that the control array had 20 or more elements. With only a small change in the For instruction (For J = 0 To 20), the three-instruction loop can still initialize the entire control array.

The capability of manipulating control arrays with loops (and with variable names inside the parentheses) is especially important in applications that add or remove elements of control arrays at run time. In such applications, you often write program code that must manipulate an unknown number of control array elements. Such code might define a variable named NumElements, which indicates the highest current Index value for the elements of the control array. Then a For loop might be written as follows:

```
For J = 0 To NumElements
```

That completes the conversion of Ted so that the application uses a control array. Use the Save File **A**s option from the **F**ile menu to save Ted with a new file name. Run the modified application. Ted should perform just as it did previously.

Printing and Running Ted from the Program Manager

Now that you have finished writing Ted and saved it on disk, you should print it. You also may want to show the program to others. You can set it up to run from the Windows Program Manager just like all "real" Windows programs.

Printing the Ted Project

Make sure that you are in the Design mode of VB and that the Ted program is loaded. Then do the following:

1 Choose **F**ile and then **P**rint.

The Print project dialog box appears (see figure 6.17).

Figure 6.17
The Print project dialog box.

2 Click the **A**ll option button.

3 Click the **F**orm, Form **T**ext, and **C**ode check boxes.

4 Click the OK button.

All the parts of your Ted project will be printed.

If you want to distribute your text editor program to someone who has Windows but does not have Visual Basic, you must first create an EXE file from your project. Then you copy the EXE file and the file VBRUN300.DLL onto a disk. VBRUN300.DLL is found in the WINDOWS\SYSTEM subdirectory. With these two files and Windows, anyone can run your application.

Producing an EXE File from TED.MAK

To create an EXE file from TED.MAK, make sure that TED is loaded into VB and a formatted disk is in your floppy disk drive. Then do the following:

1 Choose **F**ile and then Ma**k**e EXE File.

2 The Make EXE File dialog box appears (see figure 6.18).

Figure 6.18
The Make EXE File dialog box.

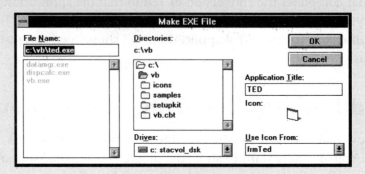

❸ In the dialog box's File **N**ame text box, type the drive on which you will store the EXE file, the path, and then the file name: **TED.EXE**.

❹ Click the OK button.

The new file is created and stored where you indicated. Now you can run the application by clicking the file name TED.EXE in the File Manager.

A "real" Windows program is run by double-clicking its icon in the Program Manager window. That's how you start VB, Paintbrush, Notepad, and all your other Windows applications, isn't it? Now you are going to learn how to run TED.EXE in the same way. This method really works best if you can store TED.EXE in a directory on your hard drive—right where all your other Windows applications are stored. But you can also store TED.EXE on a floppy disk. Then, however, you must make sure that the right disk is in the drive before you double-click Ted's icon.

Running Ted from the Program Manager

To set up a program group for your VB applications and place Ted's icon in it, do the following:

❶ Switch to Windows Program Manager.

❷ Chose **F**ile **N**ew. The New Program Object dialog box appears (see figure 6.19).

Figure 6.19
The New Program Object dialog box.

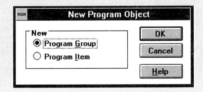

❸ In this dialog box, make sure that the Program **G**roup option button is selected. Then click the OK button.

The Program Group Properties dialog box appears (see figure 6.20).

Figure 6.20
The Program Group Properties dialog box.

Program Group Properties		
Description:		OK
Group File:		Cancel
		Help

(continues)

6

Running Ted from the Program Manager   (continued)

4 In this dialog box's **Description** text box, type **My VB Apps**. Then click OK.

The new program group window opens in the File Manager window.

5 Choose **File New**. The New Program Object dialog box appears.

6 In this dialog box, make sure that Program **I**tem is selected. Then click OK.

The Program Item Properties dialog box appears (see figure 6.21).

Figure 6.21
The Program Item Properties dialog box.

```
┌─────────────────────────────────────────────────────┐
│ ─              Program Item Properties                │
├─────────────────────────────────────────────────────┤
│ Description:      [                  ]    ┌────────┐  │
│ Command Line:     [                  ]    │   OK   │  │
│ Working Directory:[                  ]    ├────────┤  │
│ Shortcut Key:     [None              ]    │ Cancel │  │
│                                           ├────────┤  │
│                   ☐ Run Minimized         │ Browse…│  │
│                                           ├────────┤  │
│                                           │Change Icon…│
│                                           ├────────┤  │
│                                           │  Help  │  │
│                                           └────────┘  │
└─────────────────────────────────────────────────────┘
```

7 In this dialog box's **Description** text box, type **TED**, and then press the **Tab** key.

8 In the **C**ommand Line text box, type the path to your EXE file and the name of the EXE file. Note these examples:

C:**VB\TED.EXE**

A:**TED.EXE**

9 Click OK.

10 If your path points to a disk drive, Windows displays the Removable Path Specified dialog box. Click the **Y**es button if this dialog box appears.

You are finished! You should see an icon labeled TED in your program group window (see figure 6.22). Double-click that icon to begin running Ted.

Figure 6.22
The icon representing the Ted program.

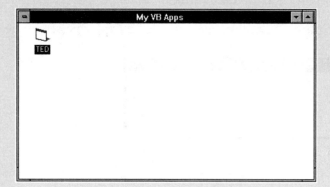

Chapter Summary

Event procedures make a Visual Basic application do things for the user. In an event procedure, you place the program instructions that execute when the event triggers. Such instructions often modify various property values to create desired effects on the form.

In this chapter, you created Ted, a functional text editor that implements Cut and Paste and selectable font attributes. By developing Ted, you have learned not only about writing event procedures but also about employing user-defined procedures, form-level variables, the Form_Load event, and the properties of a text box. You learned also how to create an access key by modifying the Caption property.

With the Code window, you can view and edit your program code. By using the Object and Proc boxes in this window, you have access to all the instructions in an application, which include the general (user-defined) and event procedures and the general declarations.

You can save a form on disk as a text file. You can view or print a textual description of an application. The description includes the property values for the form and its controls, as well as a listing of all the event procedures.

A control array groups several controls under a common name. Visual Basic uses the Index property to distinguish the individual elements in the control array. For controls that function similarly, this kind of array presents several advantages. For example, the same event procedure activates whenever the event occurs for *any* element of the control array.

You also learned how to create an EXE file from a MAK file and how to place it as an icon on the Program Manager desktop. In the next chapter, you learn about making decisions in a program and controlling the logic flow of a program.

6

Test Your Understanding

True/False
Indicate whether the statement is true or false.

1. If you place program instructions in the Form_Load event of the start-up form of an application, the instructions execute as soon as you start running the program.

2. The Proc box in the Code window displays the list of event procedures for an object.

3. Visual Basic uses the Checked property of a Check Box control to specify whether the check box is checked.

4. The term *focus* refers to the active object.

5. The syntax for a method uses an underscore to separate the object that is acted on from the action that is taken.

6. The SelLength property of a text box can be set in the Properties window.

7. You create a form-level variable by declaring it in the general declarations section of the form.

8. The Enabled property of a command button determines whether it responds to any user events.

9. A block If-Then-Else must always end with an End If statement.

10. Procedure names not associated with any event procedure are listed in the Proc drop-down list for the general object.

Short Answer

Answer the following questions.

1. Explain how to make the letter *Y* the access key for a command button.

2. After you have created a form, what must you do to view the form text with a word processing program?

3. List the three ways in which you can create a control array.

4. What is the Index property used for in a control array?

5. Why do the words Index As Integer appear inside the parentheses in the Click event of an array of command buttons? Why are the Click event parentheses empty when a command button is not part of a control array?

6. If you have three text boxes on a form and the user types a character in the first text box, does the KeyPress event occur for all three text boxes? Why or why not?

7. Assume that a text box's KeyPress event contains the following code:

```
Sub Text1_KeyPress (KeyAscii As Integer)
Print KeyAscii
End Sub
```

What will print on the form when the program is running and the user types *A* in Text1? Why?

What will print on the form when the user presses the Enter key while Text1 has the focus? Why?

8. What happens to the code in event procedures when you rename the object with which the event procedures are associated?

9. Assume that you have three Label controls (Label1, Label2, and Label3) on a form. Explain the steps necessary to place these controls in a control array named lblMyLabels.

10. When does an `If-Then` statement have to end with an `End If` statement? Is an `End If` statement always needed when you use the `If` statement? Why or why not?

11. Explain how to produce an EXE file from a MAK file.

12. What are the four techniques you can use to open the Code window? How do you close an open Code window?

13. When the Code window is open, how do you change to a different object? How do you change to a different event procedure within the same object?

14. Write the VB statement that will make a text box the active object on a form.

15. Explain the following properties, and tell how you can use them in a VB program: `SelLength`, `SelStart`, and `SelText`.

16. Write the VB statement that would explicitly declare `Count_Var1` as an Integer variable.

17. Where would you place this statement (in your answer to question 16) to declare a form-level variable? How could this statement be used to create an event-level variable?

Projects

Project 1:   Using Two Forms in a VB Project

Write a VB project that uses two forms. Name the first form `frmMain` and the second form `frmAbout`. Make `frmMain` the start-up form.

Place a label control whose caption is your name in `frmAbout`. The label's `Borderstyle` should be fixed as single and its `FontSize = 12`.

Place a command button that enlarges the label's font size in `frmAbout`. Place a command button that reduces the label's font size in `frmAbout`. Place a command button that will reduce the size of the Label control itself, as well as another command button that enlarges the size of the label itself, in `frmAbout`. When the user double-clicks on `frmAbout` (but not on any of the form's controls), unload `frmAbout`.

In `frmMain`, place a button with the caption **About...** . Make **A** the access key for this button. When the user clicks the **A**bout... button (or uses the access key), `frmAbout` should appear centered inside `frmMain` (that is, in the middle of it).

The user should be able to resize `frmMain` at run time and then click the **A**bout... button. When **A**bout... is clicked, `frmAbout` should appear *centered* in `frmMain` regardless of how the user has resized `frmMain`. Figure 6.23 shows how these forms should appear when **A**bout... is clicked.

6

Figure 6.23
The two forms.

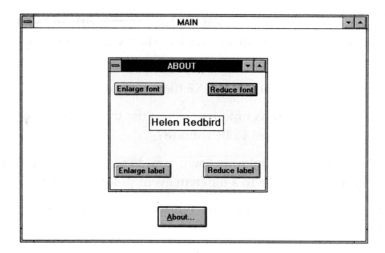

Make sure that the caption (your name) is always centered horizontally inside the label (on frmAbout). Make sure that the label itself is always centered inside frmAbout. Save the project as **C6P1** and then print the forms, form text, and code.

Project 2:   Using VB's Help on Functions

Use Visual Basic's Help to look up the use and value returned of the following functions: CVDate, Date$, Format, InputBox, Now, Time$.

Make sure that you understand the explanations given in Help and have tried out each function in little test programs of your own. Then write a VB program that first displays a form containing six command buttons. Each command button should have as its caption one of the preceding functions.

When the user clicks a button, the program should display an explanation of the use of the function and an example of VB code that uses the function. For example, if the user clicks the Date$ button, a screen should appear that explains and illustrates the use of the Date$ function. The user should be able to return to the first screen (with the six buttons) by double-clicking the explanation of the function's use.

Save the project as **C6P2**. Print the form(s), form text, and code for the project.

CHAPTER 7

Program Flow and Decision Making

Program flow, or logic flow, refers to the order in which the instructions of a Sub or Function execute. Generally, program flow proceeds line by line, from the top of the procedure to the bottom. This sequential top-down program flow is straightforward and easy to understand. Many practical procedures execute in this systematic sequence.

A limit exists, however, to what you can accomplish with such simple, linear sequencing. Frequently, the need arises to redirect program flow. From one point in a particular procedure, you might want to transfer execution to a statement a few lines away, or perhaps many lines later. This redirection usually involves some sort of decision making, or testing.

In some of the programs in earlier chapters, you saw examples of If-Then statements and For-Next loops. Both of these programming structures involve testing. And both structures involve the alteration of sequential program flow based on the results of a test. This chapter examines many different ways in which you can alter program flow from the normal sequential execution order.

Objectives

By the time you have finished this chapter, you will be able to

1. Use Unconditional Branching (GoTo statement)

2. Use Conditional Branching (On-GoTo and On Error GoTo statements)

3. End Program Execution (End statement)

4. Use Conditional Testing (`If-Then` and `Select Case` statements)

5. Use Looping (`For-Next`, `While-Wend`, and `Do-Loop` statements)

Branching

Branching
The direct transfer from one line in a procedure to another line.

Branching is the direct transfer from one line in a procedure to another line. Suppose that one line contains an instruction causing Visual Basic to jump immediately to another line within the same procedure. In Visual Basic terminology, the former line *branches* to the latter line.

Branching comes in the following two forms:

Unconditional branching
A form of branching in which program control transfers to a specific line in all cases.

- *Unconditional branching.* Program control transfers to a specific line in all cases.

- *Conditional branching.* Program control transfers to one of several lines, depending on the value of a testing expression.

Conditional branching
A form of branching in which program control transfers to one of several lines, depending on the value of a testing expression.

Labels and Line Numbers

If you want a program instruction to branch to another line, you need a way to indicate the new location. To redirect execution to a particular program line, you must name (specify) the target line. Visual Basic provides two ways to do this: line labels and line numbers. By placing a line label or line number at the beginning of a line, you give it a named identity, which can then be referenced by a branching instruction.

Note: *Don't confuse a line label with the Label control. A line label is a name that designates a line location within the code of a program. The Label control is one of the controls available from the Visual Basic Toolbox. In this chapter, the term* label *refers only to line label, not to the Label control.*

Labels

Line label
A name that designates a line location within the code of a program.

A **line label** begins with a letter and ends with a colon. Here are some valid labels:

```
CalculateSum:

HandleError:

UserMessage:
```

Each label used in a form or module must be unique. At the form level, for example, you cannot use the same label name twice—even if it is used in two different event procedures. This restriction applies to the event procedures associated directly with the form as well as with the controls placed on it. Nor can you duplicate a label name within a given procedure.

A label can contain as many as 40 characters. Upper- and lowercase letters are not distinguished in labels. Thus, `MyLabel:`, `mylabel:`, and `MYLABEL:` are equivalent.

A label can appear at the beginning of a line containing one or more instructions. In this case, when execution is redirected to the label, the program immediately executes the instructions on that line. Alternatively, a label can stand alone on a line. When you redirect execution to such a label, the program immediately executes the next line that contains instructions.

Line Numbers

Line number

A special kind of line label that consists exclusively of digits.

A **line number** is a special form of a line label. A line number consists exclusively of digits that form an integer number from 0 up to the number formed by forty 9s. Unlike a line label, a line number does not require a colon after it. The following is an example of a numbered line:

```
100 MsgBox "This line has a line number"
```

Line numbers in Visual Basic do not specify the execution order of program lines. Instead, a line number simply gives an identity to its line—a way to refer to it explicitly. You can, for example, place line number 500 between line numbers 1000 and 2000.

As with line labels, you can use a particular line number only once within a given form or module. Line numbers are entirely optional; you can include them as you see fit. If you do use line numbers, you can number every line or only certain ones.

Modern programming practice favors labels over line numbers because an alphanumeric name conveys more information than a colorless line number. Create meaningful label names, such as GraphRoutine or GetUserInput, so that your programs are easier to read and understand.

Although line numbers are discouraged in general, Visual Basic actually *requires* them when you use certain error-tracking program features. The Erl function, for example, indicates line numbers where program errors occur. Erl does not, however, report line numbers larger than 65529. For more information on Erl and error-handling routines, see Chapter 8, "Testing and Debugging Your Program."

7

Unconditional Branching with *GoTo*

Before you read about the GoTo statement, you should know that GoTo *appears* very helpful but often leads programmers to disaster. The reason is that GoTo encourages you to solve programming problems in a scatterbrained, disorganized manner. In fact, GoTo even causes you to *think* in a disorganized manner.

You can usually write a better program without using the GoTo statement. Some instructors will not accept a program that contains the GoTo statement because GoTos are a real source of problems when they creep into your programs. One form of the GoTo statement, the On Error GoTo, discussed later in this chapter, is useful when used correctly. Otherwise, avoid the use of GoTos.

If you are coding and find that you need to jump from one group of statements to another with a GoTo, *stop coding*. Think whether there isn't a better, simpler, cleaner design available to solve the problem. Don't patch together a solution with `GoTo` statements. You have been warned; you don't have to learn about `GoTo`s the hard way.

You use `GoTo` to cause an unconditional branch. You can specify the destination with a line label or a line number:

```
GoTo label

GoTo linenum
```

`label` is a label defined in the same procedure, and `linenum` is any line number in the procedure.

The destination must exist, or the `Label not defined` fatal error occurs. To get a feel for `GoTo`, look at the following example:

```
Sub Form_Click ()
    Print "I am"
    GoTo Message
    Print "not"
Message:
    Print "happy"
End Sub
```

Note: *Most program examples in this chapter consist of short* `Form_Click` *procedures. For simplicity, many examples use the* `Print` *method to display results directly on the default form.*

To try one of the examples, type the `Form_Click` *procedure as shown. Then run the program. A blank form will appear on-screen. Simply click the mouse while the pointer is on the blank form. The click activates the code contained in the* `Form_Click` *procedure. To terminate the program, choose* **End** *from the* **R***un menu or click the Stop button on the Toolbar. Visual Basic returns to the Program Design mode with the* `Form_Click` *procedure visible. Then you can modify the instructions in the* `Form_Click` *procedure to try another example.*

The following is the result that appears on the form:

```
I am
happy
```

The `Print "not"` line never got a chance to execute. The `GoTo` instruction transferred control directly to the `Message` label. The program, therefore, continues with the final `Print` instruction immediately following the `Message` label.

In a `GoTo` instruction, the label name does not include a trailing colon. In the preceding example, notice that the instruction `GoTo Message` does not include a colon after the label `Message`. The actual label, however, must be followed by a colon.

When using line numbers rather than labels, you cannot use a variable for the `linenum` parameter. That is, if `Target` is an integer variable, the following instruction is *not* legal (even if the value of `Target` corresponds to a valid line number):

```
GoTo Target
```

Using GoTo, you can branch to any location in the current procedure: to a previous or subsequent line, or even to the same line. You cannot, however, branch to a line within another Sub or Function procedure. Within a procedure, you should branch only to another line at the same level. Avoid branching to or from a multiline If construct, For loop, or similar structure. Use GoTo to control logic flow only within such structures. (These structures are explained later in this chapter.)

Remember that GoTo instructions inevitably create nasty programs with a logic flow branching in all directions. This kind of "spaghetti logic" is difficult to read and hard to debug. Experienced programmers, therefore, avoid the use of GoTo. You will be much more successful in your programming if you rarely use GoTo. You will probably never find a programming problem that cannot be easily and clearly solved without any GoTos.

The GoTo statement and the On-GoTo statement (described in the next section) are included in this chapter so that you will understand how they work in case you have to help debug someone else's program. Again, you are not encouraged to use these statements yourself.

Conditional Branching with *On-GoTo*

The On-GoTo instruction extends the GoTo concept. With On-GoTo, you branch to one of a specified set of lines, according to the value of a numeric expression. Note the following examples:

```
On numexpr GoTo labellist

On numexpr GoTo linenumlist
```

numexpr is a general numeric expression that evaluates to a value from 0 to 255. labellist is a list of one or more labels separated by commas. linenumlist is a list of one or more line numbers separated by commas.

The value of the numeric expression determines which line in the label list (or line number list) executes next. Branching occurs to the corresponding line in the list—to the first listed line if numexpr is 1, the second listed line if numexpr is 2, and so on.

If numexpr is 0 or is greater than the number of lines in the list, execution simply continues with the instruction immediately after the On-GoTo. If numexpr is negative or is greater than 255, the program terminates with the Illegal function call error.

Here is an example of On-GoTo:

```
On NumSingers% GoTo Solo, Duet, Trio, Quartet
```

The value of NumSingers% determines the line that executes next. If NumSingers% equals 1, the program branches to the label Solo: and continues from there. If NumSingers% equals 2, the program goes to the label Duet:. If NumSingers% equals 3, the program branches to the label Trio:. If NumSingers% equals 4, the branch is to Quartet:.

If `NumSingers%` is 0 or is greater than 4 (but not greater than 255), the program continues with the line that immediately follows the `On-GoTo` instruction. If `NumSingers%` is negative or is greater than 255, the `Illegal function call` error occurs. The same destination can appear in your line number list or label list more than once.

`On-GoTo` has limited use because the programming situation must be just right in order for this instruction to be practical. Like `GoTo`, the `On-GoTo` statement is outmoded. Visual Basic's `Select` statement and multiline `If` statements (discussed later in this chapter) provide better, more flexible, modern tools for conditional branching.

The *On Error GoTo* Statement

This statement is used to enable an error-handling procedure in your program. If you don't use the `On Error` statement in the program, any run-time error that occurs in the program will stop its execution. The `On Error GoTo` statement is fully discussed in the next chapter.

Ending Program Execution

The most abrupt way to alter program flow is to terminate your program. To end it, use the `End` instruction:

    End

Using `End` is equivalent to clicking the Stop button on the Toolbar or choosing the **E**nd option from the **R**un menu. The program stops execution. Any open files are closed (files are discussed in Chapter 12), and the values of all variables are cleared. If you are running the program from Visual Basic (instead of running an EXE version of the program from Windows), you return to the design environment.

No restriction exists on the number of `End` instructions you can have in a single procedure or throughout your program.

Typically, you use `End` in an event procedure that must respond to the user's request to terminate the program. For example, to terminate an application when the user clicks a command button labeled Quit, you can place an `End` instruction in the `Click` procedure associated with that button.

Unlike `End`, which terminates program execution completely, the `Stop` instruction suspends execution temporarily. When execution is suspended, you can use the Debug window and later resume execution. For more information on `Stop`, see Chapter 8, "Testing and Debugging Your Program."

Note: *What happens to program flow when a procedure terminates depends on the type of procedure and how it began executing in the first place.*

When an event procedure terminates, program flow is suspended until a subsequent event invokes another procedure. (The new event, however, might reinvoke the just-terminated procedure.) Sub *or* Function *procedures (general procedures, not event procedures) are explicitly called from another procedure. When a general procedure terminates, control returns to the procedure (the calling procedure) that invoked the* Sub *or* Function. *Program flow continues at, or just after, the invoking instruction.*

Conditional Testing

Logic juncture
A place in a program where the execution path can go different ways.

Test condition
A logical statement that the computer can evaluate as either True or False.

Decision making is a constant programming theme. A **logic juncture** is a place in your program where the execution path can go different ways. The program chooses the path based on the evaluation of a **test condition**.

Depending on the type of test condition, Visual Basic offers two flexible program structures. The If structure tests for True and False conditions, and the Select Case structure tests for values within specified ranges.

Testing with the *If* Instruction

The If statement tests whether an expression is True or False and then directs program flow accordingly. With a block If instruction, you can perform successive True and False tests.

The If instruction has many forms, but they all fit into one of two categories: single-line If or multiline If.

Single-Line *If*

Here are the two classic If-Then-Else single-line forms:

```
If condition Then thenclause

If condition Then thenclause Else elseclause
```

condition is any expression that evaluates to True or False. thenclause is the action to perform if condition is True, and elseclause is the action to perform if condition is False. The Else elseclause phrase is optional.

The following is an example of a procedure containing the simplest form of the If-Then instruction:

```
Sub Form_Click ()
    Dim Temp As Single
    Temp = Val(InputBox$("What is the temperature?"))
    If Temp > 100 Then MsgBox "It is hot"
    Print "So long for now"
End Sub
```

The Val function converts the string returned by the InputBox$ function into a numeric value.

7

Trying Out a Single-Line *If* Statement

Now try using a single-line If by following these steps:

1 Start a new project. Enter the program fragment shown in the preceding example, offering an opinion about the weather:

```
Sub Form_Click ()
    Dim Temp As Single
    Temp = Val(InputBox$("What is the temperature?"))
    If Temp > 100 Then MsgBox "It is hot"
    Print "So long for now"
End Sub
```

2 Run the program, and enter some trial temperatures.

If you enter a number higher than 100 when prompted for the temperature, the program responds by opening a box displaying this message:

```
It is hot
```

When you click the OK button to close the message box, the program responds by displaying the following message on the form:

```
So long for now
```

If you reply with a number of 100 or lower, the program displays So long for now immediately, without ever opening the It is hot message box.

The program opens a box that displays the message It is hot only if the value of the variable Temp is greater than 100. (The > character is a relational operator meaning "greater than.")

Relational operators are discussed later in this chapter.

When the test condition of an If-Then instruction is False, Visual Basic disregards the part of the instruction after Then. The program moves to the next program line immediately.

Adding an *Else* Clause to *If-Then*

Suppose that you want to execute two different instructions: one if the test condition is True, and another if it is False. A second form of the If-Then statement adds an Else clause solely for this purpose.

To see how the form works with an Else clause, you can change the If-Then instruction so that the new procedure resembles this:

```
Sub Form_Click ()
    Dim Temp As Integer
    Temp = Val(InputBox$("What is the temperature?"))
    If Temp > 100 Then MsgBox "It is hot" Else MsgBox "Not too bad"
    Print "So long for now"
End Sub
```

If you input a temperature value greater than 100, the result is the same as before. If you input a value of 100 or lower, however, the program opens a box in which the Not too bad message appears.

By adding an Else clause to an If-Then instruction, you specify what to do when the testing condition is False (the Else part) or True (the Then part). Figure 7.1 illustrates this concept.

Figure 7.1

The If-Then-Else instruction.

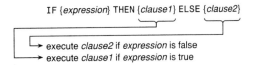

IF {*expression*} THEN {*clause1*} ELSE {*clause2*}

→ execute *clause2* if *expression* is false
→ execute *clause1* if *expression* is true

Then and Else Clauses

The Then and Else clauses can take many different forms. For starters, each clause can be any single Visual Basic instruction. Here are a few sample instructions:

```
If A = B Then MsgBox "Same" Else MsgBox "Different"

If A = B Then GoTo Identical Else GoTo Unequal

If A = B Then Beep

If A = B Then Profit = 20 Else Profit = Cost * Discount
```

The Then or Else clause can also contain multiple instructions. You simply separate each instruction with a colon, as in this example:

```
If Score > 500 Then Rate = 3.5: Num = 29: Winner$ = "Debby"
```

This instruction tests whether the value of the variable Score is greater than 500. If so, then the values of Rate, Num, and Winner$ are assigned the values 3.5, 29, and "Debby", respectively. If the value of Score is less than or equal to 500, control passes directly to the next line without assigning values to any of the three variables.

Table 7.1 summarizes the various forms of Then and Else clauses that you can use in an If instruction.

7

Table 7.1	Syntax Forms for *Then* and *Else* Clauses
Syntax	**Action Taken**
instructions	*instructions* are one or more Visual Basic directives separated with colons. After the instructions execute, control passes to the line following the If instruction.
GoTo *label*	*label* is a valid line label. Control passes to the line designated by the label. In such a clause, the Then or Else keyword is optional.
GoTo *linenum*	*linenum* is a valid line number. Control passes to the line designated by the line number. In such a clause, the Then or Else keyword is optional.
linenum	*linenum* is a valid line number. Control passes to the line designated by the line number. In such a case (when the GoTo keyword is omitted), the Then or Else keyword must appear.

Types of Testing Expressions

In an `If` instruction, the testing condition must be a **Boolean expression**, which simply means an expression that evaluates to True or False. Boolean expressions are really just numbers. Internally, Visual Basic needs a way to represent Boolean values—that is, a way to represent True and False. Visual Basic uses simple integer numbers: 0 for False and –1 for True. Boolean expressions, therefore, are really just special cases of numeric expressions.

When Visual Basic evaluates a Boolean expression, False becomes 0, and True becomes –1. (When VB converts a number to a Boolean value, 0 becomes False, and any nonzero number becomes True.)

Demonstrating Boolean Expressions

You can demonstrate this conversion with a short test:

1 Start a new project. Enter the following code in the form's `Click` event:

```
NumItems% = 0
If NumItems% Then MsgBox "Nonzero" Else MsgBox "Zero"
```

2 Run the program to see the result.

In the `If` instruction, the variable `NumItems%` is itself a Boolean expression. This example opens a dialog box displaying the message `Zero`, which demonstrates that 0 is treated as False.

3 Now change the assignment instruction so that the value of `NumItems%` has any nonzero value. Use the following example:

```
NumItems% = 22
```

4 Run the program again to see the result.

This example now displays `Nonzero` because the Boolean expression has become True.

5 Delete the existing instructions in the form's `Click` event, and enter the following instruction in the `Click` event:

```
Print 129 > 45
```

Does this instruction appear odd? What do you think the output will be?

6 Run the program to see the result.

7 Now replace the old `Print` instruction with `Print 45 > 129`.

Here are some more examples of Boolean expressions in a single-line `If` statement:

```
If Num% < 0 Then MsgBox "Number is negative"
If Num% <= 0 Then MsgBox "Number is not positive"
```

```
If Animal$ = "Dog" Then MsgBox "It's a pooch"

If (MyScore + HerScore) > YourScore Then MsgBox "You lose"
```

The first example uses the "less than" operator (<) to test the value of the variable Num%. The second example is different from the first in a subtle way, namely the "less than or equal to" operator (<=). Notice that both the first and second lines display their messages when Num% is negative. Neither line displays a message when Num% is positive. The difference arises when Num% is exactly zero. The second line displays its message, but the first line does not.

The third example demonstrates that testing expressions can be string as well as numeric. In this example, the "equals" operator (=) tests whether the string stored in Animal$ is Dog. If it is, the line displays the message It's a pooch. In relational expressions, the equal sign really means "equals" (as opposed to the equal sign in assignment instructions, which means "is assigned the value"). Notice that the expression is True only when there is an exact match. If Animal$ has the value DOG (all caps), the result is False. Dog and DOG are *not* identical strings.

The final example shows an expression involving parentheses. In this example, the values of MyScore and HerScore are added together. Then this sum is compared with the value in YourScore to determine whether the expression is True or False.

The Relational Operators

Visual Basic provides six relational operators for use in testing expressions. The operators are shown in table 7.2. Note that each example in the third column of the table is True.

Table 7.2   Relational Operators

Symbol	Name	Example
=	Equals	4 = (3 + 1)
<>	Not equal	"Dog" <> "Cat"
>	Greater than	8 > 5
<	Less than	3 < 6
>=	Greater than or equals	9 >= 9
<=	Less than or equals	"Hi" <= "Ho"

Relational operators work on strings as well as on numbers. One string "equals" another only if both strings are the same length and contain the exact same sequence of characters. But how can one string be "greater than" or "less than" another? How does the last example in table 7.2 work?

Every string character has an associated numeric value from 0 to 255. These values conform to an established code known as ANSI (American National Standards Institute). In ANSI, for example, an *A* is 65, and an asterisk (*) is 42. For more information on this topic, see the VB Help topic "ANSI Character Set."

Using ANSI, you can compare two strings character by character. Characters at the same position in each string are compared (the first character with the first character, the second with the second, and so on). As soon as one pair of characters is different, the comparison stops. The ANSI values of the two characters (in the pair) are compared. One character must have a larger ANSI value than the other. The string containing the "larger" character is considered to be the "larger" of the two.

Consider the last example in table 7.2, which compares `"Hi"` with `"Ho"`. Both strings have `H` as their first character. The second character in each string, however, is different. The ANSI value of `i` is 105, and `o` has a value of 111. Therefore, `o` is larger than `i`, and `"Ho"` is larger than `"Hi"`.

If one string is longer than the other, the same rules apply on a character-by-character basis. For example, `"Don"` is larger than `"Dance"` because `o` has a larger ANSI value than `a` (even though `"Dance"` has more characters than `"Don"`). However, if the shorter string contains the same characters as the beginning of the longer string, the longer string is considered to be larger. For example, `"Dock"` is larger than `"Do"`.

Compound Testing Expressions

Sometimes you need to test two or more conditions. Suppose that you want to assign the value `Perfect` to `Result$` only if *both* the following conditions are True:

    The value of Score% is 300

    The value of Game$ is "Bowling"

You can use the following instruction:

    If (Score% = 300) And (Game$ = "Bowling") Then Result$ = "Perfect"

This instruction uses a compound expression for the test. Note that the two conditions are combined with the logical operator `And`. Both conditions must be True in order for Visual Basic to assign the value `Perfect` to the variable `Result$`. If only one condition is True (or if neither condition is True), the test fails, and program flow proceeds directly to the next line.

The parentheses in this sample `If` instruction are not required, but they make the line easier to read and understand. In similar instructions, most programmers recommend that you use parentheses for clarity.

The Logical Operators

The sample `If` instruction uses `And` to combine the two conditions. `And` is one of Visual Basic's six logical operators. The logical operators combine Boolean expressions to create one large Boolean expression. (Remember that a Boolean expression is one that evaluates to True or False.)

The most common logical operators are `And`, `Or`, and `Not`. They work in the following ways:

And   Combines two expressions; each expression must be True for the entire expression to be True.

Or   Combines two expressions; either expression (or both expressions) must be True for the entire expression to be True.

Not   Negates a single expression.

The following is an example of Not:

```
If Not (Score% = 300) Then Result$ = "Could do better"
```

Visual Basic has three other logical operators: Xor, Eqv, and Imp. They work in the following ways:

Xor   Combines two expressions; one (but not both) must be True for the entire expression to be True.

Eqv   Combines two expressions; both must be either True or False for the entire expression to be True. (Eqv is the "opposite" of Xor.)

Imp   Combines two expressions; the entire expression is True, except when the first expression is True and the second is False.

Figure 7.2 shows the results returned by all logical operators. In the figure, A and B represent Boolean operands that have a value of T (True) or F (False). The figure has four lines because four possible "truth configurations" for the two combined expressions exist.

Figure 7.2
Results of logical operators.

OPERAND VALUE		VALUE OF LOGICAL OPERATION					
A	B	Not A	A And B	A Or B	A Xor B	A Eqv B	A Imp B
T	T	F	T	T	F	T	T
T	F	F	F	T	T	F	F
F	T	T	F	T	T	F	T
F	F	T	F	F	F	T	T

7

Nested *If* Instructions

You can nest If instructions to two or more levels. The following is the basic form:

```
If condition1 Then If condition2 Then clause
```

With Else clauses, the form resembles the following:

```
If cond1 Then If cond2 Then clause1 Else clause2 Else clause3
```

Nested `If`s provide another way to write compound tests. The example used here is the `If` instruction that appeared earlier in the chapter. The instruction contains a compound testing expression:

```
If (Score% = 300) And (Game$ = "Bowling") Then Result$ = "Perfect"
```

With nested `If`s, the following instruction is equivalent:

```
If Score% = 300 Then If Game$ = "Bowling" Then Result$ = "Perfect"
```

Avoid nesting `If` instructions in a single program line. Such instructions become confusing quickly. Things get even more muddled when nested `If` instructions contain `Else` clauses. The reason is that it's hard to know which `If` test the `Else` is associated with and how the branching occurs.

Multiline *If*

You can extend `If` instructions from a single line to a multiline block. A block structure creates more understandable program instructions when one of the following occurs:

- The *thenclause* or *elseclause* contains two or more instructions.

- `If` instructions are nested.

- An `If` instruction extends past one line.

You should use a single-line `If` instruction only when the *thenclause* and *elseclause* each contain just one instruction, and when the entire `If` instruction easily fits into one line. In these cases, the `If` instruction is easily understandable. In other cases, break the single-line `If` instruction into a multiline block.

The single-line `If` form is never mandatory. You can always write any `If`-`Then`-`Else` instruction using the multiline form. Here is the syntax of the multiline `If`:

```
If condition Then
    {instructions}
ElseIf condition Then
    {instructions}
ElseIf condition Then
    {instructions}
Else
    {instructions}
End If
```

condition is a Boolean expression (any expression that evaluates to True or False). *instructions* are a block of one or more instructions placed on separate program lines. `ElseIf` blocks are optional; you can use as many as you need. The `Else` block is optional also.

The following is a simple example of a multiline `If`:

```
If Amount > 100.0 Then
    NumLargeChecks% = NumLargeChecks% + 1
    MsgBox "Another large check"
Else
    NumSmallChecks% = NumSmallChecks% + 1
```

```
    MsgBox "Just a small check"
End If
```

The first line on the multiline If always begins with an If clause and terminates with the Then keyword. Nothing can follow Then on this first line; that's how Visual Basic differentiates a multiline If structure from a single-line If.

The last line is always End If. Notice that a space separates the keywords End and If.

You can use any number of ElseIf clauses. Notice that ElseIf is one keyword; there is no internal space. Only one Else clause can appear.

Clauses evaluate sequentially. Visual Basic first checks the initial If clause. If True (nonzero), the first set of instructions executes (that is, the group of instructions following Then), and program flow continues with the line after End If. If False (zero), each ElseIf clause is tested, one at a time.

As soon as one ElseIf clause is True, the associated set of instructions executes, and program flow continues with the line after End If. If every ElseIf clause is False, or if there are no ElseIf clauses, the instructions associated with the Else clause execute. If no Else clause appears, program flow resumes at the line after End If.

You can nest If structures to any level you want. For clarity, however, a good recommendation is that you have only three levels of If statements. If your problem requires deeper nesting, place deeper levels of nesting in general procedures and then call them. Note this example:

```
If Condition1 Then
    If Condition2 Then
        Call TestRemainingConditions
    Else
        Call TestAdditionalConditions
    End If
End If
```

The following is an example of a block If structure that demonstrates the use of ElseIf clauses:

```
If MyNumber% = 0 Then
    MsgBox "Zero"
ElseIf MyNumber% = 1 Then
    Total% = Total% + 1
    MsgBox "One"
ElseIf MyNumber% >= 2 Then
    Total% = Total% + 2
    MsgBox "Greater than one"
Else
    MsgBox "Negative"
End If
```

This program fragment evaluates the value of MyNumber% and displays an appropriate message.

When writing multiline structures such as nested If blocks, take advantage of indentation to clarify the block structure. In the sample program fragments presented here, notice how indentation makes the components of the block structure apparent.

Testing with *Select Case*

The Select Case structure tests whether the value of an expression falls within predetermined ranges, whereas the If structure tests for True and False conditions. Use Select Case to execute instructions conditionally, depending on the value of a test expression. Select Case has the following form:

```
Select Case expression
    Case testlist
        {instructions}
    Case testlist
        {instructions}
    Case Else
        {instructions}
End Select Case
```

expression is any general numeric or string expression. *testlist* is one or more test ranges, separated by commas. *instructions* are a block of one or more instructions placed on separate program lines.

Case blocks are optional. You can have as many as you need. The Case Else block is optional also. Note the following example of Select Case:

```
Select Case Age%
    Case 1 To 12
        MsgBox "Child"
        NumChildren% = NumChildren% + 1
    Case 13 To 19
        MsgBox "Teenager"
        NumTeens% = NumTeens% + 1
    Case Is > 19
        MsgBox "Adult"
        NumAdults% = NumAdults% + 1
    Case Else
        MsgBox "Impossible"
End Select
```

The testing expression can be numeric or string. The value of *expression* is tested against the ranges in the various test lists. The *expression* and the test expressions in each *testlist* must agree in type—either all numeric or all string.

Each *testlist* specifies a range of values against which the value of *expression* is compared. *testlist* has the following general forms:

testexpr1 To *testexpr2*	The test is True if the value of *expression* lies within the range from *testexpr1* To *testexpr2*.
Is *rel-op testexp*	*rel-op* is one of the six relational operators: =, >, <, <>, >=, <=. The test is True if the value of *expression* satisfies the relational expression.
testexpr	The test is True if the value of *expression* equals that of *testexpr*.

The expressions *testexpr*, *testexpr1*, and *testexpr2* are any expressions that agree in type (string or numeric) with the expression on the Select Case line. Table 7.3 shows some sample test ranges.

Table 7.3 Sample Test Ranges	
Type	**Example**
Relational	Case Is >= 39
Equality	Case Is = 21.6
Equality (implied "=")	Case 21.6
Explicit range	Case -7 To 7
Multiple	Case Is <> 14, Is < 101

Notice that *testlist* consists of two or more test ranges separated by commas. A multiple test evaluates to True if any of the individual tests are True.

Select Case evaluates each Case clause sequentially, looking for a match. The first time that *expression* is within one of the ranges specified by a *testlist*, the associated *instructions* block executes. Then control passes to the line following the End Select.

If every Case test is False, the *instructions* block following the Case Else executes. If no Case Else clause is present, program flow passes to the line following End Select.

Any meaningful Select Case structure contains at least one Case test. If you write a Select Case structure containing no Case test, however, no error occurs. In that situation, program flow passes to the line following End Select.

Select Case enables you to replace multiple If constructions with more elegant, understandable instructions. Use Select Case liberally. When you're contemplating convoluted If tests, you should use Select Case instead to make your programs more understandable.

The following program fragment displays information about the first character of a test string. The test string is stored in the variable MyString$. The expression Left$(MyString$, 1) returns the first character of MyString$.

```
Select Case Left$(MyString$, 1)
   Case ""
     MsgBox "Null String"
   Case "A", "E", "I", "O", "U", "a", "e", "i", "o", "u"
     MsgBox "Vowel"
   Case "A" To "Z", "a" To "z"
     MsgBox "Consonant"
   Case "0" To "9"
     MsgBox "Numeric Digit"
   Case Else
     MsgBox "Special Character"
End Select
```

Notice how this example works when `MyString$` begins with a letter. If the letter is a vowel, the second `Case` clause is True. Even though the third `Case` clause includes all letters (and therefore the vowels), the vowels are intercepted earlier by the second `Case` clause.

Looping

Loop
A group of instructions that executes repeatedly.

A **loop** is any group of instructions that executes repeatedly. For example, the following `Form_Load` event procedure contains a loop:

```
Sub Form_Load ()
    Show
    MsgBox "Click to begin beeping"
    Print "Now beeping incessantly"
DoBeeps:
    Beep
    GoTo DoBeeps
    Print "Why am I never executed?"
End Sub
```

Running an Infinite Loop (How to Keep a Computer Busy for Hours)

Try this exercise by following these steps:

❶ Start a new project. Enter the code shown in the preceding example in the `Form_Load` procedure:

```
Sub Form_Load ()
    Show
    MsgBox "Click to begin beeping"
    Print "Now beeping incessantly"
DoBeeps:
    Beep
    GoTo DoBeeps
    Print "Why am I never executed?"
End Sub
```

❷ Run the application.

❸ When you have seen (and heard) enough, press **Ctrl+Break**.

Why does this program not stop like a normal program? It just keeps running because it is stuck in an endless loop. Take a look at the execution of the program to see how this happens.

First, the `Form_Load` procedure obtains control, just as it should, when the form is loaded. Next, the `Show` method displays a blank form. Then the `MsgBox` instruction opens a dialog box indicating that beeping begins when you click the box. When you click the box (or press Enter), the dialog box closes, and the message Now beeping incessantly appears on the form.

The loop begins with the label DoBeeps: in the fifth line. The end of the loop is the GoTo instruction in the seventh line. This is an example of an *endless loop*— there is no programmed way for the loop and the beeping to stop. The Print instruction in the final line (just above End Sub) can never execute because the computer never gets to it. Instead, the program always branches back up to begin the loop again. To stop a program stuck in an endless loop, you press Ctrl+Break. This places your program in Break mode, and you can then end the program by clicking the Stop button in VBs Toolbar. You can see how using a GoTo statement can easily create problems in your programs.

Controlled loop
A loop that executes until a predetermined condition is satisfied.

A useful loop must have a way to end. A loop with an ending mechanism is called a controlled loop. A **controlled loop** executes until a predetermined condition is satisfied. Some form of a controlled loop occurs in many programs.

Visual Basic provides three special structures for the programming of controlled loops:

For-Next

While-Wend

Do-Loop

The characteristics of each structure are similar yet different. When programming a controlled loop, you choose For-Next, While-Wend, or Do-Loop.

As figure 7.3 shows, your choice generally depends on the answers to the following two questions:

- *Do you know how many times you must go through the loop before it ends?* In other words, is there a fixed number of times that you want the statement group (inside the loop) to execute?

Counter variable
A numeric variable that controls the number of repetitions in a loop.

- *Must the loop execute at least one time?*

Using *For-Next* Loops
A For-Next loop uses a numeric variable to control the number of repetitions. This special variable is called a **counter variable** or control variable.

7

Figure 7.3
Choosing the appropriate loop structure.

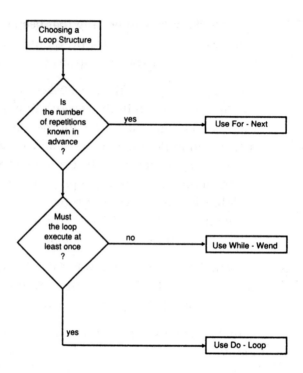

Trying Out a *For-Next* Loop

In this exercise, you display a table of the squares of the numbers from 0 to 6. (The square of a number is simply the number multiplied by itself.) This kind of task is perfect for a For-Next loop. Follow these steps:

1 Start a new project, and open the Code window.

2 Choose **View** from the main Visual Basic menu, and then choose **New Procedure**.

3 Type the name of the procedure, **ShowSquares**, in the dialog box. Close the box by pressing **Enter** or clicking OK.

4 Enter the following general procedure in the form:

```
Sub ShowSquares ()
    Rem - Display Squares of Numbers
    Print "Number", "Square"
    For Number% = 0 To 6
        Square% = Number% * Number%
        Print Number%, Square%
    Next Number%
    Print "End of table"
End Sub
```

5 Enter a `Form_Click` event procedure that calls `ShowSquares`:

```
Sub Form_Click ()
    Call ShowSquares
End Sub
```

6 Run the application, and click anywhere on the blank form.

The `Click` event triggers the `Form_Click` procedure that calls `ShowSquares`. Here is the output from `ShowSquares`:

```
Number        Square
0             0
1             1
2             4
3             9
4             16
5             25
6             36
End of table
```

In the `For-Next` loop, `Number%` is the counter variable. The value of `Number%` changes each time through the loop. The `For` instruction sets the first value of `Number%` to 0 and sets the final value to 6. The line beginning with `Next` marks the end of the loop. In a `For-Next` loop, all the instructions between `For` and `Next` are referred to as the body of the loop.

The body of a loop can have any number of instructions. Most loops are short, although loops with more than 30 instructions occur occasionally. In this example, the body of the modest loop consists of the two instructions between the `For` and `Next` lines.

The value of a counter variable, by default, increases by one each time through a `For-Next` loop. In this example, `Number%` eventually reaches 6. The body of the loop still executes because `Number%` has equaled, but not exceeded, the final value of the loop.

The `Next` instruction then increases the value of `Number%` to 7. Now, when control returns to the `For` instruction, the value of `Number%` is finally greater than the maximum loop value of 6, signaling that the loop is over. The program then proceeds to the first line after the `Next` instruction.

Using the *Step* Clause

By adding a `Step` clause to the end of the `For` instruction, you can alter the increment for the counter variable.

Trying Out *Step* in a *For-Next* Loop

To add a `Step` clause to a `For-Next` loop, follow these steps:

1 Modify the fourth line of the `ShowSquares` procedure to include a `Step` clause. Use the following code:

(continues)

Trying Out *Step* in a *For-Next* Loop   (continued)

```
Sub ShowSquares ()
    Rem - Display Squares of Numbers
    Print "Number", "Square"
    For Number% = 0 To 6 Step 2
        Square% = Number% * Number%
        Print Number%, Square%
    Next Number%
    Print "End of table"
End Sub
```

2 Run the program, and click on the form.

The output is now the following:

```
Number      Square
   0           0
   2           4
   4          16
   6          36
End of table
```

Each time through the loop, the Step clause specifies an increment of 2. As a result, Number% becomes successively 0, 2, 4, and 6.

With certain increments, you might not hit exactly the final value of the loop. Suppose that you write the For instruction as follows:

```
For Number% = 0 To 6 Step 4
```

The successive values of Number% increase by 4 (0, 4, 8 ...). Number%, therefore, never becomes 6, the designated final value of the loop. In such a case, the loop terminates whenever the counter variable becomes greater than the final value. In this example, the body of the loop executes only for Number% equal to 0 and 4.

You can specify negative increments. When the increment is negative, the counter variable decreases through the loop each time. For a proper "negative" loop, specify the final value of the counter variable to be smaller than the initial value.

Bypassing the Loop

Visual Basic bypasses a For-Next loop altogether if one of these two conditions is met:

- The starting loop value is greater than its final value when the Step increment is positive.

- The starting loop value is smaller than its final value when the Step increment is negative.

For example, you could change the `For` instruction in `ShowSquares` to the following:

```
For Number% = 5 To 2
```

This instruction specifies that the starting value of the loop (5) is greater than the final value (2). The default increment is 1 because no `Step` clause appears. Visual Basic "realizes" that you cannot count upward from 5 and reach 2! The loop, therefore, doesn't execute. The program output would now be the following:

```
Number        Square
End of table
```

Syntax of *For-Next*

You have now completed an intuitive introduction to `For-Next` loops. To specify such loops more formally, the following section presents the general syntax of `For-Next`:

```
For countervar = start To end Step increment
    .
    .       'body of loop
    .
Next countervar
```

countervar is a numeric variable acting as the counter variable. *start* specifies the initial value of *countervar*, and *end* specifies the final value of *countervar*. *increment* indicates how much to increase *countervar* each time through the loop, and *body of loop* is a block of Visual Basic instructions.

The `Step` *increment* clause is optional. Furthermore, *countervar* can be omitted in the `Next` instruction.

Using Variables in a *For* Instruction

You can specify loop limits and `Step` increments with variables or entire expressions. The following `For` instructions, for example, are all acceptable:

```
For Number% = 2 To Final%

For Number% = First% To Last%

For Number% = First% To Last% Step Increment%

For Number% = First% To Last% Step (Last% - First%) / 10

For Number% = (Value1% - Value2%) To 100
```

With the use of variables, a program can have different loop boundaries from run to run.

Allowing the User to Control Loop Boundaries

In this exercise, you modify the `ShowSquares` procedure to ask the user for the loop boundaries. When prompted, the user types values for the first and last entries in the table. Follow these steps:

(continues)

Allowing the User to Control Loop Boundaries   (continued)

❶ Alter the ShowSquares procedure as follows:

```
Sub ShowSquares ()
  Rem - Display Squares of Numbers (Get Limits From User)
  First% = Val(InputBox$("Please specify the first value"))
  Last% = Val(InputBox$("Please specify the last value"))
  Print "Number", "Square"
  For Number% = First% to Last%
    Square% = Number% * Number%
    Print Number%, Square%
  Next Number%
  Print "End of table"
End Sub
```

❷ Run the program, click the form, enter **3** for the first value, and enter **6** for the last value.

Notice how the For instruction now specifies the loop limits with the variables First% and Last%. The user supplies the values for First% and Last% by using the two InputBox$ functions.

Excluding the Counter Variable in a *Next* Instruction
In a Next instruction, the counter variable is optional. In other words, you can write the Next instruction as simply this:

```
Next
```

When you leave out the counter variable, the Next instruction automatically matches with the For instruction. It's good practice, however, always to include the counter variable in Next instructions. That way, you make the looping variables perfectly clear. When two or more loops are nested and the counter variables are included, Next instructions are much easier to understand.

Placing a Loop in a Single Line
You can specify an entire For-Next loop in one program line. You don't have to isolate the loop components into separate lines. Simply use colons to separate the individual instructions. (The body of the loop must be relatively small for a single-line loop to be feasible.) Note an example:

```
For Item% = 1 To LastItem%: Print Item%: Next Item%
```

To execute a loop in the Debug window, you must type the loop on a single line. For more information on using the Debug window, see Chapter 8, "Testing and Debugging Your Program."

Using the Counter Variable
The counter variable can be any numeric type. Usually, counter variables are type Integer (or Long). The following loop works fine, however, with a single-precision counter variable named Value!:

```
For Value! = 1 To 4
   Print Value!
Next Value!
```

The output is what you would expect:

```
1
2
3
4
```

Sometimes you need the counter variable to be Single, Double, or Currency. Suppose that the loop increment has a fractional value:

```
For Counter! = 0 To 1 Step 1 / 4
   Print Counter!
Next Counter!
```

The output now contains fractional numbers:

```
0
.25
.5
.75
1
```

If possible, use Integer (or Long) variables for your counter variables. Avoid Single or Double variables for two reasons. First, loops with integer counter variables execute faster than those with noninteger counter variables. Second, mathematical errors can occur when counter variables, or Step increments, are single- or double-precision. Remember that Visual Basic cannot represent most single- and double-precision numbers exactly, only approximately. Accuracy errors can cause the loop to execute an incorrect number of times when it contains a fractional Step clause (or fractional loop limits).

Nesting *For* Loops

You can nest For-Next loops to any level. Many practical programming projects take advantage of nested loops. When nesting loops, be sure that each loop uses a unique counter variable. Innermost loops execute the fastest (complete first). This means that the Next instructions for nested loops must occur in order, from the deepest nested loop to the outermost loop.

As an example of nested loops, the following procedure displays a multiplication table:

```
Sub MulTable ()      'Demonstrate nested loops
   Max% = 4              'Maximum value in table
   Print "Value 1", "Value 2", "Product"
   For A% = 1 To Max%
      For B% = A% To Max%
         Product% = A% * B%
         Print A%, B%, Product%
      Next B%
      Print
   Next A%
End Sub
```

7

The output resembles the following:

```
Value 1        Value 2        Product
1              1              1
1              2              2
1              3              3
1              4              4
2              2              4
2              3              6
2              4              8
3              3              9
3              4              12
4              4              16
```

The second For instruction begins an inner loop while the outer loop is still active. The counter variables for the outer and inner loops are A% and B%, respectively. Note how the second For instruction uses A% (the counter variable from the outer loop) as the lower limit of the inner loop. For that reason, Value 1 in the output table increases each time the inner loop restarts.

You can edit the second program line to change the value of Max%. By making this change, you can create larger (or smaller) multiplication tables.

When nesting For loops, if you omit the counter variable in Next instructions, each Next pairs with the most recently opened For. However, as noted previously, for program clarity and easier troubleshooting, it's a good idea to include the counter variable in each Next.

Note: *Be liberal when indenting the body of the loop. This is not a requirement of Visual Basic but merely common sense. Consistent indentation makes programs easier to read. As a result, programs are easier to understand and troubleshoot.*

The style used in this book places the For and Next keywords for each loop at the same indentation level. The body of the loop is indented three spaces. In nested For-Next loops, each level is successively indented three more spaces.

Common Traps in *For* Loops

The following are four "Don'ts" when working with For-Next loops:

- *Don't redefine the control variable inside the loop.* Never explicitly change the value of the counter variable inside the body of the loop. If you do, you are asking for problems. Beware of the common ways you might fall into this trap:

    Using the counter variable on the left side of an assignment instruction

    Making the counter variable the value requested from the user in a Text Box control or InputBox$ function

    Reusing the same counter variable in a nested loop

If you ever find yourself redefining a control variable inside a loop, throw some water on your face and then rethink your logic. A better way is bound to exist.

- *Don't depend on the value of the control variable outside the loop.* It's best to think of the counter variable as undefined after the loop terminates. You can reuse the counter variable in another place, often in a subsequent loop. Don't assume, however, that the counter variable has any particular value after the loop terminates.

- *Don't branch into or out of loops.* If it is absolutely necessary, you can use `GoTo` instructions that branch within (stay inside) the body of a loop. But don't ever branch into a loop from outside. If you do, the limits of the loop are not defined properly, and it might run indefinitely.

- *Don't use more than one* `Next` *for each control variable—pair each* `For` *instruction with a single* `Next`.

Terminating Loops with the *Exit For* Statement

Your problem solution may require you to terminate a loop before the final value of the counter variable is reached, although doing so can lead to bugs in your program. To terminate the loop, use the `Exit For` statement. Execution resumes just after the `Next` statement.

Suppose that you want to display the names contained in the array `EmployeeName$`. The array is dimensioned from 1 to 500. The exact number of employees is unknown, but it is lower than 500. The array, therefore, contains names from element 1 up to some (unknown) array element. The rest of the array values are just null (empty) strings.

The following loop displays the names. `Exit For` terminates the loop when the first null string is detected. (The upcoming discussion of `While-Wend` loops shows a more elegant way to solve this problem.)

```
For Counter% = 1 To 500
   If EmployeeName$(Counter%) = "" Then
      Exit For        'prematurely branches out of the loop
   Else
      Print EmployeeName$(Counter%)
Next Counter%
```

Using *While-Wend* Loops

`While-Wend` loops are controlled by a *condition* rather than a counter variable. Think of the condition as a True or False test placed at the top of the loop. The body of the loop continues to execute as long as the condition remains True. Here is the syntax of `While-Wend`:

```
While boolexpr
   .
   .     'body of loop
   .
Wend
```

boolexpr specifies the condition as a Boolean (True or False) expression. *body of loop* is any group of Visual Basic instructions.

The Boolean expression typically is a relational one that Visual Basic automatically evaluates to True or False. Such relational expressions are similar to the

True or False expressions you encountered in If instruction tests earlier in this chapter.

Note two examples of While conditions:

```
While TermX% < 100                      'relational expression
While (Day$ = "Mon") Or (Day$ = "Tue")  'compound logical
```

To terminate the body of the loop, use the Wend statement. In nested While-Wend loops, each Wend matches the most recently activated While.

Before executing the statements in the body of a While-Wend loop for the first time, Visual Basic evaluates the condition in your While instruction. If the condition is False, Visual Basic bypasses the loop entirely, and execution continues on the line immediately following Wend.

If the condition is True, the body of the loop executes. Control then returns to the While instruction, and the condition is reevaluated. As long as the condition remains True, the loop continues to execute.

Instructions within the body of the loop obviously must do something to affect the testing condition, or the loop is in danger of executing forever. Usually, the body of the loop modifies one or more variables that occur in the testing expression.

For an example of While-Wend, consider the following procedure that mimics a launching countdown:

```
Sub CountDown ()
    Rem Demonstrate While-Wend
    Dim TimeLeft As Integer
    TimeLeft = 5
    While TimeLeft >= 1            'Boolean condition
        Print TimeLeft
        TimeLeft = TimeLeft - 1
    Wend
    Print "Blast off"
End Sub
```

The output of CountDown is the following:

```
5
4
3
2
1
Blast off
```

The two instructions between While and Wend contain the body of the loop. Notice how the instruction immediately preceding the Wend decrements the value of TimeLeft with each pass through the loop. The condition in the While instruction is True, as long as TimeLeft has a value greater than or equal to 1.

As with For-Next loops, While-Wend loops can be nested to any level. You can write simple While-Wend loops on a single line by separating the instructions with colons.

The earlier section on For-Next loops discussed the programming problem of displaying employee names in an array dimensioned from 1 to 500. The following is a solution that uses a While-Wend loop and a compound testing condition.

The test for the end of the array is assimilated into the While condition with a logical And operator:

```
Counter% = 1
While (EmployeeName$(Counter%) <> "") And (Counter% <= 500)
    Print EmployeeName$(Counter%)
    Counter% = Counter% + 1
Wend
```

Using *Do-Loop* Loops

Do-Loop offers you the flexibility to create loops that extend the capabilities of While-Wend loops. Similar to While-Wend, Do-Loop uses a condition to control the loop. Do-Loop, however, is more flexible than While-Wend because you can place the condition at either the beginning of the loop or the end of the loop. Additionally, a Do-Loop loop can be exited without the condition being met if the End Do statement is met. The End Do statement is discussed later in this chapter.

Top-test form:

```
Do While boolexpr
    .
    .          'body of loop
    .
Loop
```

or

```
Do Until boolexpr
    .
    .          'body of loop
    .
Loop
```

boolexpr specifies the condition as a Boolean (True or False) expression. *body of loop* is any group of Visual Basic instructions.

Bottom-test form:

```
Do
    .
    .          'body of loop
    .
Loop While boolexpr
```

or

```
Do
    .
    .          'body of loop
    .
Loop Until boolexpr
```

boolexpr specifies the condition as a Boolean (True or False) expression, and *body of loop* is any group of Visual Basic instructions.

7

Notice that for both the top-test and the bottom-test forms, the loop begins with a `Do` statement and ends with a `Loop` statement.

Each testing condition must begin with `While` or `Until`. With `While`, the loop continues if the condition is True, but terminates if the condition is False. `Until` has the opposite effect: the loop continues if the condition is False, but terminates if it is True. Table 7.4 summarizes the effects of the `While` and `Until` keywords.

Table 7.4   Use of *While* and *Until* in *Do-Loops*

| | Value of Testing Condition | |
Keyword	True	False
While	Continue loop	Terminate loop
Until	Terminate loop	Continue loop

The top-test form of a `Do-Loop` is similar to a `While-Wend` loop. In fact, the following two loop constructions are equivalent:

```
Do While boolexpr
    .
    .          'body of loop
    .
Loop


While boolexpr
    .
    .          'body of loop
    .
Wend
```

A bottom-test `Do` loop must execute the loop body at least once. Such loops often terminate with an `Until` condition. The following loop, for example, asks repeatedly for a number from the user and then displays an appropriate message. When the user types *0*, the loop terminates:

```
Do
    Number! = Val(InputBox$("Type a number"))
    If Number! > 0 Then MsgBox "You're being positive"
    If Number! < 0 Then MsgBox "You're so negative"
Loop Until Number! = 0
```

In this example, note that if you enter a negative number, the words `You're being negative` are displayed. If you enter a positive number, the words `You're being positive` are displayed. And, as previously mentioned, if you enter a zero, you exit the loop.

The following example illustrates how the `While` and `Until` clauses can be used to perform the same task. The choice of when to use `While` or `Until` is usually a matter of personal preference and style.

```
x = 1
Print "The While loop example: ";
```

```
Do
   Print x;
   x = x + 1
Loop while x <= 5

Print
Print "The Until loop example: ";
x = 1
Do
   Print x;
   x = x + 1
Loop Until x > 5
```

Here is the output:

```
The While loop example: 1 2 3 4 5
The Until loop example: 1 2 3 4 5
```

The `While` portion of this example continues to loop as long as the value of x is less than or equal to 5. The `Until` portion of the example continues to reiterate until x has a value greater than 5.

The next example is the same as the preceding one, except that the initial values of x are changed from 1 to 6, which is greater than the upper limit of the loop. Because the test is at the bottom, however, the statements within the loop will always be executed at least once. Therefore, each loop will print the number 6 before exiting. This modified example is shown here:

```
x = 6
Print "The While loop example: ";
Do
   Print x;
   x = x + 1
Loop While x <= 5

Print
Print "The Until loop example: ";
x = 6
Do
   Print x;
   x = x + 1
Loop Until x > 5
```

Note the following output:

```
The While loop example: 6
The Until loop example: 6
```

In the following example, the initial values of x are set back to 1, but the `While` and `Until` conditions are moved from the bottom of the loop to the top (after the keyword `Do`).

```
x = 1
Print "The While loop example: ";
Do While x <= 5
   Print x;
   x = x + 1
Loop
```

```
Print
Print "The Until loop example: ";
x = 1
Do Until x > 5
  Print x;
  x = x + 1
Loop
```

When this programming example is executed, the output will be exactly the same as in the first example:

```
The While loop example: 1 2 3 4 5
The Until loop example: 1 2 3 4 5
```

Why? The output is the same because, once you are in the loop, whether the test is at the bottom of the current reiteration or at the top of the next reiteration does not matter—the loop will be exited before the statements are reexecuted.

The *Exit Do* Statement

As discussed earlier in this chapter, you can prematurely exit a For-Next loop with an Exit For instruction. Similarly, you can prematurely exit a Do-Loop block with an Exit Do instruction. When an Exit Do statement is executed, control is passed to the instruction immediately following the Loop statement.

Trying Out the *Exit Do* Statement

This exercise illustrates the use of the Exit Do statement. Follow these steps:

1 Start a new project, and enter the following code in the form's Click event:

```
Do While (1 = 1)
    var1 = Val(InputBox$("Enter the first number to be added"))
    If var1 = 0 Then
      Exit Do
    End If
    var2 = Val(InputBox$("Enter the second number to be added"))
    print var1;" plus ";var2;" equals ";var1 + var2
Loop
```

2 Run the program, and click the form.

In the Exit Do statement, the user is asked to enter two numbers. Once entered, the two values are added together, and the answer is displayed.

From a technical perspective, this program has two interesting points. First, the condition being tested is 1 = 1. By definition, this condition will always produce a True result, thus causing an endless loop. Second, if the user enters a zero as the first number value, the Exit Do command will be executed, and the loop will be ended. This technique of creating an endless Do loop containing programming logic that executes an Exit Do statement is a commonly used programming technique.

Even though the endless loop technique is often used by many professional programmers, other professional programmers feel that the Exit Do statement should be used only as a last resort and that the preceding example should be written as follows:

```
Do

    var1 = Val(InputBox$("Enter the first number to be added"))
    If var1 <> 0 Then
      var2 = Val(InputBox$("Enter the second number to be added"))
      print var1;" plus ";var2;" equals ";var1 + var2
    End If
Loop Until var1 = 0
```

This program runs exactly the same as the Exit Do programming example, but allows the loop to end naturally without the use of the Exit Do statement. The programming technique that you choose is strictly a matter of your preference and programming style.

Using Nested *Do-Loop* Statements

Like For-Next loops, Do-Loop loops can be nested.

Trying Out a Nested *Do-Loop* Loop

To see how a nested Do-Loop loop works, complete these steps:

1 Start a new project, and enter the form's Click event procedure:

```
        Outer = 1
        Do While Outer <= 5
            Inner = 1
            Do While Inner <= Outer
                Print "*";
                Inner = Inner + 1
            Loop
            Print
            Outer = Outer + 1
        Loop
```

2 Run the program, and then click the form.

As you review the results from this program, notice that the inner loop is run to completion during each reiteration of the outer loop. The output is shown here:

```
*
**
***
****
*****
```

In the second nested loop of the following example, the stars are replaced with the word In, and the word Out has been added to the second Print statement to illustrate further the nested loop process:

```
       Outer = 1
       Do While Outer <= 5
         Inner = 1
         Do While Inner <= Outer
           Print "In ";
           Inner = Inner + 1
         Loop
         Print "Out"
         Outer = Outer + 1
       Loop
```

Here is the output:

```
In Out
In In Out
In In In Out
In In In In Out
In In In In In Out
```

Chapter Summary

Normal program flow progresses, line by line, down a procedure. You often need, however, to alter this sequential order.

The most straightforward way to alter program flow is with branching. A branch is the direct transfer from one location in your procedure to another. With GoTo, you can make an unconditional branch. On-GoTo provides conditional branching: you branch to one of several instructions, depending on the value of a particular expression. Use of the GoTo statement is not advised because it can lead to bugs in your program.

Programs frequently need to make decisions. Often a condition is tested, and the program takes different actions, depending on the result of the test. If-Then-Else instructions and Select Case blocks provide versatile tools for conditional testing.

Loops are instruction blocks that execute repeatedly. Loops are one of the most common and useful programming structures. Many programming tasks involve repetitive calculations for which a loop is ideally suited.

A controlled loop executes a limited number of times. Visual Basic has special statements for three kinds of controlled loops: For-Next, when the loop should be executed a specified number of times; While-Wend, when the loop should be executed as long as a condition remains True; and Do-Loop, when the loop should be executed as long as a condition remains True, or until it becomes True.

In the next chapter, you learn how to track down and exterminate those pesky little critters that just seem to sneak into your program—program bugs.

Test Your Understanding

True/False

Indicate whether the statement is true or false.

1. A For-Next loop is an example of an unconditional branching statement.

2. In Visual Basic, a line label must be a number.

3. You should use the GoTo statement frequently in your programs.

4. To terminate the execution of a VB program, you should use the Stop statement in the program.

5. Multiline If statements must have an Else branch.

6. The < operator can be used only to test numeric variables or numbers.

7. The VB relational operator for "not equal" is <>.

8. For a conditional test that uses the Or operator, if *both* conditions are True, the entire expression is False.

9. If a VB program contains three or more If statements without an End If statement (that is, an "If inside an If inside an If"), the program will produce an error at run time.

10. While-Wend loops are controlled by a counter rather than a conditional statement.

Short Answer

Answer the following questions.

1. If you have a For-Next loop in which a variable I is the control variable, what will happen if you increment I inside the loop?

2. Write a nested Do-Loop in which the statements in the inner loop are executed five times for each execution of the outer loop.

3. Write a For-Next loop in which you exit the loop prematurely if a variable in the divisor of a formula becomes equal to zero.

4. Write a Do-Loop with a premature exit if a variable in the divisor of a formula becomes equal to zero. Rewrite this loop using a second loop inside the first loop. The inside loop should execute only if the divisor is not equal to zero. Which design is a better one in your opinion? Why?

5. Explain why the use of the GoTo statement—rather than the use of programming structures like If-Then-Else, Do While, and Do Until—should be avoided in proper program design.

6. If, in a series of If statements (a multiline If), every If and ElseIf clause is False, where does program flow resume?

7. Assume that a variable LastName contains an individual's last name. If an individual has a last name that begins with *A, E, I, O, U,* or *W,* that person is assigned a GroupNumber of 1. If the person's last name starts with *B, C, D, F, G, H,* or *J,* a GroupNumber of 2 is assigned. For a last name that starts with *M, N,* or *R,* a GroupNumber of 3 is assigned. All others are assigned a GroupNumber of 4. Write the Select Case statement (and any additional code) to do this group assignment.

8. Write the pair of For-Next loops (one nested inside the other) and any additional statements that would print (on a form) the multiplication table for the numbers 1 through 5. The table should be printed when the user clicks the form.

9. Explain how the comparison of "Andy" with "Anderson" would proceed in this If statement:

```
If "Andy" > "Anderson" Then Beep
```

How can one name be greater or less than another name?

10. Explain what a Boolean expression is and how VB evaluates a Boolean If-Then statement.

11. Write an If-Then statement that will cause the computer to beep if the user enters a number from 15 to 25.

12. Explain how the six logical operators are used in a VB If-Then statement. Code examples of each.

13. What is a nested If statement? Code an example of a VB nested If with four levels.

14. How is the Step clause used in a For-Next loop? Give a VB example.

15. Under what conditions will VB bypass a For-Next loop completely?

16. Under what conditions will VB bypass a top-test Do loop completely?

Projects

Project 1:   Writing a Program in Which the User Enters a Number

Write a program that enables a user to enter a number. If the number is less than 1, the program should display the message Your number is less than 1. and then request a new number. If the number is equal to 1, the program should display the message Your number is equal to 1. and request a new number.

If the number is greater than 1, the program should add all the integers from 1 to the number. Then the program should display the sum of all the integers. Use a top-test Do-While loop to calculate the sum of the integers. The program should end only if the user types the # character when the program requests a number from the user.

Save your project as **C7P1**. Print the form, form text, and code.

Project 2: Writing a Program That Prompts the User to Enter Characters in a Text Box

Write a program that prompts the user to enter from 1 to 12 uppercase alphabetic characters in a text box. Then the program should print (as output) each letter of the alphabet that was entered, as well as the number of times the letter occurred in the string of characters.

Save the project as **C7P2**. Print the form, form text, and code.

Project 3: Writing a Program That Displays the Number of Times a String Occurs

Write a program to determine (and display) the number of occurrences of the letter pair *ei* in a character string of up to 20 characters.

Save your project as **C7P3**. Print the form, form text, and code.

Project 4: Writing Program Versions That Count and Display Specified Letters in a String

Write two versions of a program to count and display the number of times the letter *C*, *D*, *E*, or *O* occurs in a string of up to 30 uppercase alphabetic characters entered by the user.

The first version of the program should use nested If-Then-Else statements (four of them) to count the occurrences of the individual letters. The second version should use the logical Or statement to count the number of times *C* or *D* or *E* or *O* occur.

Save your project as **C7P4**. Print the form, form text, and code.

Project 5: Writing a Program with Four Text Boxes

Write a program with four text boxes. In one text box, the user can enter a color. In the second text box, the user can enter a length in inches. In the third text box, the user can enter a width in inches. And in the fourth text box, the user can enter a weight in pounds. The program should continue to execute, prompting the user to enter new data sets until the user chooses a Stop button.

The program should count each occurrence of a *color+length+width+weight* entry that

> is red, from 10 to 12 inches in length and at least 5 inches in width, and from 2 to 7 pounds or is exactly 25 pounds

or

> is red or blue, 11 or 13 inches in length (or more than 8 inches wide and less than 5 pounds in weight)

or

> is not green, is not greater than 20 inches in length and wider than 3 inches, and weighs less than 4 pounds or more than 10 pounds.

When the user chooses Stop, the program should display the number of entries made, as well as the number of entries that met any (or all) the conditions. A

Print button should enable the user to create a hard copy of the program's output.

Remember that conditions written in English are subject to several interpretations (and many misinterpretations). Remember, too, that the first step in programming is to make sure that you understand the problem clearly. Check your understanding of the conditions with your instructor, and draw a flowchart (see Chapter 1) to demonstrate your understanding of the problem.

Establish a set of test data for your program that will test *all* possible combinations of conditions. This test data will demonstrate whether your problem solution is coded correctly. Make sure that all the various branches of your code are tested by the test data.

Save the program as **C7P5**. Print all the code in the project.

Project 6:   Writing a Program That Uses Integer and Prime Numbers

Write a program that accepts an integer number as input and then displays all the prime numbers less than or equal to that integer number.

CHAPTER 8

Testing and Debugging Your Program

The programming process is prone to error. No matter how carefully you plan a new project and then type the program code, you're going to find that often a complex application doesn't work quite right at first. Bugs come with the programming territory.

Fortunately, Visual Basic has many tools to help you debug programs and deal with errors. In this chapter, you learn about the testing and debugging features available from the **D**ebug menu, including tools for tracing a program and setting watch expressions. The chapter also covers error trapping. By writing an error handler, you can have your program anticipate certain errors and recover gracefully when they occur.

Objectives

By the time you have finished this chapter, you will be able to

1. Understand the Various Forms of Program Bugs

2. Systematically Test and Debug a Program

3. Use Visual Basic's Interactive Debugging Environment

4. Use the Debug Window

5. Trace the Execution of a Program

6. Set and Use Breakpoints and Watchpoints

7. Use the Calls Dialog Box in Debugging

8. Use Set **N**ext Statement, Sho**w** Next Statement, and Stop in Debugging

9. Use Error Trapping and Write Error-Handling Routines

The First Computer Bug

Bug
An error or problem in a program.

Debugging
The process of finding and correcting errors in a program.

Bug and *debug* are well-known terms in programming. A **bug** is an error or problem in a program. When an application doesn't work correctly, programmers say that the code has a bug. The process of finding and correcting the bug is called debugging the program, or simply **debugging**. How did these colorful terms originate?

When computers were in their infancy, some of their operators were having hardware problems. A computer was malfunctioning, and the operators went to take a look. They found a dead moth lodged in one of the electronic circuits. When they removed the moth, the computer resumed functioning normally. By eliminating the bug, the operators solved the problem. Thus, the earliest "bug" was, in fact, a real insect.

This first debugging was actually the correction of a hardware problem. The term *debugging*, however, has gradually evolved to mean the elimination of programming (software) errors. Errors are a fact of programming life. All programmers make mistakes, so don't feel bad when the inevitable errors occur. Recognize that errors are bound to happen, plan for them, learn from them, and continue with your programming tasks.

Good programming practices, discussed in Chapter 1 of this book, when followed in a disciplined way, will reduce the number of errors in your programs. If you find yourself spending many frustrating hours in front of the computer to remove bugs from your programs, you should examine and correct your programming practices. Plan your work carefully, and then work your plan.

Interactive Testing and Debugging

Every programmer—beginner or expert—makes mistakes. That's why testing and debugging are integral parts of developing any application. In fact, you can gauge programmers' experience by their attitude toward testing and debugging. Experienced programmers realize that for any program to work correctly, thorough testing is essential.

Some programmers despise testing and shun debugging. They would rather spend endless hours in the design and planning stages. By the time they actually type their programs, they feel confident that no bugs could have crept in.

Programmers at the other extreme say to themselves, "Let me just type something approximately close to what I need. I can fix the errors later." These programmers tend to produce sloppy, jumbled programs that are needlessly difficult to debug. A middle ground between these two extremes, of course, is preferable.

The sloppy-program trap is easy to fall into! Visual Basic's interactive nature and impressive debugging tools might lead you to think that you can readily debug your way out of any mess. Here are some of the debugging techniques you can use when troubleshooting:

- Displaying the values of variables or expressions after you stop your program (Print from the Debug window)

- Executing your program one line at a time (**D**ebug menu)

- Determining the location of nonspecific error messages (On Error GoTo)

- Repeatedly suspending and resuming execution (breakpoints, watchpoints, Stop, Ctrl+Break)

- Tracing your program's logic flow (**D**ebug menu)

The examples in this chapter are deliberately short and contain conspicuous errors. Most difficult problem-solving tasks occur in larger programs in which the errors are not so apparent. However, the main goals here are to show errors and demonstrate debugging techniques. The best teaching method for achieving these goals is to provide short, to-the-point examples.

A Debugging Philosophy

To write successful programs, you must perform the interrelated actions of testing and debugging:

- Testing refers to the actions that determine whether the program code runs correctly.

- Debugging is the subsequent action of finding and removing the errors (bugs).

Sometimes a test run shows clearly that an application has coding errors. The testing part can be easy, but the debugging process might be much more difficult. In a sense, testing and debugging never end. Every time you run a program, you are testing.

Programmers (cautious programmers, anyway) often say that every fairly large program has a bug waiting to be found. It's even possible that, despite painstaking editing, a programming error could be lurking somewhere in this book. Figure 8.1 illustrates the process of programming a project from beginning to end. As the figure lightheartedly demonstrates, you never really reach the end.

The following are some principles of a sound debugging and programming philosophy:

Algorithm
A step-by-step procedure for solving a problem.

- *Make sure that your algorithms are correct.* An **algorithm** is simply a step-by-step procedure for solving a problem. As you learned in Chapter 1, you can use flowcharts or pseudocode to design an algorithm. Or you can design an algorithm as simply a numbered series of steps that will produce the result you want.

8

Figure 8.1
The programming
process.

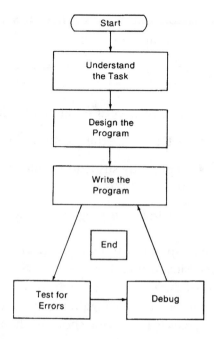

- *The easiest bugs to eliminate from your program are the ones you don't put there in the first place.* Don't just slap together some statements that "should work" and then run the program again and again until you finally say, "It works. I'm not sure why, but I'm done." Of course, it is true that the computer will find the errors eventually, and you can patch them up. This trial and error, however, is time-consuming and frustrating, and you don't really learn very much about programming. You won't become a better programmer with this approach.

  When I was learning programming at Penn State, we were allowed only five "runs" of each program assigned. The last run had to be turned in for grading. No way to get around it. No excuses. Believe me, you were very sure that you had thought through the problem and coded the solution correctly before you ever ran the program the first time. This was excellent training.

- *Use sound programming style.* Modularize your code as much as possible. Divide and conquer. The event-driven nature of Visual Basic encourages such practices. Make each of your Sub and Function procedures short and to the point. Break a large procedure into two or more smaller ones. Several smaller components are easier to understand, program, test, and debug than a larger one. Don't be tricky—keep your code as simple and straightforward as possible.

- *Always explicitly declare all variables you use, and turn on* Option Explicit. This setting ensures that variables are of the correct type. You also are alerted if you accidentally mistype the name of a variable in a procedure (creating a new, incorrect variable). Option Explicit is discussed later in this chapter.

- *Assume that your code has errors.* No one is perfect, nor does anyone write faultless code all the time. Write your code carefully, but expect to find errors later. Exposing the errors—all of them—is your purpose in testing and debugging. Enjoy the detective work.

- *No single test run can prove that an application is free of bugs.* Plan to run many test cases and use a variety of test data. A program that runs to completion and produces expected results is a good sign, but that's only the beginning of testing. And careless program design probably ensures that no amount of testing will ever identify all the problems hidden in your code.

- *Try to make your programs fail during testing.* Don't rely on "friendly" data when you test. If the program is destined to be used by others who must supply data, try all kinds of unreasonable values. Your users (or instructor) might type almost anything when prompted for input. Your goal should be an application that that cannot "crash" (produce a Visual Basic error message) or generate an incorrect result, no matter what users try.

- *While developing an application, test frequently.* After coding a new procedure, or writing just a few new lines, *test immediately.* It's best to work with small chunks of code. If you make many program changes or additions before testing, you're making your work more difficult than necessary. Do not type the whole program and then run it. The errors you have inadvertently placed in your program will compound each other. Ten errors that occur one at a time in successive test runs are much easier to figure out than ten errors happening all at once.

- *Don't try to write the final (production) version of your program first; write the development version first.* You can put all kinds of `Print` statements, `Beep` statements, and debugging statements in the first version of your program. You should add such statements to help you spot any bugs in your program immediately (as you test its parts). What you are trying to do is keep close track of what your program does *as it executes.* Make your program show you what is happening. Don't just rely on the final output statements.

  Using this approach is like dipping your program's feet in paint so that it will leave visual, on-screen tracks you can follow. Keep a tight rein on your program so that it doesn't "run away." Watch its every move, being sure that you know exactly what the program is doing at all times. Putting special output statements in your code is the only way to do this. Don't let your program just suddenly "blow up" or produce incorrect results without giving you any explanation for its failures.

  Remove all these special debugging statements before you turn in the completed version of your program.

- *If you are trying out a new statement you have never used before, test how it works before you add it to your program.* Don't use any code or techniques in your assigned program that you haven't first checked in a simple test program. Think of a series of statements that may not do anything special but will help you learn how to use the new statement. This kind of test is especially important for someone who is just beginning to learn a new programming language. You may think that this extra coding is just making more work for you. Not true. Years of experience have proved that this technique will save you much time and frustration.

- *Print troublesome chunks of code and then "play computer."* Go through the code, statement by statement. Keep track of the effect of each statement with a paper and pencil. Keep a systematic record of how values are changed inside memory locations (variables). Do exactly what you tell the computer to do in your program. Do only what your program says to do—not what you think it *should* do. This strategy will show you where the problems occur in your code.

For a minimum guide to debugging strategy, you should print the VB Help topic "Debugging Checklist."

Dealing with Run-Time Errors

Run-time error

An error not revealed until you run the program.

Errors that you don't discover until you run a program are called **run-time errors**. Three fundamental types of run-time errors can occur:

- *Syntax errors.* A syntax error occurs when an instruction doesn't follow the rules of Visual Basic. For example, you might spell a keyword incorrectly, use incorrect punctuation, combine keywords in an illegal way, or fail to provide enough parameters to a built-in function. In any of these cases, the instruction is meaningless, and Visual Basic cannot even *attempt* to execute it. The VB editor catches some syntax errors as you type statements; the remaining syntax errors are pointed out when you actually run the program.

- *Execution errors.* An execution error occurs when Visual Basic cannot perform a program instruction. The action requested by the instruction is impossible, even though its syntax is adequate. For example, you might divide a number by zero—a mathematically illegal operation. When an execution error occurs, Visual Basic enters Break mode and suspends execution. VB highlights the offending line in the program and displays an error message. The error message quickly points out the problem (although sometimes the cause is not obvious). For a list of execution errors, print the VB Help topic "Trappable Errors."

- *Logic errors.* A logic error occurs when a program runs to completion, but the results are not right. All the instructions have legal syntax, and Visual Basic executes the program and terminates normally. As far as VB is concerned, everything went well. However, the program just doesn't produce the correct results. Logic errors are the most difficult ones to debug. That's why it is so important to *think* about the problem and carefully work out your solution *before* you start typing code. Fortunately, Visual Basic's special debugging features are most helpful with these types of errors.

The following sections present simple examples of the three types of run-time errors. In practical applications, of course, your errors are bound to occur in more complex programs.

Finding a Syntax Error

Syntax errors are usually the result of simple typing mistakes. When a syntax error occurs, Visual Basic stops running the application and points out the faulty line. Take a look at an example of a syntax error now. Follow these steps:

❶ Start a new project, and type the following `Form_Resize` event procedure. Type the third line exactly as the program fragment shows, with `Print` incorrectly spelled as `Prnt`:

```
Sub Form_Resize ()
    Print "Hello"
    Prnt "Goodbye"
End Sub
```

Notice that nothing special happens when you type the incorrect line. This is an example of a syntax error that is not caught by Visual Basic until you try to run the program.

❷ Run the program.

Visual Basic immediately finds the syntax error. As figure 8.2 shows, the screen shifts back to the Code window, and a message box opens. In the box is a message indicating that a syntax error is present. The offending word, `Prnt`, is highlighted in your program code.

Figure 8.2

A syntax error occurs.

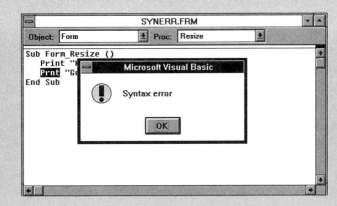

(continues)

8

Finding a Syntax Error   (continued)

❸ Click OK or press **Enter** to close the message box.

❹ You can now edit Prnt to read **Print**.

❺ Run the program. This time, no error occurs.

Visual Basic insists that you follow its rules. You might think that, given the sophistication of Visual Basic, the editor could "figure out" that Prnt should be Print. After all, the two words are very close. Prnt, however, is indecipherable to Visual Basic, and a syntax error results.

Next take a look at an example of an execution error.

Finding an Execution Error

When an error occurs during the execution of a program, Visual Basic suspends the program and displays an explanatory error message. To see how this process works, follow these steps:

❶ Start a new project, and type the following Form_Load procedure:

```
Sub Form_Load ()
    Dim NumHits As Integer, NumAB As Integer
    Dim Msg As String

    FindBatAve:
    NumHits = Val(InputBox$("Number of hits?"))
    NumAB = Val(InputBox$("Number of times at bat?"))
    Msg = "Batting average is " & NumHits / NumAB
    MsgBox Msg
    GoTo FindBatAve
End Sub
```

This procedure computes baseball batting averages. (A batting average is the total of a baseball player's hits divided by the number of times at bat.) The code uses several input boxes and one message box to get data from the user and to display the results. The code loops so that multiple batting averages can be computed.

❷ Use this program to calculate the three batting averages that follow.

A player had 128 hits in 523 at bats for an entire season.

A player had 27 hits in 79 at bats in one month.

A player had 8 hits in 30 at bats in one week.

Table 8.1 shows the program results. In this table, the first two columns represent values you type in response to the input box prompts. The third column shows the message displayed in the box that appears.

Table 8.1	Results of Batting Average Calculations	
Hits	**At Bats**	**Message Box Display**
128	523	Batting average is .2447419
27	79	Batting average is .3417721
8	30	Batting average is .2666666

❸ Now make a deliberate mistake when typing the input values. Enter **0** at bats and **8** hits.

When you try this fourth calculation, a problem develops. You entered 0 rather than 30 for the number of times at bat. This error means that the value of the variable NumAB becomes 0. In the line assigning a value for Msg, Visual Basic tries to divide by zero, which is an illegal mathematical operation.

What happens? Visual Basic enters Break mode and displays the Code window. As figure 8.3 shows, a message box opens to indicate a Division by zero error.

Figure 8.3

A Division by zero execution error.

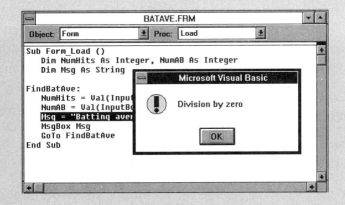

Visual Basic highlights the line in your program that caused the error.

(continues)

Finding an Execution Error   (continued)

❹ Click OK or press **Enter** to clear the error message box.

❺ Restart the program by pressing **Shift+F5**, choosing **Restart** from the **Run** menu, or clicking the Run button on the Toolbar.

❻ Verify that the program is still working correctly by entering **100** at bats and **50** hits.

❼ Break out of the loop by pressing **Ctrl+Break**, and then click the Stop button on the Toolbar.

Finding a Logic Error

As with most errors, the logic kind often results from simple typing mistakes. Consider the following user-defined procedure, named ShowCost, which contains a logic error:

```
Sub ShowCost ()
    Dim NumItems As Integer, UnitCost As Currency

    NumItems = 50
    UnitCost = 6.95
    Print "Total Cost ="; UnitCost / NumItems
End Sub
```

The following is the output produced by the Print instruction:

```
Total cost = .139
```

That answer can't be correct. The total cost is less than the cost of one item. The error is fairly obvious: the Print instruction divided by NumItems when multiplication was needed. In the program code, the division operator (/) should be replaced by the one for multiplication (*).

This program has no syntax or execution errors, only a logic error. The procedure executes to completion, but the result is just not correct. When you find that a program has a logic error, the first thing you should do is carefully check your typing. Make sure that your program code reads as you intended.

General Debugging Tips

Execution and logic errors often don't have any evident causes. Here are some general tips for debugging the less obvious types of errors:

- *Start by looking for the obvious.* Most errors result from obvious, not subtle, causes. Examine your program, and test data for simple mistakes, such as careless typing errors. Examples of common errors include nesting parentheses incorrectly, using variables of the wrong type, and interchanging the less-than (<) and greater-than (>) operators.

Usually, students "just know" where the problem is and go over and over the same piece of code without finding the error. However, the error is not where you are looking; you didn't make a mistake there. The error, small and simple, is somewhere else. Step back, stop making assumptions, and systematically search the whole program.

- *Obvious errors are often the hardest ones to find because you can't believe you could make such ridiculous mistakes.* Take heart, all programmers make them.

- *Reasonable-looking output can be wrong.* Usually, incorrect output is so wrong that it seems to leap out at you. Beware, though, of reasonable-looking output. The worst kind of error causes slightly incorrect results, which can lead you to assume carelessly that everything is working fine. Be suspicious. Check your output carefully.

- *Verify that the Visual Basic programming language works as you expect.* You might be making an incorrect assumption about how a Visual Basic statement, function, method, or event procedure works. Log, for example, works with natural, not common, logarithms. Double-clicking the mouse triggers a Click event as well as a DblClick event. Use this book and your Visual Basic documentation for confirmation.

- *Learn Visual Basic's debugging features and techniques.* These features and techniques are explained throughout this chapter.

Debugging Execution Errors

The following situation is familiar to all programmers: Your application aborts with an explanatory error message and a highlight on the offending line. But you can't figure out what's wrong. What do you do now?

This question has many answers, depending on what the error message is and what the program line contains. Here are some actions to try, along with tips about a few common error messages:

- *Look again for typing errors.* This tip cannot be stressed enough. Examine your program, and test data for simple errors that occur in your typing. Check that variable names are spelled correctly and that operators are accurate.

- *Print the current values of your main variables.* When your application aborts with an error message, you can use Visual Basic's Debug window to display (Print) the values of variables and expressions. This technique is discussed later in this chapter.

- *Split up multi-instruction program lines.* If you get a Subscript out of range error message for a line containing half a dozen subscript references spread over several instructions, you won't know which subscript is the culprit. Put each instruction on a separate program line, or split a long one into smaller components.

8

- *Search other parts of the program that manipulate the same variables*. If Visual Basic indicates that a program line is doing something illegal, the problem often stems from a previous line that erroneously computed the value of a variable. For global variables, you may need to check other procedures. The following error messages are frequently caused by incorrect manipulation of a variable elsewhere in the program:

    ```
    Illegal function call

    Subscript out of range

    Division by zero
    ```

- *Create error handlers*. With `On Error GoTo` instructions, you can branch to special routines that can process and recover from errors. Error handling is discussed later in this chapter.

Debugging with the Debug Window

One of the advantages of Visual Basic's interactive environment is that, after your program stops with an error message, you can perform your detective work from the Debug window. Most important, you can display the values of essential variables, expressions, and properties to help determine what went wrong.

In Break mode, Visual Basic retains the current values of all the variables and all property values. By issuing `Print` instructions from the Debug window, you can display the value of any variable, array element, or property.

Ways to Enter Break Mode

During program development and testing, the Debug window is available whenever Visual Basic is in Break mode. You can enter Break mode by using several methods. You can force a running application to enter Break mode with any of these actions:

- Pressing Ctrl+Break while an application is running
- Choosing Brea**k** from the **R**un menu while an application is running
- Clicking the Break button on the Toolbar while an application is running

Visual Basic itself automatically enters Break mode when one of the following conditions is met:

- A run-time error occurs.
- Program execution reaches a preset breakpoint.
- The value of a watchpoint expression changes or reaches a preset value.
- Visual Basic encounters a `Stop` instruction.

Each of these conditions is explained in this chapter.

Viewing the Debug Window

In Break mode, you can bring the Debug window to the foreground in one of three ways:

- Clicking a visible portion of the Debug window

- Pressing Ctrl+B

- Choosing the **D**ebug option from the **W**indow menu

Suppose that your program aborts with this error message:

```
Illegal function call
```

The highlight is on the following program line:

```
Length! = Sqr(Area!)
```

Apparently, the Sqr function failed because something is wrong with the value of Area!. To find out, you can activate the Debug window; type the instruction **Print Area!**, and press Enter. Visual Basic then displays the current value of Area!. You'll probably discover that Area! has a negative value. If so, that's the problem. Visual Basic's Sqr function works only with positive arguments (or zero).

Of course, if you do find that the value of Area! is negative, that's only the beginning of the whole solution. Then you must find out how the value of Area! was calculated. If Area! was manipulated several times before the line in which the error occurred, you need to backtrack to determine how the value of Area! erroneously became negative. More Print commands should narrow the problem.

Typing Instructions in the Debug Window

The Debug window executes instructions one line at a time. When you press Enter after typing a line, Visual Basic immediately executes the instructions on that line. You can reexecute any visible line in the Debug window by moving the cursor to the line and pressing Enter.

To use the Debug window effectively, you may need to place several instructions on a single line, usually when you want to execute a loop. Suppose that you want to display all the elements in an array named ClientName$. The array has eight elements. As figure 8.4 shows, you can type the following line to get the results you want:

```
For J = 1 To 8: Print J; ClientName$(J): Next J
```

You can use the Debug window for more than just Print instructions. For instance, you can assign specific values to variables or make explicit calls to procedures.

When you are in Break mode, the title bar of the Debug window shows the current form and the procedure that Visual Basic was executing. With Print, you can display the values of any variables local to that procedure, any form-level variables, or any global variables. You can't display the values of any variables local to other procedures or other forms.

8

Figure 8.4

Typing a loop in the Debug window.

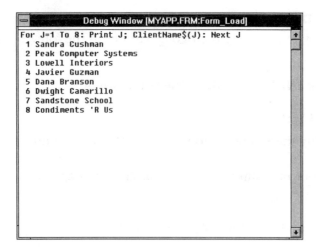

> **Note:** *If you have* Option Explicit *in effect, you cannot type undeclared variable names in the Debug window. In the preceding example,* J *must be declared in the program code. If you plan to work with the Debug window, you may want to turn off* Option Explicit *temporarily. You can do this by commenting out the* Option Explicit *instructions in the declarations section of your forms. Then you will have to rerun the application before using the Debug window. For more information on* Option Explicit *and on requiring variable declarations, see the section "Debugging Logic Errors."*

Using the Debug Window with Applications That Are Running

You can place explicit instructions in your program code to display messages directly to the Debug window. As a result, you can display the values of any variables while the application executes. Later, in Break mode, you can examine the Debug window to see what was displayed.

To display values in the Debug window, use Visual Basic's predefined Debug object with the Print method. For example, the following instruction displays the value of the variable TotalSales:

```
Debug.Print "TotalSales ="; TotalSales
```

Interrupting a Program with Ctrl+Break

When working in the development environment, you can suspend execution at any time while your program is running. Just press Ctrl+Break (or choose Break from the **R**un menu, or click the Break button on the Toolbar). Visual Basic enters Break mode, displays the Code window for the current procedure, and highlights the line currently executing. Then you can use the Debug window to test the values of variables and expressions.

Resuming a Program

With the Debug window in Break mode, you can display the values of key variables by using Print. But here's the clincher: You can resume execution of your program from the point at which it was interrupted. Simply choose **C**ontinue (F5) from the **R**un menu.

This debugging technique is quite powerful. You can interrupt execution, display variable values, and then resume the program from the place where the interruption occurred.

Breaking and resuming are useful when a program seems to be executing for an unduly long time. Often the problem is an endless loop. If your application seems to be running interminably without producing any results, press Ctrl+Break, and use the Debug window for debugging. Remember, you can avoid having a program run without producing any visible results by following advice given earlier in this chapter—placing `Debug.Print` statements in the debugging version of your program. These statements are included to print what might be called "program status log" messages to the Debug window. Then the program will leave a record of its progress as it executes.

Note: *After interrupting your program with Ctrl+Break, you can issue instructions in the Debug window and then resume execution with the **C**ontinue command. Sometimes, however, **C**ontinue does not work. If you edit an instruction that results in Visual Basic's being incapable of continuing your program, a dialog box opens to inform you of this fact. You then have a choice of going ahead with the modification or leaving the program intact so that you can continue execution.*

To clear the Debug window, you place the program in Break mode and select the text to remove by clicking and dragging with your mouse. Then you press the Delete key.

Debugging Logic Errors

Suppose that you have written an application, cleared all the syntax errors, and eliminated any errors in the executing process. The program, however, doesn't do what you intended. It runs to completion, but the results appear wrong. You have a dreaded logic error. Now what? Try the following:

- Again, examine your test for typing errors.

- Break the program at key places, and display the values of important variables.

- Search for variable conflicts. Don't use two variables with similar names, such as `Sale` and `Sales`. Make sure that you spell a variable name consistently throughout the program.

- Don't overwork a global variable by making it perform double duty. Suppose that one procedure uses a particular variable. Another procedure subsequently uses the same variable name during an independent calculation. The first procedure then regains control and needs the variable's old value—but it is no longer valid. Sometimes you might simply forget that perhaps the value of a particular variable is needed later in the execution.

- Verify that Visual Basic's statements, functions, methods, and event procedures work the way you think they do.

8

- Align troublesome parts of the program. Create more `Sub` and `Function` procedures to isolate program chunks into smaller units.

- Use the special debugging features found on the **D**ebug menu and the Toolbar. The next section discusses these features.

A good way to avoid mistyping the names of existing variables is to use the `Option Explicit` instruction. It forces every variable to be explicitly declared in a `Dim`, `ReDim`, `Static`, or `Global` instruction. `Option Explicit` instructions must be placed in the declarations sections of forms or modules, not inside individual procedures. You can have Visual Basic automatically add `Option Explicit` to your applications by selecting **E**nvironment from the **O**ptions menu and then specifying Yes as the value of the Require Variable Declaration option.

Introducing VB's Debugging Tools

The "nerve center" of Visual Basic's debugging capabilities is a set of tools available through the **D**ebug menu and the Toolbar. The following three terms are central to Visual Basic's debugging terminology:

Trace	*A* line-by-line examination of your program's logic flow.
Breakpoint	*A* designated program line on which you want execution to halt temporarily. When the program line is about to execute, Visual Basic enters Break mode.
Watchpoint	An expression whose value you want to monitor. When the value of the expression changes or reaches a specified value, Visual Basic enters Break mode.

The last five buttons on the Toolbar quickly activate some of the debugging options (see figure 8.5).

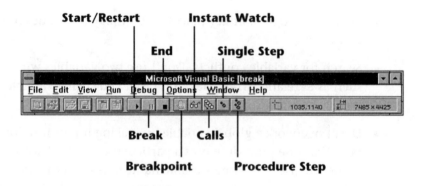

Figure 8.5
The Toolbar's debugging tools.

Tracing a Program

Tracing
The line-by-line examinination of a program's logic flow at run time.

Tracing reveals the logic flow of a program. You can request that Visual Basic pause after executing each line of your application. When VB pauses, the Code window for the current procedure opens, and the next line to be executed is highlighted. There are two types of tracing:

- *Single-step tracing.* This type executes the highlighted line of the program. Visual Basic then pauses and highlights the next line to be executed. To single-step, you can press F8, click the Single Step button on the Toolbar, or choose **S**ingle Step from the **D**ebug menu.

- *Procedure-step tracing.* This type is similar to single-step tracing except that each call to a procedure executes as a single step. To procedure-step, press Shift+F8, click the Procedure Step button on the Toolbar, or choose **P**rocedure Step from the **D**ebug menu.

When you single-step, each executable instruction executes in turn. As each procedure is called, the Code window opens to show the program code for that procedure. Visual Basic highlights the next instruction to execute by surrounding it with a rectangular frame. Tracing is especially helpful when you are confused about the order in which the statements in your program are being executed.

The Debug window is available for use at any time. One common debugging technique is to single-step through a program while displaying the values of key variables in the Debug window. Single-stepping is especially useful for debugging troublesome loop structures.

Remember that while tracing, you can resize either the Code window or the Debug window. Or to make them visible simultaneously, you can resize them both.

Figure 8.6 shows how a typical screen might appear while single-stepping. Notice the highlight on the current program instruction.

Figure 8.6
Tracing a program.

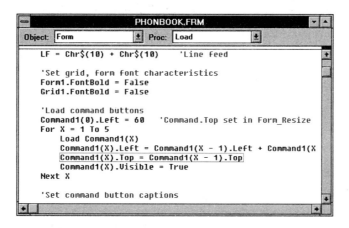

To practice tracing, complete the next exercise (although in this sample program, tracing is not much of a help).

Using Tracing to Examine a Program

Use the batting average program you entered in the preceding exercise, "Finding an Execution Error." Follow these steps:

❶ Click the Single Step button in the Toolbar until the first request for input appears.

❷ Enter **1** in the input box for the number of hits. Click OK.

❸ Keep clicking the Single Step button until the second request for input appears.

❹ Enter **4** in the input box for the number of times at bat. Click OK.

Continue to single-step through the program.

❺ For the second set of input, enter **1** hit and **0** (zero) times at bat in the respective input boxes.

❻ When the error occurs, click the OK button in the error message dialog box.

❼ Stop the trace by clicking the Stop button in the Toolbar.

Setting Breakpoints

Breakpoint
A designated program line on which you want to suspend program execution temporarily.

For many programmers, breakpoints are the best debugging allies. A **breakpoint** is a specified program line on which you want to suspend execution. When Visual Basic reaches the breakpoint line, execution halts, and the system enters Break mode.

By setting breakpoints, you can halt execution at strategic locations. After the program suspends at a breakpoint, you can set new options from the **D**ebug menu, or you can use the Debug window to display the values of variables and expressions.

To set a breakpoint, you use these steps:

1. Place the procedure containing the target line in the Code window.

2. Move the cursor to the target line.

3. Choose **T**oggle Breakpoint from the **D**ebug menu. Alternatively, you can click the Breakpoint button on the Toolbar or press F9.

Visual Basic shows the breakpoint by highlighting the line in red or reverse video.

Setting a Breakpoint in a Program

Now set a breakpoint in the batting average program you entered in an earlier exercise. Follow these steps:

1 Make sure that this program is in the Code window.

2 Move the cursor to the line that calculates the batting average.

3 Click the Breakpoint button in the Toolbar.

4 Run the program, entering **1** for hits and **3** for times at bat.

5 When the program enters Break mode at the breakpoint you set, access the Debug window, type **? NumAB**, and press **Enter**.

The value currently stored in the number of times at bat is displayed in the Debug window.

Notice that this technique tips you off when the number of times at bat is zero. Use this breakpoint-setting technique at strategic places in your program to spot problem variable values before they cause a problem. In this way, you can keep track of what the program you are developing is doing.

6 Stop the program.

7 Make sure that the Code window is displayed, and then select the program line at which the breakpoint is set.

8 Choose the Toggle Breakpoint command from the Debug menu.

This command alternately sets or removes an individual breakpoint. You can set several breakpoints simultaneously. To remove all the breakpoints in one step, choose Clear All Breakpoints from the **D**ebug menu.

Watching a Program

Watchpoint
An expression whose predetermined value, when reached, causes Visual Basic to enter Break mode.

Watchpoints are similar to breakpoints in that program execution suspends when a specified condition occurs. With a **watchpoint**, you can cause Visual Basic to enter Break mode when the value of a specified expression reaches a predetermined amount.

Specifying a Watch Expression

To specify the expression you want to watch, you use the Add Watch dialog box. To open this box, you choose **A**dd Watch from the **D**ebug menu. You can access this dialog box before running the application or whenever Visual Basic is in Break mode.

Figure 8.7 shows the Add Watch dialog box. The watch expression that you specify can be any meaningful item from your program code. The expression can

8

be a variable, a property value, a function call, or an expression combining several of these elements with suitable operators. Before choosing **A**dd Watch, if you highlight an expression in your program code, Visual Basic displays that expression as the default watch expression.

Figure 8.7

The Add Watch dialog box.

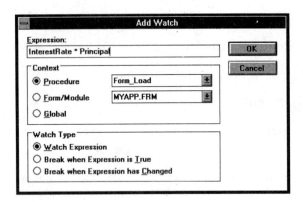

In the Context frame of the dialog box, you specify the scope of the variables used in the watch expression. The scope can be **P**rocedure Level, **F**orm/Module level, or **G**lobal.

The Watch Type frame offers three option buttons. First examine the **W**atch Expression option, as selected in figure 8.7. The other two options are covered shortly.

Viewing the Watch Pane

When you choose **W**atch Expression and click OK in the Add Watch dialog box, Visual Basic adds a Watch pane to the Debug window. This pane shows the watch expression and its current value. At the left side of the Watch pane is an icon that depicts a pair of eyeglasses (see figure 8.8).

Figure 8.8

The Debug window containing a Watch pane.

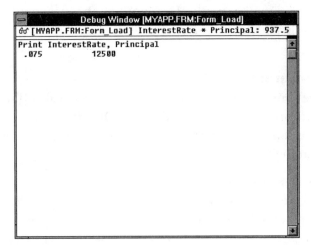

Now, as you execute the application and reenter Break mode, you can watch the value of the expression change in the Debug window.

You can specify more than one watch expression. If you do, the Watch pane displays updated values for all the watch expressions.

Editing and Deleting a Watch Expression

You can edit a watch expression with the Watch dialog box. To access it, you choose **E**dit Watch from the **D**ebug menu (or press the shortcut Ctrl+W). Figure 8.9 shows the edit Watch dialog box.

Figure 8.9

The edit Watch dialog box.

To work with any watch expression, use the arrow keys to highlight the expression. Then you can click the appropriate command button to change or erase the expression: **E**dit to edit it, **D**elete to remove it, or **A**dd to specify a new one. By clicking De**l**ete All, you remove all the watch expressions at once.

Using Watchpoints

Using a watchpoint, you can have Visual Basic suspend program execution when the value of a watch expression changes or reaches a specified amount. You create a kind of breakpoint that occurs only when the test condition in the watchpoint changes or is True. To specify a watchpoint, you select the appropriate option button from the Watch Type frame in the Add Watch dialog box (refer to figure 8.7).

If you choose the Break when Expression has **C**hanged option, Visual Basic executes the application until the value of the watch expression changes. At that point, execution is suspended. Visual Basic opens the Code window and highlights the line that caused the expression to change (or the line immediately following). The Watch pane in the Debug window shows the new value of the watch expression. With this option activated, the icon in the Watch pane is an open hand with a triangle.

The Break when Expression is **T**rue option executes the application until the value of the watch expression becomes True. (Remember that for a numeric expression, True is any nonzero value.) The icon in the Watch pane now appears as an open hand with an equal sign.

Using Instant Watch

The final watch option is Instant Watch. You can use this option in Break mode to quickly display the value of any expression. Using Instant Watch is similar to displaying the value of an expression with the Debug window in Break mode.

To use Instant Watch, you first highlight the watch expression directly in your program code. A watch expression might contain several variables and

8

operators or be a single variable name or property. The highlighted expression can be, and usually is, part of a larger Visual Basic instruction.

You then select Instant Watch in any of the following ways: press Shift+F9, choose **I**nstant Watch from the **D**ebug menu, or click the Instant Watch button on the Toolbar.

As figure 8.10 shows, Visual Basic opens the Instant Watch dialog box, displaying the watch expression and its current value. (The expression in the figure is one that might be used as a watch expression.) You can close this dialog box by pressing Esc or clicking the Cancel button. You also have the option of adding another watch expression by clicking the **A**dd Watch button.

Figure 8.10

The Instant Watch dialog box.

Using Calls

When you are in Break mode, the Calls dialog box provides a special way of looking at the execution of your program. This dialog box shows which modules and procedures are involved in the chain of execution at the time execution is suspended. Figure 8.11 shows the Calls dialog box.

Figure 8.11

The Calls dialog box.

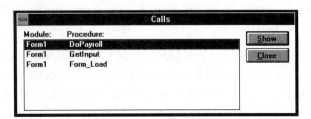

You can use any of the following techniques to access the Calls dialog box: press Ctrl+L, choose the **C**alls option from the **D**ebug menu, or click the Calls button on the Toolbar.

Calls can be a valuable debugging tool as your applications become more complex. In such applications, you frequently have one procedure explicitly calling another. Called procedures can, in turn, invoke others. Such a chain of procedures is known as nested procedure calls. Notice that, for the next instruction in the original procedure to execute, every nested procedure in the chain must first have completed its processing.

If a bug crops up in one of these procedures, tracing the execution path can be tedious and time-consuming. The Calls dialog box can help by visually displaying the nested procedure chain. If you click **S**how, the procedure highlighted in the dialog box is listed. This listing enables you to focus on suspected problems without the time-consuming effort required to trace the program execution manually. The Calls dialog box shows nested procedures in LIFO ("last in, first out") order. That is, the earliest active procedure is placed on the bottom of the list; the most recently called procedure appears at the top.

Other Debugging Tools

Besides offering the major debugging tools already discussed, Visual Basic provides some additional debugging features. This section presents the following debugging aids:

- Selecting (setting) the next instruction to execute

- Showing the next instruction to execute

- Using the Stop instruction

Using Set Next Statement

While tracing a program, or anytime in Break mode, you can designate which instruction executes next. You use the Set **N**ext Statement option in the **D**ebug menu. Instead of executing instructions, this option simply moves the highlight. When you resume execution with F5, F8, one of the continuation options from the **D**ebug menu, or the Toolbar, the newly highlighted instruction executes first. The effect is similar to that of a GoTo.

Trying Out the Set Next Statement Option

Now try using the Set **N**ext Statement option by following these steps:

1 Run the batting average program you entered in an earlier exercise.

2 Pause (**Ctrl+Break**) the program. In the Code window, the highlight (the framing rectangle) appears around the instruction to be executed next.

Now you can move the cursor to whatever instruction (within that procedure) you want to execute next.

3 Click the mouse pointer on the End Sub statement to place the cursor in that line.

4 Open the **D**ebug menu (**Alt+D**).

5 Choose Set **N**ext Statement. The highlight moves to your selected instruction.

6 Press **F5** to resume execution at this new instruction.

The procedure should end immediately.

8

Using the Show Next Statement Option

When the Code window is not visible, you can use the Show Next Statement option from the **D**ebug menu to see which instruction executes next. The Code window opens with the highlight on the instruction that executes when you resume the program. Then you can press F5 to resume execution at the highlighted instruction, or you can use the Set **N**ext Statement option to move the highlight.

Using *Stop*

Visual Basic provides the Stop instruction as a way to set a breakpoint directly in the program code. When Visual Basic encounters a Stop, execution is suspended with the highlight on it.

You can then use the Debug window, set options with the **D**ebug menu, or do anything normally associated with suspended programs. As usual, you can resume the program by pressing F5, choosing **C**ontinue from the **R**un menu, or clicking the Run button in the Toolbar. Essentially, Stop is similar to a breakpoint set at the Stop instruction itself.

The Stop instruction has one large advantage over setting breakpoints with the **D**ebug menu. While developing an application, you can save the program code between work sessions. The Stop instructions are saved along with the rest of the program code. As a result, the Stop breakpoints are retained from one work session to the next. Any breakpoints you set from the **D**ebug menu are lost as soon as you exit Visual Basic.

A Summary of Debugging Tools

Tables 8.2 through 8.6 summarize Visual Basic's debugging tools.

Table 8.2 Commands That Control Execution		
Action	**Menu**	**Shortcut**
Start	**R**un	F5
Restart	**R**un	Shift+F5
Continue	**R**un	F5
End	**R**un	
Suspend execution		Ctrl+Break
Set **N**ext Statement	**D**ebug	
Sho**w** Next Statement	**D**ebug	

Table 8.3 Tracing Commands		
Action	**Menu**	**Shortcut**
Single Step	**D**ebug	F8
Procedure Step	**D**ebug	Shift+F8

Table 8.4 Breakpoint Commands		
Action	**Menu**	**Shortcut**
Toggle Breakpoint	**D**ebug	F9
Cl**e**ar All Breakpoints	**D**ebug	

Table 8.5 Watch Commands		
Action	**Menu**	**Shortcut**
Add Watch	**D**ebug	
Edit Watch	**D**ebug	Ctrl+W
Instant Watch	**D**ebug	Shift+F9

Table 8.6 Viewing Commands		
Action	**Menu**	**Shortcut**
Activate Debug window (**D**ebug)	**W**indow	Ctrl+B
Calls	**D**ebug	Ctrl+L

Error Handling and Error Trapping

Usually, a run-time error terminates your application. If you are running from the development environment (rather than running an EXE file), Visual Basic displays an appropriate error message and enters Break mode. From there, you can use the Debug window and the various techniques mentioned earlier in this chapter to track down what happened.

Error trapping
A programming technique in which your application intercepts an error and passes control to an error-handling routine.

An alternative for dealing with run-time errors is available, however. Visual Basic provides **error trapping**, which lets your application intercept an error and pass control to an error-handling routine. In other words, when an error occurs, instead of VB's terminating your application, program control simply passes to the error handler. An error handler is a user-written block of program lines embedded in a procedure. When a program error occurs inside a procedure containing an error handler, execution branches directly to it.

8

With error trapping, you can do the following:

Error handler

A block of program lines placed in a procedure specifically to process an error.

- Pass control to an **error handler** when an error occurs
- Determine which line caused the error
- Determine what error occurred
- Correct the problem or prompt the user for information
- Resume execution at any place in the procedure

Using Error Trapping

Error trapping is most valuable in the following situations:

- You anticipate that certain errors might occur during execution of an application, especially when you know what it should do when one of these errors materializes.

- An error-producing bug has you baffled. With error trapping as a debugging tool, you can trap the error and branch to a special routine that helps you diagnose the problem.

- You write applications that request users to input data. Your users occasionally may type faulty data that causes errors. (This situation is common with coworkers in a job.) Error trapping lets you intercept possible program errors. With the error handler, you can correct the problem and continue execution. Such remedial action often involves prompting the user for new (or corrected) input data.

If nothing else, an error handler provides graceful program termination. If you cannot fix the problem that caused the error, at least you can display informative messages before the application terminates.

Table 8.7 shows the keywords used with error trapping.

Table 8.7 Error-Handling Statements and Functions	
Keyword(s)	**Action**
On Error GoTo	Enables error trapping and specifies the first line of the error handler
Resume	Branches to a designated line when the error handler finishes
Err function	Returns an error code for logic errors
Erl function	Returns the line causing the error
Err statement	Sets a value for the error code
Error statement	Simulates or creates an error
Error$ function	Returns the error message corresponding to an error code

Visual Basic's error-trapping method is a bit primitive. The techniques are inherited from QBasic and other procedural versions of the BASIC language. Branch designations and error locations use line numbers and GoTo clauses. Primitive, however, does not mean ineffective. Error trapping is a potent tool.

Enabling Error Trapping

The heart of Visual Basic's error trapping is the On Error instruction. Three forms exist:

```
On Error GoTo linenum

On Error GoTo label

On Error Resume Next
```

linenum is the line number on which the error handler begins. *label* is the line label on which the error handler begins.

The GoTo forms of On Error do two things. The forms enable error trapping; no error trap occurs until an On Error GoTo instruction executes. The forms also specify which line gets control when an error occurs.

An error handler is always local to a particular procedure. *label* or *linenum* must refer to a line in the same procedure containing the On Error GoTo instruction. That is, an On Error GoTo instruction cannot attempt to branch to a line in a different Sub or Function procedure. However, a single procedure can contain more than one On Error GoTo instruction; there is no limit on how many procedures can contain such instructions.

The TRAPERR Application

As noted, an error handler is simply a group of lines placed somewhere in a procedure. You can use error handlers in both user-defined procedures and event procedures. Visual Basic does not automatically support branching directly to a user-defined procedure when an error is trapped. Of course, the code in an error handler can explicitly invoke a user-defined procedure.

Using an Error Handler

In this exercise, the TRAPERR application shows the skeletal technique of using an error handler. The application consists of a single Form Resize event procedure. Follow these steps:

❶ Start a new project, and enter the following code in the Form Resize event handler:

```
Sub Form_Resize ()
    'The World's simplest Error Handler
    Dim NiceTry As Single

Rem On Error GoTo ErrorHandler    'Remove Rem to try handler
```

(continues)

8

Using an Error Handler (continued)

```
            NiceTry = 1 / 0
            MsgBox "No way to get here"
            End

        ErrorHandler:
            MsgBox "I think you made a boo-boo"
            End

        End Sub
```

Notice that the On Error GoTo is inactive because the line begins with Rem.

❷ Run the program.

The assignment instruction causes a run-time error because division by zero is an illegal operation. Visual Basic aborts the application and displays the error message box shown in figure 8.12.

Figure 8.12
Error message box when On Error GoTo is disabled.

❸ Remove the Rem at the beginning of the On Error GoTo instruction.

This line now activates the error-handling routine. If a program error occurs, control branches directly to the error handler at the line beginning with the ErrorHandler: label.

❹ Run the program again.

As figure 8.13 shows, you now see the message box created by the MsgBox instruction inside the ErrorHandler routine.

Figure 8.13
Message box when On Error GoTo is enabled.

Notice that, this time, the application does not display the Division by zero error message. When the assignment instruction tries to divide by zero, Visual Basic intercepts the impending error and branches directly to the error handler. In the error handler, the MsgBox instruction displays the boo-boo message. After you click OK to close the message box, the End instruction ends.the application.

In any procedure, you can have multiple error handlers and On Error GoTo instructions. The most recently executed On Error GoTo designates the active error handler. Only one error handler, of course, can be active at any time. When a procedure terminates, its error handlers are automatically disabled.

Using *On Error GoTo 0*

If your application uses line numbers, you cannot place an error handler at line number 0 because the instruction On Error GoTo 0 has special significance. An On Error GoTo 0 instruction turns *off* error trapping in the procedure. A subsequent error then halts the application in the usual way. In other words, you use the instruction On Error GoTo 0 to turn off error trapping that has previously been turned on. On Error GoTo 0 does not specify line 0 as the beginning of an error handler, even if the procedure contains a line numbered 0.

The *On Error Resume Next* Instruction

You can have execution continue uninterrupted when an error occurs. You use the following special form of the On Error instruction:

```
On Error Resume Next
```

Now, when an error occurs, Visual Basic simply continues executing the instructions in the procedure. As explained later in this chapter, your subsequent code can use the Err function to find out whether any error occurred and, if so, what it was.

When debugging a procedure, some programmers use the On Error Resume Next instruction to force execution past known errors. Remember, when you turn on error handling, *you* (your program statements) are taking over the responsibility for processing any errors the program encounters from that point on. Make *sure* that you can handle the error conditions properly. Whenever an error occurs, even though you didn't anticipate it, the error will trigger your error handler.

Returning from an Error Handler

Most error handlers include one or more Resume instructions. Resume has five forms. The form of a Resume instruction determines the place in which execution continues (see table 8.8).

Table 8.8   Return Locations of the *Resume* Instruction

Instruction	Return Location
Resume	At the line that caused the error
Resume 0	At the line that caused the error (same as Resume)
Resume Next	At the instruction immediately following the one that caused the error
Resume *linenum*	At the line designated by *linenum*
Resume *label*	At the line designated by *label*

linenum and *label* must be within the same procedure as the Resume statement.

8

Using *Resume* in an Error Handler

To use `Resume` in an error handler, follow these steps:

❶ Modify the code you entered in TRAPPER in the preceding exercise by placing a `Resume Next` instruction at the end of the error handler. Your program should now look like this:

```
Sub Form_Resize ()
    'The World's simplest Error Handler
    Dim NiceTry As Single

    On Error GoTo ErrorHandler

    NiceTry = 1 / 0
    MsgBox "No way to get here"
    End

ErrorHandler:
    MsgBox "I think you made a boo-boo"
    Resume Next

End Sub
```

Now, when the error is trapped, the handler returns control to the line immediately following the assignment instruction that caused the error. As a result, the application displays two message boxes. The first box displays the following message:

```
I think you made a boo-boo
```

The second box displays this message:

```
No way to get here
```

❷ Run the program to see how the `Resume Next` statement works.

Remember that in a `Resume` instruction, *linenum* or *label* must refer to a line in the same procedure as the error handler.

It is possible to activate an error handler located in one procedure while program control is in another. Suppose that a procedure containing an error handler has executed an `On Error` instruction to enable the error handler. Then that procedure makes an explicit call to a second procedure. While the program is executing the second procedure, the error defined in the first procedure occurs. Visual Basic returns control to the error handler in the original procedure. Notice that, in this case, the first procedure never terminated but merely transferred program control temporarily to the second procedure. If the error handler in such a case has a `Resume 0` instruction (or `Resume` without any parameters), execution would continue just after the line that called the second procedure. Again, be careful when you turn on error handling. Sometimes it can be a double-edged sword.

`Resume` instructions are valid only when error handling is active (when `On Error` is in effect). A run-time error (`Resume without error`) occurs if you execute a `Resume` instruction when error handling is not enabled. Furthermore, your application cannot simply run out of instructions in an error handler without a `Resume`. This mistake causes a run-time error (`No Resume`). However, you can use `Exit Sub` or `Exit Function` in an error handler to terminate the procedure.

Writing an Error Handler

Generally, you want to accomplish the following within an error handler:

- Determine the error and which line caused it

- Display diagnostic messages

- Correct the problem

- Resume execution, if feasible

The built-in functions `Err` and `Erl` provide information often useful for your error handler. VB's Help offers extensive information about these functions and error trapping in general.

Using the *Err* and *Erl* Functions

The `Err` and `Erl` functions enable your error handler to determine the type of error that occurred and which program line caused it.

`Err` returns the code of the error that invoked the error handler. The code is a long integer number.

Visual Basic defines more than 200 error codes. For a complete list, see the VB Help topic "Trappable Errors" or your Visual Basic documentation. Table 8.9 shows just a few of the values the `Err` function can return, along with the errors they indicate. You can print the value of `Err` in the Debug window.

Table 8.9   Partial List of Values Returned by the *Err* Function

Error Code	Error Message
5	Illegal function call
6	Overflow
7	Out of memory
10	Duplicate definition
11	Division by zero
19	No Resume
35	Sub or Function not defined
61	Disk full
68	Device unavailable

`Erl` returns the line number at which the error occurred. If the error occurs in a line without a line number, `Erl` returns the number of the last executed line that had a line number. If the procedure has not executed any numbered lines before the error, Erl returns 0.

Keep in mind that Erl works only with line numbers, not with labels. This throwback to earlier versions of the BASIC language requires you to number all program lines if you want Erl to return the most accurate information.

Using the *Err* Statement

You can assign a particular value to the Err function by using the Err statement:

```
Err = errorcode
```

errorcode is an integer from 0 to 32,768 (see the VB Help topic "Trappable Errors").

A common use of the Err statement is to create specialized error codes defined only in the application. If you look through the list of Err error codes predefined by Visual Basic, you find that there are several gaps. Many numbers do not correspond with any error. You can use any of these available numbers to define an error code specifically for the application.

Suppose that you are writing a timed-quiz application, and you want the user to reply within 20 seconds or get an error message. You notice that error code 495 is not predefined by Visual Basic. You can assign error code 495 by using the following instruction:

```
Err = 495    'No reply
```

Subsequently, in an error handler or in the normal program code, you can use the Err function to determine what error occurred. When the Err function returns 495, you know that your user has failed to respond.

You can use the Err statement also to set the value of Err to 0. If you do, Visual Basic acts as though an error did not occur.

Simulating Errors

Use an Error instruction to simulate errors or to create your individualized error codes:

```
Error errorcode
```

If errorcode is one of the error codes predefined by Visual Basic, the Error instruction causes your application to behave as though the error occurred. Control passes to the error handler from which the Err function returns the value of errorcode. If you have no error handler, Visual Basic displays the normal message associated with that error and terminates your application. This technique is a good way to test all your error-handling routines.

For example, the following instruction simulates a Division by zero error:

```
Error 11      '11 is the Err code for Division by zero
```

With Error, you can induce different errors while testing and developing an application. You can find out whether your error handler recovers adequately.

As with `Err`, the `Error` statement is suitable for defining your own codes. Just use an *errorcode* value not defined by Visual Basic. When the `Error` instruction passes control to the error handler, you can use its `Err` function inside the handler to test for the value of *errorcode* and then take appropriate action.

If your application has no error handler, an `Error` instruction that uses an invalid *errorcode* halts the application and displays the message `User-defined error`. User-defined error codes provide a way to test for special conditions or dangerous data. You can intercept potential errors and handle the problem in an error handler.

For example, the following code is the skeletal form of a procedure that asks the user to type a password. If the user types the correct password (`Swordfish`), the application displays confidential information. If the typed password is invalid, application control passes to an error handler. The application defines error 254, which is not an error number used by Visual Basic.

```
On Error GoTo ErrorHandler

    .
    .
Password$ = InputBox$("What is the authorizing password")
If Password$ <> "Swordfish" Then Error 254
MsgBox "Click to see the Strategic Plan Briefing"

    .
    .
End     'of application

ErrorHandler:
    Select Case Err
    Case 254
        MsgBox "Unauthorized request"
        Rem If possible, correct the problem here

        .
        Resume Next
    Case Else
        Rem Check for other errors here

        .
    End Select
Rem  End of error handler
```

Using the *Error$* and *Error* Functions

The `Error$` function returns the text of the error message corresponding to a given error code. Here is the form you use:

```
Error$(errorcode)
```

The *errorcode* argument is optional. For example, the following instruction displays the error message corresponding to error code 11:

```
MsgBox Error$(11)
```

`Error$` returns a string value. The corresponding function, `Error`, returns a Variant (of type string). Note this example of `Error`:

```
Dim MyMessage as Variant
MyMessage = Error(11)
```

If *errorcode* is not one of the error codes predefined in Visual Basic, the value returned is User-defined error. If you omit the *errorcode* argument, the function returns the string message corresponding to the most recent error.

A Philosophy of Error Handlers

Error handlers can be simple or complex. Use them to anticipate possible problems and to recover smoothly, especially in workplace environments.

In polished applications, most errors come from user mistakes. The likely culprits are faulty data supplied by users and mistakes with equipment, such as placing the wrong disk in a disk drive or not turning on the printer.

User-supplied numeric data often is a source of errors. Bad data typed by users can lead to errors such as Division by zero. You might write an error handler that checks for Division by zero (among other possibilities). If that's the problem, you can redisplay the user's input and ask whether the information is correct. If the information is incorrect, branch back to the place in which the data was entered, and then start over.

Disk drive errors are common when users must place a disk into a drive and enter the name of a file saved on the disk. Users can use the wrong disk or drive, forget to place the disk in the drive, or supply an invalid file name. You can check for all these errors and recover without causing the application to crash.

Error handlers often have a series of If instructions or a Select Case block. The handler checks for various anticipated errors by using Err and Erl and then executes individualized instructions that deal with each type of error.

The following is an example of such an error handler:

```
ErrorHandler:
    Print
    Print "Error number"; Err; " has occurred at line"; Erl
    Select Case Err
        Case 11
            Print "You have divided by zero."
            Print "Please rerun the program with new values."
            MsgBox "Click OK to end program"
            End
        Case 61
            Print "The disk is full."
            Print "The program will continue without writing to disk."
            MsgBox "Click OK to continue"
            Resume Next
        Case 68
            Print "The printer is probably not on or is out of paper."
            MsgBox "Check the printer and then click OK."
            Resume
        Case Else
            Print "An unanticipated error has occurred."
            Print "So long for now - Stopping the program."
            MsgBox "Click OK to end program"
            End
    End Select
```

At the least, your error handler can display diagnostic information and solicit the user to notify you:

```
    MyErrorHandler:
        Print " An unanticipated program error has occurred."
        Print
        Print "Please report the following information to"
        Print "Jill Programmer, Bldg. R8, Extension 389"
        Print
        Print "Error number"; Err; " in line"; Erl
        Print
        Print "    -Thank you"
        Print "      Jill"
    Stop
```

Chapter Summary

Experienced programmers realize that testing and debugging are necessary for successful programming. As a general rule, large programs contain bugs that must be found and eliminated. Many programmers dislike testing and debugging. Actually, these processes can be fun. Much depends on your state of mind. After all, most people enjoy solving puzzles and acting as "detectives."

Three kinds of errors can occur in programs:

- *Syntax errors*, which are incorrectly worded instructions that don't make sense to Visual Basic

- *Execution errors*, which cause diagnostic messages as the result of instructions (correctly worded) that Visual Basic cannot execute successfully

- *Logic errors*, which occur when your program runs to completion but yields incorrect results

Fortunately, Visual Basic provides several debugging features and techniques. The most important ones include the capabilities to suspend program execution, perform detective work with the Debug window, and resume the program.

With breakpoints, you can suspend a program at any line. You can display the values of crucial variables and expressions from the Debug window. You can also reassign the value of any variable. With watchpoints, you can have Visual Basic enter Break mode when the value of a specified expression reaches a particular amount.

Tracing provides a way to observe the logic flow of your program. You can see the order in which each instruction executes. While tracing, you can suspend execution and use the Debug window.

Most programming errors stem from simple mistakes rather than obscure bugs. Search for the obvious before the subtle. By far, the most likely source of any error is a simple typing mistake. When errors occur, double- and triple-check your typing.

With error trapping, your applications can take measures to intercept and recover from run-time errors. You can anticipate possible errors caused by users entering faulty input or mishandling hardware, such as the printer or disk drives. An error handler can smoothly rescue the application from these types of problems.

8

Occasionally, you can get stuck tracking down an elusive bug. If so, leave the situation for a while. Take a break and do something relaxing, such as walking or napping. It's amazing how some nagging bugs are swiftly found after a rejuvenating break.

In the next chapter, you learn how to use arrays.

Test Your Understanding

True/False

Indicate whether the statement is true or false.

1. You cannot view the contents of the Debug window at design time.

2. An algorithm is an especially difficult bug in your program.

3. One large procedure will generally contain fewer bugs than several smaller modules that, together, accomplish the same task as the large procedure.

4. The use of `Option Explicit` is a frequent source of bugs in programs.

5. Careless program design probably ensures that no amount of testing will be able to identify all the bugs in your program.

6. Entering all the code in your program before you run it for the first time is generally a good idea.

7. You should never put any statements in your program that will not be in the final version of the program you turn in for grading.

8. It is best to let the computer find the errors in your program rather than waste time finding them yourself.

9. Creating simple test programs to verify your understanding of a VB statement before you add it to a project you are developing is a good idea.

10. VB will find the syntax errors and logic errors in each program statement as you type your program.

Short Answer

Answer the following questions.

1. Explain how the `On Error GoTo` statement can be used to develop an error-handling routine.

2. How do you enter VB's Break mode?

3. Explain how to reexecute any visible line in the Debug window.

4. What is a breakpoint? How do you set one? How can setting breakpoints help you find the bugs in your program?

5. What does the `Option Explicit` statement do? Where must it be placed in a program?

6. Explain how to trace a program line by line and how to procedure-step through a program.

7. What is a watchpoint? How do you use one to help in debugging a program?

8. What is a watch expression?

9. What is the Watch pane, and what is displayed in it?

10. What is the Calls dialog box, and what is shown in it?

11. What happens when you click **S**how in the Calls dialog box?

12. Explain how to use the Sho**w** Next Statement option when you are debugging.

13. How can you use the Stop statement when you are debugging?

14. How can you use the Print statement when you are debugging?

15. How can you clear the Debug window?

Projects

Project 1: Using the Debug Window to Keep Track of a Variable's Value

In this project, you use the Debug window to keep track of the value of the variable OfInterest. Complete the following steps:

1. Start a new project. Place a command button (Command1) on the form. Enter the following code in Command1_Click:

```
Sub Command1_Click ()
For I = 1 To 4
   For J = 3 To 7
       OfInterest = I * J * 2 / 3
   Next J
Next I
End Sub
```

2. Close the Properties and Project windows to remove clutter from the screen. Make sure that the Code window for Command1_Click is open.

3. Choose **A**dd Watch from the **D**ebug menu.

4. In the **E**xpression text box, type **OfInterest**. Then click the OK button.

5. In the Code window, place the cursor in the Next J line. Then choose **T**oggle Breakpoint from the **D**ebug menu, and run the program.

6. Click the Debug window, or choose **D**ebug from the **W**indow menu. Size the Debug window to about six inches wide and two inches high. Move the window, as necessary, to see its contents on-screen at all times. Size and arrange the Code window and the program's window (it needs to be just large enough for you to see the button). You need to be able to see all three windows on-screen at once.

8

7. Click the Command1 button. The Watch pane in the Debug window should show that the value of OfInterest is 2.

8. Click the Run button in the Toolbar. The Watch pane should show that the value of OfInterest is now 2.666 (and a lot more sixes). Click the Run button again. The Watch pane should show that the value of OfInterest is now 3.333 (and a lot more threes).

Continue to use this technique to watch the calculations that occur in the program until you are sure that you know how to use the technique with any of your own programs. Stop the program.

9. From the **D**ebug menu, choose **C**lear All Breakpoints.

10. Choose **E**dit Watch from the **D**ebug menu. Then click De**l**ete All. All watchpoints are removed.

11. Click the **A**dd button.

12. In the **E**xpression box, type the following:

```
OfInterest > 9
```

Then click the Break when Expression is **T**rue option button. This expression causes a running VB program to enter Break mode whenever the value of OfInterest is greater than 9.

13. Click OK. In the Watch dialog box, click **C**lose, and then run your program. Click the Command1 button.

The program goes into Break mode when OfInterest becomes greater than 9.

14. When the program goes into Break mode, type

```
? I, J, OfInterest
```

and press **Enter**. The values of these variables show you that OfInterest is, for the first time, greater than 9 when I = 2 and J = 7.

15. Click the Single Step button (the single footprint) in the Toolbar. Notice the change in the Code window. Click the Single Step button several more times, watching the effect in the Code window.

16. In the Debug window, type

```
? I, J, OfInterest
```

and press **Enter**. Notice that this technique enables you to keep close watch on what your program is doing. Experiment with the technique as many times as you want.

Notice also that the Debug window is not cleared between runs of your program. To clear the contents of the Debug window, when the program is in Break mode (the VB window's title bar will indicate this), do the following:

   a. Click and drag over all the text (below the Watch pane) in the Debug window. The text is now selected.

   b. Click the **Delete** key. The highlighted text disappears.

17. Click the Stop Run button. Choose **E**dit Watch from the **D**ebug menu.

18. In the Watch dialog box, click the Delete All button to remove all watchpoints. Then click the **C**lose button.

Project 2:   Practicing with VB's Debugging Tools

Write a program that requests the user to enter numbers in five text boxes. These five numbers (in the five text boxes) should then be placed in five corresponding Single data type variables (A, B, C, D, and E). Place the Text1 number in A, the Text2 number in B, and so on.

Place A * 2 in a Single data type variable named F.

Place C * 3.5 in a Single data type variable named G.

If A + B + G is greater than or equal to C * D / E, the background of the form should turn red.

If A * B > C + G and F + G < E, the form's background should turn blue.

If D < 5 and (G > 10 or A < 1), the form's background should turn yellow.

If A > G, the form's background should turn green.

Use the debugging techniques and tools presented in this chapter to verify that your program is working correctly.

8

CHAPTER 9

Using Arrays and Data Structures

Ordinary variables, the kind you have used so far, store only a single value at one time. Such variables are quite useful but ultimately limiting. Many programming projects require the storage and efficient manipulation—in code—of large amounts of information.

Suppose that you want to write an inventory control program for an automobile parts company. You may need to deal with thousands of different parts. You would find it difficult to manipulate such large amounts of data with ordinary variables. To handle such sizable data requirements, you need arrays.

Arrays are like super variables, storing multiple data values under a single name. You explore arrays in this chapter. Because large amounts of data can be stored in arrays, the chapter shows you how to read data from disk files. When you are reading files, defining a record is often useful. Records, which are user-defined data types, are discussed in this chapter.

Objectives

By the time you have finished this chapter, you will be able to

1. Declare and Use Single-Dimensional Arrays and Multidimensional Arrays
2. Load an Array with Data from a Disk File
3. Understand the Differences between Fixed-Size Arrays and Dynamic Arrays
4. Use the ReDim Statement
5. Erase an Array
6. Use User-Defined Data Types (Records)
7. Pass Arrays and Records to User-Defined Procedures

Working with Arrays

In most of the program examples presented in previous chapters, the variables have been simple variables—"simple" because each variable stores a single value. In the following instructions, for example, the variables Month1$, Month2$, and Month3$ are separate variables that store separate values:

```
Month1$ = "January"
Month2$ = "February"
Month3$ = "March"
```

Simple variables can be numeric, string, or Variant. Of course, the value of a variable might change during the execution of a program. At all times, however, each simple variable "houses" a single data value. And to change the contents of one variable, you need one line of code; for 100 variables, you need 100 lines of code.

Array

A variable that stores multiple data values under a single name.

Arrays change all that. **Arrays**—or more precisely, array variables—consist of many separate data values maintained under a common name. An array is like one variable with many compartments (see figure 9.1). The compartments are referred to as the elements of the array. Using arrays, you can easily manipulate large amounts of related data. With only a few program lines, you can recalculate thousands of data values or display a large table. This chapter shows you how.

Figure 9.1

An array named MyArray.

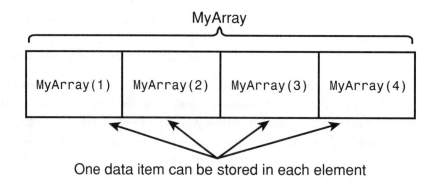

One data item can be stored in each element

Just as with ordinary variables, every array has a name that you give it. Array names follow the same naming conventions as ordinary variables, including the optional %, &, !, #, @, or $ suffix to identify the data type of the array. When you give an array a data type, every element of the array conforms to that data type.

Subscript

The index number that immediately follows the array name and identifies a specific element in the array.

Arrays, like ordinary variables, can have the data type Variant. In such a case, the individual elements (compartments) of the array can contain different kinds of data supported by Variants: numbers, strings, and date/time values. Because you must reference the individual compartments of an array when you store data in it, a distinguishing feature of an array is the **subscript** (or index number) that immediately follows the name.

Consider the following instruction:

```
Value = Cost(30)
```

Here Cost is an array. The subscript 30 is enclosed in parentheses. The parentheses "tell" Visual Basic that this is an array rather than an ordinary variable.

You can't refer to the contents of the whole array just by mentioning the array name. You must refer to each individual element (compartment) of the array.

The value of the subscript identifies a single element of the whole array. For example, the collection of month names can be written as an array:

```
MonthName$(1) = "January"
MonthName$(2) = "February"
MonthName$(3) = "March"
```

Here you have an array named MonthName$, which is a string array because the name ends with a dollar sign. Each element of MonthName$ contains a string value. The first element of the array, MonthName$(1), has the value January. The second element, MonthName$(2), has the value February. MonthName$(3) has the value March.

Remember, an array subscript is always enclosed in parentheses placed immediately after the array name. The subscript can be an explicit number, a variable, or even an expression that evaluates to a number. Table 9.1 provides some examples.

Table 9.1 Sample Array Subscripts

Array Element	Type of Subscript
MonthName$(2)	Explicit number
Salary!(Employee%)	Variable name
Cost#(23 + J%)	Simple expression
Cost#((J% - 1) * 3)	Expression containing parentheses

Subscript values must be whole numbers. Visual Basic rounds numbers that are not whole to the nearest integer. If, for example, Salary! is an array containing the salaries of a company's employees, Salary!(433.2) references employee number 433 and Salary!(228.8) references employee number 229.

A Sample Program with Arrays

The following program demonstrates how a few simple For-Next loops can manipulate groups of data.

Suppose that you own Ace Accordion Supply. Your 1995 monthly sales figures have finally arrived. Assume that the sales data is stored in a text file named YEARDATA.TXT. The file is saved on drive C in the \SALES directory. In other words, the complete file specification (path and file name) is C:\SALES\YEARDATA.TXT. The following is the text of the data file:

```
Jan, Feb, Mar, Apr, May, Jun, July, Aug, Sep, Oct, Nov, Dec,
28, 21, 14, 32, 25, 26, 20, 16, 23, 19, 29, 26
```

The first line of the file contains the abbreviated names for each month. Commas separate consecutive entries. The second line contains the number of accordions sold (by month). Again, commas separate consecutive entries.

9

Creating the ACE Application

In this exercise, you create a program, called ACE, that displays the monthly sales and computes the yearly total. Follow these steps:

1 Create the YEARDATA.TXT data file on your system. You can use a text editor such as Windows Notepad to type the text of the two-line file. Create the C:\SALES directory, and save YEARDATA.TXT in that directory.

2 Start a new project. Create a form containing a picture box and two command buttons. Assign properties for these controls, as shown in table 9.2.

Table 9.2 Design-Time Properties for ACE

Control	Property	Value
Form1	Caption	Ace Accordion Supply
	Height	5085
	Left	1035
	Top	1140
	Width	7485
Picture1	Height	4095
	Left	480
	Top	240
	Width	4215
Command1	Caption	&Show Report
	Height	615
	Left	5040
	Name	cmdShowReport
	Top	1200
	Width	2175
Command2	Caption	&Quit
	Height	615
	Left	5040
	Name	cmdQuit
	Top	2520
	Width	2175

3 Place the following two array declaration instructions in the general declarations section at the form level:

```
Dim MonthName(12) As String    'Name for each month
Dim NumSold(12) As Integer     'Number sold per month
```

④ Create the following Click event procedure for the first command button:

```
Sub cmdShowReport_Click ()
  Dim J As Integer              'Array index
  Dim Total As Integer          'Total number sold
  '
  '   Read data from data file
  Open "C:\SALES\YEARDATA.TXT" For Input As #7
  For J = 1 To 12
  Input #7, MonthName(J)  'Read string data for each month
  Next J
  For J = 1 To 12
      Input #7, NumSold(J)    'Read number sold each month
  Next J
  Close #7                    'Close data file
  '
  '  Display Report Heading
  Picture1.Print "Ace Accordion Supply - 1995 Sales"
  Picture1.Print
  Picture1.Print "Month", "Number Sold"    'Display table heading
  '
  For J = 1 To 12
  Picture1.Print MonthName(J), NumSold(J)  'Display monthly data
  Next J
  Picture1.Print
  '
  Total = 0
  For J = 1 To 12
     Total = Total + NumSold(J)  'Calculate yearly sales total
  Next J
  Picture1.Print "Yearly total = "; Total
End Sub
```

⑤ Create the following Click event procedure for the second command button:

```
Sub cmdQuit_Click ()
  End
End Sub
```

⑥ Save the form as **ACE.FRM**, and the project as **ACE.MAK**.

⑦ Run the application.

Figure 9.2 shows the output that is displayed after you click the Show Report command button. The application displays the 1995 sales data in the picture box.

(continues)

9

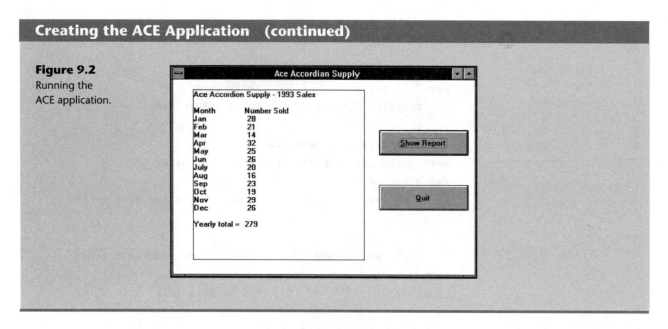

Creating the ACE Application (continued)

Figure 9.2
Running the
ACE application.

Understanding How ACE Works

By examining the program code, you get a good introduction to the use of array variables. First, consider the two `Dim` instructions in the general declarations section of the form.

You are already familiar with the use of `Dim` instructions to declare ordinary variables. The two `Dim` instructions in this program declare array variables. The instructions tell Visual Basic the names and sizes of the arrays used in the application. Because the instructions occur at the form level, these arrays are recognized in the procedures and functions associated with the form and with the controls placed on it.

The details of `Dim` are discussed later in this chapter. For now, realize that these `Dim` instructions inform Visual Basic that the project uses two arrays:

- A string array named `MonthName`

- An integer array named `NumSold`

Each of these arrays contains 12 elements. `Dim` establishes only the names and dimensions of the arrays. So that Visual Basic can distinguish between arrays and function references, you must declare an array with `Dim` or a similar instruction. You still must get data values into the individual array elements.

Note: *The arrays in this program example actually contain 13 elements, not 12. The reason is that Visual Basic includes, by default, an array element with a subscript of 0. As explained later in the chapter, you can change this default so that array elements with a subscript of 0 are not present.*

The active part of the program code occurs in the `cmdShowReport_Click` event procedure. This event procedure activates when the user clicks the upper command button.

You can place data into an array in several different ways. In this example, the data file YEARDATA.TXT contains the data values that will be stored in the array elements. The Open instruction establishes a link (data channel #7 in this case) between the application and the disk file. Two For-Next loops read the data values from the file and copy the values into the arrays.

In each loop, an Input #7 instruction does the actual reading. The first loop reads the 12 data strings expressing the abbreviations for the names of the months. The second loop reads the 12 monthly sales figures (28 accordions sold in January, 21 sold in February, and so on). After all the relevant data in the file is read, the Close instruction terminates the active link between the disk file and the application.

Notice how these two simple loops read all the data values. That's the power of array subscripting. After these loops execute, each array contains 12 data values in preparation for the rest of the program. In the NumSold array, for example, NumSold(1) is 28, NumSold(2) is 21, and so on.

The program now displays the output in the form of a two-column table. With the Print method, the program displays results in the picture box.

After the heading for the table is displayed, the ensuing For-Next loop displays the monthly sales figures. These values are the data values picked up from the YEARDATA.TXT file. But, again, notice how easily a simple loop can display a whole array full of data. By simply changing the dimensions of the array and changing the For-Next statement to

```
For J = 1 to 12000
```

you could process 12,000 items of data.

Finally, the program calculates Total, the total sales over the whole year. The ultimate value of Total is the sum of the monthly sales figures. That is, Total should be the sum of all the elements of the NumSold array:

```
NumSold(1) + NumSold(2) + ... + NumSold(12)
```

Again, a simple loop is the answer. The final For-Next loop calculates the value of Total. When the loop finishes, Total contains the desired sum, which is displayed with the Print method.

The cmdQuit_Click event procedure consists entirely of an End instruction. When the user clicks the lower command button, the application ends.

The ACE application demonstrates the power of arrays. With a few simple loops, you can easily manipulate array elements. Notice how the For-Next counter variable (J in this application) is often used as an array subscript. This practice is common in programs with arrays. Loops and arrays naturally work well together. Loop counter variables increment sequentially, which is exactly how array elements are subscripted.

Placing Data into Arrays

In any program using arrays, you must get the necessary data values into the array elements. This task is often called "loading the array." The three most common techniques to accomplish this are (1) to request the data from the user at run time, (2) to read the data from a disk file, and (3) to store the data values as part of the program code (often in the Form_Load event).

Note that Visual Basic does not support the READ and DATA statements found in QBasic and earlier versions of BASIC. (These statements facilitated the storage and retrieval of data values directly in the program code.) As a result, in Visual Basic, the data for large arrays is often contained in one or more disk files that are read during run time.

The ACE application demonstrates the techniques of opening a disk file and using Input instructions to read data from the disk file into the array elements. The AREACODE application, presented later in this chapter, further explores the reading of array data values from text files. Files are discussed in depth in Chapter 12.

Dimensioning Arrays with *Dim*

As the two instructions in the general declarations section of ACE.MAK demonstrate, you use Dim to declare arrays at the form level. Dim provides an extended syntax with several options. For now, consider only the simple form of the Dim instruction. (Extensions to the syntax of Dim are explained later in this chapter.)

This section discusses Dim instructions used for array declarations. As you learned in earlier chapters, you can also use Dim to declare ordinary variables. Furthermore, you can declare arrays with the Global and Static instructions, which are discussed later in this chapter.

The simple form of the Dim instruction (for array declarations) accomplishes four tasks:

- Establishes the name of the array.

- Establishes the data type of the array.

- Specifies the number of elements in the array.

- Initializes the value of each element of the array. Numeric array elements become zero, string array elements become the null string, and Variants become the special value Empty.

The following is the syntax of the simple form of Dim:

```
Dim arrayname(subscriptrange) AS type
```

arrayname is the name of the array. *subscriptrange* specifies the index range for the elements in the array. *type* declares the data type of *arrayname*. The As *type* clause is optional.

Note: *With Visual Basic, you must declare every array, including small arrays with fewer than 10 elements. This rule is a departure from QBasic, QuickBASIC, and other procedural versions of BASIC that permit small arrays to be used without being declared.*

Specifying the *As* Clause

The optional As clause specifies the data type of the array. To use the As clause, *arrayname* must not contain a type-declaration suffix. The *type* parameter must be one of the terms listed in table 9.3. In this table, *num* is being used as a placeholder to represent an expression that can hold many values.

Table 9.3	As Clause Data Declarations
Term	**Variable Type**
Integer	Integer
Long	Long integer
Single	Single-precision
Double	Double-precision
Currency	Currency
String	Variable-length string
String * *num*	Fixed-length string of length *num*
Variant	Variant

The *type* parameter can also be a user-defined data type (a record). User-defined data types are discussed later in this chapter.

Omitting the *As* Clause

If you omit the As clause, array names follow the same conventions as variable names. In particular, a data type suffix (!, #, %, &, @, or $) establishes the data type for each element of the array. (Recall that every element of an array must be the same data type.) If you don't use a suffix on the array name, the data type defaults to Variant.

Defining the Subscript Range

As noted, the *subscriptrange* parameter establishes the lowest and highest values allowed for the array subscript. Two forms of the *subscriptrange* parameter exist: a single value and two values separated by the keyword To.

In the former case, the single value of *subscriptrange* establishes the highest permissible value of the array subscript. Visual Basic automatically considers the lowest legal subscript value to be 0 (not 1). Note the following instruction:

```
Dim NumVotes(10) As Integer
```

This establishes an integer array named NumVotes, which has 11 elements: NumVotes(0), NumVotes(1), . . ., NumVotes(10).

In the latter case (with the To keyword), the *subscriptrange* parameter directly specifies the lowest and highest permissible values of the subscript. The lowest value does not have to be 0 or 1. For example, the following instruction declares the integer array CheckNum to have 51 elements ranging from a subscript of 100 through a subscript of 150:

9

```
Dim CheckNum(100 To 150) As Integer
```

By using the To clause, you can specify any value for the lowest and highest subscript values. Negative values are acceptable. In all instances, however, the lowest subscript value (the number before To) must always be lower in value than the highest subscript value (the number after To).

Declaring Multiple Arrays

A single Dim instruction can declare two or more arrays. In these cases, you use a comma to separate the array names. Table 9.4 shows some sample Dim instructions.

Table 9.4 Sample *Dim* Instructions	
Instruction	**Description**
`Dim Client(200) As String`	String array with 201 elements: Client(0) to Client(200)
`Dim Profit!(1975 To 1993)`	Single-precision array with 19 elements: Profit!(1975) to Profit!(1993)
`Dim Shares(-40 To 15) As Long`	Long integer array with 56 elements: Shares(-40) to Shares(15)
`Dim Tax(30), Cost(30)`	Two Variant arrays, each with 31 elements
`Dim A%(45), B%(34), C$(21)`	Three arrays: (1) An integer array with 46 elements: A%(0) to A%(45) (2) Another integer array with 35 elements: B%(0) to B%(34) (3) A string array with 22 elements: C$(0) to C$(21)

Where to Put *Dim* Instructions

A Dim instruction can appear anywhere before the first use of the array. When possible, however, you should place all your Dim instructions together near the beginning of the program. That way, you can quickly identify the names and sizes of all the arrays in the program.

Changing the Base Subscript—*Option Base*

An Option Base instruction changes the lower array subscript from the default of 0 to 1. You use the following syntax:

```
Option Base basesub
```

basesub specifies the lowest array subscript for subsequent Dim, Global, and Static instructions. The only valid values for *basesub* are 0 (zero) and 1.

Because we usually start counting from 1 rather than 0, some programmers prefer to start their arrays from 1:

```
Option Base 1
```

Consider the following program fragment:

```
Option Base 1
Dim MyArray(200) As Double
```

The first line changes the default lower array bound from 0 to 1. As a result, the `Dim` instruction creates an array with elements from `MyArray(1)` to `MyArray(200)`. If `Option Base 0` were used, an additional element, `MyArray(0)`, would be added, for a total of 201 elements in the array.

Using Variables and Constants as Array Dimensions

So far, the sample `Dim` instructions specify the number of array elements with numeric literals. You can also use variable names and constants. Variables and constants provide a convenient way to alter array boundaries between successive runs of a program.

Suppose that you have an application which displays the results of your track club's road races. The program code dimensions arrays in this way:

```
Dim LastName$(300), FirstName$(300)
Dim Age(300) As Integer
Dim Weight(300) As Single
Dim RaceTime(300) As Single
```

A more flexible solution is to use a variable name, as in the following code:

```
Dim MaxRunners As Integer
MaxRunners = 300
Dim LastName$(MaxRunners), FirstName$(MaxRunners)
Dim Age(MaxRunners) As Integer
Dim Weight(MaxRunners) As Single
Dim RaceTime(MaxRunners) As Single
```

Notice that the variable name `MaxRunners` is easier to understand than the literal `300`. Furthermore, if you need to enlarge the number 300 when your track club membership grows, all that you need to modify is the single line that assigns a value to `MaxRunners` (instead of modifying all the `Dim` instructions).

You can use this same technique with constants as well as variables.

The Scope of Array Declarations

Arrays declared with `Dim`, `Static`, and `Global` have the same scope as ordinary variables declared at the same level. The following rules apply to both arrays and ordinary variables:

- When a `Dim` instruction declares an array in the declarations section of a code module, the array is available throughout the entire module.

- When a `Dim` instruction declares an array in the declarations section of a form, the array is available in all procedures associated with the form.

9

- When you declare an array inside a procedure, the array is available only within that procedure. As explained in upcoming sections, you cannot declare an array with `Dim` inside a procedure unless the whole procedure is declared to be static. However, you can always declare an array inside a procedure with `Static`.

Declaring Arrays with *Static* and *Global* Instructions

Besides using `Dim`, you can use `Static` and `Global` instructions to declare arrays. The syntax is exactly the same as with `Dim`, except that the keyword `Static` or `Global` replaces the keyword `Dim`. All these instructions are valid:

```
Static MyArray(55) As Double

Static YearlySales@(1985 To 1993)

Global TwoD(NumRows, NumColumns)
```

As the following sections explain, the choice of the `Dim`, `Static`, or `Global` keyword affects the attributes and scope of the declared array.

Creating Static Arrays

Static array

An array in which the elements retain their values throughout the execution of the program.

An array declared with the `Static` statement becomes, naturally enough, a **static array**. As a result, the elements in the array retain their values throughout the execution of the program.

Most important, with `Static` used inside a procedure to declare an array, the elements in the array retain their previous values each time you invoke the procedure. Notice that you cannot declare an array inside a procedure with `Dim` unless the whole procedure has been declared to be static. In a static procedure, an array declared with `Dim` automatically becomes a static array.

You can use the `Static` keyword in the procedure declaration itself so that all variables in the procedure retain their values. Consider the following code fragment:

```
Static Sub GetTotal ()
    Dim MyArray(10)
    .
    .
```

Here the entire procedure is static, so `MyArray` is static even though the array is declared with the `Dim` instruction. Similarly, in the following nonstatic procedure, `MyArray` is static because the array is declared with the `Static` keyword:

```
Sub GetTotal ()
    Static MyArray(10)
    .
    .
```

Declaring Procedures with the *Static* Keyword

When you declare a procedure with the `Static` keyword, as in `Static Sub GetTotal ()`, the memory storage for the arrays (and other variables) defined within the procedure is allocated once, just before the program executes. The values of the array elements, as well as the values of the other variables, remain intact throughout the program execution.

Declaring Fixed-Sized Arrays in Nonstatic Procedures

Inside a nonstatic procedure, you must declare a fixed-size array with the `Static` keyword. As mentioned earlier, you cannot use `Dim`. The preceding example, repeated here, illustrates this technique:

```
Sub GetTotal ()
   Static MyArray(10)
      .
      .
```

Notice, though, that the following program fragment generates an error message:

```
Sub GetTotal ()
   Dim MyArray(10)
      .
      .
```

However, in static procedures (declared with the `Static` keyword), you can declare fixed-size arrays with either the `Static` statement or the `Dim` statement.

Creating Global Arrays

Arrays declared with the `Global` statement are available to every procedure in the project. "Every procedure" means just that: all procedures in every form and every module.

Recall that `Global` instructions can occur only in the declarations section of a code module. You cannot use `Global` at the form or procedure level.

Table Lookup—A Sample Program with Arrays

Suppose that you want to write a program asking the user for a telephone area code. After the user enters the area code, the program responds with the name of the state or province associated with that area code. For example, if the user enters the number *213*, the program displays `California`.

Imagine that your job requires you to respond with a state name when given an area code number. If you didn't have a computer, you would most likely tackle this task by first finding a list or table of all the area codes and the corresponding states. Then when anyone asked about a particular area code, you would scan your list for that code. If you found a match, you would respond with the corresponding state name. If you didn't find a match, you would reply that there is no such area code on your list.

This general technique is known as table lookup. You look through a table to find a specific entry. When you find it, you get the corresponding information from an adjacent "column" of the table.

9

Using the AREACODE Application

The AREACODE application does precisely the same table lookup. The data is read from a text file. The user types an area code into a text box, and the application displays the name of the state or province in a second text box. In the example shown in figure 9.3, the user has typed the area code 207. The application responded with the appropriate state name of Maine.

Figure 9.3
Running the
AREACODE
application.

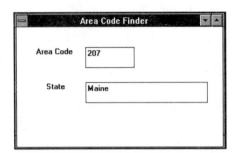

In the example shown in figure 9.4, the user has not typed a valid area code. The application responded with an appropriate message.

Figure 9.4
An invalid area code
entered.

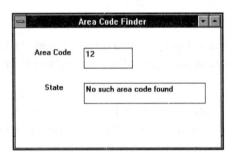

Creating the AREACODE Application

Consisting of two event procedures and some form-level declarations, this program reads its input from a text file. Construct the AREACODE application by following these steps:

1 Create a text file named AREACODE.TXT, and type the following data into it:

```
201, New Jersey
202, D.C.
203, Connecticut
204, Manitoba
205, Alabama
206, Washington
207, Maine
208, Idaho
209, California
212, New York
```

```
213, California
214, Texas
```

The AREACODE application reads the area code and state data from AREACODE.TXT. For this exercise, you type only a small portion of all the area codes. You can expand the file, however, to include as many area codes as you want.

In the file, you don't have to place the entries in numerical order. As long as each state name appears next to its area code, the application works fine, regardless of the area code ordering.

Note: *In the following code, the* Open *statement assumes that the file AREACODE.TXT is stored in the C:\VBS subdirectory. You should store the file wherever it is best for you (for example, on drive A). But remember to change the* Open *statement to reflect the location in which you saved your data file.*

❷ Create a form containing two text boxes and two labels. For these controls, assign the properties shown in table 9.5.

Table 9.5   Design-Time Properties for AREACODE.MAK

Control	Property	Value
Form1	Caption	Area Code Finder
	Height	3270
	Left	1365
	Top	1140
	Width	5190
Text1	Name	txtAreaCode
	Height	495
	Left	1680
	Top	480
	Width	1215
Text2	Name	txtStateName
	Height	495
	Left	1680
	Top	1320
	Width	3015
Label1	Caption	Area Code
	Height	375
	Left	480
	Top	480
	Width	975

9

(continues)

Creating the AREACODE Application   (continued)

Table 9.5 Continued		
Control	**Property**	**Value**
Label2	Caption	State
	Height	495
	Left	720
	Top	1320
	Width	855

3 Place the following three Dim instructions in the general declarations section (that is, at the form level):

```
Dim AreaCode(150) As Integer
Dim StateName(150) As String
Dim NumEntries As Integer
```

The first two Dim instructions declare the arrays that hold the area codes and state names, respectively. Each array holds 151 elements with index values ranging from 0 to 150.

4 Create the following Form_Load event procedure:

```
Sub Form_Load ()
  'Read data from disk file into arrays
  Open "c:\vbs\areacode.txt" For Input As #9
  NumEntries = 0
  Do
    NumEntries = NumEntries + 1
    Input #9, AreaCode(NumEntries), StateName(NumEntries)
  Loop Until EOF(9)
  '
  'Blank out initial values in the text boxes
  txtAreaCode.Text = ""
  txtStateName.Text = ""
End Sub
```

5 Finally, create the txtAreaCode_Change event procedure:

```
Sub txtAreaCode_Change ()
    'Find state name corresponding to area code
    Dim Message As String   'Text message displayed to user
    Dim J As Integer        'Index variable for For-Next loops
    Message = "No such area code found"
    For J = 1 To NumEntries
        If Val(txtAreaCode.Text) = AreaCode(J) Then
          Message = StateName(J)
```

```
              End If
            Next J
            txtStateName.Text = Message
         End Sub
```

6 Save the form as **AREACODE.FRM**, and the project as **AREACODE.MAK**.

7 Run the program. Enter area codes of **203**, **206**, and **607**. Verify that your program is working correctly.

8 Click the Stop button in the Toolbar to end program execution.

Understanding How AREACODE Works

When you run the application, the Form_Load procedure immediately activates. This procedure opens the data file and assigns data channel #9 to the link between the data file and the application. Be aware that, in the Open instruction, you can modify the path to the data file to specify the directory in which you have saved the data file.

The Do-Loop block reads the area codes and state names into the AreaCode and StateName arrays, respectively.

The EOF function tests whether the previous Input instruction read the last data in the file. If so, EOF returns True, and the loop terminates. If not, EOF returns False, and the loop continues for another iteration. The variable Entries increments by one each time through the loop. When the loop terminates, the value of Entries equals the number of area codes and state names stored in the respective arrays.

Table 9.6 shows how the area codes and state names are stored in the AreaCode and StateName arrays.

Table 9.6	Partial Contents of the Area Code and State Name Arrays	
Element Number	**Area Code**	**State Name**
1	201	New Jersey
2	202	D.C.
3	203	Connecticut
4	204	Manitoba
5	205	Alabama

The Form_Load procedure ends by blanking out the initial text in the two text boxes.

The main work of the application occurs in the txtAreaCode_Change event procedure. This procedure activates when the user modifies the text in the area code text box.

9

`Message` is the string variable that stores the response the user eventually sees. At first, `Message` is set to report that a match is not found. If a match is subsequently found, `Message` is updated appropriately.

The application expects the user to enter an area code into the `txtAreaCode` text box. The entered text is treated by Visual Basic as a string value. The `Val` function converts this string value to the actual numeric value.

The `For-Next` loop searches through the area codes in the `AreaCode` array, attempting to match the entered area code. When the loop finds a match (in the `If` instruction), the index variable `J` contains the number of the matching element from the `AreaCode` array. At this point, `Message` is assigned the proper state name from the `StateName` array. Notice that the same index value of `J` points to the proper corresponding value in the `StateName` array. That's table lookup in action.

When the `For-Next` loop finishes, the application displays the response by assigning the value of `Message` to the `Text` property of the `txtStateName` text box. Notice that `Message` contains the appropriate message whether or not a match was found. If a match was found, `Message` contains the matching state name; if no match was found, `Message` contains the no-match message originally set before the `For-Next` loop.

The application continues to process each request by the user. The program responds whenever the user modifies the value in the `txtAreaCode` text box. To terminate the program, you click the Stop button in the Toolbar or choose **End** from the **R**un menu.

Using Multidimensional Arrays

So far, the sample arrays have been one-dimensional—a list of values. For example, the array `Salary!(Employee%)` contains salary information as a function of an employee number. One-dimensional arrays use only a single subscript to span all the values of the array. Suppose, however, that you have data in the form of a table (a spreadsheet, for example). Such data has a two-dimensional, row-and-column structure.

Visual Basic supports two-dimensional arrays to represent two-dimensional data. You need two subscripts to specify an element of a two-dimensional array: one subscript for the row number and one subscript for the column number. You use a comma to separate the two subscripts.

A chessboard, for example, can be considered a two-dimensional array. Figure 9.5 shows a chess game in progress. Each square of the 8-by-8 board has a row number from 1 to 8 and a column number from 1 to 8.

For the chessboard, a two-dimensional array named `Piece` contains the name of the chess piece currently occupying each square. The following instructions represent the board shown in figure 9.5:

Figure 9.5

A chess game in progress.

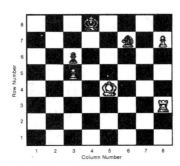

```
Dim Piece(8, 8) As String
For Row% = 1 To 8
    For Column% = 1 To 8
        Piece(Column%, Row%) = "None"
    Next Column%
Next Row%
Piece(3, 5) = "White Pawn"
Piece(8, 7) = "White Pawn"
Piece(8, 3) = "White Rook"
Piece(5, 4) = "White King"
Piece(3, 6) = "Black Pawn"
Piece(6, 7) = "Black Knight"
Piece(4, 8) = "Black King"
```

The first line dimensions the `Piece` array with a `Dim` instruction. The array is designated to be two-dimensional by the use of two subscripts. This `Dim` instruction tells Visual Basic the following information:

- `Piece` is a two-dimensional string array.

- The first dimension has subscript values ranging from 0 to 8.

- The second dimension has subscript values ranging from 0 to 8.

Notice that each dimension actually spans nine values (because the lowest value in each dimension is 0, not 1). There are 81 (9 by 9) total elements in the `Piece` array. In this program fragment, two nested `For-Next` loops initialize the value of each array element with the string value `None`. Notice how nested loops quickly reference an entire two-dimensional array.

The remaining lines assign specific string values to the array elements that represent squares containing pieces. In each array reference, the first subscript is a column number, and the second subscript is a row number. For example, `Piece(3, 5)` refers to the piece at column 3 and row 5.

Just as with one-dimensional arrays, you can use the `To` parameter to specify the subscript range of a two-dimensional array. For example, the following instruction declares that the two-dimensional string array `Title$` has index ranges from 10 to 25 and from 30 to 64:

```
Dim Title$(10 To 25, 30 To 64)
```

Arrays are not limited to two dimensions. Visual Basic allows arrays with as many as 60 dimensions! In practice, arrays with more than three dimensions are rare.

9

Fixed and Dynamic Allocation

Fixed allocation
The permanent allocation (for the duration of the running of a program) of an area of memory for a stored variable.

Dynamic allocation
The capability of a program to assign (and reassign) memory locations for a variable while the program is running.

The memory location of a stored variable can be allocated by Visual Basic either when you start the program or while the program is running (executing). The former allocation is called **fixed allocation** (or static allocation), and the latter is called **dynamic allocation**. The trade-off involves flexibility versus efficiency.

Dynamic allocation is flexible because storage is allocated and deallocated while the program runs. If a dynamic variable is no longer needed, the memory can be freed for another use.

Fixed allocation is less flexible but more efficient. Fixed variables are allocated to memory locations before the program runs and keep these addresses throughout the execution of the program. This approach is efficient because, before the program begins, Visual Basic resolves the necessary addresses. As a result, the machine language instructions produced by Visual Basic already contain the appropriate addresses.

Notice that, for fixed allocation, Visual Basic must be able to determine the variable's exact size before the program runs. The exact size of any simple variable or record is always known.

Declaring Dynamic Arrays

For some applications, you want to change the size of the array during run time. Programmers refer to this task as reassigning memory allocation "on the fly." With a `ReDim` instruction (explained shortly), you can dynamically modify the array bounds while the application executes. Sometimes you don't know the size of an array when the program begins. You know that the array needs to be present, but its size depends on a condition that occurs at run time. Usually, this condition is input from the user.

For example, a program that grades school tests might use several arrays, each dimensioned to the size of the number of students. But the number of students can vary widely—from 35 for a single classroom, to 500 for an entire school, to 10,000 or more for a school district. The user inputs the number of students, and the program dimensions the arrays accordingly.

You could dimension the arrays of a program with fixed sizes large enough to satisfy any possible practical application. The program can then simply ignore the unneeded array elements. However, this approach wastes memory and is inefficient. By using Visual Basic's dynamic array allocation, you can dimension (and redimension) arrays to precise sizes at run time.

By creating a dynamic array, you can modify the dimensioning one or more times while the program runs. To declare a dynamic array, you use a `Dim`, `Global`, or `Static` instruction, but you don't specify any dimensioning. You simply declare the array with an empty set of parentheses. For example, the following instruction declares `Score` to be a dynamic array:

```
Dim Score() As Integer
```

As with any array declaration, you use `Global` to give the dynamic array global scope, `Dim` at the module level for module-level scope, or `Static` inside a procedure for local scope.

Allocating a Dynamic Array with *ReDim*

You use the `ReDim` statement to allocate a dynamic array that has previously been declared with empty parentheses:

```
ReDim arrayname(subscriptrange)
```

arrayname is the name of an array, and *subscriptrange* specifies the dimensions for the array. For example, after declaring `Score` as dynamic, the following instruction declares `Score` to be a two-dimensional array:

```
ReDim Score(20, 40)
```

`ReDim` is an executable instruction that takes effect at run time. Therefore, `ReDim` instructions must appear inside `Sub` and `Function` procedures (including event procedures). You can specify the array bounds with variables and constants as well as numeric literals, as in this example:

```
ReDim Score(NumStudents, NumProblems)
```

Eight is the maximum number of array dimensions you can specify.

Reallocating a Dynamic Array with *ReDim*

You can redimension a dynamic array several times by repeatedly executing `ReDim` instructions. Here is the simplest syntax for the `ReDim` instruction:

```
ReDim arrayname(subscriptrange)
```

When *arrayname* is the name of a currently dimensioned array, `ReDim` deallocates the old array and reallocates the array with the new dimensions. All the old array values are lost during this process. New array values reinitialize to 0 (for numeric arrays), to null strings (for variable-length string arrays), to ANSI 0 characters (for fixed-length string arrays), and to Empty values (for Variant arrays).

`ReDim` can change the size of each dimension but cannot change the number of dimensions. Note the following typical use of `ReDim`:

```
Dim MyArray() As Single     'Dynamic array declared at module-level
    .
    .
ReDim MyArray(30, 20, 10)   'Array allocation inside a procedure
    .
    .
ReDim MyArray(50, 25, 12)   'Array is redimensioned
```

This code works because `MyArray` has three dimensions in both `ReDim` instructions. However, if the second `ReDim` instruction were `ReDim MyArray(5000)`, the result would be a `Wrong number of dimensions` error.

The syntax for the `ReDim` instruction permits the optional `Preserve` keyword:

```
ReDim Preserve arrayname(subscriptrange)
```

With the `Preserve` keyword, the existing array values can be retained when the array is redimensioned. With `Preserve`, however, only the last array dimension can change size without the loss of any array values. For a single-dimensional array, *all* the existing array values can be retained because that single dimension is the last and only dimension. For a multidimensional array, however, only the far-right array dimension can change size while retaining the contents of the array.

For example, the following program fragment redimensions MyArray while preserving the array contents:

```
ReDim MyArray(50, 25, 12)   'Dynamic array is redimensioned
      .
      .
ReDim Preserve MyArray(50, 25, 15)   'Array values are retained
```

Erasing Arrays—The *Erase* Instruction

An Erase instruction affects the designated arrays; the effect depends on whether the arrays are declared with fixed or dynamic allocation. Here is the syntax of Erase:

```
Erase arraylist
```

arraylist is a list of array names separated by commas. If an array name refers to a fixed array, the following effects apply:

1. Each element is reinitialized. That is, elements of numeric arrays are reset to 0, elements of variable-length string arrays are reset to the null string, elements of fixed-length string arrays are set to ANSI 0, and elements of Variant arrays are reset to the Empty value.

2. Each element in an array of records is reset as if it were a separate variable.

3. The effect is simply to reset the value of every array element to a default value.

If the array name refers to a dynamic array, the array is deallocated. This frees the memory used by the array.

The next program fragment reinitializes a static array:

```
Static MyArray(1000) As Integer   'Static array
MyArray(500) = 18
Print MyArray(500)
Erase MyArray                      'Reset all elements to 0
Print MyArray(500)
```

Here is the output:

```
18
0
```

When working with arrays, remember that Visual Basic requires considerable memory resources for storing large arrays. For example, VB needs more than 15,000 bytes of memory to store the following array:

```
Dim Salary(300, 12) As Single
```

When working with dynamic arrays, you can use the Erase instruction to "erase" an array from memory. The array elements become permanently lost. However,

Visual Basic can now use the array's previous memory space for other purposes, such as dimensioning a new array. It's a good idea to erase a dynamic array when the program no longer needs the array.

When you specify one or more arrays in an `Erase` instruction, use only the root names of the arrays, with no parentheses or subscripts. For example, the following instruction erases previously dimensioned arrays named `Price!` and `Client%`:

```
Erase Price!, Client%
```

Declaring a Dynamic Array with *ReDim*

You can use `ReDim` inside a procedure to declare a dynamic array initially. That is, you don't declare the array at the module level with a `Dim` or `Global` instruction using empty parentheses. Instead, you declare the array for the first time with a `ReDim` instruction inside a procedure.

In such a case, the scope of the array is limited to the procedure containing the `ReDim` instruction. The syntax for this use of `ReDim` corresponds to that of the `Dim` instruction:

```
ReDim arrayname(subscriptrange) As type,
      arrayname(subscriptrange) As type ...
```

arrayname is the name of an array, *subscriptrange* specifies the new dimensions for the array, and *type* declares the data type of *arrayname*. The `As type` clause is optional.

Using User-Defined Data Types

One shortcoming of arrays is that, with the exception of type Variant arrays, every element of an array must have the same data type. Although every element of an ordinary array must have the same data type, arrays of type Variant permit flexible data types to occur in the same array.

Sometimes you want to group data items of diverse data types together under a common name because the diverse items are associated in some way. This approach is considered good programming practice because the way your data storage is structured reflects "real world" relationships. Historically, computer data that records information on the same person, place, thing, or event has been called a record. The pieces of information are associated because they describe the same entity. For example, a given record might consist of an employee's name, social security number, department, date of hire, salary or wage, and job title. The data items in a record are commonly referred to as the record's fields.

User-defined data type
A data structure that you can create and define as a data type for use in an application.

Visual Basic lets you establish a **user-defined data type**. Other names for the user-defined data type are *record* and *structure*. Records give you a free hand to custom-design a data type for a particular application. (Records are commonly used, for example, when you read and write disk files. See Chapter 12 for information on processing files.)

9

Record
A structured data type made up of multiple elements. The elements can be of different types.

Like an array, a **record** is a structured data type made up of multiple elements. And, like the elements of an array of type Variant, the elements of a record can be of different data types.

You use a `Type-End Type` block structure to define each customized data type. Suppose that you are writing a payroll application. For each employee, you need to work with his or her name, company ID number, and salary. The following `Type` block establishes a user-defined data type called `Employee`:

```
Type Employee
    FullName As String * 35
    IDNumber As Integer
    Salary As Currency
End Type
```

`Employee` is a record made up of three pieces of information: `FullName`, which stores the employee's name; `IDNumber`, which stores the employee's identification number; and `Salary`, which stores the employee's salary. Before continuing with this example, take a more detailed look at `Type-End Type` blocks.

Defining a Record

A `Type-End Type` block must occur in the declarations section of a code module. User-defined data types have a global scope. You cannot place a `Type-End Type` block in a form module.

You place the `Type` instruction on the first line of the block, and the `End Type` instruction on the last line. Between those two lines, each component of the record appears on a separate line. Here is the syntax:

```
Type recordname
    elementname As type
    elementname As type
    elementname As type
End Type
```

recordname is the name for the data type, and *elementname* is the name for each component of the record. *type* specifies the data type of the corresponding *elementname*. You define the names for *recordname* and *elementname*. The usual variable-naming conventions apply, except that you cannot use the type-declaration suffixes (%, &, !, #, @, and $).

Notice that *recordname* gives a name to the data type itself, not to a variable having this data type. In the payroll example, `Employee` is the name of the data type. No actual variable having this data type has been created yet.

Any array declaration appearing in a `Type-End Type` block must be a static array—an array that uses literal numbers or constants to specify the number of array elements. Arrays declared with the `To` keyword are permitted. For example, the following declaration is acceptable:

```
MonthlyFee(1 To 12) As Currency
```

The requirement for static arrays arises from the restriction that the total memory size for any user-defined data type must be determinable before the program executes and must remain fixed throughout the program execution.

User-Defined Types versus Variant Type Arrays

One main advantage of user-defined data types is memory conservation. The memory required to store the data is always less with a user-defined data type than with a Variant array. A second advantage of user-defined types is that they clearly indicate associated data—data describing the same person, place, thing, or event.

Variant arrays have two main advantages over user-defined data types. First, a Variant array can be a dynamic array so that you can change the size of the array during run time. Second, you can change the data type stored in each array element at any time during program execution.

Declaring Variables of a Record Type

After you define a record with `Type`, you use `Dim` (or `Global`, `ReDim`, or `Static`) to declare a variable as having that data type. For example, the following instruction declares `Foreman` to be a variable of the user-defined data type `Employee`:

```
Dim Foreman As Employee
```

Arrays of records are permissible. The following instruction declares `Salesmen` to be an array of 75 elements:

```
Dim Salesmen(1 To 75) As Employee
```

Each element of the array has the user-defined data type `Employee`.

Referring to the Components of a Record Variable in Code

A record is a hierarchy of storage: subvariables within a larger variable. One record consists of compartments (or components) in which the items of data are stored. You refer to the individual components of a record by separating—with a period—the name of the larger variable (the higher-level variable) from the component's name. For example, the following program fragment assigns values to the three components of `Boss`:

```
Boss.FullName = "George M. Honcho"
Boss.IDNumber = 007
Boss.Salary = 3530.50
```

Similarly, you can define the 34th element of the `Salesmen` array as follows:

```
Salesmen(34).FullName = "Ed Closer"
Salesmen(34).IDNumber = 399
Salesmen(34).Salary = 2650.75
```

Passing Arrays and Records to User-Defined Procedures

In an earlier chapter, you learned how to pass variables as arguments to user-defined procedures. Remember, you cannot pass arguments to an event procedure; Windows does that. Besides passing ordinary variables, you can pass arrays and records to your `Sub` and `Function` procedures. The following sections explain these techniques.

Passing an Array

To pass an entire array to a user-defined procedure, use the array name followed by an empty set of parentheses. The corresponding formal parameter within the procedure also has an empty set of parentheses.

Inside the procedure, do not dimension the array. That is, don't use Dim, Static, ReDim, or Global to redefine the array. You can use the LBound and UBound functions to determine the lower and upper bounds of the array.

Suppose that you create the following Form_Load procedure, declaring a two-dimensional array named Sales. This procedure calls the user-defined SumArray function:

```
Sub Form_Load ()
    Static Sales(1 To 8, 0 To 10) As Integer
        .
        .      'These lines specify values for the elements of the Sales
               ➥ array.
        .
    Print "Total Sales ="; SumArray(Sales())    'Note empty ()
End Sub
```

The SumArray function appears as follows:

```
Function SumArray (A() As Integer) As Integer
    Dim Total, FirstDim, SecondDim As Integer
    Total = 0
    For FirstDim = LBound(A, 1) To UBound(A, 1)
        For SecondDim = LBound(A, 2) To UBound(A, 2)
            Total = Total + A(FirstDim, SecondDim)
        Next SecondDim
    Next FirstDim
    SumArray = Total
End Function
```

Notice that A() with an empty set of parentheses appears in the formal parameter list in the first line of the function. The empty set of parentheses identifies the argument as an entire array.

To pass an individual array element, you place the appropriate subscripts within the parentheses. For example, the following instruction calls a Sub procedure named ShowValue and passes a single array element:

```
Call ShowValue(MyArray(23))        'Single array element
```

Passing a Record

To pass an entire record, you use these steps:

1. Define the record type with a Type-End Type block declared in the declarations section of a code module, as in the following example:

```
Type BaseballPlayer
    FullName as String * 40
    BattingAverage as Single
    HomeRuns as Integer
End Type
```

2. Use a `Dim` (or `Static`, `ReDim`, or `Global`) instruction to give a variable your user-defined type. Note this example:

```
Dim Mantle As BaseballPlayer
```

3. When you invoke the procedure, pass your declared variable:

```
Call GetStats(Mantle)
```

4. In the procedure declaration, give the formal parameter your record type:

```
Sub GetStats(Person As BaseballPlayer)
```

To pass an individual record element, you can use the element descriptor when you invoke a procedure, as in the following example:

```
Call HitTotal(Mantle.HomeRuns)
```

Chapter Summary

The array is your primary tool for managing large amounts of related data. Arrays are like super variables that store multiple elements under a common array name. You refer to the individual array elements with a subscript or subscripts. Arrays can be single-dimensional or multidimensional.

Arrays and loops work well together. Inside a loop, the loop's counter variable is often used as a subscript in array references. A simple `For-Next` loop can manipulate all the data in a huge array.

Arrays can be declared with `Dim`, `Static`, `Global`, and `ReDim` instructions. The scope of an array depends on where the array declaration occurs; the scope can be throughout a code module, at the form level, or local to an individual procedure. Array allocation can be fixed or dynamic.

You can customize your own structured data type with a record, which is a user-defined data type. A record can group components of different data types under a common name.

Test Your Understanding

True/False
Indicate whether the statement is true or false.

1. An array is like a single variable with multiple, identical compartments.

2. The subscript of an array is a pointer to a particular compartment within the array.

3. Subscript values are whole numbers.

4. The only way that values can be placed in an array is to read them in from a sequential file.

9

5. A record consists of subvariables within a larger variable.

6. The statement `Dim MyArray(10)` creates a dynamic array.

7. To pass an entire array to a user-defined procedure, you use the array name followed by the number of array elements within parentheses.

8. All arrays in VB must be of type Variant.

9. The fields in a record must be of the same data type.

10. You can use the `Erase` instruction to remove any array from the computer's memory.

Short Answer

Answer the following questions.

1. Explain the use of the `ReDim` instruction.

2. Explain the use of the `Preserve` keyword. What does it do?

3. Write an event procedure that declares a five-element array and uses a `For-Next` loop to store in the elements of the array the values of the loop counter. The procedure should then call another form-level general procedure or function that sums the values in the array. The event procedure must pass the array to the procedure that does the summation. The called procedure (or function) then returns to the event procedure the total of the values in the array. Finally, the event procedure prints the sum on the form.

4. Why would a programmer use a fixed-size array rather than a dynamic array?

5. Why would a programmer choose to declare an array as being of type Variant?

6. Declare a record that contains `LastName`, `FirstName`, `Age`, and `PhoneNumber` fields.

7. Write the code that calls a procedure and passes the record you created in question 6.

8. On a sheet of paper, draw the array created by the statement `Dim MyArray(5)`. How would your drawing of the array change depending on whether the `Base` was set to 1 or 0? Label each compartment in your drawing just as you would refer to that compartment in a VB statement.

9. Assume that `Option Base 0` is in effect. On a sheet of paper, draw the series of adjacent memory locations that VB would create when you issue the statement `Dim X (9)`. Show each memory location as a box. Then enter into the series of boxes (representing the array) the values that would be stored in the array when the following code was executed:

```
For I = 1 to 9
      X(I) = I * 2
Next I
```

10. Declare a fixed-size, one-dimensional string array with 27 elements. Would your declaration change depending on where (at what level) you declare the array? If so, show each of the different statements.

11. What is the effect of the `Option Base 1` statement? Where must it be placed?

12. Declare a fixed-size Integer type array with 10 rows and 5 columns. What is the total number of elements (compartments) in the array?

13. Declare a dynamic Single type array with two dimensions.

14. Write the code that places into four separate text boxes the values in each of the four fields of the record you declared in question 6.

15. Write a statement that opens the sequential file MYDATA.TXT so that its values can be placed in an array.

16. What is the effect of the `EOF` statement? Why is it used when reading sequential files?

17. Write a statement that declares a fixed-size array in a nonstatic procedure.

18. Can a variable be used to supply the dimensions of an array? Can a constant be used to supply the dimensions of an array?

Projects

Project 1: Writing a Program That Sorts Data Items

Write a program that sorts eight data items. The data items are to be entered (by the user) into a control array of eight text boxes. The user enters eight numeric items or eight alphabetic items (for example, first names). Numbers and alphabetic characters should not be mixed. If any of the eight text boxes are empty, the program must prompt the user to complete data entry.

The user chooses an option button to indicate whether the data to be sorted is alphabetic or numeric. When the user clicks a SORT command button, the program sorts the items into ascending numeric order (smallest to largest) or ascending alphabetic order (that is, Ann comes before Bob). Then the contents of the Text Box control array are placed in an array of variables of the appropriate type. It is the array of variables that should be sorted.

Remember that if you sort digits as characters, 1000 will sort as less than 2. If when the user clicks the SORT button, the data is already in sorted order (and no sort is necessary), a message is displayed to the user. Plan the algorithm for the sort by using a flowchart, and turn this flowchart in with your program.

9

To ensure that the sort is successful, have the program convert the alphabetic data to uppercase letters, even if the user enters a mix of upper- and lowercase letters. The sort procedure(s) must be placed in a separate BAS module. When the data has been sorted, it should be displayed in a second (output form). A label on the output form displays the elapsed time between the start of data entry by the user and the completion of the sort. A button on the output form enables the user to print the output form. Another button enables the user to end the program.

A button on the output form displays the input form, clears the text boxes, and prepares for the entry of a new set of data. The array(s) of variables must be global variables. The arrays are not to be passed as arguments.

Save the program as **C9P1** and print it.

Project 2:   Rewriting the Program in Project 1
Rewrite the program you wrote in Project 1 so that the sorted array or arrays are not declared as global variables but are instead passed as procedure arguments. Save the program as **C9P2** and print it.

Project 3:   Writing a Program That Reads Letters into an Array
Write a program that reads 30 letters of the alphabet from a sequential file into an array. The program determines which letters of the alphabet are in the array and how often each letter occurs. Save the program as **C9P3** and print it.

Project 4:   Writing a Program That Stores Numbers in Arrays
Write a program that stores the odd numbers from 1 to 20 in one array, and the even numbers from 1 to 20 in a second array. The program then multiplies the first element of the first array times the first element in the second array. The result of this multiplication is stored in the first element of a third array.

This cross-multiplication of the corresponding elements of the two arrays should continue until the product of the 10th elements of the two arrays is stored in the 10th element of the third array. The program then calculates and displays the sum and the average of the numbers in each of the three arrays.

Save the program as **C9P4** and print it.

Project 5:   Rewriting the Program in Project 4
Rewrite the program in Project 4. Place the 2 columns of numbers and the third column of cross-products in one multidimensional array with 10 rows and 3 columns. Save the program as **C9P5** and print it.

Project 6:   Writing a Program That Plays Tic-Tac-Toe
Write a program that enables you (or a user) to play a game of tic-tac-toe with the computer. You use the Xs, and the computer uses the Os. Use an array with three rows and three columns to represent the grid for the game. To indicate your move, you enter the row and column references of a square in the grid. Have the computer generate its moves randomly. Have the results of each game displayed: you win, the computer wins, or it's a draw. Display an on-screen grid to show the game as you and the computer make your moves.

Have the program indicate on the form how long the game took to complete. Provide a pair of option buttons so that the user can indicate who makes the first move (the user or the computer). Unless the user indicates otherwise, the computer should always make the first move. Include a command button to clear the grid and start a new game. When the user clicks an END button, the results of all the games played during the run of the program are displayed.

Save the program as **C9P6** and print it.

CHAPTER 10

Learning to Use More Controls and Functions

In this chapter, you are introduced to more controls and shown how to use them. You also learn how to use more of VB's built-in functions. The majority of these functions are numeric functions because most Visual Basic applications manipulate numbers.

Input box
A window (dialog box) that prompts the user for desired information.

VB programs usually require user input and need to display messages to the user at run time. Often, you want the user to provide a small amount of input—perhaps a file name, a numeric value, or someone's name. In such cases, your application can open a new window over the application's main window. The new window, called an **input box**, prompts the user for the desired information.

Message box
A window (dialog box) that displays information.

An input box is one example of a dialog box. Another type of dialog box is the **message box**. A message box displays information, such as an error message or some explanatory text. After reading the information, the user clicks an OK button to close the message box, and the main application resumes. Visual Basic provides built-in statements and functions that create standard dialog boxes quickly and easily. This chapter also explains how to use these statements and functions.

Objectives

By the time you have finished this chapter, you will be able to

1. Use the List Box Control

2. Use the Combo Box Control

3. Use the Horizontal and Vertical Scroll Bar Controls

4. Use the Timer Control

5. Use the Asc and Chr$ Functions

6. Use the Format$ Function

7. Use Visual Basic's Numeric Functions

8. Generate Random Numbers

9. Use Functions to Convert Values from One Numeric Data Type to Another

10. Use the InputBox$ Function to Create an Input Box

11. Use the MsgBox Function and MsgBox Statement to Display a Message Box

The List Box and Combo Box Controls

This chapter discusses two kinds of boxes from which the user can make selections in VB dialog boxes. These boxes are list boxes and combo boxes.

A **list box** displays a list of items from which the user makes a selection. To select an item, the user clicks it. The user also can press the up- and down-arrow keys to move the highlight from one item to another. Usually, a list box is more appropriate than a group of option buttons when the number of items is four or more.

A **combo box** combines the attributes of both a text box and a list box. This control contains an edit area in which the user can usually type data, as well as a list box that displays a list of items. You typically use a combo box when the user must supply a piece of information but the application can suggest some possible values. The user can either select an item from the list or type a value in the edit area. The currently selected item in the list appears in the edit area of the combo box.

List box
An input box that lists items from which the user makes a selection.

Combo box
An input box combining the attributes of a text box and a list box. Three types of combo boxes are available.

List and combo boxes automatically add scroll bars if the number of list items exceeds the size of the control. At run time, the user can maneuver through the list of items by using the scroll bars.

Figure 10.1 shows an example of a list box on the left and a simple combo box on the right. Each box lists the same six cards in a baseball card collection. The combo box includes an edit area in which the user can type a value. The list box presents only fixed options.

Figure 10.1
Samples of a list box and a combo box.

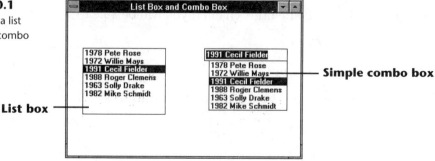

Visual Basic provides three different styles of combo boxes: simple combo, drop-down combo, and drop-down list combo. The simple combo box displays an edit area with an attached list box always visible immediately below the edit area. The drop-down combo box first appears as only an edit area with a down arrow at the right. The list portion stays hidden until the user clicks the down arrow to drop down the list portion. The user can either select a value from the list or type a value in the edit area.

The drop-down list style turns the combo box into a drop-down list box. At run time, the control looks like the drop-down combo box. The user can click the down arrow to see the list. The difference is that the edit area in a drop-down list box is disabled. The user can *only* select one of the list's items and cannot type an item in the edit area. This area, however, does display the item currently selected in the list.

Figure 10.2 shows the different kinds of combo boxes. The drop-down combo box and the drop-down list combo box appear as they do before the user clicks the down arrow.

Figure 10.2
Samples of the three types of combo boxes.

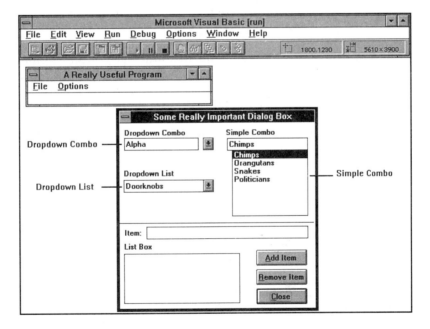

In review, here are the differences among the three types of combo boxes:

- *Simple combo box.* A simple combo box displays its list all the time (all items are visible). You can select an item from the list or enter your own item in the edit box portion of the combo box. A scroll bar appears beside the list if there are too many items to display in the list box area.

- *Drop-down combo box.* A drop-down combo box displays its list only when you click the down arrow beside the edit box. You can select an item from the list or enter an item in the edit box.

- *Drop-down list box.* A drop-down list box displays its list only when you click the down arrow. You can only select items from the list; you cannot enter your own item in this type of combo box.

Choosing between a List Box and a Combo Box

To choose between the types of box—a list box or a combo box—ask yourself how much form space is available for the control and what features it must provide. The following questions can help you decide:

- How much space is available for the list?

  A drop-down combo box initially requires only a single line of space on the form. As such, combo boxes are space efficient. (Of course, the box expands when the user drops down the list portion.) Initially, a list box requires more space to accommodate its items.

- Do you want the user to be able to type a choice instead of just selecting from a list?

  If the user may have to type a value not available from the list, a combo box is your only option. Keep in mind that many users adept at typing prefer to keep their hands on the keyboard. These users prefer to type items, even when the item they want appears in the list. The combo box is the only option that provides this flexibility.

- Do you want a multicolumn list?

  A list box can display items in a multiple-column format with horizontal scrolling. Combo boxes cannot display multicolumn lists.

- Does the user need to choose more than one item from the list?

  A list box can support multiple items selected simultaneously. Using a combo box, the user can select only one item from the list portion.

Figure 10.3 shows a list box with four names selected at once.

Figure 10.3
A list box with four names selected at once.

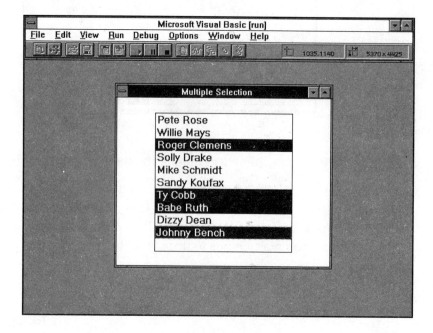

Methods for List Boxes and Combo Boxes

When discussing both list boxes and combo boxes, it's important to mention the special methods used with these controls. With the AddItem and RemoveItem methods, respectively, you can add and remove items from the list portion of these controls.

You cannot add list items at design time. Instead, you must use the AddItem method in program code so that items are added at run time. For most applications, you want the list items loaded when the application starts, so you put AddItem instructions in the Form_Load procedure.

Here is an example of the AddItem method:

```
List1.AddItem "January"
List1.AddItem "February"
List1.AddItem "March"
List1.AddItem "April"
```

List1 is the name of a List Box control. These instructions fill the list box with the names of the first four months. Each successive instruction adds a new item to the end of the current list.

You can place an item in the middle of the current list by including an optional parameter at the end of the instruction. This parameter has an integer value and specifies the place in the list at which the new item should be inserted. For example, the following instruction inserts a new item between February and March:

```
List1.AddItem "Here I am", 2
```

Visual Basic considers the first item in the list to have a ListIndex property value of 0. As specified in this instruction, a ListIndex property value of 2, therefore, indicates that the new item becomes the third one in the list. When you place a new item in the list, Visual Basic automatically adjusts the other items to accommodate the insertion.

To remove an item from a list, use the RemoveItem method. The syntax specifies the index number of the item you want to remove. The following instruction removes the fourth item (index number 3) from the list portion of the combo box Combo1:

```
Combo1.RemoveItem 3
```

You can remove all items in a list with the Clear method. The following instruction removes all items from the list box List1:

```
List1.Clear
```

Properties of Controls for Both List Boxes and Combo Boxes

The Sorted property is unique to both list and combo boxes. When Sorted is True, Visual Basic sorts list items alphabetically. When Sorted is False (the default), list items appear in the order specified with the AddItem instructions.

The ListIndex, List, ListCount, NewIndex, and ItemData properties help with list management. These property values are available only at run time. The ListIndex property specifies the index number for the currently selected item.

If the list has no items, the value of this property is –1. The List property acts as a string array that specifies the actual contents of a list item. For example, the value of Combo1.List(2) is the third list item in the combo box Combo1. The ListCount property indicates the total number of items stored in a list. The NewIndex property specifies the index number of the item most recently added to the list. For combo boxes, the Text property specifies the text in the edit area. For list boxes, the Text property specifies the currently selected item.

Special List Box Properties

List boxes have four properties not available with combo boxes: Selected, TopIndex, Columns, and MultiSelect. The Columns and MultiSelect properties are available at run time in program code and at design time in the Properties window. The Selected and TopIndex properties are available only at run time.

For any list, the Selected property specifies whether a given list item is selected. If Selected is True, the item is selected. If Selected is False, the item is not currently selected. The property uses an array syntax. The following instruction specifies that the first item in the List1 list box should be selected:

```
List1.Selected(0) = True
```

The TopIndex property specifies the index number of the item you want to appear at the top of the list.

A list box can display items in multiple columns. The value of the Columns property determines how many columns are displayed and how scrolling works. If the value of Columns is 0 (the default), the list box has a single column, and vertical scrolling is enabled. If the value of Columns is 1 or more, the value indicates the number of columns displayed. In these cases, horizontal scrolling is enabled.

A list box can let the user select more than one item from the list. The value of the MultiSelect property determines the multiselection capability. When MultiSelect is 0 (the default), multiple selection is disabled; only one item can be selected from the list. When MultiSelect is 1, you can select multiple items by clicking each item you want individually. When MultiSelect is 2, multiple items can be selected in groups by clicking and dragging or by using Ctrl+click and Shift+click, as in Windows File Manager.

Special Combo Box Properties

The following properties apply to a combo box but not to a list box: Style, SelLength, SelStart, and SelText. The SelLength, SelStart, and SelText properties work with selected text in the same way for both combo and text boxes.

As previously explained, Visual Basic supports three types (styles) of combo boxes. You use the Style property to designate which of the three types a combo box should be. The value 0 (the default) designates a drop-down combo box. This style has an edit area and a drop-down list. The value 1 specifies a simple combo box that has an edit area and a list that remains displayed. Finally, the value 2 designates a drop-down list style. This form turns the combo box into a drop-down list box.

Events of Both List Boxes and Combo Boxes

Both the list box and the combo box respond to many of the common events described in earlier chapters. See VB Help for a list of properties, events, and methods. The combo box also responds to a Change event, which occurs whenever the user types anything in the edit area or the contents of the edit area are modified in code.

The DropDown event is unique to combo boxes. This event occurs when the arrow to the right of the edit area is clicked to drop down the list portion of the control. For more information on the List Box and Combo Box controls, consult VB's Help topics.

Scroll Bar Controls

Users of Windows applications are familiar with scroll bars. Windows itself supplies scroll bars so that the user can specify such settings as the cursor blink rate in the Windows Control Panel. Scroll bars are most frequently used to enable the user to move window contents to bring into view a portion temporarily outside the visible region.

A Scroll Bar control can be a user input device to specify a value within a prescribed range. By moving the scroll box between the two arrows, the user can specify a value in an intuitive, visual manner. The scroll bar acts as a sliding input device, somewhat similar to the analog slides on professional audio equipment.

Don't confuse a Scroll Bar control with the scroll bars that Visual Basic automatically adds to other controls. A Scroll Bar control is just that—a full-fledged control you can select from the Toolbox and place directly on a form. By contrast, Visual Basic sometimes adds scroll bars to other controls. For example, when the display of the control's contents requires more space than that allocated for the list box, the control has a scroll bar.

Scroll box
A box on a scroll bar that moves as the scroll bar is used.

In Visual Basic, a Scroll Bar control consists of a bar with arrows at each end. Between these arrows is a square **scroll box**. The scroll box slides along the **scroll shaft** between the two arrows. You can create horizontal and vertical scroll bars; they both function in the same way.

Scroll shaft
The straight bar between the arrows of a scroll bar.

To work with a Scroll Bar control, you must understand the parts of the bar and their purposes. The scroll box on the scroll shaft indicates the current value specified by the bar. When the user clicks the arrow at either end of the scroll bar, the scroll box moves an incremental unit toward that arrow. When the user clicks the scroll shaft itself somewhere between an arrow and the scroll box, the scroll box moves in a larger incremental unit toward the click position. The user can also drag the scroll box along the shaft with the mouse.

Special Properties of Scroll Bars

For any scroll bar, you must determine the range of values that the control can designate. Scroll bars always specify integer numbers. The smallest permissible value is –32,768; the largest is 32,767.

The Min and Max properties are unique to scroll bars. You use Min to specify the smallest value that the scroll bar can represent, and Max to specify the largest. For example, if a scroll bar indicates a temperature scale in degrees Fahrenheit, you might set Min to 32 and set Max to 212. The default values for Min and Max are 0 and 32,767, respectively.

Value is the most useful property for a programmer. For scroll bars, the Value property specifies the current value represented by the scroll bar. The position of the scroll box along the scroll shaft graphically reflects where Value lies between Min and Max. If the user moves the scroll box, the Value property adjusts appropriately. Similarly, if you modify Value in program code, Visual Basic moves the scroll box to the appropriate position.

The SmallChange property indicates how much Value changes when the user clicks one of the arrows at the end of the scroll bar. Similarly, LargeChange indicates how much Value changes when the user clicks the scroll shaft between the scroll box and one of the arrows. The default value for both properties is 1.

You can set values for the scroll bar properties at design time or in program code. For the temperature example mentioned in this section, here is the program code you might use to initialize a vertical scroll bar named VScroll1:

```
VScroll1.Min = 32
VScroll1.Max = 212
VScroll1.SmallChange = 1
VScroll1.LargeChange = 20
VScroll1.Value = 100
```

Events of the Scroll Bars

The Change event occurs whenever the Value property changes. This change happens when the user manipulates the scroll bar with the mouse or when program code modifies the Value property.

The Scroll event is unique to scroll bars. This event triggers while the user drags the scroll box along the shaft. The difference between the Change event and the Scroll event is that Change occurs once when the scroll bar Value is updated, but Scroll occurs continuously, as long as the user drags the scroll box. As a result, you can use Scroll to update continuously the property values in other controls that must be coordinated with the scroll bar.

Vertical scroll bars are especially useful when you want the user to be able to browse through the contents of an array. You set the Min and Max properties to the upper and lower bounds of the array. You set the SmallChange property to 1. Then, in your code, you simply set the subscript of the array to the Value property of the scroll bar.

Creating a Vertical Scroll Bar

To explore the use of a scroll bar, follow these steps:

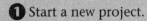 Start a new project.

❷ Create a Text box named `Text1` and an array named `DataArray` dimensioned from 1 to 100.

❸ Add a scroll bar named `Vscroll1`; size it as you like.

❹ Set `Min` to **1**, `Max` to **100**, and the `LargeChange` property to **10**.

❺ Enter the following code in the `Form_Load` event:

```
or I = 1 to 100
    DataArray(i) = I
Next I
```

This places the numbers 1 to 100 into the corresponding elements of the array and provides something to be displayed in the text box.

❻ To scroll through the array, displaying the contents of an array element in `Text1`, put the following code in the `Change` and `Scroll` events:

```
Text1.Text = DataArray(VScroll1.Value)
```

❼ Run the program, and try using the scroll bar.

Notice that when you use the scroll bar, the scroll box starts flashing. To eliminate the flashing, set the scroll bar's `TabStop` property to False.

The Timer Control

The Timer control acts similarly to an alarm clock. You specify a time interval, and when the interval elapses, the control generates a `Timer` event. The timer is designed to measure short intervals of time. One frequent use of the Timer control is to add a visible clock to your form. The time can be displayed in a Label control. You can use the timer to update the clock display continuously and display the current time.

Timers have many other uses. For example, a quiz program might give the user 15 seconds to answer a question. When 15 seconds is up, the application can take appropriate action. Windows limits the number of timers to 10. That's not a practical concern, however, as Visual Basic applications rarely use more than a single Timer control.

A Timer control is unlike any other control. At design time, the control has a fixed size, which you cannot change. The timer's location on a form doesn't matter because the timer is always invisible at run time. Furthermore, the user cannot directly access the control. The sole purpose of a Timer control is to trigger a `Timer` event at regular intervals.

Properties of the Timer Control

Timers have few properties. Because the control has a fixed size at design time and is invisible at run time, timers do not have any appearance properties. The `Interval` property, unique to timers, specifies the time interval that must elapse before the `Timer` event is triggered. You specify the value of `Timer` in milliseconds. The value can range from 0 to 65,535 milliseconds.

Notice that the maximum value specifies a time period of a little more than a minute. (You can't use timers to specify long time intervals.) If you set the value of `Interval` to 0 (the default), the timer is disabled. The following instruction specifies that the time interval for the timer `Timer1` should be one second:

```
Timer1.Interval = 1000    '1000 milliseconds equals 1 second
```

To specify longer intervals of time, use the `Now()` function (see VB Help) to calculate start and end times.

If the value of the `Enabled` property is True, the Timer control triggers the `Timer` event when the specified time interval elapses. If the value of `Enabled` is False, the timer is disabled, and no `Timer` event can occur. The default value of `Enabled` is True.

The Event for the Timer Control

`Timer` is the only event the Timer control supports. This event is triggered when the specified time period elapses. Notice that if you don't disable a timer, the `Timer` event occurs repeatedly. The countdown for the next time interval begins immediately after the preceding time period elapses.

The *Asc* and *Chr$* Functions

The functions `Asc` and `Chr$` convert data between string characters and numeric ANSI values. `Asc` returns the ANSI value for a given string character, and `Chr$` returns the string character corresponding to a given ANSI value. The syntax for these functions is

```
Asc(strexpr)

Chr$(ANSIcode)
```

In the syntax lines, *strexpr* is a string expression, and *ANSIcode* is an ANSI code value.

Notice that `Chr$` ends with a dollar sign, but `Asc` does not. `Chr$` is a string function, which takes a numeric argument and returns a string value. `Asc`, however, takes a string argument (including a variant of type String) and returns a numeric value.

`Asc` returns the ANSI value of the first character in the *strexpr* argument. If *strexpr* is a null string, a run-time error occurs (`Illegal function call`). `Chr$` complements `Asc` and returns the single-character string that corresponds to the value of *ANSIcode*. `Chr$(65)` returns *A*, for example.

`Chr$` enables you to display characters that are included in the ANSI character set but not directly available from the keyboard. Suppose that you want to display the cents symbol, ¢, as part of an output string. The ANSI value for the cents symbol is 162. The following program fragment uses `Chr$(162)` to display the cents symbol as part of a message string:

```
Message$ = "Bubble gum costs 25" & Chr$(162)
MsgBox Message$
```

Creating Line Feeds

Chr$ frequently is used to add line feeds and carriage returns to message strings. This way, a message box or multiline text box can display multiple lines of output. The ANSI values of 13 and 10 are special characters that correspond to the carriage return and line feed, respectively. You can define a form-level string variable called NewLine as follows:

```
NewLine = Chr$(13) & Chr$(10)
```

NewLine can be concatenated with other strings to form a single string that contains line feeds. Note this example:

```
MailAddress$ = "Occupant" & NewLine
MailAddress$ = MailAddress$ & "235 Oak Lane" & NewLine
MailAddress$ = MailAddress$ & "Mercer Island, Wa."
MsgBox MailAddress$
```

The *Format$* Function

Visual Basic also converts numeric data to string form with the Format$ function. Format$ is a flexible function that can format not only numeric data but also dates, times, and other strings. With Format$, you can optionally specify a formatting string that indicates the way in which the output string should appear. The Format$ function can be written in two ways:

```
Format$(expr)
```

```
Format$(expr, formatexpr)
```

In these expressions, *expr* is a string or numeric expression to be formatted, and *formatexpr* is a string expression that specifies how *expr* is to be formatted.

If you omit the *formatexpr* argument and *expr* is a numeric expression, the Format$ function converts the number to a string. The result is similar to using the Str$ function (see VB's Help), except that if the number is positive, the value returned by Format$ does not have a leading blank space. If *expr* is a string expression and you omit *formatexpr*, the Format$ function simply returns the value of *expr*.

Format$ permits many possible formatting strings. The following sections provide some examples of the available formats. The Format function (with no dollar sign) returns a value of type Variant. For more information, consult the Microsoft documentation or VB's Help system.

Note: *When used with* Print, *the* Format$ *function provides capabilities similar to the PRINT USING instruction in QBasic and QuickBASIC.* Format$, *however, contains many more options than PRINT USING.*

Formatting Numeric Values with *Format$*

The best way to understand Format$ is to study how it is used in some examples. Consider the following instruction:

```
Print Format$(4 / 3, "#.###")
```

Visual Basic displays this output:

    1.333

In the format string, the character # specifies that a digit should appear in this position (if the expression has a digit in that place). Notice that the expression to be formatted is numeric, but the format is specified with a string. You can use variables within the Format$ function, such as Format$(MyNum!, MyFormat$).

Table 10.1 shows the special characters used in the numeric formatting strings.

Table 10.1	Numeric Formatting Characters
Character	**Meaning**
#	Displays a digit (0 through 9) if one exists in the position occupied by the # symbol; otherwise, displays nothing.
0	Displays a digit (0 through 9) if one exists in the position occupied by the 0 symbol; otherwise, displays a zero.
.	Displays a period at the specified position.
,	Displays a comma between every three consecutive digits to the left of the decimal point.
%	Multiplies the expression by 100 and displays the percent sign at the position specified.
E+, E-, e+, e-	Specifies scientific format.
Other	Most other characters appear verbatim. The dollar sign ($) in the format string, for example, displays $ in the formatted output.

Suppose that you give MyNum! a value of 1234.5. Table 10.2 shows the formatted strings produced by Format$(MyNum!, MyForm$) and Format$(-MyNum!, MyForm$) for various examples of MyForm$.

Table 10.2	Examples of the *Format$* Function	
MyForm$	MyNum!	-MyNum!
"#.###"	1234.5	-1234.5
"###,#.##"	1,234.5	-1,234.5
"0.000"	1234.500	-1234.500
"0%"	123450%	-123450%
"$0.00"	$1234.50	-$1234.50
"0.00E+00"	1.23E+03	-1.23E+03

Understanding Multipart Format Strings

The format string can be expressed in two or three parts, with the parts separated by semicolons. In the two-part form, the first format applies if the number is positive, and the second applies if the number is negative. The three-part form shows the positive, zero, and negative formats.

One common use of the two-part format is to display financial numbers differently, depending on whether the numbers are positive or negative. The format `"$0.00;($0.00)"`, for example, expresses a positive number normally but encloses a negative number in parentheses. The number 1234.5 displays as `$1234.50`, and –1234.5 appears as `($1234.50)`.

Using the Predefined Formats

`Format$` defines some predetermined format names that can be used for the format string. Acceptable names include `Currency`, `Fixed`, `Standard`, `Percent`, `Scientific`, and `True/False`. `Format(1234.5, "Currency")`, for example, yields `$1,234.50`.

Formatting Dates and Times with *Format$*

In Visual Basic, numbers can represent date and time information. Dates and times are stored as serial numbers in floating-point form (Single or Double). Visual Basic includes several special formatting characters that represent date and time information.

Day, month, and year formats, for example, can be expressed with the special characters `d`, `m`, and `y`. The string `"dd"` means to display the day of the month as a two-digit number from 01 and 31. The string `"ddd"` means to display the day as a three-character abbreviation for the day of the week (Sun through Sat). VB has other day formats, as well as several different formats for month, year, and time information. The format string `"m/d/y"` displays information in the form *month/day/year*. A sample result is `10/13/84`.

Several predefined formats for date and time information include `"Long Date"`, `"Short Date"`, `"Long Time"`, and `"Short Time"`.

Numeric Functions and Statements

Note: *If you expect your programs to use only simple arithmetic, feel free to skim the following material. You can always review it later if needed.*

Numeric expression
Any expression that evaluates to a single numeric value.

A **numeric expression** is any expression that evaluates to a single numeric value. The expression can contain any combination of literals, variables, constants, array elements, and function calls. The final value can have any of the five numeric data types: Integer, Long, Single, Double, or Currency.

Note: *In the rest of this chapter, numeric variable names frequently include type-declaration suffixes, for example,* `Cost!`, `Salary@`, *and* `NumItems%`. *For the short examples in this chapter, the suffixes provide a convenient way to draw attention to the data type of the variable. In actual programming practice, variable names often do not include the suffixes. Data types of variables, however, are regularly specified with* `Dim` *instructions, such as* `Dim Cost As Single, Salary As Currency`.

As table 10.3 shows, Visual Basic provides many numeric functions and statements. Consult VB's Help topics to learn more about these functions.

Table 10.3 Mathematical Functions and Statements		
Name	**Type**	**Description**
Trigonometric		
Sin	Function	Sine of an angle
Cos	Function	Cosine of an angle
Tan	Function	Tangent of an angle
Atn	Function	Arctangent of a number
Logarithmic		
Exp	Function	Exponential
Log	Function	Natural logarithm
Conversion		
CCur	Function	Converts a number to currency
CInt	Function	Converts a number to integer
CLng	Function	Converts a number to long integer
CSng	Function	Converts a number to single precision
CDbl	Function	Converts a number to double precision
Rounding		
Fix	Function	Truncates to integer
Int	Function	Rounds to lower integer
Random Numbers		
Randomize	Statement	Seeds random-number generator
Rnd	Function	Generates a random number
Arithmetic		
Abs	Function	Absolute value
Sgn	Function	Sign of a number
Sqr	Function	Square root
Financial—Annuities		
Pmt	Function	Amount of payments
IPmt	Function	Interest payment
PPmt	Function	Principal payment
FV	Function	Future value
PV	Function	Present value
NPer	Function	Number of periods
Rate	Function	Interest rate per period

Name	Type	Description
Financial—Business Investment		
NPV	Function	Net present value
IRR	Function	Interest rate of return
MIRR	Function	Modified interest rate of return
Financial—Depreciation		
SLN	Function	Straight-line method
DDB	Function	Double-declining balance method
SYD	Function	Sum-of-years' digits method

Trying the Examples in This Chapter

This chapter contains small program fragments that use the `Print` method to display results. The `Print` instructions in this chapter do not explicitly indicate a `Print` object. (For example, a typical `Print` instruction in this chapter is `Print "Hello"`, not `Form1.Print "Hello"`.)

When you try the examples in this chapter (and later chapters), your code must designate in which place the results appear. You can indicate the destination in several ways. The two simplest approaches are to display results directly on the default form or in the Debug window.

To display results directly on the form, write code for the `Form_Click` procedure. Use the code fragment from this chapter as the body of the procedure. Begin execution of the application; then click the default form. The displayed result appears directly on the form.

The second method is to display results in the Debug window. Start an application without entering any code. Break execution (press Ctrl+Break, or click the Break button on the Toolbar). The Debug window appears. You now can type code fragments directly in the Debug window. `Print` instructions display results in the Debug window. To use the Debug window, however, you must type loops and other control structures on a single line.

Try the examples that interest you. You can experiment by changing any of the values. Experience always is the best teacher.

Using the Rounding Functions

Visual Basic has two functions that convert a numeric expression into a whole number: `Fix` and `Int`. The syntax of these functions is

```
Fix(numexpr)

Int(numexpr)
```

numexpr is a numeric expression.

Fix simply strips off the fractional part of *numexpr*. This process is called **truncation**. Fix(8.9) is 8, and Fix(-8.9) is −8.

Int returns the largest whole number that is less than or equal to the value of *numexpr*. This process is called **rounding down** or **flooring**. Int(8.9) is 8 and Int(-8.9) is −9.

CInt and CLng return the whole number closest to *numexpr*. Rounding can be up or down, as appropriate. CInt(4.2) is 4, and CInt(4.8) is 5. Fix and Int are similar functions. Each returns the same value when *numexpr* is zero or positive. When *numexpr* is negative, however, the functions produce different results.

Rounding Numbers

The following Sub procedure, RoundDemo, demonstrates the differences among values returned by CInt, Fix, and Int:

```
Sub RoundDemo ()
    Dim X As Single
    Rem Demonstrate the rounding functions
    Print "X", "CInt(X)", "Fix(X)", "Int(X)"
    For X = -2.8 TO 2.8 Step 1.4
        Print X, CInt(X), Fix(X), Int(X)
    Next X
End Sub
```

Here is the output from RoundDemo:

X	CInt(X)	Fix(X)	Int(X)
-2.8	-3	-2	-3
-1.4	-1	-1	-2
0	0	0	0
1.4	1	1	1
2.8	3	2	2

Using Random Numbers

VB's Rnd function returns a double-precision random number with a value between 0 and 1. A **random number** is simply an unpredictable number that cannot be predetermined. (The Rnd function has an optional argument, *numexpr*.) You can specify the type of random number that Rnd returns by including the optional *numexpr* parameter. Many scientific simulations and game-playing programs use random numbers regularly. As a simple example, the following instruction tosses a simulated coin:

```
If Rnd > .5 Then Print "Heads" Else Print "Tails"
```

Rnd returns values that are not truly random but are computed by a numeric formula. Such numbers are said to be pseudorandom because they simulate random numbers. The formula used to calculate the **pseudorandom numbers** is predefined within Visual Basic. The formula depends on an initial starting value, called a **seed**. By default, Visual Basic provides the same seed each time you begin an application. Unless you, the programmer, reseed the random-number generator, Rnd produces the same sequence of random numbers each time you run an application.

To reseed the random-number formula, Visual Basic provides the following `Randomize` statement:

```
Randomize seed
```

Notice that the *seed* parameter, which is optional, is *not* enclosed in parentheses.

In an application that uses random numbers, you typically execute one `Randomize` instruction before calling the `Rnd` function. In order to change the random-number sequence each time you run a particular application, you must alter the value of seed with each run. Visual Basic's `Timer` function provides a handy way to seed the random-number generator unpredictably. (`Timer` is a special function that returns the number of elapsed seconds since midnight; it is not the Timer control.)

Visual Basic uses the value returned by `Timer` as the seed if you use a `Randomize` instruction without the seed parameter. The effect is the same as for the following instruction:

```
Randomize Timer
```

`Rnd` operates in a number of different ways, depending on the value of the *numexpr* argument (see table 10.4).

Table 10.4 The Operation of the *Rnd* Function	
Value of Argument	**Action Performed**
numexpr > 0	Returns the next random number in the current sequence
numexpr omitted	Produces the same effect as *numexpr* > 0
numexpr = 0	Returns the previous random number
numexpr < 0	Reseeds the random-number generator using *numexpr* and returns the first number of the new sequence

Returning Random Numbers with *Rnd*

The following loop demonstrates the type of random numbers returned by `Rnd`:

```
Randomize

For J% = 1 To 5
   Print Rnd
Next J%
```

The following is typical output from this loop, although your results may differ because these are random numbers:

```
.9970131
.1807917
.3427377
.1339383
.6167209
```

Notice that Rnd always returns a decimal fraction between 0 and 1. You can also generate random integers using Rnd and Int. The following formula produces a random integer in the range from *lowinteger* to *highinteger*:

```
Int((highinteger - lowinteger + 1) * Rnd + lowinteger)
```

The expression Int(26 * Rnd + 10), for example, produces a random integer in the range from 10 to 35. To illustrate this technique, the following procedure calculates and displays five random rolls of two dice:

```
Sub DiceRoll ()
    Dim Roll As Integer, Die1 As Integer, Die2 As Integer
    Rem (Roll dice 5 times)
    Randomize
    For Roll = 1 To 5
        Die1 = Int(6 * Rnd + 1)
        Die2 = Int(6 * Rnd + 1)
        Print "Roll"; Roll; "is"; Die1 + Die2
    Next Roll
End Sub
```

The following results by DiceRoll are typical. (Again, your results will differ because of the Randomize instruction.)

```
Roll 1 is 8
Roll 2 is 12
Roll 3 is 7
Roll 4 is 10
Roll 5 is 4
```

The Financial Functions

The financial functions are located in a file named MSAFINX.DLL. If you distribute any applications that use the financial functions, you must distribute this file as well. Microsoft grants you the right to distribute MSAFINX.DLL free of charge. Install the file in the user's Windows SYSTEM directory, usually C:\WINDOWS\SYSTEM.

Annuity
A series of cash payments made at periodic intervals.

An **annuity** is a series of cash payments made at periodic intervals. For the purposes of the financial functions, there are two types of annuities: a loan (for which you borrow a lump sum of money and pay it off over time) and an investment (for which you make periodic payments into a fund and eventually receive back a lump sum).

The payments are made at regular intervals and are assumed to be for a fixed amount. For most annuities, the interval is monthly. However, you can specify a quarterly or annual interval, or any other period you choose. The interest rate remains fixed during the length of the annuity.

Calculating a Loan Payment

Consider an automobile loan of $15,000. Suppose that the APR is 8 percent and the loan payments are monthly over five years. Each payment is due at the beginning of a period. The following program fragment computes the amount of each payment:

```
NumPer% = 5 * 12    'Number of periods (5 years, monthly)
IR! = .08 / 12      'Interest rate per period
PresV@ = 15000      'Present value (principal) of loan
FutV@ = 0           'End value
Flag% = 0           'Payments at end of each period

Payment@ = Pmt(IR!, NumPer%, PresV@, FutV@, Flag%)
Print "Monthly payment is"; Payment@
```

The result is

```
Monthly payment is -304.1459
```

Notice that the calculated payment is negative, meaning that the payment is paid (as for a loan), not received (as for an investment).

Determining Principal and Interest

For each payment made to a loan annuity, a portion goes to pay off the principal, and a portion goes to pay interest. The PPmt and IPmt functions compute the principal and interest portions, respectively. The *period* parameter specifies the specific period in the range from 1 to the value of the number of periods.

For example, you can compute the amount paid to principal and to interest in the tenth period of the sample car loan:

```
NumPer% = 5 * 12    'Number of periods (5 years, monthly)
IR! = .08 / 12      'Interest rate per period
PresV@ = 15000      'Present value (principal) of loan
FutV@ = 0           'End value
Flag% = 0           'Payments at end of each period
Period% = 10        'Compute for tenth period

Principal@ = PPmt(IR!, Period%, NumPer%, PresV@, FutV@, Flag%)
Interest@ = IPmt(IR!, Period%, NumPer%, PresV@, FutV@, Flag%)
Print "Principal payment is "; Principal@
Print "Interest payment is "; Interest@
```

The result is

```
Principal payment is -216.7264
Interest payment is -87.4195
```

Notice that the sum of the principal and interest payments is –304.1459, the amount of each payment as calculated previously with the Pmt function. Payments are negative because they represent cash outflow.

Type Conversion

Table 10.5 reviews Visual Basic's seven data types. Every variable is one of these seven data types.

Note: *Variant variables can assume any one of the seven data types listed in table 10.5. Any Variant variable containing numeric data of a particular type behaves like any of that type's numeric variables. For example, a Variant variable containing integer data behaves like a variable of type Integer.*

Table 10.5 The Seven Data Types	
Data Types	**Sample Variable Name**
Variable-length string	MyName$
Fixed-length string	TodayDate$
Integer	MyAge%
Long integer	NumPeople&
Single precision	Price!
Double precision	Mass#
Currency	Cost@

Mixing Data Types

When you assign a value to a variable, Visual Basic checks that the value matches the data of the variable. If a mismatch occurs, Visual Basic tries to convert the value of the data to match the data type of the variable. The process in which Visual Basic converts a value of one data type into another is known as **type conversion**.

You can assign a string value to a variable of either string data type. You can also assign any numeric value to a variable of any numeric type. If necessary, Visual Basic makes the required type conversion. The following instructions, for example, are perfectly legal:

```
MyAge% = 39.9999
Tax! = 23456
Value# = Cost&
```

For each of these instructions, Visual Basic converts the numeric value on the right side of the equation into the data type required by the variable on the left. When numeric variables are involved, the type conversion is called **numeric type conversion**.

Strings and numbers, however, share the incompatible nature of water and oil: You just cannot mix them. If you try to assign string data to a numeric variable or numeric data to a string variable, program errors occur. Each of the following instructions causes a run-time error (Type mismatch):

```
MyAge% = "Too much"
YourAge& = BigNumber$
MySize$ = YourSize!
YourSize$ = 38
```

Numeric Type Conversion

The following sections explain how Visual Basic can convert a numeric value from one data type to another when assigning a value to a variable or when evaluating a numeric expression. When you assign a value to a numeric variable, Visual Basic converts that value to the data type of the variable, if necessary. As Visual Basic performs each operation, during the evaluation of an arithmetic expression, the operands must be at the same level of precision. If necessary, Visual Basic converts operands to the same level of precision.

Two problems can arise during the evaluation of expressions—loss of accuracy and overflow. If the variable on the left of the equal sign is single precision, Visual Basic computes the expression on the right side to single-precision accuracy (to seven digits of precision). This computation can result in a loss of accuracy if the variables on the right of the equal sign are double-precision variables. Overflow errors occur when the result of an arithmetic operation produces a value too large (or small if the result is negative) to be stored in the variable on the left of the equal sign. You can avoid this overflow error by using one of the type conversion functions discussed in an earlier chapter and in VB Help.

Numeric Conversion with the Variant Data Type

Variant variables containing numeric data are subject to the same type conversion rules as regular numeric variables. When an expression contains a Variant variable, the data is evaluated the same as data in a numeric variable. When the left side of an assignment instruction contains a Variant variable, VB adopts the most efficient numeric data type capable of expressing the right side of the instruction.

Explicitly Setting the Data Type of a Variant Variable

Occasionally, you may want to ensure that a Variant variable stores its numeric data with a particular data type. To guarantee the most precise calculations in a financial program, for example, you may want all Variant variables to store numbers with the Currency data type. You can do this by using the `CCur` function.

For example, if `Fee` is a Variant variable, `RatePerHour` is Single, and `BillingHours` is Integer, the following instruction ensures that `Fee` contains data of type Currency:

```
Fee = CCur(RatePerHour * BillingHours)
```

Special Variant Values: Empty and *Null*

Until your program explicitly assigns a data value to a Variant variable, it contains the special data value called Empty. If a Variant variable containing Empty appears as part of a numeric expression, Visual Basic treats the Empty value as 0 (zero) for the purpose of evaluating the expression.

However, the special data value `Null` indicates that a Variant variable contains no valid data. `Null` is a reserved word that you can assign to the value of a Variant variable. Note an example:

```
Fee = Null   'Fee is of type Variant
```

Unlike Empty, which is interpreted to have a value of 0, `Null` does not correspond to any numeric value. If an expression contains a Variant variable with a `Null` value, the final value of the expression is also `Null`. This result causes an error if the final value is stored in a regular (non-Variant) Variant variable.

`Null` indicates that a Variant variable *intentionally* does not contain valid data, but Empty means that a Variant variable has not yet been assigned *any* other value.

Testing the Numeric Data Type of a Variant Variable

You can test a Variant variable to see whether it contains data that can be interpreted as a numeric value. Use the function IsNumeric *variantexpr*. The IsNumeric function returns True if *variantexpr* can be converted to a numeric value, and False otherwise. The String type returns True only if the string value can be interpreted as a number.

The IsNumeric function is handy when you are evaluating input provided by the user. Suppose that your program prompts the user to type a value and then stores this input value in a Variant variable named UserInput. You expect the value to be numeric, but it's always a good idea to check. If the user's input is processed in a Sub procedure named Evaluate, you can use the following instruction to test whether the value is correct:

```
If IsNumeric(UserInput) Then Call Evaluate(UserInput)
```

The *InputBox$* Function

Many applications require that you design customized forms so that the user can type data values. Typically, you use a Text Box control to accept the user's input. If your program needs a single line of text from the user, however, Visual Basic's InputBox$ function provides a quick and easy alternative to creating a custom form.

Modal

A type of dialog box or window that requires the user to take some action before the focus can shift to another dialog box or window.

The InputBox$ function opens a modal input box that displays a message, two command buttons, and a text box into which the user can type a single line. **Modal** means that the input box retains exclusive focus. Until the user closes the input box, no other part of the application responds to clicks or to any other event. Therefore, you use InputBox$ when your program requires that the user provide some necessary data before continuing the application.

Understanding the *InputBox$* Function

The InputBox$ function returns the string value typed by the user. Usually, InputBox$ occurs in the following type of instruction:

```
Response$ = InputBox$(prompt$)
```

The InputBox$ function appears on the right side of the equal sign. The function assigns the text typed by the user to the variable on the left side.

For example, Response$ = InputBox$("Where were you born?") produces the dialog box shown in figure 10.4.

Figure 10.4

An example of the result of InputBox$.

10

An input box always contains a title bar with a control box at the left, the prompting message (Where were you born? in this case), OK and Cancel buttons, and a text box near the bottom.

The only required parameter is the prompt. This parameter specifies the prompting message displayed in the input box. The prompting message must be a string expression, which can be a string literal enclosed in quotation marks or a variable containing string information. The prompting message can contain as many as 255 characters. Visual Basic automatically breaks up long messages into multiple lines.

The user can type any single line of text into the text box. Clicking OK or pressing Enter closes the input box and assigns the entered text string to the variable Response$. Clicking Cancel or pressing Esc closes the input box and assigns the null string (no characters) to the variable Response$. If the user clicks OK without typing anything in the text box, InputBox$ returns the null string. This response is the same as if the user clicked Cancel.

Specifying the Optional Parameters

After the first parameter, the remaining ones are optional. The function accepts these optional parameters:

```
InputBox$(promptstr, titlestr, defaultstr, left, top)
```

The second parameter, *title*, specifies the text displayed in the title bar. If you omit this parameter, as in figure 10.4, the title bar is blank.

The third parameter, *defaultstr*, specifies initial text to display in the text box. You use this parameter when your program can anticipate the most likely response the user will make. The user can choose this default text simply by clicking OK. Of course, the user can modify the default text before clicking OK.

Consider the following program fragment:

```
Prompt$ = "What is your favorite Windows programming language?"

Title$ = "Computer Questionnaire"

Default$ = "Visual Basic"

Response$ = InputBox$(Prompt$, Title$, Default$)
```

Figure 10.5 shows the resulting input box. Notice that the input box includes a text title and a default value in the text box.

Figure 10.5

An example of InputBox$ with optional parameters.

If you skip one of the optional parameters, you must use a comma as a separator. For example, you can write the final instruction from the preceding program fragment without specifying a title bar in this way:

```
Response$ = InputBox$(Prompt$, , Default$)
```

This instruction specifies default text for the text box but does not display anything in the title bar.

The final two optional parameters specify the location of the input box on-screen. You must specify both of these parameters or omit both. Although you can specify on-screen the position of the input box, you have no control over its size or in which place Visual Basic displays the prompt message in relation to the text box. You pay this small price in flexibility for the simpler functionality that InputBox$ gives you.

InputBox$ always returns a string value. You can use InputBox$ to solicit a numeric value. Although the user can type a number, Visual Basic returns the value as a string. You can use Visual Basic's Val function to convert this text string to a numeric value.

The *InputBox* Function Used with Variant Variables

In addition to the InputBox$ function, Visual Basic includes a companion function, InputBox, which returns a value of type Variant. Recall that a variable of the Variant data type can store both numeric and string information. Except for the dollar sign omitted at the end of the function name, the syntax for InputBox is exactly the same as InputBox$. For more information, see Visual Basic's Help topic "InputBox."

The *MsgBox* Function

Both the MsgBox function and the MsgBox statement open a dialog box containing a message. This type of dialog box is called a *message box* because its primary purpose is to display a message. Unlike InputBox$, the dialog box opened by MsgBox does not accept text input from the user.

Each message box created by MsgBox contains one or more command buttons. By default, OK is the only command button. With the optional parameters in the MsgBox function, however, you can include other buttons or an illustrative icon.

The message box is modal. To close this box, the user must click one of the command buttons in it.

Although the MsgBox function does not return any text, the function does return a numeric value. This value indicates which button the user selected when closing the message box.

Message boxes are most often used to display short messages and to obtain quick feedback from the user. For example, suppose that your user tries to exit a program without saving some open files. Your program might open a dialog box to ask the user whether the open files should be saved. Figure 10.6 shows a sample message box created with `MsgBox`.

Figure 10.6

A sample message box.

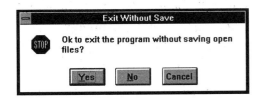

Understanding the Syntax of the *MsgBox* Function

The syntax of the `MsgBox` function is as follows:

```
MsgBox(msgstr, options, titlestr)
```

msgstr is a string expression that specifies the message displayed in the message box. *options* is a numeric expression that specifies the buttons, icon, and other attributes of the message box. *titlestr* is a string expression that specifies the text displayed in the title bar of the message box. The *options* and *titlestr* parameters are optional.

The only required parameter is *msgstr*. This string expression can contain as many as 1,024 characters. If necessary, Visual Basic automatically breaks up a long message string into multiple lines.

Specifying the *options* Parameter

The *options* parameter specifies the appearance of the message box. The value of this parameter controls the following four options:

- Which group of command buttons the message box displays.

- Which icon is present (if any). See the Visual Basic Help screen for `MsgBox` to see the icons illustrated.

- Which button is the default.

- Whether the message box is modal to all loaded applications or just to the current one.

Visual Basic associates a specific integer number with each of these options. You select the options you want, add the numbers, and use the result as the value of the *options* parameter. The CONSTANT.TXT file supplied with Visual Basic defines several constants, each with a descriptive name. This file assigns an integer (or long integer) value to each constant.

For example, CONSTANT.TXT assigns the value 4 to the constant MB_YESNO (which stands for *Message Box, Yes No*). When the *options* parameter has this value, the message box contains command buttons labeled Yes and No. If you don't specify a button group, Visual Basic displays only the OK button in the message box. VB's Help on the message box provides a list of many of the constants used with message boxes.

Once you have CONSTANT.TXT loaded into an application, you can use constant names in the program code. The result is that your programs are easier to read and understand.

The sample application at the end of this chapter demonstrates how to load and use the CONSTANT.TXT file.

Specifying the Default Button

Each group of buttons has a default. The MsgBox function returns the value of the default button if the user presses Enter instead of clicking one of the buttons. If the value of *options* does not specify otherwise, the button to the extreme left is the default. (Usually, this button is the one you want as the default button.) You can specify any button as the default, however.

Displaying an Icon

By having Visual Basic display one of the four available icons in the message box, you help the user quickly understand the type of message displayed. For example, the question mark icon informs the user that the dialog box is asking a question. Table 10.6 summarizes the four available icons.

Table 10.6	**Icons Available with *MsgBox***	
Value	**CONSTANT.TXT Name**	**Meaning**
0		No icon
16	MB_ICONSTOP	Displays a red STOP sign
32	MB_ICONQUESTION	Displays a green question mark
48	MB_ICONEXCLAMATION	Displays a yellow exclamation point
64	MB_ICONINFORMATION	Displays an *i* inside a blue circle

Changing the Modality

The message box is automatically modal to the application. Therefore, no other part of the application responds to any event until the user closes the message box. As table 10.7 shows, you can make the message box modal also to the entire Windows desktop. If you do, all other loaded applications stop and wait for the user to clear the message box. Table 10.7 shows the two values for this modality option.

Table 10.7	The Modality Values	
Value	**CONSTANT.TXT Name**	**Meaning**
0	MB_APPLMODAL	Modal to the current application
4096	MB_SYSTEMMODAL	Modal to all loaded applications

When the user selects a button, the message box closes, and the MsgBox function returns a numeric value from 1 to 7. This value indicates the selected button. Table 10.8 shows the values returned by MsgBox.

Table 10.8	Values Returned by the *MsgBox* Function	
Value	**CONSTANT.TXT Name**	**Meaning**
1	IDOK	User selected the OK button
2	IDCANCEL	User selected the Cancel button
3	IDABORT	User selected the Abort button
4	IDRETRY	User selected the Retry button
5	IDIGNORE	User selected the Ignore button
6	IDYES	User selected the Yes button
7	IDNO	User selected the No button

Most of the time, the user selects a button by clicking it. If the user presses Enter, the system selects the default button. If the user presses Esc and there is a Cancel button in the message box, the system selects the Cancel button.

Now consider the following instruction:

```
Response% = MsgBox(Message$, Options%)
```

If the user clicks OK, the value of Response% becomes 1. Similarly, if the user clicks Cancel, the value of Response% becomes 2.

The *MsgBox* Statement

The MsgBox statement works similarly to the MsgBox function. The difference is that the MsgBox statement does not return information about which button the user selects. The syntax of the MsgBox statement parallels that of the MsgBox function. You place the MsgBox statement, however, on a line by itself—you don't use this statement on the right side of an assignment instruction.

The parentheses are not used. As is the case for the MsgBox function, the *options* and *titlestr* parameters are optional. The following is an example of the simplest form of the MsgBox statement:

```
MsgBox "Top of the morning to you"
```

This instruction produces the message box shown in figure 10.7.

Figure 10.7

An example created with the `MsgBox` statement.

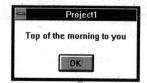

With the `MsgBox` statement, you can display the same set of buttons and icons that you can with the `MsgBox` function. The *options* parameter can have the same values with the statement as with the function.

The statement does not provide information about which of the buttons the user selects, so you rarely include any except the OK button. If you do include other buttons, the message box closes, regardless of which one the user selects.

You can add both an icon and a custom title by providing values for the two optional parameters. For example, here is the preceding instruction with an exclamation point icon and a title bar:

```
MsgBox "Top of the morning to you", 48, "Greetings"
```

Figure 10.8 shows the result.

Figure 10.8

The `MsgBox` statement with optional parameters.

The DIALOGBX Example—No Forms Needed

The following sample application, called DIALOGBX, uses both input and message boxes. With an `InputBox$` function, the program requests that you enter your name. Then the program uses a `MsgBox` statement to greet you. Finally, with a `MsgBox` function, you are asked whether you want to continue.

This project demonstrates an interesting technique—writing an application that does not use any forms or graphics controls. The user sees only the dialog boxes generated by `InputBox$` and `MsgBox`.

The program consists of a single code module. The active code for the module consists of a `Sub Main` procedure. Visual Basic looks for the `Sub Main` procedure as a start-up module whenever an application does not have any forms.

Creating DIALOGBX

Follow these steps to create the DIALOGBX application:

1 Start a new project by choosing New Project from the File menu.

2 Choose New Module from the File menu.

This step creates a code module with the default name of MODULE1.BAS.

3 Open the Project window by choosing Project from the Window menu. In the Project window, click MODULE1.BAS to highlight that item. Then click the View Code button in the Project window.

This step activates the code module for MODULE1.BAS. (This step is not necessary if the Code window for MODULE1.BAS is currently open, with the Module1.bas title bar highlighted.)

4 Choose Load Text from the File menu. The Load Text dialog box opens. Find the file named CONSTANT.TXT; it should be visible in the File Name list box. (If not, you must search through your directory files to find CONSTANT.TXT.) Double-click CONSTANT.TXT (alternatively, you can click the file name once to highlight it, and then click Merge).

5 Type the Sub Main procedure into the general declarations section of MODULE1.BAS.

The module currently consists of a copy of CONSTANT.TXT. Scroll to the end of the module and type the following procedure:

```
Sub Main ()
    Dim NewLine As String
    Dim ThreeLines As String
    Dim YourName As String
    Dim Message As String
    Dim Reply As Integer
    Dim BoxStyle As Integer

    NewLine = Chr$(10)
    ThreeLines = NewLine & NewLine & NewLine

    Do
      YourName = InputBox$("What's your name?", "Name please")
      Message = "Welcome aboard:" & ThreeLines & YourName
      BoxStyle = MB_ICONEXCLAMATION
      MsgBox Message, BoxStyle, "Hello"

      BoxStyle = MB_YESNOCANCEL + MB_ICONQUESTION
      Reply = MsgBox("Greet another?", BoxStyle, "What do you
      ➥ say?")
```

(continues)

Creating DIALOGBX (continued)

```
            Loop While Reply = IDYES
            End

        End Sub
```

6 To save the module, choose Save File **A**s from the **F**ile menu. When the Save File As dialog box opens, type the file name **DIALOGBX.BAS**; then click OK.

7 Choose **P**roject from the **O**ptions menu.

Click the Start Up Form option, moving the text Form1 to the Settings box. Click the down arrow to the right of the Settings box to open a drop-down list. Choose Sub Main from this list (see figure 10.9). Click OK to close the dialog box. This step makes Sub Main the starting point of your program.

Figure 10.9
Designating Sub
Main as the
start-up form.

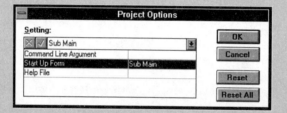

This project does not use any forms, so you can remove Form1 (currently blank) from the project.

8 Open the Project window, and click FORM1.FRM. This gives Form1 the focus. Now open the **F**ile menu, and choose **R**emove File.

9 Choose Sav**e** Project As from the **F**ile menu. When the Save Project As dialog box opens, specify the project name as **DIALOGBX.MAK**.

Now the application is completed and ready to run.

10

Running DIALOGBX

The application begins by displaying an input box that prompts you to enter your name. Figure 10.10 shows this input box with the name *Rumplestiltskin* entered in the text box. After typing your name, click OK to continue.

Figure 10.10
The Name Please input box.

The input box closes, and a message box opens (see figure 10.11).

Figure 10.11
The Welcome message box.

This box greets Rumplestiltskin by name and includes an exclamation point icon. If you have typed your name, the program will greet you by name. Click OK to continue.

The first message box closes, and a second one opens (see figure 10.12).

Figure 10.12
The second message box opens.

This new box displays the question mark icon and asks whether another user wants to be greeted. If you click either the No or Cancel button, the application ends. If you click the Yes button, however, the message box closes, and the program recycles by reopening the original input box.

Understanding How DIALOGBX Works

Sub Main contains a Do-Loop structure that executes repeatedly, as long as the user requests that additional people be greeted. The InputBox$ function opens an input box that contains a text box in which the user types a name. When the user closes the input box, the variable YourName contains a copy of the text string the user typed.

The program now displays a message box using the `MsgBox` statement. The variable `Message` contains the text displayed in the message box. Notice how the value of `Message` is constructed using the `NewLine` and `ThreeLines` variables. `NewLine` consists of the special character `Chr$(10)`, which creates a line feed. `ThreeLines` consists of three line feeds. The ampersand (&) is a string operator that joins individual strings to create a longer one.

By embedding three line feeds in `Message`, you format the displayed text in the message box. A line break appears after `Welcome Aboard:`, and three blank lines occur before the name is displayed. The program code assigns the value of the constant `MB_ICONEXCLAMATION` to the variable `BoxStyle`. This constant is one of several defined in the CONSTANT.TXT file. The CONSTANT.TXT file assigns the value 64 to the constant `MB_ICONINFORMATION`. This value corresponds to the correct value for the information icon.

Then `BoxStyle` specifies the displayed icon in the `MsgBox` instruction that follows. Notice that the `MsgBox` instruction uses the third parameter to specify a caption that reads `Hello`. The program code then assigns a new value to `BoxStyle` in preparation for the `MsgBox` function. Notice that the value of `BoxStyle` consists of adding together two constants: one to display the Yes, No, and Cancel buttons, and the other to display the question mark icon.

The `MsgBox` function asks the user whether the program should greet another person. The function returns the value of the selected button, which the program assigns to the variable `Reply`. Then the `Loop` instruction checks whether `Reply` has the value corresponding to the Yes button. If so, the program continues going through the loop. If not, the program terminates.

You can create customized dialog boxes by designing forms that contain the graphics controls and properties you require. You can load and hide these custom dialog boxes as required by your application. When used in a general sense, the terms *dialog box* and *form* become hard to differentiate. After all, most forms display information and sometimes request it from the user. At times, a form can have attributes of an input or message box, or both.

Chapter Summary

The List Box and Combo Box controls enable the user to choose from a series of alternatives. The horizontal and vertical scroll bars are useful for scrolling through arrays. The Timer control is used for measuring intervals of time within a program.

Visual Basic contains a number of built-in functions that are used to manipulate numbers and perform calculations that would otherwise require a great deal of programming. Dialog boxes provide a mechanism for displaying and receiving information. Visual Basic provides the `InputBox$` function to create standard input boxes. The `MsgBox` statement and `MsgBox` function produce standard message boxes. The dialog boxes created by `InputBox$` and `MsgBox` are modal. Until closing the dialog box, the user cannot activate any other part of the application.

In the next chapter, you learn more about creating menus for your VB applications.

Test Your Understanding

True/False

Indicate whether the statement is true or false.

1. A list box is more appropriate than a group of option buttons when the number of items is four or more.

2. List boxes cannot display multicolumn lists.

3. You can add items to a list box or a combo box at design time by setting its Text property.

4. The Sorted property of the list box and combo box enables list items to be sorted alphabetically.

5. The Selected property of a combo box specifies whether a given item in the list is selected.

6. A user can select only one item from a combo box or list box.

7. The Change event of a scroll bar occurs continuously while the user drags the scroll box.

8. If a Variant variable is empty, VB treats the Empty value as a zero when the variable is used in a calculation.

9. A message box is automatically modal to the application.

10. The Format$ function converts numeric data to string form.

Short Answer

Answer the following questions.

1. Write the VB code that displays a message box containing a Stop sign icon and the message Don't click this button.

2. Explain what is meant by the statement "Each group of buttons in a message box has a default." What difference does it make which button is the default?

3. What is meant by the term *modality*? What are the types of modality?

4. Write the VB code that enables a user to enter a length in feet into an input box. The program then displays the length in inches.

5. Write the VB code that calculates the monthly payment on a loan of $3,000 at 5% interest over three years.

6. Write the VB code that causes the numeric value in the variable Amount% to be displayed as a dollar value.

7. Write the VB code that displays the numeric value in the variable Depth with one place to the right of the decimal point. What will be displayed if the value in the variable is 3.16?

8. Write the VB code that displays the fraction 1/2 on-screen. Write the code that displays the fraction 1/4 on-screen. **Hint:** Check the VB Help for the ASCII code (128–255).

9. Write the code that causes the computer to beep if the contents of a string variable start with an uppercase *Z*.

10. Write the code that causes the name *Hillary* to be displayed in a list box.

11. Write the code that causes the name *Bill* to be removed from a Combo Box control.

12. Explain the factors to consider when a programmer must choose between using a list box or a combo box in an application.

13. Would a Timer control be appropriate to use in an application that must display the number of minutes a user has been running an application? Why or why not?

14. Explain the effect of the different settings available for the Style property of a combo box control.

15. What is the relationship that exists between the current Value property of a scroll bar and its LargeChange property? What happens to the value when a LargeChange or SmallChange event occurs? How does a user cause a LargeChange event to occur?

Projects

Project 1: Writing a Program That Displays the Time in a Label

Write a program that displays the current time in a label; the current time should be updated each second. Enable the user to set an alarm function by entering a time in a text box and by clicking a Set Alarm option button. When the system time reaches the set time, the computer beeps once every two seconds until the user clicks a Turn Off Alarm option button. Save the project as **C10P1** and print it.

Project 2: Writing a Program That Simulates a Lottery Drawing

A lottery selects its winning number by using a machine that draws six Ping-Pong balls from a box containing several hundred balls. Each ball has a two-digit number (00 to 99) written on it. The combination of the numbers on the six balls is the winning number. The balls are then replaced, and the box is stirred up before the next drawing.

Write a program that simulates the drawing. The program should produce and display the six numbers. Make sure that you have used VB's random-number generator in such a way that the numbers generated are as random as possible. The program should *not* constantly generate the same combination of numbers.

Include in the program the capability to verify that the drawing of numbers appears to be random. Do this by placing in the program a command button with the caption CHECK. When this button is clicked, a loop runs the selection process 20 times. Each set of six values produced is placed in one row of a 20-by-16 two-dimensional array.

Place a vertical scroll bar on the form along with any other controls needed to enable the user to scroll up and down through the array to see one six-ball "drawing" at a time. Clicking the scroll arrow moves up or down one drawing in the array. Dragging the scroll box should constantly update the display of the numbers—don't just update the display when the user stops dragging the scroll box. Save the project as **C10P2** and print it.

Project 3:   Modifying the Ted Application Developed in Chapter 6

Modify the Ted application developed in Chapter 6 so that the user can select one of five different fonts from a combo box. Enable the user to select one of four font sizes from a second combo box. The third combo box lets the user select bold, italic, and underline. Save the project as **C10P3** and print it.

Project 4:   Writing a Program That Contains No Forms

Write a program that does not contain any forms. The program enables the user to specify a shape (circle or square). The program prompts the user for the radius of the circle or the length of the side of the square. Then the program displays the area of the circle or square. Save the program as **C10P4** and print the code in the program.

Project 5:   Writing a Program That Obtains a Table of Monthly Payments

Write a program enabling a user to obtain a table of monthly payments. The user enters the loan amount, a low annual interest rate value, a high annual interest rate value, and the number of years in which the loan will be paid off. The program then calculates and displays a table of monthly payments for interest rates between the low value and the high value in increments of 0.1%. For example, if the user enters a low value of 8% and a high value of 8.5%, the program computes and displays the monthly payments for 8%, 8.1%, 8.2%, 8.3%, 8.4%, and 8.5%. Save the program as **C10P5** and print the project code.

Project 6:   Writing a Program That Contains a List Box and a Text Box

Write a program that contains both a list box and a text box. The items in the list box should be read into the list box from a sequential file as soon as the program starts running. Have displayed in the list box the state names used in the AREACODE application in Chapter 9.

When the user selects a state from the list box, the text box displays the corresponding area code. The area codes should be read into an array from a sequential file. Enable the user to add more states to the list box and to add area codes to the array as the program is running. Save the application as **C10P6A** and print it.

Then modify the application so that the state names and the area codes are read into a multicolumn list box from a sequential file. Set up the list box so that the user can easily see which area code corresponds to a particular state. Save the application as **C10P6B** and print the form, form text, and code.

CHAPTER 11

Designing Custom Menus

Simple applications require only a few types of controls. Check boxes, option buttons, and command buttons may be all you need for your user to select various options. As your applications become more complex and multiple windows become involved, however, this approach doesn't work. In a complex program that offers many options, the user needs a convenient way to indicate selections.

Menu
A list of alternatives from which a user can make a selection.

Using **menus** offers a solution. Most commercial Windows applications use a menu system to provide an easy way for the user to make choices. As a veteran (or almost veteran) of Windows, you have used menus many times. Visual Basic itself has several drop-down menus that have options to help you perform such tasks as saving a project, changing screen colors, or setting debugging options.

Menu Design window
A special window that enables you to add a fully functioning menu system to your application.

To add menus to your applications, Visual Basic includes a tool called the **Menu Design window**. You can easily create a hierarchical menu system that complies with Microsoft's guidelines for Windows' menus. By adding a menu system to a project, you give your finished product the look and feel of a "real" Windows application.

Objectives

By the time you have finished this chapter, you will be able to

1. Access and Understand the Menu Design Window

2. Create a Menu System

3. Designate Access Keys and Shortcut Key Combinations

4. Create Cascading Menus

5. Use the Menu Control's Checked and Enabled Properties

6. Program Application Responses to Menu Selections

Using the Menu Design Window

Visual Basic treats menus as controls. Just as with controls available from the Toolbox, menu controls—called *items* or *options*—have properties with assignable values. To open the Menu Design window, you can use any of the following techniques (see figure 11.1):

- Click the Menu Design button on the Toolbar.

- Choose **M**enu Design from Visual Basic's **W**indow menu.

- Press the Ctrl+M shortcut key combination.

Figure 11.1
The Menu Design window.

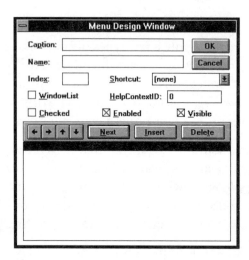

NOTE: *If your application uses multiple forms, be sure to select (activate) the form on which the menu should appear before you open the Menu Design window.*

Available Tools

To create a menu, you use the tools available in the Menu Design window. The following list provides an overview of the most important of these tools:

- *Caption.* Enables you to specify the text you want to appear on the menu. The value you specify for the caption is the menu title that the user sees when running your application. Many Windows applications have a **F**ile menu, for example. To create such a menu in your application, type **File** as the caption. When the Menu Design window opens, the cursor appears in the Ca**p**tion text box, and you can begin typing the caption immediately.

- *Name.* Enables you to specify a name for each menu option. This name is the control name recognized throughout your program code. Microsoft recommends that you name menu controls with the standard prefix mnu. You can name an **O**ptions menu mnuOptions, for example.

- *Index.* Enables you to specify the position of the menu control in a control array. Menu options, like other controls, can be grouped into control arrays. If you don't specify a value for Inde**x**, the menu option is not part of a control array. A menu control array is necessary if your application adds a new instance of a menu control during run time.

- *Shortcut.* Enables you to specify a function key or keystroke combination that enables the user to access a menu command without opening the menu. You can open the Menu Design window, for example, by pressing the Ctrl+M shortcut key. If you specify shortcut keys, the users of your application can access menu options quickly. Many experienced users and touch typists prefer to activate menu options using shortcut keys.

- *Checked.* Enables you to place a check mark to the left of a menu option. The Checked property typically indicates whether a menu choice is on or off. The default value is unchecked; if the option is checked, the menu option is on. Most applications don't turn on check marks at design time but activate the check marks when the user selects various menu options at run time.

- *Enabled.* Enables you to indicate whether a menu option is available. The default value for the Enabled property is True, which means that the menu option can be selected at run time. When the menu option is False, it appears dimmed or gray and is not available to the user.

- *OK button.* Click this button to close the Menu Design window. Choose OK when you complete your menu design rather than after you create each individual menu option.

- *Cancel button.* Click this button to close the Menu Design window without updating recent changes.

Menu Outline

The Menu outline is the large boxed area in the lower half of the Menu Design window. The Menu outline enables you to view and manipulate the order of your menus.

When you create a menu system, think of your menus as an outline. The menu options on the title bar correspond to the first level in your outline. A File menu, for example, typically is at the first level. The choices under the File menu are second-level options.

The Menu outline contains the following buttons:

- *Arrow buttons.* Enable you to change the level of a menu option and modify the place in which the menu option fits in the outline. You can have as many as four submenu levels for each main menu.

- *Next button.* Enables you to move the highlight to the next item in the Outline window or, if the cursor is positioned at the end of the menus, to add a new menu option.

- *Insert button.* Enables you to insert a new menu option above the presently highlighted menu option.

- *Delete button.* Enables you to remove the selected menu option.

Creating a Menu Application

Once you understand the components of the Menu Design window, you are ready to create your first menu. This section takes you through the process of creating a simple menu program using the different tools in the Menu Design window.

The sample application, named GREETER, greets the user with a personalized message. The user can specify through a menu system the name of the person being greeted, the salutation, and various properties of the message, such as the font and color. The application uses a single form saved as GREETER.FRM. It has two labels: one label for the salutation (greeting) and one label for the name of the person being greeted.

Creating a Simple Menu Program

To begin the sample application, follow these steps:

1 Select New Project from the File menu to begin a fresh project.

2 Place two label controls on the form: Label1 and Label2.

3 Using the Properties window, assign the form and labels the property values shown in table 11.1.

Table 11.1. Properties of *Label1* and *Label2*

Control	Property	Value
Form1	Caption	The Greeter
Label1	BackStyle	Transparent
	Caption	Welcome to
	Name	lblSalute
	Height	1335
	Left	240
	Top	960
	Width	1935
Label2	BackStyle	Transparent
	Caption	You
	Name	lblPerson
	Height	1335
	Left	2640
	Top	960
	Width	2535

The form should look similar to the form that appears in figure 11.2. After these steps are completed, you are ready to create the menu.

Figure 11.2
The initial form for the GREETER application.

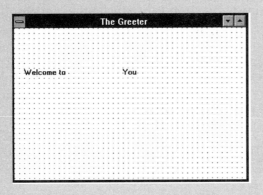

To create the menu, you have to create menu controls. The Toolbox does not contain a menu control. Instead, you use the Menu Design window.

Creating a Main Menu Option

After you have created the basic form with the labels, you are ready to create the **O**ptions menu for the GREETER application. Follow these steps:

1 Click the form to make the form window active.

2 Open the Menu Design window in one of the following ways: click the Menu Design button on the Toolbar, select the **M**enu Design option from Visual Basic's **W**indow menu, or press **Ctrl+M**.

The Menu Design window appears. You are now ready to specify values for the properties of the first menu option. Notice that a blinking cursor appears in the Ca**p**tion text box. You start by specifying a value for Caption and then proceed to specify values for the other properties.

Note: *If you access Visual Basic's* **Window** *menu and the* **Menu** *Design option is dimmed, the form window probably is not active. Click the form window again to ensure that the form is selected.*

3 Type **Options** in the Ca**p**tion text box.

Notice that Options appears at the top-left of the Menu outline. Options is the menu title that will appear on the left end of the menu bar of the application.

Remember that the caption can contain internal blank spaces, letters, and numbers.

Specifying an Access Key

Usually each menu title in Windows contains one underlined letter. This underlined letter specifies the **access key** for that menu option. By pressing Alt and the access key simultaneously, the user can activate the menu option quickly. If a conflict arises because two menu options that have the same first letter, you can use any other letter in the menu caption as the access key.

Access key
Key that enables users to take action without using the mouse; typically the first letter of a menu option; pressed along with Alt.

You use the ampersand character (&) in Visual Basic to specify an access key. When you type the Caption for a menu option, type an ampersand just before the letter that corresponds to the access key. The Caption &File, for example, makes *F* the access key, and the Caption Fo&rmat makes *r* the access key. When the caption appears on the application's menu, the access key is underlined. The ampersand character does not appear on-screen.

Specifying an Access Key for the Options Menu

To specify an access key for the **O**ptions menu in the sample application, follow these steps:

1 Position the cursor in the Caption text box, and press **Home** to move the cursor to the first letter of Options.

2 Press &.

The caption now reads &Options. The ampersand symbol indicates that the following character (*O* in this case) is the access key. The *O* will be underlined on the menu.

When you add a menu option with the Menu Design window, you are creating a control, like those selected from the Toolbox. As with other controls, a menu option needs a name so that it can be referenced in the program code. You assign a name to a menu control with the Name property.

Specifying the Control Name

To specify the name for the menu control, follow these steps:

1 Move the cursor to the Name text box by pressing **Tab**, clicking the Name text box, or pressing **Alt+M**.

2 To specify the control name for the menu option, type **mnuOptions**.

A menu control name must adhere to the same rules as other control names: the name must begin with a letter; contain only letters, numbers, and the underscore character (_); and must not exceed 40 characters. Microsoft recommends that you name menu controls with the prefix mnu, followed by the caption. Using this prefix makes it easy to remember control names.

③ To close the Menu Design window, choose OK.

The form now has a menu bar containing the single menu option titled **O**ptions. Notice that the menu title appears with the access key (*O*) underlined. The ampersand does not appear on-screen (see figure 11.3).

Figure 11.3
The Options menu.

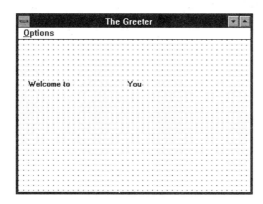

Drop-down menu

A menu that opens when the user clicks the menu title.

With the main menu title in place, you can create the drop-down (sometimes called pull-down) menu that opens when the user clicks the menu title. The **drop-down menu** presents the user with several options.

Creating a Drop-Down Menu

To create a drop-down menu, follow these steps:

❶ Open the Menu Design window.

❷ Press **Enter**, or click the **N**ext button. The cursor appears in the **Ca**ption text box, and you can create a new menu option.

❸ Type **&Background** for the caption.

❹ Press **Tab**, and type **mnuOptBackground** in the Name text box.

This name consists of the prefix mnu, an abbreviated form of the main menu name Opt, and the caption for the current menu option **B**ackground. By following this naming convention, you can easily identify the place in the Menu outline for any menu control name that appears in your code. You don't need excessively long control names.

❺ Click the right-arrow button to indent **B**ackground in the Menu outline.

Background is now the first item on the drop-down menu that opens when the user chooses the Options menu. Notice that in the Menu outline, &Background appears indented.

Understanding Indentation

For each menu option, the indentation level in the Menu outline indicates the level of that menu option. Menu options at the same indentation level represent options that appear on the same menu.

The following is the Menu outline structure at one stage in the development of the sample application. (In order to demonstrate various menu creation techniques, as you build the application, this structure will be shown in several different forms.)

```
&Message
....&Text
....&Greeting
&Options
....&Background
........&White
........Light &Blue
........Light &Gray
....&Style
........&Plain
........&Modern
```

Cascading menu

A menu displayed when a user selects an item from a menu; synonymous with submenu.

With this application, the drop-down **O**ptions menu consists of two menu options: **B**ackground and **S**tyle. The **S**tyle submenu contains the options **P**lain and **M**odern.

Using a **cascading menu** (or submenu) structure, a user can branch through a selection of choices to narrow down the desired options. In the sample application, for example, the user can choose **O**ptions, then choose to alter the background, and finally select the desired color.

Creating Cascading Menus

To create a cascading menu, use the arrow buttons to indent each menu option one more level from the level of the preceding menu. Then press **Enter**, or click the **N**ext button.

To create the cascading menu for the color selection, follow these steps:

1 To create a new menu option, click the **N**ext button.

2 Type **Light &Blue** for the caption and **mnuOptBackgroundBlue** for the name.

Notice that the caption contains a space, but no space appears in the name. The name contains the prefix (mnu), an abbreviation of the main menu caption (Opt), the drop-down menu caption (Background), and a shortened form of the caption of this item (Blue).

3 Click the right-arrow button to indent this option one level more than the indentation level for **Background**.

4 Create two more options at this menu level. Type **Light &Gray** and the name **mnuOptBackgroundGray** for the first caption. Type **&White** and the name **mnuOptBackgroundWhite** for the second caption.

You have now completed the cascading menu for the selection of the background color. To complete this application's **O**ptions menu, you need to add two more options: **S**tyle and **B**order.

Completing the Options Menu

To add the **S**tyle and **B**order items to the **O**ptions menu, follow these steps:

1 Type **&Style** for the caption and **mnuOptStyle** for the name.

2 Click the left-arrow button, and press **Enter** to move this menu option to the **Background** indentation level.

3 Type **&Plain** for the caption and **mnuOptStylePlain** for the name. Click the right-arrow button, and press **Enter** to make this option a cascading menu option under **S**tyle.

4 Type **&Modern** for the caption and **mnuOptStyleModern** for the name. Press **Enter**.

5 Type **Bor&der** for the caption and **mnuOptBorder** for the name. To move this option to the same level as **Background** and **Style**, click the left-arrow button.

6 Choose OK to exit the Menu Design window.

Note: *D is the access key for Border. You could not select B because that letter is the access key for the **B**ackground option. If two menu options share the same access key, the application recognizes the second one on the menu.*

The Options menu for the sample application is complete. Figure 11.4 shows the menu outline as it should appear in the Menu Design window. The figure shows an additional menu choice, but you have added enough choices to this submenu to see how it is done.

(continues)

Completing the Options Menu   (continued)

Figure 11.4
The menu
outline for the
Options menu.

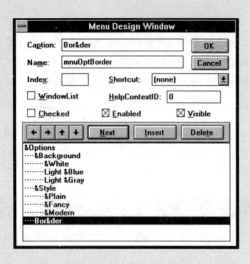

At this stage, you have created the **O**ptions menu. You now understand how to set up the fundamental menu system. Now you can run the partially completed application and see the effects of your work.

Running the Application

To run the application, follow these steps:

1 Press **F5** to run the application.

The menu bar that contains the **O**ptions menu appears under the title bar of your window.

2 Select the **O**ptions menu.

Notice that Visual Basic places right-facing arrows on the menu options that have submenus (**B**ackground and **S**tyle in this case).

3 Select **B**ackground to open a cascading menu that displays the three color options (see figure 11.5).

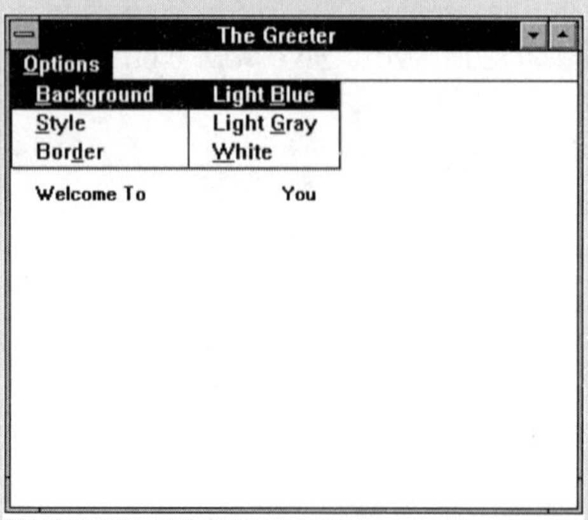

Figure 11.5
The **O**ptions
Background
menu.

```
┌─────────────────────────────────────────────┐
│ ─         The Greeter                 ▼  ▲   │
│ Options                                       │
│  Background     Light Blue                    │
│  Style          Light Gray                    │
│  Border         White                         │
│                                               │
│  Welcome To          You                      │
│                                               │
└─────────────────────────────────────────────┘
```

4 Select the color you want.

The menu option appears highlighted, and then the menu closes. The form, however, does not change color. You have designed the look of the menu system, but you must add programming code to make each menu option operate the way you want. You learn how to add the code later in this chapter.

5 Stop the application.

Designing a Menu Structure

You can create a maximum of four sublevels in a menu (see figure 11.6). Using menu levels, you can design a menu structure that leads your user through a hierarchical set of decisions one step at a time.

Figure 11.6
The submenu structure.

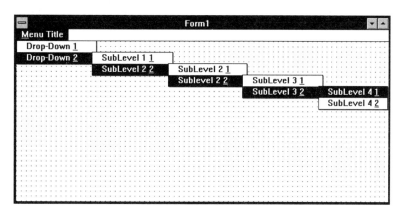

Be aware, however, that a complex multilevel menu structure may not be your best choice. Always keep ease of use in mind. Design your application to be as user friendly as possible. The following list gives you some factors to consider when designing menus:

- *Consider menu toggles instead of submenus.* If you are contemplating a submenu that contains only two items, you may want to use a single toggled menu option instead of a submenu. If the items represent two states of the same option, you can use a single toggle menu option. A toggle item uses a check mark to the left of the caption. The check mark indicates whether the toggle item is on or off. For more about menu toggles, see the section titled "Using the *Checked* Property," later in this chapter.

- *Replace crowded menus with dialog boxes.* Menus that contain too many items can bewilder a user. From a user's perspective, the menu looks crowded, which may cause difficulty in making choices. In such cases, consider a dialog box with option buttons or check boxes rather than a menu with complex sublevels. Figure 11.7 shows an example dialog box you can use in the sample application if the number of options increases.

Figure 11.7
A sample User
Options dialog box.

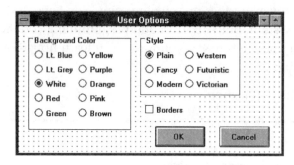

- *Decide when to use cascading menus.* You should use cascading menus only when the choices are interdependent. In the sample application, the **B**ackground and **S**tyle menus represent a good example of interdependent options. The user can choose only one background color and only one style. When choices are independent rather than interdependent, a dialog box is recommended.

- *Organize choices logically.* The relative locations of menus and the locations of items within those menus affects the time and effort necessary for the user to locate the desired task. You want your menu structure to enable the user to decide quickly where a menu option is located without searching through several menus to find that option.

Editing a Menu

You can easily modify the organization of your menus. Visual Basic provides simple ways to move menu options, delete unwanted items, and insert new menu options.

Moving Menu Options

You may sometimes create a menu and realize that you positioned a menu option in the wrong place.

Consider the **O**ptions **B**ackground menu of the sample application. The colors are organized alphabetically. Nothing is wrong with this organization; in fact, the user can scan an alphabetic list quickly. For this application, however, **W**hite is the default background. Placing a default selection at the top of a menu list often helps the user see what is selected and then scan the other options. To move **W**hite to the top of the **B**ackground menu, follow these steps:

❶ Open the Menu Design window.

❷ Click &White in the Menu outline to select it.

11

❸ Click the up-arrow button two times. Notice how &White moves up the outline to a position above Light &Blue.

To move a menu option down in the list, click the down-arrow button.

When working on a menu, you may decide that you don't need one of the menu options you created. Visual Basic provides the Delete button on the Menu Design window to remove unwanted menu options.

Deleting Menu Options

To remove the **B**order option from the menu in the sample application, follow these steps:

❶ Click the **B**order menu option in the Menu outline.

❷ Click the Delete button.

The Border option is removed from the menu.

Adding Menu Options

When working on an application, you will often want to add menu options to meet user needs. With the Menu Design window, you can add new menu options at any menu level.

For example, the sample application currently has only one main menu item—an **O**ptions menu. This menu provides ways to change the appearance of the form. Suppose that you want to add another main menu item that enables the user to change the text of a message displayed on the form.

The following steps show you how to add a new main menu item to the menu bar. This menu, named **M**essage, opens to reveal a drop-down menu that contains **T**ext and **G**reeting items. When the application is run, the user chooses the **T**ext option to type the name of the person being greeted and the **G**reeting option to specify the salutation.

Adding Another Main Item

You can add the new menu by following these steps:

❶ In the Menu Design window, click &Options in the Menu outline.

❷ Click the **I**nsert button three times to insert three spaces in the Menu outline.

❸ Click the Ca**p**tion text box to position the cursor in it.

(continues)

Adding Another Main Item   (continued)

❹ Type **&Message** for the caption and **mnuMessage** for the name; then press **Enter** to create the menu.

❺ Type **&Text** for the caption and **mnuMessageText** for the name of the second menu option.

❻ Click the right-arrow button, and then press **Enter** to make this item a submenu option under the **Message** menu.

❼ Type **&Greeting** for the caption and **mnuMessageGreeting** for the name to create the third menu option.

❽ Click the right-arrow button to move this option to the same indentation level as &Text.

❾ Choose OK to close the Menu Design window.

You can now click the **Message** menu to open the new submenu.

Adding Separator Bars

Separator bar
A horizontal line placed between menu options.

If a menu contains many items, you can break up the list into operational categories by using **separator bars**. A separator bar is a horizontal line placed between menu options.

The Visual Basic **E**dit menu, for example, contains 14 items. This menu contains horizontal lines that divide the options into groups of related choices.

To add a separator bar to a menu, you create a special menu option with a hyphen (-) as the caption. The sample application does not have crowded menus; however, to practice this technique, add a separator bar between the **T**ext and **G**reeting items.

Adding a Separator Bar between Items

To add a separator bar to the sample application, follow these steps:

❶ Open the Menu Design window (press **Ctrl+M**).

❷ In the Menu outline, select the &Greeting menu option.

❸ Insert a space for the separator bar by clicking the Insert button.

❹ Position the cursor in the Caption text box by clicking the text box. Type - (hyphen) for the caption and **mnuMessageSepBar1** for the name; press **Enter** (see figure 11.8).

Figure 11.8
Adding a
separator bar.

Note: *For each separator bar, the caption must be a hyphen; however, the name must be unique. A good convention to follow is to name the first separator bar* SepBar1 *and increment the number for each additional separator bar.*

Using an Ellipsis to Indicate a Dialog Box

You have used several devices for providing visual indicators in your menus; you have used the small arrows to the right of menu options that invoke cascading menus and separator bars that break up long menus. The next technique adds an indicator for each menu option that opens to a dialog box.

In Windows applications, an ellipsis (. . .) after a menu option indicates that a dialog box opens when the user selects that menu option. In Visual Basic, you can add an ellipsis as part of the caption for a menu option in order to indicate a dialog box.

In the sample application, because the **T**ext option on the Message menu enables the user to input the name of a person, a dialog box must open when the user selects **T**ext.

Adding an Ellipsis to a Caption

To add an ellipsis to a caption, follow these steps:

❶ In the Menu outline, click the &Text menu option.

❷ Click the Ca**p**tion text box, and press **End** to move the cursor to the end of the caption. Type three periods (an ellipsis). The caption is now &Text...

❸ Click OK to close the Menu Design window.

The **T**ext option includes an ellipsis indicating that a dialog box appears when you select **T**ext (see figure 11.9).

(continues)

Adding an Ellipsis to a Caption   (continued)

Figure 11.9
The **M**essage menu with an option including an ellipsis.

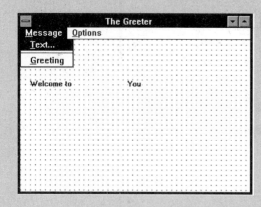

Polishing the Appearance of Menus

Experienced users appreciate quick ways of accessing the common functions, and all users like to know which menu options are active and which are available. You want your applications to meet your users' expectations. In addition to what you have already learned, Visual Basic provides three more tools that enable you to polish the look and feel of menu applications:

- Shortcut keys
- The Enabled property
- Check marks

The following sections examine these tools.

Shortcut key
Keystroke combination that provides immediate access to a menu; also called a quick-key combination.

Adding a Shortcut Key

A **shortcut key** is a keystroke combination that provides immediate access to a menu option. This method is faster than an access key because the user doesn't have to open the menu. A shortcut key is sometimes referred to as a quick-key combination. Visual Basic enables you to assign several possible shortcut keys.

Assigning a Shortcut Key

Every time the sample application is run, the name of the person greeted must be entered in the **T**ext menu option.

To save time in accessing the **T**ext menu option, you can assign a quick key to it by following these steps:

1 Open the Menu Design window.

2 In the Menu outline, click the &Text menu option.

❸ Click the **S**hortcut list box (or the list arrow) to pull down the list of possible shortcut keys (see figure 11.10).

Figure 11.10
The Shortcut list.

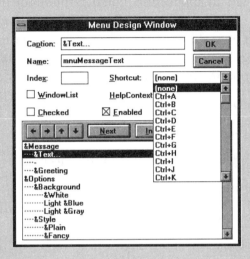

❹ Locate Ctrl+T, using the scroll bar if necessary, and click Ctrl+T to select it.

Notice that in the Menu outline, Ctrl+T appears to the right of the &Text menu option.

❺ Choose OK to close the Menu Design window.

The shortcut key appears to the right of the Text menu option on the Message menu.

When the user presses a shortcut key, Visual Basic executes the code attached to the corresponding menu option. At this point, you have not yet attached code to a menu option. You do this later in this chapter.

When you are selecting a shortcut key from the drop-down list box, Visual Basic does not immediately indicate whether the keystrokes have been previously selected. Visual Basic does, however, check for duplication when you choose OK. If the shortcut key you choose is already assigned, you get a message box like the one shown in figure 11.11.

Figure 11.11
A sample error
message indicating
duplicate shortcut
keys.

If you get a shortcut duplication error message, choose OK or press Enter to close the message box. Repeat the steps from the preceding exercise to choose an alternative shortcut. To deselect a shortcut key for a menu option, repeat the preceding steps and select (none).

Using the Checked Property

You can indicate active menu options with a check mark to the left of selected items. When you design an application, you determine the initial setting of each check mark property. The sample application, for example, starts with a white background and with no style settings (a plain style). You can indicate that these are the default settings by placing check marks next to the **W**hite menu option and the **P**lain menu option. To activate check marks, follow these steps:

1 Open the Menu Design window.

2 In the Menu outline, click the &White menu option.

3 Click the Checked box. An X appears in the check box.

4 In the Menu outline, click the &Plain menu option.

5 Click the Checked box.

6 Choose OK to close the Menu Design window.

Now when you select the **O**ptions **B**ackground menu, a check mark appears next to the **W**hite menu option (see figure 11.12).

Figure 11.12

An example of the Checked property.

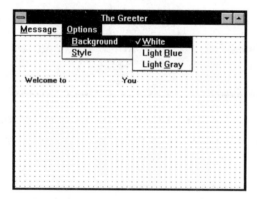

At this point, you have used check marks to indicate the defaults in effect when the user first runs the application. While the application runs, the user may change the background color. As explained later in this chapter, you must then alter the Checked property accordingly with program code.

Using the *Enabled* Property

Like the Checked property, the Enabled property can control the user's access to any menu option while the application executes. By default, a menu option is active and can be selected by the user.

Sometimes you want to deny the user access to a certain menu option. Visual Basic uses this technique itself. For example, you cannot select the **M**enu Design option from the **W**indow menu if the form doesn't have the focus.

When an item cannot be selected, it is disabled by setting the Enabled property to False. The menu option appears dimmed (or gray). A dimmed menu option informs the user that the option exists within the application but is not currently available. Clicking a dimmed item highlights it briefly before the highlight returns to the top item of the menu.

Using the **E**nabled check box in the Menu Design window, you can assign the initial state for the Enabled property of each menu option. When a menu option is enabled, an X appears in the **E**nabled check box. By default, each menu option is enabled.

For the sample application, assume that the **M**odern style can be selected only when the background color is light gray. When the application starts, the white background is the default. The **M**odern style, therefore, is not available and should be disabled by default.

Disabling the Modern Style

To disable the **M**odern style, follow these steps:

1 Open the Menu Design window.

2 Click the &Modern menu option in the Menu outline.

3 Click the **E**nabled check box to deselect it, as indicated by the X being removed.

4 Choose OK to close the Menu Design window.

Now when you run the program and select the **O**ptions **S**tyle menu, the **M**odern menu option appears dimmed (see figure 11.13).

Figure 11.13

A disabled menu option.

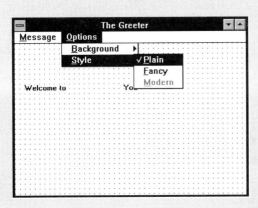

Note: *To dim an entire drop-down menu, you don't have to change the* Enabled *property for each item in the menu. Just deselect the* Enabled *property of the menu title, and the user is unable to access any of the items on that submenu.*

Coding Menu Options

In the sample application thus far, you have created only the menu structure. If you run the application and select a menu option, the menu activates, but nothing else happens. To make the application work correctly, you need to add program code.

For menu options, the Click procedure defines what happens when the user clicks a menu option with the mouse, uses the access keys, or uses a shortcut key to select a menu option. To make an application respond appropriately to the selection of a menu option, you must write program code for the associated Click procedure.

Coding a menu option is similar to coding the other Visual Basic controls. You must access the Code window for each menu option and insert your code. Be sure that the program maintains a true visual representation of your application by updating the Checked and Enabled properties in your code.

Accessing the Code Window

To program any menu option, you first must access the Code window for that option. You can access the Code window in one of three ways: click View Code in the Project window, double-click the menu option on the selected form, or select **C**ode from the **V**iew menu.

To access the Code window from the Project window, follow these steps:

1 Choose P**r**oject from the **W**indow menu, or click the Project window.

2 Select the form name (GREETER.FRM) in the Project window.

3 Click the View Code button. The Code window appears with the general declarations in view.

4 To view a list of all the objects, click the Object list arrow.

As you scroll through the list, a number of objects that start with the prefix mnu appear. These items are the menu options (see figure 11.14).

Figure 11.14
The Code window Object list.

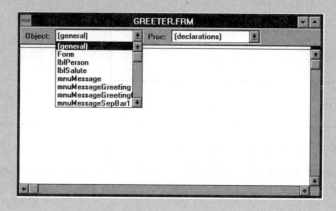

5 Click `mnuOptBackgroundBlue`. The Code window for the `mnuOptBackgroundBlue_Click` procedure appears.

6 Close the Code window.

You can also access the Code window directly from the form. In the next exercise, you learn how.

Accessing the Code Window from the Form

11

To access the Code window for the Light **B**lue menu option directly from the form, follow these steps:

1 Click the form to give the form the focus.

2 Click the **O**ptions menu.

3 Click the **B**ackground submenu.

4 Click Light **B**lue.

The Code window for the `Click` procedure appears (see figure 11.15). The cursor is blinking at the beginning of the second, line waiting for you to add code.

Figure 11.15
The Light Blue menu Code window.

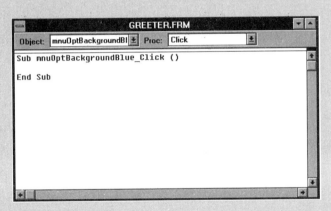

Adding Code for Menu Procedures

Basically, menus have two types of code procedures: those that take specific action and those that open a dialog box. The code procedure for the light blue background option takes action. The user chooses a color and expects the color to change. The choice does not require verification with a dialog box.

Changing the Background Color

To change the background color of a form at run time, you adjust the form's `BackColor` property. You can use the color palette available when you double-click the `BackColor` property in the Properties window to obtain the hexadecimal color values. Follow these steps:

1 Open the Code window, and type the following `Click` procedure:

```
Sub mnuOptBackgroundBlue_Click ()

    Form1.BackColor = &HFFFFC0

End Sub
```

This procedure modifies the `BackColor` property of the two labels as well as the `BackColor` property of the form. All three controls are set to a background color of light blue.

2 Run the application.

3 Select **B**ackground from the **O**ptions menu, and then select Light **B**lue.

The background color of the form and the two labels changes to a light blue color.

4 End the application.

Now create similar procedures for the other two colors: white and light gray.

5 Copy the assignment instruction from the `mnuOptBackgroundBlue_Click` procedure to the Clipboard, and then paste the instruction into the other code procedures.

6 Finally, modify the pasted code to specify the appropriate color values.

The following are the completed procedures for the other two colors:

```
Sub mnuOptBackgroundWhite_Click ()
    Form1.BackColor = &HFFFFFF
End Sub
Sub mnuOptBackgroundGray_Click ()
    Form1.BackColor = &H00E0E0E0
End Sub
```

Note: *In these procedures, the colors are specified with hexadecimal values. To determine these values, you can select the form, change the value of* Backcolor *in the Properties window by using the color palette, and then copy the hexadecimal value for each desired color. As you learned in Chapter 4, you can also change colors in other ways. You can, for example, use a* QBColor *instruction, the* RGB *function, or load CONSTANT.TXT in a separate module and use the predefined color constants in the assignment instructions.*

Testing the Application

At this point, you can save and then run the application to see the **O**ptions **B**ackground submenu at work. To see the colors change, use the **O**ptions **B**ackground submenu to select colors one at a time. When you finish testing the different colors, you can end the application.

Programming the Style Menu

You need Click procedures for each menu option of the **S**tyle menu. These procedures activate when the user clicks the **P**lain or **M**odern item. The Click procedures set the font color and font style for the label messages.

When you create your application, the default color for text is black; the default FontName is MS Sans Serif. When you decide to alter the default font, you should consider what fonts you have available. If Windows cannot locate the selected font, it will try to find a close substitute, which may create a different effect from the effect you intended.

When you first install Windows, two different sets of fonts may be included with the system. The standard Windows fonts are Courier, MS Sans Serif, MS Serif, Symbol, Modern, Roman, and Script. If you have the basic TrueType font collection, you also have these fonts: Arial, New Courier, Times New Roman, Symbol, Wingdings.

When you create your application, the fonts that are installed on your system appear in the FontName property list with the FontSize property list showing the point sizes for the selected font. For this application, the defaults are referenced as Plain and Modern (using the Modern font).

Coding *Click* Procedures for the Plain and Modern Menu Options

Create the following Click procedures for the Plain and Modern menu options:

❶ Open the Code menu, and enter the following code in the Plain menu's Click event:

```
Sub mnuOptStylePlain_Click ()

    lblGreeting.ForeColor = &H80000008

    lblGreeting.FontName = "MS Sans Serif"

    lblGreeting.FontSize = 8.25

    lblPerson.ForeColor = &H80000008

    lblPerson.FontName = "MS Sans Serif"

    lblPerson.FontSize = 8.25

End Sub
```

(continues)

Coding *Click* Procedures for the Plain and Modern Menu Options (continued)

❷ Enter the following code in the Modern menu's Click event:

```
Sub mnuOptStyleModern_Click ()

    lblSalute.ForeColor = &H80

    lblSalute.FontName = "Modern"

    lblSalute.FontSize = 18

    lblperson.ForeColor = &H80

    lblperson.FontName = "Modern"

    lblperson.FontSize = 18

End Sub
```

You cannot, at this moment, experiment with these procedures by running the application. **M**odern is disabled. In the section of this chapter titled "Programming the Additional Properties," you will add the code to activate these menu choices.

Adding Code to Access a Dialog Box

When using this application, the user must type the name of the person being greeted. The natural way for the user to input this name is in a dialog box. Rather than create a separate form for this question, you can use the InputBox$ command to create the appropriate dialog box. This dialog box opens when the user selects the **M**essage **T**ext menu option.

When the user provides a name in the dialog box, the program must update the caption of the label lblPerson.

❶ Make sure that the Code window is open.

❷ Create the following Click procedure:

```
Sub mnuMessageText_Click ()

    Msg$ = "Enter the name of the person you want to greet."

    Title$ = "Name Please"

    DefVal$ = "You"

    lblPerson.Caption = InputBox(Msg$, Title$, DefVal$)

End Sub
```

You are now ready to test your application to be sure that the code you have entered works correctly.

Testing the New Code

To test the application, follow these steps:

1 Run the application.

2 Select **T**ext from the **M**essage menu.

The menu closes, and an input box appears and prompts you to enter the name of the person the application will greet (see figure 11.16).

Figure 11.16
The Name Please dialog box.

3 Type a name in the input box, and choose OK.

The caption on the label in the middle of the form changes.

4 Stop the application.

You need to add additional code for the **M**odern option to work, as discussed in the next section.

Programming the Additional Properties

In the last section, you added code to change the settings for the application, but when you ran the application you may have noticed that the check mark and the `Enabled` properties didn't change. When designing the menu structure for this application, you used the `Checked` and `Enabled` properties to initialize the visual appearance of the menus. You now need to add procedures that change these properties at run time according to the options the user selects.

The *Checked* Property

The first thing you may have noticed when making the test runs of this application is that regardless of the color selected, a check mark remains next to the **W**hite menu option. You can change the `Checked` property of a menu option with code. When considering whether to use the `Checked` property, you must determine what type of menu option you have. If you have an option that is in one of two different states, modifying the `Checked` property is appropriate.

In the sample application, the user can toggle the message greeting on or off. When **G**reeting is selected, the message `Welcome to` appears on the form, and a check mark appears next to the **M**essage **G**reeting menu option. When **G**reeting is deselected, no greeting message appears on the form, and the check mark does not appear.

Modifying the *Checked* Property in Code

To toggle the check mark correctly, do the following:

1 Open the Code window.

2 Enter the following code in the mnuMessageGreeting_Click procedure:

```
Sub mnuMessageGreeting_Click ()

    mnuMessageGreeting.Checked = Not mnuMessageGreeting.Checked

    If mnuMessageGreeting.Checked = True Then

        lblGreeting.Caption = "Welcome to"

    Else

        lblGreeting.Caption = ""

    End If

End Sub
```

You also need to indicate that a greeting is present when the application starts.

Placing a Check Mark next to the Greeting Option

Follow these steps to place a check mark next to the **G**reeting menu option:

1 Open the Menu Design window.

2 Click &Greeting in the outline.

3 Click the Checked box.

4 Choose OK to close the Menu Design window.

5 Run the application.

6 Select **G**reeting from the **M**essage menu two or three times.

Watch the check mark toggle on and off, and the message Welcome to appear and disappear from the form.

The **G**reeting option is an example of an independent menu option. Its status doesn't depend on the status of any other option on the menu. This situation is not the case, however, with the **B**ackground and **S**tyle submenus on the **O**ptions menu. This application can display only one background color and one font style. These options are interdependent, and their event procedures are more complex than those of the **G**reeting option.

Turning Off Options

When you turn on one of the **B**ackground or **S**tyle options, you must turn off the other options. Add the following code to the indicated procedures:

1 Add to the `mnuOptBackgroundWhite_Click` procedure:

```
mnuOptBackgroundWhite.Checked = True

mnuOptBackgroundBlue.Checked = False

mnuOptBackgroundGray.Checked = False
```

2 Add to the `mnuOptBackgroundBlue_Click` procedure:

```
mnuOptBackgroundWhite.Checked = False

mnuOptBackgroundBlue.Checked = True

mnuOptBackgroundGray.Checked = False
```

3 Add to the `mnuOptBackgroundGray_Click` procedure:

```
mnuOptBackgroundWhite.Checked = False

mnuOptBackgroundBlue.Checked = False

mnuOptBackgroundGray.Checked = True
```

4 Run the application.

5 Change the background color to light blue.

6 Select the **O**ptions **B**ackground menu again to see the check mark that now appears next to the Light **B**lue menu option.

To set the `Checked` properties for the font styles, modify the `Click` procedures for the **S**tyle menu options.

The following are the updated procedures:

```
Sub mnuOptStylePlain_Click ()
    mnuOptStylePlain.Checked = True
    mnuOptStyleModern.Checked = False
    lblGreeting.ForeColor = &H80000008
    lblGreeting.FontName = "MS Sans Serif"
    lblGreeting.FontSize = 8.25
    lblPerson.ForeColor = &H80000008
    lblPerson.FontName = "MS Sans Serif"
    lblPerson.FontSize = 8.25
End Sub

Sub mnuOptStyleModern_Click ()
    mnuOptStylePlain.Checked = False
    mnuOptStyleModern.Checked = True
    lblGreeting.ForeColor = &H80
    lblGreeting.FontName = "Modern"
```

```
        lblGreeting.FontSize = 18
        lblperson.ForeColor = &H80
        lblperson.FontName = "Modern"
        lblperson.FontSize = 18
    End Sub
```

The *Enabled* Property

In this application, the **M**odern style can be selected only when the background color is gray. When the application begins, the **M**odern menu option is disabled (dimmed) because the default background color is white.

To enable the **M**odern style menu option when the user selects the gray background, you must modify code in the event procedures. Setting the `Enabled` property to True for the **M**odern menu option is only part of the task. You must also disable the **M**odern menu option when the background color is changed from gray to either white or blue. Furthermore, the program should also change the **M**odern style to **P**lain automatically when the gray background is changed to another color. The remainder of this section discusses the necessary procedure modifications:

Modifying the Program to Use the *Enabled* Property

To change your program to use the `Enabled` property, follow these steps:

❶ Open the Code window.

❷ In the `mnuOptBackgroundGray_Click` procedure, add the following instruction to the beginning of the code in order to enable the Light **G**ray menu option:

```
    mnuOptStyleModern.Enabled = True
```

❸ To disable the **M**odern style menu option and activate the **P**lain style when the user changes the background color to blue or white, add the following two instructions at the beginning of both the `mnuOptBackgroundWhite_Click` and `mnuOptBackgroundBlue_Click` procedures:

```
    If mnuOptStyleModern.Checked Then mnuOptStylePlain_Click

    mnuOptStyleModern.Enabled = False
```

Notice that the first instruction invokes the **P**lain menu option directly from the program code.

❹ Run the application.

❺ Select Light **G**ray from the **O**ptions **B**ackground menu.

Notice that the **M**odern style is now available.

❻ Select the **M**odern style.

❼ Now select Light **B**lue from the **O**ptions **B**ackground menu.

The background color changes to light blue and the font style returns to **P**lain.

8 Access the **O**ptions **S**tyle menu.

Notice that the **M**odern option is dimmed again.

Creating a Menu Control Array

Menu control array
A group of menu controls with a common name and event procedures.

An additional menu tool is the **menu control array**. Menu control arrays are just as easy to create and as useful as other control arrays. To demonstrate menu control arrays, you will add a new submenu to the **M**essage **G**reeting menu option. With this submenu, the user can change the greeting message from `Welcome` to to one of these four messages:

```
Hello
Good Morning
Good Afternoon
Good Evening
```

Changing the Greeting Message

To change the greeting message, follow these steps:

1 Select **G**reeting from the **M**essage menu.

The Code window opens showing the `mnuMessageGreeting_Click` procedure.

2 Delete all the code between the `Sub` and `End Sub` instructions.

Close the Code window.

3 Open the Menu Design window.

4 In the Menu outline, click `&Options`.

5 Click the **I**nsert button three times to prepare for three new menu options.

6 Click the **Ca**ption text box.

7 Type **&Welcome to** for the caption, press **Tab**, and type **mnuMessageGreetingChoice** for the name.

8 Press **Tab** to move to the Index text box, and type **0**.

This action establishes the menu control array.

9 Click the **C**hecked box.

(continues)

Changing the Greeting Message (continued)

10 Click the right-arrow button twice to place the new menu as a submenu option of the **Greeting** menu.

Press **Enter**.

11 Create a menu option with a caption of &Hello and a name of mnuMessageGreetingChoice.

12 Tab to the Index text box, and enter the value **1**.

13 Click the right-arrow button twice to put the menu on the same indentation level as &Welcome to, and then press **Enter**.

14 Create a menu option with a caption of &Good ?? and a name of mnuMessageGreetingChoice.

15 Tab to the Index text box, and enter the value **2**.

16 Click the right-arrow button twice, and then press **Enter**.

17 Click &Greeting in the outline window.

18 Click the **Checked** box to deselect the check mark. The x disappears from the check box.

19 Choose OK.

The **Message Greeting** menu now looks like figure 11.17.

Figure 11.17
The revised
Message
Greeting menu.

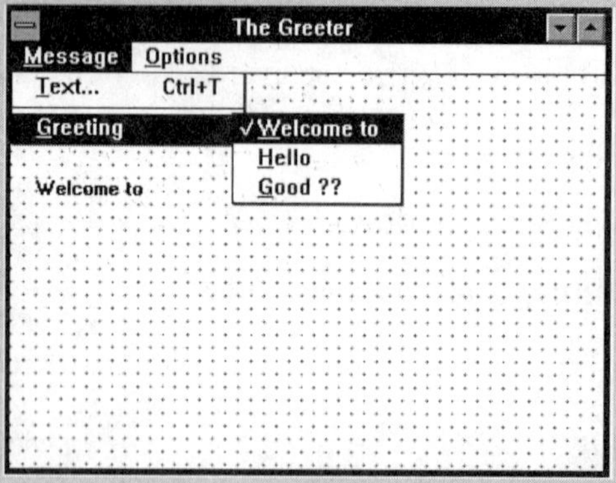

The advantage of a control array with menu options is that you can write a single procedure that specifies the actions for all the items of a submenu. This technique minimizes the amount of duplicate code and makes debugging much easier. As with any control array, you can use the menu control array to add menu options to an application during run time.

Completing the Sample Application

You need to add the code to the sample application to change the label caption for each menu choice and get the system time for the last option. Notice that instead of having three places to add code, you have to change only the `mnuMessageGreetingChoice_Click` event and the initial settings in the `Form_Load` event.

Writing Procedures to Complete the Sample Application

To complete the sample application, do the following:

1 Open the Code window.

2 Enter the following two procedures:

```
Sub mnuMessageGreetingChoice_Click (Index As Integer)

  Select Case Index

    Case 0

      lblGreeting.Caption = "Welcome to"

      mnuMessageGreetingChoice(0).Checked = True

      mnuMessageGreetingChoice(1).Checked = False

      mnuMessageGreetingChoice(2).Checked = False

    Case 1

      lblGreeting.Caption = "Hello"

      mnuMessageGreetingChoice(0).Checked = False

      mnuMessageGreetingChoice(1).Checked = True

      mnuMessageGreetingChoice(2).Checked = False

    Case 2

      lblGreeting.Caption =
➥ mnuMessageGreetingChoice(2).Caption

      mnuMessageGreetingChoice(0).Checked = False

      mnuMessageGreetingChoice(1).Checked = False

      mnuMessageGreetingChoice(2).Checked = True

  End Select

End Sub
```

(continues)

Writing Procedures to Complete the Sample Application   (continued)

```
Sub Form_Load ()

    If Val(Time$) > 0 And Val(Time$) < 12 Then

        mnuMessageGreetingChoice(2).Caption = "Good Morning"

    ElseIf Val(Time$) >= 12 And Val(Time$) < 18 Then

        mnuMessageGreetingChoice(2).Caption = "Good Afternoon"

    Else

        mnuMessageGreetingChoice(2).Caption = "Good Evening"

    End If

End Sub
```

Notice that the Form_Load procedure uses Time$ to determine the time of day and then, for Case 2, assigns the appropriate caption in the menu control array. As a result, when the user opens the **M**essage Greeting menu, the bottom option reads Good Morning, Good Afternoon, or Good Evening.

Chapter Summary

Visual Basic includes a special tool for the creation of a menu system: the Menu Design window. By using this window, you can easily create a hierarchical menu system with cascading menus, check marks, separator bars, and dimmed options.

Visual Basic treats menu options as controls. Event procedures specify the actions to take when a menu option is selected. With menu control arrays, you can save repetitive coding for related submenu options.

Menu controls have several properties, including Caption, Name, Enabled, and Checked. By manipulating these properties in program code, you can enable and disable menu options, toggle check marks next to menu options, and hide or restore menus from view.

In the next chapter, you learn more about reading and writing files in Visual Basic.

Test Your Understanding

True/False
Indicate whether the statement is true or false.

1. A menu control has only one event.

2. If you select the **C**hecked option in the Menu Design window, VB ensures that no two items within the same menu can be checked at the same time.

3. To add a separator bar to a menu, you create a special menu option with a hyphen as the caption.

4. A menu option with its `Enabled` property set to False will not appear in a menu.

5. Menu items cannot be placed in a control array.

6. A menu item that has a cascading submenu associated with it appears in the menu with a black triangle at its right.

7. A menu choice that has a dialog box associated with it automatically has three dots added to its `Caption` property.

8. Menu items at the left edge of the Menu Design window (that is, not indented) appear in the main menu of the application.

9. To remove an item from a menu, first click the menu item in the Menu Design window, and then click the Dele**t**e button.

10. You should use cascading menus only when the choices are interdependent.

Short Answer

Answer the following questions.

1. How do you access the Menu Design window?

2. How do you designate an access key for a menu item?

3. How do you create a main menu item—one that appears in the application's menu bar?

4. For what is the Inde**x** box in the Menu Design window used?

5. For what is the **S**hortcut drop-down list in the Menu Design window used?

6. What does the **N**ext button in the Menu Design window do?

7. What does the **I**nsert button in the Menu Design window do?

8. For what are the arrow buttons in the Menu Design window used?

9. What is the function of the **C**hecked box in the Menu Design window?

10. What is the function of the **E**nabled box in the Menu Design window?

11. What is the function of the **V**isible box in the Menu Design window?

Projects

Project 1:   Adding Menu Choices to Ted

Alter the Ted application that you created in Chapter 6 so that all the current options are provided only through menu choices.

Add menu options for changing the font (three font choices) and font size (three size choices). Add menu choices to change the font color to red or blue; black, the default color, should also appear as a choice in the menu. If the red font color is selected, the user should not be able to set the font color back to black again. When the user selects an option, it should be checked. Be sure to add access keys and shortcut key combinations to the menu items.

Save the modified application as **C11P1**, and print the project.

Project 2:   Adding Help and Exit Menus to Greeter

Add a Help menu and an Exit menu to the project you developed in this chapter.

The Help menu should contain at least four helpful menu items. You should have a Help menu choice for **G**reeting, **B**ackground, and **S**tyle (plus a menu choice that is up to you). Each Help menu choice should display a Help window explaining how the user can use the corresponding feature of the program. At the bottom of the Help menu, include an About choice that displays a window containing your name as the programmer. Separate the About menu choice from the other Help menu choices with a separator bar. Include access keys and shortcut keys.

Save the project as **C11P2**, and print the project.

CHAPTER 12

Processing Files

Many Visual Basic applications work with external files. After all, the most common way for an application to save information is to write it to a data file. Similarly, many applications read required information from an appropriate data file. This chapter shows you how to work with files.

First, you examine the three file controls found in the Visual Basic Toolbox: the File List Box, the Directory List Box, and the Drive List Box. Using these controls, you can build standard Windows-like dialog boxes for the selection and specification of files.

You then look at the Visual Basic statements and functions that emulate DOS-type file commands. With these statements and functions, you can manipulate files and directories. For example, you can create a new directory or copy files from one directory to another.

Next, you learn about the three types of data files supported by Visual Basic: sequential, random (random access), and binary. The discussion focuses on how to use these types of files and presents the advantages and disadvantages of each type.

Finally, you see how the Common Dialog Box control can be used to make your file-reading and file-writing programs more flexible. You can let the user select the name of a file to read or write, instead of having the file name hard coded in your program.

Objectives

By the time you have finished this chapter, you will be able to

1. Use the File Controls

2. Manage Files and Directories in Visual Basic

3. Understand the Uses of Data Files

4. Know the Advantages and Disadvantages of the Three Types of Data Files

5. Read and Write Sequential Files

6. Read and Write Random Files

7. Read and Write Binary Files

8. Use the Common Dialog Box Control When You Open and Save Files

Using the File Controls

The three file controls in the Toolbox are the File List Box, the Directory List Box, and the Drive List Box. With these controls, you can display lists of files, directories, and disk drives.

Each of the file controls works similarly to the standard list box control. In fact, the file controls share several of the properties associated with ordinary list boxes, including List, ListCount, and ListIndex.

The Toolbox icons for the file controls depict a page of paper, a folder, and a disk drive (see figure 12.1).

Figure 12.1
Toolbox icons for the file controls.

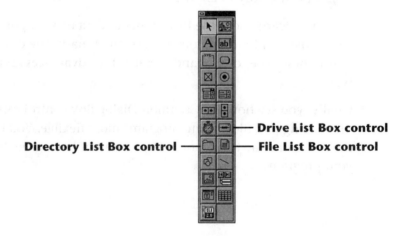

Directory List Box control —— ⎯ Drive List Box control
—— File List Box control

The file list box displays a list of files. A user can select a file with either a mouse click or a keystroke. The directory list box displays the available directories on each disk drive. The user can change directories with a few mouse clicks or keystrokes. Using the drive list box, the user can specify any available disk drive.

The file and directory list boxes have built-in scroll bars that enable the user to move up and down through the lists. The drive list box provides a drop-down list box.

By moving through the file controls in an application, the user can select disk drives, directories, and files. As explained in this chapter, these controls share related properties. With a minimum of program code, you can synchronize the controls so that they work together.

The file controls provide an interface commonly used in many Windows applications. Figure 12.2 shows a standard Windows-like dialog box used to open a file. Using the file controls, you can create such dialog boxes with relative ease.

Figure 12.2
An Open dialog box.

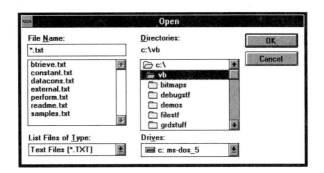

The File List Box Control

At design time, Visual Basic assigns a default name of File1 to the first file list box you place on a form. Subsequent list boxes have default names of File2, File3, and so on. Using the Properties window, you can set property values just as you do for other controls.

Figure 12.3 shows how a file list box might appear at run time.

Figure 12.3
A typical file list box at run time.

Using the Path property of the file list box, you can specify and determine which files it displays. Path can be modified only in program code at run time. The Path property specifies the current path for the file list box. For example, the following instruction sets the value of Path in File1 to the default Visual Basic directory:

```
File1.Path = "C:\VB"
```

The Directory List Box Control

The Directory List Box control displays the directories and paths on the current disk drive. Visual Basic places a small folder icon to the left of each directory name. With a directory list box, a user can navigate and select directories with the mouse or keyboard. If you are in a directory, the folder icon appears opened. For subdirectories under the current directory, the folder icons appear closed.

Figure 12.4 shows a directory list box.

Figure 12.4

A directory list box.

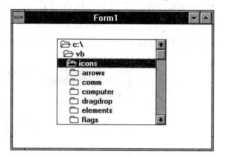

Both the directory list box and the file list box have a Path property in which you can begin to synchronize your controls. You can put code in the Change event of a directory list box to update the Path property of a file list box. Similarly, you can put code in the PathChange and PatternChange events of a file list box to update the value of Path for a directory list box.

The Drive List Box Control

The drive list box is a drop-down list box containing the names and volume labels of all available disk drives on your system. A small icon to the left of each drive name indicates the drive type: floppy drive, hard disk, network drive, or RAM disk. Figure 12.5 shows an example of a drive list box.

Figure 12.5

A drive list box.

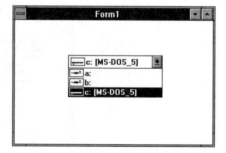

The control first displays only the current drive. When the user clicks the down arrow, a drop-down list appears, displaying all the available drives. To select one of the displayed drives, the user clicks it. When a drive is selected, the value of the Drive property for that drive list box is updated. The Drive property is a string value that specifies the selected drive.

Making File Controls Work Together

As noted, the three file controls can be synchronized to work together in an application. That way, a user can easily switch among drives and directories and select one or more files. A chain of events must be established so that this synchronization can work smoothly. When a property value changes in one control, the program code must notify the other controls, and their associated property values must be modified.

Suppose that an application has three file controls: Drive1, Dir1, and File1. When the drive in Drive1 changes, a Change event for Drive1 is triggered. In the Drive1_Change procedure, you can put code that communicates the new drive letter to Dir1. When the Path property of Dir1 changes, the Dir1_Change event can send new path information to File1. The Path property of File1 is then updated. In other words, Drive1 updates Dir1, which in turn updates File1.

File and Directory Management in Visual Basic

Visual Basic has seven statements that perform DOS-like commands (see table 12.1). You use these statements to do file and directory manipulation in your program code.

12

Table 12.1 Visual Basic's DOS-like Statements			
Visual Basic Statement	**Equivalent DOS Command**	**DOS Abbreviation**	**Effect**
MkDir	MKDIR	MD	Creates a directory
RmDir	RMDIR	RD	Removes (deletes) a directory
ChDrive	*drive:*		Changes current drive
ChDir	CHDIR	CD	Changes current directory
Kill	ERASE	DEL	Deletes a file
Name	RENAME	REN	Renames a file
FileCopy	COPY		Copies a file

The syntax of these seven VB statements is straightforward:

```
MkDir pathname

RmDir pathname

ChDrive drive

ChDir pathname

Kill filespec

Name oldfilespec As newfilespec

FileCopy oldfilespec, newfilespec
```

pathname is a string expression specifying a path, and *drive* is a string expression specifying a drive letter. *filespec, oldfilespec*, and *newfilespec* are string expressions that specify a file.

Kill deletes only files, not directories. Use a RmDir instruction to delete directories.

Here are examples of two of these statements:

```
MkDir "B:\CLIENTS"     'Note the quotation marks to indicate a string.
ChDrive "D"
```

Visual Basic's File-Processing Functions

Visual Basic provides a number of functions for processing files. The FileDateTime function returns information about the date and time for a file. The GetAttr function returns information about a file, directory, or volume label. With the SetAttr statement, you can specify attributes for a file. The CurDir$ function returns a string indicating the current path for a specified disk drive. The companion function, CurDir, returns a Variant (of type String). Dir$ returns a string indicating a file or directory that matches specified conditions. The companion function, Dir, returns a Variant (of type String).

For more information on file controls, statements, and functions, see VB's Help topics and Que's *Using Visual Basic 3*, Special Edition.

Using Data Files

As a programmer, you face an ongoing challenge: getting data into your applications and saving the information they create. Here are two of the simplest ways to get data into your applications:

- *Store the data directly in the program.* This method is the simplest. An assignment instruction such as

    ```
    City$ = "Phoenix"
    ```

    stores the data (in this case, Phoenix) as part of the program itself.

- *Ask the user for the data.* When the person running the program must supply data, the program can prompt the user to type the data. Your primary tools for this method are the text box and InputBox.

Both methods work well, but they are appropriate only when the amount of data is relatively small. Suppose that you want to write an application that manages a large set of data, such as a mailing list or the inventory of a hardware store. It's just not feasible to store all the necessary data inside the program or to ask the user to supply it when the program runs. Furthermore, the data changes with time and needs periodic updating.

The common solution to these problems is to use a data file on disk. Sequential and random files, the most commonly used types of VB files, consist of records. Each record is divided into one or more fields. The data file can be on either a floppy drive or a hard disk. Once a data file exists, your program can read the data from the file, process the data, and then write a new (or updated) data file directly to disk. By storing data in disk files, independently from the FRM and BAS files, you enjoy many tangible benefits:

- Data files can be maintained and updated.

- Large data files can be accessed conveniently.

- Programs are kept intact and relatively small.

- Files can be shared by several applications.

- Data files created from external sources (such as a word processor or spreadsheet) can be read.

Using Data Files—General Concepts and Techniques

Visual Basic supports three kinds of data files:

- **Sequential files** store data as ASCII text. Information is read from and written to the file in the form of fields made up of characters.

- **Random files** store data in special Visual Basic internal formats. Such files require a rigid file structure.

- **Binary files** store data as individual bytes. No file structure exists, and no special internal formats are assumed.

Sequential file
A file, that stores data as ASCII text characters. Individual records are fields are separated by commas.

Random file
A file that stores data in a special VB format and has a rigid file structure.

Binary file
A file that stores data as individual bytes and has no file structure.

Each file type has certain advantages and disadvantages. In general, sequential files are easy to program and understand, but reading them and writing to them are relatively slow. Random files require more programming complexity, but the I/O operations are relatively fast. Binary files provide maximum flexibility, but they impose the greatest demands on the programmer to keep track of the file organization. Upcoming sections of this chapter discuss these trade-offs.

Whether a program uses sequential, random-access, or binary files, some general techniques are commonly used with all three types. To communicate with a disk file, a program must follow these essential steps:

1. *Open the data file*. Using the Open statement, you inform Visual Basic of the name and type of the file, as well as how the program expects to use it.

2. *Read data from or write data to the file (or both)*. Visual Basic provides a variety of statements to perform I/O operations.

3. *Close the data file*. With the Close statement, your program terminates I/O operations on the data file.

Using the *Open* Statement
You must establish a communications link before using any disk file. An Open instruction serves several purposes. It

- Declares the name and path of the data file

- Establishes the file type and the I/O mode

- Opens a communications channel between the program and the file

- Associates an integer number with the data file

Using the *Close* Statement

After your program finishes its I/O activity on a data file, you use a `Close` instruction to cancel the communications link. `Close` terminates the association between the data file on disk and the corresponding file number. The `Close` statement is explored in detail in the next section on sequential files.

Reading and Writing Data

Coding the I/O activities that your program performs is the most difficult part of using files. How you perform I/O in VB code depends on the type of file you are using. Reading files and writing files are discussed in the sections that describe the three file types in detail.

Using Sequential Files

You write sequential files as ASCII (character) text. These files generally have a TXT file name extension. Many word processing programs, as well as other commercial applications, can read and write ASCII files. Furthermore, the Windows Notepad utility can work with ASCII files. In a record of a sequential file, fields are separated by commas. For example, a personnel record might consist of employee name, position, salary, office number or plant location, and phone number fields. The five fields are separated by commas, and record boundaries are maintained automatically. Visual Basic provides several statements for reading and writing sequential files conveniently. Therefore, programming is relatively easy.

Sequential files, however, have two main drawbacks:

- *You must read records sequentially.* Out of 50 records, you may want information in only the 50th record. You must first read through 49 of them. This process is slow.

- *You cannot read and write to a sequential file simultaneously.* You must open the file for either reading or writing, and then close the file before reopening it to work in the other mode.

Think of a sequential file as similar to a cassette music tape (see figure 12.6).

Figure 12.6

A sequential file is similar to a cassette music tape.

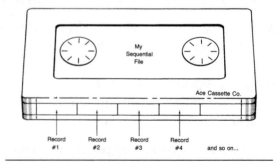

Individual songs on the tape are like records in the file. You must first play the preceding songs to listen to a song in the middle of the tape. Likewise, you must first read the preceding records to examine one in the middle of the file.

Creating a Sequential File

You can create a sequential file by writing a program to create the file and then fill it with data. When creating a sequential file using VB code, you must follow these steps:

1. Open the file as a sequential file for writing.

2. Prepare your data for writing to the file.

3. Use the `Write #` instruction to write data to the file.

4. Close the file.

Opening the File

The `Open` statement has many forms. You use the following syntax to create a new sequential file:

```
Open filespec For Output As #filenum
```

`filespec` is a string expression that specifies the name (and optionally the path) of the new sequential data file. `filenum` is an integer expression from 1 to 255 that associates a numeric value with the opened file. The pound sign (#) is optional before the `filenum` parameter.

For example, the following instruction creates and opens a sequential file named MYDATA.TXT (in the root directory of drive C):

```
Open "C:\MYDATA.TXT" For Output As #35
```

A file number of 35 is assigned to this file. Because the # is optional, you could write the instruction as the following:

```
Open "C:\MYDATA.TXT" For Output As 35   'No # before file number
```

The phrase `For Output` tells Visual Basic that this file is a sequential file to which the program writes output. (As you learn later in this chapter, `Open` accepts other phrases with additional meanings.)

When you open a file `For Output`, it does not need to be an existing file. In fact, the file often should *not* exist. Why? If the file already exists, Visual Basic completely erases the file's contents without even a warning. Don't open an existing file `For Output` unless you intend to write over the old file contents and create a new one.

The file number (35 in this example) provides a convenient way to refer to the file in later program instructions. As you will see, when you want to write data to the file, you instruct Visual Basic to write to file number 35 instead of specifying the complete file name. The `Open` instruction tells Visual Basic exactly what file you mean when you indicate number 35.

When specifying a file name in an Open instruction, you generally provide a path as part of the name. If you open a file For Output without specifying a path, Visual Basic places the file in the current directory. Be aware that the file is not placed in the root directory or the Visual Basic directory.

Writing the Data

When your program has its data ready to store, you write a record to the disk file by using the Write # instruction. Write # works with both strings and numbers. The syntax of the Write # statement is the following:

```
Write #filenum, expressionlist
```

filenum is the file number, and expressionlist is a list of expressions separated by commas. The expressionlist is the list of fields you want to write to the file. Each Write # instruction writes one record to the file. Each expression in expressionlist is the data for one field of the record.

Write # does some special formatting. A comma is placed between items in expressionlist. String values are enclosed in quotation marks. If you omit expressionlist, the instruction places a blank line in the file. Often you place the Write # instruction in a loop that writes all the records you want placed in the data file.

Closing the File

After you have written all the records to the file, you close it with a Close instruction:

```
Close #filenum
```

filenum is an integer expression that specifies the file to close. As with an Open instruction, the pound sign (#) is optional. The following instruction closes file number 35 (previously opened for output):

```
Close #35
```

Close terminates the association of the file number with the data file. As a result, the file number becomes available for a subsequent Open instruction. Close also flushes the file buffer, which means that all information written to the file is processed. Using the word Close, without a file number, closes all open files.

To see how these statements may be used, consider an array (MYDATA1) of 500 items that is written by a program to a sequential file:

```
Open "ARRAY.TXT" For Output As #1      'Opens the file as #1
For I = 1 to 500
  Write #1, MYDATA1(I)    'Writes one data item to ARRAY.TXT
Next I
Close #1                 'Closes the file ARRAY.TXT
```

Each Write # statement writes a new line of data (a record) to the file.

Because sequential files are standard ASCII text files, they are easy to examine. You can view and modify a file with most word processors and text editors. For example, from the Accessories group in the Windows Program Manager, you can launch the Notepad application. From Notepad, choose **O**pen from the **F**ile menu. Specify whatever path and file name you have used (such as A:\FILES\ARRAY.TXT). Use Notepad if you need to check the contents of a file that your program has written or will read.

Appending to a Sequential File

The process of adding new records to the end of a sequential file without over-writing the existing records is called *appending the file*. To append a sequential file, you open it in a special mode called Append. In the Open instruction, you use the phrase For Append rather than For Output. The Open instruction for a file might look like this:

```
Open "C:\COINS\MYCOINS.TXT" For Append As #1
```

Here are the four essential steps a programmer takes to append records to an existing sequential data file:

1. Open the file For Append.

2. Prepare the data for writing to the file.

3. Use the Write # instruction to write additional data records at the end of the file.

4. Close the file.

Only the first step is different from that for creating a new file. Opening a file For Append readies an existing file to receive additional records. If the Open instruction specifies a nonexistent file, one is created as though it were opened For Output.

Reading a Sequential File

Reading information from a sequential file requires the following steps:

1. Open the file For Input.

2. Use the Input # instruction to read data into variables.

3. Process the data.

4. Close the file.

The first step introduces the third way to open a sequential data file: For Input. (The other two are For Output and For Append.) By opening a file for input, you tell Visual Basic that you intend to *read from* the file rather than *write to* it. When you open a file For Input, you can only read records from it; you cannot write records to the file.

The following instruction opens the MYCOINS.TXT sequential file for input and specifies 1 as the file number:

```
Open "C:\COINS\MYCOINS.TXT" For Input As #1
```

Of course, when you open a file for input, the file must already exist. If Visual Basic cannot find your specified file, a File not found error results.

12

The *Input #* Statement

After you open a file for input, you can read records from it with an `Input #`
instruction. `Input #` and `Write #` are complementary statements. `Input #` reads a
data record from a file opened for input, and `Write #` writes a record to a file
opened for output.

`Input #` is designed for reading sequential files created with `Write #`. Like `Write #`,
an `Input #` instruction contains a variable list. `Input #` reads a data record from a
sequential file and stores the record's values in the list's variables. You use the
following syntax:

```
Input #filenum, variablelist
```

filenum is the file number, and *variablelist* is a list of variables separated by
commas.

To use `Input #`, you must know the number of fields in each record as well as the
type of data in each field. The variables in *variablelist* should match the file
data. You guarantee correct matching if the variable list in the `Input #` instruction is exactly the same as the variable list in the `Write #` instruction that created the file record.

With `Input #`, you can read numeric data into a string variable. However, you
cannot read string data into a numeric variable. Of course, Variant variables can
handle either type of data.

Even if you need only some of the information in a record, you should read all
the fields of the record to make sure that Visual Basic correctly keeps your place
in the file.

As indicated, *variablelist* usually consists of the same variable names used in
the complementary `Write #` instruction that created the file. Such consistency
ensures that the data file is read successfully.

The *EOF* Function

The `EOF` (end of file) function tests whether the end of a sequential file has been
reached. The syntax of this function is the following:

```
EOF(filenum)
```

filenum is the file number.

`EOF` returns a Boolean value: True (1) if the end of file was reached, or False (0) if
the end was not reached. For this reason, you can use `EOF` with `If`, `Do Until`, and
`While` instructions.

By using `EOF`, you don't have to know beforehand how many records are in your
data file. Be sure that you test for `EOF` before attempting to read past the end of
the file. The run-time error `Input past end of file` occurs if you try to execute
an `Input #` instruction when the last record has already been read.

Using the *Line Input #* Statement

Line Input # reads an entire record into a single string variable. Each record is read in its entirety, including any commas or quotation marks. Here is the syntax of Line Input #:

```
Line Input #filenum, stringvar
```

filenum is the file number, and stringvar is a string variable.

You use Line Input # when a file has either a special or an unknown structure. Perhaps the file was not created with Write #, or you don't know the exact Write # instruction used to create the file. Another possibility is that the number of fields varies from record to record.

In such cases, the programmer is responsible for appropriately analyzing the data in stringvar. Depending on the situation, your program might have to search for meaningful delimiters or break down stringvar into usable components.

Other Sequential File Tools

Visual Basic also has the FileLen function, which returns the length of a file (opened or not) as a long integer. The syntax is FileLen(filespec), in which filespec is a string expression that specifies the file name (with or without drive and path).

You can also write, as the first record in a sequential file, the number of data records your program will store in the file. When reading the file later, the program can read the single field in the first record. Then the program will know how many data records to read from the file. Otherwise, the only way that a program can keep track of the number of records in a file is to use a Dowhile Not EOF() loop to read the file. Outside the loop, you initialize the variable RecordCount to 0. Inside the loop, you add 1 to RecordCount each time you read a record. When the loop terminates, RecordCount will contain the number of records in the file.

Example of a Sequential File

Now look at an example of the use of sequential files. Suppose that you have in memory a type Variant array containing 50 rows and 3 columns. The name of the array is StatesData. Each row contains three data items: the name of the state, the name of the governor, and the population of the state. To write the data to a sequential file (C:\FILES\STATE.SEQ), you could use the following statements:

```
Open "C:\FILES\STATE.SEQ" For Output As #1
For I = 1 to 50
    Write #1, StatesData(I,1), StatesData(I,2), StatesData(I,3)
Next I
Close #1
```

To read the file, you could then use these statements:

```
Open "C:\FILES\STATE.SEQ" For Input As #1
For I = 1 to 50
   Input #1, StatesData(I,1), StatesData(I,2), StatesData(I,3)
Next I
Close #1
```

Using Random Files

The second kind of disk data file is the random-access file, or simply random file. Random files require more complex programming than sequential files require. Compared to sequential files, however, random files offer these significant advantages:

- *Two-way I/O activity.* When a random file is opened, you can read from and write to it.

- *Random access.* You can access any record quickly and conveniently.

- *Record modification.* You can modify (update) individual records without re-writing all the others.

As you have seen, you must read all preceding records in a sequential file to get to the record you want. If your application needs only the information in the 75th record, you must read all the information in the first 74 records. The deeper into the file the record is located, the longer the accessing takes.

A random file, however, is organized like a compact disk player, which can efficiently locate any song on a disk. Random files reference individual records by number. By simply specifying a record number, you can access that record's information quickly. The access time is virtually the same for the first record as for the 50th. Random files are the only practical choice for large applications. Furthermore, once you read a random file record, you can modify the data. You can rewrite the record directly—you don't have to close and reopen the file. Appending records is also a straightforward process.

Random files might seem the best answer for disk database programming. Why would anyone use sequential files? Computing, like life, is always a series of trade-offs. Note the following disadvantages—the price you must pay to use random files:

- *Rigid file structure.* Each record of a random file must have the same configuration. The number of fields and the data type for each one cannot vary from record to record.

- *Lack of portability.* You cannot easily read random files with applications, such as word processors, spreadsheets, and text editors. The TYPE command in DOS does not display random files.

- *Increased programming effort.* For random files, programming is more complex than for sequential ones.

Like a sequential file, a random file is a series of records, each one consisting of data fields. Unlike a record in a sequential file, each random file record has a predetermined size that cannot change throughout the file.

Designing a Random File

You might think of a random file record as being similar to a survey form, the kind in which you provide data in marked boxes. As figure 12.7 shows, such forms often provide one box for each data character.

Figure 12.7
A fixed-field data form.

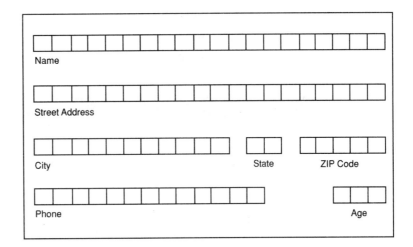

Notice that each field in the form has a fixed size. The data for one field can require fewer than the allocated number of characters. You cannot, however, use more characters than allocated. For example, the sample form has a Name field of 20 characters. You can enter a name with fewer than 20 characters, but you can't use more than 20.

This fixed-field size requirement applies to random files supported by VB. Before using a random file, you must determine a template form for each record. The number of fields and the size of each must remain constant throughout the file. You can let each field be any size, but once you specify it, you cannot make a change.

As a result, the size (number of bytes) of each record is constant in a random file. That's why Visual Basic can access any record quickly. When a record number is given, the position of the data on the disk is readily computed. For any record in the file, the computer takes essentially the same time to determine the location of the data, find it, and then read the information.

When determining the size of fields in a record, you need to treat text fields and numeric fields differently.

Creating Text Fields in a Random File

You must determine the maximum number of characters a text field can have. For each record in the file, you allocate that maximum size for the field, whether or not all the characters are actually used. For example, you can determine that a field reserved for a customer's name should be allocated 30 characters. Whether the actual data is I. M. Sly, Ace Accordion Supply, or Rumplestiltskin Meriweather, that field always occupies 30 bytes (characters) in the data file.

Creating Numeric Fields in a Random File

Random files save numbers in the internal binary formats used by Visual Basic to store numbers in memory. Therefore, for each numeric field, you designate one of Visual Basic's five numeric types: Integer, Long Integer, Single-precision, Double-precision, or Currency. Be careful that you choose the numeric type of each field wisely. The numeric type must accommodate every entry for that field. If it contains a number with a fractional component, such as 34.67, that field must be Single- or Double-precision. For whole numbers, the Integer type is limited to 32,767. Use Long Integer if your values are larger than 32,767.

Numbers are stored in binary form. Therefore, the size (in bytes) of each field is determined by the data type, as table 12.2 shows.

Table 12.2   Size of Numeric Types

Number Type	Size (Bytes)
Integer	2
Long integer	4
Single-precision	4
Double-precision	8
Currency	8

For example, a field reserved for a single-precision number is allocated 4 bytes. Whether the actual data is 10, 28.699, or 6.04E–28, the number is stored in 4 bytes, just as in the computer's RAM.

A Sample Record

Suppose that you want to design a random file for a coin collection. Each record (coin) requires four fields: Year, Category, Value, and Comment.

Year is a whole number expressed in four digits, such as 1947. The Integer type is appropriate, so the first field requires 2 bytes.

Category is a text field. Twenty characters should be enough to describe each coin's category, so the second field is 20 bytes.

Value is a numeric field expressed in dollars and cents, such as 135.50. No coin is worth more than 3,000 (three-thousand dollars). Single-precision numbers easily satisfy this data range, so the third field is 4 bytes long. (The Currency type offers more precision than necessary and requires twice as much memory storage.)

Comment is a text field. The data for this field varies widely from coin to coin. Fifty characters should be enough, so the length of the fourth field is 50 bytes. The Comment field shows the squandering of disk space that can occur with random files. For many coins, the Comment field might be short or blank, yet a full 50 bytes is still reserved. This squandering is the price you must pay to maintain rigid file structure. Typically, data stored as a random file takes more room on disk than the same data stored as a sequential file.

Figure 12.8 shows the template form for each record of the coin collection database. The total size of each record is fixed at 76 bytes.

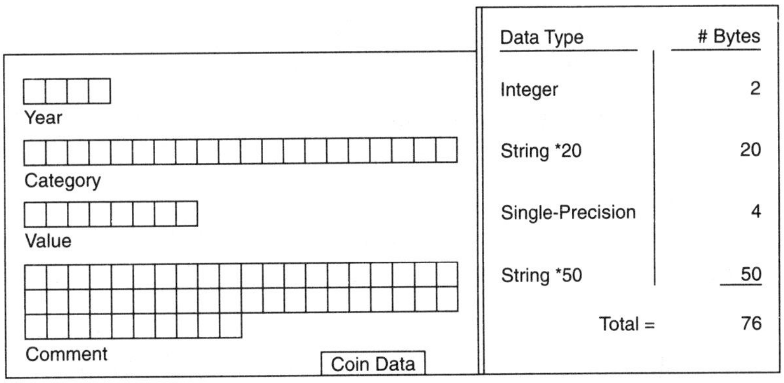

Figure 12.8
The random file record for each coin.

Data Type	# Bytes
Integer	2
String *20	20
Single-Precision	4
String *50	50
Total =	76

Using a Random File with User-Defined Data Types

The user-defined data type enables you to create data structures to describe your records (see Chapter 9, "Using Arrays and Data Structures"). After you create a user-defined data type, you can designate variables that have it. These are known as *record* variables. When you associate a user-defined variable with your record template, transferring data to and from random files is easy.

You use the following steps to process random files with record variables:

1. Define a record variable that matches your record template.

2. Open the file For Random access.

3. Use record variables in Get and Put instructions to read and write the data.

4. Close the file.

The next sections examine these steps.

Defining the Record Variable

Recall from Chapter 9 that you use a Type-End Type block to create a record data type (a user-defined data type). The following block, for example, creates the data type CoinType, which is appropriate for the coin collection database. The Dim instruction declares the record variable Coin to have the data type CoinType.

```
Type CoinType
   Yr As Integer
   Category As String * 20
   Valu As Single
   Comment As String * 50
End Type

Dim Coin As CoinType
```

Opening the File

You always open a random file For Random. The Open instruction adds a Len clause that specifies the length of each record in the file. Here is the syntax:

```
Open filespec For Random As #filenum Len = recordlength
```

filespec specifies the name and path of the data file. *filenum* is the file number. *recordlength* is an integer expression specifying, in bytes, the size of each record. The pound sign (#) for *filenum* is optional. The For Random and Len clauses are optional also. A single Open instruction opens a random file for any or all I/O activities—reading, writing, and appending.

Suppose that you design a random database file for the coin collection. You want to describe each coin (record in the file) with a variable of the user-defined type CoinType. Remember, the size of each record is 76 bytes (2 for the year, 20 for the category, 4 for the value, and 50 for the comment). So 76 is the value for the *recordlength* parameter in the Len clause of the Open instruction.

You name the file MYCOINS.RAN (here the file extension RAN is used for random files), and it is on a disk in drive B. Then the following instruction opens MYCOINS.RAN as file number 1:

```
Open "B:MYCOINS.RAN" For Random As #1 Len = 76
```

The For Random clause is optional because random is the default mode for the Open instruction. However, for clarity, it's a good idea to include the For Random clause.

As you have seen, the Len clause specifies the length, in bytes, of each random file record. For optimum efficiency, the value in the Len clause should precisely match the record length. Although wasteful of disk space, the value in the Len clause can be larger than the actual record length.

The following tip helps you specify Len clauses in your random Open instructions. The Len function calculates the length (number of bytes) of any variable, including a record variable. Using the Len function in the Len clause of the Open instruction is helpful. That way, you don't have to know or supply the exact length of the record data type. Note this example:

```
Open "B:MYCOINS.RAN" For Random as #1 Len = Len(Coin)
```

Remember that the Len clause is optional. If you omit it in an Open instruction, the record length defaults to 128 bytes.

Writing Records with *Put*

You use the Put statement to write a random file record. The syntax is the following:

```
Put #filenum, recordnum, variable
```

filenum is the file number, and *recordnum* is a numeric expression (from 1 to 2,147,483,647) specifying the record to be written. *variable* indicates the variable containing the data to be written to the file. The *recordnum* parameter and the pound sign (#) are optional.

recordnum can specify any record in the file: an old one whose data is to be rewritten, or a new one receiving it for the first time. If you omit *recordnum*, the default record number is 1, plus the last record written (using Put) or read. Thus, you can write incrementally, increasing record numbers with successive Put instructions that omit *recordnum*. You can also have a single Put instruction in a loop. When you omit the *recordnum* parameter, use two consecutive commas in the Put instruction.

The following instruction, for example, writes the next consecutive record to the coin database file, which has been opened as file number 1:

```
Put #1, , Coin
```

In a Put statement, *variable* is usually a variable of the appropriate user-defined data type. However, you can use any variable, as long as its length is not more than that of the record. Visual Basic simply writes all the bytes of the variable.

Before writing a record, you must assign the correct values to each component of the record variable. Recall that Visual Basic record variables use a period notation to identify individual components.

The following program fragment demonstrates writing a sample record of the coin database:

```
Coin.Yr = 1910
Coin.Category = "Lincoln Penny"
Coin.Valu = 70.00
Coin.Comment = "S mint mark, uncirculated"
Put #1, 5, Coin              'Write record number 5
```

Reading Records with *Get*

You use the Get statement to read a record. Here is the syntax:

```
Get #filenum, recordnum, variable
```

filenum is the file number, *recordnum* is the record number, and *variable* specifies the variable to receive the data. The *recordnum* parameter and the pound sign (#) are optional. As with Put, *recordnum* can specify any record. If you omit *recordnum*, the default record number is the last record read or written, plus 1.

The following instruction reads record number 5 from the coin data file into the record variable Coin:

```
Get #1, 5, Coin              'Read record number 5
```

Each component of the record variable Coin now contains the appropriate data.

Closing the Random File

When file read/write activity is finished, you use the Close statement as usual.

Example of a Random File Program

Suppose that you have the coin data in a random file named MYCOINS.RAN. You decide to update the database file by increasing the value of each coin by 10 percent. To write such a program, you define CoinType with a Type-End Type block. You place the following instructions in the declarations section of a code module:

```
TYPE CoinType
Yr As Integer
Category As String * 20
Valu As Single
```

```
    Comment As String * 50
    End Type
```

Now you can write the active program instructions in this way:

```
Dim Coin As CoinType
Dim RecordNum as Integer
Open "C:\COINS\MYCOINS.RAN" For Random As #5 Len = 76
For RecordNum = 1 To 3                  'File has only 3 records
    Get #5, RecordNum, Coin
    Coin.Valu = 1.1 * Coin.Valu         'Increase value by 10%
    Put #5, RecordNum, Coin
NEXT RecordNum
Close #5
```

This code fragment demonstrates one of the great advantages of random files over sequential files: You can read or write random files without closing and reopening each file. Furthermore, you can read or write records in any order. For example, you can have RecordNum loop from 3 down to 1, and the program still works well.

Using *Seek* and *Loc* with Random Files

For random files, Seek and Loc deal with record numbers. The Seek statement positions the file pointer at the next record you want to read or write. Note the following example:

```
Seek #9, 23   'Move pointer to the 23rd record of file number 9
```

After this Seek, a Get or Put instruction without a *recordnum* parameter operates on this reset file position. For example, after VB executes the preceding instruction, the following instruction writes the Coin information into record number 23:

```
Put #9, , Coin
```

The Seek function returns the next record to be read or written. The Loc function returns the last record read or written. Here is an example:

```
Dim Msg as String
Get #9, 2, Coin  'Read record number 2
Msg = "Last record read was   " & Str$(Loc(9)) & Chr$(13)
Msg = Msg & "Next record to read is" & Str$(Seek(9))
MsgBox Msg
```

The resulting message box displays the following:

```
Last record read was   2

Next record to read is 3
```

Using the *EOF* Function with Random Files

With random files, the EOF function returns True (1) if the most recent Get instruction did not read an entire record. This situation happens when Get reads beyond the end of the file.

When I/O activity is finished, you use a Close instruction as usual.

Using Binary Files

A binary file is not really a different type of file, but rather a different way of looking at one. At the most elemental level, any file is just a sequence of byte values. You can open any file in binary file mode and read or write such bytes directly. No particular structure is assumed; the entire file is treated as one long sequence of bytes.

When working with such files, you usually need to know how the file data is organized before you can make any sense of it. Does the data represent text characters, memory maps, bit mappings, or numeric formats? Something else?

Binary mode is useful for interpreting files created in formats alien to Visual Basic, such as spreadsheets or non-ASCII word processing documents. You can read or modify any part of the file, including control characters and end-of-file indicators.

A file position pointer is associated with each binary file. At any time, the pointer identifies which byte is the next to be read or written. The file bytes are considered to be numbered sequentially: 1 for the first byte, 2 for the next, and so on. You can move the pointer anywhere in the file and then read or write as many bytes as you want.

After a file is opened in binary mode, you can both read it and write to it.

Working with a Binary File

You use the following steps to work with a binary file in a Visual Basic application:

1. Open the file `For Binary`.

2. Use `Get` to read data, `Put` to write data, or both `Get` and `Put` to read and write data.

3. Close the file.

Opening the File

For binary files, the `Open` instruction simply declares the file as Binary. The following instruction, for example, opens a file residing in the root directory of drive D as file number 3:

```
Open "D:MYFILE.BIN" For Binary As #3
```

A single `Open` instruction opens a binary file for reading, writing, or appending.

Reading and Writing Data

You use `Get` to read from the file and `Put` to write to it. Here are their forms:

```
Get #filenum, startbyte, variable
Put #filenum, startbyte, variable
```

filenum is the file number, and *startbyte* is a numeric expression specifying the byte in the file where I/O begins. *variable* is any variable, array element, or record variable to receive or transmit the data values. Both the pound sign (#) and the *startbyte* parameter are optional. If you omit *startbyte*, the current file pointer establishes a default value. Successive Get and Put instructions automatically adjust this pointer. You can also use Seek to adjust the pointer explicitly.

Get reads the necessary number of bytes required to satisfy the length of *variable* (two bytes for a variable of integer type, eight bytes for a double-precision variable, and so on). If *variable* is a user-defined type or a fixed-length string, Get simply reads the number of bytes required to satisfy the length of *variable*. If *variable* is a variable-length string, the length of *variable* is considered to be that of the data currently stored in it. Similarly, Put writes the number of bytes equal to the length of *variable*.

The following instruction reads eight bytes from file number 1 into the double-precision variable MyData# (the bytes read are specified as eight because double-precision variables occupy eight bytes):

```
Get #1, , MyData#
```

The omission of the second parameter indicates that reading begins from the current position of the file pointer. After the read, the file pointer advances eight bytes. If you try to read past the end of the file, no error occurs. However, only bytes within the file are read. Bytes past the end of it are "read" as binary 0. The file pointer remains at the end of the file.

Here are two examples of Put instructions:

```
Put #1, 45, MyName$    'Writes string beginning at byte 45
Put #1, , Coin         'Writes coin record at default location
```

Use Put to modify existing data or to write new information past the end of the file.

Closing the File

You close the file in the usual way, using Close.

Using the *Seek* Statement

You use the Seek statement to adjust the file pointer. For example, the following instruction sets the pointer position to byte number 50 of file number 3:

```
Seek #3, 50
```

The position can range from 1 to 2,147,483,647.

After you use Seek, a Get or Put instruction without a *startbyte* parameter uses the new specified file position.

You can use Seek to adjust the pointer to any file position—even one past the end of the file. In such cases, Put appends data and increases the file size.

Using the *Seek* and *Loc* Functions

With binary files, the `Seek` and `Loc` functions return a file position in number of bytes from the beginning of the file. `Seek` returns the current file pointer, which is always at the next byte to be read or written. `Loc` returns the last byte read or written. Note this example:

```
Put #3, 30, MyAge%      'Last byte written is byte number 31
Debug.Print "File pointer is at byte number"; Seek(3)
Debug.Print "Last byte written was number"; Loc(3)
```

The output in the Debug window is the following:

```
File pointer is at byte number 32
Last byte written was number 31
```

Using the *EOF* Function

The `EOF` function works the same as with random files. `EOF` returns True (1) if a `Get` statement tries to read past the end of the file.

Using the Common Dialog Box Control

You have probably noticed that nearly all Windows applications use the same dialog boxes to collect the information needed to open, save, or print a document. This fact is not an accident; standard dialog boxes are available for each of these purposes. Microsoft provides a custom VB control, the Common Dialog Box control, to enable you to use these commonly used dialog boxes.

Figure 12.9 shows the location of the Common Dialog Box control in the Toolbox. If the Common Dialog Box control is not in your Toolbox, you must add CMDIALOG.VBX to your project, using the A**d**d File command on the **F**ile menu. Using a common dialog box enables the user to select which file to open or save rather than requiring you, the programmer, to code the file name in the `Open` statement.

Figure 12.9
The Common Dialog Box control.

Common Dialog Box control —

When placed on a form, just one Common Dialog Box control makes possible a standard set of dialog boxes for such operations as opening, saving, and printing files; selecting colors and fonts; or accessing a Help topic. You create common dialog boxes for your application by adding the Common Dialog Box control to a form and setting its properties.

The *Action* Property

The type of dialog box displayed is determined by the `Action` property. Table 12.3 lists the `Action` property settings.

Table 12.3 *Action* Property Settings	
Action Setting	**Action Taken**
0	No action taken
1	Displays the Open dialog box
2	Displays the Save As dialog box
3	Displays the Color dialog box
4	Displays the Font dialog box
5	Displays the Printer dialog box
6	Invokes WINHELP.EXE so that user can access Help files

The `Action` property can be set only at run time, not at design time. `Action` specifies which type of dialog box is to be displayed. At run time, a dialog box is displayed when the `Action` property is set to a valid value.

At design time, the Common Dialog Box control appears as an icon on a form. This icon cannot be sized. You cannot specify the run-time size of a common dialog box or where it is displayed at run-time in your form's window. Assume that you have placed a Common Dialog Box control named CMDIALOG1 on your form. The following statement, when executed, displays a data file Open dialog box:

```
CMDIALOG1.Action = 1
```

The following statement, when executed, displays a data file Save As dialog box:

```
CMDIALOG1.Action = 2
```

You should understand that these statements and dialog boxes do not actually open or save files. The dialog boxes simply collect the needed information from the user. When the user clicks the OK button in the dialog box, program execution continues. It is up to your subsequent program code to open the file and read the contents or to open the file and write to it.

Additional Properties of the Common Dialog Box

For the purpose of opening files for input or opening files for writing (saving a document) to them, the three properties that are most important are `FileName`, `Filter`, and `CancelError`.

The *FileName* Property

When the user selects a file name, path, and drive in the dialog box, the selection is stored in the common dialog box's `FileName` property. Thus, a programmer can use statements like these:

```
CMDIALOG1.Action = 2
Open "CMDIALOG1.FileName" for Output As #5

CMDIALOG1.Action = 1
Open "CMDIALOG1.FileName" for Input As #3
```

Notice the greater flexibility this programming technique gives the program. Now, for example, the user can open *any* file rather than the one file hard coded into the `Open` statement.

The *Filter* Property

Both the Open and the Save As dialog boxes display a filetype list box in the lower-left corner (see figure 12.10).

Figure 12.10

An Open dialog box.

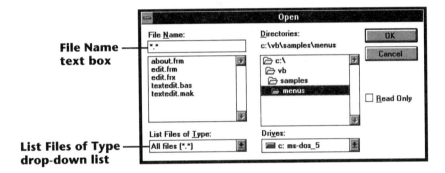

File Name text box

List Files of Type drop-down list

When the dialog box opens, the List Files of **T**ype drop-down list contains a text specification of a DOS file type. The File **N**ame text box displays the actual DOS specification. The setting that you give to the common dialog box's `Filter` property is the one that places these specifications in the actual dialog box. The `Filter` property can be set either at design time or at run time.

Suppose that, most of the time, you want to open sequential files with a TXT extension. Sometimes, however, you want to open sequential files with a SEQ extension. And once in a while, you want to open any file with any extension. You want the Open dialog box to reflect these preferences. In DOS, to say "any file name," you use the asterisk (*). For example, to indicate "any file with a TXT extension," you code `*.TXT`. To indicate "any file with a SEQ extension," you code `*.SEQ`. Finally, to indicate "any file name regardless of extension," you code `*.*`.

Here is how you would set up the `Filter` property at design time:

```
"Text files (*.TXT) ¦ *.TXT ¦ Seq files (*.SEQ) ¦ *.SEQ ¦ All files ¦
➡*.*"
```

The pipe symbol (¦) is used to delimit the text to be placed in the List Files of **T**ype list box from the corresponding DOS specification to be placed in the File **N**ame text box. In this example, when the dialog box opens, `Text files (*.TXT)` will be displayed in the List Files of **T**ype list box, and *.TXT will be placed in the File **N**ame text box. The other two pairs will be available from the List Files of **T**ype drop-down list.

To specify the same filter at run time, use the following code:

```
CMDIALOG1.Action = "Text files (*.TXT) ¦ *.TXT ¦ Seq files (*.SEQ) ¦
➥*.SEQ ¦ All files ¦ *.*"
```

Notice that, in both cases, the first specification pair is the one displayed (the default setting) when the dialog box opens. You use the same technique to set the filter for the Save As dialog box.

The *CancelError* Property

The default for the CancelError property is False. When CancelError is set to False, no error trapping can be done to verify whether the user has selected a file name in an Open or Save As dialog box.

Usually, you will want to set CancelError to True so that you can let the user know that a file must be selected before the program can continue. When CancelError is True, error number 32755 will occur whenever the user doesn't select a file and instead clicks the Cancel button in the dialog box.

Why is identifying whether the user clicked Cancel so important? If the user hasn't selected a file, the FileName property in a statement like the following (which appears after the CMDIALOG1.Action = 1 statement) will be empty, and your program will "blow up":

```
Open "CMDIALOG1.FileName" for Input As #5
```

To make sure that the user has supplied a valid file name before continuing, you can code a sequence of statements like these:

```
'THE CancelError PROPERTY OF THE COMMON DIALOG CONTROL
'MUST BE SET TO TRUE IF YOU NEED TO MAKE IT AN ERROR
'TO CLICK THE CANCEL BUTTON

10  Err = 0  ' Clear any error. 10 identifies this line

    On Error GoTo Handler     'Go to the error handling code

    CMDIALOG1.Action = 1  'File open.

    Open CMDIALOG1.Filename For Input As #1
    Do While Not EOF(1)
        'Read and process the file in here
        'No errors occured in opening the file
    Loop
    Close #1
    Exit Sub 'file reading and processing completed normally

Handler:        'The following code attempts to identify what
                'went wrong

Select Case Err ' Handle error, if any.


    Case 52 ' Bad file name or number.
        MsgBox "File name was invalid."
```

```
        Case 53 ' File Not Found.
            MsgBox "File was not found."

        Case 64  'Bad File Name.
            MsgBox "Not a valid DOS file name."

        Case 68 ' Device unavailable.
            MsgBox "The device you are trying to access is not on line or
            ➥does not exist."

        Case 71 ' Drive not ready or no disk in it.
            MsgBox "Make sure a disk is in the drive and Close the drive
            ➥door."

        Case 75 'Path/File access error.
            MsgBox " Incorrect path specification."

        Case 76 'Path not found.
            MsgBox "Path not found."

        Case 32755    'CANCEL BUTTON WAS PRESSED
            MsgBox "You must select a file. Don't just press Cancel."

        Case Else   ' Handle other cases.
            MsgBox "ERROR: Cannot continue!"    ' All fatal errors.
            Stop

    End Select

    Close #1

'YOU HAVE TO END YOUR ERROR HANDLING PROCEDURE WITH EITHER
'A RESUME OR AN EXIT SUB STATEMENT
'USE RESUME WHEN YOU WANT TO KEEP GOING BACK TO
'THE FILE OPEN STATEMENT

Resume 10              'Go back to line number 10

End Sub
```

Chapter Summary

The Visual Basic Toolbox provides three file controls: File List Box, Directory List Box, and Drive List Box. By combining these controls on a form and writing appropriate event procedures, you can create standard Windows-like dialog boxes for the selection and specification of file names.

Visual Basic has several statements that provide DOS-like file and directory management. Some of the operations your programs can carry out include deleting files; renaming files; and creating, deleting, or changing subdirectories.

When creating a disk file, you can choose from three file types: sequential, random, and binary. Sequential and random files are organized in a series of primary records, with each record containing one or more fields. A binary file, by contrast, is treated as a series of data bytes with no assumed structure.

To use any of the three file types, you open (Open) the file, read or write records (or bytes) as appropriate, and finally close (Close) the file.

Sequential files are easy to program. Reading records and writing records are relatively slow, however. For large databases, random files have many advantages. Any record in a random file can be read or written to quickly. However, the programming of random files is more complicated. Binary files provide great flexibility but demand that you keep track of both the file organization and the meaning of each data byte.

In the next chapter, you learn more about how to use graphics, buttons, and other icons in a program.

Test Your Understanding

True/False

Indicate whether the statement is true or false.

1. The VB Erase command deletes a sequential or random file.

2. Setting a common dialog box's Action property to 2 causes the file Save As dialog box to be displayed.

3. When a user selects a file in a file Open dialog box, the control's FileName property will contain the name of the file selected.

4. The CancelError property of a common dialog box must be set to False if you want to trap a Cancel button click.

5. To read data from a binary file, you use the Input # statement.

6. A user-defined data type can be of type Variant only.

7. To write a record to a random file, you use the Put # statement.

8. Only numeric type fields can be stored in a random file.

9. Once opened, a sequential file can be both read from and written to.

10. Random files are organized so that if you want to read the data in record 75, you first have to read records 0–74.

Short Answer

Answer the following questions.

1. Write the code that enables a user to browse through the directories on a disk drive and look for files. The code should show the events in which statements are placed and should use the Drive List Box, Directory List Box, and File List Box controls.

2. Write the VB code that creates a new directory on a disk.

3. What are the three kinds of data files supported by VB? What are their advantages and disadvantages?

4. Write a program that reads 100 numbers (one number per record) from a sequential file and places each number in one element of an array.

5. Write a program that writes each number in a 100-element array to a sequential file. Each record in the file should contain 10 numbers separated by commas.

6. Write a program that reads 25 numbers from a random file into an array. Each number in the array should be multiplied by itself (that is, squared) and then written back to the random file.

7. Explain how a sequential file is organized like the songs on a cassette tape.

8. Explain what happens when you write to a sequential file. Are the contents of the file affected? How is this process different from appending to a sequential file? Can you append records to a random file?

9. How is the EOF function used when reading a sequential file? How is the EOF function used when writing a file?

10. Explain how the Line Input # statement is used.

Projects

Project 1:   Writing a Seminar Registration Application

Seminars Inc. needs a VB program that will enable its secretary to enter customers for the seminars offered by S. I. every month. Each seminar has a limit of 10 participants. The secretary receives a daily "batch" of registration forms and checks in the mail. The checks in a batch are deposited at the end of each day. Each batch has an identifying number. In writing the application, take into consideration the following work flow of the secretary:

- The secretary receives a daily batch of customer registration forms and checks.

- The secretary enters customer name, address, check number, check amount, seminar requested, and batch number.

- If space is available in the seminar, have the program add the customer to the list of attendees, and then calculate and store the balance owed. If space is not available, the customer should not be registered, and a message must be displayed informing the secretary that the registration is not accepted.

- When the secretary requests it, have the program print a list of all the registrants for a seminar, the balance owed by each registrant, and a count of the registrants for the seminar.

All data should be stored in sequential files.

There are four seminars:

Seminar Number	Seminar Name	Dates	Cost
1	Agribusiness	5/15/96–5/18/96	$500
2	Mastering Change	5/20/96–5/22/96	$1,000
3	Corporate Alliances	5/25/96–5/27/96	$750
4	Retail Management	6/03/96–6/08/96	$850

The following registrant data is waiting to be entered:

Name	Address	Check Number	$ Amount	Seminar	Batch
Lloyd Elm	Seattle	3304	500	1	1
Ramona Bennett	Chicago	1010	850	4	1
John Tippeconic	Miami	2956	250	1	1
Helen Redbird	New York	1503	500	3	1
William Demmert	Dallas	5302	1000	2	1
Hattie Kauffman	Seattle	2705	300	1	1
Bill Yellowtail	L. A.	4227	1000	2	2
Martha Yallup	Atlanta	8114	750	2	2
Ben Campbell	Denver	9876	1000	2	2
Vi Hilbert	Boston	4515	500	2	3
Ada Deer	S. L. C.	5321	1000	2	3
Willard Bill	Seattle	2589	1000	2	3
David Mitchell	L. A.	3379	200	2	3

Use the Common Dialog Box control to let the secretary open and save files.

Save your program as **C12P1** and print it.

Project 2: Enhancing the Seminar Registration Application
Use the same requirements and data used for Project 1. Include the capability to add presentations (seminars) to the file of seminars offered. This time, store all data in random files. The program should print two additional reports:

- A batch report that lists all the names, check numbers, and amounts in each batch, with a count of the total number of checks in each batch and the total amount of money in each batch

- A list of the seminars and the total amount of money received so far for each seminar

Use the Common Dialog Box control to let the secretary open and save files.

Save your program as **C12P2** and print it.

CHAPTER 13

Using the Grid Control

The Grid control is a custom control available with both the Standard and Professional Editions of Visual Basic. Using a Grid control, you can display text, numbers, and pictures in ordered rows and columns, much like a spreadsheet. You can adjust the height, width, and other display characteristics of grids. You can also manipulate rows and columns individually and in groups.

This chapter explores the Grid control in detail with a full discussion of the relevant properties, events, and methods. A sample application, called PhoneBook, illustrates the use of the Grid control. This program is the first significant VB application that you have coded. This application shows you how to apply much of what you have learned in previous chapters of this text.

Objectives

By the time you have finished this chapter, you will be able to

1. Understand the Uses and Most Important Properties, Events, and Methods of the Grid Control

2. Modify the Properties of a Grid at Design Time and Run Time

3. Use a Text Box Control with a Grid Control to Edit the Cells in a Grid

4. Save the Contents of a Grid in a Data File

5. Load the Contents of a Data File into a Grid

6. Build a Large VB Application That Uses the Grid Control

Understanding the Grid Control

The Grid control is a custom control that must be part of your project before you can use the control. If the Grid control does not appear in your Toolbox, you must add the file GRID.VBX, from the WINDOWS\SYSTEM subdirectory, to your project. The Grid control is shown in figure 13.1.

Figure 13.1
The Grid control.

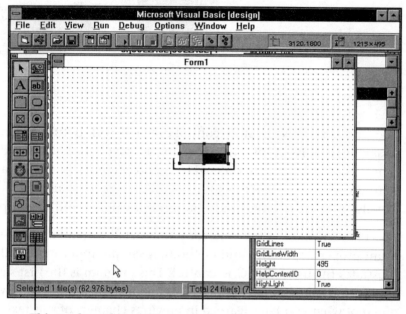

This tool produces this control.

Cell

The intersection of a row and a column in a grid.

In a grid, the intersection of a row and a column is called a **cell**. Each cell can hold a single data item—either a string value or a picture. (Numerical data is stored in string format.) You identify a cell by referring to the row and column in which the cell is located.

A grid automatically responds to user input; the user can move the cursor about the grid and select single cells or groups of cells. The user clicks a cell to select it and clicks and drags to select a group of cells. He or she can move the cell-highlight cursor around the grid with the arrow keys to change the active row and column in the grid.

You can also set the current row and column and designate cell regions by modifying property values in program code. Figure 13.2 shows a sample blank grid with the first row selected.

Understanding Grid Characteristics

The grid's Row and Col (abbreviation for column) properties identify the currently active grid cell. You can modify the values of Row and Col in program code. You can read the contents of the current cell from the grid's Text property, and the grid's Clip property references all data in the selected area of the grid. Numeric or text data is always stored in a grid cell as string data.

Figure 13.2
A grid with the first row selected.

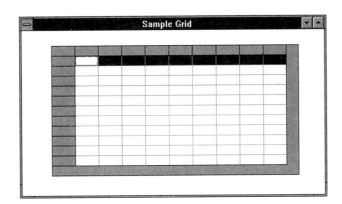

13

Tab-delimited format
A format in which the data in each cell is set off by a tab character.

Internally, the grid manipulates its string data in **tab-delimited format**. If you select an area of a grid and examine the contents of its Clip property, you will see one large string with the data in each cell set off by a tab character, Chr$(9). Each row of data is delimited by a carriage-return (CR) character, Chr$(13). This format facilitates moving data in and out of the grid, either a row at a time or in larger segments.

Displaying Pictures

Visual Basic maintains a value of the Picture property for each grid cell. Through the Picture property, you can include picture data in the grid. In code, you can read and write the value of the Picture property, which in this context refers to the current cell. You cannot, however, obtain picture data from the Clip property.

You can display both text and picture data in a single cell. Visual Basic places the picture in the top-left corner of the cell and wraps the string data around the visual image.

Controlling the Grid's Appearance

You can modify the appearance of the grid by setting various grid properties. As described later in this chapter, you can specify column height and width, column alignment (either left, right, or centered), and font characteristics. You can also determine whether cells have visible borders; you can choose a border style for the entire grid, and you can select from a variety of color options.

The grid is often the best tool for displaying data in tabular format. List boxes are faster and simpler than a grid, but they don't offer the capability to work with individual cells of data. Text boxes don't allow consistent formatting of separate, discrete rows and columns.

Setting Grid Properties

The Grid control supports approximately 50 properties (see VB's Help topic on the Grid control). Many of these properties are common to other controls. The properties covered in the following sections are unique to the grid or work in a special way with the grid.

Row, Col, and Text

The Row, Col, and Text properties are at the heart of the grid's functionality. Row and Col specify the row and column of the active grid cell. In other words, the active cell is at the intersection of the row and column specified by Row and Col. Text contains the string contents of the cell specified by Row and Col.

When the user clicks a grid cell or presses navigation keys, the active cell changes, and Visual Basic updates the values of Row and Col accordingly.

Grid rows and columns are numbered beginning with zero. Row numbering is from the top down, so the top row of a grid is row 0. Column numbering begins at the left, making column 0 the leftmost column.

Figure 13.3 shows a grid with each cell displaying its row and column numbers. Notice that the cell at the location R2C3 appears with a dotted border. (The border may be hard to see in the figure.) By default, Visual Basic uses a dotted border to indicate the active cell. In this grid, Row is set to 2 (third row counting from 0), and Col is set to 3 (fourth column). The grid's Text property is R2C3; this value appears in the form's caption.

Figure 13.3

A grid with Row and Col set to 2 and 3, respectively.

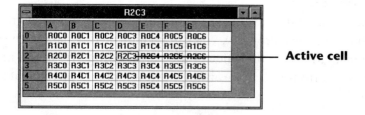

Active cell

You can use program code to modify the Row and Col properties so that an application can access grid data one cell at a time. Grid has no "cell" property; to access the contents of an individual cell, you must first set the grid's Row and Col properties. At that point, the grid's Text property holds the contents of the desired cell.

For example, to get the contents of the third cell in the second row of Grid1, you can use the following code:

```
Grid1.Row = 1
Grid1.Col = 2
Result$ = Grid1.Text
```

Result$ now contains the contents of the desired cell. Remember that the top row is 0 and leftmost column is 0. That's why the second row is 1 and the third column is 2.

By default, Visual Basic names the first Grid control in an application Grid1. Subsequent grid controls are named Grid2, Grid3, and so on. You can change a grid name by modifying the grid's Name property.

FixedRows and FixedCols

A grid can have fixed rows and columns. A fixed row or column is protected from being selected by the user. The number of fixed rows and columns is specified by the values of the FixedRows and FixedCols properties, respectively.

You typically use fixed rows and columns to construct row and column headings for a grid. Because the user cannot access a fixed row or column, the user cannot modify the values in these grid cells.

You can specify more than one row or one column as fixed, but fixed rows must start with the topmost row (row 0) and fixed columns with the leftmost column (column 0). All fixed rows must be contiguous rows. You cannot set rows 2 and 4 as fixed, for example. Similarly, fixed columns must be contiguous columns.

Fixed rows and columns appear in gray. You cannot scroll these rows and columns as you can the other rows and columns in a grid. This behavior is similar to the "freezing" rows, columns, or panes feature of many commercial spreadsheet programs.

The values of `FixedRows` and `FixedCols` indicate the total number of fixed rows and columns, respectively. For example, if `FixedCols` is 3, columns 0, 1, and 2 are fixed. Figure 13.4 shows a grid where `FixedCols` is 1 and `FixedRows` is 2.

Figure 13.4
A grid with one fixed column and two fixed rows.

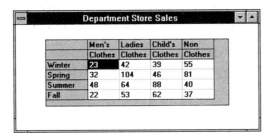

13

A grid with fixed rows and columns provides a side benefit. The user can change the height of rows and the width of columns with the mouse at run time. To do so, the user clicks and drags a grid line in the protected row or column.

Figure 13.5 shows the third column being widened. Notice that the mouse pointer appears (in the protected row) in the shape of a double-headed arrow. In the figure, the pointer is in the column labeled "Child's Clothes."

Figure 13.5
Adjusting the width of a column from within the fixed row of a grid.

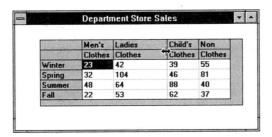

You can modify the values of `FixedRows` and `FixedCols` in code at run time, but you must always leave at least one row and one column that are not fixed. Visual Basic does not allow you to fix all the rows or all the columns of a grid. By default, a grid has one fixed column and one fixed row.

Rows and *Cols*

The `Rows` and `Cols` properties specify, respectively, the total number of rows and columns in a grid. In program code, you can modify the values of these properties to change the size of a grid dynamically at run time. For example, the following instructions set the grid to have seven rows and eight columns:

```
Grid1.Rows = 7
Grid1.Cols = 8
```

Warning!

Don't confuse the Rows and Cols properties with the Row and Col properties. Despite their similar names, these properties are different. Row and Col specify the active grid cell. Rows and Cols specify the size of the entire grid.

Creating a Basic Grid

The following sample application demonstrates the basic concepts of a grid. The contents of each cell are set to indicate the row and column occupied by that cell. As you move the cell cursor around the grid, the application displays the contents of the cell in the caption of the form.

In this chapter, you should enter all the code shown in order to complete the application properly. To create the sample application, start a new project. Double-click the Grid icon in the Toolbox to add a Grid control to Form1. The grid appears with the default name of Grid1.

Using the Properties window, set property values as shown in table 13.1.

Table 13.1   Property Values for the Sample Grid Application

Object	Property	Value
Form1	Height	2500
	Width	6000
Grid1	Left	50
	Top	50
	Height	1850
	Width	5700

Next you create the Form_Load procedure. The Form_Load procedure executes when you start the application. The procedure also establishes values for several properties not specified at design time.

Writing the Event Procedures

To set the contents of each grid cell, create the following `Form_Load` procedure.

```
Sub Form_Load ()
    Dim Temp As String
    Dim R As Integer, C As Integer   'Loop counters for row,column
    Dim TB As String, CR As String

    TB = Chr$(9)    'Tab key
    CR = Chr$(13)   'Enter key


    'Clear and reset the grid
    Grid1.FixedRows = 0
    Grid1.FixedCols = 0
    Grid1.Rows = 1
    Grid1.Cols = 1

    'Add the title row to the top of the grid
    Temp = TB & "A" & TB & "B" & TB & "C" & TB & "D"
    Temp = Temp & TB & "E" & TB & "F" & TB & "G"
    Grid1.AddItem Temp
    Grid1.RemoveItem 0   'Clear the first (empty) row

    'Fill the grid with R#C# data one line at a time
    For R = 0 To 5
       Temp = "" & R & TB
       For C = 0 To 6
          Temp = Temp & "R" & R & "C" & C & TB
       Next C
       Grid1.AddItem Temp
    Next R

    'Reset the number of fixed rows and columns to 1
    Grid1.FixedRows = 1
    Grid1.FixedCols = 1

    'Move to topmost left cell
    Grid1.Row = 1
    Grid1.Col = 1
    Form1.Show
    Grid1.SetFocus
End Sub
```

Notice that this procedure uses the following instruction to specify the contents of an entire row of grid cells:

```
Grid1.AddItem Temp
```

`AddItem` is a method recognized by the Grid control. `Temp` is a string variable. The string data in `Temp` contains internal tab (`Chr$(9)`) and carriage-return (`Chr$(13)`) characters. As described earlier in this chapter, tab characters set off the text in individual cells, and each carriage return terminates the text for an entire row.

Similarly, the `RemoveItem` method removes data from a grid row. `AddItem` and `RemoveItem` are discussed in detail later in this chapter.

(continues)

Writing the Event Procedures   (continued)

To complete this first sample application, create the following `RowColChange` event procedure:

```
Sub Grid1_RowColChange ()
    Form1.Caption = Grid1.Text
End Sub
```

The `RowColChange` event, unique to the Grid control, occurs whenever the active grid cell changes.

For this application, whenever the cell changes, this procedure displays the contents of the current cell in the form's caption.

Running the Application

Save the form as **GRIDEX1.FRM**, and save the project as **GRIDEX1.MAK**. Then run the program. Your form looks like the one in figure 13.6.

Figure 13.6

The sample grid application in Run mode.

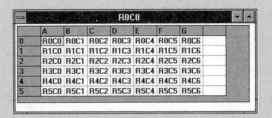

As you can see, the application places a text string in each cell. For each cell, this string indicates the row and column that the cell occupies. As you move the cell cursor around the grid (either by pressing arrow keys or clicking), you see the contents of the current cell reflected in the form's caption.

You can also adjust row heights and column widths by clicking and dragging on cell borders in the grayed row or column. Clicking and dragging works because the grid has a fixed row at the top and a fixed column at the left.

If you haven't done so already, stop the application and return to Design mode.

One of the shortcomings of the grid becomes apparent with this example: you cannot edit the contents of individual cells in the grid. For the user to modify cell contents at run time, you must add a control to the application. The best solution is a text box linked to the grid by program code. You learn that technique with the PhoneBook application later in the chapter.

Selecting Cells

You can work with a group of cells as a single block by selecting a range of cells. As is typical of Windows applications, the selected cells appear highlighted. Cells can be selected by specifying property values at run time, or the user can select cells while an application runs.

Selected cells are always in a contiguous rectangular block. As table 13.2 indicates, Visual Basic designates the selected cells with four properties whose names are fairly self-explanatory. Each property has an integer value.

Table 13.2 Properties Used for Selected Cells	
Property	**Meaning**
SelStartRow	Uppermost row in the selected block
SelEndRow	Lowermost row in the selected block
SelStartCol	Leftmost column in the selected block
SelEndCol	Rightmost column in the selected block

Adding Code to Change Selected Cells

If you modify the values of these properties in code, the grid highlights these cells. On most monitors, highlighted cells appear in a different color. Add the following instructions to the end of the Form_Load procedure in GRIDEX1:

```
Grid1.SelStartRow = 2
Grid1.SelEndRow = 4
Grid1.SelStartCol = 3
Grid1.SelEndCol = 6
```

These instructions select a block of three rows by four columns, a total of 12 selected cells. Figure 13.7 shows the result of this cell selection.

Warning!

Remember that row and column numbering starts with 0. Don't forget to count the fixed rows and columns. For example, a value of 2 for SelStartRow specifies the third row, including the fixed row.

Figure 13.7
A grid with rows and columns selected.

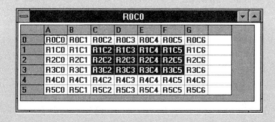

A grid maintains an active (current) cell whether or not a block of selected cells is present. The active cell can be inside or outside the selected block. Notice that in figure 13.7, the active cell is in the upper-left corner of the grid, but the selected block is near the center of the grid.

Enabling the User to Select Cells

At run time, the user can select a block of cells. To do so, the user presses and holds the left mouse button and drags over a region of the grid. Another method is to hold down the Shift key while pressing the arrow keys.

The highlighting of user-selected cells is built into the Grid control. No special coding is required. You can demonstrate the effect by rerunning the GRIDEX1 application and dragging the mouse pointer over a section of the grid. You also see that when you are selecting cells, the current cell remains unchanged.

When the user selects a group of cells, Visual Basic automatically updates the values of the four selection properties. You can read the values of these properties in code to determine the cell block selected by the user.

Understanding the *Clip* Property

The contents of the selected cell block are contained in the grid's `Clip` property. You can read or write the value of `Clip` in program code.

The value of `Clip` is always a single string quantity. Remember that this string contains a tab character (`Chr$(9)`) delimiting the contents of each cell and a carriage-return (CR) character (`Chr$(13)`) after the contents of each row.

Demonstrating Cell Selection

To demonstrate the `Clip` property in cell selection, add a `SelChange` event procedure. A `SelChange` event occurs whenever the selected region of a grid changes (either by the actions of the user or by the modification of the selection properties in code). The event triggers even when only a single cell is selected. Make the following modification to the GRIDEX1 application:

```
Sub Grid1_SelChange ()
    Dim Msg As String
    Dim TB As String, CR As String

    TB = Chr$(9)    'Tab character
    CR = Chr$(13)   'Carriage return

    If Grid1.Clip = "" Then Exit Sub   'This can't happen

    'Prepare a message to show in the message box
    Msg = "SelStartRow: " & Grid1.SelStartRow + CR
    Msg = Msg + "SelEndRow: " & Grid1.SelEndRow + CR
    Msg = Msg + "SelStartCol: " & Grid1.SelStartCol + CR
    Msg = Msg + "SelEndCol: " & Grid1.SelEndCol + CR + CR

    'Show the contents of Grid1.Clip
    Msg = Msg + Grid1.Clip

    'Show message box except during Form_Load
    If Form1.Visible Then MsgBox Msg, , "Selected Cells"
End Sub
```

Run the application with this modification. A message box displays every time you change the cells that are selected. The message box displays the values of the four selection properties and the contents of the selected cells. Press **Enter** or click the OK button to close the message box.

To display the cell contents in tabular format, the procedure uses the grid's `Clip` property. Figure 13.8 shows the message box that appears when cells R1C0–R3C1 are selected.

Figure 13.8

The message box displays information about the selected cells.

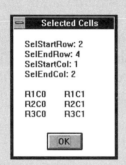

Save the modified application as **GRIDEX2**.

13

Using the *ColWidth* and *RowHeight* Properties

The `ColWidth` and `RowHeight` properties specify a column width and a row height, respectively. You can read or write the values of these properties in program code. These properties are not available in the Properties window at design time. Because each row and column of a grid can have a different dimension, you must include a reference to the desired row or column when using these properties.

The syntax for `ColWidth` and `RowHeight` is

```
grid.ColWidth(column) = size
grid.RowHeight(row) = size
```

`grid` specifies the Grid control, `column` specifies the grid column to modify, and `row` specifies the grid row to modify. `size` is a numeric expression that specifies the row or column size in twips.

For example, to set the width of column 0 in `Grid1` to 1000 and the height of row 0 to 750, you can use the following code:

```
Grid1.ColWidth(0) = 1000
Grid1.RowHeight(0) = 750
```

For multiple-form applications, you can also include the name of the form at the beginning of the instruction. For example,

```
Form1!Grid1.ColWidth(2) = 1250
Form3.Grid1.RowHeight(1) = 675
```

Notice that, as always, you can use an exclamation point or a period when separating a form name from a control name. The exclamation point is preferred to avoid possible syntax ambiguities in future releases of Visual Basic.

Remember that if a grid has fixed rows and/or columns, the user can modify the column and/or row sizes at run time. In program code, you can determine any user-modified column or row sizes by reading the values of `ColWidth` and `RowHeight`.

One technique you might want to experiment with in your programs is to use the value of the form's `TextWidth` property to obtain the exact width of a text string that is to be stored in a grid cell. You can then use the value determined by `TextWidth` to set the width for the grid column of the target cell. In this way, you make the column width no larger than necessary. For example, the following instruction sets the column width of column 2 to be just the right size for the string data stored in `MyText$`:

```
Grid1.ColWidth(2) = Form1.TextWidth(MyText$)
```

Similarly, you can use the form's `TextHeight` property to set the height of a grid column. If you use these techniques, make sure that the font characteristics of the grid match those of the form that contains the grid.

Using the *ColAlignment* and *FixedAlignment* Properties

The `ColAlignment` and `FixedAlignment` properties determine text alignment within specific grid columns. You can specify left-justified, right-justified, or centered for text entries in any column. The `FixedAlignment` property specifies the text alignment for fixed columns, and the `ColAlignment` property specifies the text alignment of columns that are not fixed.

You can set the value of `alignment` to 0, 1, or 2 to achieve the effects described in table 13.3.

Table 13.3 Values of the *Alignment* Parameter

Value of *alignment*	Meaning
0	Left-justify text (default value)
1	Right-justify text
2	Center text

For the `FixedAlignment` property, `alignment` can also have the value 3. In that case, the text justification of the column is determined by the current value of `ColAlignment` for that column.

For multiple-form applications, you can also include the name of the form at the beginning of the instruction. For example,

```
Form1!Grid1.ColAlignment(MarchCol%) = 2

Form2.Grid1.FixedAlignment(0) = 1
```

Demonstrating the *ColAlignment* Property

To demonstrate the `ColAlignment` property, add the following `Grid1_DblClick` event procedure to the GRIDEX2 sample application:

```
Sub Grid1_DblClick ()
    Dim X As Integer

    For X = 1 To Grid1.Cols - 1
        If Grid1.ColAlignment(X) = 2 Then
            Grid1.ColAlignment(X) = 0
        Else
            Grid1.ColAlignment(X) = Grid1.ColAlignment(X) + 1
        End If
    Next X

    Select Case Grid1.ColAlignment(1)
        Case 0: Form1.Caption = "ColAlignment = 0 (Left)"
        Case 1: Form1.Caption = "ColAlignment = 1 (Right)"
        Case 2: Form1.Caption = "ColAlignment = 2 (Center)"
    End Select
End Sub
```

Run the example, and widen one of the columns with the mouse so that the upcoming effects are more apparent.

Double-click the currently selected cell several times. The `ColAlignment` property for that column cycles through 0, 1, and 2, cycling the text alignment through left-aligned, right-aligned, and centered. The current alignment is displayed in the form's caption. Figure 13.9 shows column C widened and the text centered.

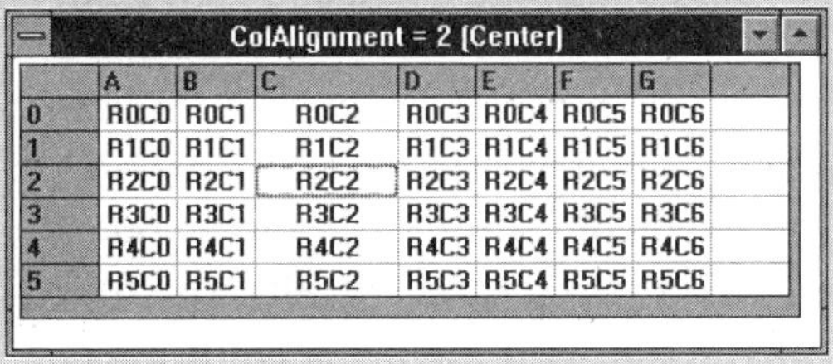

13

Figure 13.9
Demonstrating column alignment.

When running this sample application, you can avoid the pop-up message box by always double-clicking the active cell. (Recall that the message box appears whenever you change the selected text region.)

You can demonstrate the `FixedAlignment` property by replacing every instance of `ColAlignment` with `FixedAlignment` in the `DblClick` procedure.

The `ColAlignment` and `FixedAlignment` properties come in handy when you display both numeric and text data in a single grid. Often you want numbers right-aligned and text left-aligned. For some grids, you use `ColAlignment` and `FixedAlignment` to give the column headings in the fixed rows a different alignment from the data in the nonfixed rows.

The `ColAlignment` and `FixedAlignment` properties have no effect on pictures displayed in the grid.

Displaying Pictures in a Grid

As mentioned earlier in the chapter, you can display pictures as well as text in grid cells. However, picture data does not show up in the Clip or Text property. If you put both text and a picture in a cell, the text wraps around the picture.

To load a picture into a cell, you set the Row and Col properties of the grid to select the desired cell. Then you use the LoadPicture function with the Picture property to assign a picture to the grid. For example, you could use the following program code:

```
Grid1.Row = 1
Grid1.Col = 1
Grid1.Picture = LoadPicture("C:\VB\ICONS\COMM\PHONE01.ICO")
```

Keep in mind that the width of the column and the height of the row do not automatically resize to accommodate the picture. You have to set the appropriate sizes in program code. In this example, the picture is an icon. Icons are 32 pixels high and 32 pixels wide, so you can use the following code to set the appropriate dimensions:

```
Grid1.ColWidth(1) = 32 * Screen.TwipsPerPixelX
Grid1.RowHeight(1) = 32 * Screen.TwipsPerPixelY
```

Of course, you want to allow more room in the cell if the cell contains both text and a picture.

Understanding the *TopRow*, *LeftCol*, and *ScrollBars* Properties

The TopRow, LeftCol, and ScrollBars properties relate to grid navigation. When a grid is so large that it cannot show all its cells at one time, the grid can set up scroll bars that enable the user to scroll through the cells both horizontally and vertically.

Scrolling is limited, however, when the grid has fixed rows and fixed columns. If you scroll horizontally, the fixed columns do not move, but the fixed rows scroll with the other rows. Similarly, if you scroll vertically, the fixed rows do not move, but the fixed columns scroll with the other columns.

The TopRow property is a numeric value that specifies the first row displayed at the top of the grid (not counting any fixed rows). Because a grid can have more rows than it can display, you can use TopRow in program code to read or set the first visible row. The TopRow property is *not* available in the Properties window at design time. The default value of TopRow is 1.

Similarly, the LeftCol property determines the first column displayed at the left of the grid. Remember that fixed rows and columns are exempt from this sort of manipulation because they are *always* displayed.

For example, suppose that you have a small form containing the Grid control Grid1. The grid currently contains 200 lines (rows) of data. Your program may have a search routine that locates a needed data item in the cell at the intersection of row 148 and column 5. You can then set Grid1.TopRow = 148 and Grid1.LeftCol = 5. The target cell appears in the top left corner of the grid's display area.

Understanding the Limitations of *TopRow* and *LeftCol*

TopRow and LeftCol have limitations on their permissible values. You must ensure that the grid has enough rows below the TopRow and columns to the right of LeftCol to fill the space occupied by the grid—otherwise, an error occurs. For example, suppose that your grid has room to display five rows on a form, but the grid contains 12 lines of data. The highest permissible value of TopRow is 8, which displays rows 8 through 12 in the five rows available. Visual Basic generates an error if you attempt to set TopRow to 9 because, in that case, only four grid rows would be available to fill the five visible rows.

Displaying Scroll Bars

As shown in table 13.4, the ScrollBars property determines whether the grid can display scroll bars. When scrolling is enabled, the grid displays scroll bars when the full range of grid cells cannot fit within the grid boundaries.

Table 13.4   Values of the *ScrollBars* Property

Value of *ScrollBars*	Meaning
0	No scroll bars
1	Horizontal scroll bars
2	Vertical scroll bars
3	Horizontal and vertical scroll bars

For example, the following instruction enables horizontal scroll bars in Grid1:

```
Grid1.ScrollBars = 1
```

The Grid control automatically displays whatever scroll bars are enabled and required. The default value of ScrollBars is 3, displaying both horizontal and vertical scroll bars. When the value of ScrollBars is set to 0, scroll bars do not display in the grid even if more rows and columns of cells exist than the grid can currently display.

Understanding the *HighLight* and *GridLines* Properties

The HighLight and GridLines properties, which are unique to the grid, are purely for the sake of appearance. The HighLight property determines whether selected cells appear highlighted (usually in a different color). When the value of HighLight is True (the default) and the user clicks the grid and drags, the selected cells appear highlighted. (As explained earlier in the chapter, you can also select cells in program code by setting values for the SelStartRow, SelEndRow, SelStartCol, and SelEndCol properties.)

To turn off highlighting, set the value of HighLight to False. For example, the following instruction disables highlighting in Grid2:

```
Grid2.HighLight = False
```

You may want to turn off highlighting in a few situations. For example, you can discourage the user from selecting cells by turning off the visual cues provided by the highlighting. Another reason is that, with highlighting off, selection and deselection are faster because Windows does not need to redraw the affected region with different cell colors.

The GridLines property determines whether the grid displays a border around the individual cells. When the value is True (the default), a line appears between adjacent cells. When the value is False, no cell borders appear.

Most of the time, you retain the cell borders. Some grids, however, may look better without the cell lines. The decision, of course, is yours. Figure 13.10 shows the grid from the GRIDEX1 example displayed without any cell borders. The following line of code does the trick:

```
Grid1.GridLines = False
```

Figure 13.10
A grid with GridLines set to False.

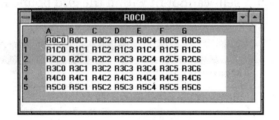

Using the Grid Events *RowColChange* and *SelChange*

The grid automatically responds to 14 different events. The only events unique to the Grid control are RowColChange and SelChange. The RowColChange event triggers whenever the currently active cell changes to a different cell. The event occurs when the user clicks a new cell or when the program code modifies the Row or Col property.

The SelChange event occurs whenever the selected area of a grid changes. As the GRIDEX2 sample application demonstrates, the SelChange and RowColChange events often happen together. However, RowColChange does not occur when you use code to change the selected range without changing the active cell.

Using the *AddItem* and *RemoveItem* Methods

You have used several Grid methods in the sample applications of this chapter. No Visual Basic methods are unique to the Grid. Some methods, however, behave differently with Grids than they do with other controls. This section discusses the two most important grid methods: AddItem and RemoveItem.

As demonstrated by the GRIDEX1 application, the AddItem method places a new row of string data in the grid. If the string contains tab characters, the data is placed in separate cells. If the string contains more data items than the grid has columns, additional columns are automatically added to the grid.

Because AddItem adds one entire row of string data to the grid, you should not put a carriage-return character (Chr$(13)) at the end of the data string. If you do, the Chr$(13) symbol is considered part of the data string. The RemoveItem method is similar to AddItem, but as the name suggests, RemoveItem *removes* a row of data from the grid. Both `AddItem` and `RemoveItem` actually change the number of rows in the grid, making the two methods very handy for adding or removing grid data.

The syntax for `AddItem` and `RemoveItem` is

> `grid.Additem` *stringdata*, *row*

> `grid.RemoveItem` *row*

grid specifies the Grid control. *stringdata* is a tab-delimited string value to add to the grid, and *row* specifies a row in the grid. For the `AddItem` method, the *row* parameter is optional. If *row* is omitted, a new row is added to the end of the current grid.

Understanding the PhoneBook Application

The PhoneBook application provides a more detailed exploration of the workings of the Grid control. Here you build a practical application that displays names, addresses, and phone numbers you can edit and save.

Using PhoneBook, you can load a file of names and addresses into a grid. You can add, copy, and delete rows in the grid; edit individual cells; and save the contents of the grid back to a file.

Not only do you use the Grid control in constructing this application, you also link the grid to a floating text box. With this text box, which appears over individual cells, you can edit the entry in a grid cell. PhoneBook demonstrates the basic techniques of data file reading and writing. Also, the application uses a control array of command buttons so that the user can select various options.

Figure 13.11 shows a sample of how PhoneBook looks when the application is completed and running. As you can see, PhoneBook even includes a phone icon in the upper-left grid cell.

Figure 13.11

An example of the PhoneBook application.

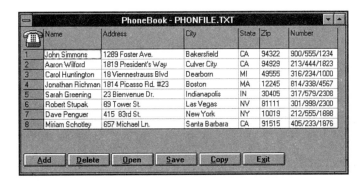

Constructing the Basic Grid for PhoneBook

Now you are ready to create the PhoneBook application. Follow these steps:

1 Start a new project, and add a Grid control (Grid1) and a Text Box control (Text1) to the form (Form1).

2 Add a command button (Command1) to the form. Move the controls on the form so that none of the controls overlaps another.

3 Make a copy of the command button using the **C**opy and **P**aste options from the **E**dit menu. When prompted by Do you want to create a control array? choose Yes. A copy of the Command1 command button appears in the upper-left corner of the form.

4 Delete the new copy of the command button. Select the new command button. (The button has the value 1 for the Index property.) Then press **Del**.

The original command button is now the only command button on the form. (The original button has a value of 0 for Index.) This technique establishes the single command button as part of a control array even though, at the moment, the command button is the only member of the array. Additional array elements are added by program code at run time.

5 Using the Properties window, set the property values shown in table 13.5. (The form's Icon property determines the icon that Visual Basic displays when the form is minimized.)

Table 13.5 Design-Time Properties for the PhoneBook Application

Object	Property	Value
Form1	Caption	PhoneBook
	Icon	c:\vb\icons\comm\phone01.ico
	Height	4605
	Width	6705
	BackColor	&H00C0C0C0& (light gray)
Grid1	BorderStyle	0 ' none
	BackColor	&H00FFFFFF& (white)
Text1	BorderStyle	0 ' none
	BackColor	&H0000FFFF& (yellow)

All other properties for the form and controls are set at run time in the program code.

Writing the *Form_Load* Event Procedure

Most of the initialization for PhoneBook takes place in the `Form_Load` procedure. A great deal is going on in this `Sub` procedure: the grid's position and dimensions are set, column headings are specified, and the control array of command buttons is loaded. The following event procedure contains quite a bit of code, but it's all pretty straightforward:

```
Sub Form_Load ()
    Dim TB As String, LF As String
    Dim X As Integer, C As Integer    'Loop counters
    Dim SetWidth As Integer
    Dim wOffset As Single, hOffset As Single

    TB = Chr$(9)                       'Tab character
    LF = Chr$(10) + Chr$(10)       'Line feed

    'Set grid, form font characteristics
    Form1.FontBold = False
    Grid1.FontBold = False

    'Load command buttons
    Command1(0).Left = 60    'Command.Top set in Form_Resize
    For X = 1 To 5
        Load Command1(X)
        Command1(X).Left = Command1(X - 1).Left +
    ➡ Command1(X - 1).Width + 30
        Command1(X).Top = Command1(X - 1).Top
        Command1(X).Visible = True
    Next X

    'Set command button captions
    Command1(0).Caption = "&Add"
    Command1(1).Caption = "&Delete"
    Command1(2).Caption = "&Open"
    Command1(3).Caption = "&Save"
    Command1(4).Caption = "&Copy"
    Command1(5).Caption = "E&xit"


    'Initialize Grid fixed rows & columns
    Grid1.FixedRows = 1
    Grid1.FixedCols = 1
    Grid1.Rows = 2
    Grid1.Cols = 7

    Grid1.Row = 0


    'Put a picture in the top left corner of the grid
    Grid1.Col = 0
    Grid1.Picture = Form1.Icon    'Use telephone icon from Form1

    'Set Height,Width based on icon size
    Grid1.RowHeight(0) = Screen.TwipsPerPixelY * 32
    Grid1.ColWidth(0) = Screen.TwipsPerPixelX * 32
```

13

(continues)

Writing the *Form_Load* Event Procedure   (continued)

```
'Add column headings and set column widths
'NOTE: Column widths set here are arbitrary.
'         You can modify the widths as desired

Grid1.ColWidth(1) = 1400
Grid1.ColWidth(2) = 2000
Grid1.ColWidth(3) = 1300
Grid1.ColWidth(4) = 500
Grid1.ColWidth(5) = 700
Grid1.ColWidth(6) = 1200

Grid1.Col = 1
Grid1.Text = "Name"

Grid1.Col = 2
Grid1.Text = "Address"

Grid1.Col = 3
Grid1.Text = "City"

Grid1.Col = 4
Grid1.Text = "State"

Grid1.Col = 5
Grid1.Text = "Zip"

Grid1.Col = 6
Grid1.Text = "Number"

'Insert a row number, then return to row 1, col 1
Grid1.Row = 1
Grid1.Col = 0
Grid1.Text = "1"
Grid1.Col = 1

'Adjust Grid1 width to show all columns
Grid1.Left = 60
Grid1.Top = 60

SetWidth = Screen.TwipsPerPixelX ' allows for borderline
➡ around grid
For C = 0 To Grid1.Cols - 1 ' add widths of all columns
SetWidth = SetWidth + Grid1.ColWidth(C) +
➡ (Screen.TwipsPerPixelX * 2)
Next C
Grid1.Width = SetWidth

'Adjust Height, Width of Form1
wOffset = Form1.Width - ScaleWidth
hOffset = Form1.Height - ScaleHeight
Form1.Width = Grid1.Width + (Grid1.Left * 2) + wOffset
Form1.Height = Grid1.Height + hOffset


'Center form on screen
Form1.Left = (Screen.Width - Form1.Width) / 2
Form1.Top = (Screen.Height - Form1.Height) / 2

End Sub
```

You have just entered a great deal of code. Don't lose it by accident. Save the form and the project with the file name **PHONE**.

The code for the initialization of the form and the grid is complete. Now you need to set the grid's height and width properties with the `Form_Resize` event procedure.

Writing the *Form_Resize* Event Procedure

The `Form_Resize` procedure resets the locations and sizes of the grid and of the command buttons in case the user resizes the form. Recall that Visual Basic invokes `Form_Resize` during the start up of any application.

PhoneBook takes advantage of that fact to set the height and width of the grid in the following `Form_Resize` procedure instead of in `Form_Load`. Add this code to your application:

```
Sub Form_Resize ()
    Dim X As Integer      'Loop counter

    'Set grid size
    If Form1.WindowState = 1 Then Exit Sub   'Form was minimized

    For X = 0 To 5
    Command1(X).Top = ScaleHeight - (Command1(0).Height * 1.5)
    Next X

    Grid1.Width = ScaleWidth - (Grid1.Left * 2)
    Grid1.Height = ScaleHeight - Grid1.Top - Command1(0).Height * 2
End Sub
```

13

Working with the Command Button Array

The `Command1()` array provides a row of command buttons with which the user can select various options supported by the application. Because `Command1` is a control array, a single block of code in the `Command1_Click` procedure is all that's necessary to control the operation of the various buttons.

Entering the Code for the Array

The completed `Command1_Click` procedure should appear as follows:

```
Sub Command1_Click (Index As Integer)
    Select Case Index
        Case 0 ' add
            AddGridLine
        Case 1 ' delete
            DeleteGridLine
```

(continues)

```
                Case 2 ' open
                    LoadFile
                Case 3 ' Save
                    SaveFile
                Case 4 ' Copy Line
                    CopyLine
                Case 5 ' Exit
                    Shutdown
            End Select
            Grid1.SetFocus
        End Sub
```

AddGridLine, DeleteGridLine, LoadFile, SaveFile, CopyLine, and Shutdown are all user-defined procedures that specify the actions taken when the user clicks one of the command buttons. These procedures are covered later in this chapter.

Adding Form-Level Variable Declarations

PhoneBook uses some variables shared by various procedures. Some of these variables are used in saving and restoring the status of the grid, and others are used for file handling and management of the text box. Because PhoneBook has a single form and no code modules, you can place the shared variables in the declarations section of the form's code. The necessary declarations are as follows:

```
'Variables for GridStatusSave and GridStatusRestore
Dim SavedStartRow As Integer, SavedEndRow As Integer
Dim SavedStartCol As Integer, SavedEndCol As Integer
Dim SavedTopRow As Integer, SavedLeftCol As Integer
Dim SavedRow As Integer, SavedCol As Integer

'Variable specifying the data file to load
Dim FileName As String

'Variable used for reverse tabbing
Dim Shifting As Integer
```

A grid application must often change the grid's row, column, and selected area in order to access target data contained in the grid. When this change happens, the rows, columns, and the selected area set by the user are changed. To ensure that the application operates in a consistent and reliable manner, you must restore the grid's status after such operations; the grid then appears unmodified to the user.

Adding *GridStatusSave* and *GridStatusRestore*

For PhoneBook, the GridStatusSave procedure saves the grid status, and the GridStatusRestore procedure restores the saved status. The parameters saved include the row and column of the current cell, the area of selected cells, and several appearance attributes. `GridStatusSave` and `GridStatusRestore` are both user-defined procedures placed in the general declarations section of the form. The `GridStatusSave` procedure is as follows:

```
Sub GridStatusSave ()

    SavedStartRow = Grid1.SelStartRow
    SavedEndRow = Grid1.SelEndRow

    SavedStartCol = Grid1.SelStartCol
    SavedEndCol = Grid1.SelEndCol

    SavedRow = Grid1.Row
    SavedCol = Grid1.Col

    SavedTopRow = Grid1.TopRow
    SavedLeftCol = Grid1.LeftCol

End Sub
```

The `GridStatusRestore` procedure uses the same form-level variables found in `GridStatusSave`:

```
Sub GridStatusRestore ()
    On Error Resume Next
    'Ignore errors generated by
    'setting selected regions
    'outside of grid boundaries.

    Grid1.LeftCol = SavedLeftCol
    Grid1.TopRow = SavedTopRow

    Grid1.SelStartRow = SavedStartRow
    Grid1.SelEndRow = SavedEndRow
    Grid1.SelStartCol = SavedStartCol
    Grid1.SelEndCol = SavedEndCol

    On Error GoTo 0

    'Restore active row & column if possible
    If SavedRow <= Grid1.Rows - 1 Then
        Grid1.Row = SavedRow
    Else
        Grid1.Row = Grid1.Rows - 1
    End If

    If SavedCol <= Grid1.Cols - 1 Then
        Grid1.Col = SavedCol
    Else
        Grid1.Col = Grid1.Col - 1
    End If

End Sub
```

Notice that the second section of `GridStatusRestore` attempts to restore the previous row and column settings. Such restoration may not be possible, however, if a row has been deleted. Although the PhoneBook application doesn't allow for the deletion of columns, other applications you write may. You can use `GridStatusSave` and `GridStatusRestore` in other applications involving the Grid control. Save the PHONE application to your disk.

13

Understanding the *UnSelect* Procedure

The UnSelect procedure is necessary because of a limitation in the Grid control. With program code, you cannot unselect every cell by using property values. You might, for example, want to unselect all cells so that no cells are highlighted.

Here's the problem. To select an area of cells, you can set SelStartRow, SelEndRow, SelStartCol, and SelEndCol. To undo a selection, you could set SelStartRow and SelEndRow to the same value and do the same with SelStartCol and SelEndCol. However, that arrangement leaves a selected area consisting of a single cell. You cannot unselect *every* cell by modifying the values of these properties in program code.

The solution is to issue a SendKeys instruction that moves the current cell right and then left, as if the user had pressed arrow keys. Remember that when an area of cells is selected, moving the current cell by using the keyboard unselects all selected cells. The purpose of the UnSelect procedure is to simulate these keystrokes. The effect is to unselect all cells while keeping the cursor at the same current cell.

Adding the *UnSelect* Procedure

Place the following procedure in the general declarations section of the form:

```
Sub UnSelect ()
    'Unselects any selected region of cells
    If Grid1.Visible = False Then Exit Sub

    Grid1.SetFocus

    Select Case Grid1.Col
        Case 1
            SendKeys "{RIGHT}{LEFT}"
        Case Grid1.Cols - 1
            SendKeys "{LEFT}{RIGHT}"
        Case Else
            SendKeys "{LEFT}{RIGHT}"
    End Select
End Sub
```

This procedure is written so that the current cell can be in the rightmost or leftmost column of the grid. UnSelect also allows for the fact that you cannot move to column 0 with keystrokes because that column is fixed.

Including the *AddGridLine* Procedure

You now must develop some of the procedures that produce the necessary results when the user clicks the command buttons. The AddGridLine procedure simply adds a row of empty cells to the grid by using the AddItem method. This procedure also puts a row number in column 0 of the new row. After the row has been added to the grid, the grid display is adjusted to show the new bottom row.

Place the following AddGridLine procedure in the general declarations section of the form:

```
Sub AddGridLine ()
    Dim Test As Integer
    Dim Dummy As Integer

    GridStatusSave

    UnSelect

    Grid1.Rows = Grid1.Rows + 1    'Add the row
    Grid1.Row = Grid1.Rows - 1     'Move to the new row
    Grid1.Col = 0                  'Insert the row number
    Grid1.Text = Format$(Grid1.Row)

    On Error Resume Next
    Test = Grid1.Row
    Do   'Find the first possible TopRow above the added row
       Grid1.TopRow = Test%
       If Err Then
       Err = 0
       Test% = Test% - 1
       Else
       Exit Do
       End If
    Loop
    On Error GoTo 0
    Dummy = DoEvents()
    UnSelect
    Grid1.Col = 1

End Sub
```

AddGridLine demonstrates the use of the TopRow property. The procedure searches for the first permissible TopRow setting above the new row and sets the value of TopRow to that setting. As a result, when you add a new line to the grid, the grid display adjusts downward so that the new row is the bottom visible row.

Understanding the *DeleteGridLine* Procedure

The DeleteGridLine procedure is the companion procedure to AddGridLine. DeleteGridLine removes the current row. This procedure does not, however, use the RemoveItem method. Normally, RemoveItem would be the way to go, but the PhoneBook application retains the line number of each entry in the phone list. Simply deleting a line results in a gap in the line numbers.

Instead, `DeleteGridLine` cycles through every row below the current row (that is, cycles through higher row numbers). The procedure selects columns 1 through 7 in each row and moves the contents of the grid's `Clip` (the selected data) up to the preceding row. At the end of this process, the last row in the grid is deleted with `RemoveItem`. The final result is that the current row is removed, and all row numbers are maintained correctly. Because deleting a row is a permanent action, a message box requests the user's confirmation before deleting the row.

Adding *DeleteGridLine*

Here's the `DeleteGridLine` procedure. Like the other user-defined procedures, it goes in the general declarations section of the form:

```
Sub DeleteGridLine ()
    Dim Msg As String
    Dim Temp As String
    Dim C As Integer
    Dim X As Integer      'Loop counter

    Msg = "Delete line " & Grid1.Row & " from grid?"
    C = MsgBox(Msg, 32 + 4, "Delete Line")
    If C = 7 Then Exit Sub    'User clicked NO.

    Grid1.HighLight = False

    Grid1.SelStartCol = 1    'Don't select the row number
    Grid1.SelEndCol = Grid1.Cols - 1

    For X = Grid1.Row To Grid1.Rows - 2
      Grid1.SelStartRow = X + 1
      Grid1.SelEndRow = X + 1
      Temp = Grid1.Clip
      Grid1.SelStartRow = X
      Grid1.SelEndRow = X
      Grid1.Clip = Temp
    Next X
    Grid1.Rows = Grid1.Rows - 1
    UnSelect
    Grid1.HighLight = True
End Sub
```

`DeleteGridLine` operates on the assumption that the currently selected row is the row to delete. You can easily modify this procedure to accept a row number as a parameter and delete that row. Save your project to disk.

Adding the *CopyLine* Procedure

The `CopyLine` procedure copies the current row of the grid to a new row at the bottom of the grid. The technique involves selecting the relevant data from the current row (columns 1 through 7), saving the grid's `Clip` data to a temporary variable, adding a new row, and then pasting the saved data into the new row. Because this process happens quickly, the procedure doesn't bother disabling the grid's `HighLight` property.

Place the following `CopyLine` procedure in the form's general declarations section:

```
Sub CopyLine ()
    Dim Temp As String

    GridStatusSave

    Grid1.SelStartCol = 1
    Grid1.SelEndCol = Grid1.Cols - 1
    Grid1.SelStartRow = Grid1.Row
    Grid1.SelEndRow = Grid1.Row
    Temp = Format$(Grid1.Rows) + Chr$(9) + Grid1.Clip

    Grid1.AddItem Temp

    GridStatusRestore
    Grid1.Row = Grid1.Rows - 1
    Grid1.Col = 1
    UnSelect

End Sub
```

13

One element that *cannot* be omitted from a program is a way for the user to exit from the program. The next procedure handles the user exiting the program.

Adding the *ShutDown* Procedure

This procedure is called by `Command1_Click` when the user clicks the Exit command button (to terminate the application). Place the following `ShutDown` procedure in the general declarations section of the form:

```
Sub Shutdown ()
    End
End Sub
```

Creating the Floating Text Box

As mentioned earlier in this chapter, the Grid control does not offer the user the capability of directly editing the contents of a cell. This lack could be a serious handicap but there are two simple "work-arounds": (1) using the grid's `KeyPress` event and (2) using a text box and grid combination.

Method 1: Using the *KeyPress* Event

When you use the grid's `KeyPress` event, you simply add each character that the user types to the `Text` property of the appropriate grid cell. For example, assume that you have set the `Grid1.Row` and `Grid1.Col` properties to point to the appropriate cell. The cell is empty, and you want to enable the user to type data into the cell. The following code would accomplish this goal:

```
Sub Grid1_KeyPress (KeyAscii As Integer)
    Grid1.Text = Grid1.Text + Chr$(KeyAscii)
End Sub
```

Method 2:   Using a Text Box and a Grid Combination

The second technique uses a text box and grid combination so that the user can edit the contents of individual grid cells. The user actually edits data that has been taken from the appropriate grid cell and placed into the text box. The user makes any changes to the data while it is in the text box (not the grid).

When the user is finished making changes to the data, the edited data is placed back in the grid cell. The user signals that she or he is finished by pressing the Enter key (ASCII 13) or the Escape key (ASCII 27). If either of these two keys is pressed, the program code must set KeyAscii to 0 so that the Enter or Escape key press is not sent to the text box.

In the PhoneBook application, that capability is enhanced by creating a floating text box. The floating text box is kept invisible until the user wants to edit the contents of a cell. The user signals a desire to edit a cell in a number of ways: double-clicking a cell, pressing Enter, or just typing letters or numbers.

When the user edits a cell, PhoneBook places the Text Box control directly over the grid cell and makes the text box visible. The text box has the same size and shape as the cell. The result is that the user appears to be editing directly in the cell, but the editing really takes place in the text box. This technique is a more elegant way to implement editing than maintaining a separate text box outside the boundaries of the grid control.

Adding the *ShowTextBox* Procedure

Determining the exact size of the text box and where to place it can be tricky. You must take into account the width of the cell column, the thickness of the lines separating each cell, and the top and left edges of the grid itself. The following procedure, called ShowTextBox, is the result of these considerations and goes in the general declarations section of the form:

```
Sub ShowTextBox ()
    Dim TestX As Integer, TestY As Integer
    Dim C As Integer    'Loop counter

    'Hide the text box and make it two lines tall and wide
    ➡ (for starters)
    Text1.Visible = False
    Text1.Height = Grid1.RowHeight(Grid1.Row) -
    ➡ (Screen.TwipsPerPixelY * 2)
    Text1.Width = Grid1.ColWidth(Grid1.Col) -
    ➡ (Screen.TwipsPerPixelX * 2)

    'Determine the X coordinate of the current cell,
    ➡ figuring in Grid1.LeftCol

    'Get the left edge of the grid plus two line widths...
    TestX = Grid1.Left + Grid1.ColWidth(0) +
    ➡ (Screen.TwipsPerPixelX * 3)
```

```
'Sum all column widths...
For C = Grid1.LeftCol To Grid1.Col - 1
    TestX = TestX + Grid1.ColWidth + Screen.TwipsPerPixelX
Next C

'Determine the Y coordinate of the current cell,
➥ figuring in Grid1.TopRow

'Get the top edge of the grid plus two line heights...
TestY = Grid1.Top + Grid1.RowHeight(0) +
➥ (Screen.TwipsPerPixelY * 2)

'Sum all column heights...
For C = Grid1.TopRow To Grid1.Row - 1
TestY = TestY + Grid1.RowHeight + Screen.TwipsPerPixelY
Next C


'Position the text box control
Text1.Left = TestX
Text1.Top = TestY

Text1.ZOrder            'Make sure it's on top!
Text1.Visible = True    'Show it
Text1.SetFocus          'Make it active

End Sub
```

Notice that the Screen properties `TwipsPerPixelX` and `TwipsPerPixelY` are used throughout `ShowTextBox`. These Screen properties ensure that the text box (`Text1`) appears *exactly* within the boundaries of the cell.

The border around the entire grid and the lines separating the cells are each one pixel wide. You must take these one-pixel line widths into account for the grid itself and for each column and row. `Text1` has no border style, so the text box fits neatly into the cell being edited. The result is that the text box masquerades as the cell being updated until the editing is completed or canceled. Save your project to disk.

Recognizing the Desire for Cell Editing

The next task is to create the code for `Grid1` so that the Grid control can recognize when the user wants to edit a cell. You must ensure that the user can cancel editing and that standard keyboard navigation rules remain in effect while the user types. Cell editing begins when any of the following situations occur:

The user double-clicks a cell.

The user presses Enter (with the focus on a cell).

The user starts typing letters or numbers (with the focus on a cell).

Cell editing terminates in the following situations:

The user presses Enter.

The user moves away from the cell using an arrow key.

The user clicks another cell.

Cell editing is canceled if the user presses Escape.

Enabling the User to Use the Tab Key

The user can navigate the cells in a grid by using the arrow keys; this capability is built into the Grid control. However, many Windows-based applications (including Visual Basic), allow the user to move between data fields by pressing the Tab key. To enable the user to use the Tab key for grid navigation and to have the program recognize when the user wants to begin editing, you can use the grid's KeyPress and KeyDown event procedures. Here is the code for the Grid1_KeyPress procedure:

```
Sub Grid1_KeyPress (KeyAscii As Integer)
   Dim Char As String

   Select Case KeyAscii
   Case 27   'Escape key was pressed
      ' Text1.Text = Grid1.Text   Add this if desired

   Case 9    'Tab: move to next column
      If Shifting Then   'Keydown event captured a shift key.
            'Move Left
         If Grid1.Col > 1 Then
            Grid1.Col = Grid1.Col - 1
         End If
      Else  'No shift key.  Move right.
         If Grid1.Col < (Grid1.Cols - 1) Then
            Grid1.Col = Grid1.Col + 1
         End If
      End If
      UnSelect

   Case Else
      If KeyAscii = 13 Then   'Show Text1 with full text
         Text1.Text = Grid1.Text
         Text1.SelStart = Len(Text1.Text)
      Else  'Send char to Text1, then show it
         Char = Chr$(KeyAscii)
         Text1.Text = Char
         Text1.SelStart = 1
      End If
      ShowTextBox
      KeyAscii = 0
   End Select
End Sub
```

Notice how the KeyPress procedure uses the form-level variable Shifting to determine whether the Shift key is being pressed. The value of Shifting is set in the Grid1_KeyDown event procedure. Here is the necessary code:

```
Sub Grid1_KeyDown (KeyCode As Integer, Shift As Integer)
    Text1.Visible = False    'just in case...
    If Shift = 1 Then Shifting = True Else Shifting = False
End Sub
```

When the user is not editing a cell's contents, the floating text box displays the contents of the current grid cell.

Adding the Text Box Event Procedures

The simplest way to keep the contents of the text box up-to-date is to use the grid's `RowColChange` event procedure. Whenever the current grid cell changes, the event procedure loads the contents of the current grid cell into the `Text` property of the text box. Here is the `Grid1_RowColChange` event procedure:

```
Sub Grid1_RowColChange ()
    Text1.Text = Grid1.Text
End Sub
```

The floating text box requires some code in order for it to determine when editing ends and how to respond when it does. Remember the keystroke guidelines: pressing Escape cancels editing; and pressing Enter, Tab, or an arrow key completes editing. The necessary code goes in the `Text1_KeyPress` event procedure as follows:

```
Sub Text1_KeyPress (KeyAscii As Integer)
    Select Case KeyAscii
        Case 13, 9    'Enter or Tab
        Grid1.Text = Text1.Text
        Text1.Visible = False
        Grid1.SetFocus
        If KeyAscii = 9 And Grid1.Col < Grid1.Cols - 1 Then
            If Shifting Then    'Keydown event captured a Shift key.
                If Grid1.Col > 1 Then
                    'Move Left
                    Grid1.Col = Grid1.Col - 1
                End If
            Else    'No Shift key.  Move right.
                If Grid1.Col < (Grid1.Cols - 1) Then
                    Grid1.Col = Grid1.Col + 1
                End If
            End If
            UnSelect
        End If
        KeyAscii = 0
        Case 27    'Escape
        KeyAscii = 0
        Text1.Visible = False
        Grid1.SetFocus
    End Select
End Sub
```

The `Text1_KeyPress` procedure responds to the Escape, Tab, and Enter keys. The text box, however, must also respond correctly when the user presses the

(continues)

13

Adding the Text Box Event Procedures (continued)

up-arrow or down-arrow key, events that KeyPress does not recognize. However, the KeyDown event can recognize the arrow keys. That's where the code to respond to the arrow keys goes.

The KeyDown event can recognize the arrow keys. The code to respond to the arrow keys goes in the KeyDown procedure. Here is the Text1_KeyDown event procedure for this application:

```
Sub Text1_KeyDown (KeyCode As Integer, Shift As Integer)
    If Shift = 1 Then
        Shifting = True
    Else
        Shifting = False
    End If

    Select Case KeyCode
    Case 38 ' up
        Text1_KeyPress 13      'Simulate Enter key
        SendKeys "{UP}"
    Case 40 ' down
        Text1_KeyPress 13      'Simulate Enter key
        SendKeys "{DOWN}"

    End Select

End Sub
```

The user's double-clicking a grid cell is a signal to begin editing the cell. The Grid1_DblClick event procedure initiates cell editing by sending the Enter key to the grid's KeyPress event:

```
Sub Grid1_DblClick ()
    If Grid1.Row > 0 And Grid1.Col > 0 Then Grid1_KeyPress 13
End Sub
```

If the user clicks the mouse, editing is over. In this case, the text box must again become invisible. Here's the Grid1_MouseDown procedure:

```
Sub Grid1_MouseDown (Button As Integer, Shift As Integer,
➥ X As Single, Y As Single)
    Text1.Visible = False
End Sub
```

Writing and Reading the Data File

At this point, you can try running PhoneBook. The application starts with an empty grid (see figure 13.12). Notice the phone icon displayed in the upper-left corner. This icon is an example of a grid cell containing picture data. (The icon is copied from the data in the Form1.Icon property. Recall that the form's Icon property specifies the icon which appears when the form is minimized.)

Figure 13.12
The PhoneBook
application with
blank data fields.

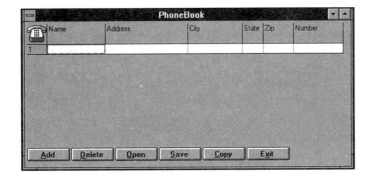

You can add rows, edit individual cells, and delete grid rows. Try entering some data to see how the floating text box works. Notice that you seem to be typing the data directly into the grid cell.

Storing and Loading Large Amounts of Data When You Use a Grid

Hard coding
Writing program code to supply values rather than reading the values from user input or from a file.

Small amounts of data can be loaded into a grid using **hard coding** at design time. This method was illustrated in the Form_Load procedure of the GRIDEX1 program developed earlier in this chapter. This technique works well for small amounts of unchanging data—for example, row or column headings. However, when the amount of grid data that needs to be saved at the end of a program run (or loaded at the start of a run) is large, hard coding is not appropriate.

Furthermore, if the contents of the grid can be altered by the user at run time, another method of saving and then loading grid data *must* be used. As you know from Chapter 12, files are designed to store large amounts of data. As you learn in Chapter 14, databases are also used for this purpose. Therefore, the method used with grids is to save the data in a file (or a database table) at the end of a run. Then at the start of the following run, the data file (or database table) is read back into the grid. Any previous additions, modifications, or deletions of data that you made to the grid will be available for the following session.

The PhoneBook application does not yet contain any code to save or load data files. (The Open and Save command buttons are not operational.) That's where the user-defined SaveFile and LoadFile procedures come into play. Before typing these procedures, click the Exit command button to terminate the application and return Visual Basic to Design mode. Then make sure that you have saved the project on disk.

Understanding the *SaveFile* Procedure

The SaveFile procedure places a copy of the grid data into a text file and saves that file on disk. Although the code for SaveFile may appear complex, in reality, the procedure is divided into three sections that are fairly easy to understand.

First, if no file name has been previously specified by the user, the procedure prompts the user for a file name. The file is saved with this file name. To get the file name, SaveFile uses the InputBox function. (Other choices would be to use a customized dialog box or the Common Dialog custom control, but InputBox is used here for simplicity.) Be aware that SaveFile does little error checking here.

13

If a file specification error occurs, the user is alerted, and the application terminates. The form-level variable FileName holds the specified file name without the path.

Second, SaveFile must determine the data to save and prepare that data to be written to a file. SaveFile accomplishes this step by selecting all the rows and columns of the grid and copying the Grid1.Clip property to a temporary string variable named Contents.

Third, SaveFile must actually write the data in Contents to the disk file. Here, the Print# statement is used. Save your project to disk if you have not already done so.

Coding the *SaveFile* Procedure

The following code is for the SaveFile procedure. Place this procedure in the general declarations section of the form:

```
Sub SaveFile ()
    Dim Contents As String, Msg As String

    'Get a filename using the InputBox function.
    If FileName = "" Then    'Get a filename
        P$ = "Enter filename to save to:"  'prompt
        T$ = "Save File"                   'title
        D$ = "PHONBOOK.TXT"                'default name
        FileName = UCase$(InputBox(P$, T$, D$))
        If FileName = "" Then Exit Sub     'user canceled
    End If

    Form1.Caption = "PhoneBook - " & FileName

    'Prep grid, screen for activity
    Screen.MousePointer = 11    'hourglass
    Grid1.HighLight = False
    GridStatusSave
    UnSelect

    'Select grid data (minus row numbers) and
    'copy grid contents (Grid1.Clip) into temp variable
    Grid1.SelStartRow = 1
    Grid1.SelEndRow = Grid1.Rows - 1
    Grid1.FixedCols = 0
    Grid1.SelStartCol = 0
    Grid1.SelEndCol = Grid1.Cols - 1
    Contents = Grid1.Clip
    Grid1.FixedCols = 1

    On Error GoTo SaveFileError

    'Open and write the file
    Open App.Path + "\" + FileName For Output As #1
    Print #1, Contents  'Write variable contents to saved file
    Close #1
    On Error GoTo 0

    GridStatusRestore
    Grid1.Visible = True
```

```
            UnSelect
            Grid1.HighLight = True
            Screen.MousePointer = 0

        Exit Sub

        SaveFileError:
            Msg$ = "Error " & Err & " saving " + FileName + ": " +
        ➥ Error$ + "."
            MsgBox Msg, 48
            Close
            Screen.MousePointer = 0
            Exit Sub

        End Sub
```

Understanding the *LoadFile* Procedure

The LoadFile procedure reads the contents of a disk file and places the data into the grid. LoadFile works correctly only with data files previously saved with SaveFile. (You can load other data files into the grid with LoadFile, but if the tab and carriage-return characters aren't properly formatted in the data file, the resulting grid display won't make much sense.)

SaveFile copied the grid data by assigning Grid1.Clip to the string variable Contents. The proper Chr$(9) and Chr$(13) characters (tab and CR, respectively) are automatically included in Grid1.Clip. As a result, the Contents variable and the disk file are properly formatted.

LoadFile uses an input box to request from the user the name of the file containing the stored data. The data in the file is read one line at a time; each line of data is appended to the grid using the AddItem method. The tabs, which set off the data value for each cell, are already embedded in the data read from the disk.

Coding the *LoadFile* Procedure

The following code is the LoadFile procedure. It must be placed in the general declarations section of the form:

```
Sub LoadFile ()
    Dim Ctr As Integer
    Dim Msg As String

    'Get the file name
    P$ = "Enter filename to load:"    'prompt
    T$ = "Load File"                  'title
    D$ = "PHONBOOK.TXT"               'default file name
    NewFileName = UCase$(InputBox(P$, T$, D$))

    If NewFileName = "" Then Exit Sub 'user canceled

    Screen.MousePointer = 11
    Grid1.HighLight = False
    UnSelect
```

(continues)

Coding the *LoadFile* Procedure (continued)

```
                'Remove every row except row 0 (column headings)
                Grid1.FixedRows = 0
                Grid1.Rows = 1


                'Read file one line at a time and add to grid

                If InStr(NewFileName, "\") = 0 Then  'Assume current dir
                    FullFileName = App.Path & "\" & NewFileName
                Else
                    FullFileName = NewFileName
                End If

                On Error GoTo LoadFileError

                If Dir(FullFileName) <> "" Then        'Check if file exists.
                    Open FullFileName For Input As #1  'If it does, open it.

                    Screen.MousePointer = 11

                    Ctr = 1                      'Initialize the line counter
                    Do While Not EOF(1)          'Read file data until you're done
                        Line Input #1, TextLine  'Get complete line.
                        Grid1.AddItem TextLine   'Add it to the grid at the proper
                        ➡ line
                        Ctr = Ctr + 1            'Increment the line counter
                    Loop
                    Close 1
                    Screen.MousePointer = 0
                Else
                    MsgBox "File " & FullFileName & " not found.", 48
                End If

                'Reset fixed rows to 1, and move to the
                'top left corner of the grid
                Grid1.FixedRows = 1
                Grid1.Row = 1
                Grid1.Col = 1
                Grid1.HighLight = True
                Grid1.SetFocus

                FileName = NewFileName    'Update form-level variable
                Form1.Caption = "PhoneBook - " + FileName 'Update form caption
                On Error GoTo 0

            Exit Sub

            LoadFileError:
                Msg = "Error " & Err & " Loading " & NewFileName
                Msg = Msg & ": " & Error$ & "."
                MsgBox Msg, 48
                Close
                Exit Sub
            End Sub
```

Your application is now complete. Well done! Make sure that you have saved the complete application on your disk. Try it out, and correct any bugs you may have entered in error. Then save the project to disk.

Chapter Summary

The Grid control can quickly and conveniently display tabular data in a form familiar to spreadsheet users. The Grid's Row and Col properties can be read or set to highlight an individual cell. The SelStartRow, SelEndRow, SelStartCol, and SelEndCol properties work with groups of cells. With the Text property, you can obtain the contents of a single cell, and the Clip property provides the data in the grid's selected region.

A grid can display both text and pictures. Text data is represented internally with a tab (Chr$(9)) separating the data in adjoining cells and a carriage return (Chr$(13)) ending each row. This internal data arrangement provides a convenient mechanism for inserting and extracting data to and from the grid.

A grid also has a number of display-related properties that you can set or read at run time. These properties include column width, row height, TopRow, and LeftCol. The value of the HighLight property determines whether selected cells appear highlighted, and the value of the GridLines property determines whether cell borders appear.

In the next chapter, you learn how to use the Data control to access databases.

Test Your Understanding

True/False

Indicate whether the statement is true or false.

1. Numerical data is stored in string format in a Grid control.

2. You can display both text and picture data in the same Grid cell.

3. Visual Basic, by default, uses a dotted border to indicate the active cell.

4. You cannot scroll a fixed row.

5. A Grid must always have at least one fixed row and one fixed column.

6. When an application is running, you can adjust column width and row height by clicking and dragging cell borders.

7. To enter data into a grid cell, the user must first enter the data into a Text Box control.

8. The highlighting of user-selected cells is built into the Grid control.

9. The LoadPicture function can be used to assign a picture to a cell in a grid.

10. The font or font color of text in a Grid cell cannot be changed.

Short Answer

Answer the following questions.

1. Write a `Form_Load` procedure that will place the integers from 1 to 5 in a column of a Grid control.

2. Modify the procedure in your answer to question 1 so that the grid also displays, in a second column, the square of the five integers in the first column.

3. What are the crucial property settings of a Grid control with two fixed rows, one fixed column, ten total rows, and five total columns?

4. Explain the difference between the `Col` and `Cols` properties. For what is each used?

5. Explain the difference between the `Row` and `Rows` properties. For what is each used?

6. What is the `Clip` property of a Grid control? Explain how it can be used in a program.

7. Explain the `SelEndCol`, `SelStartCol`, `SelEndRow`, and `SelStartRow` properties. How can they be used in an application?

8. What is the `SelChange` event? Give an example of how it could be used in a program.

9. What do the `AddItem` and `RemoveItem` methods do to a Grid control? Do they add rows or columns to a grid?

Projects

Project 1: Modifying a Program to Allow a User to Enter Data

Modify the program that you created in the first project at the end of Chapter 12 so that the secretary enters the registration data in a Grid control. When the secretary selects Save **As** from the program's **F**ile menu, the data should be saved in a sequential file. The program should also be modified so that it displays the participants in each seminar in a grid control. Save the program as **C13P1** and print the project.

Project 2: Writing a Program to Create a Spreadsheetlike Application

Write a program that uses the Grid control to create a spreadsheetlike application. The layout is shown below:

ITEM	JAN	FEB	MAR	APRIL	MAY	JUNE
Rent						
Phone						
Staff						
Supplies						
TOTAL						

The user should be able to enter numbers for each item for each month. At the bottom of each month's column, the total expenses for that month should be displayed and updated as the user enters values. Save the program as **C13P2** and print the project.

Project 3:   Writing a Program for a Game

Use the Grid control as the user interface for a program that enables the user to play a game of Tic-Tac-Toe against your program. Your program should try its best to defeat the user; your reputation as a programmer will be at stake. Save the program as **C13P3** and print it.

13

CHAPTER 14

Using the Data Control to Interact with Databases

Microsoft's Access and FoxPro, Borland's Paradox and dBASE, and Novell's Btrieve are popular data storage and retrieval programs. Perhaps you have already used one or more of these application packages. Visual Basic includes the database engine from Microsoft Access. VB enables you, the programmer, to store and retrieve data in the format used by these popular programs. Access is a representative and powerful piece of database software. Visual Basic includes considerable database functionality and is particularly compatible with Microsoft Access.

The VB Data control attaches to an existing database, providing a link between your application and your data. Various controls—such as labels, images, text boxes, check boxes, and picture boxes—can be made data-aware by binding (connecting) to the Data control. In this way, a Visual Basic application can communicate with a database. For example, the Text property of a bound Text Box control can link with a string field in the database.

You can easily navigate through data with little or no programming by clicking the Data control buttons to move from one record to another. Of course, you can also add commands to control your database access at run time. In this chapter, you learn the basics of databases. You learn how to create tables, add data to the tables, and retrieve data. In short, you learn how to use VB to create a "database front-end" that will enable users to access a database easily. To learn the use of the Data control, you construct a database application.

Objectives

By the time you have finished this chapter, you will be able to

1. Understand the Concepts of Databases, Linked Tables, Records, Fields, and Indexes

2. Know the Advantages That Database Systems Offer over Systems Based on Files

3. Understand Where Visual Basic Is Used in a Client/Server Environment

4. Use Visual Basic's Data Manager to Create and Edit a Database

5. Understand the Uses of the Data Control and Its Most Important Properties, Events, and Methods

6. Bind Data-Aware Controls

7. Add the VB Code Necessary to Use Data Controls at Run Time

8. Become Familiar with Structured Query Language (SQL)

9. Use Multiple Tables and Queries

10. Demonstrate Database Techniques by Creating an Access-Compatible Database and Developing a Sample Application That Manipulates It

Understanding Databases

Database
A collection of data related to a particular topic or purpose and organized into one or more tables.

Database management system (DBMS)
A program that organizes data in a database, providing information storage and retrieval capabilities.

A **database** is a collection of data related to a particular topic or purpose. The collection is further organized into tables that present information on a particular subject in the familiar column (field) and row (record) format. Two examples of databases are the registration data for students and the inventory of a bookstore.

Databases are usually created and maintained by a type of prewritten application software called a **database management system (DBMS)**. Access, FoxPro, and Paradox, for example, are all DBMSs. Relational databases are currently the most common type of database on microcomputers, minicomputers, and mainframe computers. In relational databases (such as Access, FoxPro, and Paradox), data is stored and retrieved in tables. Databases can efficiently handle large amounts of data.

If a database contains information about a business, the individual tables may contain data on products, customers, suppliers, sales, and employees. Mail order companies maintain mailing lists in databases. Airline databases contain information about customer registrations and available flights. The U.S. Federal government maintains large databases that enable the collection and rapid retrieval of information on any of its citizens and their lives.

Structure
The organization of a database.

Field
A specific category of information in a database table.

The organization of a database is called its **structure**, and it includes tables, field names, types, sizes, and indexes. The structure must be defined before data can be stored in the database. To function satisfactorily for a business or organization, a database (and its structure) must be carefully planned and designed. Each **field** in a table is a specific category of information. For example, typical fields in a Customer table include Name (such as John Q. Public), Address, Phone Number, and so on. A **record** stores all the information about one particular person, place, thing, or event (such as a sale to a customer). Each record contains the same fields, and tables consist of a collection of the same type of records (see figure 14.1).

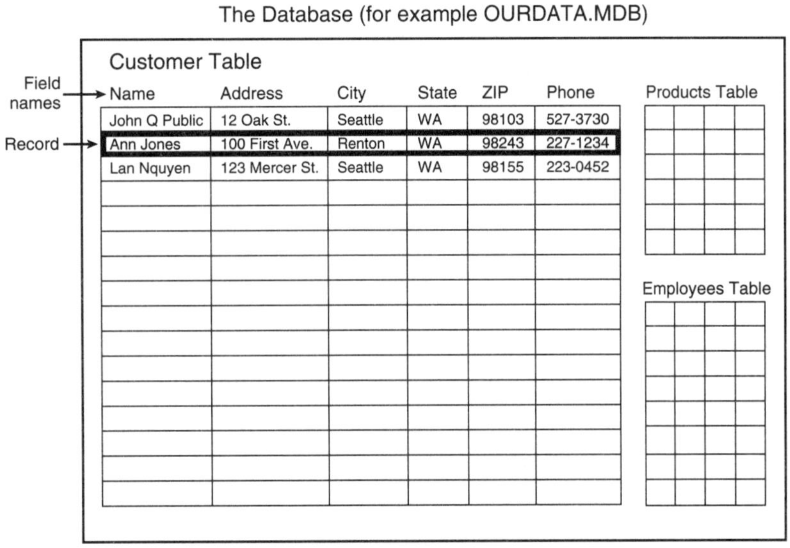

Figure 14.1
An example of a database.

The Database (for example OURDATA.MDB)

Record
A set of related information stored in named data fields.

A specific data value is stored at the intersection of a field (column) and record (row). For example, John's address is located in the Address field of John's record. You can search records to see whether the data values for a field have a particular value. To search, you use a query. A **query** is, in essence, a question you ask about the data in your database. Structured Query Language, or SQL (pronounced "sequel"), is a commonly used language for expressing database queries.

Query
A question asked about the data in a database.

Index
A structure created via the DBMS that organizes a database and makes possible more rapid access to data.

You can speed up your search for data by creating an **index** on one or more fields. For example, a customer name index for the Customer field contains the customer names in alphabetical order. For each name, the index includes a pointer to the corresponding record in the Customer table. If you want to query the database for the record of a particular customer, it's much faster for the DBMS's database engine to search just the customer name index rather than the entire table. That way, you have immediate access to the table record for the customer name.

Primary key
A unique identifier for each record in a table.

A table can have one or more indexes (or none), but if the table grows to more than 50 records, you may want to create a primary key field and index the table on that field. A **primary key field** is a unique identifier for each record in a table. In other words, only one record in the table can have that value. Student numbers, social security numbers, and part numbers are examples of unique record identifiers that can be used as key fields. If you designate a primary key field for a table, each record in the table must have a data value for that field, and there can be no duplicate key field values. Primary keys are useful when you want to join two tables, as you do later in the chapter.

Storing information in databases has two advantages over storing information in separate files:

1. *Database management systems do much of the work that you would have to do as a programmer when you code your VB program.* Database management systems can perform the editing of input fields, enforce constraints on the data values that can be entered in a field, and ensure that the user does not enter duplicate values for a key field. A DBMS can maintain indexes and can simplify the addition, deletion, modification, storage, and retrieval of records. When you design and write a file-based application, you have to do *everything* yourself by writing code. A DBMS is a program, written by other people, that does much of your work for you.

2. *Unlike a file-based system, a database enables you to extract related information from different tables in the database.* A file-based system tends to produce "walls" between your data files—unless you create a design and write a great deal of code to avoid this problem. In a file-based system, for example, the manager of a store may be able to retrieve data on customers only, sales people only, or items sold only. But the manager cannot see which salespeople sold what items to which customers because the data is stored in three separate and unrelated files. The linkage of related data is exactly the kind of information that managers often need. But file-based systems do not lend themselves to this kind of retrieval. Databases do.

Join
The extraction of related data from two database tables; requires that the tables contain link fields.

If, when designing your database, you create common "link" fields in tables, you can easily extract related data from different tables. This extraction is usually performed by what is called a **join** of the data in the linked tables. Therefore, if you design your Customer, Salesperson, and Sales tables with the appropriate link fields, you can easily write code to let the store manager quickly find out which salespeople sold what items to which customers.

Corporate databases are usually stored on mainframes or minicomputers. Visual Basic is often used to create a user interface (a "front end") to the corporate database. This interface gives the user easy access to a complicated database system. The Visual Basic program performs as a client application, and the mainframe or minicomputer DBMS is the data server. This kind of system is referred to as client/server computing. In a local area network (LAN) environment, a VB program often runs on a user's workstation as the client (database front end) application. A combination of hardware and software (for example, Microsoft's SQL Server) functions as a database server.

Note: *If you are interested in working in any area related to computer information systems, a knowledge of database theory, software, and technology is important. To* *learn more about databases, consult Que's* Using Access 2.0 *or* Using FoxPro 2.6 for Windows, *Special Edition, or Sams'* Database Developer's Guide with Visual Basic, *Second Edition.*

In the next part of this chapter, you complete the necessary tasks in building a sample application. The first task is to build the database.

Building the Database for the Sample Application

To develop the sample application, you first need to create a database, using VB's Data Manager utility. Both the Standard and Professional Editions of Visual Basic include this utility. With the Data Manager, you can create databases in Microsoft Access format. That is, databases you create can be imported into Microsoft Access. Similarly, databases created with Microsoft Access can be accessed and manipulated with Visual Basic's Data Manager.

The following sections take you through the steps of using the Data Manager to create the sample database. This database contains one table, several fields, and an index.

Starting the Data Manager and Creating the Database

To avoid potential file-sharing conflicts, you should load and run SHARE.EXE whenever you use a database. This program is supplied with DOS and runs as a TSR program (a terminate-and-stay-resident program).

To load and run SHARE.EXE, you can type the command **SHARE** from the DOS prompt. However, a simpler method is to have your AUTOEXEC.BAT file automatically run SHARE every time you boot your system. Place the following line in your AUTOEXEC.BAT file:

C:\DOS\SHARE.EXE

SHARE.EXE must be running in order for the Data Manager to access a database while any project is loaded in the Visual Basic environment. SHARE permits the sharing of data and files among applications. You don't need to run SHARE if you close any other VB project before working with the Data Manager.

Do the following to use the Data Manager:

❶ Start Visual Basic. Then choose D**a**ta Manager from the **W**indow menu. When the Data Manager window appears, open the **F**ile menu, and choose **N**ew Database. Then choose either the **A**ccess 1.0 or A**c**cess 1.1 file format from the submenu (see figure 14.2).

(continues)

Starting the Data Manager and Creating the Database   (continued)

Figure 14.2
Creating a new
database with
the Data
Manager.

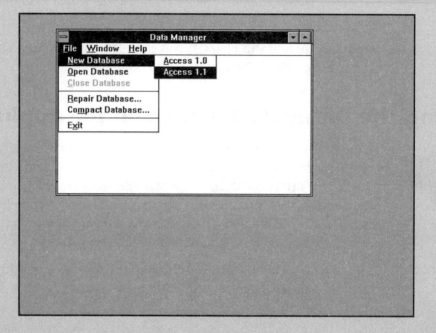

Note: *Some versions of Visual Basic cannot read or write databases created with the newest release of Access (Version 2.0). However, all versions of VB can read and write databases in Access 1.1 format. This situation holds true whether the Data Manager created the database or the Access program itself created the database.*

❷ When the New Database dialog box opens, type **Country** in the File Name text box.

The path is C:\VB, assuming that you installed Visual Basic (and therefore DATAMGR.EXE) in the default directory. You can specify a different directory path when typing the file name. In that case, you must modify the subsequent C:\VB code references to reflect your specified path.

❸ In the New Database dialog box, click OK.

The database is created and saved as a disk file. The file extension MDB is automatically added to the file name. The next task is to create a table.

Using the Tables Window

After you click OK, the Data Manager opens the Database window and displays the Tables window. Click the New button. The Create New Table dialog box opens.

In this dialog box, you create the structure of the table. Elements include the names, types, and sizes of the fields in the table. After you have defined the structure of the table, it is ready to store data. In the text box, type the table name **Country**, as shown in figure 14.3. (In this figure, the Tables window is maximized to fill the Data Manager window.)

Figure 14.3

Creating a new table.

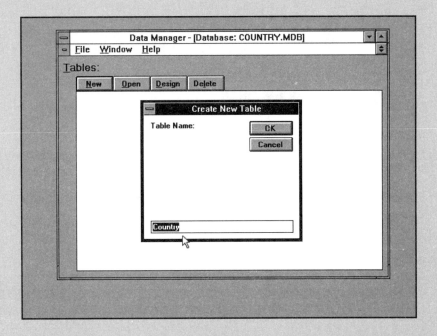

Notice that the caption of the title bar reads `Data Manager-[Database: COUNTRY.MDB]`. Click OK to accept the new table name. Then close the Create New Table dialog box. The Table Design window now appears (see figure 14.4).

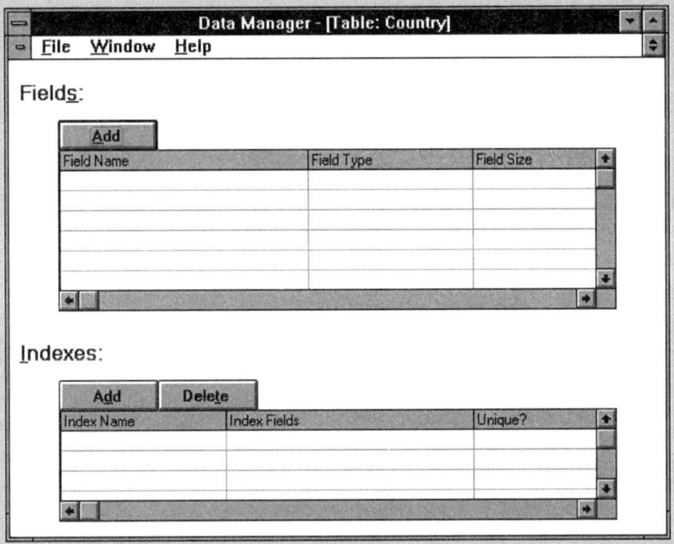

Figure 14.4

The Table Design window.

Click the **A**dd button in the Field**s** section to display the Add Field dialog box. In the Field **N**ame text box, type **Country Name**. Then click the down arrow to the right of the Field **T**ype combo box. A drop-down list opens so that you can select the field's data type. Scroll down the list, and click the Text type. By

(continues)

Using the Tables Window (continued)

selecting the Text type, you indicate that the Country Name field contains text (string) data.

In the Field Size box, type **20**. Now the data for this field is limited to 20 characters of text. Figure 14.5 shows the completed data entry for this first field.

Figure 14.5
The completed data entry for the first field.

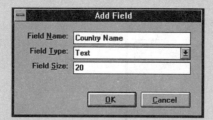

Using the data in table 14.1, repeat the preceding steps to specify the rest of the fields in the database.

Table 14.1 Country Table Design Data for the COUNTRY Database

Field Name	Field Type	Field Size (for Text Fields Only)
Capital Name	Text	20
Population	Long Integer	
Flag	Binary	
Comments	Memo	

Figure 14.6 shows the Table Design window when all the fields have been added.

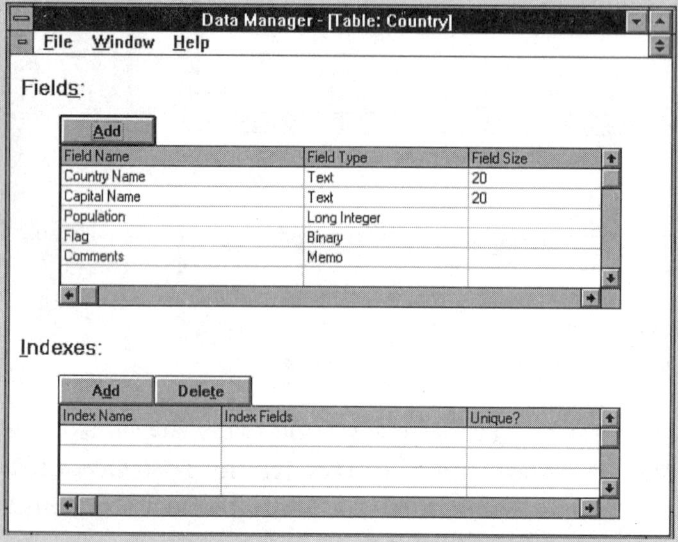

Figure 14.6
All the fields are specified.

As you see, you can add fields to a database table with the Data Manager. However, you cannot rename, modify, or delete the fields individually. If you make any mistakes, you must delete the entire table and start over. Later in this chapter, you learn how to add a field to this table. You also learn how to create an additional table in the COUNTRY database.

The next task is to create an index for the Country table.

Creating an Index

To create an index for the Country table, click the Add button in the Indexes section of the Table Design window to display the Add Index dialog box. The Fields in Table list box displays three of the five fields: Capital Name, Country Name, and Population. The other two fields are not displayed because Memo and Binary fields cannot be indexed.

Type **CntryName** in the Index Name text box. In the Fields in Table list box, click Country Name to select it (see figure 14.7).

Figure 14.7
Adding an index for the Country Name field.

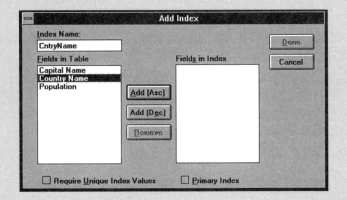

14

Then click the Add (Asc) button to create an ascending (Asc) index. The Country Name field is now removed from the Fields in Table list box and placed in the Fields in Index box. Click the Primary Index check box at the bottom of the dialog box. Finally, click Done to create the index.

The design of your database is complete and ready for you to add some actual data.

Adding Data to the Database

Before you add data, you should first close the Table Design window. Just click the Control-menu box in the window's upper-left corner. When the Control menu appears, choose Close. The Database window reappears. Click the Open

(continues)

Adding Data to the Database (continued)

button to display the Table Access window. Then click the Add button so that you can enter the data shown in table 14.2.

Table 14.2 Table Data for the COUNTRY Database

Country Name	Capital Name	Population
Canada	Ottawa	25652000
France	Paris	55632000
Germany	Berlin	78420000
Great Britain	London	57142000
Mexico	Mexico City	81163000
Russia	Moscow	284500000
Spain	Madrid	38900000
United States	Washington, D.C.	241078000

Figure 14.8 shows the data record entered for Canada, the first country in the database.

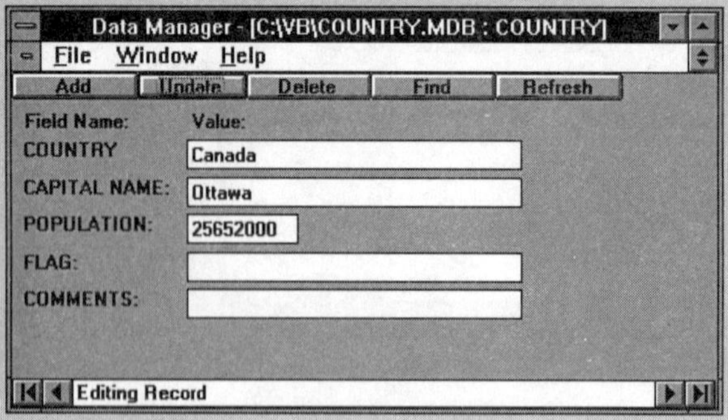

Figure 14.8 The data entered for Canada.

After entering each data record, click Update. When the Commit Changes dialog box opens, click Yes to save the data record. You can also trigger the save sequence by using the arrow controls at the bottom of the display. Instead of clicking Update, click an arrow button to move away from the current record. When you do, the Data Manager opens the Commit Changes dialog box.

The next task is to create the Flag field. The Flag field is a binary data field in which you can store bit-mapped graphics. You use this field to display an icon of each country's flag. You can add the data for the Flag field while you are inputting the data for the other fields or after the other entries are complete. The following exercise assumes that you have already entered the data for the other fields.

Creating the Flag Field

To add the Flag field, follow these steps:

1 Click the left-arrow button that displays a vertical bar at the bottom of the window.

The Canada record comes into view.

2 To add the flag icon image for a country, double-click in the blank Flag field.

The Enter Picture FilName dialog box opens.

3 For the Canadian flag, type the appropriate path and file name, as shown in table 14.3. Then click OK.

Figure 14.9 shows Canada's flag icon added to the database.

Figure 14.9
Adding Canada's flag icon to the database.

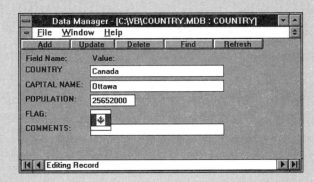

Table 14.3   Flag Field Data for the COUNTRY Database

Country Name	File Specification for Flag Field
Canada	C:\VB\ICONS\FLAGS\FLGCAN.ICO
France	C:\VB\ICONS\FLAGS\FLGFRAN.ICO
Germany	C:\VB\ICONS\FLAGS\FLGGERM.ICO
Great Britain	C:\VB\ICONS\FLAGS\FLGUK.ICO
Mexico	C:\VB\ICONS\FLAGS\FLGMEX.ICO
Russia	C:\VB\ICONS\FLAGS\FLGRUS.ICO
Spain	C:\VB\ICONS\FLAGS\FLGSPAIN.ICO
United States	C:\VB\ICONS\FLAGS\FLGUSA02.ICO

Click the right-arrow button (not the one with the vertical line and the arrow) to move to the next record. When the Commit Changes dialog box opens, click Yes. The France record opens so that you can add that country's flag icon.

(continues)

14

Creating the Flag Field   (continued)

In a similar manner, step through each record, and add the applicable flag icon. For the file specifications shown in table 14.3, a normal installation of Visual Basic is assumed. If your icon files are in another directory, specify the appropriate path instead.

The database is now complete. Your final task is to close the Data Manager.

Closing the Data Manager

To close the Data Manager, open the Data Manager's File menu. Choose Exit to end the Data Manager application.

Understanding the Data Control

As noted earlier, the Data control is the link between Visual Basic and a database. This control enables you to access data, for the most part without writing code. After you have attached a Data control to a database, you **bind** data-aware controls to the Data control. The data-aware controls display the contents of the fields of each record as you navigate with the Data control. If you make changes in a bound control, the updates are saved as you move to another record.

Bind
To connect a control to a Data control.

You place a Data control on a form just as you place any other control, either by double-clicking the Toolbox control or by selecting its icon and drawing the control directly on the form (see figure 14.10). Visual Basic gives the default name of Data1 to the first Data control you place on a form. Subsequent Data controls are named Data2, Data3, and so on.

Figure 14.10
The Data control.

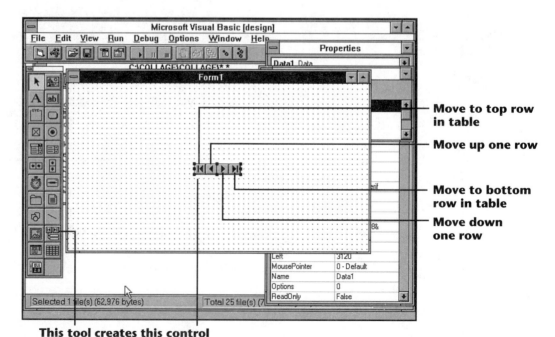

This tool creates this control

Adding a Data Control to a Form

Start a new project, and add a Data control to the form. Click the control to select it, and then open the Properties window. Notice that the name Data1 appears in the Object box. Select the DatabaseName property, and then click the ellipsis (. . .) button at the right edge of the Settings box. You see the Database Name dialog box, in which you can choose a database. (You can open the dialog box in one step by double-clicking the DatabaseName property.)

In the dialog box, select the COUNTRY.MDB file, and click OK. Notice that the full path and name of the database is now displayed in the Properties window (see figure 14.11).

Figure 14.11
The Properties window for Data1.

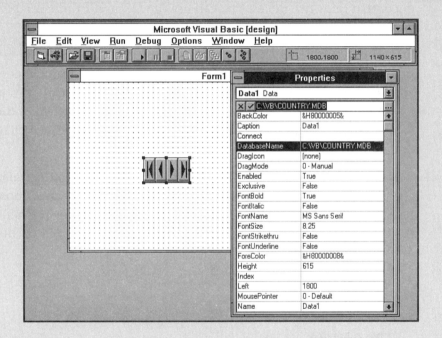

With the DatabaseName property now set, Visual Basic is prepared to access the database file and populate (or fill) the RecordSource property list. The RecordSource property specifies the underlying data source of the records that the bound controls on the form can access and display.

Scroll through the Properties window, and double-click the RecordSource property; you hear the hard disk engage as Visual Basic determines what tables exist in the database. In this case, there is only one, the Country table, which displays in the Settings box. If you have multiple tables, you can select one by clicking the down arrow next to the Settings box and then clicking your choice. Repeatedly double-clicking the RecordSource property enables you to cycle through the tables in the database.

Several other Data control properties exist, including Exclusive, Options, and ReadOnly. With these properties, you can control access to the database in multiuser environments. You can define who can have access, when, and for how long. SHARE.EXE must be loaded when access to the database will not be limited to just one user. If only one user at a time will have access to the database when your VB application is reading or writing the database, SHARE.EXE doesn't need to be loaded. Generally, you should load SHARE at all times if you are using a database. If you are running out of RAM, however, and access to a database table is always `Exclusive`, you don't need SHARE.EXE when your VB application is running.

Using Bound Controls

When the database is opened by the Data control, it creates a dynamic set of records called a Dynaset object. Similar to a table, a Dynaset has information in records and fields. The difference is that a Dynaset can also be the result of a query that joins two tables. You can use the Dynaset to add, modify, and delete records from the underlying table or tables.

The set of records created in the Dynaset object is represented by the `Recordset` property of a Data control. You access this information through controls on your application's form by binding (attaching) data-aware controls to the Data control. A bound control can display the data contained in a field of the current record, enable the user to edit the value, and save the modified data back to the underlying database.

A bound control is said to be *data-aware* because it links to the Data control. You can bind five types of controls: labels, images, text boxes, check boxes, and picture boxes. To bind a control, you set the appropriate property values. Visual Basic 3 defines the following new binding properties for each of the five data-aware controls:

    DataSource

    DataField

    DataChanged

The value of the `DataSource` property specifies the Data control being bound to. After adding a data-aware control to your form, you display the Properties window and then select the `DataSource` property. As with the `RecordSource` property, you can double-click to cycle through the available Data controls. Alternatively, you can select a Data control from the drop-down Settings list. Visual Basic then examines the set of records as defined by the Data control and determines what fields are available for binding. To complete the process, you select the `DataField` property and click the down arrow in the Settings box. Finally, you select a field from the drop-down list.

You don't have to bind a control in the order just explained. You can choose the `DataField` property first, but you need to know the name of the field. Then you type the field name in the Properties window. You can set the `DatabaseName`, `RecordSource`, and `DataField` properties at both design time and run time. However, the `DataSource` property can be set only at design time.

The `DataChanged` property is available only at run time. This property indicates whether data in the bound control has been modified. When a Data control moves to a new record, Visual Basic sets the value of this property to False. If the program or user modifies the data, Visual Basic sets the value of `DataChanged` to True. When the Data control moves to a new record, Visual Basic updates the data in the underlying database only if the value of `DataChanged` is True. Your program code can set this property value to False to prevent Visual Basic from modifying the data in the database.

Building the Sample Application

In the next several sections, you develop a sample application named COUNTRY.MAK. This application uses a Data control and bound controls to manipulate the COUNTRY.MDB database you created earlier in the chapter. With COUNTRY.MAK, you can display and move through all the information you stored about each country, including the text data and the flag icons.

When the application is complete, you will be able to edit individual fields, add and delete records, and even integrate data from another table. In the first sections, you get things working without writing a single line of program code. Later in the chapter, you add code to create a robust, interactive program.

Setting the Property Values

You should now have a form containing a single Data control. If not, start a new project, and add a Data control to the form. Using the Properties window, set the property values shown in table 14.4.

Table 14.4   Design-Time Property Values for the Form and Data Controls

Control	Property	Value
Form1	Caption	Country Database Demo
	Left	1005
	Top	1155
	Width	7485
	Height	5085
Data1	Caption	Countries
	DatabaseName	C:\VB\COUNTRY.MDB
	Exclusive	False
	Height	375
	Left	600
	Options	0
	ReadOnly	False

(continues)

Setting the Property Values   (continued)

Table 14.4   Continued

Control	Property	Value
	RecordSource	Country
	Top	3960
	Width	3495

The Exclusive, Options, and ReadOnly properties of the Data1 control are set to their default values.

The next step is to add bound controls.

Adding Bound Controls

To add the bound controls, follow these steps:

1 Add four text boxes and an Image control to the form.

These objects are the data-aware (bound) controls that become associated with various fields in the database.

2 Assign the property values listed in table 14.5. The four text boxes and the Image control are all bound to the same Data1 control.

Table 14.5   Design-Time Properties for Bound Controls

Control	Property	Value
Text1	DataField	Country Name
	DataSource	Data1
	Height	285
	Left	1680
	Top	240
	Width	1335
Text2	DataField	Capital Name
	DataSource	Data1
	Height	285
	Left	5400
	Top	720
	Width	1575
Text3	DataField	Population
	DataSource	Data1

Control	Property	Value
	Height	285
	Left	5760
	Top	240
	Width	1215
Text4	DataField	Comments
	DataSource	Data1
	Height	1095
	Left	600
	MultiLine	True
	ScrollBars	Vertical
	TabIndex	0
	Top	2160
	Width	2775
Image1	DataField	Flag
	DataSource	Data1
	Height	1575
	Left	5160
	Stretch	True
	Top	1800
	Width	1815

Note: *You can quickly specify the appropriate property value for each of the five controls by using multiple selection. After placing the controls, click the upper-left corner of the form. Drag the expandable selector box until it includes all the data-aware controls but not the Data control itself. Press F4 to open the Properties window; then double-click the* DataSource *property. Choose* Data1 *(the only Data control on the form) to assign that property value for all five data-aware controls.*

The Text4 text box permits the user to add comments. This text box is unique in that the MultiLine property is set to –1 (True), with a vertical scroll bar added to handle text that extends beyond the bottom of the control. The value of Text4's TabIndex property is set to 0 so that this text box has the focus when the application is first run.

The Image control displays the flag icons. This control's Stretch property is set to –1 (True) so that the small flag icons included with Visual Basic can be enlarged in the application. (Recall that Image controls do not have the AutoSize property of Picture controls. This property enables a Picture control to alter its size to match exactly any bit-mapped graphics. Image controls, however, display much faster than Picture controls.)

Adding Labels

The next task is to add labels. Follow these steps:

1 Add five labels to the form.

These labels identify the bound fields.

2 Assign the property values shown in table 14.6.

Table 14.6 Design-Time Properties for Labels

Control	Property	Value
Label1	Alignment	2 'Center
	Caption	Country
	Height	255
	Left	720
	Top	240
	Width	855
Label2	Alignment	2 'Center
	Caption	Capital
	Height	255
	Left	4440
	Top	720
	Width	855
Label3	Caption	Population
	Height	255
	Left	4560
	Top	240
	Width	975
Label4	Alignment	2 'Center
	Caption	Comments
	Height	255
	Left	1440
	Top	3480
	Width	975
Label5	Alignment	2 'Center
	Caption	Flag
	Height	255
	Left	5760
	Top	3240
	Width	735

3 Save the form as **COUNTRY.FRM**, and save the project as **COUNTRY.MAK**.

Now you're ready to see the Data control in action.

Running the Application and Editing Fields

To see how the VB Data control works, follow these steps:

1 Start the application.

When COUNTRY runs, the Country Name, Capital Name, Population, Flag, and Comments data of the first record (Canada) in COUNTRY.MDB display on the form, as shown in figure 14.12.

Figure 14.12
Starting the COUNTRY application.

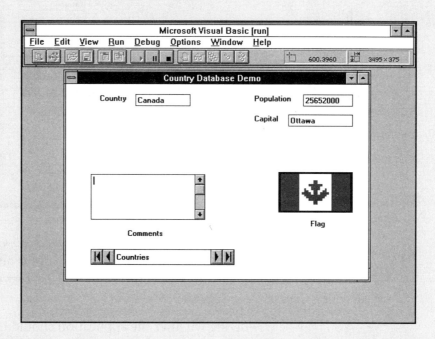

2 Click the arrow buttons on the Data control to move through the records of the database; you can move to the next, previous, first, and last records.

3 When you are satisfied that all the information you entered earlier is now accessible, return to the first record (Canada) by clicking the arrow button at the far left.

At the moment, the Comments field is blank because you didn't enter any information in this field when you created the database. Notice that the cursor is blinking in the Comments field. The Text4 control (Comments) has a TabIndex value of 0. So Text4 gets the focus when the application begins.

4 Now add the following text to describe Canada, the first country in the database:

Filled with lakes, both big and small, Canada could be called the "Lake" country. Canada has more than 40 lakes 50 miles long.

(continues)

Running the Application and Editing Fields (continued)

As you type, the text wraps at the edge of the control and scrolls down as you reach the bottom of the text box (see figure 14.13).

Figure 14.13
Adding comments to the Canada record.

You can cut, copy, and paste text by using Ctrl+X, Ctrl+C, and Ctrl+V, respectively. Notice that by simply setting the MultiLine and ScrollBar properties of the text box, you have a full-featured, mini-text-editor tied into your database.

You may be wondering whether the application should have a Save button. The answer is no. The capability to save a record is built into the Data control's functionality. When you click any arrow button to move off the current record, its contents are saved. You can confirm the save by moving back to the Canada record and checking that your comments have been preserved.

You can edit any of the other fields in much the same way that you edit the Comments field. Just click a data field to give it the focus. For example, you might change Russia's name to the Commonwealth of Independent States or use some other name. The only control whose contents you cannot edit at run time is the Image control, which displays the flag icons.

5 Now stop the application, and return to Design mode.

Next, you add code to improve the application's picture-adding capability.

Improving the Image Control

Recall that when you originally added the flag images to the database, you had to double-click the Flag field and then type the complete path and file name in the dialog box. Here you add program code that makes editing a Flag icon at run time easy. The code uses a Common Dialog control (or Common Dialog Box control) to create a standardized file-selection dialog box for the specification of a flag's icon file. Follow these steps:

1 Using the Toolbox, place a Common Dialog control on the form for the COUNTRY application. The default name for the control is `CMDialog1`.

2 Click the Common Dialog control to make sure that it is selected.

3 Using the Properties window, assign the property values shown in table 14.7.

Table 14.7 Design-Time Properties for the Common Dialog Control

Control	Property	Value
CMDialog1	Left	3960
	Name	CMD1
	Top	2520

4 Open the Code window and create the following `Image1_DblClick` event procedure:

```
Sub Image1_DblClick ()
    CMD1.Filter = "Bitmaps (*.bmp)¦*.bmp¦Icons (*.ico)¦*.ico¦
    Metafiles (*.wmf)¦*.wmf¦All Files (*.*)¦*.*"
    CMD1.DialogTitle = "Select a Picture File to Load"
    CMD1.FilterIndex = 2   'Sets default filter to *.ico
    CMD1.Action = 1        'Sets dialog type to Open File
    If CMD1.Filename <> "" Then
        Image1.Picture = LoadPicture(CMD1.Filename)
    End If
End Sub
```

5 Save the project on disk.

6 Run the program, and edit the Flag field by double-clicking any flag icon.

The Common Dialog springs to action, opening a file-selection dialog box named Select a Picture File to Load.

7 Using this dialog box, you can access the C:\VB\ICONS\FLAGS directory and choose an icon file.

(continues)

By default, the `FilterIndex` property is set to `Icons`, but you can change this value to any of the other graphics formats. Moving to another record saves the image to the database.

Using Code with Data Controls

The Data control and its bound controls handle all the work of moving through, editing, and saving records of your database. To add a new record or delete an outdated one, however, you must write code for the Data control.

You can duplicate the functionality of the Data control without having to use its arrow buttons. You can confirm this duplication by setting the value of `Data1`'s `Visible` property to False and adding a command button for each of the four arrow buttons. Then you add code to the appropriate button for each navigational command. For example, the code to move to the next record is

```
Data1.Recordset.MoveNext
```

Understanding the *Recordset* Property

The Recordset is the current set of records, created when you attach the Data control to a database, using the `DatabaseName`, `RecordSource`, and `Connect` (if needed) properties. The `Recordset` property is a reference to the Data control's underlying Dynaset object. A Dynaset is a dynamic set of records. You can use the Dynaset to add, change, and delete records from the underlying table(s). A Recordset has all the same properties and methods as the Dynaset; the `MoveNext` method is one example. Other methods you learn about here include the following:

```
MoveFirst, MoveLast, and MovePrevious
Edit
AddNew
Update
Delete
FindFirst, FindLast, FindNext, and FindPrevious
```

The `Move` methods (`MoveFirst`, `MoveLast`, and `MovePrevious`) correspond to the rest of the Data control's arrow-button actions. They move to the first, last, or preceding record of the Recordset to change the current record.

The `Edit` method opens the current record for editing by duplicating it in the copy buffer. This method is most often used with the Recordset's `LockEdits` property to enable changes to the current record while preventing other users from making alterations. The `AddNew` method sets all fields in the buffer to `Null` in preparation for creating a new record. The current record becomes this cleared-out record.

After you use `AddNew` or `Edit`, the `Update` method saves the data from the buffer to the database, replacing the current record. As you have seen, using one of the Data control arrow buttons automatically invokes `Update` when you move off the current record. The `Delete` and `Find` methods are discussed shortly.

Adding a New Record

To enable the user to add a new record in the COUNTRY application, do the following:

1 Add a command button to the form.

2 Set the property values shown in table 14.8.

Table 14.8   Design-Time Properties for a New Command Button

Control	Property	Value
Command1	Caption	New
	Height	495
	Left	4920
	Top	3840
	Width	975

3 Create the following `Click` event procedure for this first command button:

```
Sub Command1_Click ()
    Data1.Recordset.AddNew
    Text1.SetFocus
End Sub
```

Now you should run the program to verify that the new code is working properly.

Running the Application

Run the program, and then click the New button. The current record's fields are cleared from the bound controls, and a new record is added to the end of the Recordset. The `Text1.Setfocus` method places the cursor in the Country Name text box. Enter the data for a new country in the appropriate fields, as shown in table 14.9.

(continues)

14

Running the Application   (continued)

Table 14.9   New Country Record Data

Field Name	Value
Country Name	Japan
Capital Name	Tokyo
Population	123778000
Flag	C:\VB\ICONS\FLAGS\FLGJAPAN.ICO

Your form should resemble that in figure 14.14.

Figure 14.14
Japan joins the COUNTRY database.

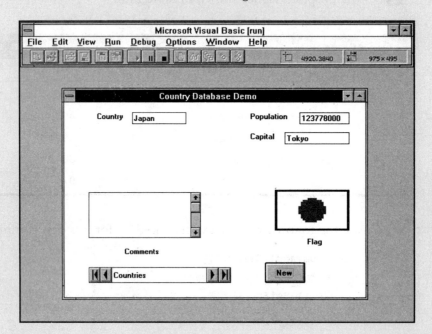

To move to the last record, click the right-arrow button at the far right of the Data control. The new record is saved and is now a new member of your database's family of nations.

You've always been able to edit and update existing records with the functionality built into the Data control. To delete a record, you need to add a new button and write additional program code.

Deleting an Existing Record

To add the capability to delete a record, follow these steps:

1 Return to Design mode.

2 Add a second command button to the form, and assign the property values shown in table 14.10.

Table 14.10	Design-Time Properties for the Delete Command Button	
Control	**Property**	**Value**
Command2	Caption	Delete
	Height	495
	Left	6240
	Top	3840
	Width	855

❸ Create the following `Click` event procedure for the second command button:

```
Sub Command2_Click ()
  Dim MSGBOX_TYPE As Integer
  Dim Msg As String
  MSGBOX_TYPE = 17     'Stop icon, OK & Cancel buttons

  Msg = "Are you sure you want to delete" & Chr$(10)
  Msg = Msg & Text1.Text
  If MsgBox(Msg, MSGBOX_TYPE, "Delete Record?") <> 1 Then
  ➥ Exit Sub

  Data1.Recordset.Delete
  Data1.Recordset.MoveNext
    If Data1.Recordset.EOF Then Data1.Recordset.MovePrevious
End Sub
```

14

Now you can save the project and then test the application again.

Running and Testing the Application

To run the application and test it, follow these steps:

❶ Run the sample application.

❷ Move to the record you just entered—Japan.

❸ Click Delete.

A message box asks you to confirm that you want to delete the current record (see figure 14.15).

(continues)

Running and Testing the Application (continued)

Figure 14.15
Deleting a record.

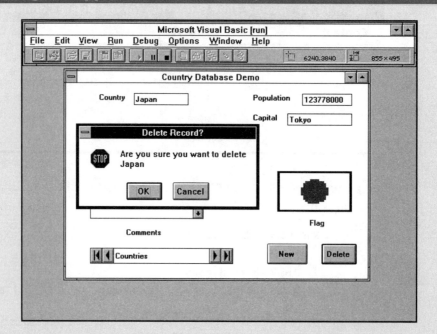

④ Now you can either delete the record or leave it intact.

If you click OK, the record is deleted, and the preceding record becomes current. To leave the Japan record intact, click Cancel.

Understanding How the Delete Button Works

The Delete method works by setting the Recordset's current record to Null and removing the current record from its underlying table(s). The deleted record remains current but becomes invalid. Any references to it produce an error. That result may not be a problem here, but sometimes you need to refer to the current record to do other things in your code. It's always a good idea, therefore, to use the MoveNext method to go to a new current record.

Using Queries with Single and Multiple Tables

Queries are another way to manipulate and extract data from a database. You can use a SELECT query that asks the database for a set of records matching specified criteria. You create these queries with Structured Query Language (SQL). If you intend to work with databases, learn SQL; it is virtually a universal database language. Good references are Que's *Using Access 2 for Windows* and Sams' *Access 2 Developer's Guide* and Sams' *Database Developer's Guide with Visual Basic 3*. The SQL syntax used in Visual Basic and Access is similar to that used internationally with many other software applications on microcomputers, minicomputers, and mainframe computers.

Structured Query Language (SQL)
A standardized language for querying, updating, and managing relational databases.

Furthermore, Visual Basic has facilities for connecting directly to external databases, using the appropriate SQL syntax for each. You can enter a SQL statement, instead of a table name, in the Data control's RecordSource property. The discussion here concerns SQL statements that you can define either at design time or run time with the Standard or Professional Edition of Visual Basic. You can use a SQL statement to define a set of records from single or multiple tables.

All SQL query statements have a standard format. With SQL, you can specify exactly what you want shown in the table that is the result of the query. The word *SELECT* is followed by a list of the fields you want shown in the result. If you want to see more than one field, separate the field names with commas. The asterisk (*) means "all the fields in the specified table(s)." The word *FROM* is followed by the name of the specific table(s) from which you want to extract data; separate multiple table names with commas. The selection criteria for the records that you want to see in the result table follow the word *WHERE*. This selection condition is used to "filter out" any records in the database that do not meet your criteria. Only the records that meet the condition are placed in the result table.

In Design mode, you can use a SQL statement, instead of a table, as the value of the RecordSource property. If you do, the WHERE clause identifies the specific data you want to retrieve. You can also use SQL SELECT statements in code at run time. For example, to create at run time with COUNTRY.MAK a Recordset that contains all fields from only the countries with a population greater than 100 million, you can use the following instruction:

```
Data1.RecordSource = "SELECT * FROM Country WHERE Population >
➥ 100000000"
```

You then follow this instruction with a Refresh method to re-create the Recordset. The resulting Recordset includes Japan, Russia, and the United States, if you have built the sample application as indicated earlier.

Adding a New Table and Field to COUNTRY.MDB

By tying together (linking) multiple tables with a query, you can greatly expand the power and efficiency of your database application. To explore this capability, use the Data Manager to create a new table.

Warning!

Remember, the DOS program SHARE.EXE must be running in order to access a database with the Data Manager while an application is loaded.

To activate the Data Manager, choose **D**ata Manager from the **W**indow menu.

Choose **O**pen Database from the **F**ile menu. Then choose **A**ccess from the submenu.

(continues)

Adding a New Table and Field to COUNTRY.MDB   (continued)

Now open the COUNTRY.MDB database you created earlier. Click the New button to open the Create New Table dialog box. Name the new table **Language** (see figure 14.16).

Figure 14.16
Creating the new Language table.

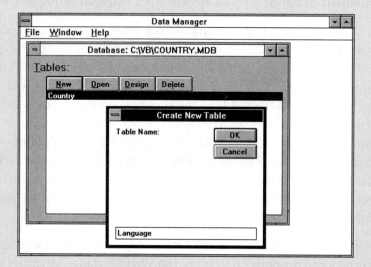

When you click OK, the Table Design window is displayed. Click the Add button in the Fields section to display the Add Field dialog box, as shown in figure 14.17. Enter **Language ID** as the first field's name, and then click the down arrow to select the field's data type. When you choose the Long Integer type, a small Counter check box appears. Check that box to select it (see figure 14.17).

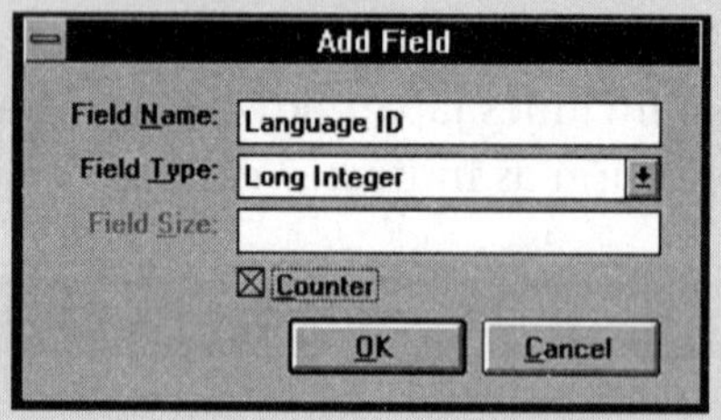

Figure 14.17
Completing the Add Field dialog box.

By checking the Counter box, you stipulate that the values for the Language ID field should be consecutive increasing integers. The value of Language ID is 1 for the first record. The value is automatically incremented by one as each new record is added. A field created with Counter makes an excellent primary key index.

Click OK, and click the Add button again to define another field. Name this field **Language Name**, and select the Text data type. Then give the field a size of **20**. Notice that when you select the Text type, the Counter box does not appear. The reason is that only fields created with a numerical data type (not Text) provide the option of choosing Counter.

Now create an index for the new table just as you did for the Country table. This time, enter **LangID** in the **I**ndex Name text box; then click Language ID to select it. Click **A**dd (Asc), and check the **P**rimary Index box (see figure 14.18).

Figure 14.18
Adding the LangID index.

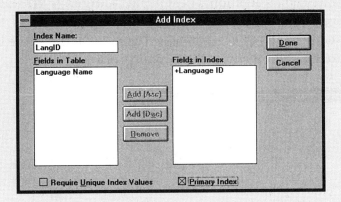

Click **D**one to create the index. Close the Fields Design window. Click the Language item in the Field**s** section of the table to make sure that it's selected. Then open the Table Access window for the Language table to add the data shown in table 14.11. You don't have to enter the Language ID value, because it auto-increments when you save each new record's data. (This is the reason you marked the **C**ounter check box when you defined the field type.)

14

Table 14.11 Language Table Data for the COUNTRY Database	
Language ID	**Language Name**
1	English
2	French
3	German
4	Russian
5	Spanish
6	Japanese

Figure 14.19 shows a data value that is entered.

Figure 14.19
Adding the Spanish language data value.

Data Manager - [C:\VB\COUNTRY.MDB : LANGUAGE]
File   Window   Help
Add   Update   Delete   Find   Refresh
Field Name: Value:
LANGUAGE ID: 5
LANGUAGE   Spanish
Entering New Record

(continues)

Adding a New Table and Field to COUNTRY.MDB   (continued)

With the new table created and filled with data, close the Table Access window. Click the Country table, and then click the **D**esign button to open the Table Design window. Add an additional field named **Language ID** and a field type of Long Integer. Do not check the **C**ounter check box in this case, because you are about to enter the ID values manually. Figure 14.20 shows the Language ID field added to the Fields section of the Country table.

Figure 14.20
The Language ID field added to the Country table.

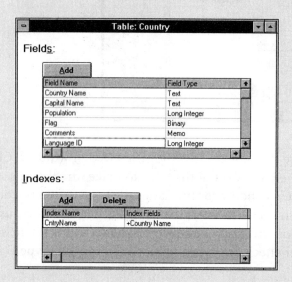

Close the Fields Design window. Then open the Table Access window on the Country table. Add the data shown in table 14.12. (Note that you need to add only the Language ID field data; the first field is the existing Country Name data.)

Table 14.12 Additional ID Field Data for the Country Table	
Country Name (Already Entered)	**Language ID**
Canada	1
France	2
Germany	3
Great Britain	1
Japan	6
Mexico	5
Russia	4
Spain	5
United States	1

Figure 14.21 shows the Language ID value of 5 that is added to the Mexico record.

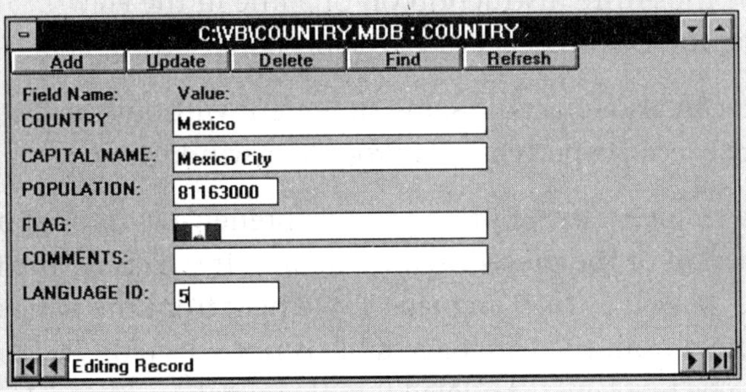

Figure 14.21
Specifying the
Language ID for
Mexico.

To close the Data Manager, choose Exit from the File menu.

Add both a Label (Label6) and a Text Box control (Text5) to the form. The text box will be made data-aware. Assign the property values given in table 14.13.

Table 14.13   Design-Time Properties for Additional Controls

Control	Property	Value
Label6	Caption	Language
	Height	255
	Left	4560
	Top	1200
	Width	855
Text5	DataSource	Data1
	Height	285
	Left	5520
	Top	1200
	Width	1455

Relating Two Tables

You may have guessed the reason for adding this new table and the additional field in the existing table. Now you can display the language for each country in your database, by *relating* information from one table to another. You establish a relationship between two tables by having fields in both tables that share a common value (the link field), such as student number, social security number, or part number.

In this case, the Language ID fields are the linking fields. You use this relationship with a SQL statement to *look up* the Language Name in the Language table. You then relate this language to the appropriate country in the Country table. This technique is referred to as a *table lookup*. It serves a vital purpose in database design, by reducing the duplication of data.

Here is the SQL-like instruction that links the fields from both tables:

```
Data1.RecordSource = "SELECT Country.*, [Language Name] FROM Country,
➥Language, Country INNER JOIN Language ON Country.[Language ID] =
➥Language.[Language ID] Order by [Country Name]"
```

You must type the entire instruction on one line in the `Form_Load` event procedure, replacing the existing `RecordSource` property setting.

Note that you can also enter the same statement without the quotation marks for the `RecordSource` property in the Properties window.

Although this chapter cannot provide a comprehensive tutorial on SQL, here is a brief explanation of the preceding instruction: It selects all the fields from the Country table, as well as the Language Table field from the Language table. (The Language ID field from the Language table is not selected.) Field names with spaces need to be bracketed. An INNER JOIN operation connects the Country and Language tables. The operation combines records from the two tables whenever there are matching values in a field common to both. The Language ID fields qualify on that score; in fact, the fields don't need to have the same name, as long as they are of the same data type. Finally, the resulting Recordset is ordered (`Order`) by the Country Name field, so that the records are sorted alphabetically.

Changing the *DataField* Property and Running the Application

The Visual Basic Help system contains descriptions of the various statements in the SQL. Remember that you can set the `DataSource` property only at design time. However, you can set the `DataField` property at either design time or run time. Here, you set the `DataField` property in the `Form_Load` event procedure, using the following instruction:

```
Text5.DataField = "[Language Name]"    ' Set field for text box.
```

The steps for making these changes are as follows:

1 If you are in Run mode, return to Design mode.

2 Enter the following in the `Form_Load` procedure:

```
Sub Form_Load ()
    Data1.DatabaseName = "C:\VB\COUNTRY.MDB"
    Data1.RecordSource = "SELECT Country.*, [Language Name] FROM
    ➥ Country, Language,
    Country INNER JOIN Language ON Country.[Language ID] =
    ➥ Language.[Language ID] Order by [Country Name]"

    Loading = True    'Set the global variable

    Data1.Refresh     'Open database & recordset
    Text5.DataField = "[Language Name]"    'Set field for text box
    Loading = False   'Turn off global variable
End Sub
```

3 Save the project.

Now you are ready to run and test the application.

❹ Run the application.

❺ Move through the records with the Data control's arrow buttons.

Each record now displays all the original data, as well as the language of each country. English is spoken in Canada, Great Britain, and the United States; Spanish is the language of both Spain and Mexico. In these instances, the application looks up the Language Name field in the Language table and displays the result on the form. This method saves the space that normally would have been taken up by the repetition of the language text. The savings are small here. However, they can add up quickly in actual database applications.

❻ Correct any errors in your program, and save this project as **COUNTRY**.

Other Database Tools

Although the Standard Edition offers much in the way of programmability, the Professional Edition is a vital tool for anyone interested in developing serious database applications. The programmatic data-access layer gives you tools to create new databases and modify the structure of existing ones. Three more data-aware controls are included.

The Professional Edition also includes Crystal Reports 2.0, a report writer that uses the Microsoft Access 1.1 engine for data access. Crystal Reports 2.0 includes a custom control to embed reports in applications. Also included are full ODBC support, additional code examples, and expanded documentation for creating data-aware controls.

If you also own Microsoft Access, you will find it invaluable for learning about database design and techniques. Databases created in Access or Visual Basic work interchangeably. Some early copies of Visual Basic 3 Standard Edition cannot interact with Access 2.0 databases. If your copy of Visual Basic cannot open an Access 2.0 database, call Microsoft for a copy of the Visual Basic Compatibility Layer Software for Access 2.0.

Chapter Summary

Visual Basic enables you to read and write data to databases as easily as you can read or write to files. You can create databases and tables by using the Data Manager. The Data control and the bound data-aware controls work together to provide powerful tools for manipulating databases. You can view all the data in a table or use a SQL query to obtain a subset of the data. You can obtain related data from two different tables (if they contain link fields) by joining the tables with a SQL query. You can develop a wide variety of data-aware applications, including easy-to-use visual front ends for existing databases. Typically, only a minimum of programming is necessary.

Test Your Understanding

True/False
Indicate whether the statement is true or false.

1. A database is a collection of data related to a particular topic or purpose.

2. The organization of a database is called its structure.

3. Each record in a table stores the information about one particular person, place, thing, or event.

4. All records in a table contain the same fields.

5. An index is a question you ask about the data in your database.

6. A secondary key field is a unique identifier for each record in the table.

7. Unlike file systems, database systems do not enable you to extract related information from different tables in the database.

8. You can join two tables only if both tables contain at least one field that is the same.

9. VB's Data Manager creates databases similar to those created in dBASE IV.

10. VB cannot access a database unless SHARE.EXE has been loaded.

Short Answer
Answer the following questions.

1. Write a SQL statement that makes the RecordSource of a Data control be all the fields in a table named Accounts.

2. Explain what properties you must set so that a Data control can access the data in the January table in Months, an Access 1.1 database.

3. What is meant by a data-aware control? What data is the control "aware" of? What properties are set to make it aware?

4. What controls are classified as bound controls? What properties does this group of controls have that make them "bound"?

5. What is a Dynaset?

6. What must be done so that VB can update a record in the database when the Data control moves to a new record?

7. Can you bind a text box to a Data control on another form? How?

8. If you want to access two different tables, must you have two separate Data controls? Why or why not?

9. What is a link field?

10. Explain how you can cause VB to perform an INNER JOIN of two tables. Sketch two linked tables, each with eight records. Show how VB would join the two tables. What would the resulting table look like?

Projects

Project 1:   Entering Data into an Access 1.1 Database

Use the VB Data Manager to enter the registrant data (from Project 1 of Chapter 12) into an Access 1.1 database. For this project, you need to create a database containing one table with six fields. Name the table **REGISTER**. Then write an application that displays the six data fields in bound Label controls. Each Label control should be labeled with the corresponding name of the field from the database. The user should be able to browse through the data by using the Data control's arrow buttons. Save the project as **C14P1**.

Project 2:   Adding Capabilities to the Seminar Registration Program

Now add to the capabilities of the program you created in Project 1. Include the capabilities to add, delete, and modify records in the REGISTER table. Save the project and the form as **C14P2**.

Project 3:   Adding the Capability to List Registrant Data for All Seminars

Add another feature to the program you created in Project 2. Include the capability to list the data for registrants in each of the four seminars. Save the project and the form as **C14P3**.

Project 4:   Adding Other Listing Capabilities

Add to the seminar registration program the following capabilities: (1) to list the data for records in each of the batches; (2) to list the data for individuals who have paid less than 50 percent of the charge for the seminar they will attend; and (3) to list the name of each registrant, each registrant's address, the name of the seminar that each registrant will attend, and the dates for the seminar.

To add these capabilities, you will need to add another (linked) Access 1.1 table to your database. This second table will contain the data for the four seminars and should be named **SEMINAR**. Your program should also allow a user to add, delete, and modify seminar records. Use a join to associate related data in the two tables. Save the project and the form as **C14P4**.

Project 5:   Placing a Second Data Control on the Form

Modify the application you created in Project 1 by placing a second Data control on the form. The RecordSource for this second Data control should be the SEMINAR table that contains the four records for the seminars—their numbers, titles, dates, and costs. The second control should not be visible. Add Label controls that can display data from the second table.

The user should be able to scroll through the REGISTER data (using the original, visible Data control) and see the associated (linked) data from the SEMINAR table. No SQL statements should be involved in the project. (*Hint:* The solution involves using the FindFirst method in the first Data control's Reposition event.) Save the project and the form as **C14P5**.

Index

Symbols

& (ampersand character) and access keys, 356
= (equal sign) and assignment statements, 18
0 data type, 135

A

About Program Manager dialog box, 113
Access, 455, 459, 487
access
    databases, 467
    dialog boxes (menus), 374
access keys
    ampersand character (&), 356
    captions, 76
    menu bar, 35
    menus, 356-357
    Options menu, 356
    text editor project, 184-185
ACE sample program (arrays), 285-290
Action property (Common Dialog Box control), 408
activating
    fonts (text editor project), 170
    menus, 35
Add Field dialog box, 461, 482
Add File command (File menu), 31, 407
Add Index dialog box, 463
Add Watch command (Debug menu), 261
Add Watch dialog box, 261
AddGridLine procedure, 439
AddItem method
    combo boxes, 319
    grids, 421, 430-431
    list boxes, 319
AddNew method (Recordset property), 476
algorithms, 10
    debugging, 245
aligning grids, 426-427
Alignment property, 78
allocating dynamic arrays with ReDim, 303
ampersand character (&) and access keys, 356
And (logical operator), 217
animation, 109-111
annuities, 332
ANSI (American National Standards Institute) code, 215
    Asc( ) and Chr$( ), 324-325
apostrophes (comments), 17
appending sequential files, 395
applications, *see* programs
AREACODE application (arrays), 296-300
arguments, 152-153
arrays, 283-285
    ACE sample program, 285-290
    AREACODE application, 296-300
    As clause, 291
    compartments (elements), 284
    constants as dimensions, 293

control arrays, 111-112
    text editor project, 189-197
    data entry, 288-290
    declaring, 290
    Dim instruction, 288, 290-292
    dynamic arrays, 302-305
    elements, 284
    Erase instruction, 304-305
    fixed allocation, 302-305
        in nonstatic positions, 295
    global arrays, 295
    menu control arrays, 379-380
    multidimensional arrays, 300-301
    multiple arrays, 292
    naming, 284
    Option Base instruction, 292-293
    output, 289
    preserving, 303
    procedure declarations with Static, 294
    scope, 293-294
    sizing (dynamic arrays), 302-304
    static arrays, 294-295
    subscriptrange parameter, 291-292
    subscripts, 284-285
    table lookup program, 295-300
    two-dimensional arrays, 300-301
    variables as dimensions, 293
As clause (Dim instruction), 291
Asc( ) function, 151, 324-325
ASCII (American Standard Code for Information Interchange)
    files, 392
    values (character values), 150-151
assignment statements, 18
attaching code to objects, 47
AUTOLOAD.MAK file, 125
AutoRedraw property, 108

B

BackColor property, 58, 372
    Shape controls, 107
background color, 102
    menus, 372
backgrounds (Shape controls), 107
BackStyle property (Shape controls), 107
backups, 50
binary files, 391, 405-407
binary systems, 2, 40
bit maps, 64
BlankText procedure
    invoking from event procedures, 179-182
    text editor project, 177-182
BMP files, 64
Boolean expressions, 214-215
    logical operators, 216-217
BorderColor property, 58
    Line controls, 104
borders
    cell borders (grids), 430
    Options menu, 359
    Shape controls, 107
BorderStyle property, 61
    Line controls, 104-105
BorderWidth property (Line controls), 104

bound controls, 468-469
    COUNTRY.MAK, 470-471
branching, 16, 206-210
    conditional branching, 206
        On-GoTo statement, 209-210
    For-Next loops, 231
    line labels, 206-207
    line numbers, 207
    On Error GoTo statement, 210
    unconditional branching, 206
        GoTo statement, 207-209
Break command (Run menu), 256
Break mode
    Ctrl+Break, 256
    Debug window, 254
breaking up code, 132
breakpoints (debugging), 260-261
    Stop instruction, 266
bugs, 3-4, 243-281
    algorithms, 245
    breakpoints, 260-261
    calls, 264-265
    comments, 17
    Debug window, 254-257
    debugging tools, 258-265
    development, 247
    execution errors, 253-254
    interactive testing, 244-245
    logic errors, 257-258
    modules, 246
    Option Explicit setting, 246
    output, 253
    run-time errors, 248-252
    Set Next Statement option, 265
    Show Next Statement option, 266
    Stop instruction, 266
    testing, 245, 247
    tools, 266-267
    tracing, 258-260
    watchpoints, 261-264
business-related programming, 8
buttons (clickable buttons and Toolbars), 115-118
bypassing For-Next loops, 226-227
ByVal keyword, passing by value, 153

C

calculator, 65-67
calls (debugging), 264-265
Calls command (Debug menu), 264
Calls dialog box, 264
Cancel button (menus), 353
CancelError property (Common Dialog Box control), 410-411
Caption property, 59
    access keys, 76
    controls, 76-77
    ellipses, 365
    forms, 28, 47
    menus, 352
carriage returns and Chr$( ), 325
cascading menus (submenus), 358-359, 362
case statements, 20

Case testing (Select Case statement), 220-222
case-sensitivity, 49
cells (grids), 416
   borders, 430
   editing, 443-446
   selecting, 422-424
   user-selected cells, 424
central processing unit (CPU), 2
Change event procedure, 180
   combo boxes, 321
   scroll bars, 322
character values, 150-151
   selecting for text boxes, 163
check boxes, 94-95
   Click procedures (text editor project), 172-173
   events, 95
   initializing (text editor project), 169
   properties, 94
check marks
   Greeting menu option, 376
   menus, 353, 368, 375-376
   toggling, 376
Checked property (menus), 375-376
Chr$( ) function, 324-325
Chr( ) function, 151
CInt( ) function, 330
Click event procedures, 22
   attaching code to objects, 47
   check boxes (text editor project), 172-173
   control arrays, 196
   menus, 370
   Modern menu options, 373-374
   Plain menu options, 373-374
   text editor project, 170
clickable buttons (Toolbar creation), 115-118
Clip property (grids), 416-417, 424-425
Clipboard, 112
CLng( ) function, 330
Close statement
   data files, 392
   sequential files, 394-395
closing
   binary files, 406
   Data Manager, 466
   forms, 28
   random files, 403
code, 3
   attaching to objects, 47
   breaking up, 132
   comments, 131-132
   Data controls, 476-480
   entering in Code window, 47-50
   event procedures, 48-49
   menus, 370-379
   placing, 127
   pseudocode, 11
   source code, 4
   tabbing, 132-133
   writing, 131-133
Code command (View menu), 167, 370
code modules, 124-125
   multiple code modules, 131
code procedures (menus), 371-373
Code window (menus), 370-371
Col property (grids), 418
ColAlignment property (grids), 426-427
color
   background color, 102
      menus, 372
   DrawMode property, 105
   FillColor/FillStyle properties, 107-108
   foreground color, 102
   properties, 58-59
color palettes, 58
Cols property (grids), 419-420
Columns property (list boxes), 320
ColWidth property (grids), 425-426
combo boxes, 316-321

command buttons, 82-83
   design, 43
   disabling (text editor project), 177-179
   enabling, 177
      text editor project, 180-181
   events, 83
   grids, 435-441
   properties, 83
Command1( ) array, 435-441
commands
   Debug menu
      Add Watch, 261
      Calls, 264
      Edit Watch, 263
      Instant Watch, 264
      Procedure Step, 259
      Set Next Statement, 265
      Show Next Statement, 266
      Single Step, 259
      Toggle Breakpoint, 260
   Edit menu
      Copy, 112
      Cut, 112
      Paste, 112
   File menu
      Add File, 31, 407
      Exit, 50, 126
      New, 199
      New Database, 459
      New Form, 56
      New Project, 43, 162, 354
      Open Database, 481
      Open Project, 65
      Print, 36, 117, 189, 198
      Remove File, 31
      Run, 26
      Save File As, 172
      Save Project, 50
      Save Project As, 172
   Message menu
      Text, 375
   Options menu
      Environment, 40
      Project, 41
   Run menu
      End, 39
      Start, 39, 49
   View menu
      Code, 167, 370
      New Procedure, 130
      Toolbar, 39
   Window menu
      Data Manager, 459, 481
      Menu Design, 352
      Project, 370
comments, 16-17
   apostrophes, 17
   code, 131-132
   COUNTRY.MAK, 474
   debugging, 17
   remarks, 17
commercial programming, 8
Commit Changes dialog box, 464
Common Dialog Box control, 407-411
   COUNTRY.MAK, 475
compartments (array elements), 284
compilers, 4
compound testing expressions, 216
concatenating strings, 147
conditional branching, 206
   On-GoTo statement, 209-210
conditional statements, 16, 19
conditional testing, 211-222
   Boolean expressions, 214-215
   compound testing expressions, 216
   If statement, 211-220
   If-Then statement (Else clause), 212-213
   logical operators, 216-217
   multiline If statements, 218-220
   relational operators, 215-216
   Select Case statement, 220-222
   single-line If statements, 211-212

   Then and Else clauses, 213
constants
   as array dimensions, 293
   declaring, 153-154
Continue command (Debug window), 257
control arrays, 111-112
   Click event procedures, 196
   creating, 190
   Index property, 190
   loops, 197
   text editor project, 189-197
Control menu, 62-65
control variables, redefining in For-Next loops, 230
controlled loops, 223
controls, 31-34, 55-122
   Alignment property, 78
   bound controls, 468-471
   Caption property, 76-77
   check boxes, 94-95
   combo boxes, 316-321
   command buttons, 82-83
   Common Dialog Box control, 407-411, 475
   copying, 111-112
   custom controls, 31
   Data control, 455-490
   deleting, 34, 70
   directory list boxes, 386-387
   drawing, 32
   drive list boxes, 386, 388
   Enabled property, 79
   event procedures, 75, 128-129
   file control, 386-389
   file list boxes, 386-387
   focus, 79
   frames, 100-101
   Grid control, 416-453
   Image controls, 96-98, 471, 475
   labels, 83-85
   Line controls, 102-105
   list boxes, 316-321
   menu names, 356-357
   MousePointer property, 81
   moving, 70
   Name property, 73-77
   option buttons, 95-96
   picture boxes, 98-100
   placing in forms, 31-33, 70-71
   prefixes, 76
   properties, 71-77
   resizing, 70
   scroll bars, 321-323
   selecting, 70
   Shape controls, 102, 106-108
   sizing, 33-34
   tab order, 80-81
   Tab_Order property, 79-81
   TabStop property, 79-81
   text boxes, 85-88
   Text property, 77
   timers, 323-324
   Toolbox, 70-77
   Value property, 79
   values, 72
   Visible property, 79
converting
   data types, 333-336
   numeric variables, 334-336
Copy button
   refining (text editor project), 181-182
   text editor project, 174-175
Copy command (Edit menu), 112
copying controls, 111-112
CopyLine procedure (grids), 440-441
corporate databases, 458
counter variables (For-Next loops), 223, 228-229
COUNTRY.MAK (databases)
   bound controls, 470-471
   comments, 474
   Common Dialog control, 475

Image control, 475
labels, 472
linking tables with queries, 481-485
property values, 469-470
records
    deleting, 478-479
    inserting, 477
    starting, 473
CPU (central processing unit), 2
Create New Table dialog box, 460, 482
creating
    animation, 109-111
    control arrays, 190
    databases, 459-466
    drop-down menus, 357
    forms, 56
    grids, 420-422
    indexes, 463
    menus, 354-361
    sequential files, 393-395
    tables, 461
    Toolbars with clickable buttons, 115-118
Crystal Reports 2.0 (database tool), 487
Ctrl+Break (Debug window), 256
CurDir$( ) function, 390
CurDir( ) function, 390
Currency data type, 135
cursors (text boxes), 162
custom controls, 31
custom menus, 351-384
Cut button
    refining (text editor project), 181-182
    text editor project, 174-176
Cut command (Edit menu), 112

D

data, 390-391
    binary files, 391, 405-407
    Close statement, 392
    entering in arrays, 288-290
    inserting in databases, 463-464
    LoadFile event procedure (grids), 449-451
    loading (grids), 447
    Open statement, 391
    random files, 391, 398-404
    sequential files, 391-398
    storing (grids), 447
data awareness (bound controls), 468
Data control, 455-490
    bound controls, 468-469
    code, 476-480
    placing on forms, 467
    property values, 469-470
    Recordset property, 476-480
Data Manager, 459
    closing, 466
    Flag field, 464-466
    SHARE.EXE, 459
    starting, 459-460
    Table Design window, 461-462
    Tables window, 460-462
Data Manager command (Window menu), 459, 481
data types, 134-135
    0, 135
    converting, 333-336
    Currency, 135
    Double, 135
    integers, 135
    Long, 135
    mixing, 334
    Single, 135
    strings, 136-137
    user-defined data types, 305-307
    Variant, 137
database management systems, *see* DBMSs
Database Name dialog box, 467
databases, 456-459
    Access, 459, 487

access, 467
bound controls, 468-471
building, 459-466
comments, 474
corporate databases, 458
COUNTRY.MAK, 469-475
Crystal Reports 2.0, 487
Data control, 455-490
Data Manager, 459
Dynasets, 468
fields, 457
Flag field, 464-466
Image control, 475
indexes, 457, 463
inserting data, 463-464
labels, 472
link fields, 458
primary key fields, 457
queries, 457, 480-487
records, 457
    deleting, 478-479
RecordSource property, 467
relational databases, 456
SQL (Structured Query Language), 457
structures, 457
Table Design window, 461-462
table lookup, 485
tables, 456
Tables window, 460-462
DataChanged property (bound controls), 469
DataField property (bound controls), 468
DataSource property (bound controls), 468
dates and Format$( ), 327
DblClick event procedure (grid text boxes), 446
DBMSs (database management systems), 456-458
Debug menu commands
    Add Watch, 261
    Calls, 264
    Edit Watch, 263
    Instant Watch, 264
    Procedure Step, 259
    Set Next Statement, 265
    Show Next Statement, 266
    Single Step, 259
    Toggle Breakpoint, 260
Debug window, 254-257
debugging, 3-4, 243-281
    algorithms, 245
    breakpoints, 260-261
    calls, 264-265
    comments, 17
    development, 247
    execution errors, 253-254
    interactive testing, 244-245
    logic errors, 257-258
    modules, 246
    Option Explicit setting, 246
    output, 253
    run-time errors, 248-252
    Set Next Statement option, 265
    Show Next Statement option, 266
    Stop instruction, 266
    testing, 245, 247
    tools, 258-267
    tracing, 258-260
    watchpoints, 261-264
decision making (conditional testing), 211-222
declarations, 138-139
    arrays, 290
    constants, 153-154
    dynamic arrays, 302-304
        with ReDim, 305
    fixed-sized arrays in nonstatic positions, 295
    form-level variables, 175
    multiple arrays, 292
    procedures with Static keyword (arrays), 294

variables, 133, 138-140
default buttons and MsgBox( ), 340
defaultstr parameter and InputBox$( ), 337
defining
    control variables (For-Next loops), 230
    interfaces, 44-46
    problems, 42
    record variables (random files), 401
Delete button (text editor project), 173
Delete method (Recordset property), 480
DeleteGridLine procedure (grids), 439-440
deleting
    controls, 34, 70
    menu options, 363
    records (COUNTRY.MAK), 478-479
    watch expressions, 263
design
    Command Button control, 43
    Label control, 42
    menus, 361-362
    programs, 9, 42-43
    random files, 399-401
    Text Box control, 42
design-time properties, 57
    PhoneBook, 432
development (debugging), 247
dialog boxes
    About Program Manager, 113
    access (menus), 374
    Action property, 408
    Add Field, 461, 482
    Add Index, 463
    Add Watch, 261
    Calls, 264
    CancelError property, 410-411
    Commit Changes, 464
    Common Dialog Box control, 407-411
    Create New Table, 460, 482
    Database Name, 467
    Edit Watch, 263
    ellipses, 365-366
    Enter Picture FilName, 465
    Environment Options, 40
    FileName property, 409
    Filter property, 409-410
    Instant Watch, 264
    menus, 361
    Name Please, 375
    New Database, 460
    New Procedure, 130
    New Program Object, 199
    Print, 36-37, 117
    Print project, 198
    Program Group Properties, 199
    Program Item Properties, 200
    Project Options, 41, 67
    Save File As, 172
    Save Project As, 172
    View Procedures, 183
DIALOGBX sample application, 342-346
DIB files, 64
digits (string conversion), 146-147
Dim instruction, 290-292
    arrays, 288
    As clause (arrays), 291
    placing, 292
    scope (arrays), 293-294
    variable declarations, 138-139
dimming drop-down menus, 369
Dir$( ) function, 390
Dir( ) function, 390
directory management, 389
directory list boxes, 386-387
disabling command buttons (text editor project), 177-179
disk drive errors (error handlers), 276
displaying
    pictures in Image controls, 97
    values in the Debug window, 256
Do-Loop loops, 233-238
Double data type, 135

drawing controls, 32
DrawMode property (Line controls), 105
drive errors, 276
drive list boxes, 386, 388
drop-down combo boxes, 317
drop-down list boxes, 317
drop-down menus
    creating, 357
    dimming, 369
DropDown event (combo boxes), 321
dynamic arrays, 302-305
Dynasets, 468
    Recordset property, 476-480

E

Edit menu commands
    Copy, 112
    Cut, 112
    Paste, 112
Edit method (Recordset property), 476
Edit Watch command (Debug menu), 263
Edit Watch dialog box, 263
editing
    cells (grids), 443-446
    fonts, 77-78
    forms, 56-62
    menus, 362-366
    text, 77-81, 189
    watch expressions, 263
elements (arrays), 284
ellipses, 365-366
Else clause, 213
    If-Then statement, 212-213
Empty value (Variant variables), 335
Enabled property, 79
    command buttons, 177
    menus, 368-369, 378-379
    timers, 324
enabling
    command buttons (text editor project),
      180-181
    error trapping, 269
    menu options, 353
End command (Run menu), 39
End Function statement, 130
End Sub statement, 130
ending programs, 210-211
endless loops, 222
Enter Picture FilName dialog box, 465
entering
    code in the Code window, 47-50
    data in arrays, 288-290
Environment command (Options
    menu), 40
environment options, 40-41
Environment Options dialog box, 40
EOF( ) function
    AREACODE application, 299
    binary files, 407
    random files, 404
    sequential files, 396
equal sign (=) and assignment state-
    ments, 18
Eqv (logical operator), 217
Erase instruction (arrays), 304-305
Erl function, 273-274
Err function, 273-274
error codes (Err statement), 274
error handlers, 276-277
    disk driver errors, 276
    numeric data, 276
    Resume instructions, 271-273
    writing, 273-275
error handling, 243-281
    debugging, 3-4, 244
    execution errors, 248, 250-252
      debugging, 253-254
    logic errors, 3, 249-281
      debugging, 257-258

On Error GoTo statement, 210
On Error Resume Next instruction, 271
run-time errors, 248-252
syntax errors, 3, 248-250
Error instruction, 274-275
error trapping, 267-277
    CancelError property, 410-411
    enabling, 269
    input, 268
    On Error GoTo 0 instruction, 271
    On Error instruction, 269
    programs (line numbers), 207
    TRAPERR, 269-271
    turning off, 271
Error$( ) function, 275
Error( ) function, 275
event procedures, 128-129
    BlankText procedure, invoking, 179-182
    Change, 180, 321-322
    check boxes, 95
    Click, 22
      attaching code to objects, 47
      control arrays, 196
    coding, 48-49
    command buttons, 83
    DblClick, 446
    DropDown, 321
    Form_Load, 167-169, 433-435
    Form_Resize procedure, 435
    forms, 67-69
    frames, 101
    grids, 421
    Image controls, 98
    Index parameter, 194
    KeyDown, 446
    KeyPress, 151, 441, 445
    labels, 85
    Load, 67-69
    LoadFile, 449-451
    MouseDown, 446
    naming (controls), 75
    option buttons, 96
    picture boxes, 100
    RowColChange, 422, 430-431, 445
    SaveFile, 447-449
    Scroll, 322
    SelChange, 430-431
    text boxes, 87-88
    text editor project, 167-182
    Timer, 324
    Unload, 69
    viewing (text editor project), 182-184
event-driven programming, 21
events, see event procedures
examples (Help), 38
execution errors, 248, 250-252
    debugging, 253-254
Exit command (File menu), 50, 126
Exit Do statement (Do-Loop loops),
    236-237
Exit For statement (loops), 231
exiting Visual Basic, 50
explicit declarations, 138-139

F

fields
    link fields, 458
    primary key fields, 457
    random files, 399
    tables, 457
file controls, 386-389
file list boxes, 386-387
File menu commands
    Add File, 31, 407
    Exit, 50, 126
    New, 199
    New Database, 459
    New Form, 56
    New Project, 43, 162, 354

Open Database, 481
Open Project, 65
Print, 36, 117, 189, 198
Remove File, 31
Run, 26
Save File As, 172
Save Project, 50
Save Project As, 172
file position pointers, 405-406
FileDateTime( ) function, 390
FileLen( ) function and sequential
    files, 397
FileName property (Common Dialog Box
    control), 409
files
    ASCII files, 392
    binary files, 391, 405-407
    CurDir$( ) function, 390
    CurDir( ) function, 390
    data files, 390-391
    Dir$( ) function, 390
    Dir( ) function, 390
    FileDateTime( ) function, 390
    GetAttr( ) function, 390
    managing, 389
    processing, 385-414
    random files, 391, 398-404
    sequential files, 391-398
    SetAttr( ) function, 390
FillColor property, 58
    Shape controls, 107-108
FillStyle property (Shape controls),
    107-108
Filter property (Common Dialog Box
    control), 409-410
financial functions, 332-333
Fix( ) function, 329
fixed arrays, 302-305
    declaring in nonstatic positions, 295
    random files, 399
FixedAlignment property (grids), 426-427
FixedCols property (grids), 418-419
FixedRows property (grids), 418-419
Flag field (tables), 464-466
floating text boxes
    DblClick event procedure, 446
    grids, 441-443
    KeyDown event procedure, 446
    KeyPress event procedure, 445
    LoadFile event procedure, 449-451
    MouseDown event procedure, 446
    PhoneBook, 442
    RowColChange event procedure, 445
    SaveFile event procedure, 447-451
flow of programs, 16
flowcharts, 11
focus (controls), 79
    SetFocus method, 171
fonts
    activating (text editor project), 170
    editing, 77-78
    initializing (text editor project), 169
    Style menu, 373
    TrueType fonts, 77
For loops (control arrays), 198
For-Next loops, 223-228
    AREACODE application, 300
    array sample program, 285-290
    branching, 231
    bypassing, 226-227
    counter variables,
      excluding, 228
      redefining, 230
    Exit For statement, 231
    indenting, 230
    negative increments, 226
    nesting, 229-230
    single Next statements, 231
    single-line For-Next loops, 228-231
    Step clause, 225-226
    syntax, 227
    variables in For statements, 227-228

ForeColor property, 58
foreground color, 102
form files, 124
form-level variables
    command button array (grids), 436
    declaring, 175
    scope, 140
Form_Load event procedure
    grids, 420
    initializing code, 167-168
    PhoneBook, 433-435
    text editor project, 167-169
Form_Resize procedure (PhoneBook), 435
Format$( ) function, 325-327
formatting files, 40
forms, 55-92
    background color, 372
    BorderStyle property, 61
    calculator, 65-67
    Caption property, 28, 47, 59
    closing, 28
    color properties, 58-59
    control placement, 31-33, 70-71
    creating, 56
    Data control placement, 467
    editing, 56-62
    event procedures, 67-69, 128-129
    Load event, 67-69
    location properties, 60
    Name property, 28, 47, 59-60
    Picture property (picture placement),
        113-115
    program development environment,
        27-28
    properties, 56-58
    Properties window, 28
    size properties, 60
    sizing, 28
    start-up forms, 125
    text files, 185-189
    text properties, 59-60
    Unload event, 69
    Visible property, 61-62
    WindowState property, 64-65
frames, 100-101
Function procedures, 130-131
functions
    Asc( ), 151, 324-325
    Chr$( ), 324-325
    Chr( ), 151
    CInt( ), 330
    CLng( ), 330
    CurDir$( ), 390
    CurDir( ), 390
    Dir$( ), 390
    Dir( ), 390
    EOF( ), 299, 396, 404, 407
    Erl, 273-274
    Err, 273-274
    Error$( ), 275
    Error( ), 275
    FileDateTime( ), 390
    FileLen( ), 397
    financial functions, 332-333
    Fix( ), 329
    Format$( ), 325-327
    GetAttr( ), 390
    InputBox$( ), 336-338
    InputBox( ), 338
    InStr( ), 148
    Int( ), 329
    IsNumeric( ), 336
    Len( ), 148, 402
    Loc( ), 404, 407
    LTrim$( ), 147
    LTrim( ), 147
    Mid$( ), 149
    MsgBox( ), 338-341
    Now( ), 324
    numeric functions, 327-332
    Rnd( ), 330-332
    rounding functions, 329-330

RTrim$( ), 148
RTrim( ), 148
Seek( ), 407
SetAttr( ), 390
Str$( ), 147
Trim$( ), 148
Trim( ), 148
Val( ), 147
variable passing, 152-153

G

general procedures, 129-130
    BlankText, 177-182
Get statement
    binary files, 405-406
    random files, 403
GetAttr( ) function, 390
global arrays, 295
global constants, 154
global variables
    logic errors, 257
    scope, 140, 142
GoTo statement
    spaghetti logic, 209
    unconditional branching, 207-209
graphical user interfaces (GUIs), 5
graphics, 93-122
    AutoRedraw property, 108
    background color, 102
    bit maps, 64
    displaying in Image controls, 97
    file formats, 64
    foreground color, 102
    grids, 428
    icons, 64, 101
    Line controls, 101-105
    metafiles, 64
    methods, 101
    persistent graphics, 108-109
    picture boxes, 98-100
    pictures, 101
        moving at run time, 109-111
        placement, 113-115
        properties, 62-64
    Shape controls, 101-102, 106-108
GREETER (menus), 354-361
    access keys, 356-357
    completing, 381-382
    drop-down menus, 357
    indentation, 358
    Options menu, 355, 359
    running, 360-361
    submenus (cascading menus), 358-359
Greeting menu option (check marks), 376
GRIDEX1.MAK, 422
GridLines property, 429-430
grids, 416-453
    AddGridLine procedure, 439
    AddItem method, 421, 430-431
    alignment, 426-427
    cells, 416
        borders, 430
        editing, 443-446
        selection, 422-424
    Clip property, 416-417, 424-425
    Col property, 418
    ColAlignment property, 426-427
    Cols property, 419-420
    ColWidth property, 425-426
    command button array, 435-441
    Command1( ) array, 435-441
    CopyLine procedure, 440-441
    creating, 420-422
    data, storing/loading, 447
    DblClick event procedure, 446
    DeleteGridLine procedure, 439-440
    design-time properties (PhoneBook), 432
    event procedures, 421
    FixedAlignment property, 426-427

FixedCols property, 418-419
FixedRows property, 418-419
floating text boxes, 441-443
form-level variables (command button
    array), 436
Form_Load procedure, 420
    PhoneBook, 433-435
Form_Resize procedure (PhoneBook), 435
GridLines property, 429-430
GridStatusRestore procedure, 437
GridStatusSave procedure, 436
HighLight property, 429-430
KeyDown event procedure, 446
KeyPress event procedure, 441, 445
LeftCol property, 428-429
LoadFile event procedure, 449-451
MouseDown event procedure, 446
navigation, 428-429
PhoneBook, 431-435
Picture property, 417, 428
pictures, 416, 428
property values, 420
RemoveItem method, 421, 430-431
Row and Col property, 416
Row property, 418
RowColChange event procedure, 422,
    430-431, 445
RowHeight property, 425-426
Rows property, 419-420
SaveFile event procedure, 447-449
ScrollBars property, 428-429
SelChange event, 430-431
ShowTextBox procedure, 442-443
ShutDown procedure, 441
strings, 416
Tab key, 444-445
tab-delimited format (strings), 417
text boxes, 442
Text property, 416, 418
TextHeight property, 426
TextWidth property, 426
TopRow property, 428-429, 439
UnSelect procedure, 438
user-selected cells, 424
GridStatusRestore procedure, 437
GridStatusSave procedure, 436
grouping option buttons, 95
GUIs (graphical user interfaces), 5

H-I

Height property, 60
Help, 37-38
    examples, 38
    SQL (Structured Query Language), 486
    tutorials, 38
hiding the Toolbar, 39
HighLight property (grids), 429-430

I/O (input/output) activity in random
    files, 398
Icon property, 63
icons, 64
    graphics, 101
    MsgBox( ) function, 340
IconWorks, 63
If statement
    conditional testing, 211-220
    multiline If statements, 218-220
    nested If statements, 217-218
    single-line If statements, 211-212
If-Then statement (Else clause), 212-213
Image control, 96-98
    COUNTRY.MAK, 475
    events, 98
    Stretch property, 97, 471
Imp (logical operator), 217
implicit declaration, 138-139
indentation
    loops, 230
    menus, 358

independent programmers, 7-8
Index property
    control arrays, 190
    event procedures, 194
indexes
    creating, 463
    databases, 457
    menus, 353
infinite loops, 222
initializing
    check boxes (text editor project), 169
    code with Form_Load, 167-168
    fonts (text editor project), 169
input, 5, 10, 14
    error trapping, 268
Input # statement (sequential files), 396
input boxes, 315
    DIALOGBX sample application, 342-346
input screen, 10
input statements, 18-19
InputBox$( ) function, 336-338
InputBox( ) function, 338
inserting
    data in databases, 463-464
    menu options, 363-364
    records (COUNTRY.MAK), 477
Instant Watch command (Debug menu), 264
Instant Watch dialog box, 264
Instant Watch option (watchpoints), 263-264
InStr( ) function, 148
Int( ) function, 329
integers, 135
interactive testing (debugging), 244-245
interest calculations, 333
interfaces, 5
    defining, 44-46
    Properties window, 28-29
    text editor project, 164-167
    Windows standards, 6
interpreters, 4
Interval property (timers), 323
investments, 332
invoking BlankText from event procedures, 179-182
IsNumeric( ) function, 336

J-K-L

keyboard (focus), 79
keyboard shortcuts, 366-367
KeyDown event procedure (grid text boxes), 446
KeyPress event procedure, 151
    grid text boxes, 445
    grids, 441
labels, 83-85
    CONTRY.MAK, 472
    design, 42
    events, 85
    line labels, 206-207
    properties, 84-85
languages (programming), 2-4
LargeChange property (scroll bars), 322
leading spaces, trimming from strings, 147-148
Left property, 60
LeftCol property (grids), 428-429
Len( ) function, 148
    random files, 402
Line controls (graphics), 101-105
line feeds and Chr$( ), 325
Line Input # statement (sequential files), 397
line labels, 206-207
line numbers, 207
link fields (tables), 458
linking tables with queries (COUNTRY.MAK), 481

list boxes, 316-321
List property, 320
ListCount property, 320
ListIndex property, 319
listing 1.1. QBasic program example, 6
Load event procedure, 67-69
LoadFile event procedure (grid text boxes), 449-451
loading data (grids), 447
loan calculations, 332-333
Loc( ) function
    binary files, 407
    random files, 404
local constants, 153
local variables (scope), 140-141
location properties, 60
    Line controls, 103-104
    Shape controls, 107
logic errors, 3, 249, 252
    debugging, 257-258
    global variables, 257
logic flow, *see* program flow
logic junctures, 211
logical operators, 216-217
Long data type, 135
loops, 20, 222-238
    control arrays, 198
    controlled loops, 223
    Do-Loop loops, 233-238
    Exit For statement, 231
    For-Next loops, 223-228
        AREACODE application, 300
    indenting, 230
    infinite loops, 222
    sequential files, 397
    While-Wend loops, 231-233
LTrim$( ) function, 147
LTrim( ) function, 147

M

MAK files, 29
managing
    directories, 389
    files, 389
manipulating strings, 148
math operators, 145-146
mathematical functions and statements, 327-332
Max property (scroll bars), 322
memory (variables), 15
menu bar, 34-37
menu control arrays, 379-380
Menu Design command (Window menu), 352
Menu Design window, 352-354
Menu outline (Menu Design window), 353-354
    indentation, 358
menus
    access keys, 356-357
    activating, 35
    background color, 372
    Cancel button, 353
    captions, 352
    check marks, 353, 368, 375-376
    Checked property, 375-376
    Click procedure, 370
    code procedures, 371-373
    Code window, 370-371
    coding, 370-379
    Control, 62-65
    control names, 356-357
    creating, 354-361
    custom menus, 351-384
    deleting options, 363
    designing, 361-362
    dialog boxes, 361
        access, 374
    drop-down menus, 357
        dimming, 369

editing, 362-366
ellipses (dialog boxes), 365-366
Enabled property, 368-369, 378-379
enabling options, 353
fonts, 373
GREETER, 354-361
indentation, 358
indexes, 353
inserting options, 363-364
Menu Design window, 352-354
Modern style option, 378
moving options, 362-363
naming, 352
OK button, 353
Options menu, 40-42, 359
    access keys, 356
    GREETER, 355
separator bars, 364-365
shortcut keys, 353, 366-367
Style menu, programming, 373
submenus (cascading menus), 358-359, 362
switching off options, 377-378
text, 352
toggles, 361
Window menu, 37
message boxes, 315, 338-341
    DIALOGBX sample application, 342-346
    modality, 340-341
Message menu commands
    Text, 375
metafiles, 64
methods
    AddItem, 319, 421, 430-431
    combo boxes, 319
    graphics methods, 101
    list boxes, 319
    RemoveItem, 319, 421, 430-431
    SetFocus, 171
Mid$( ) function, 149
Min property (scroll bars), 322
mixing data types, 334
modality in message boxes, 340-341
Modern menu options (Click procedure), 373-374
Modern style menu option, 378
module-level constants, 153
module-level variables (scope), 140-142
modules, debugging, 246
MouseDown event procedure (grid text boxes), 446
MousePointer property, 81
Move methods (Recordset property), 476
moving
    controls, 70
    menu options, 362-363
    pictures at run time, 109-111
MSAFINX.DLL (financial functions), 332-333
MsgBox statement, 341-342
MsgBox( ) function, 338-341
msgstr parameter, 339
multicolumn lists (list boxes), 318
multidimensional arrays, 300-301
Multiline property
    If statements, 218-220
    text boxes, 163
multipart format strings, 326
multiple arrays, 292
multiple code modules, 131
MultiSelect property (list boxes), 320
MYCOINS.RAN (random file program), 403-404

N

Name Please dialog box, 375
Name property, 59-60
    controls, 73-77
    forms, 28, 47
    Line controls, 103
    Shape controls, 107

naming
  arrays, 284
  conventions, 129
  event procedures (controls), 75
  menus, 352
  procedures, 131
  reserved words, 129
navigating grids, 428-429
negative increments (For-Next loops), 226
nesting
  Do-Loop loops, 237-238
  For-Next loops, 229-230
  If statements, 217-218
  procedure calls, 264
New command (File menu), 199
New Database command (File menu), 459
New Database dialog box, 460
New Form command (File menu), 56
New Procedure command (View menu), 130
New Procedure dialog box, 130
New Program Object dialog box, 199
New Project command (File menu), 43, 162, 354
NewIndex property (combo boxes and list boxes), 320
Next statement (single statements), 231
Not (logical operator), 217
Now( ) function, 324
Null value (Variant variables), 335
numeric fields (random files), 400
numeric functions and statements, 327-332
numeric type conversion, 334-336
numeric values
  error handlers, 276
  Format$( ) function, 325-326
  programs, 133-147
  random numbers, 330-332
  rounding, 330
  string conversion, 146-147
numeric variables, 135-136

O

objects, attaching code to, 47
OK button (menus), 353
OLE (Object Linking and Embedding), 74
On Error GoTo 0 instruction (error trapping), 271
On Error GoTo statement, 210
On Error instruction (error trapping), 269
On Error Resume Next instruction (error handling), 271
On-GoTo statement (conditional branching), 209-210
OOP (Object Oriented Programming), 21-22
Open Database command (File menu), 481
Open Project command (File menu), 65
Open statement
  binary files, 405
  data files, 391
  random files, 401-402
  sequential files, 393-394
  Write # statement, 394
Option Base instruction (arrays), 292-293
option buttons, 95-96
Option Explicit setting (debugging), 246
Options menu, 40-42, 359
  access keys, 356
  borders, 359
  environment options, 40-41
  GREETER, 355
  project options, 41-42
  style, 359
Options menu commands
  Environment, 40
  Project, 41

options parameter and MsgBox( ), 339-340
Or (logical operator), 217
organizational programmers, 8
output, 5, 10, 14
  arrays, 289
  debugging, 253
output statements, 19

P

palettes, color, 58
passing variables, 152-153
Paste button
  text editor project, 174-176
  verifying (text editor project), 181
Paste command (Edit menu), 112
persistent graphics, 108-109
PhoneBook (grids), 431-435
  AddGridLine procedure, 439
  CopyLine procedure, 440-441
  data, storing/loading, 447
  DblClick event procedure, 446
  DeleteGridLine procedure, 439-440
  design-time properties, 432
  floating text boxes, 442
  form-level variables (command button array), 436
  Form_Load procedure, 433-435
  Form_Resize procedure, 435
  GridStatusRestore procedure, 437
  GridStatusSave procedure, 436
  KeyDown event procedure, 446
  KeyPress event procedure, 445
  LoadFile event procedure, 449-451
  MouseDown event procedure, 446
  RowColChange event procedure, 445
  SaveFile event procedure, 447-449
  ShowTextBox procedure, 442-443
  ShutDown procedure, 441
  Tab key, 444-445
  TopRow property, 439
  UnSelect procedure, 438
picture boxes, 98-100
Picture property, 63-64
  grids, 417, 428
pictures, 93-122
  bit maps, 64
  displaying in Image controls, 97
  file formats, 64
  graphics, 101
  grids, 416, 428
  icons, 64
  metafiles, 64
  moving at run time, 109-111
  properties, 62-64
  see also graphics, 101
placing
  code, 127
  controls in forms, 31-33, 70-71
  Data controls on forms, 467
  Dim instructions (arrays), 292
  pictures into Picture properties, 113-115
Plain menu options (Click procedure), 373-374
pointers, 405-406
portability of random files, 398
positioning menu options, 362-363
predefined format strings, 327
prefixes (controls), 76
preserving arrays, 303
primary key fields (tables), 457
principal calculations, 333
Print command (File menu), 36, 117, 189, 198
Print dialog box, 36-37, 117
Print project dialog box, 198
printing
  Format$( ) function, 325
  text editor project from Program manager, 198
  text files, 188

problem definition, 9-24, 42
problem solving, 9-10
Procedure Step command (Debug menu), 259
procedure-step tracing, 259
procedures, 21, 128-131
  AddGridLine, 439
  BlankText, 177-182
  Click, 170, 370
    Modern menu options, 373-374
    Plain menu options, 373-374
  code procedures (menus), 371-373
  CopyLine, 440-441
  declaring with Static keyword (arrays), 294
  DeleteGridLine, 439-440
  Function procedures, 130-131
  general procedures, 129-130
  GridStatusRestore, 437
  GridStatusSave, 436
  naming, 131
  nested procedure calls, 264
  ShowTextBox, 442-443
  ShutDown, 441
  Sub Main procedures, 126
  Sub procedures, 130-131
  UnSelect, 438
  variable passing, 152-153
  see also event procedures
processing files, 385-414
Professional Edition (Visual Basic), 26
program development environment, 27-31
  forms, 27-28
  Project window, 29-30
  Properties window, 28-29
  Toolbox, 30-31
program flow, 16, 205-242
Program Group Properties dialog box, 199
Program Item Properties dialog box, 200
Program Manager, 198-200
programmer-defined procedures, viewing, 183
programming, 123-160
  algorithms, 10
  arrays, 283-285
  assignment statements, 18
  binary systems, 2
  branching, 16
  case statements, 20
  character values, 150-151
  Click events, 22
  code placement, 127
  coding, 3
  comments, 16-17, 131-132
  conditional statements, 19
  controls, 31-34
  CPU (central processing unit), 2
  event-driven programming, 21
  flowcharts, 11
  independent programmers, 7-8
  input, 5, 10, 14, 18-19
  interfaces, 5
  languages, 2-4
  loops, 20
  math operators, 145-146
  menu bar, 34-37
  OOP (Object Oriented Programming), 21-22
  Options menu, 40-42
  organizational programmers, 8
  output, 5, 10, 14, 19
  problem definition, 9, 42
  problem solving, 9-10
  procedures, 21, 128-131
  pseudocode, 11
  random files, 398
  recreation, 7
  scope (variables), 140-143
  source code, 4
  Style menu, 373
  Toolbar, 39
  users, 2

utilities, 7
variables, 14-15
    declarations, 133, 138-140
    passing, 152-153
Windows, 1-24
writing code, 131-133
programming statements, 13-21
programs, 1-2
    AUTOLOAD.MAK file, 125
    code modules, 124-125
    constants, 153-154
    data types, 134-135
    design, 9, 42-43
    form files, 124
    initializing code (Form_Load event
        procedure), 167-168
    numbers, 133-147
    resuming (Debug window), 256-257
    running, 49-50
    start-up forms, 125
    stopping, 126
    strings, 136-137
    Sub Main procedures, 126
    systems software, 2
    terminating, 210-211
    testing, 49-50
    text, 133-147
    translation programs, 2, 4
    variables, 133-134
    Variant data type, 137
Project command
    Options menu, 41
    Window menu, 370
project options, 41-42
Project Options dialog box, 41, 67
Project window (program development
    environment), 29-30
projects (MAK files), 29
prompt parameter and InputBox$( ), 337
properties
    Action, 408
    Alignment, 78
    AutoRedraw, 108
    BackColor, 58, 107, 372
    BackStyle, 107
    border properties, 107
    BorderColor, 58, 104
    BorderStyle, 61, 104-105
    BorderWidth, 104
    CancelError, 410-411
    Caption, 59, 76-77
    check boxes, 94
    Checked, 375-376
    Clip, 416-417, 424-425
    Col, 418
    ColAlignment, 426-427
    color properties, 58-59
    Cols, 320, 419-420
    ColWidth, 425-426
    command buttons, 83
    controls, 71-77
    DataChanged, 469
    DataField, 468
    DataSource, 468
    design-time properties, 57
    DrawMode, 105
    Enabled, 79, 177, 324, 368-369, 378-379
    FileName, 409
    FillColor, 58, 107-108
    FillStyle, 107-108
    Filter, 409-410
    FixedAlignment, 426-427
    FixedCols, 418-419
    FixedRows, 418-419
    ForeColor, 58
    forms, 56-58
    frames, 101
    GridLines, 429-430
    Height, 60
    HighLight, 429-430

Icon, 63
Index (control arrays), 190
Interval, 323
labels, 84-85
LargeChange, 322
Left, 60
LeftCol, 428-429
List, 320
ListCount, 320
ListIndex, 319
location properties, 60, 103-104, 107
Max, 322
Min, 322
MousePointer, 81
Multiline, 163
MultiSelect, 320
Name, 59-60, 73-77, 103, 107
NewIndex, 320
option buttons, 96
Picture, 63-64, 417, 428
picture boxes, 99-100
picture properties, 62-64
Recordset, 476-480
RecordSource, 467
Row, 418
Row and Col, 416
RowHeight, 425-426
Rows, 419-420
run-time properties, 57
ScrollBars, 428-429
Selected, 320
Shape, 106
size properties, 60
SmallChange, 322
Sorted, 319
Stretch, 97, 471
Style, 320
Tab_Order, 79-81
TabIndex, 80-81
TabStop, 79-81
Text, 320, 416, 418
text, 59-60, 78-81
text boxes, 86-87, 162
    text editor project, 162-164
TextHeight, 426
TextWidth, 426
toggling (text editor project), 170
Top, 60
TopIndex, 320
TopRow, 428-429, 439
Value, 79, 322
Visible, 61-62, 79, 105
Width, 60
WindowState, 64-65
Properties window, 28-29
property values
    Data controls, 469-470
    grids, 420
    text editor project, 165-166
pseudocode, 11
Put statement
    binary files, 405-406
    random files, 402-403

Q-R

QBasic, 6
queries, 480-487
    databases, 457
    linking tables (COUNTRY.MAK), 481
    relating tables, 485-487
    SELECT queries, 480
quick-keys (menus), 366-367
quitting Visual Basic, 50

RAM (random-access memory) and
    variables, 15
random files, 391, 398-404
    closing, 403
    designing, 399-401

EOF( ) function, 404
fields, 399
Get statement, 403
I/O (input/output) activity, 398
Len( ) function, 402
Loc( ) function, 404
MYCOINS.RAN, 403-404
numeric fields, 400
Open statement, 401-402
portability, 398
programming, 398
Put statement, 402-403
records, 398-401
Seek statement, 404
text fields, 399
user-defined data types, 401-403
random numbers, 330-332
reading sequential files, 395-397
reallocating dynamic arrays with ReDim,
    303-304
record variables, defining, 401
records
    deleting (COUNTRY.MAK), 478-479
    Get statement (random files), 403
    inserting (COUNTRY.MAK), 477
    Put statement (random files), 402-403
    random files, 398-401
    tables, 457
Recordset property (Dynasets), 476-480
RecordSource property (databases), 467
recreational programming, 7
redefining counter variables in For-Next
    loops, 230
ReDim statement (dynamic arrays),
    303-305
refining Cut and Copy buttons (text editor
    project), 181-182
relating tables (queries), 485-487
relational databases, 456
relational operators, 215-216
remarks (comments), 17
Remove File command (File menu), 31
RemoveItem method
    combo boxes, 319
    grids, 421, 430-431
    list boxes, 319
reserved words, 129
resizing controls, 70
Resume instructions (error handlers),
    271-273
resuming programs (Debug window),
    256-257
retrieving values from variables, 145-147
Rnd( ) function, 330-332
rounding functions, 329-330
Row and Col property (grids), 416
Row property (grids), 418
RowColChange event procedure
    grid text boxes, 445
    grids, 422, 430-431
RowHeight property (grids), 425-426
Rows property (grids), 419-420
RTrim$( ) function, 148
RTrim( ) function, 148
Run command (File menu), 26
Run menu commands
    Break, 256
    End, 39
    Start, 39, 49
run time
    editing control properties, 72-73
    errors, 248-252
    pictures, moving at, 109-111
    properties, 57
running
    GREETER, 360-361
    GRIDEX1.MAK, 422
    programs, 49-50
    text editor project from Program
        Manager, 199-200

S

Save File As command (File menu), 172
Save File As dialog box, 172
Save Project As command (File menu), 172
Save Project As dialog box, 172
Save Project command (File menu), 50
SaveFile event procedure (grid text boxes), 447-449
saving
    text editor project, 172
    to disk, 50
scope
    arrays, 293-294
    form-level variables, 140
    global variables, 140, 142
    local variables, 140-141
    module-level variables, 140-142
scope (variables), 140-143
scroll bars, 321-323
    Change event, 322
    combo boxes, 316
    LargeChange property, 322
    list boxes, 316
    Max property, 322
    Min property, 322
    Scroll event, 322
    SmallChange property, 322
    text editor project, 164
    Value property, 322
    vertical scroll bars, 322-323
scroll box, 321
Scroll event (scroll bars), 322
ScrollBars property (grids), 428-429
seed parameter (random numbers), 330
Seek statement
    binary files, 406
    random files, 404
Seek( ) function, 407
SelChange event (grids), 430-431
Select Case statement, 20, 220-222
SELECT queries, 480
Selected property (list boxes), 320
selecting
    cells (grids), 422-424
    characters (text boxes), 163
    controls, 70
    text (text editor project), 173-174
separator bars (menus), 364-365
sequential files, 391-398
    appending, 395
    ASCII, 392
    Close statement, 394-395
    creating, 393-395
    EOF( ) function, 396
    FileLen( ) function, 397
    Input # statement, 396
    Line Input # statement, 397
    loops, 397
    Open statement, 393-394
    reading, 395-397
    Write # statement, 394
Set Next Statement command (Debug menu), 265
SetAttr( ) function, 390
SetFocus method (text editor project), 171
Shape controls, 101-102, 106-108
Shape property (Shape controls), 106
SHARE.EXE (Data Manager), 459
shortcut keys
    menu bar, 35-37
    menus, 353, 366-367
Show Next Statement command (Debug menu), 266
ShowTextBox procedure (grids), 442-443
ShutDown procedure (grids), 441
simple combo boxes, 317
simulating errors, 274-275
Single data type, 135
single Next statements (For-Next loops), 231

Single Step command (Debug menu), 259
single-line For-Next loops, 228-231
single-line If statements, 211-212
single-step tracing, 259
size properties, 60
sizing
    arrays (dynamic arrays), 302-304
    controls, 33-34, 70
    forms, 28
    text boxes, 162
small utilities, 7
SmallChange property (scroll bars), 322
snapshots, 112
software, 1-2
Sorted property (combo and list boxes), 319
source code, 4
space (combo and list boxes), 318
spaghetti logic (GoTo statement), 209
SQL (Structured Query Language), 457, 480-487
Standard Edition (Visual Basic), 26
Start command (Run menu), 39, 49
start-up forms, 125
starting
    COUNTRY.MAK, 473
    Data Manager, 459-460
    Visual Basic, 26
statements, 13-21
    assignment statements, 18
    branching, 16
    case statements, 20
    comments, 16-17
    conditional statements, 16, 19
    input statements, 18-19
    loops, 20
    output statements, 19
    Select Case statement, 20
    variables, 14-15
static arrays, 294-295, 302-305
static variables, 143-144
status bars, 118
Step clause (For-Next loops), 225-226
Stop instruction (debugging), 266
stopping programs, 126
storing
    data (grids), 447
    values in variables, 145
Str$( ) function, 147
Stretch property (Image control), 97, 471
strings, 136-137
    Asc( ) function, 324-325
    Chr$( ) function, 324-325
    concatenating, 147
    grids, 416
    InStr( ) function, 148
    Len( ) function, 148
    manipulating, 148
    Mid$( ) function, 149
    multipart format strings, 326
    numeric conversion, 146-147
    predefined formats, 327
    relational operators, 215
    tab-delimited format (grids), 417
    trimming, 147-148
Structured Query Language, see SQL
structures (databases), 457
style
    combo boxes, 320
    Options menu, 359
Style menu
    fonts, 373
    programming, 373
Sub Main procedures, 126
Sub procedures, 130-131
submenus (cascading menus), 358-359, 362
subscriptrange parameter (arrays), 291-292
subscripts (arrays), 284-285
    Option Base instruction, 292-293
synchronizing file controls, 388
syntax errors, 3, 248-250
systems software, 2

T

Tab key (grids), 444-445
tab order
    controls, 80-81
    text files, 188
tab-delimited format for strings (grids), 417
Tab_Order property, 79-81
tabbing code, 132-133
TabIndex property, 80-81
Table Design window, 461-462
table lookup
    arrays, 295-300
    databases, 485
tables
    bound controls, 470-471
    comments, 474
    creating, 461
    databases, 456
    Dynasets, 468
    fields, 457
    Flag field, 464-466
    Image control, 475
    indexes, 457, 463
    labels, 472
    link fields, 458
    linking with queries (COUNTRY.MAK), 481
    primary key fields, 457
    queries, 480-487
    records, 457
        deleting, 478-479
    RecordSource property, 467
    relating (queries), 485-487
Tables window, 460-462
TabStop property, 79-81
Ted, see text editor project
terminating programs, 210-211
testing
    conditional testing, 211-222
    debugging, 245, 247
    If statement, 211-220
    interactive testing (debugging), 244-245
    programs, 49-50
    Select Case statement, 220-222
testing expressions, 214-217
text, 150
    Alignment property, 78
    concatenating strings, 147
    editing, 77-81, 189
    Enabled property, 79
    fonts, 77-78
    formats, 40
    forms, 185-189
    menus, 352
    MousePointer property, 81
    numeric conversion, 146-147
    printing, 188
    programs, 133-147
    properties, 59-60, 78-81
    selected text, 173-174
    Tab_Order property, 79-81
    tab order, 188
    TabStop property, 79-81
    trimming strings, 147-148
    Value property, 79
    Visible property, 79
text boxes, 85-88, 162-163
    character selection, 163
    cursors, 162
    DblClick event procedure (grids), 446
    design, 42
    events, 87-88
    floating text boxes (grids), 441-443
    grids, 442
    KeyDown event procedure (grids), 446
    KeyPress event procedure (grids), 445
    LoadFile event procedure (grids), 449-451
    MouseDown event procedure (grids), 446
    Multiline property, 163

PhoneBook, 442
properties, 86-87, 162
text editor project, 162-164
RowColChange event procedure
(grids), 445
SaveFile event procedure (grids), 447-449
ShowTextBox procedure, 442-443
sizing, 162
word wrap, 163-164
Text command (Message menu), 375
text editor project, 161-204
access keys, 184-185
BlankText procedure, 177-182
check box initialization, 169
Click procedures, 170
check boxes, 172-173
command buttons, enabling, 180-181
control arrays, 189-197
Copy button, 174-176
refining, 181-182
Cut button, 174-176
refining, 181-182
Delete button, 173
disabling command buttons, 177-179
event procedures, 167-182
viewing, 183-184
font activation, 170
font initialization, 169
form-level variables, declaring, 175
Form_Load event procedure, 167-169
Index parameter, 194
Paste button, 174-176
verifying, 181
printing from Program Manager, 198
programmer-defined procedures,
viewing, 183
property values, 165-166
running from Program Manager, 199-200
saving, 172
scroll bars, 164
selected text, 173-174
SetFocus method, 171
text box properties, 162-164
toggling properties, 170
user interface design, 164-167
value properties, 169
viewing, 185-188
available events, 182-184
word wrap, 163
text fields (random files), 399
Text property
combo boxes, 320
controls, 77
grids, 416, 418
list boxes, 320
TextHeight property (grids), 426
TextWidth property (grids), 426
Then clause, 213
third-party custom controls, 31
Timer event, 324
timers, 323-324
times and Format$( ), 327
title parameter and InputBox$( ), 337
Toggle Breakpoint command (Debug
menu), 260
toggling
check marks, 376
menus, 361
properties (text editor project), 170
Toolbar, 39
creating with clickable buttons, 115-118
hiding, 39
Toolbar command (View menu), 39
Toolbox
controls, 70-77
custom controls, 31
program development environment,
30-31
Top property, 60
TopIndex property (list boxes), 320
TopRow property (grids), 428-429, 439
tracing (debugging), 258-260

trailing spaces, trimming from strings,
147-148
translation programs, 2, 4
TRAPERR (error trapping), 269-271
Trim$( ) function, 148
Trim( ) function, 148
trimming strings, 147-148
troubleshooting, 9-10
TrueType fonts, 77
turning off
error trapping, 271
menu options, 377-378
tutorials, 38
Twips, 60
two-dimensional arrays, 300-301
type conversion, 333-336
type-declaration characters, 139
typing
combo boxes, 318
in the Debug window, 255-256

U

unconditional branching, 206
GoTo statement, 207-209
Unload event, 69
UnSelect procedure (grids), 438
Until keyword (Do-Loop loops), 234
Update method (Recordset property), 476
user interfaces, see interfaces
user-defined data types, 305-307
random files, 401-403
user-selected cells (grids), 424
users, 2
utilities, 7

V

Val( ) function, 147
Value property, 79
scroll bars, 322
text editor project, 169
values (controls), 72
retrieving from variables, 145-147
storing in variables, 145
variables, 14-15, 133-134
arrays, 283-285, 293
declarations, 133, 138-140
Dim statement, 138-139
For statements (For-Next loops), 227-228
form-level variables
declaring, 175
scope, 140
global variables
logic errors, 257
scope, 140, 142
local variables (scope), 140-141
math operators, 145-146
module-level variables (scope), 140-142
numeric variables, 135-136
passing, 152-153
scope, 140-143
static variables, 143-144
type-declaration characters, 139
values
retrieving, 145-147
storing, 145
Variant variables, 137
Empty value, 335
InputBox( ) function, 338
Null value, 335
numeric type conversion, 335-336
verifying the Paste button, 181
vertical scroll bars, 322-323
View menu commands
Code, 167, 370
New Procedure, 130
Toolbar, 39
View Procedures dialog box, 183

viewing
Debug window, 255
event procedures (text editor project),
182-184
programmer-defined procedures (text
editor project), 183
text editor project, 185-188
Watch pane, 262
Visible property, 61-62, 79
Line controls, 105
Visual Basic, 6-7
arrays, 283-285
AUTOLOAD.MAK file, 125
calculator, 65-67
case-sensitivity, 49
code modules, 124-125
Control menu, 62-65
controls, 31-34, 81-88
custom menus, 351-384
Data control, 455-490
debugging, 243-281
examples, 38
form files, 124
Grid control, 416-453
Help, 37-38
loops, 222-238
menu bar, 34-37
naming conventions, 129
Options menu, 40-42
processing files, 385-414
Professional Edition, 26
program development environment,
27-31
program flow, 205-242
programming, 123-160
quitting, 50
Standard Edition, 26
starting, 26
text editing, 77-81
text editor project, 161-204
Toolbar, 39
tutorials, 38

W

watch expressions, editing, 263
Watch pane, viewing, 262
watchpoints (debugging), 261-264
Wend statement (While-Wend loops),
232-233
While keyword (Do-Loop loops), 234
While-Wend loops, 231-233
Width property, 60
Window menu (menu bar), 37
Window menu commands
Data Manager, 459, 481
Menu Design, 352
Project, 370
Windows, 1-24
Click events, 22
Control menu, 62-65
event-driven programming, 21
interface standards, 6
OOP (Object Oriented Programming),
21-22
procedures, 21
WindowState property, 64-65
WMF files, 64
word wrap, 163-164
writing
code, 131-133
error handlers, 273-275

X-Y-Z

X1/X2 properties (Line controls), 103-104
Xor (logical operator), 217

Y1/Y2 properties (Line controls), 103-104